128
218

British Transport

British Transport

An economic survey from the seventeenth century to the twentieth

H. J. Dyos and D. H. Aldcroft

Leicester University Press

1971

First published in 1969 by
Leicester University Press
Second impression 1971

Distributed in North America by
Humanities Press Inc., New York

Copyright © H. J. Dyos and D. H. Aldcroft 1969

Designed by Arthur Lockwood

Set in Monotype Spectrum and Univers Condensed
Printed in Great Britain by
Unwin Brothers Ltd, Old Woking, Surrey

SBN 7185 1081 X

Contents

Maps

Tables

Acknowledgments

We are grateful for the help we have received from colleagues in our own and other universities in the preparation of the maps, and in particular we wish to record our large debt to Terry Garfield and David Orme, who drew them with such skill and care. The principal sources for the maps are included among other references in the Bibliography, but we wish specifically to acknowledge the valuable information derived from the following: Ordnance Survey Maps of Roman Britain (1928) and of XVII Century (1930) as well as the One-Inch Ordnance Survey—Maps 2, 3, 8 and 9 respectively; Lewis A. Edwards (compiler), *Inland Waterways of Great Britain and Ireland* (Imray, Laurie, Norie & Wilson, Ltd, 2nd edition, 1962)—Map 10; H. G. Lewin, *The Railway Mania and its Aftermath, 1845–1852* (The Railway Gazette, 1936)—Maps 11 and 12; W. E. Simnett, *Railway Amalgamation in Great Britain* (The Railway Gazette, 1923)—inset to Map 13; G. C. Dickinson, "Stage-Coach Services in the West Riding of Yorkshire between 1830 and 1840", *Journal of Transport History*, iv, No. 1 (May 1959)—Map 14; Mersey Docks and Harbour Board, "The Plan of the Liverpool Dock Estate in 1900" contained in S. Mountfield, *Western Gateway: A History of the Mersey Docks and Harbour Board* (Liverpool University Press, 1965)—Map 19; Royal Geographical Society, "Discussion on the Geographical Distribution of Industry", *The Geographical Journal*, xcii, No. 1 (July 1938)—Maps 20–23; J. Stroud, *Annals of British and Commonwealth Air Transport, 1919–1960* (Putnam & Co. Ltd, 1962)—Map 24; "All the World's Air Lines", *The Aeroplane*, lvi, No. 1458 (3 May 1939)—Map 25. In addition, we wish to thank the following: Mr F. Neal for permission to use certain material from his thesis, "Liverpool Shipping, 1815–1835" (unpublished M.A. thesis, University of Liverpool, 1952); Dr C. H. Feinstein of Cambridge University for supplying some data on capital investment; Mr W. Forsyth of Glasgow University for providing cartographical material on the Monkland Canal; Mr G. Ottley of Leicester University Library for unstinted help with the Bibliography; the Carnegie Trust for a small travelling grant.

To

Jack Simmons

who has done more than anyone
to advance the study and enjoyment
of transport history

Preface

No-one has ever tried to write a full length general survey of the development of transport in Britain in modern times. This book is such an attempt. It does not aim at uncovering much new evidence about the history of transport but seeks particularly to draw into a connected account the many writings that have accumulated on the subject in the last century and more. Naturally, even in a book of this length there must still be some gaps. We have not made any serious attempt, for example, to deal with labour or trade union history. Some material is being presented in print for the first time, but we make no pretence at sustained originality in this work. It is designed primarily to meet the needs of students and others who want a full synopsis of the main developments set in the context of Britain's general economic history. The draft of Chapters 1–4 and 6–7 was prepared by the first-named of us and Chapters 5 and 8–13 by the second.

Careful attention has been given to the bibliography, for transport history is composed of innumerable monographs, most of which are read only by experts or enthusiasts and too seldom by students of wider issues. We hope that this book will be found useful as a guide to the literature. We have omitted all references in order to avoid distracting readers by what would have had to be an unduly tiresome apparatus of footnotes, but every work which we have used in writing the book will be found in the bibliography. We would like to take this opportunity of paying our particular tribute to the patient and scholarly work of the host of amateur historians, past and present, who are to be found in this field and whose labours have so often been of immense value to us.

We owe a still greater debt to one man from whom the idea for the book derived and whose encouragement brought it to fruition—our colleague, Jack Simmons. He has read and criticized the whole text in detail, given us generously of his own researches, and opened up to us a number of new insights. We are very grateful. Such errors as may still be found are all our own.

We write this at the very end of a unique era in the history of transport.

Today, the last train to be hauled on a scheduled run by a steam locomotive on British railways has made the journey from Lime Street, Liverpool to Carlisle and back. It is a reminder that transport history is still being made and we would like to think that this volume will give historical perspective to the far-reaching changes now taking place and to those that will succeed them.

H. J. Dyos
D. H. Aldcroft

Leicester, 11 August 1968

1

The transport system of pre-industrial Britain

In a world made so small by highly developed forms of transport, it is difficult to visualize a state of affairs in which the movement of men and materials was once undertaken only for the most pressing purposes and with the greatest effort. Nor is it easy nowadays to make the kind of calculation of cost and risk which once had to be drawn up, even in a peaceful and settled country, before quite short journeys were undertaken, or small consignments of goods put in hand. Yet, apart from the extraordinary requirements of war or the sheer necessity of staving off hunger or escaping from disease, it has invariably been these costs and risks of moving goods and people which have governed the amount of that movement. And it has been through attempts to lower those costs and to increase that mobility that the changing needs of a developing economy have usually expressed themselves. The economic condition of Britain and its transport system have always been most intimately and directly related. Not surprisingly, the history of transport in Britain is primarily an economic one, and the economic history of Britain since the beginning of the eighteenth century has as one of its major themes the creation and the modification of a system of internal and external communications.

Even at the beginning of the eighteenth century, the points at which physical or administrative barriers to the free movement of people and goods across the face of Britain or around her coasts had been pierced corresponded exactly with the points at which the commercial pressures and administrative needs of earlier generations had been most urgently expressed. The transport system which had been pressed out in this way, imperfect as it was in many respects, was unquestionably the most vital single component in an economic mechanism which was annually growing more comprehensive and more complex. Whether one looks at the numberless tracks and the rather fewer metalled roads which laced together the rural parts of the country; or at the deeply penetrating, though shallow, rivers that gave access to the open sea; or at the chain of ports around

B

Britain's heavily indented coasts, it is plain that in all of them there were symptoms of underdevelopment just as there were indications that much had already been done. By the beginning of the eighteenth century Britain was already becoming in essence an interlocking system of trade routes, large and small, which ran between centres of production and consumption —between village and village, between countryside and town, between port and hinterland. The volume of that trade, and the directions it took, were fundamentally controlled quite as much by the efficiency—that is to say, the costs—of existing forms of transport as they were by the sheer productive energies and human needs of her people and of those with whom she traded abroad.

To study the different forms of transport which were evolving in this way is, therefore, to watch the changing reflection of a maturing economy and to identify some of the social and political implications of these changes. It was this vital connection which so impressed W. T. Jackman when he was writing his great seminal study on the development of transportation in modern England: the relationship between transport and the development of agriculture, the growth of markets for home-produced foodstuffs, the growing complexity and power of industry, and the effects of all this on the welfare of the country as a whole. These were matters which had not much concerned historians during the period when Jackman was writing his work before the First World War, and he understandably concentrated on his central theme of the evolution of transport as such. Since then the researches of economic historians have demonstrated more clearly the significance of some of these conditions and have given to'the history of transport a more general importance in the economic and social history of the country than Jackman's more limited theme appeared to acknowledge. It is this body of historical research which is being tapped in this book, and it is this relationship between the development of different forms of transport and the economic condition of the country which provides its main theme.

At the beginning of the eighteenth century, Britain was still quite literally an under-developed country. The land was sparsely and patchily populated by some seven million people, three-quarters of whom were still living and working on the land. Manufacturing industry and corporate forms of business organization were still very much in their infancy, and the common basis for the greatest part of economic activity was still the family and the village community. Manufacturing, mining, and building taken together probably accounted for no more than a fifth of the national income at that time, and measured in such terms manufacturing industry itself was as yet of merely fractional importance in the national economy. As little as half-a-million pounds had by then been invested in joint-stock enterprise, and most of that was committed to trading overseas. Viewed as a whole, the economy was not yet capable of sustaining a very high rate of investment in new forms of productive enterprise. Probably no more than 5 per cent per annum of the national income was available for new investment, and to accumulate capital at such a rate was not sufficient to produce from one year to the next more than a very modest addition to the wealth-producing equipment of all kinds which was at work in the country.

In short, the economy had not yet begun to experience the almost irresistible surges of economic progress which are thought normal in the advanced countries of the world in the middle of the twentieth century. On the other hand, it would be a mistake to regard the British economy as in a stagnant condition. It is true that the production of wool almost alone —especially in its new manufacturing areas in the West Riding—was expanding with any speed, and that it was not until the 1740s that the rate of growth of the output of some other industries first equalled and then outstripped that of wool. Yet judged by reference to the contemporary achievements of other countries Britain already stood among the leaders of economic development. It is probable that the Dutch alone were in 1700 enjoying a higher general level of material welfare than had then been realised, on the average, in Britain, and this was also substantially higher than that of numerous under-developed countries today. The situation simply was that, as yet, the economy was not in a condition to mount such a heavy programme of investment in new forms of wealth that the process could give the appearance of being a self-sustaining one.

1   Regional and inter-regional trade

The most stubborn limitation to more rapid economic expansion was undoubtedly that of transport. Inland transport was still very much in the grip of geography, and the lie of the land or the intervention of physical barriers virtually decided which way and how far traders and other travellers should go. But natural limitations of this kind also produced geographical regions sufficiently different in weather or subsoil to create some primitive specialization of crops and livestock. The wetter, hillier parts of the country to the west, for instance, had long been identified with cattle-raising; the comparatively low-lying clay soils of the Midlands with wheat, and the less fertile and drier zone to the east and southeast with sheep and barley. By the beginning of the eighteenth century this simple pattern had become complicated by the growth of towns, particularly by one or two metropolitan markets, and by the enlargement of some of the existing continental markets for grain. Communication between these geographical regions of the country had developed far enough by the eighteenth century to allow more particular specialization. Fatstock-grazing, dairy-farming, fruit-growing, and market-gardening were tending to diversify the agrarian pattern more and more, and were beginning to cause quite sharp breaks to appear in the prevailing type of husbandry, not only between counties

Map 1   *The distribution of economic activity about 1700*

but between districts within them. This did not show that existing forms of transport were adequate to sustain an inland trade in certain foodstuffs so much as it revealed transport as its most important limiting factor. Grain was more widely distributed than any other product and it was the imperfections in inland transport as much as anything which virtually divided the kingdom into a number of distributive zones for it. The movement of grain, though not wholly circumscribed by them, took place within six or seven major regions where land and water carriage were more coherently organized than they were with the regions bordering them: the Thames basin; a great arc of southern England within easy reach of the Channel between Dartmoor and the Weald; the counties of Cambridge and Bedford and most of the country lying to the east of them, an area broadly held together by the Great Ouse and numerous smaller rivers; practically the whole of the area lying between the Thames, the Trent, and the Severn; the country lying to the north of the Trent, divided in two by the Pennines and perhaps subdivided still further; and the west and southwest, between the Severn valley and Cornwall on one limb, and between the Wye and Pembrokeshire on the other. (*See Map 1*, p. 20.)

Within such regions, constricted as they were by imperfect means of communication, hundreds of market towns up and down the country still drove their weekly trade in the products of the locality in very much the same way around 1700 as they had done in the Middle Ages. In East Anglia, for example, there were over ninety such market towns around the middle of the seventeenth century. To them the surrounding villages and hamlets consigned their surplus foodstuffs and rudimentary manufactures, and in this way brought into being little localized systems of bridle-paths and roads which were adequate enough for their normal traffic of ox-carts, pack-horses, and local people on foot or on horseback, but which were usually incapable of sustaining very heavy loads on long journeys. The market towns were themselves part of a larger distributive system which had evolved hundreds of years beforehand to meet the transport difficulties of the Middle Ages. Some of the great annual fairs of medieval England— King's Lynn, Gainsborough, Beverley, and Sturbridge—were still in existence at the beginning of the eighteenth century. Sturbridge fair at Cambridge was, in Defoe's view, when he visited it in 1724, the greatest fair in the world: to it came West Country, East Anglian, and West Country clothiers, London wholesale dealers in woollens, hop factors, hosiers, horse dealers, ironmasters, shopkeepers, and merchants of all kinds out of virtually every country of Western Europe. Merchants attending the fair overflowed Cambridge and the surrounding towns and caused some fifty hackney carriages and numerous wherries and wagons to come up specially from London to provide local transport. To it came vast consignments of goods of every sort: a thousand horsepacks of wool out of the North Country alone, supplies of stockings from Leicester and Nottingham, edge-tools from Sheffield, wrought iron and brassware from Birmingham, hops from

Kent and Surrey, tin from Cornwall, lead from Derbyshire, iron from the Weald, and a miscellany of other goods. All converged on temporary warehouses and tents arranged in streets on a large cornfield on the banks of the Cam. Communications had by this time improved enough to allow still more specialized fairs to come into being all over the country: for cattle at St Faith's, Norwich, herrings at Yarmouth, cheese at Atherstone and Ipswich, poultry at Dorking, sheep at Weyhill, horses at Barnet, Penkridge and Northampton, and corn at Farnham and Warminster. More than this, regular markets were already beginning to establish themselves for particular commodities, either at the main centre of consumption or at some collecting or distributing point where navigable water met an overland route, or at a coastal port.

There had also already begun that process of urban concentration of a growing population which had revealed itself unmistakeably by the seventeenth century and which has yet to come to a halt. Such growing towns depended for their provisioning and for their livelihood not merely on their own rural neighbourhoods but upon supplies of foodstuffs and industrial raw materials from further afield. Perhaps the most conspicuous topographical feature of many of the principal towns of the provinces—Bristol, Norwich, Exeter, Chester, York, for example—was the convergence at those places of radial networks of roads which had been developed to perform just this function. Nor was the trade carried by them purely regional. There is some evidence that even before the close of the Middle Ages road haulage was taking place regularly over very long distances. In the middle of the fifteenth century, for example, road hauliers at Southampton were already dispatching cartloads of wine and woad fairly regularly to destinations as far off as Gloucester, Oxford, Coventry and even Kendal.

Even more tangible evidence of the development of an inter-regional trade which had sprung up to cater for the needs of the growing towns was that in livestock of all kinds. Cattle which had been bred in one region were transferred on the hoof to another in order to be fattened and moved again by road to market for slaughtering. Livestock was widely scattered throughout the country and apart from short journeys to local markets its movement was always towards the large towns and, above all, to London. The traffic often began on the borders of the kingdom and the driven herds were enlarged as they progressed at twenty miles a day or so towards the grazing areas. The black Highland-bred cattle, which converged on Falkirk and Crieff and were driven in such large numbers over Cheviot after the Act of Union in 1707, moved south in one stream to Westmorland and Cumberland and in another, with the herds augmented in crossing the Yorkshire dales, to East Anglia, whence they were later driven to Smithfield: at the St Faith's cattle fair just north of Norwich some 40,000 Scots cattle were sold annually. The Anglesey cattle, made to swim the perilous Menai Strait, concentrated on Abergele fair before trekking on to Barnet fair

and Londoners' tables. Leicestershire and Northamptonshire were other
fattening areas; and there were numerous other well-marked routes taken
by the West Country cattle into the home counties. The great sheep-breed-
ing areas were the Midlands and the West Country, so London's supplies
of mutton had less ground to cover, but within this region there were
considerable transfers of flocks: something under half-a-million sheep
changed hands annually, for instance, at Weyhill fair near Andover, the
majority of them ewes which were driven into the neighbouring counties
as store-sheep. Some of this movement was localized in small markets
but the metropolitan demand for mutton was very strong and the main
tendency of all this movement was towards London. It is difficult to be
precise about the volume of it all because the Smithfield sales of cattle on
the hoof may not have been more than half the total turned into meat for
consumption in London, for carcass butchers also bought stock all round
London and slaughtered it outside the capital. On the average, some
80,000 cattle and 610,000 sheep converged on Smithfield annually in the
first half of the eighteenth century, though the numbers of both were
liable to fluctuate a good deal. Turkeys and geese also moved in on London
in hundreds of thousands from Sussex, Surrey, Suffolk, and Norfolk, though
these were often driven for long distances across the open country: Defoe
calculated that 150,000 Norfolk turkeys were driven in 300 separate droves
down the Ipswich road towards London each year. Much poultry also
travelled live in special four-tiered wagons; those which went from Peterborough to London twice a week were so heavily loaded as to require
teams of twelve horses to pull them over the roads. From the Lincolnshire
fens even live fish were carried in waterbutts by waggons to London.

London already contained over half-a-million people, almost a tenth of
the population of England and some twenty-five times the population
contained in the next largest cities of Bristol and Norwich. During the
sixteenth and seventeenth centuries the population of London had probably trebled and its share of total foreign trade doubled. In the circumstances it was inevitable that London should in the course of the seventeenth
century have begun to influence the whole pattern of inland trade. In
organizing its own supply-lines London tended to magnetize the whole
transport system and virtually to give to many provincial towns the rôle
of collecting centre in the great co-operative task of meeting its needs. This
was particularly plain in the organization of the inland trade in grain,
especially after 1663 when an old law against speculating in stocks of cereals
was repealed. The influence of London was enhanced still more in 1689
when corn exports were encouraged by bounty and London merchants
engaged vigorously in the export of grain. From an early date the London
corn markets had been supplied by road from Cambridgeshire, Huntingdonshire, Bedfordshire, and Hertfordshire, but by Tudor times these sources of
supply could no longer match the growth of the population of London,
and the London corn-merchants were reaching much deeper into the

provinces. They were also increasing their capacity for doing so by using navigable water to bring in supplies from every part of the country.

The Thames had always been used to some extent to provision London with grain and by the end of the seventeenth century a chain of regular loading-points had come into being at Kingston, Henley, Great Marlow, Reading, and Abingdon. There was also in existence by this time a still larger network of road and river connections which drew in supplies from Ware, Farnham, Guildford, Warminster, Devizes, and Gloucester. In some cases this entailed the improvement of tributaries. One of the principal reasons for the improvement of the River Lea late in the sixteenth century, for example, had been to make it the main artery for the great grain-producing region behind Ware. Before this time the corn had been carried overland to Enfield, an expensive operation which was probably made still more so by the operations of the London corn "badgers", the itinerant middlemen of the corn trade at that time, who were able to monopolize the London supplies. When a passage was forced through its unnavigable stream late in the sixteenth century it was done in the main at the instance, though not at the expense, of the London merchants. The entrepôt being moved from Enfield to Ware in this way, the London corn-factors shifted their grip and monopolized the river barges instead of the wagon trade. Similarly, the Wey was made navigable between Guildford and the Thames in the middle of the seventeenth century in order to open a vent for the timber and corn of the area. This tapped the greatest corn market in England outside London, at Farnham, whence the grain was carried seven miles overland to the River Wey, where it was ground and dressed before being shipped by barge to London. In all these areas the London price was beginning to moderate, if not to rule, the prices asked and given in the corn-growing areas, and the system of collection was becoming so sophisticated that it was already normal for the grain to be bought by sample, moved by common carriers, and milled before shipment. By the early eighteenth century there were regular weekly and twice-weekly schedules of barges to and from a number of towns below Oxford, carrying corn, malt, and meal downstream and coal, salt, groceries, and other goods upstream from London. By mid-century smaller barges were reaching as high as Lechlade.

Down to 1660 London had also imported foreign corn from abroad but its corn merchants had been so successful in tapping the great granaries of the fens, the upper Thames, and the southern home counties that the flow could now begin to be reversed. This was made possible by augmenting the river traffic with a coastal one, which brought vessels of up to 50 tons displacement up the Thames in such numbers that a new market had to be made for them at Bear Key below London Bridge. Inevitably, this quickly established itself as the principal market for corn in the country, taking its supplies first from Kent, but by the middle of the seventeenth century also from East Anglia, the northeast coast, from the south and west coasts, and even from South Wales. The eagerness of the London corn-factors to increase supplies had led them into supporting the Don navigation scheme in 1704 because they hoped the wheat-producing area around Doncaster could be exploited. By 1680 nearly 200,000 quarters of corn were being brought into London by coaster, a figure that had more than doubled in thirty years. This represented well over a thousand shipments of corn a year during the last quarter of the seventeenth century, mainly from King's Lynn, Hull, and Great Yarmouth: almost everywhere these shipments were still on the increase throughout the first half of the eighteenth century. To these must be added the huge annual shipments of cheese and butter consigned to London by water by this time, though some cheese did travel overland, for instance from Warwickshire to London, whence it was redistributed by river and sea to the home counties. A large part of the Cheshire cheese trade also went overland much of the way to London and the east coast towns before being embarked on Trent barges to Hull and thence by coaster. As with so many other supplies, the last stage was almost always undertaken by water. Butter, too, came mostly from the eastern counties by similar routes. The cheesemongers of London, who handled this trade, had by the beginning of the eighteenth century placed their factors in practically every port through which it passed, and these agents obtained supplies from the surrounding countryside: as early as 1670 the London cheesemongers had completely monopolized the trade between Chester, Liverpool and London, and were even operating a fleet of coasters of their own.

We have slipped at this point into the same kind of easy relationship between the rivers and coastal waters of Britain which was literally theirs. In a vital functional sense the two were uniform. The seas was already being used by a great fleet of small ships as a continuous stretch of navigable water connecting the estuaries and mouths of the inland waterways and their hinterlands. Britain has more sea-coast per square mile of land than any other European country, and her coastal waters were in those days of difficult overland transport an inestimable economic benefit. Not all of the score of English headports had behind them navigable inland waterways, but there were some, above all London, Bristol, Hull, and King's Lynn, which were indeed gateways to the interior. By 1700 there existed nowhere in the country a navigable stream on which vessels could be bottled up by a stretch of unnavigable water between them and the sea, and the process of pressing back the unnavigable frontier never altogether relaxed. King's Lynn, for example, near the mouth of the Great Ouse, was the natural collecting and distributive centre for water-borne corn and numerous other commodities for ten counties, and it was at the same time their natural outlet to the Wash and the North Sea. By the last quarter of the seventeenth century King's Lynn was handling, apart from that required for its own consumption, about 47,000 quarters of corn a year which had been collected by the Great Ouse and its tributaries. Half of this was sent abroad and the other half shipped up or down the coast: about a fifth of it went to other provincial ports, especially Newcastle and Hull, the rest to London. Great Yarmouth, Ipswich, Rochester, Chichester, and Southampton were all engaged in varying degrees in the same kind of trade, exporting and importing corn and its various products to London or to some other outport. In the west, the Severn was performing a rôle similar to that of the Great Ouse in the east. Here it was Gloucester which was the clearing centre, the natural vent for the whole water-borne produce of England's mightiest river of the day. Gloucester, as much a sea-port as a river-port, had by this time developed a special subordinate trading relationship with Bristol, though one which was not to last, taking and receiving most of her trade from there. In the outward cargoes shipped in 1690–1 went over 65,000 bushels of rye and wheat, more than 8,000 hogsheads of cider and perry, and considerable quantities of malt, cheese, meal, industrial raw materials, and domestic goods of all kinds. Bristol did not consume all of this but was itself the centre of a coasting trade in foodstuffs with South Wales (chiefly with Chepstow and behind it with the Wye valley), and with the other ports of southwest England.

Though London undoubtedly occupied an outstanding position in this internal and coastal trade in foodstuffs it was not, strictly speaking, a dominant one, except in one or two commodities like butter and cheese, nor was the movement all one way. The smaller consignments tend to escape notice, but it should be remembered that London was a distributive and industrial centre as well as an area of consumption. Some of the grain which had been sucked into London made a return trip into the provinces in the form of flour, meal, starch, beer, and spirits; livestock in the form of leather, fell-wool, glue, tallow, bacon, and so on. And this criss-crossing of internal trade was even more pronounced in the movement of industrial raw materials and manufactured goods.

It is true that concentrated manufacturing industry occupied as yet only a tiny fraction of the population, but the largest industry, cloth-making, was widely dispersed. In one sense this was natural because the manufacture of woollen cloth fitted easily into the agrarian pattern. The natural, broken rhythms of agriculture had always allowed those working on the land to turn their hands from time to time to spinning yarn or weaving cloth, and to drop those tasks when the demands of field-work became peremptory once again. In one sense it could be said that this traditional, almost self-sufficient economy had little need of elaborate forms of transport, but such a state of affairs was also an acknowledgment of the inadequacy of what was available. By the end of the seventeenth century these widely-dispersed activities had had the paradoxical effect of creating new demands for transport services because the regional specialization which had grown up naturally on the basis of the varying fineness and treatment of the raw material in different parts had led to the growth of an inter-regional trade both in wool and in the cloth which was made of it. In the middle of the seventeenth century only five counties were regarded as important in the production of the raw material though a dozen made considerable use of it. Between them lay a gap which had to be bridged, and the bridging of it was one of the most important functions that the various forms of transport had to perform in the seventeenth and early eighteenth centuries, for woollen manufacture probably accounted for no less than a fifth of the national income and earned some £2 million in exports.

Just as the sheep themselves were moved in large numbers between breeding and grazing areas, their fleeces, whether taken annually from their backs or finally from their carcasses, performed another, perhaps even more circuitous, series of journeys. The first took them in the direction of one of the great annual fairs or to one of the specialized markets like Warminster, Leicester, Lincoln, or Cirencester. The last-named was the meeting place for wool-men and woollen manufacturers for half of England: wool broggers who had canvassed for the wool from farm to farm and brought it in; wool jobbers and merchants from the magazine of English wool, Leicestershire; woollen manufacturers from Devon and the Cotswolds; Somersetshire clothiers whose cloths combined yarns from Wales, Ireland, Lincolnshire, and Spain; fellmongers from shambles in Southwark, Kent, East Anglia, and the Midlands, much of whose fleeces shuttled weekly on the last stage of their journey up from London in the wagons which had carried the products of the Witney blanket-makers down. According to Defoe, the total trade of this one town was over 500 packs of wool a week. The wool then passed into the complex web of the clothing industry to be sorted, spun and woven in villages and towns which usually performed only a single process before handing the raw material on to the next. Repeatedly it was carried back and forth in small consignments and large, by packhorse or by wagon, gradually making its way out of one region into another, and so normally on to London and its great cloth market of Blackwell Hall. There was no simple pattern in an industry which was so widely spread and intricately organized. Much wool and cloth also went by river and coastal vessels. Some of the west of England trade, which was in this respect more localized than in other parts of the country, was carried by coasters from Gloucester, Exeter, Lyme, and Southampton, but it was also being exported directly from Bristol without going to London; Faversham, Ipswich, Colchester, King's Lynn, Boston, and Hull all had a heavy wool and cloth trade either between themselves or with London, or with other towns.

Less important than wool as an industrial raw material in 1700, but far more important in the stimulus it gave to the coasting trade, was coal. Though coal was carried all round the English coasts, it was the trade between the northeast coast ports of Newcastle and Sunderland and London which overshadowed the rest. Between 1661 and 1710 Newcastle shipped coastwise about 21 million tons of coal, some 70 per cent of which was bound for London, while the rest was distributed among 45 ports as far south as Guernsey and as far west as Plymouth, though about half of this provincial trade was with two of them, King's Lynn and Great Yarmouth. As with corn, the coal trade with London owed much to the rapid growth of population in the capital in the seventeenth century, but as well as a purely domestic demand there was also a rapid expansion in the demand for coal by a number of London industries. The vital factor in its use was the low cost of transporting an easily handled commodity in bulk across water which presented none of the impediments offered even to river vessels. It would have been impossible, as things were at the time, to develop the coal trade on such a scale without sea transport. Although there was no comparable concentration of trade in coal on the west coasts, the traffic between Swansea and Gloucester and the other West Coast ports was not inconsiderable, and the Severn itself was in 1700 carrying more coal downstream from the Shropshire pits than was being borne by any other inland waterway.

The influence of London on the internal trade of pre-industrial Britain was so great in some respects that it tends to obscure the growing import-ance of those provincial centres of trade and industry which were to be of such importance in the subsequent industrialization of the country. The truth of this could not be better illustrated than by reference to the way in which the whole basin of the Trent had been formed into a single economy in which the mining and quarrying industries of the west of the region dovetailed commercially with the basically agricultural part of the region to the east and south of them. Here was an area in which complementary industrial materials wanted only a modest means of communication to form the basis of thriving industries which could cater both for the needs of the region and for much wider markets. Even in the seventeenth century this was a function which the River Trent had begun to perform with an unusual efficiency. Though the industry depended for its full development on an industrial genius not yet born, the potteries of Staffordshire were already in a lusty infancy in 1700. The necessary clay, coal, lead, and salt were all within usable range of each other, and the Trent thirty miles away to the nearest navigable point at Willington, just below Burton, provided an export outlet and a means of bringing in flints from Gravesend for the manufacture of earthenware. Using local coal and iron, smiths at Notting-ham in the middle of the seventeenth century were turning out agricultural implements of all kinds not only for the surrounding country but for Leicestershire, Lincolnshire, and Rutland as well. The valley of the Tame, a tributary of the Trent, where old corn-mills were being converted early in the seventeenth century into slitting-mills by local landowners quick to exploit the decline of the Wednesbury iron trade, was already humming with a nascent iron industry and its products were being exported down the Trent. In south Derbyshire forges and slitting mills found a similar outlet down the Derwent, while lead mined in the north of the county travelled overland to Chesterfield and on to Bawtry before being shipped down the Idle and so into the Trent. By 1700 the quantity of coal mined on the Nottinghamshire-Derbyshire border may have been approaching 150,000 tons a year and this was being moved by river to serve a variety of local industries and domestic purposes.

The high value to the region of its means of communication is clearer still from the efforts being made to improve them even before the seventeenth century, and from the 1630s schemes were being mooted for enlarging the system by improving the navigation of the Soar and the Derwent. Throughout the second half of the century a well-organized lobby was at work to secure the improvement of the Derwent and this was supported not only by local manufacturing interests, London merchants, and shipping interests on the Trent, but by others in the Cheshire salt towns and in Stafford, Lichfield, Birmingham, and Coventry. But to improve a river, or any other form of communication, was seldom to improve the economic welfare of all who were touched by it, and the reflex action of established transport and other commercial interests was sometimes bitter and even violent.

Nothing could illustrate better the subtlety of the well-established commercial relations that existed in regions like the vale of the Trent than the counterblasts of protest which so often withered the pleas of the improvers. Seven bills were presented to improve the Derwent between 1638 and 1702 and all were silenced in this way. Nottinghamshire colliery owners feared cheap Derbyshire coal; Northamptonshire farmers thought they would lose their market for corn in Derby whence they obtained their coal; Derby innkeepers dreaded an impending fall in corn prices which would keep local farmers from coming to market; and every transport interest connected with the overland movement of lead, salt, malt, and other goods between Leicester and York added more complaint. As one region after another pressed closer to the workable limits of its existing transport systems in the course of the seventeenth century and new proposals were made for perfecting them, so in almost every case the growls of men who feared the loss of some less efficient carrying trade revealed the existence of local and long-distance transport systems quite as intricate as that already in being in the wide basin of the Trent.

2 Road transport

Long before 1700 the great traffic which had been put upon the roads by all this commercial activity was quite literally more than they could bear. Of course, much of the movement of foodstuffs, livestock, and manufactures which Defoe observed about this time took place over roads originally made for local use, but there were other roads which, even in the Middle Ages, had been entitled to be regarded as trunk roads. Their main basis was the Roman road system which had originally been designed as a highly complex framework of skilfully engineered direct routes between strategic points, mainly for the rapid movement of military units. In the course of over a thousand years this remarkable system had been partially dismembered and the rest allowed to decay, but there were still the bare bones of it in existence at the beginning of the eighteenth century. Watling Street, Ermine Street, Stane Street, Akeman Street, the Icknield Way (which antedated the Romans themselves), and a number of other roads still provided the basis of the trunk road system in linking London with its provinces and the North of England with the South and West. The centralized administration of the Romans had depended on the maintenance of an efficient system of internal communications which was conceived as a whole, and it was the re-appearance in England of a highly centralized monarchy in the thirteenth and fourteenth centuries—a phenomenon unique in Western Europe—which effectively resuscitated some part of this comprehensive network. A national system of administration once again required a system of adequate roads radiating from the seat of political power in London. Though seldom coinciding precisely with the Roman alignment, many of them pursued the same routes, and in broad outline these were also the roads travelled by Celia Fiennes and Daniel Defoe two hundred years later. When John Ogilby published in 1675 his meticulously descriptive road-book, *Britannia* (the very first of its kind and the pattern for others for a long while to come), he could display an elaborate cobweb of eleven main roads leading out of London deep into the provinces, and an extensive system of cross-roads which tied them together at many points. But it was essentially the same system which had been portrayed by an anonymous cartographer who traced and roughly measured it some three hundred years before. (*See Maps 2 and 3, p. 32.*)

What chiefly distinguished the road system of the early eighteenth century from that of Roman times were its engineering and administration. Since the Romans had left there had been no development nor—if travellers' tales are any guide—even the retention of the principles of road-making which they had used. In the Middle Ages the improvement of communications had been concentrated almost entirely on relatively few key points, especially bridges. Many of these were timber constructions, which continued to be used even for some of the widest rivers until the eighteenth century, but an increasing number was built of stone, sometimes to much more advanced designs than had been necessary to serve the Roman legions. By contrast, the condition of the roads was determined haphazardly. Their administration was no longer directly controlled by a centralized government whose stability and efficiency depended on a network of military and civil roads. It had passed instead into the hands of local communities whose interests seldom transcended their own parish boundaries and who were rarely able to develop an administrative system to answer for more than their own transport needs. The common law recognized the responsibility of local people in maintaining their own roads, and the upkeep of the highways had naturally enough come within the jurisdiction of the same authority as for local roads, the manorial courts. By the middle of the sixteenth century the manorial organization of rural life was rapidly breaking down under various economic pressures and new kinds of local official therefore had to be appointed. One of these was the Surveyor of Highways, who was brought into being by the Highways Act of 1555, the first legislation ever passed applying to roads in general in England. The Surveyor was elected annually by his parishioners and charged with the responsibility of supervizing the annual stint of four days' work which each of them was obliged to render on the parish roads which served local markets; seven years later, when the initial trial period was extended (it actually remained operative down to 1835), the stint of "statute labour" was increased to six days and the Surveyor was authorized to requisition road-repairing materials. The arrangement was inherently weak, for neither the parishioners nor the Surveyor could be made to give good service, though they could be punished by fines for any serious neglect of their tasks; and the Surveyor himself, who normally had no technical qualifications for the job, was all too vulnerable to selfish pressures. In 1575 the status of the Surveyor was raised, and in 1691 his appointment was transferred to the Quarter Sessions, while the parishes themselves were empowered to make a rate to cover the costs of repairing their roads and to hire the labour to perform it. The derelictions of the Civil War and the much greater personal mobility and commercial activity now going on meant that local arrangements like these tended to press disproportionately on different communities, not according to the multiplication of their own transport needs but to meet the arbitrary demands of others. Already, with the growth of internal trade, many parishes found themselves being made to bear some of the real costs of transport which might more equitably have fallen either on the users of the roads themselves or upon the country as a whole. The system was clearly outdated and the condition of the roads which it had been intended to improve was frequently more deplorable than ever. This was particularly so on the great bed of stiff clay at least fifty miles across, which any traveller heading north was bound to encounter within thirty miles of leaving London, or in the deep slough of Sussex. The subsequent history of the administration of the roads has been concerned with attempts to regulate the increasing traffic and to divide the increasingly irksome financial responsibility for the upkeep of the roads between their users and the community at large.

Local authorities began to apply their own remedies. In Kent in 1604 the Quarter Sessions imposed a premium of five shillings on cart-loads above a ton and directed that this money should be spent on repairing the very roads that were being broken under such heavy loads. Later, after vainly attempting in 1621 and 1629 to restrict loads to a ton by proclamation alone, the government resorted to subtler but equally ineffectual means of trying to fit the traffic to the roads. In the Highways Act of 1662 for example,

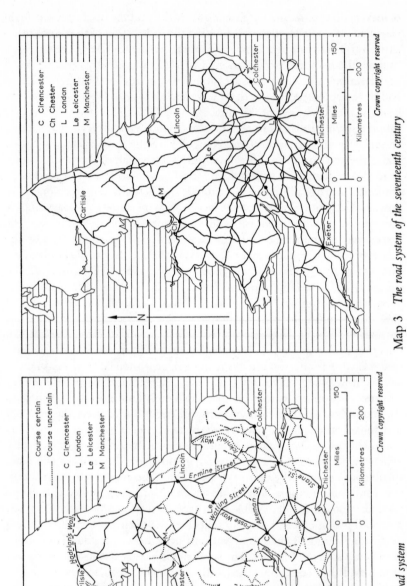

Map 3   The road system of the seventeenth century

Map 2   The Roman road system

wagons drawn by more than seven-horse teams or fitted with wheels less than four inches wide were prohibited. These measures failed as completely to halt the irresistible growth in road traffic as did others of the same period and kind which tried to put a straitjacket on London, and for very similar reasons.

But the year after the Highways Act another purely local one was passed in which, having lamented the failure of the attempt of 1555 to keep in good repair by the use of statute labour alone that part of the Great North Road which ran through Hertfordshire, Cambridgeshire, and Huntingdonshire, the local justices obtained powers to convert it into a toll-road and to use the tolls to increase the amount of repairs. Imposing a toll in order to defray the costs of road repairs was not new but there had been no royal grant of the right to levy *pavage* since the fourteenth century, and the only tolls for this kind of purpose were collected on certain bridges. It is quite clear from the first tolls imposed what traffic was bearing hardest on the road: each horse was charged a penny and each coach sixpence, but carts were charged eightpence and wagons a shilling; for each score of pigs the charge was twopence and for oxen and cattle fivepence, but for the same quantity of sheep 1s. 2d. This first turnpike act of 1663 was to remain in force for eleven years but it was largely beaten by the clay and was not immediately imitated beyond Hertfordshire; in any case its provisions were never properly applied and were easily evaded by road-users. The road itself was scarcely altered from its original dangerous and impassable condition. But the possibilities of such measures had been demonstrated, and in time the device was used elsewhere, first on the ancient road between Colchester and London in 1695 and in four other instances in Essex, Norfolk, Sussex and Gloucestershire before the turn of the century. In all of them the administration of the roads was left to the Justices themselves.

Within ten years the old practice of vesting authority for such turnpikes in the local Justices was being abandoned in favour of one creating independent bodies of trustees, formed for the most part of local men. The first of these were established by two private acts in 1706 to govern separate stretches of the Holyhead road, one between Hockliffe in Bedfordshire and Stony Stratford in Buckinghamshire, the other between Old Stratford and Dunchurch in Warwickshire. Not infrequently, Justices were numbered among the trustees but within a few years the administration of the toll-roads was completely divorced from that of the other local roads, including the superintendence of the statute labour which had to be performed on the new roads as on the old, and the authority of the Quarter Sessions was limited to imposing penalties for infringements of the general highway acts. By 1720 the system was beginning to be used so widely that legislation assumed the form of public, as distinct from the earlier private, acts. Originally created for a term of 21 years, the trusts were normally given longer life by further legislation; their powers of raising capital on the security of the tolls were usually left unrestricted and their ways of using it were not

c

prescribed; nor were they directed how to appoint their own toll-gatherers or whether or not to auction the proceeds of their toll-gates to tenants. All the early acts applied to short lengths of road, and the scope given to the trustees to administer them well or badly, or to put money in their own pockets while doing so, were clearly not insignificant even in an age full of such opportunities. This was the pattern of turnpike administration right through the period in which the roads were made to bear much of the weight which the new industrial system was presently to thrust upon them, and it was not changed until the very eve of the railway age. All the same, by making wear and tear or obstruction on the toll-roads the basis of a cash contract between the users and the administrators of such roads, the invention of the turnpike trust made it possible for the roads to be equipped to handle the traffic which was beginning to come on to them. Whether or not the opportunity was taken is a matter for another chapter.

The kind of traffic using the roads at the beginning of the eighteenth century depended partly on the condition of their surface and partly on the economic and social development of the regions they served. Sometimes the two factors worked together, as on the terrible clays around London, which a wet season could turn into a quagmire thick enough to hold fast a troop of horse or a king's coach; and land which was justified in being worked intensively often yielded few flints and other materials for good road metal. One of the most striking features of English roads at the beginning of the eighteenth century beyond thirty miles from London was the number which were unenclosed by hedges or fences. These roads were sometimes little more than uncertain tracks that could be varied or lost altogether without difficulty. It was partly for this reason that, apart from one remarkable map of the road system in the fourteenth century and a few guidebooks to London which appeared in the second half of the seventeenth century, road maps as such scarcely yet existed in sufficient detail and compactness to make travel on any but the most frequented highways at all certain. John Norden's *An Intended Guide for English Travellers*, which had first appeared in 1625 and been re-issued several times, was one of the earliest roadbooks, but John Ogilby's more accurate maps, though published separately from their descriptive matter in 1675, were too large to be easily consulted on the road.

There were few who travelled for pleasure, but the growth of commerce and the needs of public administration, not to mention military operations, increased the volume of travel very considerably in the seventeenth century. Most of it was done on horseback at speeds of around thirty miles a day, though it was often possible to go two or three times as fast if need be. Horses could be hired from postmasters on the main roads since the sixteenth century. In 1635 four regular mail services were established between London, Oxford, Bristol, Colchester, and Norwich. A supplementary postal service was also available along some of the crossroads. The lowest letter-rate was 2*d*. for distances up to 80 miles, the highest 8*d*. for, say, the five day journey to Edinburgh.

It was about this date that the stage-coach began to supersede the wains or long wagons which had served as long-distance transport for rich and poor passengers alike since the middle of the preceding century and which were already being used on regular scheduled journeys between London and the provinces. These wagons, drawn by teams of six or more horses at two or three miles an hour, were usually capable of carrying around twenty passengers in addition to miscellaneous goods. To judge by John Taylor's remarkable little guide to these services, *Carriers Cosmography*, which was published in 1637, there were over two hundred carriers, wagoners and others who were regularly embarking passengers, letters and goods at the London inns for all parts of England; by the last quarter of the century their numbers had grown by at least half as much again, and they were not entirely superseded until the railways arrived. Wool-merchants and others were also operating their own fleets of wagons between provincial collecting centres and London, but they also depended very much on pack animals. Packhorses or mules were usually saddled with wicker panniers or bales and tethered together in a single file, sometimes forty or fifty together.

By 1700 such pack-trains were being used by common carriers wherever roads were too bad or loads too light for wagons, and by this time there was also coming into being, mostly in the north, the wholesale travelling merchant who supplied retailers with cloth and other goods from the stock carried in his pack-train. Chapmen were also on the move in large numbers, men scarcely distinguishable at their most affluent from the travelling merchants but sometimes counting for little more than hawkers. The packhorse persisted much longer in the north of the country, where the roads were poorer, than it did in the south, thanks perhaps to the widespread use of stone causeways just wide enough for a single beast but inadequate for wagons. Private carriages had also been in use since the middle of the sixteenth century, but the stage-coach was becoming of much more general importance, especially after 1662, when the drivers of hackney-coaches—four-seaters which had been giving a kind of taxi service in London since about 1625—dispersed to the nearby towns in order to escape the licensing system that had been introduced to limit their numbers in London. By the last quarter of the century virtually every town within 25 miles of London had coach services to and from it; there were three coaches a week to York and Newcastle, Chester and Kendal, Exeter and Plymouth; a one-day "flying coach" to Oxford had also been inaugurated in 1669, though even this crack performance was relaxed to two days during the winter. Each road had its own features and it is impossible to generalize very much. Fifty years after the Oxford coach had first flitted the sixty odd miles to London in 13 hours Defoe watched a perfectly sane old woman drawn in her carriage to church near Lewes in Sussex by six oxen because horses could not make any headway in the mud.

3   River improvement

If, as Defoe supposed, the cost of reinstating the roads of England in their
Roman condition was beyond the means of his generation, capital could
still be used to the same end but with much greater profit on inland waterways. There were few rivers in England which were naturally navigable
over much of their course before the seventeenth century. Almost everywhere they tended to be cluttered up by mills and fish-garths or inter-
sected by weirs—sometimes up to ten feet high—which impeded the passage of barges or boats. Some of them were also barred by toll-gatherers or
infested by river-pirates, both of whom took their own income from the
river trade. The Thames was a watercourse rather than a properly navigable river above Richmond throughout the Middle Ages, and it was not
until the early seventeenth century that a clear passage was regularly open
as high as Oxford. The Trent was obstructed by shifting gravel shoals above
Burton, and even in a wet season was not regularly open for river traffic
above this point until well into the eighteenth century. Even the Severn,
whose tidal reaches were so effectively scoured by the Bristol Channel, and
whose upper waters were naturally navigable to Bewdley and by small
craft as high as Shrewsbury, had probably not been entirely rid of its pre-
dators by 1700. Bewdley watermen had tried to reinforce their natural
hold on the trade of the upper Severn in the fifteenth century by acts of
virtual piracy, and armed scuffles sometimes took place between river
users in different towns lower down when vital interests seemed threatened.
Despite the river's legal immunity from tolls there was no continuous
towpath between Gloucester and Shrewsbury before the beginning of the
nineteenth century; and there had been since the sixteenth century, when
the practice was legally permitted, numerous points at which a toll was
levied for the use of a tow-path.

It was in the course of the seventeenth and early eighteenth centuries
that interest in the improvement of English rivers first became widespread,
but it was by no means the period in which such ideas were first carried
into effect. It is more than probable that the little canal known as the Fossdyke, which connected the Trent and the Witham at Lincoln, was cut for
drainage and even navigation in Roman times—there are grounds for thinking that the Witham was already navigable over its whole course from
Boston; and there is also the possibility that the Romans had cut a canal,
the Cardyke, between the Nene at Peterborough and the Witham just below
Lincoln. The Fossdyke was reopened early in the twelfth century and this
led to a vigorous trade centred on the town of Torksey where it joined the
Trent, but the channel silted up some time in the late Middle Ages. The
River Itchen, which emptied into Southampton Water, was also made
navigable to Alresford by the Bishop of Winchester very early in the
thirteenth century.

There had also been the building of the first true canal of modern times in the British Isles, a purely artificial lateral cut of deadwater which was dug out in 1564–6 between Topsham and Exeter, after vain attempts had been made to improve the main stream of the Exe between these two points. The Exeter lighter canal was of far-reaching significance, not for the city it served but for the whole future development of English waterways. Technically, Exeter itself became once more a seaport, though this opportunity was insecurely grasped at the time because the channel was made too shallow and the city quay too small, and Topsham remained the main disembarkation point for Exeter; the cut became much more useful commercially a hundred years later when the channel was deepened and extended, and seaborne cargoes no longer needed to be handled twice. But, more important, this was almost certainly the first occasion that the continental pound-lock was brought into use in England. This was an invention of hardly less importance for economic development than the later use of steam power.

Hitherto, the relatively inefficient flashlock, a device by which an operator could release a pent-up flood (a "flash" or "stanch") of water and float a boat, or even a dozen at a time, over shallows, had been the only means of dealing with changes of water-level. It could equally well be used for boats going upstream as down, though against the current it was usually necessary to use winches. Its drawback was that it was a method which used a scarce resource prodigally, and it also involved long delays: as much as a couple of hours while the river was resuming its normal level after a "flash", or two to three days if grinding was in progress at the mill. The device was basically a technical compromise between the conflicting demands of boatmen and millers and was used extensively. There had been flashlocks on the Thames, for example, since the thirteenth century, and by 1585 there were 23 of them in existence on the 62-mile stretch between Maidenhead and Oxford, all but four of which were in the weirs of mills; many of them, incidentally, were still in place in the middle of the eighteenth century.

The technical significance of the pound-lock which eventually completely replaced it in England was that, by raising or lowering the water level within an enclosed chamber, which was its essential characteristic, an artificial waterway could overcome a gradient in the ground it was crossing, and it could also make an easy entrance on to tidal water. The efficiency of the pound-lock had already been increased by the highly important invention —attributed to Leonardo da Vinci—of the double mitre-gate, which replaced the inconvenient portcullis type. The pound-lock did not have all the technical advantages: for example, the water in it was liable to freeze up more quickly in winter and to thaw more slowly than it did in the current of the stream; and it also tended to require extensive dredging operations. But the pound-lock had the immense advantage of neutralizing the unending struggles of different river-men for command over particular stretches of the stream. The collisions of interests of river traders and riverside communities occurred on the great rivers as on the small because undredged and uncanalized streams seldom contained enough water to give full draught to large river craft as well as the power to turn water-wheels, or to keep undisturbed adequate catchments for fish. The pound-lock was the means of ending this tension on terms of immense potential advantage not only for the river-traders but for all who stood to benefit by a fall in the cost of inland transport.

Before the seventeenth century the improvement of rivers by the removal of obstacles placed in the stream by local communities in their own interests, or by shoring up river-banks, or by deepening channels which had silted up, was a spasmodic and ineffectual process. For a time it was not difficult for sheer parochialism to thwart any scheme which did not yield an obvious and immediate benefit locally, but the demands of traders could in the end usually be given the appearance of serving more desirable national interests, and petty sovereignties were gradually pared away. In this way the rivers were gradually fitted to carry a larger and less localized trade. In some places water which had been made navigable supplemented the existing over-land routes, in others it superseded them.

The process had really begun with a half-hearted attempt to make the Kentish Stour navigable as high as Canterbury very early in the sixteenth century, but the scheme was long delayed and ineptly done. Entirely different was the improvement of the Lea—already the subject of legis-lation early in the fifteenth century—between London and Ware in the years 1571 to 1581, when the channel of the stream was widened, cleared of obstructions, and sealed off by sluices. It included at least one pound-lock, at Waltham Abbey, with both upper and lower mitre-gates, and this in-novation became typical of so much subsequent improvement in other places. By 1635 three such locks were in existence on the Thames, at Iffley, Sandford, and Abingdon, and they were also installed on the Warwick-shire Avon when it was improved in the next few years. When the Wey was made navigable by extensive lateral cuts in 1651-3 ten pound-locks were used to step down the water level 86 feet in the fifteen miles from Guildford to Weybridge. (*See Map 10 for the location of all river improvements*, pp. 104-5.)

River improvement in the opening decades of the seventeenth century was advanced very tentatively by the Commissions of Sewers—royal com-missions with local personnel—who were trying to use their authority in clearing rivers that had become cluttered up. Their success depended in the last resort on the co-operation of the riparian owners to whom the non-tidal stretches of rivers severally belonged, and these were seldom won over. Although there were cases in which the Commissions had their way right into the eighteenth century, it was already clear by 1650 that they were neither the appropriate bodies nor did they have adequate legal powers to make the rivers navigable. Navigation schemes could not be undertaken without disturbing the river-banks, and if (as was usually the case) lateral cuts had to be made across adjoining land, the interference with private property was even more extensive. All this required specific authority from parliament, or directly from the Crown.

Non-parliamentary developments were comparatively unimportant. Except for an isolated instance referring to the Warwickshire Avon in 1619, letters patent granted to private individuals for river improvement—of the Great Ouse, Lark, Tone, Stour, and Soar—were concentrated in the years 1634–8. When river improvement was next in spate, following the Restoration, authority was derived from parliamentary legislation. In the four years 1662–5 more than a dozen navigations were authorized. The most important to be carried out were for some of the smaller rivers in the Severn basin (the Wiltshire Avon, Stour, Salwarpe, Wye, and Lugg), and for two falling into the Wash (the Welland and Great Ouse); among the others were the Itchen and the Mole. This burst of legislation was partly a reaction to long inactivity and partly a welcome to the return of peace at home and abroad, but it was probably also a response to a number of other influences. There had been some vigorous and imaginative pamphleteering thirty years before which had raised the scent of opportunity, and now others were beginning to visualize the possibilities of a systematic interconnection between the river systems of the compact island of Britain. There was also the sustained example of continental engineers. Above all, there was the expansion of the demand for agricultural products, especially grain.

More legislation followed in the 1670s touching the Fal, Wey, Witham, Waveney and the Bedfordshire Ouse, but in 1697–1700—that brief interval of peace in the long period of war from 1689 to 1713, at a time when capital was cheap—there was another much more concentrated round of parliamentary activity concerning a dozen more river schemes. Now, almost for the first time, there were some bills for rivers further north, the Aire and Calder, the Trent, the Dee, while two others for the Derwent and the Don did not pass into law; in the south, the Yare, Tone, Lark, and Bristol Avon all had successful schemes. By now the total mileage of navigable waterways which had been sanctioned by one means or another had risen to close on a thousand. Another interval passed and the last big batch of navigation schemes came in the years 1719 to 1721, when money was once again cheap, and parliament, as much infected by the speculative fever of joint-stock promotions which was being bred in the South Sea Bubble as the investing classes themselves, was ready to authorize almost anything. Again, some of the most important schemes were in the north: the Douglas, Derwent, Idle, Irwell, Mersey, Weaver, Dane, and Eden. There were still some important navigations to come—the Don and the Stroudwater, for instance—and several much smaller schemes, but the scope for river improvement on its own was by now almost played out, and to provide more navigable water meant the building of entirely man-made waterways in the form of canals. In general, it was not until this was done and the further possibilities of inland waterways opened up that the rivers were subject to any further substantial improvement to fit them better into the canal system.

Though legislation spaced itself out into these three major bursts of improvement, the intervening periods were not years of inactivity. Obtaining an act of parliament for this purpose was seldom less protracted than the execution of the works it authorized, and normally very much longer. Local opposition had first to be overcome and financial and engineering difficulties had ultimately to be met. Thus the first proposal to make the Derwent navigable for the export of North Derbyshire lead had come direct from the king to the burgesses of Derby as early as 1638. Three bills were laid before parliament among the other promotions of the 1660s and 1670s, and another three in the next round of improvements at the turn of the century, but it was not until the third instalment of successful navigation schemes that an act was passed in 1719 and the works carried out in the two years that followed. Nottingham, then virtually the head of the navigable stretch of the Trent, was also at the head of the opposing forces to the Derwent navigation, as it was indeed of those against the navigation of the Trent itself. As early as 1675 its Corporation had engaged counsel to thwart any such scheme, and although acts were obtained despite this in 1699 and 1714 there was still no clear passage to Burton for the next 70 years. Similarly, it took a quarter of a century for Doncaster to get the powers it obtained in 1727 to open up the Don, and another 12 years before the channel was satisfactorily scoured; the Weaver was the subject of nine bills between 1663 and 1721 and its navigation took another eleven years to accomplish; the Stroudwater required four acts and three-quarters of a century before its gestation came to an end in 1776.

The driving force behind a number of the early navigation schemes was clearly the aim of catering, either directly or indirectly, for the profitable trade of provisioning the capital. But as time went on it is clear that the increasing traffic in foodstuffs was simply one of the side-effects of improvements aimed at cheapening the collection and distribution of industrial raw materials and manufactured goods. Whatever the precise intention of their promoters, river navigations could scarcely help providing joint services. To the extent that they lowered freight charges they were bound to influence the prices of any bulky goods, even the cheapest, which would not deteriorate on protracted journeys, and most agricultural products that entered trade at all came into that category. The gains in the mechanical efficiency of water transport were already recognized as impressive, for whereas a packhorse could carry no more than about $2\frac{1}{2}$ cwt, a single horse could tow up to 30 tons in ordinary conditions on an improved river. By the early eighteenth century it had become possible to move bulk cargoes which involved long journeys for as little as a penny per ton-mile on the improved rivers: the average was probably nearer $2\frac{1}{2}d$. but by road the figure was around a shilling. Even allowing for the more direct routes usually taken by roads, the relative cost of water transport was certainly no more than half that for land carriage. What the effect of such low rates actually was on the volume of water-borne agricultural products from one period to the next it is not possible to say in precise terms, though there are some statistical scraps of information which do suggest that in particular areas improved rivers were of the greatest importance for this reason alone. In one year at the end of the seventeenth century, for example, the Lea bore nearly 4,000 tons of malt from Ware to London, and even the great river system which fell into the Humber—which was so much more important for another kind of traffic—handled each year thousands of tons of wheat, oats, barley, malt, cheese, timber, and groceries of all kinds.

The major reason for the indefatigable efforts of the promoters of navigation schemes, especially the later ones, was to secure or to distribute supplies of coal, wool, iron, lead, timber, and cloth. Rivers which carried agricultural products downstream were used to carry industrial raw materials and products upstream. But easily the most important countervailing commodity in this two-way traffic was coal, and it was the cheap movement of coal, either as an industrial or as a domestic fuel, which was deliberately sought above all. The Aire and Calder, the Don, the Weaver, and the Mersey were made navigable primarily in the interests of industries in which coal was a crucial factor. It is generally true to say that coal was the dominant influence on the development of the whole programme of inland waterways, of the rivers as well as the canals.

The promoters of navigations like these, whether acting corporately or individually, were the trading class in the towns most directly affected. This was the class in whose hands capital was beginning to accumulate fastest, and their own business interests naturally dictated the forms in which it should be used. The sums invested in navigation schemes were small and generally confined to the locality in which they were raised. Perhaps these are the reasons why they were on the whole well spent, for although the money subscribed did not always get squarely applied to the purposes intended, there seems to have been no flagrant case of financial irregularity. This was remarkable at a time when the forms of business undertaking were largely experimental and distinctions between private and public enterprise were not always easy to draw. Usually, the Act named the undertakers along with the commissioners (who were local men of property having a generally supervisory function for the scheme), but the appointment of an undertaker or undertakers was sometimes left to the commissioners themselves. Some were joint-stock companies possessing limited liability, others partnerships or individual undertakings: there was no standard practice.

One of the most remarkable features of river improvement was that, although the engineering problems involved were in some respects more formidable than most of those raised in the cutting of canals, they were first met by men who had had no training in hydraulics. The profession of civil engineer did not yet exist, and from one point of view it might be said that river improvement helped to create one. Some of these pioneers were simply landed gentlemen, like Arnold Spencer who carried out the navigation of the Great Ouse from St Ives to St Neots in 1618, or William Sandys who expended £20,000 on making some 32 miles of the Warwickshire Avon navigable in 1636–9, or Sir Richard Weston, the noted agriculturist, who "improved" the Wey; among the others were an ironmaster and a tanner. Towards the end of the century experience of hydraulics was accumulating: John Hadley, for example, the engineer for the Aire and Calder navigation, was already very experienced in designing and building waterworks; and George Sorocold, the engineer for the Derwent navigation, had not only been even more widely engaged in waterworks in London and the provinces, but had already designed the first wet dock in England and the great water-wheel that drove the machinery in Sir Thomas Lombe's silk mill at Derby, the first successful power factory in the country.

It does not appear that there was any set pattern in the organization of the carrying trade itself. The undertakers of river navigations were not legally forbidden to become common carriers, but the opportunity was little used and the undertakers mostly relied on the tolls (statutorily fixed at various maxima) which were collected on the operators' boats. The same division of the work between independent carriers and merchants carrying their own goods that had already occurred on the roads, and was to become one of the salient characteristics of the organization of modern transport, seems to have come into operation on the rivers by the early eighteenth century. The boats used were mostly small, square-rigged, open sailing barges which probably depended more on teams of "halers" or of horses on the towpath and on oars and poles aboard than they did on a favourable breeze. On the Severn and the Thames the barges were much bigger, more elaborately rigged, and capable of carrying up to about 80 tons; the Thames grain barges were the largest in use and some carried as much as a hundred tons or more. Boats on this scale brought large economies in operating costs, especially in comparison with land carriage, even though they did little to accelerate the speed at which cargoes were moved. At the end of the seventeenth century it was said that it was possible to send 300 miles for tenpence on the Thames goods which would have cost three shillings for the thirty miles overland from Hitchin to London. There were, it is true, some exorbitant charges on the rivers and they were naturally higher on the upper than they were on the lower reaches of a particular river, but freight rates were no more than half of those for land carriage and frequently a very much smaller fraction still, perhaps even a tenth in some places. It was their capacity to cheapen the cost of transporting goods which were in elastic demand, particularly coal and other industrial raw materials, which was of paramount significance in these navigation schemes. They demonstrated the possibilities that the canals were to realize even more fully, and in the largest sense of the word they prepared the way for them.

4   Seaborne trade, ports and shipping

All rivers lead to the sea and it was natural that the English should have used it so much in their commerce. By the beginning of the eighteenth century they had become one of the principal maritime nations in Europe, possessed not only of a large coasting trade but of well-established connections in the North Atlantic, the Mediterranean, the Baltic and the North Sea. Before the second half of the sixteenth century the principal seafaring nations had been Spain and, to a lesser degree, the Low Countries. It was chiefly under the combined stimulus of the Newfoundland cod fisheries and the trade which developed in the period that followed that the English put to sea in any considerable numbers. It was this, too, which helped so much in the schooling of English sailors, and when the commercial opportunity was presented of assuming the rôle vacated by the southern Netherlanders (following the sack of Antwerp and the closing of the Scheldt in the last quarter of the century) English merchants could seize it readily. By the beginning of the seventeenth century English sailors were able to challenge even the Dutch, both in northern waters and in pioneering new trade routes into the Levant and round the Cape of Good Hope to India. Despite competition from the Dutch, and in one sense because of it, the English merchant fleet grew rapidly almost to the end of the seventeenth century: in three successive wars against them between 1652 and 1674 it was very substantially enlarged by the taking of Dutch prizes, and the English carrying trade, including in particular that between England and her colonies, was reserved for native ships by a policy of commercial protection. It was in the timber trade with the Baltic and in the sugar and tobacco trade with the West Indies and the southern American colonies that much the greater part of the increase in shipping in the thirty years after 1660 took place.

This growth was not continued, for in the long period of war with the French that now followed from 1689 to 1713 the English merchant shipping routes were much more directly threatened than they had ever been by the Dutch, and even the coasting trade was harried considerably by privateers. The growth of overseas trade slackened and the merchant shipping afloat at the end of the period was probably no greater than it had been at the beginning. By the end of the wars the very long period of growth of the east coast coal trade had also come to an end. The most accessible seams had now been worked out and coal had to be dug from deeper pits and hauled greater distances to the staithes on Tyneside; much of the coal required by the new industries of the Midlands and the North was beginning to come from local fields and fed to them by the improved rivers; and the growth of demand in London itself temporarily abated with the rise in coal prices that accompanied the exhaustion of the riverside seams. For these various reasons it might be said that in the second and third decades of the eighteenth century the shipping industry was marking time. This is not to say that the whole of English commerce was in a stagnant condition, though the Continental wars and confusions of the period did create special difficulties in foreign trade. It is also important to notice that the experience of particular ports—Whitehaven's, for instance, which depended on trade with Ireland—ran counter to the general tendency. The situation simply was that the initial phase of ebullient commercial growth had ended and it was not until the second half of the century that another was to open.

That new phase of commercial expansion was based on a different distribution of trade among the various ports of Britain, and it might therefore be added that a commercial phase of another kind had also by now closed. Since the Middle Ages London had been easily the greatest port in the kingdom. In Elizabethan times it was already handling something approaching three-quarters of the country's foreign trade, and even a thriving medieval port like Southampton or Boston could fall into decay in the course of a single generation or so as a result of this concentration of commercial power. Even King's Lynn was gradually losing its place. The trade of London was already greater than that of all other ports put together, and this state of affairs continued well into the eighteenth century. Indeed, there was a period late in the seventeenth century, as we have already seen, when London was becoming a veritable commercial vortex, sucking in an increasing share of the available trade. By 1700 London's share in the total commerce of England and Wales had grown to 69 per cent of home-produced goods, 80 per cent of imports, and 86 per cent of re-exports, but in each case there was subsequently a long steady decline in these proportions as the industrial development of the North and Midlands began to swing the commercial centre of gravity another way. Its geographical position, the improved pilotage of its tricky estuary following the establishment of Trinity House in 1513, and the existence in London of easily the largest centre of consumption in the country, all helped to give a metropolitan axis to English commerce. Moreover, London had already developed substantial port facilities which could be used by any trade not having a natural centre: wool in particular (still accounting for 57 per cent of home-produced exports in 1700) was just such a case.

It had not been until very late in the seventeenth century that the commercial pre-eminence of London had in any sense been mitigated by the rise of other ports, but it was then that the port of Bristol rose to a position of real maritime importance. This was partly based on a long-standing trade with Ireland which, apart from the coasting trade, still accounted for about a third of its outgoing vessels. To a considerable extent the rise of Bristol may be attributed to its being the natural outlet for the rapidly developing industrial hinterland of the Severn valley, but increasingly its prosperity was also to be explained in the context of a trade in rum, sugar, tobacco, and slaves with West Africa, the West Indies, and the English colonies of North America. By 1700 the volume of shipping entering Bristol from the West Indies was approaching three times that of 30 years before, and since

1696, when the monopolistic hold which London had tried to assert over the African slave trade was broken, Bristol merchants had been free to participate in this highly lucrative, if risky, trade. This was also an opportunity for Liverpool, which only as recently as 1666 had emerged from the status of a mere creek in the port of Chester. The growth of the port was so rapid that when Celia Fiennes visited it in 1700 her view of it was that "it's a very rich trading town . . . London in miniature". Compared with Bristol, Liverpool's Irish trade accounted in 1717 for a much larger number of outgoing vessels, and this also occupied a much larger proportion of the total shipping which it engaged in overseas trade. Of 402 ships of all sizes trading overseas from Liverpool in that year, 284 were bound for Ireland and the Isle of Man and only 32 for North America, 21 for the West Indies, 16 (allegedly) for Madeira, and most of the rest were bound for European ports, particularly in the Netherlands; in terms of tonnage the Irish trade took about half. From Bristol in the same year some 235 ships divided themselves evenly between the West Indies, North America, and Europe, while eight were bound direct for Africa.

Each of these ports was also important in different degrees in the coasting trade. The functions of coastal and oceanic shipping were closely linked, for the former helped to make up the shipments of the latter and were also involved in the distribution of imports from overseas. For this reason, apart from some obvious differences in the shipping of corn and coal, the provincial trade differed from the metropolitan in degree rather than in kind. In none of the smaller ports were these branches of the shipping industry entirely divorced from each other and each of the 21 headports of England were at the beginning of the eighteenth century engaged in some foreign trade, the direction of which was largely determined by their respective geographical positions. For example, some of the south-western ports which had originally been heavily involved in North Atlantic fishing were around 1700 trading with Ireland and the North American colonies; and the east-coast ports traded with northwest Europe and Scandinavia. The significance of these shipments coastwise and abroad was not normally in their volume but in the immense scope they gave for the economic development of the hinterlands of the ports in which they were handled.

One element which was significant in terms both of volume and economic potential was the coal trade, which accounted for a very high proportion of the tonnage registered in the outports: in 1701 four out of the ten leading provincial ports were primarily coal ports or collier-owning ports. By this time there were some 1,400 ships engaged in the coal trade—more than three times the number there had been early in the seventeenth century —and these were mostly colliers of 300 or 400 tons. Not surprisingly, the tonnage of colliers represented over a third of all English shipping by 1695. Newcastle accounted for most of the home trade in coal, though it was overtaken by Sunderland and Whitehaven in the export trade during the eighteenth century. The colliers themselves were owned by ports all along the coast but especially by Whitby and Scarborough, where large numbers of them had been built.

By the closing years of the seventeenth century the pressure of this trade round the English coast and into foreign parts had begun to put a strain on existing port facilities which called for extensive improvements. Schemes for the improvement of harbours by the setting up of new authorities or by the rebuilding or extension of piers and quays were set going on an unprecedented scale between 1697 and 1719 in Bridlington, Whitby, Sunderland, Grimsby, Yarmouth, Whitehaven, Bristol, Minehead, Watchet and Dover. There were also some quite new developments, in particular the building of wet docks; there were already several dry docks in the port of London. The very first of the wet docks, the Brunswick Dock, a small area of 1½ acres designed for the fitting out of vessels after launching, had been built in 1661 at Blackwall. The second, the Howland Great Wet Dock, covering 10 acres, was opened in 1700 and remained the largest dock in the port for a hundred years. As with the first, it was probably not intended to handle cargo. Indeed, it was sited at Rotherhithe on the opposite side of the river to the legal quays and may have been intended to take government contracts from the nearby Admiralty dockyard at Deptford. Between 1701 and 1717 three other wet docks were opened, at Liverpool (which was the first to be publicly-owned), Bristol, and Portsmouth.

A word needs to be said here about some important changes in design and operation of English merchant ships which were taking place at the end of the seventeenth century. Except for more elaborate rigging and increased size the technology of English shipping had changed little since the disappearance from general use of the single-masted square-rigged ship which had sailed European waters and the Atlantic before 1500. It had been replaced in the course of the sixteenth century by three- and four-masted vessels in which the keel was lengthened from less than twice, to three times the beam. Such vessels, which could be handled with considerably more dexterity than the old round ships, had suited merchants well for they were capable of carrying bulkier cargoes and more cannon, two distinct commercial assets on the longer voyages which English ships were now undertaking to the Levant and to India. The average size of ocean-going ships was about 200 tons but much bigger vessels were already being built in English yards. The tradition of building defensible ships began to die out in the seventeenth century. Adequate defence meant heavy manning but by the second half of the seventeenth century the Dutch had given a convincing demonstration of the way to build lighter, bulk-cargo ships. These met very well the needs of the trade they pursued in North European waters, where they could afford to reduce armament to an insignificant amount. These flyboats required little more than half the crew which English ships of comparable tonnage needed, and inevitably this meant a substantial reduction in operating costs. The changes which were occurring in the English merchant fleet from the third quarter of the seventeenth century had first been induced as a result of taking so many Dutch fly-boats as prizes of war, but by the close of the century some English ship-wrights were beginning to build their own versions of them. There seem to be good reasons for believing that the ship-building ports in which these new ideas were being put into practice were on the northeast coast, and this implied the decline of some of the traditional ship-building ports like Ipswich and Shoreham which Defoe had noticed being overtaken. But the change in technique was important for a more significant reason: in helping to make English sea transport cheaper it helped to maintain an important element in the expansion of the whole economy.

2

Transport and the industrial revolution (1)

The economic expansion of Britain, for which all the transport improvements of the sixteenth and seventeenth centuries had helped to make her ready, did not become both marked and sustained before the very end of the eighteenth century. Before then, the productive gains of one generation tended to be smothered by the setbacks of the next, or to be so imperceptible that they left too little evidence for historians to assess. The most recent spurt had come in the 1740s. So far as the evidence goes, it is probable that the growth in total output of the economy per head of the population had never averaged more than 3 per cent for a whole decade together before that time. Economic growth, as we have come to know it today, just did not exist. In the mid-1740s this scarcely noticeable growth in output more than doubled itself, then briefly flattened out, before rising, this time significantly, in the last twenty years of the century.

The population of the country was growing rapidly at the same time, and the demands for food, clothing, shelter, and the means of locomotion to which these gave rise played a crucial role in bringing economic expansion about. Numbers had grown little during the first half of the century and probably did not exceed 7½ millions around 1750, but within thirty years another 2 millions had been added. This growth in the population did not slacken but in the last two decades of the eighteenth century the expansion of production outstripped it so fast that output per head rose by something like 9 per cent per decade. By 1801 the population of Great Britain was approximately 11 millions and was now growing so fast that it had risen about half as much again by 1831.

By the beginning of the nineteenth century these trends in production, the new methods used to attain them, and the adjustment of society to new patterns in sharing the gains and losses which they entailed, had all gone so far that it became, and still is, feasible to speak of an industrial revolution as taking place. The economy could be said to be displaying for the first time that capacity for self-sustaining growth which subsequently

D

became the normal characteristic of all industrialized countries. The most tangible evidence of this was to be seen on the ground, though not everywhere, in the new appearance of the enclosed countryside, in the growth of the towns, in the multiplication of powered workshops of many kinds, and in the thin uneven web of new roads and winding canals. These showed, more conclusively than anything, a capacity for putting resources towards building up future production that was entirely new in its range and amount. At the beginning of the eighteenth century the proportion of the national income which had been available for new investment had not exceeded 5 per cent at any time; in the last two decades of the century this proportion was lifted to 8 per cent or more, where it remained more or less until the coming of the railways thirty years later.

These few figures are, of course, some of the benchmarks of the economic historian and would not have been recognized, nor indeed would they have been discoverable, at the time. They mark in the simplest and most general way the level of economic achievement in Britain during the Industrial Revolution. Yet it ought to be recognized that they tend to conceal the fact that the approach to industrialism in Britain was in reality a process of considerable complexity and length. The changes that occurred in the productive functions of society were the products of a vast concatenation of circumstances that lie far beyond the scope of this book. Framed in too simple and dramatic a setting the significance of the invention of new ways of transporting men and materials to accomplish these ends, which are the subject of this and the next chapter, are liable to be misunderstood. The truth of the matter is that the transformation of Britain from an underdeveloped to an industrialized country was a very protracted process, which was neither begun nor completed in the eighteenth century, nor yet by the time the railways came. It is important to remember that the improvements to the roads and inland waterways that we shall be discussing in these two chapters were part, in some ways perhaps the most important part, of the build-up of the general facilities of the economy—what economists call its infrastructure—and are therefore to be regarded as a preparation for general economic advance.

Unfortunately, it is impossible to measure their contribution to it at all satisfactorily. Yet it can be recognized straightaway that all the most important changes in internal transport that we shall be discussing for the time being occurred *before* industrial advance became at all marked, certainly before the factory became the characteristic form of production. By the last quarter of the eighteenth century the main road network had been laid out and was in operation. During the last quarter of the century the main components of the canal system were being assembled. As we shall see, there was also some definite response to the changing demands of the economy for extensions to these systems at the turn of the century but their basic functions were performed as pre-requisites to economic advance, not as by-products of it. It may be as well to recognize at the same time that every innovation in transport did not necessarily make for economic advance. The application of steam-power to road transport early in the nineteenth century did not do so, for example. Nor can it be taken for granted that new forms of transport, whatever their costs of installation, not only covered them but justified the effort of doing so. It cannot even be assumed that the real costs of transport were always lowered by new techniques. Haphazard additions to an ill-conceived network of roads or canals could actually raise the real costs of making economic progress or frustrate all but the most draconian attempts at improving it. The most persistent tendency in the history of transport is creeping obsolescence. Hence the drama of the wholesale abandonment or drastic curtailment of one form of transport in favour of another.

1   Shipping, ports and foreign trade

Before we become immersed in the opening phase of this process by looking at the development of the roads and canals it is as well to take a little farther the account which was given at the end of the last chapter of the development of shipping and trade. We need not concern ourselves to any extent with one question to which economic historians have not yet given very satisfactory answers, namely the contribution which overseas trade made to the quickening of economic expansion at home. What must be recognized, however, is the way in which the concentration of the growth of foreign trade, both in time and place, produced a disproportionately large impact on particular ports and their hinterlands.

There were two periods in which overseas trade just about doubled in value in the course of the eighteenth century. The first came in the period 1735–60 and the second in 1785–1800, though both expansions were not based on the same markets and the same composition of exports and imports. What stood out in the first period was the trade with England's colonies, including Ireland, and the very wide range of manufactures that was called for, giving opportunities to shipping chiefly in the western outports, including those of small size. But in the second period the expansion of trade was based upon an altogether narrower range of commodities, over eight-tenths of the increase in the value of home-produced exports being accounted for by cotton, wool, copper, brass, and iron, of which the first two were overwhelmingly important. The repercussions of this expansion in key commodities on the feeder services in the industrial hinterlands of Liverpool, Hull, Glasgow, and London were correspondingly far-reaching and go a long way towards explaining the construction of the road and canal developments we shall be examining presently.

It was, of course, a two-way effect. There is an undeniably close correlation between improvement of the interior and growing volumes of trade in every port for which records exist during this period. The huge investment which presently took place in port improvement down to 1830 can properly be regarded as a lagged response not only to new commercial opportunities overseas but to the improvement in internal communications. It was derived also from a significant increase in re-exports in this second period and after it which reinforced the pressures building up very strongly in the largest ports, especially London, and these were augmented still more all round by the coasting trade.

The big problem facing most ports, large and small, before 1830 was how to manage bulk cargoes handled in ships which were increasing much more in number than in size. One notable advance which bore this out was the invention of the steamboat. In the last decade of the eighteenth century one or two people were already thinking of applying steam power to navigation and, quite soon after the turn of the century, some promising experiments were being conducted to propel ships by steam. The first steamer, the *Charlotte Dundas*, paddled along the Forth & Clyde Canal in 1802 towing two barges, and the earliest commercial steamship, the *Comet*, was sailing the Clyde seven years later, precipitating a little flurry of steamer competition in the Irish Channel after that. It was certainly a later generation of shipbuilders who made steampower feasible, not only technically but commercially, for ocean-going ships: the earliest ocean steamship company, the P. & O., was not formed till 1837. But by 1810–20 or so, steam navigation was adding greatly to traffic problems on the Thames as well as the Clyde as the new craft flitted about with an unfamiliar disdain for wind and tide.

There were no really dramatic technical advances in ship design until well into the nineteenth century. In the meantime, ships continued to be built of timber and had to rely on sails alone. Some exceptionally large ships, East Indiamen especially, were beginning to come out of the yards, but there was a strict limit of a few hundred tons at the most if vessels were to be handy and economical in carrying cargoes of many kinds into ports of every sort. The average size of British merchant ships increased only from 80 to 100 tons throughout the eighteenth century, and the average tonnage of British shipping engaged in the Atlantic trade was probably not more than 250. The most notable technical innovation of the late eighteenth century was copper sheathing of ships' bottoms, which protected them from damage by weeds, barnacles, and worms. There were also some successful attempts at building simple hulls in iron.

An expansion of trade without any corresponding increase in the capacity of the average cargo ship imposed severe problems on the ports. What was important almost everywhere was to find some way of increasing the area of water on which ships could ride without being grounded, for the relatively long periods in which they were being loaded or unloaded by laborious rope-hauling and back-bending methods. The answer to this problem was more wet docks and basins, whose acreage was doubled in the course of the big trade expansion in the last quarter of the eighteenth century. In the thirty years that followed, the boom in dock-building was of a different order of magnitude altogether as the dock areas that had existed in 1800 were enlarged to over 4,700 acres.

Apart from the standstill in ship technology at a time of rapid commercial expansion, this enormous enlargement may be explained by the nature of the cargoes that were being handled. It is customary to think of British eighteenth-century trade primarily in terms of an exotic colonial and oriental traffic which did not yield pride of place to more humdrum cargoes until Britain was well in the grip of industrialism, with its growth of mass consumer demand, in the nineteenth century. It is certainly true that sugar was easily the most valuable single import and engaged much shipping owing to the long distances that had to be covered; and there were some commodities, such as silk, which took up the merest fraction of such tonnage while adding quite disproportionately to the trade returns. The fact that an almost sensational leap occurred in the nineteenth century in the volume of mundane traffic—raw materials, foodstuffs, finished products, passengers—gives the impression that these kinds of traffic were of no consequence before that. This is not so. The demand for shipping space is a function of mass, not value, and the big job of the shipping industry even before the full advent of industrialism was to move by the most economical means the commonplace, heavy cargoes of coal and corn which had to be shipped around Britain's coasts in very large amounts, and to a somewhat less extent abroad, and to bring in the bulky awkward cargoes of Norwegian and Baltic softwood and iron.

The great majority of ships were thus engaged in carrying goods which were very cheap in relation to their weight: in the middle of the eighteenth century, for example, neither European timber nor English coal were valued much above one pound sterling per ton, as compared with, say, linen or woollen cloth which came within the range of £200–£1,000 per ton. Yet about half the volume of English imports and a third of exports was to be accounted for by timber and coal respectively. According to some estimates made by Professor Ralph Davis, probably four-fifths of all inward shipping tonnage in 1752-4 was engaged in carrying timber, iron, flax, hemp, pitch and tar from Northern Europe, wine and brandy from Southern Europe, and sugar, rice and timber from the Americas; the overwhelming demand for outward shipping space was for coal and corn to nearby Europe.

Just how much shipping there was in existence at various dates, how many individual ships there were and of what types, how they were distributed among the ports of Britain, and what voyages they made, are matters on which our knowledge is still very imperfect. Taken as a whole, it is probable that the volume of shipping using British ports remained fairly stationary during the greater part of the first half of the eighteenth century. The figures for coastal and foreign trade suggest that in the port of London, which was still handling at least as much traffic as all other ports combined, this volume was growing almost imperceptibly. This was in sharp contrast to London's own experience in the late seventeenth century, and it did not match at all the spurt which was being made by Liverpool and by Glasgow (mainly on account of its booming trade in sugar and tobacco) and, to a lesser extent, by Bristol. The principal ports engaged in the coastal coal trade, and the East Anglian grain ports, were also much busier than the aggregate shipping figures would suggest. Yarmouth, which had become the main outlet for fenland corn, thrived on the great trade which the export bounty steered abroad down to the 1760s, while Ipswich, which had traded with the Baltic and the Low Countries in the seventeenth century, watched its commerce being engrossed during the first half of the century by London and some of the other east-coast ports. In the southwest, the little ports that had been set humming by the West Country cloth trade before 1700 lost their commercial impetus as their main customers fell away after that date, while Bristol, not yet the loser to Liverpool in the transatlantic trade, was the hub of a great metropolitan and industrial region and its port a forest of masts.

Such changes were further complicated by war, which tended to move some trade away from London to provincial ports, while at the same time repatterning the country's overseas commerce. Some of these effects were short-lived but the whole commercial position of the country was being re-orientated permanently as her traditional markets on the Continent were being replaced in order of importance by those in the East, the West Indies, and North America.

To trace the impact of all these changes on the relative position of the country's ports from one phase of the operation to the next is not possible. The volume of traffic handled in foreign trade, both exports and imports, probably roughly quadrupled in the course of the eighteenth century, but no comparable figure can be offered for the coastal trade, and the statistics for shipping registrations in particular ports and the tonnage cleared in them are notoriously unreliable guides to the actual quantities shipped. The proportion of foreign shipping entering British ports is another complication for it varied quite sharply, and in the closing years of the century was sometimes over 40 per cent of the tonnage cleared. The most that can be said here is that the port of London accounted for about a third of all British tonnage afloat at the beginning of the century and almost two-fifths at its close, and that, in descending order of importance, the first three to come after it in 1700 were Bristol, Yarmouth and Liverpool, and in 1800 Liverpool, Newcastle, Hull and Sunderland; Bristol had by then fallen to eighth. It was in these ports that commercial congestion was most conspicuous and here, too, that some of the most important improvements to port facilities were made in the period down to 1830.

Bristol, the very toy of commercial circumstance in the eighteenth century, epitomizes some of these changes. Until the 1760s the vast multifarious trade of the wide Severn valley was irresistibly concentrated at that point, and it was also a natural focus, though not the major one, for both the Irish and the transatlantic trades. No doubt foreign and colonial mattered rather more than coastal trade in resuscitating Bristol and bringing it to the position of second port and city in the kingdom by 1700, but all were clearly at work in producing the congestion of traffic which put it in the van of port improvement, and it was their general collapse which forced the port into relative decline.

Access to the port up seven miles of the Avon was never convenient, for the river had a great tidal range (39 feet on spring tides) and was beset by sharp bends and a shallow stream at neap tides. The cost and delays of working shrouded ships through the gorge probably helped in the end, along with high port charges, to stifle traffic. The third wet dock in the country which was built there in 1712–17 was a wasting asset that had quickly become a base for privateers, then for whalers, before being abandoned completely after the 1750s owing to its inconvenient site. Continuous extensions to quays and moorings were much more valuable. Yet the problem of achieving a quicker turn-round in a congested river, which became very acute during the unevenly expansive years before the Seven Years' War, still dogged the port authorities right into the era of decline.

The desultory attempts that were made from 1758 to make the river itself into a wet dock (a small one had come into use in 1765) culminated, more in fear than in hope, in William Jessop's scheme of 1802 to dig a new course of over two miles for one stretch of the river. When this was finally done for an outlay of £600,000 over the next seven years Bristol possessed a fine floating harbour of 130 acres. To use it to capacity was another matter. Bristol could not make of this opportunity any more than she had been able to do of the general revivals of trade after 1753 and 1785. The floating harbour scheme had been repeatedly postponed by parsimony and timidity in the mercantile community, and now that it was ready trade winds and broad rivers mattered less than the location of the pace-setting industries and their canal links with other ports. Internal commerce had acquired a new centre of gravity. And it was the old rival, Liverpool, which Defoe had already described as "the Bristol of this part of England", that demonstrated this fact without any equivocation.

The Mersey was the only estuary of consequence between Milford Haven and the Clyde and though it was often fog-bound and a rough anchorage outside the ancient tidal basin, strong currents kept the channel well-scoured, and it was a comparatively easy matter to enlarge the capacity of Liverpool as a port. Steers' "Old Dock", which literally replaced the old pool and was an entirely different scheme from Sorocold's which had formed the basis for the 1709 Act, was brought into use by 1715; a dry dock was added in 1718, and a wooden pier in 1725. These were the earliest signs of the benefits wrung from the wars of 1689–1713 but even more of the rapid exploitation of Cheshire salt and the ending of the Africa Company's monopoly of slaving. Very soon Lancashire fustians also entered this trade and the North Atlantic triangle, which was the basis of Liverpool's roaring prosperity, had been completed. The trade with Ireland, which was for so long subject to all the frustrations of colonial commerce, grew appreciably with the relaxation of restrictions after 1780 and Liverpool was the chief gainer from this, too.

According to Edward Baines, the Lancashire historian, who based his view on the tonnage of vessels cleared, the increase in the commerce of Liverpool was four times that of the rest of the country from 1716 to the end of the century. It is certainly the case that from 1725 to 1830 the numbers of ships using the port and the acreage added to the docks rose roughly in step, a multiplication of eleven times, half of the increase coming before the 1770s and half after them. A new tidal basin was opened in 1743, the second wet dock (Salthouse) in 1753, and three more (George's, King's and Queen's) in 1771, 1788 and 1796; after the French wars the latter had to be extended, and the Prince's Dock, the largest of all, followed between 1811 and 1821. By this time the acreage of the whole dock area was 47, puny enough when compared with the sevenfold increase which was to ensue in the next sixty years, but as the result of a continuous accretion of one dock after another it was a phenomenon which was in every way exceptional in the eighteenth century. (*See Map 19*, p. 252.)

Some other ports were certainly enlarging their installations from time to time during this period. Hull, for example, which had just reached parity with Bristol in terms of the volume of overseas trade, built a wet dock (Queen's) of nearly ten acres in 1775–8, which was not supplemented till 1807–29, when two more were built covering 13 acres. In half-a-dozen other places where the handling of coal or corn demanded proper facilities and a safe sea passage piers, harbours, lighthouses, and numerous other installations were being made or extended. In Sunderland, for example, the establishment of the River Wear Commission in 1717 had been the prelude to a very lengthy programme of pier, harbour, and lighthouse construction which was continued into the nineteenth century; and at Ramsgate the idea of a haven for ships rounding the North Foreland in a storm was translated into a harbour and dry dock under great engineering difficulties that taxed even Smeaton between 1749 and 1791.

But this was not a period in which all the old out-ports were continuously forced to renovate themselves, nor were those that made the attempt always successful. Even Whitehaven, which under pressure from the Lowther's colliery workings was quintupling its coal-trade with Ireland in the course of the century, and had made some moves to handle it properly, did not respond until 1824–41 to Smeaton's proposal of 1768 to enlarge the harbour. The improvement of Tynemouth was not tackled seriously until after Rennie's report of 1813. At Shoreham, where a new harbour entrance was built in 1760–3, the work was so badly done that it needed renovating long before it was finally put in hand in 1816. When that had been done, it had to be done all over again in 1823, and yet again a few years later.

2   The port and streets of London

In many places the chief difficulty in the way of port improvement seems to have been lack of capital, but this was certainly not the case with the most striking of all cases of delayed improvement, that of London. The port of London, which occupied a river basin peculiarly favourable to the formation of docks, continued unaltered throughout the century despite a trebling of the tonnage of shipping it cleared. Congestion in the Pool was severely aggravated by the seasonality and annual variations of both coastal and foreign trade and by the sheer mass of coal, timber, corn and wool which was carried to or fro by lighter to the Legal Quays, which had remained unchanged since 1558, and the Sufferance Wharves, at which goods carrying lighter duties could be landed. There was little more quay space all told than there was in Bristol at the same date, and by the end of the century the river was often so crowded that, according to an Admiralty surveyor, a wherry could scarcely squeeze between the ships at anchor. The Howland Dock, renamed the Greenland Dock when it became a fitting-out basin for whalers in 1763, and the small Brunswick Dock (primarily a privately-owned ship-yard used by the end of the century exclusively by the East India Company), could not alleviate the congestion because neither was a licensed quay. (See Map 4, p .58.)

Cargoes were brazenly pilfered on an immense scale, which the establishment of the River Police in 1798 did little to reduce, and the real costs of using the port were raised still more by interminable delays in unloading —for much more came into the port than went out. According to Patrick Colquhoun, the contemporary authority on mercantile affairs, over 10,000 persons took a nefarious living from the Pool around 1800, not to mention whatever proportion of the 120,000 persons officially employed in the port was hand-in-glove with the thieves. What inhibited improvement of port interests so long was, in fact, an informal consortium of port interests ranging from the City Corporation itself to the porters' tightly organized fellowships, then at the height of their power, a mutual interest that included virtually all port workers and officials as distinct from merchants and ship-owners.

For almost a hundred years there had been a crescendo of criticism from traders in the port about its inefficiencies but it was not until the all-powerful Committee of West Indies Merchants threatened in 1793 to transfer their trade to another port that the first steps were taken to remedy the situation. The outcome was a sudden explosion of interest in port improvement, reinforced no doubt by the parallel canal "mania" (of which more will be said later) which resulted in the first dock boom the country had known. Obtaining parliamentary consent to the first two undertakings to appear took another six years because the resolution of their apparent incompatibility carried political overtones, and it was also clouded by the appearance of five other independent schemes.

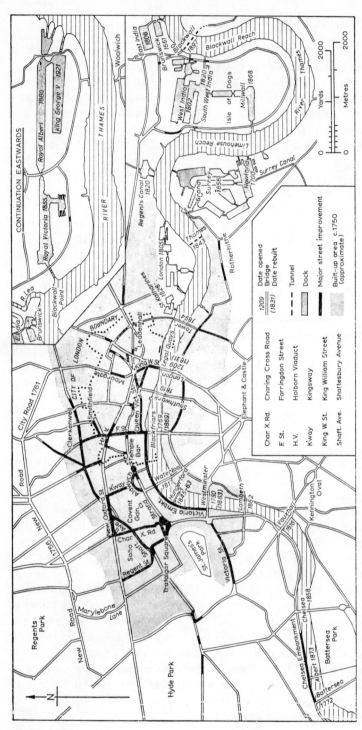

Map 4   London port and street improvement

The prime mover in all this was a ship's architect and merchant, William Vaughan, who not only indicated in his first dock tract, On Wet Docks, Quays, and Warehouses for the Port of London (1793), the Wapping site of the future London Docks but unerringly picked three more as well. Two of these, the Isle of Dogs (a marshy tract forming a great loop in the river), and Rother-hithe on the right bank, were the basis of the other major proposals made, more in self-defence than conviction, by the City Corporation itself. All the schemes were deadlocked in a parliamentary select committee from 1796 to 1799, but with astounding sagacity the commissioners reported in favour of both the main contenders on the grounds that the dearer Wapping proposal would cater best for the small vessels which made up the majority of shipping in the river, and the Isle of Dogs would conveniently take the large; the Wapping docks, it was also recognized, would make it possible to bring the costliest merchandise within closer protection of the merchant-houses. The West India Docks Act was passed first in 1799, probably because this deferred to the Corporation's interests, and both its basins, plus a canal of less than a mile, which was of value, for the timber trade (converted in 1829 into South-West India Dock), were completed by 1806. The London Docks, which cost nearly three times as much, largely owing to the extensive demolitions of existing property, were completed between 1800 and 1805.

Before the end of the war more schemes had been promoted, of which the most important were the East India Dock (1803–8) and the Commercial Dock, which began in 1807 as an enlargement of the old Howland Dock and ended in an extravagant proliferation of neighbouring docks by four highly competitive companies controlling 160 acres of water and nearly five miles of quays. The final instalment in the first great building of docks in London came with the completion of the St Katharine's Dock, even closer to the City than its sister dock, the London, in 1825–8. The total initial outlay on all these schemes was over £7 million. By 1830 investment had produced an installation which did not need any important extensions, apart from jetties and warehouses, for another twenty years, when the long London water-front was brought, in thirty-five years more, to its logical culmination of a dock in every usable bend of the river from Wool-wich to the Tower.

The river and street traffic of London completely dwarfed that of any other town in England throughout the eighteenth century. At its beginning the population of London already stood at about 600,000 while the largest towns in England—Bristol and Norwich—contained a mere 20,000 people each. At its close London contained about a million inhabitants and the next largest places were Manchester-with-Salford, Liverpool, Birmingham, Bristol, and Leeds, all of which had between 50,000 and 100,000 inhabitants; in Scotland, only Edinburgh and Glasgow came within this bracket. Lon-don's predominance in size has continued to our own day but by the 1830s the coming of industrialism had brought five towns—Birmingham, Leeds, Sheffield, Liverpool, and Manchester-with-Salford—to more than 100,000 inhabitants and another eight towns had by then topped 50,000. London's population in 1831 was over 1,300,000.

Two things have to be recognized in this situation. One is that the provisioning of London and its absorption of such a large part of the country's foreign trade, to say nothing of its varied manufactures and its role as the seat of the government and of the court, put it into a position of extraordinary command over the whole English economy. Defoe, we noted, was detecting the signs of this control in the way in which the grain trade was being centred on London and in the manner in which farmers', traders', manufacturers', and miners' interests in so many places in the realm were refracted by London markets, London sources of supply, London skills. The situation naturally did not remain unchanged. Cotton supplies, for example, did not go on reaching Lancashire through London once Liverpool had taken hold of the trade towards the end of the eighteenth century, nor did the silk trade remain centred on Spitalfields for long after its beginning. But the overall influence of London on her provinces did not diminish on this account for it became still more important as a source of finance and as the largest retail market in the world. It is not clear how this influence was modified as provincial manufacturing towns like Birmingham or Manchester or Leeds began to exercise something of a metropolitan hold on the economies of their own regions. But until they did so, London's predominance over the economy meant that hers was the vital impetus for the whole programme of road improvements and was probably also the largest single influence on the development of the canals.

The second thing to be seen in this situation is that London was anticipating urban traffic problems to a remarkable degree from very early in the eighteenth century. The opportunity that had come with the Great Fire of 1666 to replan the whole city and to replace its medieval lanes by a system of wide straight roads had been frustrated by dilatory surveying and too little capital. Instead, the capacity of the street plan to throttle any growth in traffic was largely recreated by the retention of the original building lines, and the rising chorus of complaint about streets jammed with opposing flows of vehicles of all kinds, people on foot and on horseback, and livestock being driven to Smithfield and Leadenhall went on in every form throughout the century. Private coaches and carriages did most, perhaps, to aggravate this situation. By the middle of the eighteenth century there were over 7,250 of these registered in London plus 800 hackney carriages and another 400 public sedan chairs—a French invention introduced to this country a century before in the forlorn hope of unstopping streets cluttered with hackney and other carriages. Their justification and their popularity waned as the streets became better lit and paved, and they had virtually disappeared by Regency times.

Most streets were no better metalled than country roads and too ready a receptacle for rubbish of every conceivable sort for the surface to be kept up to condition for wheeled traffic. The principal streets were cobbled but few were paved so grandly as the Strand, and it was not until the Westminster Paving Act of 1762 that the ancient obligation of each householder to pave and keep his own stretch of street in repair was publicly recognized as ineffectual. The Westminster Paving Commissioners laid flat Purbeck stone in the roadways (elsewhere Aberdeen granite was also used), overhauled the system of scavenging, and removed any hanging signs or projections that were a danger to traffic. They soon began to control street nuisances in general and even to undertake repairs to sewers and drains. Other Paving Acts followed and were augmented by Lighting and Watching Acts, though these never succeeded in piercing whole nests of streets occupied by the lower classes. The street system was normally augmented by private building speculation—happily conducted for the most part on a coherent ground plan by substantial landowners—but gradually public and semi-public authority intervened to improve the street alignment, to build new ones, or even to bridge the Thames.

London Bridge, the only available bridge over the tidal reaches of the river since the twelfth century, remained a narrow cluttered street of houses until it was rebuilt in 1824-31. The river, much more used then as a major highway than it was even in Victorian times, could be crossed by ferry at innumerable stairs and jetties, but the great bend in it around Lambeth marsh extended the distance that wheeled traffic had to cover between Westminster and the south bank an unconscionable way. A bridge at Westminster was therefore built first (1736-50) but it did nothing to relieve the traffic at the centre, so a second bridge was conceived at Blackfriars (1760-9) with a double purpose: not only to relieve London Bridge but to let some air into the infamous purlieus of the river Fleet, which had long lost its high-bred aspect and become an open sewer bordered by slums that raised the death rate and a contingent of the London mob more effectively than the civic finances.

Street improvement and slum clearance have in fact always gone hand-in-hand, and in the City of London there was a kind of geographical logic in the succession of works to enclose sewers and to make better avenues for traffic right through to mid-Victorian times. The new London Bridge led to the formation (at a cost of a million pounds) of Moorgate and King William Street (1824-46); old Blackfriars Bridge led to Farringdon Street (1826-30) and the new one (1869) to Holborn Viaduct, Victoria Embankment, and Queen Victoria Street (1869-71). Occasionally, street improvement became a civic or a regal gesture: forlorn at Temple Bar (1793-1817); triumphant in Regent Street (1812-23). It was all a matter of cash. Royal coffers and not municipal rates gave London the one great plan for the city as a whole that has ever been fulfilled. Nash's "metropolitan improvements" (1811-35) embraced Regent's and St James's Parks, Trafalgar Square, and the west end of the Strand, as well as Regent Street, and they anticipated the "western improvements" forty years later, from which Charing Cross Road and Shaftesbury Avenue were to come. Almost all of these new streets punctured or contained unwanted slums and where they did not they could hardly fail to pick at their seams. In the provinces, too, were numerous towns in which various kinds of Improvement Commissioners had been at work more or less since the last quarter of the eighteenth century, notably Liverpool, Manchester, Birmingham, Glasgow. Most of them were concerned with street maintenance but a few of them with the building of new streets. In Edinburgh, the process had started even earlier and much more magnificently with the planning and sweeping execution of the New Town (1766–1840).

The attempt to deal with traffic problems at the centre by street improvement was a minor exercise before 1815, but it was becoming annually more urgent as a result of the rise of suburbs, especially in London. They had been growing there despite official constraints throughout the seventeenth century, and the Great Fire made merchants think even more about moving upwind, first to Soho, Covent Garden and Clerkenwell, and thence to the great grid of squares being steadily opened up on the Bedford, Portland, Portman, and Westminster estates beyond this throughout the eighteenth century. This was helped unintentionally by the building of the arterial New Road beyond the built-up area between Paddington and Islington in 1756–7. South of the river, Blackfriars Bridge, built by the Corporation of the City of London, also gave swift impetus to new roads reaching out to Walworth and New Cross. Much later, once bridge-building no longer seemed foolhardy to both capitalists and generals, three more were built in quick succession at Vauxhall, Waterloo and Southwark (1816–19), and important new roads were formed at great speed. "Rows of houses shoot out every way like a polypus", wrote Horace Walpole as early as 1776, and if he stayed at Strawberry Hill for a fortnight he always looked about him for new houses as he went into town. It was to be the experience of far-flung Londoners ever after.

3   Parish roads, turnpikes, and bridges

The roads which carried the traffic that sustained London and its suburbs were of two kinds: parish roads and turnpikes. Of these, the parish roads were numerically superior, as they were in the country at large throughout the eighteenth and nineteenth centuries. At no time did the ordinary roads of the kingdom fail to outnumber the turnpikes in terms of mileage by less than five to one, and in many places turnpikes were scarcely known. One traveller from London to Falmouth in 1752 never saw one beyond 50 miles from the start. As we have already seen, the age-old responsibility of the community for its own roads was put into specific terms in the Highways Act of 1555 and that this continued in force down to 1835. There had also been some forlorn attempts to obtain by legislation the kind of traffic which the locally maintained roads could bear. These also continued.

They culminated in the first General Highway Act of 1767 and a more effective measure in 1773, which tried to clarify and improve the conflicting demands of earlier legislation: cartways into market towns had to be at least twenty feet wide; little-used cross roads could be abandoned and the materials used on busier routes; statute duty was graded progressively so that the heaviest users paid most and the poor gave nothing but their labour; parish assessments could be called for by the justices if statute labour and duty failed to keep the highways in repair; the loads of wagons with wheels six inches across had to be kept down to that of a six-horse team, but if the wheels were fitted so as to roll nine inches of road surface a seventh horse could be added. Yet more attempts at using road traffic to repair rather than subject the roads to ordinary wear and tear and at distributing the burden of upkeep more fairly followed, but the final verdict of the Highway Act of 1835 on all these efforts was that they were either excessively cumbersome or ill-advised. The Act completely abolished all regulations relating to loads and the design of wheels, and it substituted for the system of statute duty a highway rate and the amalgamation of parishes into highway districts with competent surveyors to serve them.

One reason for turning highway surveyors' backs on the efforts of generations to keep traffic light simply was that it had been proved impossible to do so. It was moreover futile to legislate in general when soil conditions and road metal varied so much in particular. It must also be remembered that there were by that time cheaper ways of transporting heavy goods for long distances. But the chief reason for the change of attitude was that the parish roads and highways themselves were being appreciably improved. There was certainly much room for improvement in their administration so long as the surveyors were appointed annually by rotation, remained ignorant of elementary principles of road-building and maintenance, and were hobbled by social constraints. Statute labour was often so scantily done that six days on the roads began to look like a holiday, and, when paupers were used, more like a gesture of despair or even a symptom of corruption.

The nub of the matter was simply drainage. The worst roads suffered by virtue of the subsoil, by lack of any camber, by excessive gradients, by flooding, and by becoming so deeply rutted and pot-holed that the slightest deterioration in the weather made them into a morass. It was easy to be wrong-headed in theory when the practice was so patchy and there were roadmenders who went so far in the right direction by keeping the section convex that vehicles toppled over, or so far in the wrong as to flush roads by streams in the hope of washing out the mud. There were apologists, if not advocates, of undulating, corrugated, hollow, and even "pantile roof" roads. Administrative makeshifts could do little to change this state of things, though one proposal in 1808 by a committee of the House of Commons that all the roads in the kingdom be subject to direct parliamentary control might have worked changes in time. What was wanted above all was the application of principles of road construction which were like the Romans', as readily applied to gravel as to clay soils, and as firmly administered. In terms of engineering that is very close to what happened. In terms of administration it could not have been farther removed. But to understand both we must look at the spread of the turnpikes.

Before doing so, it is important to look briefly at the important matter of the history of bridges. There had survived from the Middle Ages—and do still—a considerable number of stone and a few wooden bridges, though very few indeed were of the size and structural refinement of that, say, of Bideford (1315) whose 24 arches supported a carriageway, though very narrow, 677 feet long. Another long stone bridge was built at Berwick-on-Tweed in 1611–37. Bridges were so narrow that angular recesses had to be provided for people on foot to shelter from the traffic, and they had a distinct propensity for falling down. Ferries and fords were widespread. No laws had ever been passed for the construction of bridges, the first of which was not enacted till 1888, when the Local Government Act made them the responsibility of the county councils. But during the eighteenth century, particularly towards its close, the growing volume of traffic required a large increase in bridge-building and rebuilding and considerable numbers were built, the largest as toll-bridges, smaller ones by means of a special rate ("bridge money") levied locally, or by private means. The modern bridge, in which the clustered arches of medieval builders gave way to much wider spans and a wider, flatter carriageway, was an innovation of the eighteenth century. Such bridges were mostly of stone, like that over the Taff at Pontypridd (1746–55) or, more notably still, the 37 structures which Thomas Telford, stonemason, put up in Shropshire in the half-century after his appointment as County Surveyor in 1786. The world's first cast-iron bridge was built across the Severn near Coalbrookdale by John Wilkinson and Abraham Darby III in 1776–9, having a single span of a hundred feet. Within twenty years, two more iron bridges had been built, one at Sunderland and the other a little further up-river from Ironbridge itself; Telford later put up another four. The administration of bridges had been laid down in the Statute of Bridges of 1531 which put the onus for repairing those in towns on its citizens and all others on the counties, though without making such provisions unequivocal and binding. In the circumstances it is not surprising that the history of bridges should have oscillated between the local justices and the turnpike trustees, the former indicting the local inhabitants for failing to keep their bridges intact, while the latter looked hopefully at them to secure the upkeep of the bridges they had built.

The most formative years for the turnpike system lay in the middle of the eighteenth century. During the period in which Defoe was exploring their possibilities and for some years after that the average number of turnpike Acts passed by Parliament each year was just over eight, but in the twenty years after 1751 there were some 870 Acts passed, an average five times that for the preceding period. The Webbs wrote in their *The Story of the King's Highway* (1913) that "a perfect mania" seemed to have set in. Not all of these were for construction purposes and some referred to roads already authorized: it would moreover be foolish to treat these figures as though they referred to schemes of equal size and importance. Yet they do suggest unmistakably a marked shift in the whole scale on which new roads were being made or old ones made usable which corresponds with an abundance of other evidence that confirms this as the period in which the great transfer of responsibility for the major roads of the country was taking place. (*See Map 5*, p. 66.)

The parochial system of road administration and development had plainly failed to match the needs of society and of the economy, and the alternative of taking this form of transport out of its customary mould and fitting it into a contractual one was being tried. There were only slightly fewer Acts in the period that followed, 1771–90, before road legislation leapt to new heights around the turn of the century. It must be remembered that the total tended to be cumulative so long as the powers granted by the Acts were of limited duration and had to be renewed, and that any significant variation in the trustees' powers also needed further authority. The upshot of all this legislation was the creation of some 1,100 separate turnpike trusts by the 1830s, operating under powers derived from around 4,000 individual Acts, and controlling about 22,000 miles of road, some of it major trunk routes, some of it by-roads and suburban streets, a little of it still operating at comfortable profits, most of it at a steadily mounting loss.

The administration of these assorted bodies had but few basic elements in common. They were governed by a self-perpetuating body of named trustees who had absolute powers to erect toll-gates on their stretch of road, or to let them off to contractors, but who were authorized to levy tolls only within the tariff specified in the Act—a latitude which produced some striking differences in the level of the tolls for various types of traffic on different roads. The trusts had and used the prerogative of any monopolist to grant preferential rates. There was never any restriction placed on their borrowing powers nor on the way the earnings should be used. At the beginning the justices were free to dismantle the gates once the trust had fulfilled its purpose by recouping the trustees for their outlay in putting the road into good repair, but it is difficult to find a single case of that ever happening, and there are obvious reasons why that state of affairs was seldom, if ever, reached. Indeed, the main tendency was for turnpike trustees to go some way beyond the original intention and acquire powers through general legislation to buy land compulsorily, to stop up ancient highways, to erect gates in side-roads, and to force traffic onto the turnpikes. In fairness, it ought also to be said that many trusts undertook more or less continuous improvements to their roads, removing unnecessary corners

E

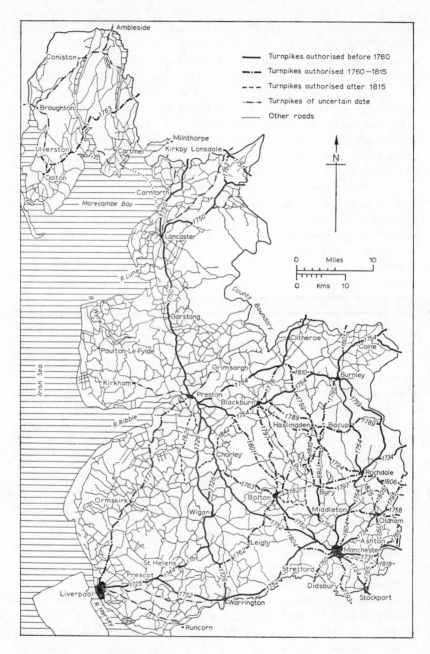

Map 5   *The roads of Lancashire*

and sometimes going so far as to lower hills, though the compulsory acquisition of land for these purposes was not a popular way of doing so. The trusts had paid officials to do the day-to-day work and these invariably included a surveyor (who was obliged to report regularly to the trustees), a clerk, a treasurer, and collectors. Apart from statute labour, the road surface was repaired either by the trust's own gang or by a sub-contractor, though it generally proved difficult to maintain the quality of work done in this way.

The turnpike trusts were included in a certain amount of general legislation, including all that relating to loading and the design of vehicle undercarriages. One measure of this kind which was peculiar to them was passed in 1741 to give trustees powers to set up weighbridges which could be used to assess an extra toll of 12s. per hundred-weight on loads above three tons. Ten years later the Trusts within thirty miles of London were actually required to instal them and to levy an extra £1 per hundredweight for all wagons having six horses. These extra costs were cut back under the terms of another Act, passed in 1753, which made nine-inch tyres mandatory, under stiff penalties, though without preventing altogether the use of narrow wheels disguised as broad ones which had been made conical in section. It should not be thought, incidentally, that the broad wheel was acknowledged everywhere as the better design. For one thing, its success depended greatly on local soils and available road metal. Not surprisingly a real controversy raged round this point to the very end of the century, if not beyond it. Within two years more, wagons having nine-inch wheels escaped toll altogether for a period of three years. A new law of 1765 clapped comparable premiums on wagons whose wheels were not mounted on axles of different lengths, so making each staggered pair roll sixteen inches of road. All these and other provisions were codified or modified in the General Turnpike Act of 1773, which also made their repetition in each separate turnpike Act unnecessary. What was more important about the Act of 1773 was the fact that it removed altogether from the local magistrates the remnant of legal authority that remained to them in relation to the trusts, and required any legal action that should be brought to be taken to Quarter Sessions. It also established some fairly substantial property qualifications for turnpike trustees.

The only other important general legislation of the period was contained in the Turnpike Act of 1822 following three searching inquiries into the road laws in 1810, 1819, and 1821. Much of this was simply the culmination of the wheelwright legislation of the previous sixty years but there were now, ominously enough, more demanding regulations about finances. There had been no parliamentary inquiry into the condition of the trusts since 1752 when the relation between toll receipts and outgoings had first been examined. The 1822 Act made a number of cautionary provisions about keeping of proper accounts, including their auditing, and regulated the action of mortgagees who had taken over toll-gates to obtain payment of their dues from the trustees. Like much other legislation of the time relating to money matters such regulations were too often passed over by the very trusts who needed to observe them most closely, as their winding-up was so often to show.

The financial position of the trusts can never be fully known. What is known is that their management was often notoriously inept and not infrequently fraudulent, their funds sometimes subject to excessive interest charges, inordinate wages bills, and not a few acts of embezzlement, their control of the tolls and of statute labour too variable or lax and both subject to petty jobbery. One notorious case reported on by the 1752 committee, for example, was the Kensington trust, whose income in the three years 1749–51 was approaching £10,000. It had a mere fifteen miles of road that were capable of being maintained for no more than £100 per mile. Yet this trust found itself at the end of these years in debt for £3,300.

On the other hand, there were trusts which were managed conscientiously and energetically even where the problems of doing so were specially complicated by being located in densely populated urban districts. The Bermondsey, Rotherhithe & Deptford Trust, for example, which was established in 1748, was faced by exceptional difficulties in collecting toll and keeping their roads—they were really more like streets—in good repair, but it prevented every escape from toll so successfully that it faced violence instead. It was then ingenious enough to get legal authority in 1803 to levy a rate of up to £160 on local inhabitants as a collective levy for their use of the roads. It was even more inventive in carrying out a conversion of its mortgage loan from 5 per cent to 4 per cent when money became cheap in the 1790s, even though it had difficulty in reducing its overall size or preventing the jobbery in roadmending which helped to keep it in debt. Yet this trust was also performing tasks for the common good that might otherwise have been left undone, such as the cleansing and arching over of common sewers and the prosecution of anyone committing a public nuisance by flinging rubbish on the road or lining it with privies. Happily enough, leasing the tolls tended to become more profitable, rising from £850 for the year 1780 to £3,100 for that of 1811.

This was not always the trend and many trusts were handicapped by the loss of income that followed when parishes compounded their tolls at a fraction of what it would have cost them under a normal tariff, or where local farmers used the local turnpikes more cheaply than the parish roads to which they had once made their contribution. Of course, parliamentary costs were high and recurrent, and if road metal had to be brought any distance it was likely to be in an area where much of it was needed and therefore expensive. There was also damage to be made good in some places, especially in the early days, after bands of local men had demolished gates and tried to destroy altogether what they regarded as an extra tax on their daily lives. This was a menace that never quite expired and it flared up menacingly and to great cost in the Rebecca Riots in South Wales in the 1840s.

Whether the turnpikes paid financially depended on so many factors and it makes little sense to generalize at all widely, yet public toll auctions, which became the regular way of disposing of the management of the gates, suggest that some trusts were yielding very high returns and that the professional toll farmers who took them over were sometimes men of substantial capital: one of them was reputed to have contracted at one time for a sum equal to about a third of the whole toll income of the country. A single short section of the Holyhead road was let at an auction in 1831 for £7,530 a year. But the most flamboyant scraps of information on such matters tend to live on while the ordinary business of running the roads is forgotten. All the same, it is difficult to believe that most turnpikes were not paying their way in some form or another during their long hegemony in inland transport. Their real difficulties arose when toll receipts began to fall with the shift of passenger traffic on to the railways. It was not till then that the debts of the worst placed rose to irretrievable heights, with the interest payable on mortgaged tolls almost brimming the level of the tolls themselves. By the time the railway overtook them many trusts were facing debts that their incomes could not hope to cover in fifty years, some never.

4   The contribution of the turnpikes

What was the real contribution of the turnpikes to the transport system of England as she underwent the Industrial Revolution? If early travellers' tales were all there were to go upon, it is doubtful if it could be regarded as a particularly positive one. The state of the roads entered conversation and letter-writing like the weather, always under judgment but never by the same judge, with the truth of the matter necessarily including the tergiversations of the witnesses themselves.

Arthur Young, whose language was among the most vivid, kept the best of it for the worst journeys and is inclined to deceive the casual reader of his *Tours* into thinking that his travels must have been almost uniformly bad. He cursed bad roads so splendidly that his expletives ring on in almost every account written of his travels. The murmurs of approval are seldom heard. Young's movements through the south of England, especially Sussex, seem to have angered him most, though it is noticeable that he managed to get his light chaise across a hundred miles of these roads per week. On a 1,460 mile tour he made in 1768 through the Midlands, Yorkshire, Northumberland, and Cumberland, before returning to his farm in Hertfordshire, he gave his verdict on more than half the turnpikes he used (930 miles of them in all) as good, while the rest were divided between middling and bad; on the other hand, well over half the crossroads he regarded as bad and nearly a third of them only middling. Yet he found some excellent parish roads which he quietly praised and a few turnpikes which obviously pleased him greatly. Later on (1813), he found substantial improvement had taken place, even in Sussex, and commended especially the road that ran from Horsham to London. This, in his view, had very few equals, and had done the trick of raising agricultural rents and breeding "a general spirit of mending the cross roads" round about. A few years before that he was finding it "impossible to say too much in praise of the roads of most of the districts of Essex". His less flamboyant and in some respects more authoritative contemporary, William Marshall, had always had fewer faults to find and was correspondingly less open-handed in his praise.

Whatever the English thought of their own roads, foreigners were beginning to find them a source of real envy. Parson Moritz in his *Travels through England* (1782) spoke often of firm, smooth roads. On the other hand, de Saussure, a Frenchman who wanted to impress his countrymen with the advantages of the turnpike system in preference to the *corvée*, had been gushing about the magnificent high roads of England sixty years before that. Yet it was an understandable reaction to roads which, despite their imperfections, were incomparably better than these travellers could find at home. What can we say, though, of an Englishman who only England knows? Henry Homer, writing after 1760, claimed in his *Enquiry into the Means of Preserving and Improving the Publick Roads* (1767): "There never was a more astonishing revolution accomplished in the internal system of any country. The carriage of grain, coals, merchandize, etc. is in general conducted with little more than half the number of horses which it formerly was . . . Everything wears the face of dispatch and the hinge which has guided all these movements, and upon which they turn, is the reformation which has been made in our public roads". Which way to turn was in truth one of the things which travellers often found it difficult to decide. Happily, signposts were becoming more numerous and helpful and in 1771 the local squire in one desolate spot on the southern approaches to Lincoln had put up a lighthouse for a landmark.

The real point is that the road system then, as now, had its black spots as well as its stretches of dry, open highway, and the impression one has of it depends entirely on where and when one looks. This patchiness was perhaps the greatest defect in the turnpike system. In some places it was like a return to the erratic particularism of the Middle Ages on a reduced scale. Good road was interspersed with bad road, insignificant places found themselves interconnected, important places were almost held apart, and turnpike trustees fought any upstart scheme that threatened to drain their traffic away. The changes that occurred on the turnpike roads were accordingly not swift, any more than the growth in road traffic was steady and unfluctuating throughout, but comparisons of road conditions prevailing in almost any part of the country at, say, twenty-year intervals after 1750 would undoubtedly show tangible improvements, expressed in terms of less intermittent use, shorter travelling times, more substantial traffic, and more generally felt effects of widespread communications.

Such views may safely be stressed for there has been something of a tendency to underrate the significance of the turnpikes. They cannot be said to have nursed any new industries of importance nor provided such a range of productive investments that they became, in the modern jargon, a growth sector. Nevertheless, they did marshal resources for a vital improvement that could not conceivably have happened in any other way. Sir Henry Parnell wrote in his *Treatise on Roads* (1833) that no other scheme could have induced parliament to lay out the £1½ million a year which was being collected on the toll-roads of the country at that time. The turnpike trusts tapped local initiative and served local interests in a singularly appropriate way. It is a striking testimony to the aptness of their enterprise that, with all its command over the resources of the modern state, government nowadays turns occasionally to the idea of a toll route when the capital cost of an undertaking on the scale, say, of the Forth Bridge can fairly and acceptably be met to some extent by the direct users of it. In the United States the idea is even more widely accepted to this day and turnpike remains a word in everyday use.

The turnpike trusts were financed by borrowing and by the proceeds of the gates, with a limited amount of bank finance (mainly to meet initial and parliamentary expenses), and individual backing that seldom amounted to more than a gesture of local patriotism. Sometimes the costs of building the road could be quite high—up to £800 or £1,000 per mile—but in the majority of cases in which trusts took over existing roads in order to improve them, the outlay could increase as revenue accrued, and some trusts could begin their operations merely by erecting the gates and scraping the road. In this way, capital was being formed in its most natural manner, out of the earnings of the enterprise. If the form of the undertaking had been different and allowed for more open earning and allocation of profits, it is probable that the trusts would have amalgamated naturally and avoided the more wasteful of their activities. It would certainly have been possible to invest the undistributed profits with an eye to creating more business, and there is no telling what might have come of that. As it was, some of the resources of the trusts were undeniably wasted and it was rare for them to be conducted as business enterprises even after the time when demonstrable efficiency was no longer liable to work its own destruction in the termination of the trust.

In more tangible terms, there can be little doubt that the road system as a whole performed the indispensable function of simply bearing a considerable traffic in all kinds of industrial materials and merchandise that could not otherwise have been moved about. Andrew Yarranton, before the end of the seventeenth century, had told how Forest of Dean pig iron was being transported not only up the Severn and into the Stour Valley but overland from there to the heart of the South Staffordshire coalfield. To and from Bewdley scores of carriers hauled coal, pig iron, and charcoal from the forges along the Stour Valley right down to the time when the Staffordshire & Worcestershire Canal brought them better service in 1770, though the charge for pig from Bewdley to Wolverley (a distance of about four miles) was only 3s. 3d. per ton. In the 1760s, the pottery towns of Burslem and Newcastle-under-Lyme were exporting a hundred tons of pots a year by pack-horse and another eight tons by wagon each week to Bridgnorth and Bewdley for embarkation in Severn barges; and they made their return journeys laden with white clay, iron and groceries. Manchester, at the same date, was sending some 150 pack-horses and a couple of wagons each week to Stafford alone and had regular overland connections with Bristol, Edinburgh, and London, as well as with towns in the vicinity.

It is significant that the first road to be turnpiked out of Liverpool in 1725 was that to the collieries at Prescot, and that it should have been carried on to St Helens later, though this did not prevent coal prices from fluctuating with the weather. About 1780, Leicester was the junction for weekly waggons between London, Leeds and Manchester, and to Birmingham, Bristol and beyond; within the next fifty years its traffic in hosiery and other goods justified at least a score of wagon services to Bristol, Birmingham, Nottingham, Stamford, and Cambridge, as well as some 250 carriers, some operating twice a week, serving the surrounding villages. Even before being turnpiked, the roads from Birmingham to Dudley and Wolverhampton were said, in 1727, to be heavily used for the transit of coal and iron, and although much of this was eventually transferred to the canals the traffic in other goods replaced it sufficiently to enable the trust which was formed in 1760 to go on paying its way right down to 1840. Similarly, the Bristol road out of Birmingham was described in 1707 as being almost impassable owing to the heavy traffic in salt, iron and coal. In another direction, 80 pack-horses a day were carrying greengroceries between Evesham and Birmingham, though this road appears never to have become suitable for carriages in the eighteenth century.

Pack-horses or mules, each carrying five or six hundredweights, could form caravans capable of crossing the wildest country or picking their way along the paved causeways that were so common on both sides of the Pennines as far south as Derbyshire. Sheffield had a weekly traffic of this kind with London. Yet this more primitive form of transport appeared to be dying out towards the very end of the eighteenth century, except in the hilliest parts and in the West Country. Instead, wagon services were becoming so numerous as to be subject to timetables. These stage wagons were great, lumbering, canvas-hooded vehicles hauled by up to eight horses that normally moved at a slow walking pace but could, given the right roads and a good team, pick up a little more speed and keep going for days. Some were even styled "flying waggons", though the kind of "caravan on springs and guarded" that Pickford's ran, which was scheduled to cover the distance from London to Manchester, say, in 35 hours—a third of the time taken by the fastest wagons—did not take to the roads in any numbers till after 1815. Twenty years after that this firm was using these four-horse vans on daily services from London to Liverpool and to Nottingham.

The wagons that were in use in the eighteenth century carried practically anything and everything, including passengers too poor for coaches, at rates which varied at least as much by commodity as by bulk, weight or distance carried. The justices had had the power in Quarter Sessions to curb excessive charges since 1692, but used this too little before it lapsed as no longer operative in 1827, to permit us to estimate at all closely what road carriage costs were on the average. The most general impression they give is of carriage rates of 12d. or more per ton-mile, though the upper limits varied very widely between districts and seasons of the year. These variations probably suggest more or less primitive road conditions rather than sheer arbitrariness. The Leicestershire justices' ruling in the 1780s on rates from London, a distance of about a hundred miles, which allowed for small variations around 5s. per hundredweight according to destination, fixed a relatively low rate. There does not seem to have been anything like a flat rate ruling at any time either within the counties or among them all. Just how much was actually charged rather than assessed, much less enforced, is more problematical, for advertised charges were expressed in all kinds of measures and varied without reference to weight alone. Pickford's were still using a tariff in 1830 in which the maximum rates for plate glass and gunpowder were five or six times greater than those for sacks of grain or casks of ale.

Long before then, substantial carrying firms like Pickford's—which had originated in the North early in the seventeenth century—were already being established, some of them with their own warehouses and a regular clientèle, ready to provide through services that even included partial transit on the canals. Despite their ubiquity curiously little is know about the operations of these firms in any detail. Their outgoings included wagoners' and stable-hands' wages, fodder, rent for stables and hay-lofts, shoeing the horses, refitting harness, repairing or hiring outright the wagons on a mileage basis, paying toll, and withstanding losses by theft or fire. On one stretch of road 41 miles long between Manchester and Sheffield, Pickford's running costs for a daily service of four six-horse wagons working two legs of the journey, and two four-horse wagons the third, totalled almost £2,500 for the year 1835, of which tolls alone accounted for nearly half. Long-distance carriers were supplemented by others who kept to the locality or did round trips through outlying villages. By the second half of the eighteenth century long lists of wagoners were appearing in town directories and in London special guides to these services were being published annually. By 1835 *Robson's London Directory* was listing over 14,000 regular wagon services each week in all parts of the country and more than 800 public carriers operating from London alone.

The volume of goods in transit by road by this date was formidable. One

set of returns for the Shenfield turnpike gate 22 miles from London illustrates this vividly. On one Sunday in March 1838—there is no evidence that
this was ever a day of rest for the roads—some 21 broad-wheeled wagons
alone, of which seventeen were drawn by six horses or more apiece, carried
between them 88 tons of general goods from London to various towns in
Essex and Suffolk; one six-tonner passed through *en route* for London from
Norwich. It is unthinkable that the inland industrial towns, above all,
could have existed for long without the paraphernalia of mobility which the
turnpikes had brought into existence, long before the end of the eighteenth
century. One of the features of transport history is that all major improvements rapidly become indispensable and it almost becomes irrelevant to
inquire whether they were always so.

As to passenger travel by road, this did not become markedly important
before the last few years of the eighteenth century. The first stage coach
had appeared on the roads around the middle of the seventeenth century
but it was not until the late eighteenth and early nineteenth century, that
a real boom in coaching occurred. Then the major provincial towns could
begin to measure their coach services not in so many per week but in terms
of dozens or scores per day, and when road-books began appearing in
annual editions, even tourism may be said to have begun to move into its
popular phase. The coach was a tiny vehicle capable of carrying four inside
passengers and a dozen outside at the very most, and a great growth in numbers scarcely altered the ratio which their total capacity bore to the population of even a small town. However, whereas there was but one coach
a week between London and Birmingham in 1740, there were 30 in 1783,
and 34 a day in 1829. In Leicester in the 1760s two coaches crossed each day
on their runs to and from Manchester or Leeds out of London; at the end
of the 1820s between forty and fifty coaches were leaving each day for
destinations on every point of the compass—London, Birmingham, Manchester, Derby, Nottingham, Sheffield, Leeds, and Stamford. Between
Manchester and Stockport, which caught all the Birmingham, Nottingham
and London coaches, there were as many as a hundred of them going in
each direction per day at the height of the coaching boom. On the giddiest
route in the country for competition, from London to Brighton, 21 coaches
were travelling daily in each direction in the 1820s; by the 1830s this number
had risen to 50. Out of London itself scores were leaving from every coaching
inn in the City and West End, not only into the country but now into
London's own suburbs. By 1835 there were 50 daily coaches to Brighton,
22 to Birmingham, 15 to Dover, 12 to Exeter, 10 to Leeds, 11 to Manchester,
and 16 to Portsmouth.

The improvement of the roads as well as of the coaches themselves
reduced travelling times, if not its discomforts. The journey from London
to Edinburgh, which had occupied ten days in summer in 1754, was cut by
"flying coach" to four days, and by 1836 the mail coach was making the
run in less than half this time. The same kind of acceleration was taking

place in practically all directions: London and Manchester stood three days apart in 1750 and a mere eighteen hours in 1836; York, which had been four days out of London in the 1750s could in the 1830s be reached in twenty hours; Bristol, which had been two days' journey from London in 1754 could in the end be reached in under twelve hours. These were the biggest savings in time and neither the coaches following the cross routes nor the "accommodation" coaches which were maids-of-all-work achieved such dramatic reductions in travelling time. Movement between the major towns was four or five times as fast around 1830 as it had been in 1750, and almost everywhere else it was at least twice as fast. No-one after Sydney Smith seems to have kept a log of the bruises sustained in the process. His tally for the journey he regularly made between Taunton and Bristol was between ten and twenty thousand.

Competition brought lower fares and provided the opportunity for large firms to move in and crowd competitors off the road or into their own yards. Chaplin & Company of London was the largest coach proprietor in existence in the early 1830s, having something approaching 1,500 horses, 64 coaches, and an annual turnover estimated at half-a-million pounds. There were other firms of substantial size in London as well as in the provinces, though there were also some one-coach partnerships and owner-driver firms. The cost of running a coach is difficult to compute for it depended so much on the condition of the roads, the number of gates to be passed, the skill or recklessness of the driver, and the demands made on the horses. They normally ran a single stage of about twelve miles before being changed but different stages made such different demands. Replacing them altogether at least every six years was the largest recurrent cost and could be doubled on the most demanding roads, where the going was hard or competitors pressing and the horses were driven off their legs at twice that rate. Around 1830 horses were costing anything between £20 for a broken down nag to a hundred guineas for a fine gelding in tip-top condition, though the average tended towards the lower end of this range. The margin for errors of judgment in driving was never wide and was too often cut down severely by tippling on the road, by racing, by overloading on the driver's account (despite stringent legislation), or by drivers falling asleep. Coach proprietors not infrequently had to meet legal damages following injury to passengers. Highway robbery was a continuous threat and on occasions something rather more than a pest to the passengers, especially where it was organized in gangs. It continued to a surprisingly late date. More lucrative and easier prey, however, were both the stage-wagons and the post-boys who carried the mail. The mail-bags often had valuables in them.

At its height, coaching was having to bear duties which added appreciably to its costs: the stagecoach duty which was levied by the Stamp Office varied according to seating capacity, and when it was introduced, in 1776, it stood at £5 per coach and $\frac{1}{2}d$. per mile, soon to be raised to 1d. From 1804, the mileage rate was raised to 2d. per mile for a coach with seats for four inside, but the upper limit was 5*d*. a mile if over ten seats. These charges had to be met whatever the actual load, and were not abated until 1838. Some coaches could carry up to eleven passengers on top (something that was not possible before the coming of smooth roads), though seating capacity was severely restricted. For coach proprietors who did not own the coaches themselves —there is no way of telling how many of these there were—there was also a mileage duty of between 2*d*. and 3*d*. per mile to be paid to the coachbuilder. Tolls on stage-coaches could aggregate sums up to 25*s*. per coach per day on the Brighton run and nearly £6 on the road to Manchester. The coach proprietor who got a net return of anything between £4 and £8 a mile on a good route was doing very well indeed. However, the returns could be very much lower than this. The receipts and expenses of one coach working to capacity between London and Edinburgh in 1830 were: 4 inside passengers at £6 15*s*. each, and 11 outside passengers at £3 10*s*. each, producing £65 10*s*.; passenger duty, £4 19*s*. 3*d*., hire of coach £4, hire of horses (four at 3*d*. per mile) £4 19*s*. 3*d*., turnpike toll (216 gates at 4*d*. each) £6 12*s*., wages and other running costs £12, amounting in all to £32 10*s*. 6*d*.

There was no official ceiling on fares and these could apparently always be adjusted to cover costs. Yet the demand for travel never became sufficiently elastic for the cost of travel alone to make a substantial difference to its volume. Competition certainly increased the capacity of some routes appreciably but many coaches were running half-empty long before the passengers they sought turned to the railways. To judge by the public blandishments of coach proprietors in competition with each other—as by the very names of their coaches—they offered speed, safety, and good company before lower fares. These varied in terms of mileage rates all over the country but as a general guide it can be reckoned that around 1800 fares were averaging 2*d*. or 3*d*. a mile, rather more for winter journeys and about double the basic rate for travelling inside. By the 1830s they were rather higher than that, reaching 5*d*. in some places. The cost of tipping and meals could raise the basic cost of a long journey by more than a third: one recorded journey from London to Newcastle in 1836, for which the fare for an outside seat was £3 10*s*., was increased to £4 17*s*. 3*d*. by tips and refreshments. This represents something of the order of £30 at present day prices. Travelling by road was therefore far from cheap, and within the reach of a tiny fraction only of the total population, as a comparison of the seating capacity available to the inhabitants of any sizeable town shows. Posting, either on horseback or by chaise, was more exclusive still and very much more expensive, especially on account of the charges at the inns *en route*. These varied enormously in quality, of course, and Dean Tucker's observation that their condition was a kind of pulse by which one may tell the riches or poverty of a country was even more true then than now. The historian Somerville carried his own knife and fork.

5   Some innovations and innovators

The public mail continued to be carried between towns on the system which
Ralph Allen had introduced in 1720 and which he kept in his own hands
until he died in 1762. By this time the system of carrying the mails by chaise
or on horseback was becoming demonstrably inadequate when compared
with the speed of the ordinary stage-coaches. Mail coaches, adequately
armed, and carrying four passengers inside, travelling at higher speeds than
the ordinary coaches, were introduced following John Palmer's suggestions
to this effect in 1783. He was himself installed in the Post Office in London
to superintend the reform of the service on the Bristol road and it was not
long before his ideas spread to the country at large. One outcome of this
was to give the Postmaster General a keener interest in the state of the roads,
and his inspectors provided him with reports that he used in criticizing
shoddy turnpikes and even indicting negligent road authorities. In one
direction he very nearly succeeded in applying public money to the wholesale improvement of the Great North Road, with a new section of dead
straight road all the way from Peterborough to York, but the Bill did not
reach Parliament in time. It came up in 1830 and was soon lost altogether
in the stampede of people willing to spend their own or other private
money on schemes which had more of the touch of fire, and of steam.

This tendency towards the centralization of limited authority was, however, strengthened in another direction by the necessity to improve communications with Ireland after the Act of Union in 1801. The Holyhead
road assumed a crucial political importance which its 23 existing trusts
in England could not be allowed to frustrate, though they were not amalgamated as were the seven on the other side of the Welsh border. This was the
nearest thing to a national highway ever built and the road of the Shrewsbury–Holyhead Turnpike Trust which was formed in 1823 was popularly
referred to as "the Parliamentary Route". The improvement of this road
closely resembled in its administrative form the Commission for the Highland Roads which had been formed in 1803. Scotland had always tended to
set a different pattern of road development because the second Jacobite
rising in 1745 had brought a reaction in the investment of public money
in military roads and bridges to forestall further rebellion. General Wade's
engineers, whose work was largely completed by the early 1750s, had brought
improvements to the Highlands as far north as Fort William and Inverness.
Under the 1803 Commission they were being brought up to coaching
standards under a scheme which divided the cost equally between the
government and local landowners. The improvement of the Holyhead
road, searchingly examined by eight parliamentary committees between
1810 and 1822, was also financed by parliament following the appointment
of a special Commission to superintend the works in 1815. By the time it was
completed in the early 1830s, the cost to the English taxpayer, including
the harbour works at Holyhead, was some three-quarters of a million

pounds. It was the only substantial public investment in road-building until the arterial roads of the twentieth century.

There are two, or perhaps three, names missing from this review of road developments whose holders illustrate particularly aptly some of the achievements as well as the failures of this system of communications. The first is John Metcalfe (1717–1810), who first brought scientific principles to bear on road-building and left his own testimony to this not only in the 180 or so miles of turnpike he built, mostly in Yorkshire and Lancashire, between 1765 and 1792, but in his autobiography. Not the least remarkable thing about him as a road engineer is the fact that he had been blind since childhood. He had been many things before becoming a carrier in Knaresborough and then sub-contractor for a short stretch of new turnpike from Harrogate to Boroughbridge in 1755, and he went on to build up a road-contracting business which had a pay-roll at one time of 400 men. His basic principle of road-making was to lay a firm foundation, to build solidly to a smooth convex surface, and to make ditches below the level of the road to complete the drainage. John Loudon McAdam (1756–1836), a native of Ayr, built on these ideas as well as those of other Scottish road engineers whose work became familiar to him as a road commissioner from 1783. He took even greater pains to get good drainage, though without paying very much attention to the road-bed itself, on the argument that providing the surface was well drained it was not important to have solid foundations, nor even to have much of a camber. What was in his view vital was a standard method of road engineering applied with scrupulous care under the direction of a competent surveyor and the effective oversight of parliament. His road-building technique was astonishingly simple and effective and McAdam's ideas have rightly been perpetuated in the terms derived from his name—macadam and tarmacadam—which give the reason for the excellence of English road surfaces down to the era of concrete and asphalte.

McAdam repaired, in fact, more roads than he built and it was his administrative efficiency at least as much as his abilities as an engineer—by 1819 he had been instrumental in the repairing of some 700 miles of road in 15 counties—which advanced him from the surveyorship to the Bristol Trust to a position of great authority in public circles in London down to 1836. There he wrote and gave advice to public bodies and evidence before parliamentary select committees that were beginning to meet with almost feverish regularity—in 1819, 1820, 1823, 1825, with at least a dozen more on metropolitan street improvements alone between 1831 and 1851. But for the whole shift in emphasis that was imminent with the coming of the railways, McAdam's influence would have been more far-reaching still. His touchstone was efficiency, an unfamiliar enough attribute in the administration of the roads so far, and he took every opportunity of advancing the arguments for consolidating the trusts around London into a single controlling body. This plan was only partly executed in the consolidation of those in London north of the Thames in 1826 and was continued by his third son and disciple, James, who held the post of General Surveyor to the Metropolitan Turnpike Trust until his death in 1852. The Trust itself expired twenty years later. It had had real promise as a road system capable of being developed on a national scale. The intervention of the railways stopped that.

Thomas Telford (1757–1834), renowned as a bridge-builder, especially in Scotland which he toured first in 1801, was a road engineer of great distinction too. The poet Southey aptly nicknamed him the "Colossus of Roads". He was operating in effect on a totally different level from McAdam. His methods were very much more expensive mainly because his standards were much higher than McAdam's needed to be. "Now the principle of road-making I think the most valuable", he was quoted as saying by McAdam himself, "is to put broken stone upon a road, which shall unite by its own angles, so as to form a solid hard surface". His more expensive principle, it might be added, was solidity, the strength of masses of stone properly joined, which would provide a basis for the kind of smooth, dry roads on which not only the steam carriages of Telford's own vision might go at speed but the heavy, pounding traffic of the modern motorway. There are stretches of the Holyhead road (A5), north of Shrewsbury, that are still substantially in the form that Telford engineered them. What is even more to the point here was his genius in using stone and iron in relation to earth and water. This was a still more massive contribution to the fulfilment of the country's natural endowments. The two great aqueducts of his which lie so close to the A5 provide, with the road itself, some of the great monuments of that day. They belong, of course, to another system of inland communications—the canals. To these we now turn.

Rapid Transit
Urban Transit

3

Transport and
the industrial revolution (2)

1 The first canals

The chief highway of the English during the turnpike era was not the road at all but navigable water. The controlled application of water to industrial and commercial purposes was indeed the basic and most potent technology in Britain's early economic advancement. Nothing could have contributed more to that phase of her development than the skilled manipulation of her rivers and their commercial connection to her coastal waters. The technique of channelling and controlling a large volume of moving water was, in fact, the first major breakthrough in the industrial revolution, and the second was the natural sequel to it, that of providing artificial navigable channels which could be made available to any point required. This was vital to economic progress because by 1720 or so the potential capacity and efficiency of the natural system of inland waterways had been almost fully realized.

It is true that some important navigations had yet to come—for example, the Douglas, completed at last in 1738–42, and the Calder in 1759–64—and even a hundred years later hardly a major river could fail to have been improved either by more efficient locks, more lateral cuts, or systematic dredging, but there were inevitable limits to their development as a flexible system of internal communications. Most importantly, they could not be used for unbroken cross-country journeys nor even for exploiting cheaply or unaided the resources contained in their own basins beyond a very few miles, and for certain resources even a few hundred yards, from the main stream. This was particularly the case in the new industrial regions of the north where an overland distance of fifteen miles could double or even treble the cost of some crucial bulky raw material such as coal. (*See Map 6*, p. 84). It was above all the multiplication in the uses that could be made of coal in the course of the eighteenth century which exposed this

F

limitation in the existing transport system in the starkest commercial terms and justified the engineering of the canals.

The logicality of proceeding next to the extensive cutting of deadwater canals had, of course, already struck a number of Englishmen well before the possibilities of river improvement had been fully played out, though very much later than it had appeared to their predecessors on the Continent and in the East. Defoe was not the only writer to press for a canal joining the Forth and Clyde; and the idea of bisecting England by joining her major rivers had long played on men's minds. One such notion depended on connecting Bristol and Oxford by a canal between Malmesbury on the Avon and Somerford Keynes on the Thames. This had first been explored in a practical spirit in Elizabeth's reign and probed twice more before the end of the seventeenth century. Another proposal, more sophisticated than the rest, fed on the possibility of connecting the Trent at Burton with the Severn at a point just below Bewdley, a waterway of some 70 miles, which was laid out on paper by a Dr Thomas Congreve of Wolverhampton in 1717. It faced the problems of crossing a watershed of 500 feet with a pioneer's innocent confidence and its financial calculations were almost recklessly ambitious. This was a proposal to reduce the inaccessibility of some of the midland counties. It was based on a detailed assessment of the potential markets for water-borne products of local agriculture and industry. There were 71 market towns and 42 mills and forges which were thought of as likely customers, and the traffic in coal, lead, lime, iron, stone, timber, and wool was expected to amount to thousands of tons per week. The scheme (though revived with a peevish air in 1753) came to nothing. It represented in effect, however, a transitional stage between the navigation of existing streams and the cutting of extensive new channels and was a step towards the true canal. But for its current, the Wey had already been made to resemble a canal by the middle of the seventeenth century, for two-thirds of its length was composed of lateral cuts across bends in the river. When the Mersey and its tributary, the Irwell, were being made navigable in the 1720s the river was so criss-crossed by lateral cuts of this kind that it appeared to its first historian, writing in *The Gentleman's Magazine* in 1821, to have become a veritable canal—the first, he was mistaken enough to claim, to have been made in England.

It was, of course, as natural for those engaged in the engineering of one type of water undertaking to shift their attention to another as the basic conditions confronting them altered as it was for the experience gained in solving one problem of hydraulics to be drawn upon in meeting one of another type. Thus it was in 1708 that the town authorities of Liverpool, when faced with the task of improving their harbour, should have turned to George Sorocold, the most versatile engineer of his day and the renowned designer of the Great Howland Dock. In this way they became introduced to another London engineer, Thomas Steers, who had been engaged in the works at Rotherhithe. Steers not only drew upon this experience to build

Liverpool's first dry dock but he became a fountain-head of ideas in the planning of the Mersey-Irwell Navigation, in making the Douglas navigable for getting out Wigan coal, and in lending advice on the navigation of the River Weaver for the carriage of Cheshire salt. He it was, moreover, who between 1730 and 1742 really did open the canal age in the British Isles by crossing to Ireland and building, across the most unhelpful terrain, the Newry Canal to bring the coal of Tyrone cheaply to the sea.

This was one source of the canal idea in England. But the historical and geographical associations between improved rivers and canals were so intimate and direct that to be too precise about the ending of one era and the beginning of another would be as pedantic as too narrow a view of the separate components of the communications system of an area would be pointless. This is particularly plain in the circumstances leading to the cutting of what has come to be acknowledged as the first English canal of modern times. What brought the Sankey Navigation into being against the background we have been considering were economic pressures that in the opening decades of the eighteenth century had successively touched off every kind of transport response in Liverpool's hinterland and would continue to do so long after they had culminated in the first genuine canal of the industrial age.

Until the end of the seventeenth century, Liverpool had been connected uncertainly with the interior of the country by bad roads, a wide but treacherous estuary, and contorted rivers. Even as late as 1750 the road between Warrington and Liverpool was not fit for coaches, though the Mersey had been made navigable to this point under an Act of 1694. This scheme was primarily an acknowledgment that though the Mersey was naturally far less helpful for trade than the lower reaches of most of England's rivers, it had already outclassed the silt-laden Dee as a commercial outlet for the region. The re-orientation of the country's overseas trade with the development of the North American colonies and Ireland was giving to Liverpool a position second only to Bristol among the western ports. Making the Mersey navigable as far as Warrington was to take a sizeable step towards reaching Manchester in the same way. To arrive there by water was another matter, and the contentions and delays *en route* occupied almost thirty years. The first survey of the Mersey and Irwell took place in 1712 and the final navigation of the route was completed in 1740, twenty years after the passage of the Act which authorized the work.

The other main tributary of the Mersey, the Weaver, had had an even longer history as a navigation scheme and led on sooner to the cutting of an authentic canal than the navigation of the Irwell did. The critical elements in this situation were the difficulties in maintaining an expanding triangular trade between the South Lancashire coalfield around Prescot and St Helens, the saltworkings of the Weaver basin, and the port of Liverpool. A proposal to bring the Weaver into commercial use above its tidal reach had been made, rather timidly, as early as 1663, though the failure of the

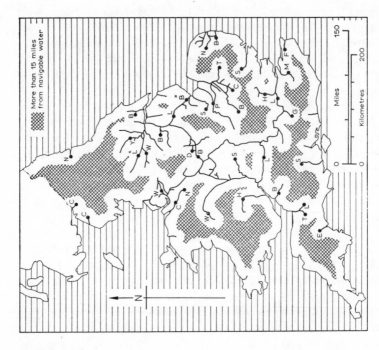

Map 7 *Distance from navigable water, 1790*

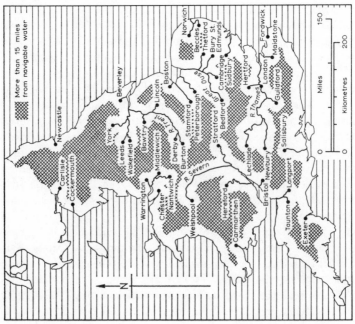

Map 6 *Distance from navigable water, 1700*

seven bids which were made for parliamentary approval down to 1720 was much less the result of indecision than of clashes of interests. There were minor rivalries between the colliers of South Lancashire and Staffordshire and between the road hauliers and rivermen, but the major collision occurred between those who produced salt from the brine-springs of Northwich and those who did so from the rock-salt mines at Marbury nearby. The former refined the salt before consigning it overland to the nearest tidal water and the latter did not do so until its arrival there. The rock-men had therefore more to gain and the brine-men a comparative advantage to lose by the navigation of the river beyond the tidal reach of Frodsham Bridge. However, the brine-men were divided against themselves by the sheer extent of the saltfields stretching away upstream to Middlewich, Winsford, and Nantwich. What the brine-men on the upper reaches gained over those lower down in the cheaper carriage of coal from Staffordshire they lost to them on the longer trek their finished products had to make to Merseyside. Beyond the point to which Lancashire coal could be carried as cheaply as the Staffordshire more of the advantages of distance passed into the hands of those nearest the Mersey. The alignment of these interests to the various proposals which were made might have been drawn with a protractor, so accurately did they measure the costs of moving these bulky raw materials and finished products by land and water towards their collecting centre at Liverpool. Once the scheme had been enlarged to include the Witton Brook and the main stream as high as Winsford the importunate clamour of the Liverpool merchants for some means of increasing the output of salt could not be shouted down by the few brine-men who still had little to gain and much to lose. But it was another eight years before the first concrete proposals were agreed and work begun. By the beginning of 1732 the navigation had been brought to Northwich and it was carried up to Winsford by the following spring. Nantwich alone stood beyond the pale. The river had been given a new mouth and the channel straightened here and there, but as an engineering feat coming towards the close of a long era of such improvements it was otherwise unremarkable.

The agitation for a navigable short cut to the salt-fields had stemmed from the commercial centre of Liverpool because with the winning of highly-prized and expanding markets for salt in Ireland and Northern Europe, the problem of freeing this trade from the restrictions of the pack-horse trains which moved both the salt and the coal that was needed to refine it had been growing annually more urgent. The navigation of the Weaver was only a partial solution to this problem however. As at least one ton of coal was required to refine three of salt it did not take long before the expansion of the salt trade was threatened by a fuel crisis produced by relying solely on pack-horses to transport Lancashire coal to Merseyside, where refineries were beginning to be set up in preference to locations on the other side of the Mersey on the salt-fields themselves. The other industrial and domestic needs of Liverpool for coal and foodstuffs were multiplying rapidly in step with the three- or four-fold increase in the town's commercial activities between the 1720s and 1760s. These had been met only to a very limited extent by the turnpiking of the road to Prescot and St Helens between 1726 and 1749, and by the coastwise movement of coal which had been made possible by the navigation of the Douglas. It therefore seemed to the town authorities in Liverpool when they considered the matter in 1754 that the logical solution to these difficulties would be found in the navigation of the Sankey Brook, which meandered across the flat land between the coalfield and the navigable reach of the Mersey below Warrington.

By this date the Corporation's first engineer, Thomas Steers, had died and his post taken by his clerk and apprentice, Henry Berry, who was now commissioned to survey the Sankey Brook with a view to applying the same techniques as had been used on the Weaver. The technical problems were in fact as different as they could be. To soothe parliamentary prejudice by appearing to obey convention was one thing, but to have done so literally would have been futile, and Berry made instead the logical response of a single deadwater cut, a veritable canal, which used the Brook merely as a reservoir and overflow, nowhere as a navigable channel, and was separated from it by a lock. The Sankey Navigation was opened in November 1757 to the highest navigable point of the Brook, half-a-mile from its mouth, and five years later to the Mersey itself, in order to overcome shallows at neap tides; to avoid this trouble altogether the canal had later to be carried another four miles to Widnes. There were also some tidal difficulties on the upper reaches but these did not interfere seriously with the canal's basic commercial function of enabling Liverpool to surmount both its own fuel crisis and that of the Cheshire saltfields as well. It was essentially a complement to the Weaver Navigation and the means of expanding the outlet for a valuable return cargo of salt out of Liverpool, by using the same 35-ton sailing barges on each leg of the triangular trade between the Lancashire coalpits, the Cheshire salt-wiches, and the Liverpool quays. One sequel to it was that during the ensuing decade the Weaver had to be widened in some places in order to conform to the width of the canal for which it had been the logical premise. Another result may well have been that the whole project encouraged the fulfilment of an idea (just as it had pioneered some of the necessary techniques) for another canal which had been evolving long before in the vicinity of Manchester. There the uselessness of the Mersey & Irwell Navigation as a means of tapping another seam of the self-same south Lancashire coalfield was becoming more and more obvious.

Manchester was almost ringed by coal but it sold in the town at double the pit-head price owing to the cost of carrying it most of the way there by pack-horse or cart. The Mersey & Irwell Navigation—the Old Quay Company, as it was known locally—bore some of it on the final stretch, but its own course disqualified it from doing more. It had been dug out originally to the specification of Thomas Steers in order to make a vent for trade with Liverpool, but this promise was slowly being suffocated by the confusions produced by alternately undredged or flooded channels and the shiftlessness of carriers. A scheme for making the Worsley Brook navigable had got through parliament in the headlong days of 1720 and something of the kind was much later the subject of discussion between the Old Quay Company and the first Duke of Bridgewater, and an Act was even obtained for that purpose in 1737. The time proved unripe in many ways and the idea of a speculation to bring cheap coal to Manchester by this means dissolved completely. Actually, this commercial problem of high transport costs was less acute than the production problem of preventing the flooding of underground coal workings, and it was the familiar expedient of tapping these by an adit or sough which would run the water off at a lower level that now came into play as the logical step towards using that very source for transporting the coal which could as a result be safely mined. This was the essence of the famous Worsley Canal, which was the first to be built in Britain entirely independently of an existing river.

When he took possession of the Worsley Park estate in 1757 nine years after succeeding to the title as a minor, Francis Egerton, third Duke of Bridgewater, had already begun to form that knowledgeable passion for hydraulics and that adventurous opportunism which were to govern his life and make him the first entrepreneur of the canal age. He had inspected some of the most celebrated Continental canals while on the Grand Tour and though he did not discover for himself the formula that combined the ideas necessary for his grand design he did exploit them with consummate skill. The notion of a sough enlarged to a canal was really due to his agent, John Gilbert, who was primarily a mining engineer and was responsible for all the early surveying and overall direction of the construction of the canal. What was also crucial to the enterprise was the unlettered, empirical genius of the Staffordshire millwright, James Brindley, who took charge of the forward operations. No less vital was the duke's own wholehearted commitment and resourcefulness. Theirs was a collective engineering triumph. For although the works that were begun following the Acts which were obtained, with deceptive ease in 1759 and 1760, covered a mere ten miles and were of the simplest conception in following a single contour, they demonstrated at once and with incredible *panache* almost the whole range of technical possibilities that now lay within the grasp of the engineers of that day and the next two generations.

The original scheme was for a canal that would enable coals from Worsley to be dispatched down one arc of the canal to Salford and down another to a point on the Mersey just below its junction with the Irwell. This was a project which entailed a complete range of novel problems in tunnelling, crossing bog, embanking, cutting, and making all kinds of elaborate earthworks. To these was presently added, by varying the original line, the ineffable wonder of that age, the Barton aqueduct, which carried the new canal clean across the Irwell and in midsummer 1761 brought the duke's first cheap coals triumphantly to Stretford in the suburbs of Manchester. The Old Quay Company which had in the past embarked the duke's coals at Barton Bridge and had confidently awaited the gratuity of Worsley water in their navigation, now provided a side-show of inefficient transport as seven or eight bargees struggled to get their vessel to breast the stream of the Irwell while a single horse almost effortlessly shifted 50 tons at 4 miles an hour through the treetops overhead. Four years later the canal was brought to a fittingly capacious terminus with the Medlock at Castlefield, where the coal could be had for 3½d. a hundredweight, half the old cost. Within a year, after rejecting the idea of working arrangements with the Old Quay Company (as well as the alternative of buying them out) the duke pressed his advantage still harder against them by what was perhaps the hardest fought private bill in the history of transport, and thus got into a position to claim the through traffic to Liverpool.

The last 24 desperately difficult miles from Stretford to Runcorn, all on the same level and to the original 14-foot gauge, were completed in 1767, though it took another nine years to clear the financial and legal obstacles and make the cut that locked the Bridgewater Canal to the Mersey—using for the first time in England a flight of ten locks—and yet another fifteen before the whole work was consummated by a new dock alongside. By then, these refinements did no more than reiterate the fact which the first stretch between the Worsley soughs and the Barton aqueduct had long made plain, that, given an adequate supply of water, canals could be carried almost anywhere.

2   Completion of the trunk routes

Already the beginning of the canal age in Britain had had its end and the possibilities of canal-building were being fulfilled, even before the prototypes of the Sankey and Bridgewater Canals had been articulated in their final form. The second phase of canal development lasted till 1790. It opened with a meteoric burst of promotions between 1766 and the crisis of 1772, which also marked the death of Brindley, and this was followed by a much longer period of consolidation and more detailed modulation of the system, interrupted only by the depression of 1778–84. This was the period in which all of England's great river systems—the Severn, Thames, Great Ouse, Trent, Humber, and Mersey—were made to subscribe to a single system of navigable trunk routes; it was also the period in which the conjunction of the Forth and the Clyde was planned and executed. (*See Map 7*, p. 84.)

The Seven Years War (1756–63), it is true, sapped a little of the impetus which the work of the pioneer canal builders had imparted, but once the war debts had been funded private credit could expand and interest rates fall. It was on the crest of the post-war boom in construction of all kinds which now followed that the first major elements of an integrated system of waterways could be hauled into place. The great wave of legislation began in 1766, but in one sense canal promotion had never ceased since the Sankey Brook had been surveyed. As early as 1755 the first exercises in bisecting the country by its first trunk canal had been made by two Liverpool surveyors (at the Corporation's expense), and three years later another had been undertaken by Brindley, this time primarily at the instance of the Duke of Bridgewater's brother-in-law, former guardian, and parliamentary ally in canal enterprise, the lord lieutenant of Staffordshire, Earl Gower. His and his collaborators' scheme was to circumvent the Pennines, yet link the Mersey and the Humber, and thread together some of the most important industrial regions of the North Midlands and the North. This latest eruption of an idea that had been aired before probably took place among the members of the Lunar Society in Birmingham, with which Dr Erasmus Darwin, Matthew Boulton, and Josiah Wedgwood were particularly concerned. It was certainly the tireless advocacy of the idea by Wedgwood and his friend, Thomas Bentley, a Liverpool merchant, that saw it successfully through.

This was the start of the Trent & Mersey Canal, or the Grand Trunk Canal as it was also known from its earliest days, in the hope that other canals would soon attach themselves to it as branches to a tree. The scheme was, quite simply, to make a narrow cut of 93 miles—except for six locks at the eastern end the rest were only 7 feet wide against 14 feet on the Bridgewater Canal—from Wilden Ferry on the Trent just above its junction with the Derwent, and to carry this north-west across the watershed at Harecastle beyond the Potteries, and so down to the Mersey. It was far more ambitious than anything yet done and Earl Gower, for one, hesitated to go on until the politically innocuous Bridgewater Canal had shown the way. Just the same neither its advocates nor its enemies left the field clear, and the scheme had to be brought through one fierce encounter after another—mainly with river interests on the Trent and Weaver who would have curtailed the line at each end and made it vulnerable to neap tides and their own control—until it won parliamentary approval in 1766. The year before the Duke of Bridgewater had altered the line of his Runcorn cut by agreement with Wedgwood so as to receive the northern end of the Grand Trunk.

In the same day's parliamentary business that launched the Grand Trunk an entirely independent scheme for a canal that covered half the distance and slighted fewer established interests was authorized much more quickly. This was the Staffordshire & Worcestershire (or Wolverhampton) Canal, which was meant to form a junction with the Grand Trunk and be connected with the Severn near Bewdley. Actually, local merchants there later cut off their own noses by opposing the scheme and deflecting the line a few miles downstream where the mushroom town of Stourport was planted and flourished instead. Both these canals were engineered by Brindley, and the crucial truss to support the whole structure of the canal system which he had visualized was visibly moving into position.

The main purpose of both canals was industrial. The promoters of the Grand Trunk mentioned the rock-salt deposits in the valley of the Dane (which had never been made navigable under the Act obtained in 1720), building materials, limestone, marl, and agricultural products, but they had their eyes primarily on Staffordshire coal and iron and the multifarious needs and commercial opportunities which the canal would cater for in the Potteries. Its raw materials were brought by sea and river barge either up the Trent to Willington, the Weaver to Winsford, or the Severn to Bewdley, and thence up to 40 miles by pack-horse. The trading area had expanded very considerably in the preceding thirty years and the finished pots, instead of reaching merely the annual market fairs of Staffordshire or being hawked further afield only occasionally, now made the same return journeys over- land and downriver. The stimulus of a rising population and the growing habits of drinking tea and beer meant an expansion in the demand for earthenware and a potential national market for the Potteries.

To Wedgwood, who in 1763 was already beginning to lift himself above his fellow-potters by perhaps the most remarkable flair for salesmanship and distribution in the business annals of the eighteenth century, the canals were the vital means of meeting not only this popular demand but the many changes of fashion that he deliberately created over the next forty years with such tact and determination. What attracted Wedgwood to the canal idea were plainly its commercial possibilities. Among these was one goal that to a potter was exceptionally desirable: the prospect of getting his pots to his customers without breakage, something that straw- filled crates on pack-horses could never guarantee. Understandably, when the Staffordshire & Worcestershire Canal was completed in 1772 and the Grand Trunk in 1777, Wedgwood, who had become the latter's treasurer, was engaged in using the new means of transport to the full and in doing so achieved success for himself and prosperity for the Potteries at large. One sign of this was the extent to which he was already eliminating the middle- men who were in the eighteenth century the symbols of an archaic system of communications.

The centre of gravity of the canal system was beginning to shift southwards and the next few years saw it envelop Birmingham and reach for London. The Birmingham Canal, authorized in 1768, was appropriately enough the first to give to the town its claim to be regarded, as Jackman has put it, as the Kremlin of canals, for it immediately provided a link with Liverpool, Bristol, and Hull, and became in time the basis for the Birmingham Canal Navigations which controlled almost all the cuts which radiated from the town. Again the surveyor was Brindley, and though the line that was pro- posed was locked on the narrow gauge and straggled badly over the 22 miles from Broad Street wharf through Wolverhampton to a junction with the

Staffordshire & Worcestershire at Aldersley, it was entirely adequate for the coal traffic that was intended. The first load from Wednesbury was carried in 1770 and the whole work was completed two years later.

So began the process of interlocking the network by the formation of canals between canals. Two vital elements in this process were the Coventry Canal, conceived and authorized in 1768 as an artery for coal traffic between the town and the partially completed Grand Trunk at Fradley Heath, and the Oxford Canal, which emerged from a welter of opposition the following year with permission to latch this line to the Thames and so, it was hoped, open the way to London. Both were soon halted miles short of their termini, the former by the crisis of 1772 and the latter by that of 1778. It was then that the Birmingham & Fazeley Canal, which aimed at breaking the Birmingham Canal's local monopoly by an alternative cut to the Grand Trunk *via* the Coventry Canal, thus making the first link by water with London, managed to stimulate them all into a drive for completion. The following year the Birmingham & Fazeley was merged with the monopolist and its very name soon obliterated, but all works continued, and in 1790 every connection was finally made. By this date, too, some new cuts had been started in other directions, most notably in 1776 by the Dudley and Stourbridge Canals, which together made a shorter line between Birminghan and the Severn by way of the Staffordshire & Worcestershire at Stourton.

During these years the classic cut to connect the Thames and the Severn was also carried through at last. It was a relatively easy and rewarding matter, as the promotion of the Droitwich Canal had shown in 1768, to open a blind cut to the Severn, and by 1779 this had also been done lower down the river by the Stroudwater Canal. Its very line and easy profitability soon rallied widespread support for covering the remaining thirty miles to the Thames, and the Thames & Severn Canal, brought into being in 1783, was by 1789 passing 30-ton coal barges into the Thames at Inglesham just above Lechlade *en route* for London. Unfortunately, except for the erection in the 1770s of some ten locks by the Thames Commissioners (a body created in 1751 to control the river above Staines), its stream remained in much the same condition as it had been in the middle of the seventeenth century. Thus the Commissioners thwarted the purpose of the Thames & Severn Canal (and denied them their profits) by insisting that the traffic that could find its way downstream did not justify improvements. Goods from Birmingham which reached the river by the Oxford Canal were in 1790 regularly carted by road to London instead.

In the North and in Scotland the main canals under construction during this period were designed to cross the country like great transoms between east and west. In the north of England the major barrier of the Pennines was more formidable than most promoters had supposed and work begun in this period was mostly completed long after it. The most ambitious and costly was the Leeds & Liverpool Canal which between 1770 and 1777 began to make its 127 mile course through Wigan, Burnley, Skipton, and Shipley (where the little Bradford Canal was attached in 1774). Work was held up during the long depression of these years and when it was resumed in 1790 it took until 1816 to finish. The Huddersfield Canal, which was authorized in 1774, did not span the Pennines between Huddersfield and Ashton-under-Lyne before 1811, partly owing to the need to pierce the highest ground by a prodigiously long tunnel of 5,456 yards and to construct 74 locks—all but ten of them in flights—as well as other engineering works in the course of barely twenty miles. (*See Map 9*, p. 93.) The first to get satisfactorily across the back of England was, in fact, the Rochdale Canal (1794–1804): although this included 92 locks in the 33 miles between Sowerby Bridge on the Calder & Hebble Navigation and its junction with the Bridgewater Canal in Castlefield, Manchester, it required only two short tunnels of less than a hundred yards each. By contrast, though the Chesterfield Canal, which was surveyed by Brindley in 1769 with the object of bringing the coal, lime and lead of North Derbyshire cheaply to the Trent, involved 65 locks and a tunnel of over a mile-and-a-half in its 46 miles, it was not held up for money and was completed in only five years (1788–92). Three other shorter but important cuts started in the north Midlands at this time were the Shropshire Canal (1788–92), which was promoted by the Darbys and Reynolds, ironmasters of Coalbrookdale, the Cromford Canal initiated in 1789 and subscribed for, among others, by Richard Arkwright, and the Chester Canal which, in linking the Mersey tideway and Nantwich between 1772 and 1780, reached beyond the old Weaver Navigation and made in effect the opening cut of the hopeful and glorious flop of the Ellesmere Canal.

In Scotland, the Forth & Clyde Canal, a project aimed at shortening the hazardous sea-route through the Pentland Firth, was gestating for a century before being built to John Smeaton's designs between Leith and Greenock in the years 1768 to 1790. Like its limb, the Monkland Canal, which had been started in 1770 in order to move Lanarkshire coal down the winding contours of the Clyde Valley, it soon ran into financial difficulties and work was halted for some years. (*See Map 8*, p. 93.)

3   The canal mania and its aftermath

The third phase of the canal era opened with the exhilaration of a spectacular boom in construction of all kinds in 1790 and closed 40 years later in the ominous gaiety that marked the opening of the Liverpool & Manchester Railway. It was a period heavily charged by war and its aftermath, but it was also the period in which the power stroke of the industrial revolution lifted output to unprecedented heights and threw a great new load of industrial raw materials and manufactured goods upon the transport system. The canal boom of 1791–6 included a brief period in 1792–3 when the re-

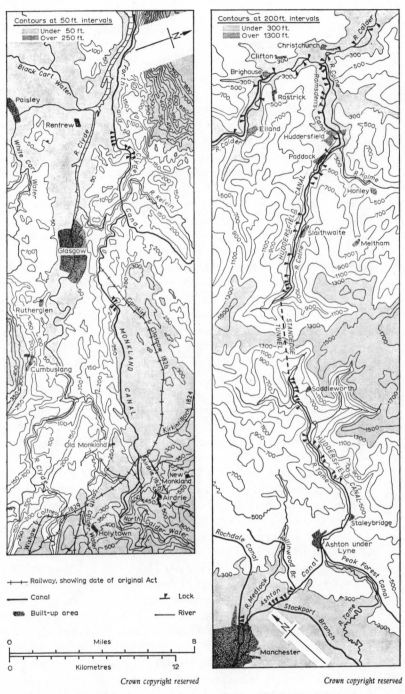

Map 8 *The Monkland Canal*   **Map 9** *The Huddersfield Canal*

sponse to these ebullient conditions almost became an investment bubble—a "canal mania": "perseverance having vanquished prejudice, the fire of speculation was lighted", wrote Richard Fulton, the American authority on inland navigation, in 1796, "and canals became the subject of general conversation".

In general the boom of the 1790s was no more than an uninhibited acknowledgment by the investing classes that canals were the only form of transport that could accommodate this expansion and that canals would therefore pay. The financial and operating successes of the earlier canals had not all been very convincing, it is true, but those that had had difficult days now began to share in the easier conditions that came with an expansion of the currency, more bountiful harvests, and a widespread surge of manufacturing production. Some of the most important canal undertakings were already undeniable successes: the ability of the Birmingham Canal to pay out 23 per cent in 1789 after two or three years of recession was rapidly reflected by a mark-up in the value of its shares, and by 1792 one £140 share fetched £1,250, another £130 share in the Staffordshire & Worcestershire went for £1,100, and the market price of Grand Trunk shares was more than treble their nominal value. No doubt the inclination of inexperienced investors to misconstrue particular successes for a general lift in prospects was as rife then as it has ever been. Investment in public undertakings was too recent a development for the signs to be read correctly, anyway.

Between 1791 and 1796 the authorized capital of the 51 new canal companies which secured an Act was over £7½ million. Total authorizations reached their peak in 1793-4, but although the outbreak of the war with France had already affected canal promotions along with other capital projects, plans already set going took time to fulfil and even in 1796 three new canals were being authorized at a total capital outlay of over half a million pounds. It is certain that, even if disenchantment did not come quickly, a substantial part of this investment was misconceived. The inflationary tendency which their own massive outlays helped to initiate was soon accelerated by the circumstances of war, and a number of canal companies never surmounted the difficulties which this entailed.

Easily the most important undertaking to be launched during the mania was the Grand Junction Canal, a scheme for a barge canal that would redress the inefficiencies of the Thames Navigation and the narrow artery of the Oxford Canal, through which London's waterborne commerce with the Midlands and the North passed with difficulty. The collapse of two schemes for by-passing long stretches of the Thames by canals that would take the largest barges—the first London Canal (1770) and the London & Western Canal (1792)—left the field open for the Marquess of Buckingham's proposal for a much more direct cut of about 93 miles (scarcely longer than the overland route) between Brentford and the northern stretch of the Oxford Canal at Braunston. This was authorized in 1793 along with a scheme for the Leicestershire & Northamptonshire Union Canal, a potential link that would continue its line by means of the Soar (the Loughborough Navigation, which had just been completed) to the Trent and that highly productive area beyond; this was already being tapped by the Erewash Canal (1777-9) and probed deeper still by the Cromford, Nottingham (1792-1802) and Derby Canals (1793-4).

Despite some taxing problems in engineering, the Grand Junction Canal itself, bristling with branches, was finished with some alacrity by 1805. It immediately opened up new routes to the Black Country and the lower Severn through the Warwick & Napton (1794-9), the Warwick & Birmingham (1793-9) and the Stratford-upon-Avon Canals (1793-6); the Worcester & Birmingham Canal (1792-1815) and a short but difficult cut to it by a branch of the Dudley Canal (1793-1801) removed the last major hindrance along this line—the low level to which the Severn just below Stourport could drop in dry weather. The Grand Junction's promise of a route to the Trent had been denied for a time by the abandonment of the Leicestershire & Northamptonshire Canal in the crisis of 1797, where work did not resume until 1810-14. A new undertaking, the Grand Union Canal, then took over and set about justifying its name. The Grand Junction dominated canal promotion to the end of the French wars in 1815, but its function as a barge canal was frustrated by two flights of narrow locks on the Grand Union and the narrow gauge of the Birmingham network: however, the broad channel was well adapted to speedier use by narrow boats and it became the conscious policy of the company to foster this kind of traffic. The canal's usefulness to Londoners was greatly enhanced when the branch to Paddington (1795-1801) was supplemented by the Regent's Canal (1812-20), which brought it into the heart of the new Docks to a basin at Limehouse.

Though London never became a canal metropolis in the sense that Birmingham did, it was her needs more than anything which governed the promotion of canals throughout the south of England. War-inflated prices and virtually guaranteed, as well as expanding, markets for home-grown foodstuffs made many small schemes for penetrating agricultural and mining areas beyond the reach of tidal water or river navigations look self-assured. Yet this was not, with one or two exceptions, an important arena for canal enterprise. The Kennet & Avon Canal, built between 1794 and 1810 as a barge canal to link London and the West more efficiently than the deprived and half-stifled Thames & Severn Canal had been able to do, did develop a large and reasonably lucrative traffic, owing partly to its being fed by the much more prosperous Somersetshire Coal Canal (1794-1805). In the south, too, was the largest canal in the country and perhaps the only one of its vintage to pick up profits with the coming of the railways, the Gloucester & Berkeley Ship Canal. This was built between 1792 and 1827 to give ships up to 600 tons an alternative to the treacherous reach of the Severn below Gloucester. But even at their busiest the waterways of southern England probably did not carry more than about 15 per cent of the country's total water-borne traffic and they could never match the earnings of those in the Midlands and the North.

To Wales canals came almost entirely in one burst of promotion in the last decade of the eighteenth century. They were successful only in the south, where the heavily trenched valleys of Glamorgan and Monmouthshire contained the essential ingredients of the industrial revolution, coal and iron, and one centre in it, even in the 1790s, held something approaching nine-tenths of the country's copper production and a substantial part of its tin-plate. Canal promotion was the firmly grasped means of releasing the enormous potential of this natural bounty at just the moment in time when new industrial processes were becoming available—notably Cort's puddling furnace—and the demand for ferrous products was being very rapidly expanded by war; the dominant element in the economy of South Wales throughout the canal era was iron. Four canals—the Glamorgan, Neath, Monmouthsire, and Swansea—which were built between 1790 and 1799, and another two, the Brecknock & Abergavenny and the Aberdare, which were open by 1812, were virtually the only means of moving practically all the iron and coal used in South Wales throughout the first half of the nineteenth century. Though some trade did take place with the southwest, exports of coal were relatively unimportant until after 1850. Owing to the configuration of the valleys, these canals did not form a system as they did in England, but became more intimately identified with the fortunes of a single valley and its complement of collieries and ironworks than was possible almost anywhere else in the country. They also became the arteries for numerous colliery tramroads which covered ground inaccessible to the canals. These, and the existence of some 176 locks in a total of a mere 72 miles, made a precarious basis for the prosperity of the canals in that region.

In the north of England and in Scotland the mania and the years that followed spawned many more small fish than big. For the most part, this was more a period of detailed modulation of the existing canal framework than it was of the conception and execution of new trunk routes. Apart from the Rochdale Canal, which we have already noticed, only the Birmingham & Liverpool Junction Canal, built in a financially unpropitious period, 1826 to 1834, in order to make a negligible saving in mileage (though a sizeable one in lockage), could properly be regarded as offering new trunk facilities in England. In Scotland, both the Crinan Canal (1793–1801), which contrived to save time on the sea route to the Western Isles but caused a good deal of financial and navigational trouble, and Telford's triumphant feat of a ship canal through the Great Glen, the Caledonian Canal (1803–22), were also in this category, though the rapid development of steamships which were less at the mercy of the weather diminished their usefulness almost from the start. For the rest, the canals of this period were mostly either tributaries of existing ones or ingenious intersections with navigable rivers. These were canals which were mainly designed either to reach land-locked sources of coal or limestone or to shorten some existing line between the principal cities. Among the most important of these were the Lancaster (1792–1816), Barnsley (1793–9), Peak Forest (1794–1800), and Macclesfield Canals (1826–31).

By 1830 the great building was over and there were in existence in Britain over 4,000 miles of navigable waterway. (*See Map 10*, pp. 104–5.)

4   Finance, construction and management

Unlike the turnpikes, almost all canals were owned by private incorporated bodies of shareholders and administered by management committees which, instead of discharging the functions of disinterested trustees serving the needs of the locality, aimed at making a profit and distributing a dividend. In the scope this gave for speculative investment they closely resembled the railway companies which were soon, quite literally, to replace so many of them, but, unlike the railways, canals were not the subject of speculative promotion: their promoters did not launch them for the quick and easy profits that could be made later on from the sheer act of doing so. They were mostly local men—leading social figures, landowners, farmers, industrialists, traders, and country bankers—men who were as often concerned to meet their own local needs for improved transport as they were to profit directly from the canal. There were some important exceptions to this tendency: the Forth & Clyde Canal, for example, was largely financed in England. Wherever local enterprise was the dominant force it tended to give way, once the canal became a commercial success, to more geographically diffused ownership, if only because of dealings on the Stock Exchange. The Ellesmere Canal, which was oversubscribed four times when it was projected in 1793, was probably exceptional in the extent to which this process was carried. By 1822 (it had become the Ellesmere & Chester Canal in 1813), less than a third of the shares was held in the counties through which it passed and the rest were diffused throughout almost the whole of England and North Wales: the biggest concentration of 20 per cent was in Leicestershire, and London proprietors held 15 per cent of the shares.

The preliminary agitation for a canal in a locality, in which hopes were raised and fears were, if possible, soothed seldom reached beyond the area intended to benefit from the canal until sufficient support had been found. Even at this tentative stage costs were being incurred, and it was vital to collect subscriptions that would cover both the surveying and other initial expenses and the capital sum thought to be required for the main works. Almost inevitably, such schemes frequently cut across incompatible economic interests, not only in the same locality but farther afield, mostly those of existing canals, river navigations, turnpikes, towns that faced the diversion of trade, and landowners who feared for the catchment of their

G

water supplies. Unless they were outmanoeuvred at every turn of the running battle to which each private bill was liable, its opponents might kill it outright or spoil its intentions by deflecting the canal's course or depriving it of some of its water. Once the canal had been authorized, the shareholders elected the committee, appointed the various officers (chairman, treasurer, and secretary), paid over whatever proportion of their shares was wanted to meet immediate expenses, and settled down to the long programme of construction and to meeting further calls on their shares, sometimes even in excess of their nominal value.

The financial history of the Peak Forest Canal for which, incidentally, Samuel Oldknow, the cotton manufacturer, was the leading promoter, typifies the kind of difficulty which was encountered by the promoters of even a moderate sized undertaking. The Act of 1794 authorized a capital of £90,000 in £100 shares, and £8 per cent was immediately called up, making a total initial subscription of £15 per share including the original deposits. The company was also authorized to raise a further £60,000 by mortgaging the tolls, but in the stringent period at the end of the 1790s, when an attempt was made to raise these loans, only £36,540 could be obtained. This, and the failure to raise the last £9,400 of the authorized capital, made for serious difficulties and by 1796 the company had run into a bank overdraft of £40,000, a quarter of which had to be guaranteed by the management committee itself. This also had to produce the further £4,000 which was apparently necessary to complete the works at the summit level between Whaley Bridge and Buxworth. By 1800 funds were quite exhausted and a further Act had to be obtained authorizing the company to raise by new shares or promissory notes up to £150,000 including previous subscriptions. Oldknow, who had first taken 52 shares, now raised his holding to 261.

The cost of construction was difficult to predict because although the main line of the canal was only about fifteen miles long, it involved an aqueduct of 90 feet to cross the Mersey and a flight of 16 locks to raise the level by some 212 feet in order to connect with the Macclesfield Canal at Marple; the original plan to carry the canal on from Buxworth to Chapel Milton had been discarded for financial reasons, but the seven-mile railway which was substituted to cover the whole distance thence to Limestone Rock in the Peak Forest was not cheap to construct and it involved a fairly steep inclined plane of 600 yards. The additional authorized capital could not all be raised, but the £70,000 or so that was subscribed was soon fully committed, and at a shareholders' meeting in 1801 it was agreed to make an additional call of £10 per share, which was to be repaid with interest before dividends on the main stock could be paid. By 1803–4 the construction of the Marple locks and the other works had used up all but £573 and the company was forced in 1805 to seek a third Act, which now authorized a last instalment of £60,000 share capital. Perhaps it was not surprising that, whatever value it had as a means of connecting the heavily industrialized valley of the Goyt to its markets, it should have rewarded its shareholders so little: in 1830 it was paying 3 per cent and its £100 shares were selling for £88.

Most canals, in fact, cost more to build than had been expected, and only one tiny undertaking, the Pocklington Canal (to connect the town of that name in the East Riding to the Derwent) seems to have been built below its estimate. Some of the larger undertakings exceeded estimates by very wide margins: Brindley had estimated that the Leeds & Liverpool Canal would cost £260,000 but it absorbed £1¼ million, and the Kennet & Avon cost more than double the original figure of £420,000.

It was customary to pay nominal dividends out of capital before working receipts came in, a practice which may have been necessary in order to maintain faith in the enterprise but undoubtedly contributed in the long run to the severe financial difficulties of a number of companies. Except for the prolonged support given to the Scottish canals and the direct assistance given by the Poor Employment Act of 1817 (which was first intended to alleviate unemployment but initiated the continuous allocation of public money to capital projects of this kind), the government seems to have remained aloof from canal enterprise. The size of the government's contribution to transport undertakings at large in the first half of the nineteenth century—for docks, harbours, bridges, turnpikes, as well as canals—was considerable, and in the 35 years during which the 1817 Act was operable the canals benefited most: the Regent's, Thames & Medway, North Wiltshire, Montgomeryshire, and the Edinburgh & Glasgow Union Canals were among those that received grants.

The share capital of canal companies was generally subdivided into £100 ordinary shares, though a small part of it was sometimes raised in the form of debentures, or in the entirely novel form of preference shares. This was a form of share capital first developed in canal enterprise. It originated in the need to obtain large sums from an investing public which was still chary of trusting too heavily to the ordinary stock. A fixed rate of interest which was payable after any debenture payments had been met was often thought better, especially during the critical construction phase, than the pie-in-the-sky of ordinary shares. On the other hand, it could happen that the ordinary shares were enhanced in value far beyond their face value and they were then usually sub-divided into quarters or even into eighths to facilitate dealings in them.

Relatively little is known about the sources of the short-term capital of which canal companies must at times have stood in more urgent need than share capital or mortgage loans. It is more than probable that the main source of short-term accommodation was the banking system. London bankers as well as those in the provinces committed their own funds and undoubtedly strongly influenced the investment of their clients' in canal shares, but it is clear from the records of the Oxford Canal that bankers were ready enough to go further and make ordinary loans.

The construction of the canals with simple manual tools and horse-power, often across the most difficult and inaccessible terrain and much of it years ahead of the Ordnance Survey (whose one-inch maps did not appear until 1801 nor cover the whole of Great Britain until 1870), was a herculean task. Canals had a plasticity denied to river navigations and the mere recognition that they could be carried almost anywhere stimulated engineering ambitions and increased the whole scale and complexity of their operations. Aqueducts became commonplace, tunnels a standard alternative to steep flights of locks, and a variety of technical devices—new designs of lock, inclined planes and lifts—was developed to meet particular problems.

If river navigation gave birth to the profession of engineer the canals provided most of its schooling, and when the Institution of Civil Engineers was chartered in 1818 it was fitting that Thomas Telford (1757–1834), whose canal work even outshone his roads and bridges, should have been elected its president. His canal masterpiece was a pair of exhilarating aqueducts exactly suited to their function at Pontcysyllte and Chirk on the Ellesmere Canal, but his work is to be traced quite as tangibly not only along the many miles of canals that he personally engineered but in the work of his contemporaries whom he undoubtedly influenced. Since James Brindley (1716–72) had begun his restless and resourceful career in canals—excluding the Bridgewater Canal, he planned and started work on seven canals covering no less than 340 miles between 1768 and 1772—almost all the leading engineers of their day had either been drawn into canal work or started their careers there.

John Smeaton (1724–92), probably the greatest civil engineer of the eighteenth century and one of the very few canal engineers to have matriculated first on river navigations, was one of the lords of appeal in the early part of the canal age when untried men were proposing some daring things: he is reputed to have scorned the notion of the Barton aqueduct. He performed some of his greatest work on the Calder Navigation and the Forth & Clyde Canal, but it was probably in his own small club for engineers which he founded in London in 1771, The Smeatonians, the forerunner of the Institution with which it was merged, that his influence was at its most solid. Ten years before that he had become the guardian of the son of his former resident engineer during the building of the third Eddystone Lighthouse, Josias Jessop. William Jessop (1745–1814), who became one of the leading engineers of the canal period, made his debut as an engineer under Smeaton's tutelage, then formed a partnership with Benjamin Outram which resulted in the formation of the remarkable coal-and-iron firm, the Butterley Company; and finally, when he was appointed consulting engineer to the Ellesmere Canal in the heat of the mania, he came into close working association with Telford, which lasted for the rest of his life. Among the principal canals which he built were the Barnsley, Erewash, Cromford, and Nottingham Canals, and the Leicester Navigation.

John Rennie (1761–1821), who set himself up in London in 1791 primarily as a canal engineer, built the Crinan, Kennet & Avon, Rochdale, and Lancaster Canals, while developing an even bigger reputation as a builder of docks and bridges. It was in Rennie's employment that James Green (1781–1849), himself the son of an engineer, obtained a training in canal construction which led to his important work on the canals of southwest England. Such personal connections were the vital means of transmitting the skill of one generation to the next before the industrial revolution itself enlarged and diversified the whole matter of technical training.

There were other contributors, not all of them lesser ones, to the building of the canals, men who belonged to this same tradition but of whom we mostly know little more than their names and the schemes they undertook: Hugh Henshall, Brindley's brother-in-law, Robert Whitworth and Thomas Dadford, both of whom had been Brindley's assistants and whose sons learned from them, Josiah Clowes, Ralph Dodd, and Nicholas Brown.

As for the actual execution of canal building by the armies of "navigators", too little is known about them to say at all confidently just how they were organized. It is probable that some of the work, perhaps even the bulk of it, was performed *ad hoc* by whatever labour could be attracted to it by its promise of apparently continuous employment and good pay, though more specialized work must generally have been given to contractors. When the Sapperton Tunnel (the second largest in the country) was being built on the Thames & Severn Canal between 1783 and 1789 the contract was let, after open tendering, to a Manchester mason and miner who sub-contracted part of the work to others, some of whom took over from him when he failed financially. It seems likely that large contractors, like Edward Banks, whose methods clearly foreshadowed those of the railway period, began to make their appearance in the early days and took over more and more of the work after about 1790.

Down to 1845 canal companies were almost invariably forbidden under their Acts to operate barges of their own (though not from trading on their own cuts) because canals were regarded as common highways open to all users prepared to obey their by-laws and to pay the tolls. Unlike the generally smaller charges that canal users had to meet for haulage, tolls were *pro rata* per ton-mile (a form of measurement, incidentally, that the railways did not adopt for accounting purposes before 1922). Tolls were generally tapered down as the mileage increased, but were precisely limited to varying maxima by the Act. Discriminatory practices were expressly forbidden but as no minimum rates were laid down this did not prevent the development of the common practice of allowing drawbacks, nor did it prevent collusive agreements between canal companies, or full-scale mergers. As the canal network developed it became in fact a cat's-cradle of conflicting interests in which the established concerns were usually able to defend their trading position by obtaining compensation payments from rival companies whose lines threatened to lower their own tolls. The carrying trade does not seem to have been basically different from that which had grown up on the river navigations, except perhaps for the more marked appearance of firms operating fleets of boats and more elaborate schedules of services.

There were, for example, 34 firms operating as canal carriers in Birmingham alone about 1830. The craft themselves had obviously been adapted from river work, but the sailing flat which had inaugurated the Bridgewater Canal had soon given way almost everywhere in England to the narrow boat of about 70 foot keel and 6′ 10″ beam: this fitted the normal lock as a bobbin in a shuttle or, paired together, quite as snugly in a broad one. Such a boat carried an average load of 25 tons with a laden draught of nearly three feet, and was usually towed by a single horse at two or three miles per hour. Just how many such boats there were in their heyday, how the carrying business was organized, and what were its returns is not known in detail.

5 The economic significance of the canals

What were the economic results and overall significance of the building and operation of the canal system before 1830? It would be possible, quite simply, to regard the canal period merely as a transitional episode in the history of industrial technology, falling as it does between the phases in which the natural resources of easily canalized rivers and of coal were in turn exploited to the full. That would be a correct but limited view of their place in economic history. There are three aspects of the economic significance of canals which this view tends to disregard and which may be noted straight away in very general terms before we consider their results in a little more detail.

The first is that they dramatically enhanced the efficiency of the whole economy. That bad roads produced a kind of sterility in the country was a matter for common observation towards the end of the eighteenth century, and canals could be considered, as John Phillips in his *General History of Inland Navigation* pointed out in 1792, "as so many roads of a certain kind, on which one horse will draw as much as thirty horses do on the ordinary turn-pike roads." A much earlier writer, Nehemiah Grew, a scientist of sorts, had calculated that canals had a differential advantage over wheeled traffic of 1:12 and over the packhorse of 1:16. In economic terms, this improved efficiency was at once the product and agent of a much larger process which was at work, that of substituting relatively plentiful for relatively scarce factors of production. The essential characteristic of almost all contemporary industrial development was simply the introduction of labour-saving machinery capable of increasing the returns to effort. Put another way, labour was being replaced to some extent by capital, more or less rapidly according to their respective availability and the trading prospects in each industry. The canal system was the extension of this process of increasing the power and versatility of the human arm by the investment of proportionally greater amounts of capital per unit of output. It was at the same time a means of increasing the productivity of capital itself by keeping it more regularly and economically employed than had been possible in a less efficient system.

The second general point of significance is that the canals were the means of overcoming a fuel crisis which threatened to limit very sharply further industrial development: cheap, abundant supplies of coal were crucial to an increasing number of industries whose production techniques had been transformed, first by its high suitability as a fuel, and then by the potentialities of steam-power. The canals alone could have coped with the demands created in this way at that stage in the history of technology. Writing in 1803, Phillips claimed that 90 of the 165 Acts obtained for canals since 1758 had been to serve collieries and another 47 on account of iron, lead, and copper mines and works.

Thirdly, the building of the canals, as distinct from their operation, gave massive employment and created spending power at a time of strategic consequence for the growth of industries looking to mass markets. In this the canals supplemented the effect of other construction industries, including road-building, and though they were also partly responsible for increasing the fluctuations in economic activity which were becoming apparent, their general developmental contribution to economic expansion was undoubtedly very considerable. It is clear that in a number of ways the canals can be regarded, not merely as a brief adventure in hydraulics with a hang-over of obsolescence and nostalgia, but as the vital prerequisite of the railways and of the great Victorian boom which attended them.

The total capital invested in canals and river navigations cannot be computed with certainty. No select committee inquired into their general condition before 1883, nor were they subject in any respect to the oversight of the Board of Trade, which would have led to the accumulation of a variety of data; when asked by parliament for the first time in 1870 to declare their capital position the companies' returns were often vague or incomprehensible. The actual capital raised in shares or debentures, or by long-term loans, remains unknown. One estimate of the capital committed to the inland waterways of England and Wales in 1882 is over £19 million, and the sum invested even fifty years before, when the canal system had grown to its maximum extent, cannot have been much below this. How well employed all of this was is no easier to discover. It is worth noticing in passing here that the market for canal shares was not a perfect one: their Stock Exchange prices were not widely or systematically publicized during the main building period—*The Gentleman's Magazine*, for example, did not add this information to its regular quotations of government funds and commercial stock before 1810. Not surprisingly perhaps it was possible for one writer in the *Quarterly Review* for 1825 to say: "It is frequently asserted that the produce of the whole of the canals in this kingdom

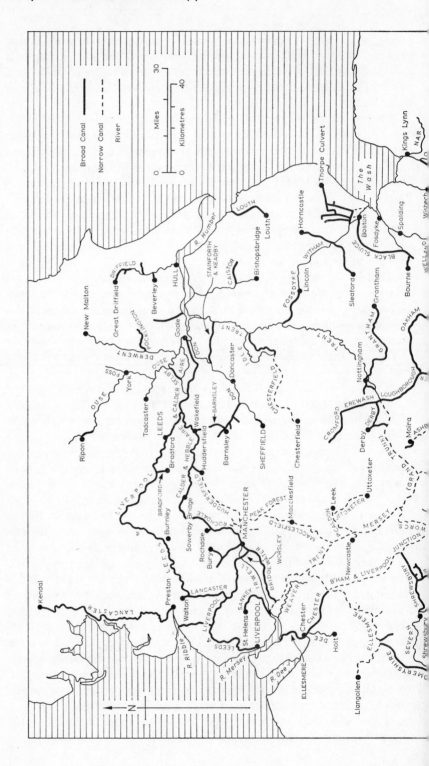

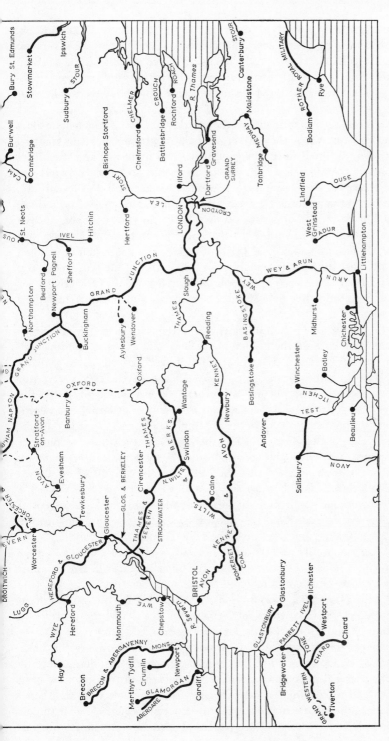

Map 10   *The principal waterways, c. 1830*

does not amount to nearly the legal interest on the whole of the sums expended in forming them." It would, in fact, be as great a mistake to suppose that all of this capital was productively employed as it would be to think that the contribution of canals earning little or nothing for their shareholders was necessarily insignificant in terms of general economic well-being.

The record of profits made by the canals does come somewhere near bearing this out when they are regarded in aggregate, but the financial history of individual undertakings was often so mercurial and the differences between the financial position of companies so great that aggregate figures tend to be even less informative in this matter than they usually are. According to the writer in the *Quarterly Review* in 1825, of about £13¼ million invested in 80 canals and which was then producing on the average 5¾ per cent, a quarter was rewarded by dividends of 10 per cent or more, but almost £8 million paid only 2½ per cent or less, and about half of this had not up to that time produced any dividends at all. At one pole were a top ten capitalized at a mere £1¼ million averaging dividends of nearly 28 per cent, and at the other pole were 37 companies which barely met their expenses.

It is difficult to verify such statements and to neutralize the special pleading that often entered them. One of the difficulties of the economic historian, especially in the period which now followed, arises from the growing use of statistics as propaganda. In this particular case the canals were not made to appear over-profitable. Why, then, ran the message between the lines, should their businesses be made any more difficult to run by new competitors—more canals or, more threateningly, railways? According to another estimate in the summer of 1829 there were 31 companies paying 6 per cent or more, of which the Loughborough Navigation, the Birmingham, Erewash, Coventry, Mersey & Irwell, Trent & Mersey, and Oxford Canals distributed dividends of between 32 and 140 per cent; and there was still a number of canal companies paying dividends handsomely in excess of 30 per cent as late as 1838. The outstanding successes were mainly in the industrial Midlands and the North, the capital sumps in the South.

Whether financially successful or not, all canals had the initial effect of lowering the costs of overland carriage by at least a half. On the most efficient canals costs could fall to a quarter of what they had previously been, though the average was more like a third. This was the canals' critical contribution to general economic growth for it widened the horizons of both internal and external trade. Lime and marl could rectify soil deficiencies more cheaply for farmers and, with the help of the turnpikes, the canals could also begin to break down the regional segregation of agriculture along with the regional price differentials in perishable foodstuffs that had been its chief feature. Although some of these effects on prices were smothered by inflation, the relative improvement in the supply of perishables in under-supplied places like London, Liverpool, and Manchester, where food riots now subsided if they did not disappear, was inescapably counterbalanced by dearer prices in the areas supplying them. This was naturally accompanied by loud and sometimes violent protest by the consumers in those areas, and those farmers who had had urban markets virtually to themselves took unkindly to a lowering of prices which simply ate into their monopoly profits. Producers' and consumers' interests could scarcely avoid conflict at either end of the supply line when changes were so radical. To industrialists like Josiah Wedgwood, Samuel Garbett, Matthew Boulton, Samuel Oldknow, and many others, cheap carriage by canal was the master key to markets everywhere and neither fragility nor bulk was any longer a disqualification to their products entering trade. "Until the middle of the century", observed a Frenchman in 1790, "there was not one Birmingham trader who had direct relations with foreign centres: London merchants' warehouses had exported Birmingham goods. Now Russian or Spanish firms order what they want direct from Birmingham."

How much the canals were used for normal passenger services it is not possible to say with any precision. That there were such services from the very beginning and that they continued well into the railway period is clear enough. A passenger service had opened at fares of a penny a mile on the Bridgewater Canal in 1766 and by 1800 its net income was approaching £5,000 a year. Some operators divided the accommodation into classes and the traffic itself was classified in terms of speed. Ordinary packet-boats towed by a pair of horses, changed at intervals of four to six miles, normally averaged 8 or 10 miles per hour, and there were in some places fly-boats which improved even on this. But however fast the passage on an unlocked stretch, locks were bound to slow progress down quite appreciably. One such run, for example, on the Leeds & Liverpool Canal between Liverpool and Wigan involved five locks and took from 8 a.m. to 4 p.m. to cover the 35 miles. However, the canals never provided a national passenger transport service as they did, for example, in Holland.

In view of the high profits made by the leading canal companies it is reasonable to ask whether the cost of carriage was lowered to its practicable limits. Canal companies were usually in a monopolistic position and were free to vary the tolls below the statutory maxima, but there seem to be no authenticated cases of rate-cutting nor, apart from a Bill that came to nothing in 1793 to limit canal companies' profits, were they subject to any general legislation in the interests of canal users. Having secured control of a trade route, not infrequently by breaking a monopoly of road and river interests, canal companies were always liable to exercise the prerogative of the monopolist themselves. The Sankey Canal proprietors did so unblushingly after promising to stabilize their charges, and the owners of the Loughborough Navigation, mainly Loughborough traders, exploited their position to the full before the opening of the Leicester Navigation forced their prices down. On the other hand, the Duke of Bridgewater more than kept his pledge of bringing coal to Manchester at half the cost of land carriage for forty years, despite the huge growth in his personal debt, and maintained a very modest tariff, without any collusion with the Mersey-Irwell Navigation, to the end; it was after his death in 1803 that the old charges were trebled, a price-ring organized, and the ground for an alternative, cheaper form of transport unconsciously prepared. It should be added that even the duke's record is marred by his ruthlessness in running down a proposal for a canal in Cheshire which would have competed with his own.

Even without more overt acts of monopolistic pressure to go upon it is easy to see that the very disjointedness of the canal system was bound to keep prices needlessly high. There were some isolated attempts to make various common working arrangements, but full-scale operations like the organization of the Shropshire Union (1846)—a mere prelude, in fact, to its being leased the following year to the London & North Western Railway Company—or the Birmingham Canal Navigations (1784–1846) were exceptional. The varying gauges of channels and locks and constant changes in the permissible draught, or the slowly deteriorating river navigations which were in some places the only means of holding the canal system together, tended to keep the average size of consignments small. The narrow boat could go virtually anywhere, except on the tub canals of the West Country, which were in any case unconnected to the main canal system, but the larger barges of the northern and southern canals were limited to their own regions.

It may seem curious that in an age quite used to the concerted action of traders there should have been so little attempt by the canal companies to combine, however loosely, in their own interests. The whole economy had not yet fully emerged from a condition of regionalism and it was still natural enough to think first of purely local requirements. What was conspicuously lacking was some kind of pooling arrangement to share tolls and to make the passage of through traffic easier and cheaper: it was not until 1897, for example, that the four companies covering the route between London and Birmingham made joint arrangements that made it possible for through tolls to be quoted even by the owner of the greater part of the route, the Grand Junction Canal. With profits coming easily to the leading concerns and no inclination on their part to dilute them by mixing their operations with unprofitable concerns there seemed to be little need to do more. In particular, the notion of a clearing-house, which would have made the companies themselves more efficient and have lowered the real costs of canal transport for their customers, did not commend itself. Nor were canal users helped in calculating the money costs of shifting their goods owing to the almost total failure of the canal companies to publish books of rates.

It is clear from all this that it is not easy to generalize satisfactorily about the scope that existed for lower prices on the canals. It would be wrong, for example, to suppose that the big reductions which canal companies were forced to make in the face of railway competition are an exact measure of earlier overcharging. One of the biggest reductions that then took place was made by that old monopoly, the Loughborough Navigation, whose tolls of 2s. 6d. a ton fell to 4d. after 1836. But it is valid to regard the reductions which were then made of between a third and a half as an approximate indication of the scope that existed. In the public's mind, the canals had by 1830 assumed the mantle of monopoly and this odium was a powerful element in their destruction.

Many of the benefits conferred by the canals cannot be quantified nor even isolated. How many head of cattle and other livestock, or loads of muck scavenged from London mews and streets were carried by them, or precisely what subtle mutations they caused in local marketing, or how much the prosperity of one place or the hard times of another are to be attributed to them no-one can tell. They clearly gave to the existing river navigations a new significance. But they also complemented and protected the turnpikes by accepting heavy, bulky loads that were damaging to the roads. They also gave to the coastal trade, not the weakening blow it had feared, but the benevolence of its greatest prosperity. In unsuspectingly pioneering horse-drawn railways as their own feeders among the collieries or as both temporary and permanent links in their own system, they also pioneered some of the early railways. Perhaps more important still, the canals familiarized a much wider class of lenders with the opportunities of investment in equities, advanced engineering skill, and gave a preliminary exercise in the logistics of large-scale contracting—all of which made a handsome legacy for the railways.

4

The creation of
the railway system

1 The early railways

If water-power and the navigation of waterways provided the technical basis for the opening phase of Britain's industrialization, iron and steam were clearly the means of entering the second. Yet the railway, which was the very embodiment of this development, had antecedents very remote from their use. The notion of arranging for the wheel to travel on a narrow smooth surface is almost as old as the wheel itself, and some historians claim to be able to recognize the rudiments of the modern railway in the rutted tracks and grooved streets of ancient civilizations. But the essential step of placing the wheel on a raised rail does not appear to have been taken before the Middle Ages, when wooden tracks were installed in the silver and gold mines of Central Europe. It was roughly in this form that the practice was also soon developed in England, not in underground workings nor to get out precious metals, but at the pit-heads of collieries having no cheap access to navigable water.

On the Trent, then the Severn, and then on the Tyne and Wear, the technique was widely adopted in the course of the seventeenth century as a means of winning coal from relatively shallow pits set back from the river, rather than from greater depths at the river's edge where difficult and expensive pumping operations were needed. Coal-mining, despite the fitful expansion of demand since the sixteenth century, was being conducted within very narrow physical limits both above and below ground, and until Newcomen's steam-engine drastically revised the scope of operations at the coal-face from the 1730s the only practical way of holding costs and prices within commercial limits while expanding output was to find a cheap substitute for the pack-horse and the wain as the first step in putting the coal on the market. The colliery wagonway was the result. In its most primitive form it comprised short oak or fir rails around six inches thick pegged to sleepers and bedded directly on the undulating ground; the wagons were simply four-wheeled hoppers capable of discharging a load of about two tons through a hinged bottom directly into a coal-barge, and were man-handled or propelled by a combination of horse-power and gravity. In time the rails were strengthened by extra strips of beech or plane, or even of wrought iron at points of extreme friction, and supplemented by light bridges, turn-tables, and so on. Despite their high initial costs—one built at Ravensworth in 1726 cost £785 per mile—and their heavy wear and tear, the wagon-ways handsomely justified themselves to colliery owners substantial enough to build them, for they were capable of raising the productivity of wagon drivers five times or more, and were less vulnerable to bad weather than the ordinary roads. What often sapped their profits and sometimes led to violence and frequently to legal action, were the high wayleaves exacted by landowners whose ground had to be crossed to reach the staiths and the waiting keels.

The growing scarcity of timber in the eighteenth century and the increasing loads that had to be carried soon put these almost wholly wooden wagon-ways at a premium. In 1731 the cast-iron wheel had been patented and flanged wheels were soon in use on wagons of strikingly modern design on the railway which Ralph Allen had had built to carry stone from his quarries above Bath to the Avon. In 1767 the first iron rails were laid at Coalbrookdale, where the Darbys had begun to produce heavy castings for engine parts in place of the kitchen utensils on which they had been concentrating, and therefore had need of a more robust, yet cheaper track: between 1768 and 1771 they manufactured 800 tons of cast-iron rails, and by 1775 had laid nearly 20 miles of them for their own use. William Jessop's fish-bellied cast-iron rails a yard long, which were laid for the first time to the canal dock at Loughborough in 1788 and Thomas Barnes's modification nine years later, which made them abut rigidly in chairs on stone blocks instead of wooden sleepers, meant that although the raw material was as yet too brittle for heavy loads travelling at any speed the basic elements in the design of a railway and its rolling-stock had definitely evolved.

The parallel development of the plate-way of cast-iron with a flange on each inside edge was also taking place in the collieries of the North Midlands and presently to a great extent in South Wales, and its simple section soon enabled it to be made in the more durable but costly material of wrought iron: the earliest case known occurred at Alloa in 1785, but such rails were rare for at least twenty years. The advantage of the plate-way was that ordinary carts could become railway wagons without adaptation and use the track on payment of a toll, which was the manner in which a number of canal companies developed some of their feeder services, following the example of the Trent & Mersey Canal from its very inception. But it was the edge-rail which was eventually made of lasting importance by John Birkinshaw's discovery in 1820 of a way of rolling wedge-shaped wrought iron rails. This was a distinct advance on the slender square bars lapped together and held by a pin that had been the subject of earlier experiments. Within the next few years the wrought iron edge-rail established its superiority beyond doubt, though it was many years before cast-iron or even wooden track was completely abandoned.

The adaptation of the steam-engine to these railways was relatively slow, despite the simplicity of its basic technology and the prior work of James Watt and his predecessors on low-pressure steam engines. Watt's difficulties in perfecting the standards of workmanship required for the installation of his engines may have kept the possibilities of deriving steam-power from a much more compact, even transportable, design of high-pressure engine to the back of his mind. Raising the pressure to, say, two atmospheres was not so much dangerous as unnecessary, given the volume of work in hand. His patent rights to all types of condensing engine did not expire until 1800, but it was around this time that the advantages of engines with smaller cylinders of at least comparable power were becoming apparent. With the cost of horse fodder rising rapidly during the French wars an alternative form of traction had special merit, particularly in areas where a new source of power could be had in abundance. It is not surprising that it was a mining engineer, Richard Trevithick, who first took the step of designing a steam locomotive specifically for the railway. He had already built and demonstrated a steam-carriage for use on the roads but the site of his new experiments was Samuel Homfray's colliery at Penderyn near Merthyr Tydfil, where he demonstrated his unnamed locomotive in 1804; he showed another at Gateshead a few months later. Heavy enough to give its smooth wheels full purchase on the rails, it was not light enough to avoid breaking them; powerful enough in getting steam up, and even to using its own exhaust to augment the boiler fire, it was not capable of maintaining the pressure and keeping on the move. Thus the main problems to be solved were how to increase power without adding to the overall weight, and how to strengthen the rails without greatly raising their cost. These were the problems occupying a handful of men, mostly in the north-east, whose labours over the next twenty years to make the locomotive work efficiently made their names household words—John Blenkinsop, William Hedley, Timothy Hackworth, and George Stephenson—and whose efforts produced in the end a commercial railway capable of depending on steampower and an iron road. The principal means of doing so were the multi-tubular boiler and the wrought iron rail.

The idea that the railway could exist as an entirely independent institution was crystallizing at the same time. As with all new forms of transport, the railway had come into being as an economical modification of an existing mode of transport. In the 1790s, for example, the Lancaster Canal Company had closed an already built-up gap between two stretches of their canal in Preston by a railway five miles long, and the Ashby Canal, which used dry land to avoid costly locking, had become little more than a railway with canal appendages. Quite properly, for at least twenty years

H

to come railways were inclined to be classified topographically—as in Rees's *Cyclopaedia* (1819)—under "canals". The building of a railway that could offer effective competition to the canals, much less the turnpikes, barely antedated Trevithick's prototype of the locomotive itself, though the Duke of Bridgewater had long anticipated this threat. One of the flings barely thwarted during the canal mania had been a scheme to connect Cardiff and Merthyr Tydfil by a railway which would have rivalled the Glamorgan Canal; and an even more ambitious proposal, fortified by military considerations, came up in 1799 in a scheme to carry a horse railway from London to Portsmouth, an alternative route to that offered by the Basingstoke Canal which had been opened three years before. More modestly, its immediate practical result was the first public railway to obtain parliamentary approval, the Surrey Iron Railway, authorized in 1801 to carry a pair of plate-ways from Wandsworth to Croydon and subsequently to Godstone, though that point was never reached. Before it had been opened in 1803 the original aim of reaching Portsmouth was revived in plans drawn up by William Jessop for an outlay of £430,000, an unprecedented sum for a railway, and this proposal now directly confronted the still more costly alternative schemes prepared by John Rennie for either a broad or a narrow waterway to carry the Croydon Canal to the dockyard at Portsmouth. Victories at sea and persistently dear capital at home slowly blunted the whole exercise, but in the claims and counter-claims over capital and running costs were signs of a bitter struggle to come.

Elsewhere other public plate-ways were coming into use, mostly in South Wales and the Severn Valley, all of them having at least one terminus alongside navigable water; and with the opening in 1807 of the Oystermouth Railway on the Mumbles beyond Swansea passengers were carried in a regular railway service for the first time. These were all puny undertakings: sixteen only were established for an aggregate outlay of much less than a million pounds during the first twenty years of public railways, and the longest line to be built, the Hay Railway (notable also as including the earliest railway tunnel in the country) covered a mere 24 miles. With so little to see on the ground it was understandable that, despite the publishing success in 1821 of the most credible vision yet of the railway's potential scope, Thomas Gray's *Observations on a General Iron Railway*, few men could foresee such fragments ever being collected into a general railway system which did not merely wheel around navigable water.

These possibilities were sharpened presently by the active development of a scheme for a conventional horse plate-way to run between Stockton and Darlington as a means of exploiting the Durham coalfield through one of its natural outlets, the Tees. The idea had germinated in the mind of Edward Pease, a Darlington merchant and banker, as early as 1810, when the river had been improved by a lateral cut below Stockton, but it had been held in suspense between 1812 and 1815 while the alternative of a canal was being thoroughly explored on the advice of Rennie, a scheme which eventually foundered with the failure of a big local bank. The first bill for a horse railway, based on a survey made by George Overton, the engineer for the works at Penderyn, was defeated in effect by the local hunt in 1819, though a second voluminous bill for a new line, which kept clear of the foxes, struggled through in 1821.

It would be a little melodramatic to date the beginning of the railway age from this very day on which the Stockton & Darlington Railway was authorized. That was the precise moment at which Pease met George Stephenson, already an engineer of some standing, and was persuaded by him to go for steam locomotion on edge-rails. It is true that railway technology was such that the promise of steam was still a long way from being consummated and that the Stockton & Darlington Railway turned out in practice to be a hybrid of muscle and steam. It might also be said that the railway system was still a rather blurred vision in one or two men's minds and that it was not at all certain of becoming a concrete reality. But all that now followed was in fact the culmination of this initial stroke.

The decision first required another Act and this was obtained in 1823. Finally, and with some sense of natural drama, the whole main line of 27 miles was duly opened in September 1825. The track was laid with Birkinshaw rails only in part and Stephenson's own *Locomotion* which drew the first bedecked train gave way to a great extent to both horses and winding engines on ordinary working days: a horse had, indeed, preceded the locomotive even on the opening day, and such passenger traffic as there was was hauled by horses. But among the hundreds who came to see the new railway in operation were potential imitators by the score. These were struck less by the lack of a more powerful boiler in the engines than by the sheer business possibilities which horses and steam engines together could now realize. Without doubt this was a great theatre of commercial operations.

This railway built up its first traffic by following established usage. It took tolls, for example, from competing users of the track, just as the turnpikes did. This made commercial sense. The insignificant passenger receipts —no more than 3 per cent of the total in the first three full years of operation —were completely overshadowed by the volume of the coal traffic. The demonstration that steam locomotives could run cheaply enough to haul goods—a proposition which one leading authority, Henry Fairbairn, doubted as late as 1836—was as yet only half-proved to the outside world, but in some figures of costs per ton-mile for locomotives and fixed engines which Stephenson had required one of his resident engineers to compile in 1826 lay a comparison of some importance to Stephenson himself. Locomotives, according to Thomas Storey's figures, cost less than a farthing per ton-mile and fixed engines about a penny more: more significant, perhaps, was Storey's calculation that locomotives were cheaper by 30 per cent than horses—two comparisons which were less important for their accounting accuracy than for the strong hint they gave of the general direction in which costs were now moving and of the watchful attention they were getting.

That the same readiness to scrutinize costs was probably widespread is well illustrated by the Stratford & Moreton Railway, whose directors were taking pains to gather authentic information of the same kind in 1821–2. They rejected the advice of their engineer, William James, that when fully employed one of Stephenson's original Killingworth engines—which long ante-dated the *Locomotion*—would work at less than a quarter of the expense of horses, because they found on inquiry that locomotives required a much heavier track and would not work an adequate pay-load up an incline greater than 1 in 72 nor run appreciably faster than a horse-drawn train on the flat. Actually, their railway would never thoroughly justify investment in steampower and they rightly chose instead horses, light cast-iron rails, and a level route. Local circumstances governed everything. On two short plate-ways serving the Forth & Clyde Canal over flat ground— the Monkland & Kirkintilloch Railway and its extension (1826–8)—loco-motives were used effectively enough with horses; but on another much more ambitious line interconnecting two English canals over high ground —the Cromford & High Peak Railway (1830)—the locomotive yielded entirely to the fixed engine and the horse. Seven other new railways relied on horses alone in these years. At best the locomotive was still no more than a kind of courier to the vastly more powerful stationary engines that over-came gradients too steep for cuttings and too gentle for tunnels. Its in-glorious archetype was, perhaps, Stephenson's *Invicta*, which hauled the first passenger trains to be put into normal service with steam. This was on the level northern section of a couple of miles on the diminutive Canter-bury & Whitstable Railway, begun in 1825 in order to side-track the un-dredged Stour and completed under difficulties five years later with three laborious inclined planes.

Understandably, the builders of short local railways were right to dither between the horse, the locomotive, and the stationary engine until the efficiency of the locomotive had improved or railway plant given some promise of being used at full capacity. A real choice between these various forms of traction did not last for very long, though it did not end abruptly. On the Newcastle & Carlisle Railway, where the directors had had to change their minds several times since first deciding to connect the Tyne and the Solway by a canal, a final choice for the locomotive had still not been made when the rails came to be ordered as late as 1834. Where there was little dithering was in devising new directions in which railways, whatever the form of traction, might now go, and this promotional activity reached a peak for the first time in 1824–5. Some of the most important developments of the 1830s, such as the London & Birmingham and the Birmingham & Liver-pool Railways, were first mooted at this time but were suspended in the panic with which 1825 closed or were obliterated by the recession that occurred in the later 1820s.

The dramatic episode which set the railway boom going again also symbolically closed the first tentative phase in the development of the railway. This came in 1829 with the holding of the celebrated ordeal, as its organizers regarded it, on the Rainhill level of the almost-completed Liverpool & Manchester Railway, and with the unequivocal triumph of Stephenson's *Rocket*. When it opened almost a year later, in September 1830, this became the first substantial railway to rely completely on steam power. Behind it lay years of bitter resistance by landed interests and a whole generation of thinking about ways of breaking the local navigation monopoly, which was immune to competition in kind for lack of water to fill another cut. It should not be forgotten at the same time, that the descent into Liverpool raised difficult problems of the kind which the Canterbury & Whitstable Railway had only just solved completely a few months before. Yet the more persistent problem was the political one. The earliest railway projects had stirred in 1797–8, but the idea had not become emphatic till 1822, when the luckless William James surveyed a route through St Helens for a group of Liverpool merchants. With a prospectus arraigning the canal interests already out in 1824, the project had risen easily on the speculative tide of the following year, though Stephenson's uncritical adoption of James's survey reduced it at first to a parliamentary fiasco. It appears to have been retrieved from this by the rare political stroke of an adversary, the Bridgewater Trust, switching sides in the public interest rather than its own. Despite the implacable opposition of their agent, the Trustees were silenced by their own beneficiary, the Marquess of Stafford, who had been induced to invest £100,000 in the new railway, a fifth of the total capital required, and by the local M.P., William Huskisson, as a gesture of support for the unfranchised mercantile classes. The new line now selected by the Rennies also led more directly to a suburban terminus at Liverpool, offended fewer land-owners, and was defensible in engineering terms.

Apart from demonstrating so convincingly the paces of the locomotive, the Liverpool & Manchester Railway led the way in establishing the whole administrative apparatus of the modern railway; it broke decisively with the business practices of the turnpikes and canals which had left such clear marks on the earlier railways. It owned outright and operated its whole installation within a single undertaking, employing a regular staff to run it, neither sub-contracting any of its operations nor allowing others to use its plant on payment of a toll, and it lifted the whole scale of railway investment to an entirely new order of magnitude. In many coal districts collieries were already working their own wagons on the local railways, and although the Stockton & Darlington Railway kept the coal and goods traffic in its own hands, it continued down to 1833 sub-letting the passenger traffic to several coach proprietors; in the case of the Bolton & Leigh Railway, which opened in 1831 to link the Manchester, Bolton & Bury and the Leeds & Liverpool Canals, the operation of the whole line was leased entirely to a local carrier.

What also marked off the Liverpool & Manchester Railway from earlier undertakings was its clear emphasis on passenger traffic, from which it drew about half its revenue at the start; none of its predecessors had done more than cater incidentally for them. Apart from the fatal accident to poor Huskisson on the opening day, the railway halved the time and cost of travel between the two cities with perfect safety, and in its first three full years' operation it averaged well over a thousand passengers a day. The full journey one way over the thirty or so miles took about an hour-and-a-half, for which the average fare amounted to five shillings. Here, then, was a major railway between the two most important industrial and commercial cities in the provinces, solidly engineered despite great difficulties, completely mechanized, creating a demand that had not been thought to exist, working to full capacity with unparalleled efficiency, and distributing to its shareholders year after year with the same measured power that drove its engines a dividend of $9\frac{1}{2}$ per cent.

2   The first railway boom

Apart from nudging into existence some small branch railways and extensions, the Liverpool and Manchester Railway quickly energized two or three of the most important projects that had been half-dormant in the late 1820s. The earliest of these proposals were for railways linking Liverpool and Birmingham, for which two quite separate companies acting in collusion had issued prospectuses in 1824, but whose bills had easily been frustrated by canal interests fortified by the start of building operations on Telford's last trunk waterway, the Birmingham & Liverpool Junction Canal. Attempts at reducing the scale of one of the railway projects to that of a local line merely joining Birmingham and Wolverhampton and other desultory manoeuvres came to nothing, but by 1832 the various promoters were ready to consolidate in a single undertaking, the Grand Junction Railway Company, which was incorporated the following year with powers to start building the longest but least complicated line yet in existence over the 78 miles between Birmingham and Warrington; here a short link was to connect with the Liverpool & Manchester Railway at Newton-le-Willows.

The idea of a railway from London to Birmingham had also germinated among the promotions of the mid-1820s, but, despite sporadic interest in the idea in 1827 and 1829 culminating in the formation of another pair of companies favouring different routes, the first bill was not ready till 1830 and was soon thrown out. This procedure was repeated in 1832 when a consolidated company's first attempt to overcome the most intransigent opposition yet encountered by a railway bill succeeded in the Commons but not in the Lords. To only a small fraction of the land it had to cross did the company have undisputed access, and parliament itself was predictably hostile to any substantial interference, without compensating advantages, with an institution on which its own structure of power was still very largely based—the private ownership of land. The directors of the Grand Junction Canal and the Oxford Canal no less than the coach proprietors, wagon masters, and turnpike trustees who were directly threatened, also now had the vivid object-lesson of the Liverpool & Manchester Railway in front of them, and in their counter-petitions they were fighting for dear life. Others whose turn must soon come were also easily alarmed, and the whole issue tended to be stoked into a general argument. In the event, the land-owners whose basic complaint was that they were not getting enough for their land were handsomely bought off or avoided altogether, and the existing transport interests brushed aside in the lobbies by the putative rail-way interest now forming from the Liverpool party of merchants which was heavily backing the enterprise. The third bill went through in 1833 and all 112 miles were opened five years later, a year behind the Grand Junction Railway, at a total cost of £5½ million, more than double the original estimates.

London had already got its first passenger line working—the London & Greenwich Railway (1836)—if only as far as Deptford until 1838, but the line to Birmingham was its first inter-city connection. London had been assailed and a triumphal Doric portico was fittingly erected in Euston Square; but on the incline of 1 in 70 that led behind it to Camden Town a winding engine still had to overcome the deficiencies of locomotives down to 1844. Authorizing this first trunk route out of London was the prelude to two other acts of the same kind, one for the London & Southampton Railway, obtained with mere whimpers of opposition in 1834 owing to its discreetly chosen route, and the other for the Great Western Railway between London and Bristol, for which the Act of 1835 was the product of an ineluctable struggle of herculean proportions; they were fully in use by 1840 and 1841, respectively.

These three trunk routes were great imaginative feats of enterprise. They drew their inspiration directly from the pioneering work which had been done in Durham and Lancashire, but the promotion of railways was by the mid-1830s beginning to develop a momentum that owed rather less to tangible evidence of commercial success than it did to the sheer availability of capital and the hunches of businessmen. One of the striking impressions made by this period is the growing readiness with which capital was being subscribed without any very clear idea how it was to be used, whether it would be adequate, or whether it was being put into safe hands. It is true that the railways which had first captured the imagination of the lending public were beginning to repay that trust handsomely enough. The Stock-ton & Darlington Railway's dividend, which had risen to 6 per cent in 1831 and 8 per cent in 1834, soared to 14 per cent in 1837 and took with it the hopes of other shareholders than its own. But not all lines were by any means so encouraging to investors as they were to local merchants and industrialists, whose measure of success was often the size of the construction

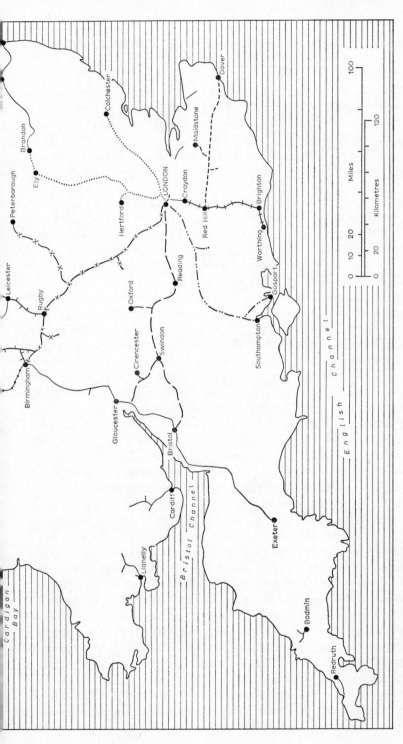

Map 11   *The railway system in 1845*

job and the cut to be made in freight rates. Though railway share prices were rising moderately enough during the early 1830s the rate of return on the capital invested in new lines frequently seems to have been a secondary consideration.

The acid test of a railway was not everywhere being applied in terms of distributed profits alone, and it was indeed the case that even the most sensibly conceived local lines can have done little to puff up the general expectations of investors. On the Leeds & Selby Railway, which was the rump of a much bigger scheme drawn up in 1824 to connect Leeds and Hull, the first dividend to be paid ten years later when the railway opened was a scanty $2\frac{1}{2}$ per cent and this petered out completely within three years. Perhaps the best illustration of modestly adequate returns is the Leicester & Swannington Railway, the first tiny component of the future Midland Railway. The promoters were led by John Ellis, a local Quaker landowner, and the line had been built under the eyes of both Stephensons between 1830 and 1832 as a means of getting local coal into Leicester cheaply enough to undo the monopoly which canal transport had conferred on the Nottinghamshire and Derbyshire collieries. This it certainly did, as the elder Stephenson thought it would when he invested in the line and bought a coal-pit himself, as well as a small country house nearby. In its first year the railway handled about 20,000 tons of coal and 13,000 tons of building materials; over the next ten years the latter remained fairly stable but the coal traffic multiplied about seven times. Receipts, however, grew less than four times and dividends averaged under 5 per cent throughout, though for the first three years, 1833–5, this was barely their aggregate.

This was not a line which had been conceived rashly or developed irresponsibly: indeed, its management was in some respects strikingly resourceful, though when the directors offered the first annual meeting of shareholders an explanation of the difference between their first estimates and the actual costs of developing the line as a going concern they had to admit their failure to include the cost of locomotives, rolling stock, and parliamentary expenses. If local investors, who could generally outvote the rest in an enterprise of this kind, were prepared to exercise such docile credulity, how much readier might they be to do so in one of more imaginative proportions? In this case the shareholders might have been more awake for much of the capital had been subscribed by solicitors in Lincoln. The new exhilarating optimism which began to sweep the railway market by 1836 owed nothing to the cautious pragmatism and modest earning power of dogged little lines like the Leicester & Swannington. Soon nothing succeeded like the promise of success and investors were prepared to plunge wildly into a rising market for railway capital, hopefully regarding every new proposal as a stereotype of the best.

Cheap money and a relative political calm both helped. The civil and political disturbances of the early 1830s had partially spent themselves, and two government stock conversions in 1830 and 1834 had helped to increase the supply of capital looking for higher returns than $3\frac{1}{2}$ per cent Consols. The prices of two crucial raw materials, copper and iron, had also been falling very appreciably. The low earnings on safe investments coupled with the rather ebullient tendencies of bankers when trade was visibly picking up inclined investors to seek more speculative openings. But the groundswell to the burst of investment which occurred in railways in the mid-1830s, as in a wide variety of other undertakings abroad and at home, was provided quite simply by the real growth in the wealth of the country which had occurred since 1821. This was the period in which the power stroke of the Industrial Revolution can be timed by the most rapid growth in industrial output to be achieved in the whole of the nineteenth century, and by the general level of investment in manufacturing industry, docks and harbours, and in the working apparatus of the industrial towns. It had not all been smoothly done, it is true, and expansion had been blotched by unemployment and agricultural depression, but by 1832 labour and capital were being rapidly absorbed once more by widespread heavy investment, which was augmented the following year by the customary expansionist effects of a short series of good harvests. All this did not react directly on railway investment straight away, but from the late summer of 1835 promotions began to boom rapidly in sympathy with buoyant economic conditions, and during 1836 parliament almost doubled the railway capital it had authorized in the preceding three years. In the following year the rate of promotion slackened, but for the two years 1836–7 the mileage of track authorized was more than three times the amount actually built—around 450 miles—in the four years from 1832 to 1836.

The railway map was still virtually blank, and almost any pair of towns, including some highly improbable ones, was now liable to be linked, not infrequently by more than one scheme: one promoter had three parallel projects for Durham, three companies competed for the opportunity to link London with Norwich, five to connect it with Brighton, and across the map of London itself the projected lines made a veritable lattice-work. Many of the proposals were mere confidence tricks and others dangled on such slender financial threads that they were liable to snap at any time, but the railway bubble alone was not responsible for the crisis that ultimately developed in 1837. The financial situation had become precarious almost from the start of the mania itself, and when the boom broke it did so largely under pressures created by an external drain of gold to the United States (whose economy had in effect become the complement of Britain's, principally through the cotton trade), and by the over-development of joint-stock banks and discount houses in this country. The triggering mechanism of the crisis, at least, was imported.

The decade 1833–43 witnessed the authorization of about 85 per cent of all railway capital raised so far and provided for as much as £73 million in new issues for the building of over 2,300 miles of track. That is the measure of this great cycle of promotions, but in fact a large part of it came to nothing simply owing to the difficulty of raising such large sums in the time. The amounts provided for in the Acts of 1835-7 had merely been subscribed and had now to be called up for the completion of the works. This meant that, although the main trunk routes authorized before the mania were still under construction during the promotional phase, its own main expenditures did not build up until 1838-40, when they were running, according to one estimate, somewhat beyond £10 million a year. The physical culmination of this growth cycle came in 1840 with the complete drying up of new railway bills—five only had been introduced since 1838—and the commissioning of well over 500 miles of new line in a single year. Its force was even then not fully spent, for, despite the general depression of 1841-2, railway building contracts were still being fulfilled at a rate not very different from that prevailing during the mania's promotional phase. By 1843 the national mileage of public railway track had multiplied about ten times for a total outlay which was computed, by a select committee reporting in 1844, at £54 million, and over 2,000 miles of railway were now in use, three-quarters of it having been built in the previous five years. Not all these figures are entirely beyond statistical reproach but they do represent reasonably accurately the net results of a process which can only be described as a gigantic demonstration of the commercial possibilities of steam railways that had first been realized with faltering efficiency in 1825 and then with real power in 1830.

This prolonged building operation could scarcely have been telescoped, though there was hardly one company which was not delayed at some stage either by unexpectedly difficult terrain or the demands of landowners or simply through their own miscalculations or mismanagement. The most notorious case of a railway being crippled by its finances is the Eastern Counties Railway. This was authorized with great expectations in 1836 as a line of 126 miles right through East Anglia to Norwich and Yarmouth, but the company raised its initial capital with some difficulty and then spent a million pounds in four years barely clearing London; it was utterly exhausted in another three, when it made Colchester its terminus and left the line beyond to another company, the Eastern Union, to be completed later. Even the soberly managed London & Birmingham Railway could not master the versatile geological strata along its route without more than doubling the estimated cost, and very probably shortening the life of its indefatigable engineer, Robert Stephenson. Apart from engineering and financial problems, both of which merit more attention in detail later on, many of the difficulties that arose were the natural result of the highly competitive conditions in which companies were being formed. Within obvious geographical limits every new mark on the railway map was making business possibilities more subtle and the collision of interests more violent, for lines were no longer localized but were beginning to form a system—disjointed as yet, awkwardly distended, with no common organization to articulate its parts, but without doubt a system capable of organic

growth. The railways were even now more consciously adapting themselves
to their total environment, changing their lines, their financial basis, their
internal organization, and their commercial policy, to suit circumstances
that could not be finally stabilized until the whole railway economy had
evolved. The railways had become, and were long to remain, highly volatile.

Their lines had now been ramified mainly across the Midlands and the
North, around London, and into the West Country. Bristol could be reached
from London over the broad tracks of the Great Western Railway by 1840,
and by 1844 it was possible to go by rail (though not on the same train
throughout) from Birmingham to Exeter. Rennie's London & Brighton
Railway was completed in 1841 and to it at Redhill was attached the following
year the South Eastern Railway, which was taken on to Dover by 1843.
From Crewe it was already possible to go on to Birkenhead or to Fleetwood
by 1840, to Manchester by 1842. Relatively small but vital connections had
also been made independently of the rest in the industrial parts of South
Wales and Scotland: the Taff Vale Railway connected Merthyr Tydfil and
Cardiff by 1841; Edinburgh, Glasgow, Greenock and Ayr were all linked
by 1842. (*See Map 11*, pp. 120–1.)

The system was a veritable house-that-Jack-built. The first element in
one complex—to choose but one example for closer examination—was the
Birmingham & Derby Junction Railway, formed in 1836 and opened in
1839. Almost at once its northern terminus was used as the southern end
of another scheme by the North Midland Railway which aimed at completing a line to Leeds, which was actually done by 1840; but wedged between
these two schemes in the parliamentary calendar of 1836 had been a third
company, the Midland Counties Railway. This had first been planned in
1832 as a direct response by Derbyshire colliery owners to the Leicester &
Swannington Railway's threatened closure of one of their important
markets, but which had been modified when the London & Birmingham
Railway had obtained their Act in 1833 so as to make the line run on to
Rugby to join it. The price which the Midland Counties Railway had to
pay for entering the ring was the dropping of its original intention at its
northern end of penetrating the Erewash Valley, which would have opened competition with the other two lines. A short link from the Birmingham
& Derby to the London & Birmingham lines southeast of the town finally
enabled the North Midland to circumvent the Midland Counties tracks
altogether. On the same day that the Midland Counties was authorized a
fourth component in this interlocking series was enacted as the York
& North Midland Railway, which was itself the successor to two other
dauntingly expensive proposals to connect York directly with London.
One of these, the Northern & Eastern Railway, had deliberately been cut
down in favour of the other Midlands companies we have been considering,
and it was not allowed beyond Cambridge, which it did not reach till 1845.
The York & North Midland Railway joined its 25 miles to the main trunk
of the North Midland Railway at Normanton in 1840, by which time

it had already begun its insidious conquest of a vastly greater territory. Yet another two companies authorized in 1836 meanwhile attached themselves to the network. One of these was the Great North of England Railway, which was initiated by the directors of the Stockton & Darlington Railway with the object of joining Newcastle to York, an undertaking not completed till 1844, nor without substantial modification, owing to the heavy cost of making the line as far as Darlington. The other was the Manchester & Leeds Railway, a veteran of 1824 now revived, which, having pierced the Pennines near Todmorden, joined the North Midland very conveniently at Normanton in 1841, a junction which parliament had forced upon it rather than allow it to duplicate the North Midland's tracks into Leeds. Among other branches and connections it made subsequently was one with the old Liverpool & Manchester Railway in 1844. Potentially, the last great rib to the North Midland Railway of this period was the Sheffield, Ashton-under-Lyne & Manchester Railway, formed in 1837 to tackle the most formidable physical obstacle of all. Tunnelling for three miles under the Pennines, it did not emerge to complete its line to Sheffield until 1845. Among the lines actually undertaken in the heat of 1835–7, it was virtually the last to be completed. Yet it was still separated by half-a-mile from the Sheffield & Rotherham Railway which had for five years attached Sheffield to the North Midland Railway. Closing this gap was the tiniest part of the hectic parliamentary business of 1845–6, two sessions of unparalleled importance in the history of the railways.

3   The railway mania

There had been several signs during the preceding eighteen months or so that the completion of the first great burst of railway enterprise had left both the money market and the labour market considerably under-employed. The ruling rate for discounting bills of exchange had never kept so low for so long, and 3 per cent Consols rose to par for the first time in eighty years. Cheap money was once more at work. In September 1844 its reign appeared moreover to have been extended immeasurably when the Bank of England's schizophrenic personality of central and commercial bank was enhanced by the Bank Charter Act, and the Bank itself now came more open-handedly into the money market than almost any of its competitors handling first-rate bills. Monetary confidence understandably suffused the whole scene. Railway shares came on to the floor of the Stock Exchange for the first time in a bull market, and the prices of the leading companies were marked up month by month. By the end of the year those of all but two of the companies which had fifty miles or more of track in use stood at a premium: the Great Western's £100 shares (of which £25 had not yet been called up) were fetching £150, even though the current dividend was nominally 7½ per cent; both the London & Birmingham's and the Grand Junction's fully paid-up shares almost reached £230 and both were paying 10 per cent. The apparent earning power of the railway companies was such that the government had already legislated, even if somewhat confusedly, for the eventuality that companies' distributed profits might exceed 10 per cent for long periods. Who could reasonably doubt that the last great spate of investment had paid off and that another was due? In February 1844 Gladstone spoke in parliament of an unprecedented abundance of unused capital and of his conviction that it would soon be employed building more railways, a theme which the leading newspapers echoed in one way or another a number of times during the rest of that year.

The deceptively gentle slopes of the share market boom that was soon to assume mountainous proportions had, in fact, already come into view during 1844. In that year 49 Acts had been passed authorizing the expenditure of over £20 million, mostly on the 805 miles of new line which were the subject of 37 of these Acts. The following year, 1845, the number of Acts for new lines alone totalled 94, representing an addition of 2,700 miles, and new capital authorized rose by over £59 million, a figure almost exactly coinciding with the size of the national income. This was a huge undertaking given the existing transport requirements, but beyond the parliamentary scene as yet lay a great penumbra of railway schemes in the making, many hundreds of them, for ostensibly sensible or plainly crackpot lines. The previous November one share list—Spackman's—had entries for projected railways that totted up to £563 million. This overall bid to double, perhaps to multiply still more, the length of line already open was not, however, such a firm declaration of intent as it appears, for much of it was a purely speculative exercise in making money fast out of 'scrip'—the subscription receipts which would be exchanged for ordinary equity on incorporation. This aspect of the railway mania was not always distinguishable in practice from the more genuine speculation based on the earning prospects of proposed lines, especially as both were stimulated by the level of current railway dividends, which in turn were kept up at almost all costs by directors infected by the buoyant mood. The chain reaction weakened appreciably during the summer of 1845 as the size of the impending capital requirements for the new promotions and the wild unreason of share prices became recognized. Railway shares reached the top of their market in August and by October a minor panic had developed as speculators tried to unload commitments they could no longer sell at a profit nor meet themselves. Some 600 schemes never even arrived at a first reading. In its warning of the pitfalls awaiting the honest man with money to put into railways the experience was a mildly salutary one. Railway promotion was a long way yet from being purged of its sharp practices.

Money became intermittently tighter after this and companies were beginning to have difficulty calling up their capital, but the general momentum of railway building did not slacken, nor was the main wave of railway investment broken by the crisis in the share market. During 1846 parliament was inundated by railway bills. Out of it issued by the end of that year 219 Acts, covering 4,538 miles of new line, and the new capital outlay authorized altogether approached £133 million. Even this did not fully appease the gargantuan appetite of the railway world and in the following year a dessert of another 112 Acts was tabled to bring 1,354 extra miles of track into existence; £39 million more was added to the capital. In terms of Acts passed 1847 was a much less active year than 1845, though in terms of railway mileage authorized it was exactly half as important. It is surprising that the boom did not abate more quickly in view of the now much more obvious difficulties in making calls on capital and the general deterioration in the condition of the economy which was showing itself long before the close of 1846. Financial stringency was expressing itself forcibly in terms of rising bank-rate as bullion stocks were depleted by outflows of gold to pay, among other things, for the large imports of grain made necessary by the crop failures of 1846, and for abnormally high cotton imports; a new source of instability was also revealing itself in the financial dealings of the big corn merchants. In two scarcely unexpected movements during the spring and autumn of 1847 the financial crisis came dramatically to its head, bank-rate moved almost to panic level, and the whole frenzied mood of an overstretched market was finally relaxed.

So far as the railways were concerned this, too, was the end for the time being of their tearaway promotion of the previous four years. In 1848, only 37 Acts for new lines were passed, and over the next two years another 16. What was significant was not the aggregate mileage of under 400 which these Acts authorized but the fact that the railway companies were now asking for an extra £33 million largely to enable them to complete the lines which had already been sanctioned. The culmination of the physical process of creating these lines was only now taking place: during 1848 alone the operational scope of the railways was extended by nearly a third.

It would be futile in a book of this kind to disentangle piece by piece the different strands in the tightly knotted network that was now being put together. The heroic era of single lines pioneering every step of the way was passing very quickly indeed and the possibility of watching every move they made was fading with it. The tentative first steps of promoters were in any case now becoming a more confident routine, and the towering opposition of threatened property interests were tending to dissolve into tacit, well-greased alliance. Interest must therefore now be fixed not so much on the chronology of a movement in which literally everything was happening at once, as on some of the underlying factors at work and the general pattern that was evolving. What the country was in fact trying to do was to complete its railway system in a single final bound. In the event it temporarily overshot its mark by a very wide margin. In purely physical terms this aspect of the process can be described quite simply. Though still-born schemes would have raised the totals very much more, parliament passed in the period 1844-48 about 720 railway Acts and gave its authority for raising £267 million. If all the railways which had been authorized had been built they would soon have covered a distance of 12,000 miles. In fact, by 1852, when the constructional phase of the railway mania may be said to have virtually worked itself out, something less than 7,500 miles of track were in use. These comprised a basic system of trunk routes and the greater part of all the subsidiary line they would ever really need. (*See Map 12*, pp. 136-7.) But before we can take stock of this achievement it is necessary to consider two other related aspects of the railway boom: the balance of power between the companies and that between them and parliament. These helped to govern the shape and the workability of the railway system.

The first of these soon became critically important. Given a free market for railway enterprise within such a narrow commercial box as Great Britain the keenest rivalry between companies was bound to spring up almost at once. The greatest potential traffic existed in and between highly concentrated industrial areas and the number of railway links that could usefully be made between them was strictly limited. In these circumstances the railway system very quickly became a kind of parallelogram of forces in which its very shape was the product not only of the underlying commercial requirements of the economy but of the political tactics and deeper strategy of the protagonists themselves. Across the surface of the investment bubbles of two decades there had certainly swum many blind and purposeless schemes, and even among the survivors were some who fumbled badly with their opportunities. But among them also were some exceptional business leaders whose dominance soon expressed itself in schemes for the outright amalgamation of companies or simply for working agreements between them. Their common object was not so much that of securing some narrow territorial monopoly—though that was to come later—as defeating lines in competition with theirs by a policy of aggrandizement through the end-on attachment of lines already built further afield. The struggles for power that now went on in board rooms and in parliamentary committees were not parish squabbles but epic contests for control of the great trunk routes—a species of imperialism, no less—and no region of the country remained immune from them.

The elements in this situation were the 104 railway companies which had a separate legal existence in Britain by the end of 1844, plus another 110 companies which were incorporated over the next six years; on some grounds it might also be reasonable to include the fifty or more companies which were sanctioned by parliament but whose powers of construction were allowed to lapse or were deliberately abandoned under later Acts. Most of the companies in existence at the end of 1844 were small undertakings, and eleven only, which between them accounted for over half the track in use, were operating more than fifty miles of line apiece. Such

I

a structure could not last. Merely keeping the accounts straight on through-traffic, both passenger and freight, which was being handled on a growing scale at the beginning of the 1840s, was a relatively simple matter. This was met to some extent by the establishment in London of the Railway Clearing House by nine companies in 1842. By the time it was legally authorized in 1850 it included in its membership virtually all the railways of importance, except for a number in the south of England, of which the Great Western, the London & South Western, the South Eastern, and the London & Brighton were the most conspicuous. Though it aimed at removing one of the penalties of dispersed control of railway operation, the Clearing House probably tended in practice to demonstrate some of the advantages which amalgamation would bring, and it is arguable that its very existence hastened the process for which it had been designed as an alternative. It could of itself confer fewer benefits than would follow from complete uniformity in operation of the kind already demonstrated, as early as 1834, by the creation of the North Union Railway out of two companies serving the coal town of Wigan; and in the Grand Junction Railway's end-on amalgamations of 1835 and 1840 was an obvious pattern for widespread imitation once railways began to touch one another at numerous points.

Perhaps the most conspicuous intersection of interest was at Derby, which we have already noticed as the duelling ground of the Midland Counties and the Birmingham & Derby Junction Railways as they struggled for what they knew to be the rich dowry of the coal traffic that was to be brought down from the northeast by the North Midland Railway. For a time their competitive rate-cutting was allayed by an agreement reached late in 1840, but by 1843 the struggle was resumed. It was clear nevertheless that the only beneficiary of the situation was the North Midland Railway, which maintained its rates as its traffic was swollen by users taking advantage of the rate war being waged by the other two companies. Another flicker of interest in joint working occurred in 1843, but the two competitors were only brought to terms under the strongest pressure by the professedly disinterested bystander, the North Midland, which brought about the unison of all three companies in 1844.

The chairman of the North Midland was the ruthless, vulgar, spectacularly successful genius, George Hudson, unquestionably the greatest railway entrepreneur ever to operate in this country. His perception of the possibilities of railways and his skill in the strategy of realizing them brooked no financial scruples whatever and his whole dizzy career down to 1849 became a single-minded pursuit of railway power. It brought him a huge personal fortune, a seat in parliament, the adulation of society, bankruptcy, and disgrace. His distinctive contribution to the growth of the railway system was to be in the welding together in his own person practically overriding control over the whole network of lines that really mattered on the eastern side of England between the Tweed and the

Thames. The creation of the Midland Railway out of the three lines joining at Derby was Hudson's first great bid for the crown of the railway
kingdom. Characteristically enough, it was a move in a wider game in
which the other players were the Great Western Railway and the putative
Great Northern Railway. The Great Western was at this time planning to
bring its broad-gauge system into the Midlands, a move which Hudson
neatly checked by absorbing into the Midland Railway one by one over
the next two years the lines between Birmingham and Bristol. The Great
Northern's proposal to bring an entirely separate main line to London
from York threatened to divide Hudson's intended kingdom in two at
Peterborough and to undermine his monopoly of the traffic from the
northeast. No compaign in the history of railways was more bitterly nor
more prodigally fought than the passage, in 1845–6, of the bill to authorize
the longest line yet submitted for parliamentary scrutiny, nor was any
triumph more critical for the vanquished: fully half-a-million pounds and
seventy days of committee time were spent on it in parliament alone.
When the struggle with the Great Northern began Hudson already controlled over a thousand miles of railway and had begun to push a line from
Syston on the old Midland Counties line across to Peterborough in order to
link up with another which the Eastern Counties, whose chairmanship
Hudson took late in 1845, was building west from Ely. The link was not
completed until the year of Hudson's downfall, an event precipitated in
part by the parlous finances of the Eastern Counties Railway.

4   Amalgamation and state intervention

As with the promotion of new lines, 1846 was the year of years for amalgamations—twenty in all. The formation of the London & North Western
Railway in that year was of even greater importance in terms of the track
involved, some 280 miles of it, than that of the Midland Railway. Its nucleus
was the Grand Junction Railway, which had absorbed the Liverpool &
Manchester the previous year, and its strategist was the Grand Junction's
remarkable general manager, Mark Huish. By giving parliamentary support
to the Midlands-probing schemes of the Great Western Railway in 1845—
the Oxford & Rugby Railway and that supreme catalyst of trouble, the
Oxford, Worcester & Wolverhampton Railway—and even giving general
support to it in the larger battle of gauges, the Grand Junction succeeded
in devising a situation in which the London & Birmingham was ready to
combine, not with the Manchester & Birmingham Railway alone, as it
had been trying to do, but with the Grand Junction as well, and on terms
particularly favourable to its own shareholders. Further north, the
Manchester & Leeds Railway and five smaller undertakings came together,
adopting the following year the name of the Lancashire & Yorkshire

Railway; four other companies formed the Manchester, Sheffield & Lincolnshire Railway; the London & Brighton and the London & Croydon combined to form the London, Brighton & South Coast Railway. In 1847, another nine amalgamations occurred, of which the East Anglian Railway and the York, Newcastle & Berwick Railway, in which the powers of eight companies were concentrated as a prelude to the larger creation of the North Eastern Railway in 1854, were the most important. After 1847 the consolidation of companies abated markedly until the 1850s.

This was also a period in which a series of joint purchases and leases was made, especially among the companies of southern England which remained outside the Railway Clearing House, and these had the effect of concentrating the control of railway operations into still fewer hands. These agreements did not all need parliamentary approval, though the volume of legislation for purchases and leases greatly outweighed that for amalgamation in the period as a whole. This was a process enabling a resolute company to extend its operations quickly and relatively cheaply: to take one example, the South Eastern Railway had by 1853 bought or leased its way across seven adjoining companies' lines, one only of which had succumbed to complete amalgamation by that time. On the other hand, some of these working arrangements, especially those made at the height of the mania, were recklessly expensive in terms of guaranteed dividends, sometimes being fixed even higher than those being paid by the bidding company. With some astuteness it was occasionally possible to plant a small company in the path of a larger one so as to take a kind of ransom from the traffic it would wish to carry through. It must be recognized that it was in business operations of this kind, as in the complex planning of more permanent consolidations, that some of the most profitable chicanery in railway promotion was possible. None of the companies performing these operations had any really detailed cost accounts upon which decisions could be based, and it took a cunning eye as well as hot-and-cold diplomacy to spot and hang on to the best opportunities. Often vague yet shrewdly successful as commercial offensives, such working arrangements could also be desperate, mistimed lunges in self-defence, and the lengths to which they were taken in this period are some measure of the inherent necessity of co-ordination in a system which had been devised almost completely without it.

The irony of the situation was that parliament had originally given railways their head in the belief that competition between them would block the formation of monopolies of the kind which many canals were believed to have become. Statute law had scarcely noticed the railways as yet and too little litigation had occurred before the 1840s to define their opportunities and responsibilities in the courts. Some early railway enterprise had been subject to nominal control of maximum rates per ton-mile, coupled even with limitations on the dividends that could be paid without compensating reduction in freight charges, as in the case of the Liverpool

& Manchester Railway. Yet these sanctions were not enforced and were, indeed, not strictly enforceable, any more than a variety of other provisions in private railway bills were in practice subject to judicial control. The railways were on a legal honeymoon, and it was not altogether surprising that the dangers of monopoly should grow unchecked. That this should have continued into a period in which the railways had fully developed legal personalities and even a certain commercial notoriety may seem more remarkable. The chief explanation is that parliament, which was fast becoming a judge in its own cause, was in the dilemma of finding some formula which would curb the abuse of commercial power without disturbing the sanctity of private property: putting the matter another way, one might say it was simply undergoing the ordinary difficulties of any arbiter with an interest in the outcome of an issue. This forced some early critics of the railways like James Morrison, the member for Ipswich, into a seemingly ambivalent position. His argument, which he developed for the first time in 1836, rested on the premise that railways had a natural monopoly conferred upon them by legislation and that parliament should therefore have some means of guarding against its consequences, including the waste of capital; private enterprise was at the same time to remain unimpaired. The argument was not doctrinaire; perhaps it would have been more convincing if it had been. Nothing broke the surface immediately but the notion that parliament must provide some executive machinery, not merely a mandatory act, had been well aired. The government remained inert until 1839, but when some allegations were made in the Lords about monopolistic practices by the London & Birmingham Railway, they led straight to the appointment of the first Select Committee to look generally into the railways; it was re-appointed to complete its work the following session.

Six rapid reports followed, with warnings of the impending failure of competition to offset monopoly, unaided by the State. Notice had been taken of the fact that certain companies—the Leeds & Selby Railway, for instance—were in the monopolist's position of having no ruling market price to accept but being able instead to increase their net revenues by increasing fares and freight charges and running fewer trains. The Select Committee on Railway Communication (1839–40) therefore recommended that companies should make returns as required of their traffic and finances to a Railway Department in the Board of Trade, which should also have powers of inspection and prosecution; the letter of this was carried out omitting finance from the returns, under the Acts of 1840 and 1842. In practice, the controlling hand on monopoly, and even on the legal enforcement of its own inspectors' reports, withered; and the slighter, though valuable and overdue, even extra-legal, exercises of drafting regulations affecting the safety of passengers, and of discovering the facts about third-class travel, were undertaken instead. A new President of the Board of Trade, W. E. Gladstone, taking note of the impending Midland amalgamation bill, obtained a fresh inquiry in 1844 from which he clearly hoped to forge a better instrument of parliamentary control. The new committee worked swiftly and thoroughly, authenticating the facts about monopolistic pricing, and even evoking near unanimity among its witnesses for some form of State control; the stubborn witnesses were Charles Saunders, Secretary to the Great Western, and, not surprisingly, George Hudson.

Legislation was ready before its sixth and final Report was out, but the bill itself was politically inept. It was easily riddled by arguments that it discriminated unfairly against the railways and that it implied a fundamental and unsupported disbelief in the effectiveness of competitive enterprise; too few amalgamations and working agreements yet existed to contradict it. The bill also touched insensitively on an antipathy to the centralization of governmental powers that had been growing since the inception of the Factory Act and New Poor Law in 1833 and 1834. The arguments themselves were far less important than the fact that parliament now contained, principally in the Commons, a very substantial railway interest which could stomach nothing so uncompromising, and the teeth of the bill were quietly drawn in private by the Prime Minister himself, Sir Robert Peel, who does not seem to have bargained for so radical a bill. The original intention of providing for the nationalization of any new company after 15 years' existence, with compensation of 25 years' purchase of its distributed profits to a maximum of 10 per cent per annum, was discarded without serious argument. Instead, the Railway Act of 1844 provided that purchase might be made only after 21 years and that if the average profits were less than 10 per cent purchase would be by arbitration instead; if they were over 10 per cent their full value would be counted in the 25 years' purchase. Nationalization immediately looked very distant, dubious and costly: emasculated with this part of the bill were the clauses fortifying the Board of Trade, and the contrast between the liberal covenants under which the railways could operate and the restraints which held back the State now looked sharp indeed. The "parliamentary train", a requirement that one daily train should run every weekday in both directions over any new lines at not less than 12 miles in the hour, including stops at all stations, at a maximum fare of a penny a mile (no passenger duty payable), was one of the very few tangible results of the sole attempt made in the nineteenth century at giving the State effective control of the railways. For almost a quarter of a century little more was added to that power.

Gladstone almost immediately turned his back on the Board of Trade and, for the time being, on the railways, and the Railway Board (the Railway Department with a new face) which he had set up in August 1844 in the hope of winnowing out unsatisfactory railway bills deposited the following session, crumpled within months of his going. Lord Dalhousie's Board, nick-named the "Five Kings", was actually a not inglorious failure, and it is arguable that it was a healthy influence on both parliament and promoters which might have stemmed some of the mania's excesses had it remained. It worked under serious handicaps, especially after Gladstone's departure: it was a censor without a veto, a referee without any clear rules, and its recommendations that mattered were too easily overlooked by a diffident government and an overworked parliament. It was a joint demonstration of both against the Board's recommendation on the Oxford, Worcester & Wolverhampton Railway's bill in June 1845 which brought this to a head and led to the winding up of the Board a month later. Its disinterested if not impartial scrutiny had had to take place in a furore of impatient promotion and it simply had to give way, as Dalhousie came to recognize, to the demand that the fittest should secure their own right to survive.

Parliament was now inundated with railway bills, private bills which tended still to be regarded as private contests between promoters and their particular antagonists. "That the whole society was interested in having a good system of internal communications seemed to be forgotten," Macaulay told the House early in the summer of 1846, "nobody applied to be heard on behalf of the community." During that year of big public issues and heavy general legislation some 64 Private Bill Committees sat for 867 days on railway bills alone; the following year 52 Committees met on 635 days. Despite the attempt made in the Railway Clauses Consolidation Act of 1845 to standardize railway bills, and the furious work of the Select Committee for the Classification of Railway Bills in sorting them regionally, the Private Bill Committees, even when pruned of their hefty and partisan membership, had absurdly little time for matters of much moment. Likewise, the Committee on Standing Orders, whose business it normally was to ensure the obedience of promoters to basic parliamentary requirements about deposits, plans, subscription registers, and so on, was often driven to the most cursory formalities: even their hand-written minutes betray their inordinate haste. Meanwhile, four more sleect committees in one House or the other and one royal commission ferreted for the facts on the actual implementation of railway legislation, the management of companies, the progress of amalgamation, the case for a standard gauge, and the condition of railway labourers.

Not until the overwhelming bulk of this technically private bill legislation had gone through was parliament ready to accept—more from exhaustion, perhaps, than from conviction—that it had all along been concerned in fact with public affairs, and that these really needed a permanent and effective commissariat. Wilson Patten's Committee on Amalgamations and James Morrison's more powerfully packed Committee on Railway Acts Enactments had recognized all too clearly during 1846 that although competition in railway matters was an indulgence that the companies allowed themselves with reluctance, their struggles for control of a route all too frequently began in a flurry of wasted resources and ended in a serious—and in some respects permanent—loss to the public. Yet these committees' recommendations were nugatory still, for the Railway Com-

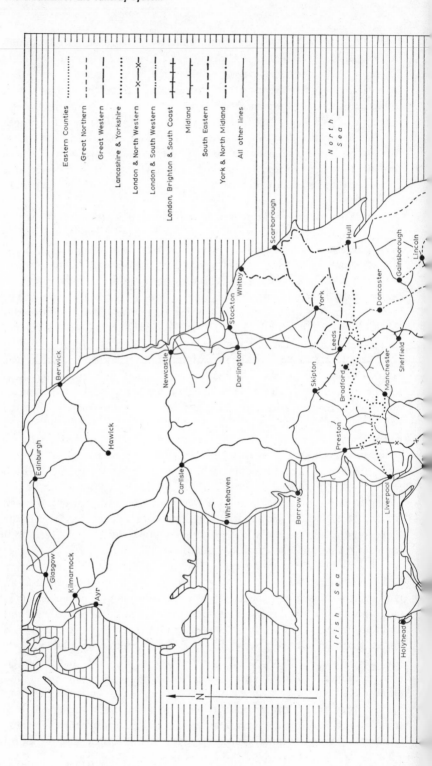

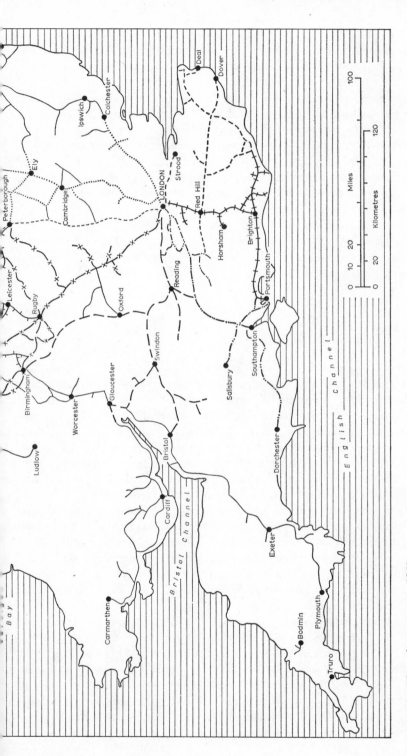

Map 12   *The railway system in 1852*

missioners who were appointed almost at once to meet the case, now independent of the Board of Trade, were scarcely better empowered nor more loyally abetted by parliament, and much less coherent as a body, than Dalhousie's Board had been, and within five years they, too, were abandoned. To be quite fair to the Commissioners, they had repeatedly drawn parliament's attention to difficulties and potential abuses among the expanding activities of the railway companies. Many of those reported on in 1847, for instance, were connected in one way or another with water— leasing river navigations, investing in steamships, lending to harbour authorities, supplying water. They found numerous objections in principle to clauses contained in railway bills and it was up to parliament to respond during the Committee stage of any bill. Such work had to be done by a responsible body and when the Railway Commissioners were disbanded responsibility for the railways reverted to the Board of Trade.The Railway Department was resuscitated once more and kept active above all implementing safety measures and conducting routine inspections.

5   Completion of the system

The disbanding of the Railway Commissioners in 1851 helps to accentuate the watershed which was reached in the development of the railways in the early 1850s. The system had reached physical maturity and the formative influences of its adolescence had left their ineradicable marks. The real costs already incurred in the headlong criss-crossing of the railway map in the later 1840s were as yet a latent force in the economics of railway operation. So, too, the full benefits of a network which had not yet become an efficient mechanism remained largely unrealized. A great deal had still to be done, yet the railway system was in all essentials already complete. At the heart of it was London, and the first great trunk route that had been carried into the English provinces was still its aorta. A second of the three great lines eventually to reach the North, the Great Northern Railway, had been opened in 1852, and from its terminus at Kings Cross the Queen herself embarked on a journey for Scotland in that very year. But the most heavily used trunk line out of the capital still ran directly to the Black Country and the industrial North-West.

At Rugby, which had become a major junction for lines from the north and east though not from the southwest, this road now forked to Birmingham in one direction and to Lichfield in the other, so going directly to Stafford, Crewe, Preston, Carlisle, Glasgow, Edinburgh, and even Aberdeen. At points along the route wholly new minor networks had been looped or branched on to it, as for example in Buckinghamshire, North Staffordshire, and Lancashire, so that hardly a town of importance had failed to secure a rail connection, inconvenient though it might be, with London and with its more important neighbours. Nor were these interconnections any longer localized. From Crewe it was now possible to reach another all-round distributing point at Leeds and beyond it many of the most important industrial towns of the West Riding as well as Hull and Newcastle; looked at from the other end, Leeds now had two separate routes to Birmingham, Manchester, Liverpool and London. From Crewe in another direction it had just become possible to travel by rail to Holyhead along the coast of North Wales and across the Menai Straits, and southwards by a sweeping series of separate lines to double back on Birmingham through Wrexham, Oswestry, Shrewsbury, Wellington, and Wolverhampton, which offered a choice of two, presently three, routes. Birmingham, first among the great cities to do so, also now had a second route to London, though on a different gauge of track, through Oxford and Reading. With the West Country its links were still relatively tenuous. It was possible, certainly, to make roundabout journeys solely on the broad gauge of the Great Western through Didcot, but the more direct route still lay through Gloucester with its break of gauge. Here, under the same constraint, it was now possible to reach Carmarthen via Newport, Cardiff and Swansea, though Wales as a whole remained desperately bare of railways, and the line northwards through Hereford and the Welsh marches was still incomplete. The bottleneck of Gloucester was a serious one for it impeded Welsh traffic bound for London through Swindon, as well as choking movement between the industrial regions of the country and the southwest.

Bristol's metropolitan connection was superb, as were its links with Exeter and Plymouth, but in general the West Country was still very patchily served. The line to Southampton from London had five years previously been taken on to Poole and Dorchester, where it terminated still in 1852, but Salisbury had as yet only a circuitous connection with London and Exeter none save through Bristol; apart from the Bristol connections, the railway system west of Salisbury had not yet emerged from the confusion of half-completed or abandoned schemes to which it had commonly been reduced by inter-railway rivalry or poor commercial prospects.

Mountainous regions apart—the Scottish Highlands, the North Pennines, and Wales—it was, in fact, south of a line between the Bristol Channel and the Wash that the most substantial additions to the railway system still had to be made. This is not altogether apparent from a small-scale map. It is true that the Fens had now been laced quite adequately with railways but one line only crossed the whole country between King's Lynn and Yarmouth, and movement across the rest of East Anglia was still impeded by unfinished contracts. One serious impediment removed in 1844 was the re-laying of the Eastern Counties line to Colchester, as well as one other to Bishop's Stortford, which had both been built originally to a different, slightly broader gauge than the rest. The whole coastline of East Anglia was touched at only two points by rail and, indeed, this landlocked feature of the railway system still prevailed round much of the east and south coasts. Apart from places which would later become important as seaside resorts, it is worth noticing that Harwich, Chatham, Lymington, Weymouth, and Exmouth were all places of actual or potential maritime importance which lay beyond convenient rail-heads in 1852, while Portsmouth was still awaiting the arrival of a direct line to London through Godalming. It is noticeable, too, that although some of the main lines out of London provided incidental suburban services and that two or three lines in London itself had been among the pioneers of steam passenger railways, there had been very little deliberate attempt made in this period to provide specifically suburban railways.

After the completion of the lines sanctioned during the mania of the 1840s no landmark of comparable significance was reached in the creation of the railway system until the very close of the nineteenth century. The last gesture which may be said to have signalled their ultimate physical development was the building of the last main line to London, the Great Central Railway, between 1893 and 1899. The railways' climacteric had probably come in the 1870s, when the vigorous growth of the earlier years began to decline, though it was not until the opening years of the twentieth century that the net annual addition of new mileage to the system really began to taper off completely. In 1900 the total had practically reached 22,000 miles; it rose a fraction above this for another five years before levelling off almost entirely for the remaining period down to 1914. This culminating phase in the building of the railways which took the whole of the second half of the nineteenth century to work itself out was remarkably undramatic in its general character, although some of the railways' finest engineering achievements were made in this period. If the railway system can be said to have come of age about 1852, its active and useful life was a very long one, not reaching old age until 1890 or so.

Maturity was spent filling the gaps, or more correctly of perceiving gaps which might be filled, and associating companies into larger undertakings, some of which could no longer conceal themselves as territorial monopolies. So fast was this process that by 1870 the only English towns that lacked railway stations were places as small as Tenterden, Shaftesbury, Lyme Regis, Chagford, Burford, Abbot's Bromley, Clun. Yet the towns, too, were growing fast and insignificant places were springing into prominence, and the railways raced to connect up all they could. Thus, the legislative programme did not abate to any extent. The number of railway Acts passed in the 1850s, for instance, was scarcely smaller than that for the 1840s—831 against 863—but there were now a great many small connecting lines to be authorized, a growing number of amalgamations, and the raising of more capital. Railway promotion still tended to rise and fall with the hardening and easing of the share market, and to produce its own feedback effects, but except for a disproportionate burst of activity, some of it reckless, in the mid-1860s the second half of the nineteenth century saw none of the widespread speculation of the kind that had occurred in the

1830s and 1840s. The effects of such over-investment as did occur tended
to be smothered by the rapid expansion in traffic and net receipts, and the
relatively high-cost rail transport that resulted from this proliferation of
lines did not appear to have been dearly bought until the fixing of railway
rates and a resurgence of interest in costs per ton-mile began to throw
doubts upon the value of some of them.

The main construction work to be done on the trunk routes in this
long period was either at their extremities or fixed on London. The London
& South Western Railway opened its direct route from London to Salisbury
in 1857 and to Exeter, much delayed by finance, in 1860; still more handicapped by economic conditions, the northern circuit of Dartmoor was
not completed to Plymouth until 1876 and to Padstow by 1899. The Great
Western reached the south coast with the opening of its meandering line
to Weymouth in 1857, and two years later, by virtue of Brunel's last great
railway achievement, it crossed the Tamar at Saltash to join the Cornwall
Railway with its connection to Truro; through trains from Paddington
to Penzance were not possible until the West Cornwall Railway had completed the laying of a mixed gauge track in 1867.

In Wales, the Taff Vale Railway, which had been incorporated as early as
1836 and opened between Merthyr Tydfil and Cardiff in 1840, was established
already as the leading railway in the country, and its great traffic in coal—it
carried as much coal over its 124 miles as the Great Western did over the
whole of its tracks in the late 1890s—was bringing it into wider amalgamations and more extensive running powers in the interval. Apart from this,
the principal railways in Wales—notably the Rhymney Railway and the
Brecon & Merthyr Railway—were built in the ten years after 1859. Yet
in some ways the greatest was still to come. The Barry Docks & Railway
Company was formed in 1884 in response to the obvious need for another
outlet for coal, despite the completion of the Bute Dock at Cardiff in 1882.
The Barry Dock, which formed part of the scheme, covered 73 acres, and
when the line from Pontypridd was opened in 1889 it was deluged with
an enormous traffic of coal that never yielded the shareholders less than
10 per cent per annum and sometimes almost twice as much. The connection between South Wales and London was improved markedly by the
opening of the Severn Tunnel, a prodigious feat, in 1886.

Before 1885 no railway had reached beyond the Central Lowlands of
Scotland, though Edinburgh and Glasgow were connected both with the
south and each other, and some potentially useful lines had been built
in southwest Scotland. A number of purely local lines had also appeared
elsewhere—one, the Morayshire Railway, as far north as Lossiemouth,
which was connected with Elgin in 1852. Work had started on the rather
irresolute Great North of Scotland Railway beyond Aberdeen in 1852 and
was carried with the help of others to Inverness by 1858, though a more
direct line (the Highland Railway) was carried with great audacity over
the mountains between Perth and Inverness by 1863; beyond Inverness

the line reached Wick and Thurso by means of the Sutherland & Caithness Railway by 1874. What shortened the east coast route to Inverness still more was the bridging of the Tay in 1878 and again, after this structure collapsed disastrously, in 1887; even more important was the opening of the Forth Bridge in 1890.

The link with the south was closed more slowly in the west of Scotland, though Glasgow was connected with Ayr by 1840 and with Dumfries two years later. On this side of the country the crucial link with the south, already complete in physical terms, was made effective in 1876 when the Midland Railway's formidable line over the North Pennines from Settle to Carlisle provided a much more direct approach. The Midland had already formed a line through the Peak District between Derby and Manchester in 1867, and it had over rather a longer period, since 1853, also been making its approach to London by a line between Leicester and the Great Northern's tracks at Hitchin, which it reached in 1857, and then, by means of its very own metropolitan extension, coming to St Pancras by 1868: Hudson's dreams of empire had been practically fulfilled. Two other important connections to be made in the north in this phase were the Great Northern's between Doncaster and Leeds, opened in 1866, and the North Eastern's between Doncaster and Hull, opened in 1869; the Lancashire & Yorkshire was also hard at work in the 1860s and 1870s bringing remaining industrial towns on to the railway map.

It was here especially, and in the densely developed Midlands, that competition between the large companies produced many minor structural refinements to their systems. It was here, too, that the largest and most hapless undertakings of the whole of this period are to be found. The Hull & Barnsley Railway, capitalized at £4 million in 1880, was a remarkable attempt by the commercial and civic leaders of Hull to break the hold on them of the North Eastern Railway, which had had a virtual monopoly of its hinterland for over a quarter of a century; financially calamitous, its survival ultimately depended more than anything on coming to terms with the very company it had hoped to brush aside. Under its deluded chairman, Edward Watkin, the Manchester, Sheffield & Lincolnshire Railway, which had undertaken some of the most costly works in the country and knew penury all too well, worked up to a still more ambitious and debilitating swipe at three well-nigh impregnable companies with London termini as part of a quixotic plan to form a single undertaking serving the North, Midlands, London, and the Channel ports. It failed. The ordinary stock of the Great Central Railway, as it had become during the constructional phase, never yielded a dividend.

The southeast was the scene of yet another struggle with disastrous financial consequences. The South Eastern Railway had developed a tight grip on the Kentish lines since the 1840s, but this was prised open to some extent from 1853 when its line to Strood was carried on to Canterbury by another company, the East Kent Railway, and more still by the authorization two years later of its extension to Dover. In 1859 the East Kent Railway became the London, Chatham & Dover Railway, and two years later it justified its title by opening the line to Dover and, by arrangement with the South Eastern's principal competitor on its western flank, the London, Brighton & South Coast Railway, carrying it into a London terminus at Victoria. This was the opening move in a decade of bitter competition for the continental traffic which put the Chatham company into Chancery for five years and led later to a celebrated working union between the two contestants.

Few indeed of the major lines built after the 1860s found commercial success, and it is also noticeable that the era of large-scale amalgamation was coming to an end at about the same time. The consolidation of railway companies threatened at the beginning of the 1850s to assume very large proportions indeed with the fusion of several companies which had already swallowed others: the London & South Western and the Brighton Railways; the Midland, the North Staffordshire, and the London & North Western Railways; the York & North Midland, the Leeds Northern, and the York, Newcastle & Berwick Railways. The Select Committee on Amalgamations (Cardwell's), which was appointed in 1852 in response to these developments, soon declared itself opposed to amalgamation in principle, but parliament was not equally intransigent and it promptly approved one of the schemes that Cardwell's Committee had suspended and thus created, in 1854, the most complete case so far of a territorial monopoly, the North Eastern Railway. Three other small companies were quickly added and by 1863 its writ was made absolute throughout its area by the absorption of the Stockton & Darlington (itself now enlarged by four other companies added in 1858) and the Newcastle & Carlisle. The North Eastern's complete tally was 37 separate lines. This amalgamation probably succeeded because the founding companies had had good relations with their neighbours and could placate their opponents; others, like the Great Western's absorption of the Shrewsbury & Birmingham, the Shrewsbury & Chester, the West Midland and the South Wales Railways—469 miles in two instalments in 1854 and 1863—took place in the teeth of a rival, the London & North Western, unable to muster extra support; another, the fusion of the Midland and the North Western, failed because an antagonist, the Great Northern, was too strong; yet another, the Great Eastern, formed in 1862 out of five companies which had partially come together in 1854, succeeded because no-one was sufficiently interested in blocking such a financially dubious enterprise. In all of this the recommendations of Cardwell's Committee were an irrelevance.

The consolidation of companies was almost certainly more influenced by the balance of commercial power and the compulsion to imitate than it was by doctrinaire arguments, or even by practical concern for cheap working. The Royal Commission on the Railways, appointed in 1865 to consider, among other things, their cost structure, reported two years later that amalgamation had been more a "matter of offensive and defensive policy than a question of economy in working the lines". The degree of concentration was clear from the figures they collected: 2,100 miles of railway owned by 70 companies in 1843 and 11,451 miles of railway owned by 78 companies in 1865; by 1871, 28 companies were in control of about 80 per cent of the track in use. The 1865 Commission took a neutral view of this tendency, but in the aftermath of the crisis of 1866 there was a very general attempt by the large companies to reinforce their holdings and to maintain the balance of power. In particular, the prospect of an alliance between the strategically exposed Midland Railway with the Great Northern, the Glasgow & South Western and the Manchester, Sheffield & Lincolnshire was matched by one between the London & North Western and the Lancashire & Yorkshire. Eleven amalgamation bills were before parliament in 1871, and these along with many more schemes for working arrangements covered every important company in Britain.

The following session the whole question was reopened by another Select Committee on Amalgamation, which led to an unusually powerful Joint Committee of both Houses in 1873. To what extent this body was swayed by the special pleading to which it was inevitably subjected, and to what extent it was simply dumbfounded by the scale of the problem of acting in the public's best interests when so much had already been decided independently of them, it is impossible to say. They decisively rejected the two biggest amalgamations without even hearing the opposition, but found it impossible in their long report to evaluate the basic principles which would have had to be embodied in the general legislation for which it asked. This aspect of railway policy had to be pragmatic. The amalgamations which had raised again the issues of 1844 were dead: long live amalgamation! Some that came along later, like the Great Western's absorption of the Bristol & Exeter and South Devon Railways in 1876 and 1878, succeeded; others, like the proposal to merge the Great Northern, Great Central and Great Eastern in 1909, failed; one or two that made excellent sense, like the absorption of the Manchester, Sheffield & Lincolnshire by the Midland and Great Northern in 1877, collapsed through human foibles; another that came only after a long war of attrition, the working agreement made between the South Eastern and the London, Chatham & Dover Railways in 1899, was a triumph for the weak.

What was now being kindled indeed was a more active interest on the part of the companies in working together where they could, and on the part of the government in seeing that they did so on the right terms. The railway interest which had dominated parliamentary attitudes towards the railways since the 1840s now waned. The background to this had its economic and its political aspects. With the revival of the Conservative party twenty years after its disintegration over free trade in the mid-1840s and the widening of the franchise in 1867 parliament became, as it had never been, an arena for popular opinion and party politics, and the government benches were looked to more squarely for the controlling influence on the railways. The last third of the nineteenth century was also one in which the high rate of economic growth which the country had experienced around mid-century was slowing down, and Britain's long commercial hegemony was coming under review not only in world markets but in her own. Economic portents and a changing political climate helped to make the old distinctions between competition and monopoly among the railways an academic one and to bring into greater prominence the question of costs and charges. On this score the government now felt obliged and able to intervene.

K

5

The economics of
railway operation

1 The growth of traffic

By 1870 the railway mania was over and the companies were able to settle
down to enjoy a steady growth of traffic and at the same time fill in the gaps
that remained. The main line network was all but complete and few major
extensions were required in the years before 1914. Only a few main lines
were added to the system. (*See Map 13*, pp. 152–3). The most important of
these were the Midland line from Settle to Carlisle, opened for all traffic in
1876, the Hull & Barnsley and Barry Railways which were constructed in
the 1880s, and the West Highland line to Fort William opened in 1894. The
last important main line to be built in Great Britain was the London extension of the Manchester, Sheffield & Lincolnshire Railway, better known as
the Great Central, to which it changed its name in 1897. The original M. S.
& L. Railway had never been very prosperous and the Company under
Watkin had tried many things to revive its fortunes. Unfortunately building
the London extension provided no solution to the problem. The line, which
was sanctioned in March 1893 after fierce opposition from rival companies,
proved a financial failure since it competed with three more powerful
companies for traffic from the North and Midlands. It is not surprising to
find, therefore, that after 1899 when the line was completed the Great
Central paid no dividend on its ordinary stock. In fact few of the major
extensions made after 1870 were commercially successful except the Barry
Railway, the prosperity of which was based upon the flourishing coal export
trade of South Wales.

Though spectacular railway constructions were few and far between
in the half century or so before 1914, railway development was by no means
negligible. Roughly one third of the route mileage remained to be built for
by 1912 total mileage open for traffic amounted to 23,441 compared with
15,537 in 1870. Though most of this additional track consisted of branch or

local lines, loop lines or cut-offs, many of the extensions were of vital importance at a time when few other forms of transport existed. All over the country and particularly in Scotland numerous branch lines were built either to act as feeders to the main lines or to serve outlying communities. Some of them tapped new industrial centres such as the Bury, Bacup, Oldham and Hellifield extensions of the Lancashire & Yorkshire Railway in the 1870s. The Great Western found that cut-offs not only solved the problem of congestion on some of its routes but also shortened the distance by rail on many routes to the west country and south Wales. Some notable attempts were also made in this period to shorten routes by the construction of bridges and tunnels. In 1886, after nearly 13 years of construction, the Severn Tunnel was completed which greatly shortened the route from London to south Wales and enabled faster services to be run from the west country to the North. A year later the second Tay Bridge was opened—the first one having collapsed in a storm in December 1878 when 73 people lost their lives—to be followed by the Forth Bridge in 1890 which shortened substantially the route from Edinburgh to Dundee and Aberdeen. These bridges led to the famous, though sometimes dangerous, set of races to Scotland in the late 1880s and 1890s.

As the Table below shows, a remarkable growth in traffic took place on the railways in the period 1870–1912. Undoubtedly the extension of the network and the growth in trade, industry and population was a vital factor

Table 1   *Railway traffic and finance, 1870–1912*

Year	Length of line open for traffic	Total number of passengers carried (exclusive of season-ticket holders)	Weight of goods and minerals conveyed	Gross receipts	Working expenses	Net receipts
	miles	no. millions	tons millions	£m.	£m.	£m.
1870	15,537	336·5	—	45·1	21·7	23·4
1880	17,933	603·9	235·3	65·5	33·6	31·9
1890	20,073	817·1	303·1	79·9	43·2	36·8
1900	21,855	1,142·3	424·9	104·8	64·7	40·1
1912	23,441	1,294·3	520·3	128·6	81·2	47·3

accounting for the expansion in traffic. A contributory factor was the steady reduction in rates and fares as an increasing number of special fares and exceptional rates were introduced. The rapid growth of passenger traffic, for example, was fostered in no small part by the progressive reduction in in the price of third class travel, particularly after 1883 when the passenger duty was abolished, and by the expansion in the number of cheap travel facilities in which the North Eastern Railway Company was a pioneer. Even before 1870 this company had introduced weekend and tourist tickets, excursion facilities and reduced fares for workmen, servicemen and soldiers, and their example was soon followed by other companies. By the early twentieth century the average third class fare was around $\frac{1}{4}d$. per mile or nearly one half its former level and all but 5 per cent of passengers carried went by third class compared with only 41·0 per cent in 1845. Though an increasing number of exceptional rates were granted for freight traffic it is unlikely that the growth in the latter was stimulated unduly by rate reductions.

Changes in the cost of transport were not of course the only factor which caused the growth in traffic. Rising real incomes, the growing popularity of new forms of entertainment and of holidays and the growth of town suburbs led to an increasing demand for travel facilities. In fact the last quarter of the nineteenth century saw a rapid development in longer distance suburban travel as more people began to live further away from their place of work and this in turn was made possible by the extension of the railway network into the outlying areas. Suburban travel became a marked feature of some of the larger towns, particularly London where by 1895 40,000 people were using the Great Northern's suburban services every day. Moreover, as railway companies grew larger and agreements between them became more prolific there was a strong tendency for price competition to be replaced by competition in travel facilities. This was particularly the case in passenger traffic where companies sought to foster the growth of the travel habit and "vied with each other in offering new facilities for the attraction of passengers". Considerable efforts were made to improve the speed, comfort and safety of railway travel particularly for third class travellers who had been largely neglected in the past.[1] The initiative in this respect came from the Midland Company which in 1872 announced its intention of providing third class accommodation on every train at the Parliamentary fare of 1d. per mile. Two years later the same company decided to abolish its second class and raise its third class accommodation to the level of the second. Though at the time regarded as revolutionary and foolish steps by the other companies its example was quickly followed elsewhere, though not all companies abolished their second class facilities. As a result third class travellers were soon enjoying the many improvements which were made in the ensuing decades. These included the famous American Pullman cars, dining and sleeping carriages, corridor trains, lavatories and washing facilities, steam heating and gas and electric lighting. In 1910 the London & North Western introduced the first British train to carry a typists's office on its "City to City" express from London to Birmingham. Not all travellers of course enjoyed such luxuries and innovations were always adopted initially on the first class. Moreover, standards of

[1] In some cases improvements in travelling facilities and station accommodation were long overdue. According to Dow in his history of the Great Central the station arrangements at Regent Street, Barnsley (c. 1890s)) violated "the most ordinary requirements of decency"; one small room served a number of different functions whilst the ladies' room was so small that one lady of moderate dimensions would occupy a very considerable proportion of it!

accommodation varied greatly between companies, according to Hamilton Ellis, even down to the water closets "from excellent valve and washdown types to zinc 'pans' and beastly cast-iron hoppers flushed by a paltry trickle". Yet there was no denying the remarkable improvements made, and these, together with fare reductions and special concessions, certainly encouraged people to travel by rail. As the *Jubilee of the Railway News* commented in 1914 "British railways have met the demand for luxury travel in a generous spirit, their only reward lying in the extraordinary growth in the number of people travelling induced by the improved conditions and low special fares."

At the same time the speed and frequency of train services on both main-line and suburban routes were improved considerably especially from the 1880s onwards. The opening of the Severn Tunnel in 1886, for example, enabled the Great Western to improve the facilities it offered. Between 1886 and 1912 train services between London and Cardiff were doubled and the running time reduced by one half. By October 1888 the best train of the London & North Western had reduced the journey time between Euston and Manchester from 5 hours to 4 hours 15 minutes and almost one hour was clipped off the Liverpool run. The famous races to Scotland between the east and west routes brought a reduction of nearly 3 hours in the journey time between London and Edinburgh and Glasgow though speeds were reduced somewhat later on account of the safety factor. Competition in speed in these years was fierce and many new main-line express trains were inaugurated. By 1907 there were 157 non-stop runs over 100 miles in Great Britain of which the London & North Western had 50 and the Great Western 33. The longest was the "Cornish Riviera" to Plymouth via Westbury (225¾ miles) and the fastest was the crack express of the Great Western between Paddington and Bristol via Bath (118¾ miles) which made the journey in 2 hours.

Nor were the short-distance, suburban or cross-country services neglected for the sake of improvements in main-line travel. As early as 1877 the Cheshire Lines Committee began an hourly service between Manchester and Liverpool which did the journey in 45 minutes with one stop at Warrington. By October 1902 the Lancashire & Yorkshire, one of the pioneers in electric traction for suburban passenger services, had reduced the timing on this run by a further five minutes. Perhaps most notable, however, were the number of new cross-country services that were started. In the first decade of the twentieth century the North Eastern introduced cross-country services between Leeds and Glasgow and Newcastle and Liverpool. After its arrival in London the Great Central did much to foster similar services since it was in the unique position of providing connections with nearly all the major railway systems in England. In July 1902 a through train was put on between Newcastle and Bournemouth via Oxford and four years later a service between Newcastle and Cardiff via Banbury appeared on the time-table. At times of course competition for the travellers' custom led to much waste and unnecessary duplication of facilities, the classic example being the Manchester–London route on which four companies ran 81 trains a day. On the other hand, the railway traveller had plenty of choice and the benefits of better services. As Ellis has pointed out the great virtue of British railways was in the relatively high speeds of their ordinary trains including some of the outer-suburban services and the short-distance inter-city and inter-urban services of areas like Lancashire. In comparable services "foreign railways frequently shone very dimly indeed".

Many of these achievements were only made possible by continued technical progress on the railways. Improvements in the design and construction of rolling stock, the use of better and more powerful locomotives and the replacement of iron by steel rails all helped to increase the speed, comfort and safety of railway travel. Above all the general adoption of the block system of signalling and the continuous brake made high speeds compatible with safety for the first time. Before the 1870s the absence of powerful brakes and efficient signalling methods had made it difficult to increase train speeds beyond a certain point without enhancing the danger to safety of the passengers. In 1870 only about one fifth of railway mileage in Britain was fitted with the block system whilst continuous brakes had only just got beyond the experimental stage. Henceforward the companies made rapid progress in extending the use of these new safety devices so much so that by the time they were made compulsory in 1889 it was only a matter of "whipping in the laggards". By the turn of the century British railways were said to be the safest in the world and indeed not one passenger life was sacrificed through a railway fault in 1901.

For freight traffic technical progress was far less conspicuous when compared with the developments which took place on the passenger side. Freight trains were speeded up, the loading of trains was increased in some cases and a few companies such as the North Eastern, Great Western and Lancashire & Yorkshire experimented with high capacity wagons.[1] But the small 8- or 10-ton wagon remained the standard down to 1914 since it was often found difficult to get sufficient loads of merchandise to keep the larger wagons fully employed. Moreover, roughly one half of the wagons used on the railways belonged to private owners (mainly coal merchants) who were against the use of larger wagons. Only the Midland Railway managed to purchase all the private wagons used on its railway though it found to its dismay that many of them were only fit for the scrap heap. No doubt substantial economies could have been achieved had not traders blocked reform.

On the other hand, the rapid growth in freight traffic sometimes forced the companies to improve their methods of handling in order to relieve congestion on their lines. This was apparently the case at Liverpool, for example, where by the 1870s the siding accommodation had failed to keep

[1] As far back as the 1860s 30-ton wagons had been put into service by one Scottish company.

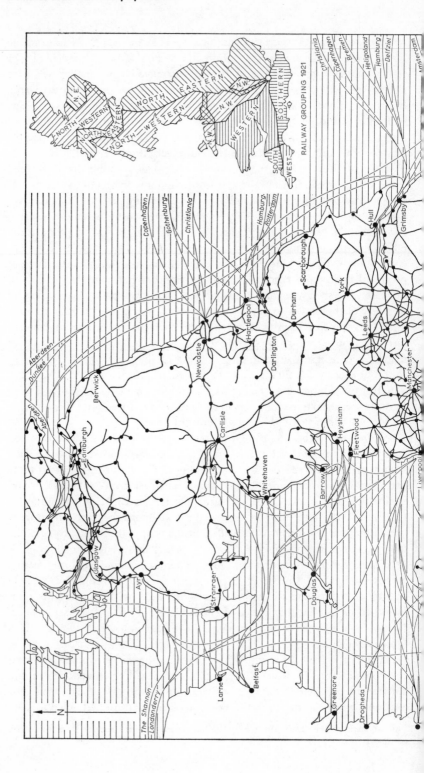

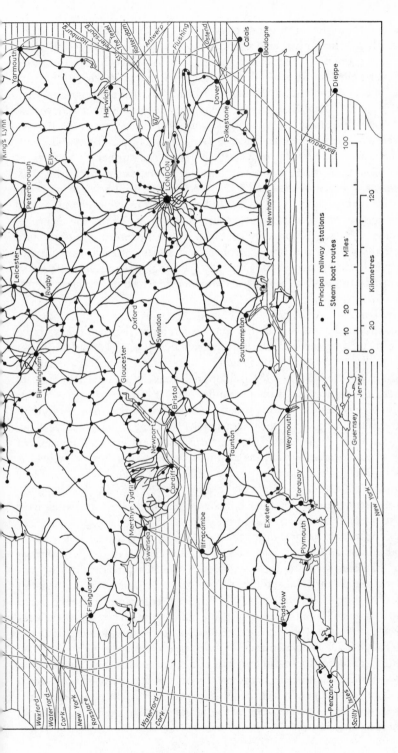

Map 13 *The completed railway network, 1914: inset, railway grouping, 1921*

pace with the growth in goods traffic. To solve the problem the London & North Western constructed a unique marshalling yard at Edge Hill where outward traffic from the various goods depots and docks was concentrated and marshalled for despatch all over the system. It was worked on the principle of gravitation and by the early 1880s the yard was clearing more than 2000 wagons a day. Similarly, an extensive remodelling of Crewe was undertaken in the late 1890s to avoid congestion. The capacity of the terminal was greatly expanded and as far as possible passenger and goods traffic were separated by providing underground tunnelling for freight trains. Another great marshalling yard for coal capable of clearing 7000 wagons a day, was opened in 1907 by the Great Central at Wath. This was part of a larger scheme, which included the construction of the port of Immingham, designed to improve the facilities offered for the export of coal from the South Yorkshire coalfield. It was the forerunner of modern marshalling yards and was controlled by a system of electro-pneumatic, route-indicating semaphores. Generally speaking, however, improvements in freight handling were notably absent in a field which offered considerable scope for economies.

The construction of new mileage and the improvement in facilities involved a considerable increase in capital expenditure. Between 1870 and 1913 the total paid-up capital of the railways rose by £815,231,000. Only just over £516 million of this sum represented new investment for railway purposes, whilst roughly £150 to £200 million represented nominal additions to capital. The railways used the remainder of their capital to invest in a wide range of activities which were usually ancillary or complementary to their main undertaking. Thus their acquisitions included hotels, road vehicles, horses, canals, docks and harbours, steamboats and even an amusement park at Cleethorpes which was acquired by the Manchester, Sheffield & Lincolnshire Railway Company in the 1880s. By the end of the century more than £100,000 had been spent on the resort and it proved to be one of the best investments made by the Company. These non-railway activities have not so far received the attention they deserve.

A considerable proportion of the extra-railway investment was made in canals, docks and steam-boat services and by 1914 around £75 million or more had been spent on these activities. As we have already seen, the railways acquired control of about one third of the canal network in the latter half of the nineteenth century. Most railway companies also recognized at a fairly early stage the value of good marine connections, and their interests in this field were rapidly extended in this period. Between 1847 and 1909 roughly 200 Parliamentary Acts were passed empowering the railways to build or acquire docks and purchase and operate steamships. By the latter date some 72 harbours, docks and piers were leased, controlled or operated by railway companies. In fact the railways became the chief dock and canal owners and they operated one of the largest fleets of short-sea steamboat services in the country.

Canals and docks have been dealt with elsewhere and it is intended here merely to say a few words about railway steamboat services. Early attempts of the railway companies to provide cross-channel shipping services for their passengers were frustrated by opposition from both existing shipowners and parliament, since the bulk of these services were then provided by private companies or Admiralty packets. To overcome the difficulty the railway companies either contracted with private owners to run a service in connection with their trains or they assisted in the formation of subsidiary undertakings for the same purposes. It was not until the 1860s—by which time the Admiralty had relinquished its mail service to the continent to private owners—that a committee of the House of Commons reported in favour of the railways owning steamships. Henceforward the railway companies began to acquire powers to operate their own steamers. Between 1862 and 1864, for example, the Great Eastern, the London & South Western, the London Brighton & South Coast and the Manchester, Sheffield & Lincolnshire railway companies all acquired powers to run steamboat services to various places on the continent. Ten years later the Great Western began running steamships to Ireland when it took over the existing service between New Milford and Waterford. Eventually most of the major railway companies extended their activities into the maritime field either by building their own ships or buying out the existing private operators. By 1914 many of the short-sea crossings between England and Scotland and Ireland and the continent were represented by railway steamers. On some of the routes, notably the English channel-crossings to France, the railways soon monopolized the field. Until the early 1860s these routes were still being operated by private shipping concerns or joint rail and shipping undertakings. Most of them were quickly taken over by the railway companies as soon as they acquired their permanent powers and from 1870s onwards they dominated the cross-channel routes. Of the 103 new vessels built for these services between 1870 and 1914 no less than 73 were on account of British railways and most of the rest were for Belgian and French operators. Traffic expanded rapidly in these years and by 1914 1,550,072 passengers passed over southern railway routes to the continent compared with only 270,763 in 1870.

The railways undoubtedly rendered a great service to the public in supplying co-ordinated rail and steamship services. The number and frequency of crossings had increased considerably by the end of the century. The standard of accommodation on many steamers was often very good and time schedules were sometimes better than those of today. By 1896 the Dover to Calais trip of the London, Chatham & Dover was made in one hour. Some of the companies were pioneers in the use of the latest marine techniques; the South Eastern & Chatham's *Queen*, for instance, was the first turbine steamer to be used in the English Channel. The railways' steam passenger services were not, of course, confined solely to the continental routes. They also had considerable interests in the short-sea crossings to Ireland and the

Channel Islands, and, to a somewhat lesser extent, in those to Scandinavia and the Baltic countries. In addition, they operated many special holiday steamers in the summer months, the most notable being the services around the islands of Western Scotland.

Many of the railway companies also operated cargo steamers, most of which were engaged in the near continental trades. This is particularly true of the companies with access to the Humber region, and there is no reason to believe it was not the same in other areas, though information on this aspect is very scanty. By the end of the nineteenth century the marine activities of Hull, Grimsby and Goole were dominated by three railway companies, respectively the North Eastern, the Manchester, Sheffield & Lincolnshire (by then the Great Central) and the Lancashire & Yorkshire. Not only had these companies gained control of the ports in question but they also operated rival freight steamer services to a large number of continental ports. The main objective was to attract traffic through the ports and hence on to the railways, and in this respect they seem to have been quite successful. Traders, however, often alleged that the railways exercised monopolistic powers and that the rates charged for the shipping services were unnecessarily high largely as a result of the conference rate structure devised by the participating companies. On the other hand, it has also been argued that many of these steamer services were put on as "loss leaders" in order to attract traffic to the railways. There is, of course, a strong element of incompatibility in these assertions and in the present state of knowledge it is impossible to resolve the problem. It is worth noting, however, that recent research on the Lancashire & Yorkshire's steamer operations in the early twentieth century suggests that the Company costed its services fairly carefully, and that as a result considerable profits were made. One swallow, of course, does not make a summer and it would be dangerous to draw any general conclusions until we know more about the steamship enterprises of the railways.

2 Monopoly and the state

From the very beginning parliament attempted to limit the powers and activities of the railway companies. Apart from the private Acts of incorporation which conferred separate powers on each company, numerous committees of both houses were established in the nineteenth century to inquire into various aspects of railway management whilst general Acts of Parliament were passed to regulate their affairs. Select Committees for such purposes were appointed either by the House of Lords or the House of Commons in every year between 1835 and 1840 and further committees sat in 1843, 1844, 1846, 1849, 1853, 1863, 1864, 1872, 1881–2 and 1893, while two Royal Commissions reported in 1846 and 1867. Many of these investigations often led to fresh legislation which attempted to circumscribe the powers or limit the freedom of the companies. It is probably no exaggeration to say that by 1914 the railways were the most regulated form of economic activity in Britain for by that time over 200 general statutes had been passed relating to the railways.

Generally speaking, throughout the nineteenth century parliament's main concern was to protect the interests of the railway users from the monopolistic tendencies on the part of the railway companies. Initially the State sought to achieve this by authorizing the construction of competitive lines. Despite such efforts it proved impossible to prevent a movement towards combination between the companies which was more often than not in the interests of both the railways and the railway users. Combination, in fact, was the logical outcome of the futile atomistic competition which parliament initially sought to promote. Many of the early companies were too small to maintain an independent existence and were soon absorbed by their wealthier neighbours. Excessive competition between rival lines inevitably led to a fusion of interests by outright amalgamation. Another factor encouraging railway companies to combine was the greater efficiency and economy in working which could be secured from doing so. Moreover, since concentration increased the territorial coverage of individual companies it was possible to provide better through services for traders and passengers. Improvements in facilities were also increased by the inevitable growth of working agreements, leases, and traffic pooling arrangements among the companies.

Thus during the 1850s and particularly in the 1860s large scale amalgamation or the leasing of the lines of one company to another proceeded rapidly and largely unchecked. In 1863 the Great Western added nearly 400 miles to its system by taking over the West Midland and the South Wales and a couple of years later the Caledonian and the North British absorbed many hundreds of lines in Scotland. Similarly in the decade 1860–70 the London & North Western increased its route mileage from 929 to 1506, such was the rate of absorption of satellite companies. During the same period no less than 187 Acts were passed containing provisions for amalgamation and another 383 were passed to establish working agreements. By 1871 amalgamation had been effected to such an extent that little more than 100 major companies remained and 28 of these worked 12,414 out of 15,537 miles of track open for traffic. Many of these large companies were the result of numerous fusions and legislative action and parliamentary pressure had done little to prevent the natural trend towards consolidation. As the Select Committee of 1872 observed: "Committees and commissions carefully chosen have for the last thirty years clung to one form of competition after another; it has nevertheless become more and more evident that competition must fail to do for the railways what it has done for ordinary trade and that no means have yet been devised by which competition can be permanently maintained."

Despite the high degree of concentration that had been achieved by this time there was still plenty of scope for competition. Fusion had not eliminated competition but merely transferred it "from small bodies to large, powerful, wealthy corporations capable of large undertakings and large policies". Certainly much waste and duplication of facilities still remained. Nevertheless both parliament and public were becoming increasingly apprehensive about the position especially when in 1871 a large flurry of Bills for amalgamations and working arrangements were presented for legislative sanction.[1] Among these was the famous proposed combine between the London & North Western and the Lancashire & Yorkshire, which together worked one-eighth of the railway mileage and owned one-seventh of the railway capital. As a result of agitation and petition from traders in particular, a Select Committee was appointed to review the whole position.

If the critics of monopoly expected an unfavourable report they must have been sadly disappointed by the Committee's findings. In fact the Committee went out of its way to exonerate the companies. In their opinion combination was both inevitable and desirable. "It is generally easy to show that the public will gain largely by harmonious arrangements; and considering how doubtful is the extent of competition, or of the facilities it produces, the balance of advantage, to the public as well as to the shareholders, may often well be thought to be on the side of amalgamation". They felt that past amalgamations had not produced the evils anticipated and sought to prove this point by reference to the North Eastern railway which though "the most complete monopoly in the United Kingdom" had the lowest fares and the highest dividends of any English railway. Moreover, the Committee thought that combination was bound to increase and that it was impossible to lay down any general rules determining the limits or character of future amalgamations. It was, however, suggested that a special commission might be appointed to exercise a greater degree of supervision over the railways. Accordingly in the following year the Railway and Canal Traffic Act (1873) was passed which strengthened the government's powers of control. The Act set up a three-member Railway Commission whose duties were extensive but powers narrow.The Commission was not only entrusted with the task of examining and preventing if necessary all future proposals for amalgamations and agreements, but it was also given the task of investigating all complaints made under the Act of 1854 relating to the refusal of reasonable facilities and undue preference. Unfortunately, the nature of its appointment and the lack of adequate executive powers rendered the Commission a fairly impotent force. Initially it was established for five years after which it was renewed annually until reconstituted and made permanent in 1888. On the whole its powers were too weak to be really effective; in the words of one contemporary it had "power enough to annoy the rail-roads but not power enough to help the

[1] Altogether 11 amalgamation Bills and 71 Bills for working arrangements were submitted in that year.

public effectively". The Commission had little authority to require the companies to observe the provisions in their private Acts, whilst if the companies chose to disregard the Commission's recommendations regarding reasonable facilities and undue preference then there was little they could do about it. In fact, in the early years of the Commission's existence the companies often defied its findings. Though intended to be cheap, litigation before the Commission was often quite expensive and it was said that a complainant became a "marked man" in the eyes of the railway companies. Nevertheless, the Commission was not entirely useless. It served to curb the more blatant activities of the railways, and the companies became somewhat reluctant to give occasion for appeal to the Commission. Moreover, the establishment of a separate body of control marked the beginning of a more direct and extensive era of parliamentary control over the railways of Great Britain.

Whether the institution of stricter control or the rejection of two important amalgamation Bills, including that of the London & North Western in 1873, dampened the enthusiasm of the railways for amalgamation or not, it is a fact that the trend towards combination slackened off considerably after 1872. No doubt the obvious reason was that the scope for further concentration was very much less by this time anyway. A few important amalgamations still remained to be completed however. The most notable were the Great Western's absorption of the Bristol & Exeter and the South Devon railway companies in 1876 and 1878, and the acquisition of the Lancashire, Derbyshire & East Coast Railway by the Great Central in 1906. In addition, a number of important working unions, which secured the benefits of unified management and operation whilst retaining the companies separate identity, were concluded in these years. Perhaps the most famous was the full working union established between the South Eastern and the London, Chatham & Dover in 1899, which brought to an end nearly half a century of bitter rivalry. For the most part, however, it was merely a case of the larger companies acquiring control, either by lease, joint working or outright absorption, of the small, short railways of limited significance designed to give outlying towns and villages connection with the main traffic arteries of the country. Few of these smaller companies were financially strong; many of them had maintained a precarious existence from the beginning and were unable to render an adequate service to the public. Yet though the amalgamations themselves may not have been large, the number of companies involved was substantial. By 1906, 223 of the 351 companies which existed in 1881 had disappeared from the scene, most of them having been absorbed by larger neighbours. In 1913, 15 major companies controlled about 84 per cent of the railway mileage of Great Britain. Many of these great undertakings were the result of numerous acquisitions. The Great Western alone was the product of 115 separate companies, and six of the major railways had absorbed more than 300 companies. The extent to which amalgamations and working unions had occurred is illustrated by the fact that the 110 separately operated railways (excluding light railways) which existed in 1910 consisted of more than 1,100 separately authorized undertakings.

Formal amalgamation was not the only way in which the railway companies sought to limit the degree of competiton. Since the very early days alliances and traffic agreements had been concluded by certain companies and these had often paved the way for complete fusion of interests. Similar though more elaborate agreements between the larger concerns became more common later in the nineteenth century and early in the twentieth century for a number of reasons. In the first place fierce competiton between the companies at various points still prevailed, and since the scope for fusion was by the 1870s limited and frowned upon by Parliament, the companies sought to circumscribe the area of competition by collusive action. The willingness to co-operate was strengthened by the fact that during the 1880s competition in facilities and service became more severe. Moreover, after the legislation of 1888–94[1] rate adjustment became increasingly inflexible at a time when costs began to rise and the only way in which the companies could economize was to eliminate unnecessary waste and duplication of facilities. There were a variety of ways in which an identification of interests could be secured but the most common forms adopted were working agreements, pooling agreements and conferences for settling rates. None of these required direct parliamentary sanction (whereas amalgamations, working unions and leases did) though railway users had the right to appeal against them to the Board of Trade and Railway Commission, and in the case of working agreements the Commission had power to revise them if thought to be against the public interest. Oddly enough there was much less opposition to such agreements than over amalgamations, and the official attitude was often one of mild indifference. Between 1873 and 1910 for example, 67 working agreements were submitted to the Railway Commission for approval, only nine of which were rejected. For companies seeking economy by co-operation, therefore, it was a question how far they could go with unobtrusive agreements without raising the wrath of the public or parliament in the process.

Clearing House Conferences for regulating the general principles upon which railway companies conducted their undertakings and agreements to facilitate transactions relating to joint traffic were by no means new. In the early years of railway development many companies had found it necessary to settle joint claims on traffic by agreement and the Clearing House Classification of the 1840s had provided for co-operation on a national scale. In order to avoid cut-throat competition in price, formal meetings of representatives of various companies began to be held for purposes of settling rates between competitive points in various parts of the country. The earliest of these was the London, Liverpool and Manchester conference

[1] See below, pp. 167–70.

formed in 1860, and the Normanton conference established in 1865 to deal with a mass of competitive rates in Britain. Other conferences, mostly on a regional basis, were established, such as the English and Scottish conference of 1869, the West Riding conference of 1875, and the Humber Ports conference of 1906. Though these conferences reduced the number of competitive rates considerably, competition in facilities continued for some time as railway agents sought to attract traffic by offering special concessions. In time fewer conveniences were given gratis and there was more agreement about charges to be made for them. By the turn of the century competition had been very much reduced though it was by no means completely absent; according to Milne and Laing, the position was one of "collusive oligopoly in respect of price and certain aspects of quality of service, with points of fierce competition in the selling of similar transport services by 'transport drummers' to a market of smaller size than the capacity of the services devoted to the rail industry."

Towards the end of the nineteenth century the development of joint working agreements or pooling agreements providing for the sharing of traffic and pooling of receipts between the major companies became a marked feature of railway history. Neither of them were new but at this time they assumed a new importance since they permitted the companies to secure economies by reducing wasteful competition at a time when costs were rising rapidly. Traffic pooling became very common after 1900 and such agreements were concluded between the Scottish companies, between the London & North Western, the Lancashire & Yorkshire and the Midland companies and between the Great Western and the London & South Western. The movement did not go unchallenged. In 1907 a proposal by the Great Central and the Great Northern to form a working agreement, with a joint managing committee and a division of net receipts on the basis of 1906, was contested and thrown out by the Railway Commissioners. Whereupon the two companies, in association with the Great Eastern, presented a Bill to parliament in 1909 for a working union by which it was proposed to "district" nearly all the railways in Eastern England east of the Great Northern main line to Doncaster. The Bill was hastily withdrawn, however, when the strength of the opposition, both in Parliament and outside, towards it was revealed.

The battle of the Great Northern, the Great Eastern and the Great Central was sufficient to animate the fury of the traders once again. The Government diligently responded by setting up yet another departmental committee to consider what changes, if any, were required in the law relating to agreements and whether any additional safeguards were necessary to protect the public against the possible abuse of railway monopoly. The committee were clearly on the side of the railways, and in part their report echoed the findings of the Select Committee of 1872. Not only were they unanimously in favour of "more perfect understandings and co-operation" but they could see little benefit to the public in the limited degree of

L

competition which still remained. The era of competition was clearly passing away and it was recognized even by witnesses on behalf of traders that this could not be prevented for, in the words of the committee: "the natural lines of an improved and more economical railway system lie in the direction of a more perfect co-operation between the various railway companies; and we accept the growth of co-operation and the more complete elimination of competition as a process at once inevitable, and likely to be beneficial, both to the railway companies themselves, and, if properly safeguarded, to the public also"; and "that the protection required by the public cannot be afforded by any system of sanctioning or regulating agreements, but that such protection must in the main be given by general legislation dealing with any injurious consequences of the co-operative action of particular railways, or the assimilation of railway practice, independently of whether they occur as the results of formal agreements or not."

Consequently the committee offered few startling recommendations but merely suggested that a greater degree of general supervisory control should be exercised over the railways. Needless to say the outbreak of the First World War prevented the Government from taking further action.[1] The conclusions of the committee were justified both on theoretical and empirical grounds. One of the cardinal errors of British railway policy was that it attempted to apply at one and the same time the economically incompatible principles of monopoly and competition. It was never fully realized that the ordinary principles of competition, which the State applied to other commercial undertakings, were not appropriate to the railways where fixed costs formed roughly half of the total and much of the capital was irredeemable. Consequently any dissipation of traffic between competing companies was bound to increase unit costs at least in the short run unless competition produced an increase in total traffic. There was a limit, however, to the volume of transport required and beyond a certain point the demand for transport facilities became relatively inelastic. At this stage any further increase in competition, either by way of a reduction in fares or better facilities, merely raised unit costs without adding to net revenue. In any case, any policy which brought about a duplication of facilities, e.g., track, sidings, stations, etc., in order to provide an alternative service, was a waste in itself unless it could be justified on the grounds that a single monopolist would exploit his favourable position. In short, the movement towards unification was based simply on economic expediency.

Though the management of British railways before 1914 is not above criticism, there is no doubt that the public benefited from the trend towards unified working. Competitive canvassing, conveyance by circuitous routes, duplication of equipment and facilities, management and administrative expenses and other sources of waste were reduced or eliminated. For example, an agreement between the Midland and the London & North

[1] The war interrupted the sittings of a Royal Commission appointed in 1913 to study the question of Government relationship with the railways.

Western saved the former company 3,000 train miles a week in the carriage of meat between London and Carlisle. Passengers were able to enjoy greater inter-availability of tickets, more through routes and less changing and re-booking. Traders could secure quicker and more economical delivery of goods through shorter routing, fuller wagon and train loads and less transhipment of freight. Very often amalgamations or agreements led to a reduction in charges for the simple reason that it was possible to calculate rates on a through basis. In evidence before the departmental committee of 1911 spokesmen for the railways pointed out that pooling arrangements had not raised a single rate and had lowered some. Pratt was in no doubt about the advantages: "that the conveniences of travel and the advantages to traders have been greatly enhanced by the substitution of these few great companies for a large number of small ones is beyond question, and actual experience has shown that the fear of grave evils resulting from prospective abuses of the railways, 'monopoly' brought about by amalgamations such as these have been mainly imaginery, notwithstanding the fact that they have formed the basis of so much of the policy of the State in its dealings with the railways."

Of course nothing in the nature of a real monopoly existed so there was little possibility of outright exploitation, and certainly no British railway company ever made very large profits. Even in cases which approached near monopoly, there is little evidence to suggest it led to abuse. In fact, rather the contrary. As we have seen the North Eastern had the lowest fares and the highest dividends. Neither did the Great Eastern abuse its privileged position in the Eastern counties of England; in fact the company pioneered the movement for offering exceptionally low rates and other special facilities for the transport of agricultural produce and it probably did more than any other railway company to enable working men to live in healthy suburbs in London. Moreover, competition, though much reduced, still existed at various points on the system and companies still continued to vie with each other in types of service offered. The railways' position was also influenced by competition from other forms of transport, especially by water. Indeed a large number of railway rates for freight traffic were influenced by coastal sea transport which was said to affect about three-fifths of the railway stations in the United Kingdom. Pratt maintained that the rates for traffic between any two ports "will necessarily be influenced, if not controlled, by the possibility of the commodities going by a coasting vessel if the railway company should try to get more than, in these particular circumstances, such traffic will bear." Finally, it should be remembered that if a company charged excessive rates or gave inadequate facilities for traffic it would soon find that, in the case of goods traffic at least, the markets which it had been in the habit of serving, were drawing their supplies from elsewhere. In the long run, therefore, it was the companies, not the traders, who stood to lose from poor railway services.

If traders failed to appreciate the position they could scarcely complain that they lacked adequate protection against possible abuse. In the first instance they could always challenge any proposed amalgamation, working union or lease, all of which required statutory sanction before they could be brought into operation. It is true that Parliamentary approval was unnecessary for pooling or working agreements, but in such cases traders had the right to appeal to the Board of Trade or Railway Commissioners. By law the railways were subject to many regulations; they had to carry all traffic offered to them, provide reasonable facilities, avoid giving undue preference, and in the latter half of the nineteenth century a much greater degree of control was imposed on their rate-making powers. Failure to observe these conditions would more than likely produce an appeal. Thus any interested party could bring a railway company before the Railway Commission requesting that reasonable facilities be provided as regards any particular point. It may be argued that this was an expensive proposition for an individual and that since the Commission's scope and powers were rather limited it was unlikely to be able to effect railway policy a great deal. On the other hand, in the last resort Parliament itself could step in and pass legislation requiring a company to improve its facilities in any respect in which they were found to be inadequate. Furthermore, the powers of the Railway Commission were strengthened by the Railway and Canal Traffic Act of 1888.[1] The jurisdiction of the Commission was extended to cover a wide range of matters including traffic facilities, private sidings, undue preference, through rates, etc., and it was given power to enforce obligations under special Acts. Henceforth the Commission exercised a greater degree of control over railway matters than previously and it provided a convenient, if expensive, form of appeal for dissatisfied railway clients. Traders' interests were further safeguarded under the Conciliation Clause of the 1888 Act whereby the Board of Trade could settle complaints (mainly concerning rates) informally thus saving the expense of a case being brought before the Commission. Though the Board of Trade had no powers to enforce a settlement its efforts at conciliation met with a fair degree of success. Between 1894 and 1911, 3,396 complaints were submitted to the Board, 2,647 of which were either settled or not followed up. This procedure undoubtedly saved much costly litigation and it appears that every reasonable complaint of traders was very carefully considered, not only by the officials of the Board of Trade but also by the railway companies themselves. There seems little evidence to suggest that any serious grievance was left uninvestigated. The most surprising thing is that the number of complaints was so small, and many of them so trivial in nature, and one wonders to what extent the outcry against railway rates was really justified. Whatever the position, it certainly left its mark on the statute book.

[1] In that year the Commission was made permanent and its title changed to Railway and Canal Commission.

3   Pricing policy

Though the railways had cheapened the price of transport appreciably, traders never ceased to complain about railway charges. This dissatisfaction grew as the railway companies became larger and more powerful and competition in price diminished, and ultimately it led to inquiries which resulted in the parliamentary legislation of 1888–94. Traders alleged that the railways misused their powers by charging unequal mileage rates, discriminating in favour of foreign goods and granting special rates or discounts to certain traders. More generally it was reckoned that railway rates were too high and compared unfavourably with those abroad. Some of these complaints were no doubt valid, others were simply based on a misinterpretation of the facts. However, one fact was incontrovertible: that the basis of rate-making was exceedingly complex and unscientific. British railway rates were, according to Kirkaldy and Evans, based on no set of clearly defined principles but were "evolved empirically as traffic has grown from year to year, and consequently there is much about them that, on the surface, may appear illogical, inconsistent, and, sometimes, even unjust." Thus whatever justification there was for the other allegations there was no denying the fact that by the 1870s the reform of the railway rate structure was long overdue.

Following the precedent of the canals the original Railway Acts had contained simple classifications of goods expected to be carried by rail and maximum charges were prescribed for each class of goods. In the early years, therefore, maximum mileage tolls were fixed on the basis of a rough "value" classification according to what the traffic would bear. The position was unsatisfactory in many respects. Classifications and maximum charges varied from company to company and it was often difficult to discover what the charge would be for traffic passing over several companies' lines. The difficulties increased enormously as the volume and variety of traffic grew and the original classifications soon became obsolete. Moreover, though the companies were obliged to charge rates within the maxima laid down in the Acts, there was nothing to prevent discrimination between traders by quoting unequal charges. To make matters worse the Acts authorized the railways to make three separate charges, one each for the use of the track and locomotive and another for the actual conveyance.

It was not long before attempts were made by both Parliament and the companies to improve the system of charging. The "maximum rate clause" of the Act of 1845 combined the three separate tolls into one flat rate and introduced the principle of equal mileage rates to check discrimination. In an effort to prevent the companies from exploiting their powers parliamentary control was strengthened by the Railway and Canal Traffic Act of 1854 which defined the duties of the railways to the public. This laid down the terms and conditions on which traffic was to be conveyed, forbade any undue preference and directed the railways to offer reasonable facilities for all traffic. These measures failed to allay the dissatisfaction of traders. Though maximum charges for conveyance were prescribed, charges for collection and delivery and terminal services were not statutorily limited and so the companies could charge what they liked for these facilities. The practice was to lump all the charges together so that the shipper could not discern whether he was being overcharged for conveyance as distinct from additional charges for extras. The law against undue preference or discrimination remained very much a "dead letter" for the simple reason that traders could not compare charges for similar traffics because the railways were not required to publish their tariffs. Subsequent legislation sought to remedy the worst of these anomolies. Acts of 1868 and 1873 required charges to be disintegrated and itemized on request and all rates in force were to be published. The second of these two Acts set up the Railway Commission which, among other things, was to settle inter-railway disputes and adjudicate all complaints touching railway and canal charges. Initially, however, the Commission lacked adequate powers to inspire confidence in traders.

Meanwhile the railway companies themselves had been trying desperately to simplify and make consistent the classification and to reduce as far as possible the number of rates they were authorized to charge. In 1842 a few companies had established a Railway Clearing House whose task was to facilitate through traffic and adjust the debts arising from through booking. By 1850, when it received statutory blessing, it included most of the main railway companies and within the area affected, through booking and through movement of wagons were universal. One of its most important achievements was the preparation of a more elaborate classification for goods traffic applicable to all railways in the clearing system to replace the original lists which were found to be crude and inadequate. Initially, the Railway Clearing House Classification contained about 300 articles, but by 1887 it had been expanded to 2,753 articles grouped under seven distinct classes. Some idea of the miscellaneous descriptions of goods carried by rail can be gathered from the fact that there were more than 200 items grouped under "Explosives and other dangerous goods" and nearly as many under "Hardware".

Despite the efforts made by the railways to standardize and unify their methods of charging, the position was still far from satisfactory. The Clearing House Classification divided traffic up only into very broad classes on which charges might be levied. It never applied to every company and it did not deal directly with rates to be charged. It merely sorted out commodities into various classes and left the companies to levy charges in accordance with their charging powers embodied in the separate Acts of Parliament. Consequently a multiplicity of rates and charges continued to exist. Nearly every company levied rates under several Acts applicable to different portions of its own system. The Midland company, for example, was empowered in one Act to charge 1*d*. per ton per mile for coal, and in another $1\frac{1}{2}d$.; for grain in one Act it might charge $1\frac{1}{2}d$., in two more $2d$. In one case reference had to be made to more than 50 Acts to determine the approximate charges. Altogether there were some 900 different Acts which dealt with charging powers. Some idea of the total number of different rates possible can be gathered from the fact that there were 18,000 railway stations and some 40,000 pairs of stations between which business could be transacted in regard to the 2,753 articles included in the Railway Clearing House Classification. The rates in force on the London & North Western alone numbered 20 million and those on the Great Northern over 13 million. The situation was made more confusing by the fact that maximum rates authorized by statute did not necessarily indicate the charges made in practice, since terminal charges remained uncontrolled and the companies granted many exceptional rates. There were still no general economic criteria on which railway rates were based other than the simple value classification and the force of competition. Indeed the railways themselves were at a loss to know exactly what factors determined pricing policy. One railway manager referred to the absence of any "general principles or system for fixing rates", and of charging "as much as could be got . . . without reference to the cost of the company of performing the service".

In 1881 and 1882 Select Committees were appointed to make a thorough investigation into the system of railway charging and to examine the validity of traders' complaints. Not surprisingly, they were unable to find any general principles on which maximum charges had been fixed in the past. However, the railway companies were absolved of any "grave dereliction of their duties to the public". Whilst acknowledging the fact that complaints about discrimination were often well founded, the 1882 Committee felt unable to recommend any new legislation to enforce equality of charging for the simple reason that differential charging was not always against the public interest. On the other hand, the Committee did suggest the adoption of a uniform classification for the whole country and the recognition of terminal charges since it considered that discrimination and a multiplicity of rates would continue to prevail so long as Parliament did nothing to introduce a uniform classification and maxima charges for terminals.

Six years later the first general codification and review of railway charges by Act of Parliament was made. The principal object of the Railway and Canal Traffic Act of 1888 was to make uniform the classification and maximum charges over the whole railway system of Great Britain. Within six months of the passing of the Act the companies were required to submit to the Board of Trade a revised classification and new schedules of maximum rates applicable thereto, including maxima charges for station terminals. The Board of Trade was to consider objections to them and, failing agreement, to impose the new schedules by statutory order. By the appointed date, February 1889, the new lists had been prepared, but unfortunately the process of revision was so laborious, owing partly to the large number of complaints received, that the task was not completed until

1892. The revised classification proved to be the least controversial aspect of reform. It was based on the original Clearing House Classification and contained eight categories of merchandise compared with seven under the old system. The task of framing the new schedules of maxima rates was more complicated and took far longer. Over 4,000 objections were made by traders to the new schedules of charges and conferences had to be arranged between representatives of traders and railway companies to reconcile the differences. Finally, after protracted bargaining, the Board of Trade was able to produce a report containing the schedules of charges and revised classification, which came into force on 1 January 1893, under the Railway (Rates and Charges) Order Confirmation Acts of 1891 and 1892.

The reform produced a considerable simplification of railway rates. Practically uniform maximum scales and a uniform classification were substituted for the separate and varied scales and classifications contained in the companies' private Acts. Conveyance and terminal charges had to be distinguished separately and both were subject to maxima; charges for collection and delivery and other special services fell outside the scope of the new schedules and were left to the discretion of the companies. Within the maxima laid down railway companies were legally free to charge what they liked provided that no undue preference was shown. The law regarding undue preference was made more explicit, however. Differential rates in favour of foreign merchandise were prohibited but competition was recognized as a justification for differential charging so long as the public interest was secured thereby. The burden of proving that any difference in treatment did not amount to undue preference lay with the companies. To adjudicate on such matters the Railway Commission was made permanent and given extended powers of investigation. In addition, the Board of Trade was empowered to settle informally disputes about railway rates.

The adoption of the tapering rate was the most notable innovation made in the method of calculating charges. Instead of charges increasing with each mile of distance beyond a maximum of six miles as hitherto, the principle was adopted that the rate per mile for conveyance of freight by rail should diminish with increased distance. The tapering scale imposed a certain rate per mile for the first twenty miles, whereafter it diminished as the distance increased. This meant that for the first time it was openly acknowledged that rates charged should bear some relation to operating costs. It was, however, the only concession to cost criteria. Neither the railway companies nor the Board of Trade attempted to be theoretical when framing the new schedules of maximum rates. To a great extent they were based on existing rates and the time-honoured principles which had determined these in the past.

As soon as the new schedules were put into force there was a great outcry from traders. They did not object to the new classification nor to the fact that about 30 to 40 per cent of the rates had been lowered, but they did object when they found that some rates were higher than they had been previously. This situation arose simply from the fact that the companies had had insufficient time to revise many of the exceptional rates which had been granted in the past. Consequently, they had merely charged the full maximum rates which they were legally entitled to do until the new special rates could be worked out. Thus, traders who had been used to paying 12s. per ton for certain freight were now obliged to pay the full rate of 18s. or 20s. with no explanation. They refused to pay the higher rates and demanded further parliamentary action. Another committee of the House of Commons, appointed to investigate the matter, reported against the companies for "they failed to see that any increase was justified, that the action of the companies had unreasonably disturbed the trade of the country, and that it ought to be placed out of their power to act in a similar manner of future" (Kirkaldy and Evans). The upshot of the report was the passing of the Railway and Canal Traffic Act of 1894 which prevented the companies from raising charges above those in operation at the end of 1892 unless they could justify the increase to the satisfaction of the Railway and Canal Commission.

The effect of the Act of 1894 was to reduce the flexibility of charging powers even further. "Although permitting in principle the discretion of the companies to vary their charges within the statutory maxima, the Act tended to make the actual rates in force become both the maximum and minimum rates" (Milne and Laing). The companies were put in difficulties. They were reluctant to demand increases in rates since, if challenged, they had to prove that there had been an increase in the cost of working the railway, excluding the cost of carrying and dealing with passengers. Of course this was a very difficult task since it was almost impossible to segregate joint costs whilst the method of charging adopted by the legislation provided little incentive to determine rates on the basis of operating costs alone. Consequently the companies found difficulty in raising their charges just at a time when costs were beginning to rise. In order to overcome this difficulty the companies resorted to securing economies by joint action in various ways, a policy which proved unpopular with traders. No relief was afforded until 1913 when they were allowed to raise their goods rates by 4 per cent to cover recent wage claims. It has also been argued that it prevented a general lowering of rates since, if any reductions made proved unprofitable, the railways would find it difficult to get them increased again. It is doubtful, however, if this rigidity in the downward direction was quite as strong as often imagined. Traders took every opportunity to secure reductions where possible and the competition from coastal sea transport often forced the companies to lower their rates. If the number of exceptional rates is anything to go by then rates were still being reduced after 1894. In the short space of twelve months one company alone arranged 63,000 new special rates. By 1914 something like 80 per cent of the rates quoted by the railways were exceptional.

Perhaps the most pernicious effect of the new legislation was that, apart

from the one concession of tapering mileage rates, it provided little opportunity or incentive for the companies to base their rates on costs of operation. According to Findlay, rates continued to be governed, in much the
same way as canal rates had been, "by the nature and extent of the traffic,
the pressure of competition, either by water, by a rival route, or by other
land carriage; but, above all, the companies have regard to the commercial
value of the commodity, and the rate it will bear, so as to admit of its being
produced and sold in a competing market with a fair margin of profit."
Admittedly the cost principle was a difficult concept to apply to railway
working and has remained a problem right down to the present day.
Nevertheless, failure to take the initiative in this respect, together with the
restrictive provisions of the 1894 Act, encouraged the companies to retain
the benefits of cross-subsidization far longer than was desirable. "The
failure of revenue to cover costs in some directions", say Milne and Laing,
"was made good in others by the exercise of monopoly power to make
revenue there much more than cover costs." It was not until the growth of
road transport threatened seriously the fortunes of the railways that the
futility of their pricing policy was fully realized.

Even after the stricter control of railway rates had been instituted traders
continued to complain that rates were either too high or compared
unfavourably with those abroad. Some of these complaints were justified
but it is only fair to remember that many of the comparisons made by
traders between English and foreign railway rates were highly misleading.
Traders who alleged that American or German railway rates were lower
than the British often failed to take account of the fact that they were
not comparing like with like. Certainly the average rate per ton on German
and American railways was often lower than that on British railways, but
then the nature of the service was not always the same. American freight
rates were low partly because the tapering rate, when applied to large
volumes of traffic conveyed over great distances, reduced the unit cost
considerably and terminal charges in such cases formed only a very small
proportion of the total cost. In contrast, charges on British railways were
calculated for short hauls of small consignments and terminal charges
accounted for a relatively high proportion of total costs. As Pratt observed:
"there was, and could be, no basis of comparison between huge consignments, carried long distances on comparatively unexpensive lines, and
small average consignments, carried short distances on the most costly
railway system in the world. The element of 'the same or similar circumstances' was obviously lacking." Moreover, precise comparison was made
difficult by the fact that foreign railways, particularly those on the continent, quoted special export rates or combined rail and shipping tariffs
which had no parallel in this country. The practice abroad was usually to
quote simple haulage rates which included no additional services such as
cartage and delivery, demurrage or warehousing, services which were
often provided free or at very low cost by British railways. Unless proper

allowance can be made for these factors it is very doubful whether any valuable comparison can be made between British and foreign railway rates. According to Pratt "a comparison of British with Continental, or even with American, railways is altogether delusive, and in the one case, as in others, judgment must be based on individual merits and national circumstances. If this be done, most of the grievances, real or imaginary, between British and foreign railway rates become untenable." In fact, it is highly probable that for shorter hauls British railway rates were lower than those quoted abroad. After an exhaustive study the Caledonian Railway Company found that for short distances (50 miles or less) their rates were lower than those for equivalent hauls in the United States of America but were higher for longer distances. Further investigation into the problem would no doubt produce a more conclusive answer.

Passenger fares were not reviewed by the 1888–94 legislation and no general revision was made at all in the nineteenth century. On the whole they gave far less occasion for dispute, partly because of the lack of an organized pressure group on behalf of the passengers. Consequently the railways were allowed a much greater degree of freedom in varying passenger fares than goods rates. As with the latter, however, passenger fares were fixed more according to what the traffic would bear rather than on the cost of service rendered.

Initially the bulk of the railway passenger traffic represented the more wealthy members of society transferring from stage coaches and paying fares averaging 2d. per mile or more. There were few third-class travellers since little provision was made for them and the fares charged (averaging round 1½d. per mile though there was considerable variation from company to company) were often outside the means of many of the poorer members of the community. But throughout the nineteenth century there was a steady growth in third-class travel and by the early twentieth century nearly 95 per cent of all railway passengers were travelling third class. This increase was largely due to a steady reduction in fares and improved facilities. An Act of 1844 made provision for one train daily along every new passenger line stopping at every station and carrying third-class passengers at 1d. per mile. Though this brought an increase in third-class travel the facilities for this class were still limited and the imposition of a railway passenger duty, by an Act of 1842, on all passengers including third class (except those on parliamentary trains) prevented any further reductions being made in standard fares. The extension of third-class travel facilities and the introduction of special cheap fares from the 1860s onwards brought into existence an entirely new class of traffic. This was facilitated by the remission of the passenger duty in 1883; in return for this concession the railways were required to provide a service of trains at very low fares for workmen and to carry members of the Armed Forces and Police at reduced fares. Prior to the Act many companies had been charging more than 1d. per mile for third-class passengers except on parliamentary trains where 1d. was compulsory. After 1883 the standard third-class fare was reduced to 1d. on most trains and, eventually, with the introduction of many more concessionary fares, the average fare charged had fallen to $\frac{1}{2}d$. per mile by the early twentieth century. On some lines in the greater populated areas such as London, cheap workmen's tickets accounted for one quarter or more of the total passenger tickets issued.

4   The efficiency of the railways

If, as traders alleged, British railway rates were higher than they should have been the companies could never be accused of making extortionate profits as a consequence. If anything, the profitability of the railways was declining throughout the period though most concerns continued to make a fair return down to 1914. Though gross receipts increased steadily, working expenses rose more rapidly and the operating ratio (that is, working expenses expressed as a percentage of gross receipts) rose, particularly after 1890. The operating ratio increased from just below 50 in the 1860s to 54 in 1890 and then to a peak of 65 in 1908. In the light of these figures it is not surprising that both traders and contemporaries accused the railways of inefficiency and bad management. Two notable students of the industry, the American E. B. Dorsey and the English economist, George Paish, made detailed comparative studies of American and British railway operation and came to the conclusion that there was considerable scope for improvement in the British system. Even Acworth, who was an ardent supporter of British railways, felt that by the turn of the century foreigners had little to learn from British experience as far as railway administration was concerned.

The deterioration in the operating ratio was not necessarily a true reflection of a decline in efficiency on the part of the railways. In the first place working costs rose rapidly towards the end of the nineteenth century. In the 1890s the cost of labour in the running part of the locomotive department rose by 43 per cent whilst rates and taxes doubled and in the five years 1896–1901 the cost of coal doubled. Secondly, though railway traffic was increasing rapidly much of it was now of a kind which required a greater proportionate outlay in capital and working expenses than the increase in revenue derived from it. An increasing proportion of it consisted of the cheaper grades of traffic such as passenger and goods at special fares or rates, and a greater proportion of coal which was carried at a very low margin of profit. More traffic was being carried on branch lines, some of which were relatively costly to operate because of the lower density of traffic particularly on lines serving remote areas. Suburban line traffic was also less profitable than had been anticipated, for a good deal of it consisted of workmen travelling at reduced fares the return from which was fairly small, whilst at the same time the peak-hour nature of this traffic necessitated a heavy outlay in rolling stock part of which remained under-utilized during the slack periods. And as the Great Northern found when dealing with the large daily traffic flow to London, suburban traffic could become an embarrassment if it began to interfere with more profitable main-line traffic. Moreover, in this period the railways were providing a far wider range of facilities than ever before, sometimes with little additional costs to the consumer. To improve the safety and comfort of passenger travel, for example, the railways were obliged to introduce more expensive rolling stock, the maintenance and running costs of which were relatively greater. Whereas in 1863 a railway carriage cost the Great Western company £250 at the most, by the 1890s the company had to pay over £1,000 for an eight-wheeled, gas-lit coach, upholstered throughout. Finally, the nature of goods traffic was changing towards a greater number of small consignments and short hauls which tended to increase the unit cost of handling. A chief goods manager of one of the leading railway companies reported that "In order to work with as little capital as possible and to minimize the risks from changes of market conditions, the retailers and local agents keep but little stock on hand and depend upon quick transit for the execution of the orders they receive. As a consequence, instead of large consignments as formerly, the railway companies are called upon to convey small separate lots at more frequent intervals, and with extreme expedition and regularity of service." All these factors tended to raise the cost of operation at the very time when railway charging powers were being made increasingly inflexible by Parliamentary control.

Critics of the railways contended that considerable savings in working expenses could have been achieved had more efficient methods of handling traffic been adopted. Dorsey and Paish were appalled at the high unit cost of moving freight and passengers on English railways compared with American railways. They concluded that the difference in cost was partly attributable to the less economical methods of handling traffic on the British system. In 1900 the majority of passenger and goods trains were probably loaded no more heavily than in 1880 and large trucks and modern marshalling yards were conspicuous by their absence. "Our railways have been content to go on working by the antiquated methods of thirty or forty years ago, and have neglected to take advantage of the experience of the American Lines." Paish also maintained that not only had British railways effected few economies in the cost of moving traffic, but that in 1900 unit costs of operation were much greater than in 1880, whereas American railroads had achieved considerable reductions over the same period. In a detailed comparison between the London & North Western and the Pennsylvania Railroad, he found that the cost of moving a ton of goods one mile on the former system rose by 24 per cent between 1880 and 1900 whereas a reduction of 33 per cent was secured by the latter; over the same period the cost of conveying one passenger one mile rose by $11\frac{1}{2}$ per cent and fell by 13 per cent respectively. These differences were no doubt due to some extent to the fact that the London & North Western made little progress in improving its methods of handling the traffic. In 1900 the average passenger train load was still no more than sufficient to fill one carriage whilst freight trucks were often run with loads of less than one ton. The average freight train load of the Pennsylvania Railroad was 484·6 tons compared with only 68·6 tons for the North Western, and the latter's train loads were heavier than those of any other British company barring the Lancashire & Yorkshire. Compared with the Pennsylvania the London & North Western ran 45 per cent more trains over one mile of its road to carry 79 per cent less traffic per mile. Had the North Western in 1900 carried as heavy train loads of freight and passengers as the Pennsylvania its expenses would have been only £3·5 million as against £8·1 million and its net earnings would have increased by £4·5 million.

The railways were not oblivious to the fact that substantial economies could be made by improved methods. In fact a few companies such as the Caledonian were using American methods by the end of the nineteenth century and in the decade before 1914 greater progress was made in this direction by other companies, particularly the North Eastern. That the advance was slow and faltering was due not so much to the lack of initiative on the part of the railway companies as to the fact that there were a number of factors which hindered the adoption of modern methods. For one thing it is only fair to remember that American methods of handling traffic were not wholly applicable in Britain where the nature of the traffic was totally different. The pattern of traffic on British railways—short hauls and small consignments—provided less scope for the introduction of such methods, particularly as regards introducing new equipment when there might be little prospect of it being used to full capacity. In fact it has been suggested that some of the alleged shortcomings of British railways were due as much to the nature of the traffic as to bad management. This argument can be stretched too far however, for, as Paish pointed out, even when allowance is made for lower density of traffic, smaller consignments and the shorter hauls of the English compared with the American lines, "there can be no doubt that our lines are woefully behind. All the considerations that can be thought of, and which should be made for our English lines, cannot justify a train load of only 68 tons against the Pennsylvania's 484 tons. Everyone who gives careful consideration to the subject will admit that with the expenditure of a relatively small amount of capital upon reducing gradients and upon increasing the size of our toy trucks, and by the exercise of reasonable care in the loading of trucks and trains, an enormous improvement can be effected."

Given favourable circumstances drastic reform could have been achieved but only at a price which in terms of capital was fairly high. Fixed capital equipment was highly interrelated and innovation in one sector would not only have required the adaptation of other parts of the railway system but would also have demanded an alteration of some of the installations outside the railways. Thus the height of bridges, the short radius of curves and the layout of stations, docks and staithes set the limits within which an increase in the size and weight of locomotives, wagons and coaches could be made. In this respect Britain suffered from being a pioneer. In America, where the shipping ports and iron and steel and other works had grown up at the same time as the railways, the appliances at the ports and works had been made to fit in with the modern appliances of the railway companies. But in Britain the railway companies had to adapt their appliances to the old and crude conditions already existing or started whilst the railways were still in their infancy. Thus innovations on the railways tended to be determined very much by the rate of progress elsewhere. Sir James Thompson, Chairman of the Caledonian Railway, was not exaggerating when he observed that "there is not, at the present time, a single shipping port, iron or steel work, or gaswork, or any work in Scotland, capable of dealing with a waggon of a carrying capacity of 30 or even 20 tons of coal, and there are not half a dozen collieries in Scotland whose appliances for separating coal are capable of admitting a waggon of the height of a 30 ton waggon."

Finally, it should be recalled that railway users themselves hindered the development of more economical methods of handling traffic. The retention of the privately owned railway wagon, a legacy of the early days when traders were expected to provide their own rolling stock, involved the railway companies in much expensive shunting and hauling since they had to be sorted and returned empty to the owners, and, of course, this delayed the adoption of larger wagons. As Sherrington observed: "Traders who cry out that the level of British railway rates is too high should remember their own continuous opposition to the adoption of a system which has always been the practice on railways abroad." Moreover, railway users in this country enjoyed a far wider range of services and facilities than their counterparts in other countries. Only the British railways tolerated such conveniences as separate dining cars for different classes, or low demurrage charges which encouraged traders to use wagons as warehouses. Such facilities were no doubt one aspect of qualitative improvement but many of them were expensive to provide and the additional cost fell on the railways rather than on the users. Thus whatever their defects, in terms of service British railways were probably unsurpassed anywhere in the world by 1914, but to achieve this distinction they sacrificed much in the way of economies.

6

Railways and the expansion of the economy

By the end of the period we have just been considering, the railway system had become a high-cost industry, whether this be measured by comparison with the freight charges made in other countries, or in terms of the general failure of the railway companies to maintain their earlier earning power. New investment and the ploughing back of undistributed profits to improve rolling stock and traffic facilities still went on heavily, without any very conspicuous fluctuations, down to 1914; yet operating costs began to rise faster than revenue and the ratio of net receipts to paid up capital slipped substantially below 4 per cent for the first time in 1891, and never climbed back. There was much anxiety being felt by companies whose lines served the suburbs of the large cities that they were being faced by a serious competitor in the form of the electric tram, which was joined from about 1906 by the motor-bus. Neither was of significance for inter-city traffic, nor was it yet conceivable that the internal combustion engine would soon begin that inexorable process of commercial attrition which was to last so long and have such dire consequences for the railways. Some of these problems could be met for a time, at least, by the companies themselves, and the possibilities that were open to them here will be examined presently.

What we need to do now is to assess the quite different situation as it existed for a large part of the nineteenth century, in which the building and running of the railway system, abroad as well as at home, provided a kind of strategic presence not only in relation to industry and commerce but within the fabric of society itself. For one or two decades around mid-century the railway had been the dominant influence on affairs and it took some time for the momentum it had imparted then to be taken over by other forces. The steam locomotive itself had multiplied steadily throughout the second half of the century to reach 21,000 in commission in 1901, but a hint of its own ultimate demise came with the fall in numbers added from 4,844 in the decade 1891–1901 to less than a thousand in the decade that followed. What we see here perhaps, at the beginning of the

M

twentieth century, is the zenith of the railways' commercial power, a point
that coincides closely with much broader economic attainments, and we
ought now to consider the contribution which the railways had made to the
general economic expansion of the period that preceded it.

1 The impact of the railways

Once it had been translated from an idea to a business proposition with
parliamentary approval a railway began to make its impact, quite literally,
on the communities through or to which the line was to be taken. The
full historical significance of the railway, when that comes to be assessed, will
have to be based, not only on national statistical aggregates which smother
such idiosyncracies, but on the local history of the places touched by it.
There is clearly not room for an extensive treatment of that kind here, nor
is it necessary perhaps to insist so much on regional and municipal differences as it would be in the evaluation of the rôle of railways in much larger
countries, like the United States, for example, where it is so prone to under-
estimation when subjected to methods of analysis which rest on large
statistical assumptions. But it is important to recognize the highly localized
character of much that must be referred to here in more general terms.

Though the railways quickly nestled into the English countryside in
a way that they never did in the towns, they often gashed the fields, and
imposed a new scale on any scene they came upon above ground level.
These intrusions now seem astonishingly discreet and often graceful,
especially the structures of brick and masonry—much more so, indeed,
than the less accommodating lines of modern apparatus, and less draconian
in their impact than the upheavals of the enclosure movement. The
railways seem to have been accepted as part of the rural landscape with
more goodwill than the blasts of invective levelled at them in the planning
stage could conceivably have allowed. The provincial press and, to a
markedly less extent, parliamentary proceedings, gave vent to both sober
and hysterical anxiety about what would happen to farm livestock, game
and other wild life, the layout of farms, the drainage of the land, and the
social stability of communities so recklessly laid open to influences they
had never known. It was not only that the opportunities for complaining
tapered off when the line was built, nor even that human indignation
tends so often to be short-lived, but that the evils that were so much feared
either evaporated or were more than counterbalanced by the advantages,
both economic and aesthetic, that had looked small in advance. Perhaps
it is significant that the best of everything came near the beginning and
that tone and economic prospects tended to fall off together.

Much of the noise that was made seems also to have been quietened by
the liberal rates of compensation for the land that was taken. Before 1845,

when the Lands Clauses Consolidation Act began the expensive process of
assuaging landowners' fears in the only practical way, compensation had
depended on such flimsy, piecemeal provisions as could be got into each
bill, and a noisy reception to a new proposal was one way of raising the
promoters' bids. There was less need of this once the courts had established
that the basis for compensation was not the market price of the land but
the value of it to the owner plus his costs of being severed from it. Agricultural land, especially if it provided a fine prospect from a gentleman's
seat, could cost the promoters of a new railway a great deal. But it was in
the towns, heaped as they were with inter-locking property rights, that
the law's increasing tenderness towards property showed itself more, and
it was here that the disturbance of railway building was in every way greater.

The upheaval was great enough in the open countryside. The canals
had made earlier generations familiar with navvies' encampments and all
the paraphernalia that was necessary for moving mountains by hand. It
may even be that part of the labour force recruited for railway building
had served a rough apprenticeship in digging the canals. The gangs were
not usually brought together by the main railway contractors themselves
but by the sub-contractors who took a section of the line and engaged fore-
men called "gangers" to work a kind of butty or sub-contracting system,
either by the piece or by the day. Too little is known about the men who
carried this whole industrial hierarchy through these great engineering
works, partly because the risks of this enterprise were so often overwhelming. Of thirty main contractors on the London & Birmingham Railway, ten
seem to have failed financially owing to unpredictable rises in costs and the
failure of the greatest of them all, Samuel Morton Peto, though complicated by his other financial interests, was not unconnected with his
contract work. This was an industrial hierarchy very similar to that then
operating on large contracts in the building trade, except that it also
entailed some responsibility (though generally not nearly enough) for
the problems of colonization: food and drink was often supplied retail
by truck-shops run for their own profit by gangers, sometimes by the
contractors or sub-contractors themselves, less often it appears by a local
grocer; shelter was usually communal, improvised, overcrowded, insani-
tary, run by a kind of *concierge;* clergymen, doctors, schoolmasters and
magistrates appeared in almost inverse order to the need for them, though
some contractors appear to have been providing coffee-houses, reading
rooms, hospitals, mission houses, and schools by the 1870s. Not surprisingly,
Edwin Chadwick, appalled at the misery and degradation experienced by
the navvies at work on the first Woodhead Tunnel, obtained the appointment of a Select Committee to look into the whole question in 1846 but
its report, disturbing as it should have been, did not raise a hair, and conditions continued unabated for many years.

The men they recruited were not merely a residue of the building
trade, nor did they simply give temporary employment to local labour.

The pick-and-shovel man may almost be said to have had a craft of his own, a set of skills and attitudes which could not be built up inside twelve months nor lightly abandoned once held, and a gang would tend to hang together till the line was done, emptying or filling its ranks with navvies on the tramp for fresh work. The work was exceptionally severe, the occupational risks high, the whole way of life reckless, rude, riotous. Under the best conditions an individual navvy might shift twenty tons of earth a day, removed in small wagons running on rails; on cuttings the work was organized around a series of steep plank inclines on which the loaded wheel-barrows and those running them could be helped perilously to the top by those coming down for another load; tunnels were cut from a series of shafts worked by horse-gins, with both men and material being hauled up and down in baskets. The steam shovel did not come into general use on railway contracts before the 1880s, by which time most of the major work had been done. The last contract to be carried out in the traditional manner was for the Midland Railway in the wild region between Settle and Carlisle. This was completed between 1869 and 1875, with such privation and panache that the *Daily News* sent its reporter to the spot in 1872 to see how the navvies and their families had created shanty towns like great raw lumbering camps in all but name and were driving the line through the bog and boulder clay of that region with a purpose to be envied. When the last main line came to be built to London by the Manchester, Sheffield & Lincolnshire Railway between 1893 and 1897 some 39 steam navvies were used.

It is easy to see why the navvy gangs should have been so widely feared and why one sober historian of the time, John Francis, should even have suggested in 1851 that they were "at war with all civilized society". In the cities the navvies were far less conspicuous but railway works were not. Almost every yard of projected line pressed against some obstacle and bringing the railways into or near the major centres of population meant redrawing the street plan, to some extent at least, in almost every case. They threw down some of the old barriers to movement within the cities by cutting through the tangled streets that embodied generations of varied response to the legal, social and economic possibilities facing the landed proprietors. They also created some entirely new obstacles and bottlenecks of their own, and tended to limit the scope for subsequent redevelopment. The railways were not the first disturbances of this kind, of course, to London—to take the case of most widespread demolitions—many hundreds of houses and other buildings having had to be removed for the bridge-building, dock construction, and street improvements that had been going on there since the middle of the eighteenth century. However, the impact of the railways in this way far exceeded that of all other improvements combined and contributed more than anything, both directly and indirectly, to the repatterning of the physical and social texture of London as a whole over the remaining years of the nineteenth century. One of the earliest lines to involve demolition on any scale was the London & Blackwall Railway which threatened nearly three thousand houses in 1836; the same process was at work on a still larger scale thirty years later as the Midland Railway cleared the way to St Pancras and swept four thousand houses from its path. It is difficult to be precise about the overall scale of these operations but in about seventy schemes declared to have affected the working classes in the second half of the century, at least 76,000 such people were turned out of doors, about half of them in the eight years 1859 to 1867.

Nothing illustrates more clearly than this the impact of the railway on densely settled districts. Largely because compensation could be kept down by steering a new line through slums and working-class districts without adding to the expense of the operation by being forced to rehouse those they displaced, at least before 1885, the railway companies tended to produce the maximum adverse effect on the housing problem. They decreased the supply of houses at the centre while adding to the commercial pressure which was already building up there. This also increased the demand for labour, mainly of a casual sort in docks, warehouses, distribution, and the building trades. The direct result of this was higher rents and new levels of overcrowding for all those who could not afford to live more than a short walking distance from their work. In destroying some of the worst slums of Victorian London the railways immediately helped to create the conditions in which still worse could follow. Yet the railways had it in their power to distribute the population of the major cities, the working as well as the middle classes, in their own suburbs. This did not happen to any extent until the last few years of the century when cheap fares were deliberately used to achieve that result, and it will be necessary to return to this point later on. What was true of London in these respects was also true of a number of provincial cities, in which it was not possible to site new termini on the edge of the built-up area in the way in which it was possible to do for many medium sized towns. Nor was the programme of slum demolition by the railways confined to an early period, for the Manchester, Sheffield & Lincolnshire Railway's progress through Nottingham and Leicester in the 1890s was just of this kind.

2   Railways and economic expansion

The question must now be asked: what contribution did the railways make to the economic expansion of Britain down to 1914? Any answer is bound to be curiously unsatisfying for although it has almost been taken for granted for many years that the railways were the very sinews of industrialization, and that their development tended to settle the tempo and direction of economic change, this view has more recently been seen to be resting on somewhat uneven foundations. Recent research by Fogel has suggested that in the case of America at least the contribution of the railroads to economic growth has been somewhat exaggerated. This might be even more true of Britain, since this was a country which already possessed reasonable transport facilities before the railways arrived. Thus it may well be that the nineteenth-century growth of the economy could have been achieved with a few strategic extensions to the existing transport network. But this proposition must await verification. The more vigorous demands of scholars recently for statistical measurement of the contribution of the railways to the growth of the national income, coupled with the suggestion that this was probably very much less, or was important for a much shorter period, than was once thought, would require research on an immense scale, a task clearly outside the scope of this volume.

There are in particular two related historical problems here. One is to define accurately the relevant measures of railway growth and efficiency and their social product; the other is to establish empirically the extent to which the railways reduced transport costs or achieved real savings to the community, either directly or indirectly. Apart from the general difficulties of building up and interpreting the aggregates that must be set against other statistical series in any attempt to answer broad questions about the economic rôle of the railway system as a whole, there are those which occur when trying to discriminate between the repercussions that took place in different industries or regions. It is obviously also desirable at some points to relax our pre-occupation with aggregate data and consider individual undertakings. If we want to consider whether railway development involved the most efficient use of resources in the nineteenth century we are also faced by the problem of determining the marginal phase beyond which investment in entirely new plant was yielding decreasing returns. These difficulties are mentioned here, not in order to introduce new approaches or data that would go beyond the purpose of this book, but to draw attention to the very real difficulties that exist in interpreting the rather patchy information we do have on the behaviour of one element in economic development which clearly had multiple consequences.

In a manner which was never wholly true· of the canals, the railways were built primarily for an existing traffic. There was very little genuine enterprise without careful assessment of the movement of passengers or merchandise by road or by water. Though a new line might be expected to create its own additional demand, it was not regarded, even in remote parts of the Kingdom, as performing the kind of pioneering rôle which could be justified only by the planting of new settlements and industries along its route. The only frontier where this might be held to be partly true was the suburban one, where railway stations tended sometimes to be regarded as little more than advertisements in wood and iron. The initially uneconomical commuting facilities which they provided comprised a kind of loss leader which would ultimately bring the altogether more lucrative traffic of provisioning the suburban communities.

On the other hand there were a number of important urban communities or townships which were virtually created by the railways. Some of these were of course created by the railways primarily for their own use— the most notable examples being New Swindon and Crewe which became great centres of rolling stock construction. But others sprang up as a result of the railways providing access to hitherto unexploited raw materials. The rise of Middlesbrough and Barrow as industrial towns can be attributed almost solely to the influence of the railways. The Furness Railway (opened 1846) played a decisive rôle in the opening up of a backward area in the latter half of the nineteenth century. Largely as a result of the efforts of the railway the Furness district became one of the most important iron districts in the north of England, and its directors virtually created Barrow. By 1881 the population of the town was over 47,000 compared with a mere 250 forty years earlier, whilst the region's production of ore exceeded one million tons. Many smaller, semi-rural towns, as for example Redhill and Surbiton, also owed their birth to the railway though it is significant that such towns often developed as a result of neighbouring towns' resistance to the intrusion of the railways.

But except in one or two cases it is often difficult to say how much the development that occurred in such towns and regions would have taken place in any case. The synchronizing of colliery with railway development was sometimes so close as to make the connection quite plain: this was so on Tyneside in 1836–7, on the vast anthracite field behind Llanelly, Swansea and Neath in the 1840s, and in the Rhondda Valleys farther east in the 1850s. To illustrate this point in more detail: the Taff Vale Railway between Cardiff and Merthyr Tydfil had been conceived by Brunel primarily as an outlet for Sir John Guest's iron at Dowlais, but two branch lines were quickly added to the scheme before it opened in 1841 so as to make pit development possible, and it was the coal traffic which was soon providing the bulk of this highly profitable line's revenue and turning Cardiff into the chief coal-port of the region. The Bute Dock was handling the coal mechanically the year after the railway opened and over the next thirty years dock accommodation at Cardiff expanded five times. It is easy to see how much the railway contributed to this by glancing at the collapse of the trade in water-borne coal on the Usk farther east. Newport handled only 21,000 tons a year when ten years before the figure had been 30,000–40,000 tons. The capacity of the railways to develop an unlooked-for return traffic was also sometimes clear enough, as on the Stockton & Darlington Railway after 1850, when the Cleveland iron deposits began to be worked.

More directly than this, the railways expanded the demand for coal, iron and mechanical engineering products to fulfill their own requirements. Their effect on the demand for coal is impossible to assess with any kind of accuracy because coal was used in the manufacture of all other railway material as well as being required to raise steam in locomotives; and no statistics ever seem to have been collected that might illuminate this point. So far as the direct demand is concerned it seems likely that this was quite modest. Lardner estimated in 1849 that the annual consumption was 750,000 tons, which has to be set against the total output of probably 50 million tons. There is no particular evidence that the conditions of supply and demand were disturbed to any marked extent by railway developments during the main construction period.

As for the iron industry, it is possible to be more specific. The weight of iron used for rails and chairs increased rapidly with advances in the design of locomotives, rolling stock and fixed installations, all of which permitted heavier loads, faster journeys, and more condensed timetabling; the switch from wrought iron to steel rails following their introduction in 1860 simply intensified and sustained this process. Just the same, the effect it had on the growth of the iron and steel industries is difficult to calculate. It has been estimated by B. R. Mitchell that over the period 1844–51 the total demand for pig iron for rail manufacture was 28·6 per cent of that available in the country and thereafter down to 1869 this averaged 16·0 per cent, or about 8 per cent of the total make. During the 1830s, when the weight of metal required per mile of track probably doubled, the average railway demand for pig iron had probably not risen above about 20,000 tons a year. During this period the output of the industry as a whole had multiplied about three times to $1\frac{1}{2}$ million tons. The impact of the railways on this was obviously marginal, but in the next decade the railway demand was of overriding importance. At its height it accounted for by far the greatest part of the increase in total pig iron production, temporarily slowing down even the growth in exports. As we saw in the last chapter but one, it did not take long to develop the basic structure of Britain's railway system, most of which was in place by the early 1850s, and thereafter the home demand for railway iron and steel cannot be regarded as being of leading importance for the economy as a whole.

This is not to say, of course, that it was not important for particular towns and regions. It is arguable, for example, that the iron industry of South Staffordshire, which had originally depended on local supplies of ore, would have declined rapidly without the help of the railways in supplementing them. This applied equally to the pig and wrought iron branches of the industry of the region after about 1860. On the other hand, the switch from iron to steel rails undoubtedly depressed some centres of production while it made others prosperous, though this was more on account of the loss of an export than of a home trade. The transition was actually very swift and the iron rail trade was virtually dead by 1876. The collapse of the market in iron rails was the beginning of the end for the Welsh wrought iron industry. Though iron rails were still being marketed grimly at falling prices, local output fell by more than a fifth between 1869 and 1877. The Cleveland manufacturers of iron rails who had refused to sacrifice themselves on this

altar of steel tried to move into other branches of the wrought iron trade—
mainly girders and plates for ships—but this was not then a sufficiently
expanding market and firms failed rapidly, 20 out of 44 puddling firms
controlling about 40 per cent of the furnaces of the district having to cease
production by 1879.

The direct effect of railway development on the mechanical engineering
industry is clearer in technological, perhaps even in aesthetic, terms than
it is in economic ones. With only the crudest figures of employment in the
engineering industry and of the railways' outlays on rolling stock to go
upon it is scarcely possible to measure even the order of magnitude of the
railways' contribution to the development of this nascent industry during
the early railway age. The best guess is that the railways, in spending something of the order of £20 million on rolling stock between 1844 and 1851,
probably took about one-fifth of the total output of the engineering industry at that time. It seems unlikely that the railways' total outlay on rolling
stock did anything more than double before the 1860s, when it was probably
running at between £5–£6 million a year, half of which may be computed
as representing orders for the engineering industry as such. What was
certainly coming to be important by that period was the foreign demand for
locomotives, which were being exported to the value of £1 million a year.
By then the railways had certainly established a new branch of the engineering industry, but it was becoming more and more the domain of the companies themselves, the largest of which had already started to manufacture
their own rolling stock. The engineering firms were inclined to look to
foreign railways for their orders.

In more general terms, the perfection of the steam locomotive was
unquestionably an important element in the general advance of technology in the nineteenth century. It cannot be claimed very conclusively,
however, that this was a progressive development which threw up a whole
series of substantial technical achievements which led indirectly to general
economic expansion. What seems surprising in retrospect is that so many
of the major technical advances should have been made so early. All the
basic problems were solved within twenty years of the Rainhill Trials
and the performance of trains had reached a very high pitch almost as soon
as the main network had been completed. It is true that with the greater
strength of steel rails trains could become heavier, and this led directly to
attempts in the last quarter of the century to perfect the compound engine
as a means of economizing on fuel, and to the designing of much larger
locomotives. By 1870, too, it had become possible to substitute coal for coke
as locomotive fuel, which raised a higher head of steam. The compound
locomotive was tried out with great thoroughness, chiefly by the London &
North Western Railway during the 1880s and 1890s, but it never seemed
capable of such satisfactory performance as simple engines, which were
judged to be easier to drive and cheaper to build. It was used extensively and
profitably on the continent, however, and was adopted by other companies

in Britain after the turn of the century. A device that did not come in till then was the superheater. Almost the only really significant technical innovation before 1914 was, in fact, electrification, though even this was of far greater importance after the war.

One important reason for the lack of greater advance in the design of locomotives (without wishing to deny that there was any) is that the railway companies just did not know what existing equipment was costing them to run, if not to build. The interpretation of railway accounts is a special mystery which too few historians have attempted to master. Yet even a cursory glance at the books of any of the major companies shows how much their directors were compelled to go by personal inclination or rule-of-thumb. The form in which railways had to make their statistical returns to the government did not help in removing this attitude. The operating costs of specific types of traffic hauled by locomotives of different types, on work schedules making a variety of demands on personnel, just were not known in sufficient detail to enable mounting costs to be recognized clearly where they were occurring, and for effective measures to be taken to offset them.

At first sight this is a little surprising. When the locomotive was in its infancy some quite elaborate data on the basic economics of railway design were being assembled. Often these calculations were more promotional in character than anything else, and one of the more significant aspects of F. W. Webb's sustained testing of the principle of compounding on the London & North Western tracks is that it was directed rather exceptionally towards elucidating the facts about actual performance. Even so, it may be doubted whether the crucial question was cost rather than speed on the tracks and time out of service. This leads on to a question of ignorance of another kind about operating and capital costs. By the last quarter of the nineteenth century there were some fifteen companies having works of their own in which they built locomotives and other rolling stock, as well as a good deal of other equipment, including in some cases rails, chairs, and the like. The manufacture of their own equipment was no more governed by the principles of cost accounting, which was still very much in its infancy, than traffic management, and the allocation of resources to this branch of their enterprise as little governed by needs of strict economy. The tendency to throw off branch lines without proper regard to all the supplementary costs of doing so is evidence of the same kind.

Any knowledge about the division of costs would for a long time have been of purely academic interest. "Opinions differ", wrote George Boag in his tentative little *Manual of Railway Statistics*, published in 1912, "as to the merits of a control by means of statistical units, some of which cannot be available until some considerable time after the period to which they relate." In his view the scope that existed for making economies in working expenditure probably amounted to something less than 30 per cent of gross receipts, but although he detected more general recognition recently of the value of statistics in railway operation he insisted that they were not being used to anything like their full extent. The Railway Companies (Accounts and Returns) Act of 1911, with its demand for more detailed returns than had ever been required, was likely to lead in that direction. Until that time the whole system was expanding so fast, and the traffic that it carried growing at least as quickly, that it was unnecessary to ask how costs could be clipped so as to do more business still. Questions like these were deferred with the same kind of readiness that other businessmen were postponing more careful reckoning of their true costs of production even in the face of foreign competition.

Such questions did not come to be important on the railways until they, too, faced effective competition, not among themselves but from a new direction altogether. For them this was not a nineteenth-century phenomenon at all but a twentieth-century one. And in one way the companies were right to behave as they did. It is important to keep in mind the benefits as much as the costs of proceeding in this way, and to recognize the companies' own priorities. Throughout the period we have been considering the railway system was still in a state of growth, in which the whole effort of the railways was thrown into completing their lines, making them run, getting the traffic, holding on to it. Estimates came first, the outlay second, counting the costs third. The pioneering of a wide range of locomotives had to precede the selection of the basic types, and there was never sufficient demand, nor a clear view of the need, nor even the justification, for standardizing all production of this kind. This experimenting had far-reaching effects on mechanical engineering in general, of course. So long as there was a persistent demand for faster and more comfortable passenger services, moreover, locomotives capable of providing them remained in a developmental stage. It is true that such rolling stock was not only more and more expensive to build but dearer in operation. The system itself was costly when compared with others abroad (where government finance was widely available) but its benefits must be counted in terms of speed of operation, flexibility in use, capacity, accessibility, reliability.

To what extent were the railways less directly, but perhaps more fundamentally, responsible for the growth of the Victorian economy? Did they affect incomes or institutions in any significant respects? In terms of their specific income-generating power there seems little question that in the main construction phase they were of strategic importance in expanding the economy. This they did primarily through the huge task-force that had to be assembled to move the earth and rock and build the line. The personal incomes generated in this way rippled through a whole series of transactions, creating more employment in the fields and factories, in just the same way as the manufacture of railway plant was also doing. For every mile of track under construction in the 1850s the average labour force was around 50 men and there is no reason to think that the figure had been very different during the feverish activity of the preceding decade At its height, in 1847, when gross investment in railways was running at about £30 million, well over a quarter of a million men, or 4 per cent of all working males, were employed on railway contracts. The wages bill must have absorbed something over half of the total annual outlay and accounted for nearly 3 per cent of the national income.

The rate at which this labour force was built up reinforces the view that it generated a quite exceptional surge of spending power, and it seems likely that its direct and indirect multiplier effects must have been very pronounced both at the national and regional levels, though only extensive research would establish this point beyond doubt. Only four or five years before, the great wave of activity which had been launched in the first railway boom of 1836–7 had petered out completely and contractors must have laid off almost all their men. There were numerous signs of widespread under-employment of labour in the early 1840s. The recruiting began again in 1844–5 and was brought to its climax in less than a couple of years; it declined almost as rapidly. The total numbers employed during the 1850s fluctuated only slightly around 50,000, much of the balance presumably either melting away into other forms of construction in the towns or going abroad to build railways in Europe or the United States.

The importance of the railways in priming economic expansion in the early period, and the way in which this fell off after the 1840s, is clearer still from the figures for railway capital formation, even though these are bound to be subject to a wide margin of error. According to Mitchell, total gross capital formation reached a peak of almost £44 million in 1847, of which over £7 million went on the purchase of land; the other major peaks occurred in 1839 (£11 million), 1865 (£28 million), 1874–5 (£24 million). At no time in the Victorian period did railway investment drop to really insignificant proportions, though it was only in the 1840s and 1860s, when it accounted for between 20 and 30 per cent of total gross domestic investment, that it was in a position of outstanding importance in the national economy. Although the proportion of total capital resources absorbed by the railways fell sharply towards the end of the 1860s there still continued to be a fairly large demand for replacement investment so that even by the end of the century railway investment accounted for around 10 per cent of total domestic investment. In terms of its contribution to the national income, excluding the transactions in land, expenditure on railway building did not reach beyond 2 per cent of the total before 1845 and remained above this for only four years more; it did so again, though at a much lower average level, in 1863–6.

The build-up in the mid-1840s was quite exceptional in every way, reaching 5·7 per cent of the national income in 1846 and 6·7 per cent in 1847. There can be no doubt about the importance of this achievement in terms of the economy as a whole. Railway investment was, however briefly, in a dominant position, and the outlay on railways in the peak year of the decade was almost equal to the current value of exports of cotton, wool, linen, and silk goods. For the years 1845–9 it amounted to more than three-quarters of the quantity of currency and bullion in the Issue Department of the Bank of England. The building of the railways came very near to absorbing for this brief spell virtually all the free capital that was available in the country for new investment. Indeed, it probably went beyond this. To have reached this level so rapidly suggests that there must have been some transfers of assets and that some of these had probably even been repatriated from abroad for the purpose. Foreign investment certainly abated, and it may even be the case that the dislocation which railway investment caused to the existing flow of resources helped to induce that alternation in the cycles of home and foreign investment which has been so often remarked upon for the period that followed. This is substantiated to some extent by the fact that waves of railway investment were accompanied by similar swings in other domestic investment, particularly in residential building, giving rise to a transport-building cycle. This long-wave cycle was probably more prominent in the United States but there is certainly evidence to show that it was not entirely absent in Britain.

Whether the intermittent character of railway investment also induced the major cyclical fluctuations of the economy has been disputed. It was at the most a contributory factor to other financial and commercial circumstances, and if an excess of railway investment increased the general dimensions of crises from time to time, the continued laying-out of capital on the actual works was a counteracting influence which maintained employment and helped to reduce the general impact of the ensuing depression. So it certainly was in the second half of the 1840s, as well as in the depression in the second half of the 1850s, following on the decline in government spending on war material after the cessation of the Crimean war.

3   Railways and the capital market

Where did railway capital come from and how was it raised? The early companies tended very often to rely heavily on local sources, but the subscription lists that were drawn up to accompany the two parliamentary bills for the Liverpool & Manchester Railway reveal very clearly how widespread was the catchment area for railway capital even in the 1820s. Less than 47 per cent of the shares were taken up in Liverpool and 3 per cent in Manchester: about 20 per cent was raised in London, nearly 24 per cent came from the Marquess of Stafford, and about 6 per cent from other places. Lancashire, and Liverpool in particular, may well have been the principal source for capital down to the 1840s, though the subscription lists do not make it easy to establish this point unequivocally. Thomas Tooke stated that seven-eighths of the capital for the London & Birmingham and the Grand Junction Railways came from Lancashire, and there is much evidence of this kind to support the view that capital from this quarter was of dominating importance in a wide range of undertakings at this time: the Leicester & Swannington, the Midland Counties, the North Midland, the London & Southampton, the Great Western, and the Eastern Counties Railways exhibited very well this pervasive influence. After the mania the position tended to change and London capital became more important, even in the industrial north. It had occasionally reached far afield already. In the original subscription contracts for the Preston & Wyre Railway and Docks in 1835–7 London capital made up well over two-thirds of the total. The Lancashire & Yorkshire Railway, of which these later became two small components, did not echo this sounding at all before 1845, and in all but one of the remaining fourteen companies which eventually formed the Lancashire & Yorkshire Railway, Lancashire capital was in a quite dominating position, most conspicuously of all in the Bolton & Preston Railway (1837) and the Blackburn, Darwen & Bolton Railway (1845), which were financed practically entirely by Lancashire. But on the more substantial Manchester & Leeds Railway there were signs that London capital was already becoming more important before the mid-1840s, and this was a tendency which appears to have continued.

As with most industrial investment, railway capital was not formed with the aid of the institutions of the money market; but, unlike industry, the railways did not have sufficient turnover in the early days to form their own capital from undistributed profits. This came much later. At the start, earnings had to be paid out as dividends on the stock as fast as, and not infrequently faster than, they were made in order to convince investors that an undertaking was financially viable. Almost all railway promotion occurred under boom conditions and there was usually little to be done than to advertise a new line and appeal for subscriptions. There are many instances of schemes being vastly over-subscribed. In such circumstances the promoters did not have to go through the full procedure of holding public meetings in order to drum up subscriptions and allot the scrip but could get all they wanted simply by issuing a prospectus. This explains why railway promoters should have made so little use of underwriters or other investment agencies, and it also helps to explain why some companies should have experienced real difficulty in collecting together all the funds they needed once a boom had collapsed. It was not at all usual for companies to resort to stockbrokers, even as agents for the allocation of shares, and they appear to have used bankers and solicitors at least as much, or to have undertaken to act entirely as their own agents. The way in which railway shares were marketed, not only down to the mania of the 1840s but right into the second half of the nineteenth century, strongly suggests that railway promotion had the effect of supplementing very considerably indeed the whole apparatus of the capital market. In just the same way it was also augmenting the structure of the legal profession, through such heavy parliamentary business in private bills, property dealings, patents, and litigation.

There is abundant evidence to show that a substantial amount of railway capital raised at this time came from new saving and from a new type of investor. In one sense this was probably the railways' biggest single contribution to economic expansion. Certainly, at the beginning of the 1840s the money market had become very slack and swollen with idle capital. "Money was very abundant", wrote John Francis of 1844. "The great discount houses were full, the bank discounted at two-and-a-half per cent, consols were above par, and everything promised a continuance of the golden age." By the following spring railway investment was at full flood. "There has certainly never before been any one object of speculation", commented *The Economist* in February 1845, "into which all classes and ranks of men have entered so warmly as at this time into railways." The mania coaxed new capital from classes which had never invested before as well as providing astute financiers with a bonanza of unparalleled opportunity. Forty years later the American, C. F. Adams, could write in his *Railroads, their Origin and Problems* (1886) that England awoke one day from dreams of boundless wealth to the reality of general ruin, but not only had new wealth been created for discriminating investors but a new kind of situation had been established in which small savings could be as safely put to use in joint-stock undertakings as any large fortune. The new institution which made this possible was general limited liability for registered companies.

The railways greatly advanced joint-stock company development both by their example and by the demand they induced in potential investors in other enterprises for railway-type security of investment. It should not be forgotten that before the company legislation of 1855 to 1862 the principal means of establishing a limited company had changed very little in its fundamentals since the eighteenth century and that, despite the movement in the 1830s to liberalize the conditions on which full corporate status was granted to undertakings, there was still a certain arbitrariness in granting this privilege. It was this which railway promotion did so much to change. The proliferation of so many companies in the conventional parliamentary way helped to establish a more general expectation of proper corporate status by undertakings outside the field of public utilities. What led still more emphatically towards a change in the law of incorporation was a demand for it by investors who had grown accustomed to the advantages of limited liability in railway investment but who, in the early 1850s, found that opportunity drying up along with some of the more traditional ones.

The railways had done more than anything to prepare the way not only for general limited liability but for the means of implementing it more fully. Thus, although the stock market had not been the means of initiating railway enterprise, the Stock Exchange had been prised open for dealings in shares as distinct from bonds by the railway promotions of the 1840s, and these had also led straight to the appearance of provincial stock exchanges. These developments were part of a general movement to create the institutional framework within which long-term capital could move with greater freedom between its alternative employments, and it is difficult to conceive a more valuable contribution to the economic development of the country in the circumstances of the time. It is not easy to believe that the only regulator of these transfers was the expected rate of return from the invest- ment that had been made, nor even that money was always put where profit and safety were nicely balanced. The market for long-term capital was not free from convention and irrational choice but railway investment at home as well as abroad did offer very readily comprehensible and com- parable opportunities which small and substantial savers alike were prepared to weigh up. Railway property was as negotiable as gilt-edged and the market for it was perhaps even more democratized after the 1840s. In a particularly striking phrase the American historian, L. H. Jenks, once referred to the investing public as having "matriculated in the school of Hudson" and as being more prepared thereby to lend "blind" to the great impersonal undertakings which were later to become so characteristic of highly de- veloped capitalist economies.

The inexorable separation of the ownership of such corporations from their control, which is nowadays taken so much for granted, was advanced by railway promotion in a singularly striking way. Canal promotion had been essentially localized, and, to a considerable extent, personal. It is true that this had not been so invariably but there was generally a close identifi- cation between an undertaking and the region it served, as there appears generally to have been between their boards of directors and the share- holders—though too little is known about the internal affairs of canal companies to make many comparisons. There certainly did not emerge the kind of modern managerial element which became so conspicuous with the later railways, though there were signs of it, for example, in the agents to the Bridgewater Trust. The general manager did not become important until undertakings achieved a certain scale and range of operations, nor was a hierarchy of management possible before the amalgamation movement had built up the large railway companies. Its appearance signalled an im- portant phase in the wider development of depersonalized investment, just as the growth of large, complex organizations also produced a whole new range of industrial occupations, with significant repercussions on organized labour.

The likeness between the financial aspects of canal and railway legislation is particularly striking when we consider the form of the capital stock. Apart from the ordinary shares, both canals and railways introduced prefer- ence shares, particularly in order to induce reluctant investors to invest when construction was proving unexpectedly costly or the counter-attrac- tions of alternative investments too strong. More important, it was the preference share which appealed so strongly to the ordinary investor, especially down to the Railway Regulation Act of 1871, which palpably improved the basis of railway accounting, and took some of the uncalcu- lated risks out of holding ordinary railway shares. It had first become important in 1839 and over the next five years over 30 per cent of all railway share issues were of this type. During the relapse of railway investment after the mania of the 1840s, preference shares at one time accounted for two-thirds of all new issues. Perhaps the extreme case of a railway resorting to this means for raising capital was the Brecon & Merthyr Railway, the building of whose 66 miles of track had by 1864 long since exhausted the original authorized capital of £700,000 and caused the issue of shares and debentures to the contractor totalling a further £2 million: these issues included ten kinds of preference share and fourteen issues of debentures, all of them ranked by date; yet more powers were granted in 1864 to raise £570,000 in new preference stock and £190,000 by debentures, but to no avail.

The debentures mentioned here were normally regarded as the safest investment of all, though not on the strongest grounds because a debenture was strictly a mortgage on the income of the undertaking, not on its general property. This was not the least devastating revelation in the Chancery judgment on the London, Chatham & Dover Railway's land case of 1866–7, when it debentures were found to be valueless. The knowledge was very disturbing to the credit of the whole railway system, especially as the railway mania of 1865–7 had been largely developed by these means, and at least 100,000 people were still holding vast amounts of debenture stock: over 27 per cent of the £450 million of railway capital in 1867 was said to be in this form. Steps were, however, soon taken to strengthen the position of debenture-holders vis-à-vis other creditors, and they climbed very rapidly in popularity. In 1870 debentures accounted for less than 10 per cent of paid-up capital but five years later about 20 per cent was held in this form. By 1890 the proportion had settled down somewhat above 25 per cent, roughly on a par with the proportion held in preference shares, though these had changed their standing very little in the interval. What had declined in importance throughout this period were loans and, to a much less extent, ordinary shares.

There were the best of reasons for this switch because the ordinary shares of the leading railway companies no longer justified any hopes of high dividends. There had been some big dips in ordinary railway shares before this, notably following the mania of the 1840s, when Midland Railway shares, as recorded in *The Economist*, fell between 1846 and 1850 from 140 to 33½ and the Great Western Railway from 149 to 58¾: according to one calculation, the average dividend on ordinary capital stood at 1·88 per cent in 1849. Another calculation was that, just as share prices touched bottom in 1855, 28 railways in the United Kingdom, incorporating £22 million, paid no dividends whatever; only nine paid 5 per cent or more. Even the paying lines averaged less than 4 per cent between 1850 and 1854, a period described as one of "almost unexampled commercial prosperity". One reason for this was that branch-line building was already beginning to soak up capital.

Big differences in profitability were soon being smothered to some extent by the recrudescence of amalgamation which occurred in the 1860s. This

N

had the effect of saddling the low-cost lines with the high-cost ones without the system of railway accounting spot-lighting the differences clearly enough to lead towards any significant closure on grounds of economy and higher profits. Even the most successful lines were having to cut back dividends on their ordinary stock by the 1880s. The Furness Railway, for example, now paid 10 per cent for the last time; the Maryport & Carlisle Railway, one of the steadiest earners of all, turned the same corner in 1882, though it managed to keep its dividend above 6 per cent down to 1912; the Lancashire & Yorkshire dropped well below this figure after 1877; the Great Northern, which had averaged almost 7 per cent for the ten years before 1873 could only manage half this for the decade after 1900. Some railways which had never done well financially, like the Great Eastern and the North Stafford-shire, contrived now to do no worse and even to pick up fractionally in the Edwardian period; one or two which had a weak record now did disastrous-ly, none more so than the Great Central which after a decade averaging little more than 1 per cent failed to declare a dividend at all from 1899 to 1913. The steadiest of all at around 7 per cent for a full half-century before 1914, was the London & North-Western, though the short coal lines, like the Rhymney, the Barry, and the Taff Vale averaged much more.

When the rate of return on capital invested could vary so much it is pointless to try to strike any kind of average, especially as individual rail-way stocks altered their composition so much, but the general expectation at the end of the 1880s was probably no more than 4 per cent. How good this was depended on returns from other investments. Bank rate was then exceptionally low and had touched 2 per cent in each of the years from 1884 to 1888. Consols, which had been holding to 3 per cent from 1881 to 1888, dropped below this figure for the first time since they had been put on the market 133 years before, and stayed there right through to 1907. In those circumstances, Home Rails were still worth holding, even if the ordinary stock had fallen rather badly, and the only justifiable alternative in the same field was to invest in railways abroad. Even so, the extra gains were in most cases quite marginal.

4   Some measure of costs and benefits

The financial failure of some schemes and the unprofitability of others as going concerns raises the question whether the railways wasted a significant part of their assets. Did they not also, perhaps, divert some resources from more useful employment in other fields? Some early critics certainly made these points but it seems doubtful whether there is very much substance in them, if they are interpreted in the light of actual fulfilment of plans. Had all the schemes projected in the mid-1840s been built, or, still more to the point perhaps, all those of the mid-1860s, when railway contractors' own lines entered the lists in a way which they had not done before, there would have been every reason to think that resources ran to waste on a large scale. Speculation seems to have over-reached itself sufficiently rapidly to prevent this from happening.

All the same, there is the common charge that the railways were inordinately expensive to build, largely owing to the compensation paid to the owners of the land they took for their lines, and that this was a perpetual drag on their enterprise. E. D. Chattaway, a director of the North British Railway, insisted in 1855 that land taken for railways had been realising between £2,000 and £10,000 an acre and that railway companies had in the majority of cases paid anything between ten and a hundred times too much for the property they acquired. There are certainly some reasons for thinking that the railways as a whole were over-capitalized but this cannot be explained solely in terms of their outlay on land, despite a number of individual cases of exorbitance. The picture that emerges from a study of the ratio between expenditure on land and total outlay by all railway companies taken together is that during the initial wave of development down to 1844 land absorbed no more than 13 per cent of railway capital but that this increased appreciably over the remainder of the nineteenth century before tapering right off again down to 1914: between 1845 and 1856 land took 14·4 per cent; in 1857–69, 17·6 per cent; in 1870–93, 17·5 per cent; and in 1894–1910, 12·0 per cent. What does seem to have happened is that the filling in of the main network was somewhat more expensive in this respect than the basic system that had been completed by the early 1850s. Looked at in more general terms, however, the issue becomes a less important one. Of the £1,300 million which approximates to the total gross capital formation in the railways of the United Kingdom between 1831 and 1914, the purchase of land took altogether less than £200 millions, or under 15 per cent.

There is no way of disentangling parliamentary and legal costs, which were reputedly high, from the general expenses of enough companies to be able to say whether these items made unreasonably large additions to the total bill for the railways. On Chattaway's reckoning, each mile of railway cost about £1,000 in parliamentary and legal expenses, or £9 million all told; some lines greatly exceeded this rate of expenditure, and the Great Northern, which had had some notable battles in putting together by 1858 its 283 miles of line, had laid out about £1·4 million out of its total authorized capital of £9·6 million. This was understandable enough. This particular battle for incorporation in 1845–6 was the biggest ever fought on one railway, for it involved not only the largest railway yet conceived in one prospectus but the most combative adversary in the field, George Hudson and his newly-formed Midland Railway. A more direct coal line from Durham and the West Riding to London was a threat to a vast network of lines either in existence or in prospect, and the orchestration of the opposition to it could not be done cheaply nor perhaps guilelessly. Such detachments of counsel, troops of witnesses, interminable plots, agitations, rumours, and intrigue were never more elaborately staged, more desperately financed, more bitterly aborted. The cost to the successful promoters can be reckoned up without difficulty but how much such campaigns cost all told cannot be known. The Great Northern was conspicuously expensive at birth and some of the promotional costs of particular concerns certainly looked high in the early phase of development, but a more sober reckoning is that they normally did not exceed 5 per cent of total outlay. Yet these were heavily overshadowed by the sheer costs of construction.

There can be little question that the main reasons why British railways were by 1914 so heavily capitalized were, first, that engineering the railways had presented a series of difficult and costly feats and, secondly, that the system had been greatly elaborated by the construction of branch-lines and other installations. As we have seen in an earlier chapter, the benefits of such a versatile structure capable of handling traffic at high speed probably justified the costs of building it, but we cannot be sure of this any more than the directors of the railway companies of the time could know the true extent of their operating profits and losses and the connections these had with the capital structure of their undertakings. Substantial re-investment of earnings in new equipment proceeded with very little sophisticated knowledge of the relation between the costs and earnings to be expected from these marginal additions. For despite the return of certain data annually by each company to the Board of Trade and the publication of numerous treatises and handbooks on the economic and financial aspects of railways, there was no way of discerning their true position with complete accuracy. The reasons for this obscurity are partly to be found in the way the system had developed.

Railway promotion was inclined to be conducted with comparatively few rules, and companies were sometimes managed in the early days in a reckless fashion, but those which were formed and worked with probity and good sense undoubtedly outnumbered the rest by a wider margin than is sometimes recognized. It is probably true that the railway era did give larger scope to shady business practices than ever before, and there were some notable frauds. "If the ledger was then the bible of the people of England", wrote Francis on the mania of the 1840s, when duplicity was at its height, "let it be remembered that the base, bad acts were the work of the scum on the surface. . . . The evil which was performed was not by our merchantocracy." This was in his view just the current outlet for swindlers. "As I find railways much more profitable than law, I have cut the latter", wrote one man in proposing himself as a railway director, and D. Morier Evans in his two books *Facts, Failures and Frauds* (1859) and *Commercial Crisis 1847–1848* (1848) gives ample detail on this kind of activity.

Yet some at least of the defects of business administration must be attributed either to the sheer inexperience of promoters and railway directors or to shortcomings in the law. The widespread inclination to pay dividends out of capital, for instance, first arose when the characteristic equity was the large uncalled share, on which it was not always easy to get calls answered; and the payment of interest began to be made before the completion of a line had allowed traffic receipts to accumulate. Such a procedure had been prohibited as early as 1837 on the Croydon Railway but the pressures of the 1840s held the rule in general abeyance and even when it was stipulated in the Companies Clauses Act of 1845 it was interpreted as meaning that it did not apply to the construction period. Even the Companies Act of 1862 and the Railway Companies Act of 1867 did not make this provision water-tight because parliament failed to define "working expenses" and railway accounting therefore continued to be a variable practice. As late as 1882 a select committee could report that paying interest out of capital was based on sound financial principles. It is not therefore surprising that railway companies should have continued this practice even though it was bound to create friction and dispute. There were, in fact, numerous features of railway company management that are quite out of keeping with more recent ideas, or even with the demands of their own time. Probably the best example of this that might be noted in passing is the dogged use of "train-mile" statistics instead of the altogether more realistic "ton-mile" basis which was being urged on the railway companies as a step towards greater efficiency, particularly at the end of this period.

Though the railways absorbed vast amounts of capital, and may have used some of it prodigally, it is important to keep in mind in assessing the general contribution they made to economic expansion that they also economized it to an incalculable degree. The railway, like other transport improvements, was essentially capital-saving for it reduced transit and travelling times and thereby released resources which would otherwise have been unproductive. Manufacturers and housewives alike need no longer carry such large stocks, with obvious economy. There was a number of more subtle repercussions, not least in making the middle-class domestic economy more efficient and requiring less labour in the home. Many companies saved traders part of their normal warehousing and demurrage costs by allowing them extra time in unloading from their wagons, and some began to provide special containers.

The railways had in these and other ways a considerable impact on retail distribution and assisted the widespread emergence, first of small shops, which became conspicuous almost everywhere during the second half of the nineteenth century, and then the organization of chain stores, which became marked in the food and clothing trades from the 1890s. In the large towns the multiple store could effectively serve a much larger area through suburban railways and these helped it to enlarge its influence in the 1860s and afterwards. H. G. Wells recalled in his *Experiment in Autobiography* (1937) how the business of his father's china shop at Bromley was undermined by the railway in this way: "An improved passenger and goods service, and the opening of a second railway station made it more and more easy for people to go to London for their shopping and for London retailers to come into competition with the local traders. Presently the delivery vans of the early multiple shops, like the Army and Navy Co-operative Stores and the like, appeared in the neighbourhood to suck away the ebbing vitality of the local retailer. The trade in pickling jars and jam pots died away. Fresh house-keepers came to the gentlemen's houses, who knew not Joseph and bought their stuff from the stores." In a different context it is worth noticing that it was in this period that local fairs and markets ceased to have their old significance, and that the sphere of influence of the large cities was widened quite appreciably: London in particular grew more and more important. Yet there were some metropolitan influences that now began to fade: Bristol's position as the "Welsh metropolis" (which had depended primarily on the coasting trade between the ports of South Wales) was now taken from it by the South Wales Railway which was open from Gloucester to Haver-fordwest by 1855. There was here a tendency of still wider meaning, for the very marked improvement in transport helped to create conditions in many parts of the country in which manufacturing and commercial interests had more interest in and opportunity for limiting competition.

The agrarian economy was thrown open to the most diverse influences. The initial effect of a new line was to alter entirely the limits of local markets and to bring distant producers unexpectedly into competition with those close to the main areas of consumption. Farm produce did not immediately form a national market but prices did begin to equalize and T. E. Cliffe Leslie, the economist, wrote in *Macmillan's Magazine* in 1864 of a "complete revolution in the scale of local prices in the United Kingdom", which rail-ways tended to lift towards the metropolitan level. The contribution of the railways to the prosperity of English farming in the middle decades of the century was three-sided. First, by providing a basis for the growth of manu-facturing industry they created an expanding market for home-grown food-stuffs and certain industrial raw materials, despite the abandonment of agricultural protection between 1846 and 1860. There is a good deal of evidence to show that industrial real wages were beginning to rise appreci-ably and that urban working-class diets were being improved by the inclu-sion of more protein foods. Secondly, the railways made the dissemination of improved techniques easier to accomplish by the cheaper transport of farm machinery, fertilizers, and drainage materials; it is conceivable, too, that they brought about the wider spread of improved ideas. Thirdly, they provided a source of employment in themselves as well as a means of marshalling it better. Many agrarian communities were undoubtedly still under-employed in the 1850s and 1860s, and it is clear from studies of migration into London and some other large towns that this reservoir of only partially-used labour was being tapped well before the 1870s. Long before Joseph Arch, the farm-workers' leader, told them to make themselves scarce so as to raise their wages, the railways had begun to move labour off the land. This was also partly cause, partly effect, of the movement towards the consolidation of land holdings which in some parts of the country was to have important social repercussions before the end of the century.

There were, of course, other influences helping to produce the era of "high farming", but it would not be an exaggeration to say that the railways marked a more important turning point in the general history of British agriculture than did the period of parliamentary enclosure of the open fields which had preceded them. It is also true that the railway was the principal agent of agrarian depression after 1879. It was then that the compensation of high prices which farmers might have expected following one of the worst harvests of the whole century was utterly lacking as cheap prairie wheat flooded into the country. The capacity of transcontinental railways and steamships to bring the costs of marketing the grain grown so far away below the price ruling in the home market of the most productive farms in Europe had a devastating effect. In the course of the next quarter of a century millions of acres returned to rough pasture, and the farmers themselves turned to dairy-farming, fruit-growing, market-gardening, anything to avoid competing with the cost-reducing effects of foreign railways and their allies, the steamships.

These were not the only changes to appear in the village. The decline of village handicraft industries had begun in many places before the railway arrived but its appearance invariably accelerated change, as the writings of George Sturt (*pseud.* George Bourne), especially *The Wheelwright's Shop* (1923), make plain. By the 1860s the railways were also making redundant many local quarries of building stone by concentrating production to a growing extent on a smaller number of brickworks and on the blue slate quarries of North Wales. Before long the same building materials were finding their way to every part of the railway system, though there was still some local bias in cost terms as well as outright choice in favour of local bricks, especially when they could be made on the building site itself.

The tendency in all these matters was towards standardization, the normal means of reducing the cost of almost anything. To what extent this was also true of the standardization of Greenwich time for every part of the country is problematical but this was almost as essential to the economical operation of the railways as was the adoption of the standard gauge. The great Western Railway had adopted Greenwich as the standard time by 1840, though it does not seem to have been implemented thoroughly before the 1850s. How long this convention took to steal into ordinary social intercourse everywhere is not clear, though R. M. Robbins has pointed out that the clock at Christ Church, Oxford, still resists the adoption of railway time. This kind of uniformity stopped short of passengers, whose distinctions of class, if anything, hardened when travelling by railway.

The original two classes that corresponded to the inside and outside of the stage-coach were soon supplemented by a third and even a fourth class on some lines, with another tariff imposed upon this one according to the speed of the train. The categorization was very perplexing. One impediment to more widespread adoption of third-class fares had been the insistence by the Inland Revenue that trains claiming exemption from the railway passenger duty had to stop at every station, under the terms of the Railway Regulation Act of 1844. This interpretation was corrected in the Finance Act of 1863 and twenty years later passenger duty on all fares up to a penny a mile repealed altogether. The "parliamentary train" now disappeared. The Midland Railway had already announced, in 1872, that third-class seats were to be had on all trains and, three years later, that second-class was to be abolished altogether. It was not the first company to have done so experimentally but it now led the way in a general abandonment of the second class. From the 1870s one company after another dropped it, brought their fares more generally into line with each other, and provided accommodation for passengers of each type on every train. When the City & South London Railway—the "twopenny tube"—was opened in 1890 passengers even found that there was one class only on all trains. The statistical progress of these developments is a dramatic one: in 1845, over 40 per cent of passengers held first-class tickets, over 42 per cent second-class, and 17 per cent third-class; by 1875, these proportions had changed to 9 per cent, 14 per cent, and 77 per cent, respectively; by 1911, almost 96 per cent of all passengers went third-class and the remaining 4 per cent divided themselves evenly between the other two classes. Such changes tell, however, only a small part of the story of how the railways were not only responding to social pressures but helping to form them. Railway carriages were the embodiment of certain social distinctions to such an extraordinary degree that to study such rolling stock is to study some of the most telling archaeological remains of Victorian society. The impact of the railways on society will require a book to itself, and we must look instead at their repercussions on other parts of the transport system.

7

Railways and the transport system

1 The eclipse of the canals

The interference by the railways with the physical layout of towns and country was scarcely more direct and immediate than their threat to established transport interests of every kind. No form of transport was immune from their influence for long, though the responses which their challenge evoked varied very much.

The canals were the most obvious though by no means the most vulnerable of the railways' competitors. There certainly were some sensational cuts in canal revenues. The connection of Manchester and Leeds by rail in 1840, for example, led directly to a 70 per cent collapse in bulk cargo revenue on the Rochdale Canal within two years; the Grand Junction Canal's revenues were nearly halved in the six years after the opening of the London & Birmingham Railway in 1838; and falls in revenue of a third to a half in four or five years were not uncommon. Share values tended to slump even more dramatically wherever this kind of rot seemed to have set in. But there were others which held their position indefatigably for a much longer period than is commonly supposed.

The essential feature of the situation was that both the railways and the canals were incipient or actual monopolists, capable in the long run of supplementing each other's facilities economically to only a limited extent, and therefore bound in the end to dispute the right to be the universal common carrier of the overwhelming bulk of the goods which the industrial system required handling. This did not show itself fully at the start despite the expressions of anguish on one side and cockiness on the other, and there was a tendency, before the mania at least, for the railways to look to the passenger traffic and the canals to the goods traffic for their major revenues. Some two-thirds of all railway revenues were drawn from passenger traffic in the early 1840s and though the proportion continued to fall it never fell as low as 40 per cent in the nineteenth century. This may help to explain not only why the decline of a particular canal did not begin abruptly on the appearance of a railway in the vicinity but also why the public campaign carried on by advocates of the canals against the railway should have been so curiously muted. Another reason for this was, of course, that there must have seemed to be few convincing things that could be said, and still less that could be done, to efface the railways' dazzling image of vitality and efficiency and to rejuvenate the undemonstrative, sluggish spectacle of the canals. There is a sense, too, in which the railways came to be regarded from their earliest days not only as giant-killers but as champions of a new order in society, and the conflict between the railways and the canals had undertones almost of class animosity: "You can scarcely fail to see", wrote the future Baron Dunfermline to James Loch, Lord Stafford's agent, at the end of 1824, "that the conflict between canals and railways is also a conflict between two classes of society and that the 'middling' (and lower orders probably) will take part with the merchants and manufacturers, who are opposed to the grandees". A campaign of these dimensions was unlikely to be concluded quickly.

All this was made plain from the first decade of the railway era and in the very part of the country in which the canal idea had germinated. There should have been no irony in the fact that it was the earliest and most entrenched canal undertakings which first felt the competition of the railways, and it is not easy to see at first why the railways did not bite deep and hard into canal profits. Their own early capture of road traffic by undercutting wagoners' rates had conferred on many canals an almost natural monopoly which they found difficulty in the end in using really expansively; such absolute power tended to corrupt commercial relations in various ways, and the commercial interests which did not profit from it strove to escape from its power. "What remedy remains for the commercial public of Manchester, Liverpool, and their great connected population against the circuity, danger, monopoly, and defective accommodation of the existing canal and river navigations?" asked the anonymous author of a pamphlet entitled *Observations on the General Comparative Merits of Inland Communication by Navigations or Rail-roads*, published as early as 1825. "Answer, Rail-road only."

What was the real force of that final word? The Liverpool & Manchester Railway, which was the answer to this plea, was saved, as we saw in an earlier chapter, by the investment of capital that was, in a sense, transferred by the local canal interest; and the battle of rates for the goods traffic between Manchester and Liverpool was not joined for twenty years after the opening of the railway. Why was this? Personal factors almost inevitably played a significant part in the curiously phoney war that was played out between 1830 and the end of the 1840s, though the effects of these did not all pile up on one side. The only satisfactory explanation for the series of rate agreements, not retaliatory cuts, between the railway and the canal down to 1845 must be that the canal, which had much the best of these bargains, was still in the stronger competitive position. Despite expectations, the two towns were not quite far enough apart to make delivery times and the unit costs of transport really critical. One of the last schemes to be contemplated between the rival concerns, put up in 1845, was for a pooling agreement under which two-thirds of the goods traffic would go by water. What ended this period of collusion was the absorption of the Liverpool & Manchester Railway into larger concerns which were not so specifically concerned with this one link, particularly in the London & North Western Railway in 1849. Not surprisingly, perhaps, the profits of the Bridgewater Trust went higher in 1844 than they had ever gone since the prospectus of their major competitor had first appeared, and although canal traffic began to fall off in the 1850s the rates themselves and the profits that accrued were remarkably slow to follow suit.

It would be rash to assume that this buoyancy in one canal's affairs was repeated everywhere. Many of the smaller undertakings, especially those depending mainly on a rural traffic, had little or no resilience and capitulated to the railways without any commercial fight: their only defence was a couple of debating points and the thicket of paraliamentary procedure. One somewhat remarkable exception was the Lancaster Canal which for a few years in the 1840s was the lessee of a railway—the Lancaster & Preston Company. Even in their heyday many of these undertakings had been struggling to pay their way, with over-elaborate installations and too little traffic to cover the capital and running costs. Their last real kick often came with the carriage of building materials for the very railway that would soon eat into their regular traffic.

One undertaking which conducted its affairs in something of an imperative mood, the Thames & Severn Canal, illustrates quite well how much and how little could be done by such canals to stay in business. Its fortunes had never matched the vision of its promoters because the chalk hills it had to step over or through soaked up capital and water alike, without ever providing the kind of artery for coal as well as agricultural products and other supplies that had once been imagined. Understandably, the proprietors became mercurial. A false attempt to force the whole undertaking on the Cheltenham & Great Western Union Railway in 1835 was succeeded by an interval of strenuous independence as it encountered railway competition virtually along its whole length: two abortive attempts followed in 1866 and 1882 to convert itself into a railway; then an almost immediate acquisition by the Great Western Railway of a controlling interest through nominees, followed by partial closure in 1893; it was formed into a Trust in 1895, adopted by the county council in 1900, closed permanently in 1911, and survives now, wherever it is not totally abandoned, as an escape channel for flood water.

There were perhaps a dozen canal companies still making worthwhile profits as late as 1888, mainly the short, heavily-used canals of the industrial areas. The competitive position of the rest was pretty forlorn and could not be bolstered up in any way, not even by giving them the same statutory right that the railways had to become carriers themselves, and thus to profit directly by the traffic from which they had formerly merely taken a toll. Parliament had originally expected the railways to conform to the practice of the canals in having competing carriers working across their systems, though this idea was allowed to expire. Now the canals, with rather less justification, were to correspond with the railways. This was done under the Canal Carriers' Act of 1845. This Act gave to the canal companies the powers to become carriers themselves, to make joint working arrangements, and to lease themselves to other undertakings—without, of course, restricting their rôle as toll-takers to private carriers. Some—like the Thames & Severn—had long done so without warrant, if only because private carriers were sometimes slow to appear, and a few others had obtained parliamentary powers to do so. A second Act in 1847 encouraged this activity by permitting canal companies to borrow capital for the purpose. The Grand Junction Canal was one to do so and raised £100,000 in 1848. It did well enough to enable it to make a rate-fixing agreement with the London & North Western Railway three years later, though it was forced to close down after the disastrous explosion of one of its barges while it was carrying gunpowder along the Regent's Canal in 1874. The Acts of 1845 and 1847 do not seem to have been very widely used.

Nevertheless, more general concentrative tendencies were being given more scope, for the 1845 Act, though intended as a bulwark to canals prepared to collaborate among themselves, permitted railway companies which had acquired one canal undertaking (thus becoming a "canal company" itself within the meaning of the Act) to take control of others by outright purchase, lease, or a variety of working agreements, without recourse to Parliament or the Board of Trade. Before this measure, amalgamations were not always visible and companies sometimes came to Parliament only to legalize a secret agreement. The arrangements made in some cases seem to have been concluded in a panic, without waiting for real evidence to build up relating to the competitive power of either the canal company or the railway company concerned. One reason for this was that the profitability of a new undertaking could not be properly assessed when capital and running costs were not always kept apart; another was that many of these capitulations occurred during the mania, when judgment was suspended on so many aspects of railway development. The Canal Carriers' Act simply added to these possibilities in ways which favoured, for example, the leasing of the Trent & Mersey Canal by the putative North Staffordshire Railway in 1845.

The new possibilities opened up were Machiavellian by comparison. One example will serve. Three of the largest railway amalgamations of the later 1840s—the London & North Western, the Lancashire & Yorkshire, and the Midland—who were wanting to bring an end to canal competition for ordinary goods traffic in the area, made an agreement with the Leeds

& Liverpool Canal in 1851 to prohibit this traffic by raising its charges well above railway rates, in return for an annual payment of nearly £42,000. Actually, the canal had halved its tolls in the face of the railway competition and was now agreeing to raise them to the original level, a step which led to closure of the canal. The legal basis for this was a lease of the canal tolls under the terms of the 1845 Act, whereby the three railway companies could make the agreement as proprietors of the Huddersfield, the Bolton & Bury, and the Ashby-de-la-Zouch Canals, respectively; a fourth railway company, the East Lancashire Railway, had also wanted to participate in the bargain, but it owned no other canal and could not figure in the final agreement: perhaps the benefits it obviously received were recognized in other ways.

The extent to which canal and railway interests merged during this period was very considerable. According to the secretary to the Canal Association, there were in existence in 1865 some 109 canals comprising 2,552 miles and 49 river navigations covering 1,339 miles, a total length of nearly four thousand miles of navigable waterway throughout the country. By that date, 37 of these undertakings had been amalgamated with railways, five small ones had themselves been converted into railways, and two had been taken on lease by railway companies. These totalled 1,271 miles, or just over a third of their whole length, a proportion which increased by 1883 to something over a half, as more and more undertakings gave up their separate existence. There is little doubt what the immediate benefits were to transport users, either of these mergers and working agreements or simply of railway competition, when this was offered to the canals at close range. The careful researches of Jackman on this point show quite clearly that canal freight rates were very rapidly lowered by anything between a sixth to six-sevenths, depending on the proximity of the railway and the degree of monopoly profit that was being taken by individual canals. The broad truth is that the average reduction was at least of the order of one-third to a half of the former rates.

There were isolated exceptions to this where it was the railway which was compelled to lower its charges for sections of its line where a canal was threatening its traffic. This it normally found quite easy to do by recouping itself on other lines where it was in a monopolistic position, a characteristic exercise of monopoly power. Alternatively, it was possible to maintain relatively high fares for passengers and much lower charges for freight. It followed that when amalgamation occurred between railway and canal in these circumstances it normally led to somewhat higher rates all round. How much higher, and how widespread this tendency was, it is not easy to say in general because rates varied so much between commodities, though there is evidence that it did take place. Pig iron being shipped from Runcorn to destinations in Lancashire was charged at two or three times the old rate on the Lancaster and the Leeds & Liverpool Canals once they had been leased by the railway. Perhaps it is not insignificant that a pamphlet literature was already growing up complaining of the new powers-that-be: "that leviathan monopolist" was said to be the general view held by the merchants and bankers of Liverpool of the London & North Western Railway in 1865.

It was this kind of reaction which led in another quarter to the building of the greatest artificial waterway ever known in this country, the Manchester Ship Canal. This was a direct response to what traders considered to be the exorbitant charges made not only by the docks at Liverpool but by the railways and the Bridgewater Canal, which came under their control in 1872. It was built between 1886 and 1894, at a cost of £14 million, to take ships of up to 12,500 tons straight to Manchester. Its early days were precarious and it gave one of its backers, Manchester Corporation, good reason for postponing any serious expenditure on the city's acute street traffic problem, but it was an artery of quite exceptional importance which was to turn the city into the third port in the country.

From this almost incredible flowering of canal enterprise long after the waterways were thought to be done, we must pass ironically enough to some consideration of the reasons for the decline of the canals in the face of the railways. There were three main reasons for it. First, the canals were in a weak strategic position. Despite their greater triumphs of civil engineering they were incapable of taking advantage in full measure of the growing efficiency of the machine. Getting more power out of the locomotive was bound to mean a very rapid narrowing of the economic advantage which water-transport had initially had over all forms of land transport—especially as the commercial demand for faster deliveries of practically everything in transit was growing more and more imperative. In this purely technical sense canal transport could not compete for the carriage of the full range of raw materials, goods in process, finished products, and foodstuffs which its capital outlay demanded, and the loss by a canal of any substantial part of its traffic tended to have cumulative effects on the whole enterprise. It was their inherently inferior technology, too, which put them at the mercy of the weather, though interruptions due to ice, floods, or drought may have been more of a talking point than a commercial hindrance in a slow-moving age. It should also be recognized that it was basically the canals' technical inability to compete for speed with the railways that denied them passenger traffic of any significance. This possession was strategically vital to the railways for it not only gave them greater financial stability from the start but enabled them to develop a flexible structure of rates which could be used to balance low returns from freight, especially where canal competition was of any effect.

Secondly, the canals were weak in both organization and administration. They did not comprise a unified system in any but a purely topographical sense. As we saw in an earlier chapter, the canal system was an improvisation aimed mostly at meeting a series of quite specific local needs rather than regional or national ones. These congenital defects were aggravated very often by unexpected stringency in the supply of capital and of the water itself sometimes, with the almost ludicrous results that different sizes of lock or channel were built on the same canal. There were some trunk routes that had been deliberately organized for long-distance traffic and other relatively short lengths that had hooked local systems on to the main network. Yet no organizing genius of the kind thrown up by the railways had pulled these connections taut in really effective comprehensive organizations. So far as can be seen, one major undertaking only, the Staffordshire & Worcestershire Canal, made a real effort to organize any joint action when the railway menace was at its height, in 1845, and this was essentially a negative exercise to defeat railway bills threatening the Birmingham canals.

Their particularism was medieval. For example, whichever of the three routes were taken by canal barge from London to Liverpool in the 1880s there were nine separate undertakings which had to be dealt with; similarly, from the very metropolis of the canal system, Birmingham, the most direct routes to, say, London, Liverpool, and Hull involved six, seven, and nine different waterways respectively, the last two routes also requiring transhipment of cargoes at one point. The presence on these numerous canals of so many independent carriers complicated matters still more and made inland shipping a strikingly unbusinesslike affair when compared with the zeal and dispatch of the railway. All this was telling. It was undoubtedly the private carriers on the Bridgewater Canal who gave it its major support when railway competition stiffened. There were some exceptions, of course. The Grand Junction Canal, which had by 1850 become the largest canal carrier under the terms of the 1845 Act, provides the best-documented case of resourcefulness rewarded, for its failure to form a consortium of carriers from the canal proprietors between London and Birmingham did not deter it from going ahead itself and actually increasing the volume of traffic using its canal. Just the same, its performance could not match the returns which the London & North Western Railway got from an altogether heavier, more varied, and lucrative traffic.

Not without significance, it was the Select Committee on Railway Amalgamations of 1872 that first took detailed account of the failure of the canals to develop a standard gauge: the width and depth of the largest were at least three times greater than those of the smallest. It was this weakness which was so easy for the railways to exploit on the tactical level. Not only was it possible for them to demonstrate a facility for organizing through traffic over independent systems which shared a standard gauge, but the ability of the canals to respond could be entirely frustrated by the railways' gaining control of a vital link. There was no special subtlety about this. The intention of the railway companies was simply to drive canal traffic as much and as fast as possible on to their rails. Thus, the Great Western Railway had by 1881 spent almost a million pounds on acquiring control of canals and drew a net annual revenue from this investment of only £276, which was utterly offset by the rent charges it had agreed to pay of £8,243: by this date the traffic receipts on those of the canals it had acquired in 1848 had been cut by an average of nearly 80 per cent.

The third reason for the swift advance of the railway over the canal can only be described as psychological. The railways had in every sense a presence. Their very appearance quickly kindled a kind of awe and sense of poetry that seems to have been shared to some degree by people of every class: steam, speed, controlled power, new sounds, spontaneous movement—there was an excitement here that communicated itself to the press, the board-room, the stock market, the arts, and everyday speech in a way that was almost oblivious of the canals. In retrospect it certainly appears that their obsolescence was too readily taken for granted, perhaps even before their latent capacity had been realized. Yet it must be recognized that this tacit acceptance by the Victorians of a situation in which an asset of these proportions was allowed to waste before its time is strikingly modern in its approach. It is a capacity that showed itself even more vividly perhaps in relation to the roads. Before looking at them it is important to reflect for a few moments on the repercussions which the railways may be said to have had on the prosperity of transport undertakings using that other major waterway of Britain, her coastal waters.

2   Coastal shipping and ports

Traditionally, there had been a close rivalry between inland and coastal trade, particularly in coal. A number of the canals had been developed, among other things, as a means of distributing coal inland more cheaply than it could be had after passing through the hands of the Newcastle hostmen. The coasting trade had kept a jealous eye on these developments for a long time, and the memorials presented to Parliament in 1846 by shipping interests on the north-east coast, asking to be protected from the threat of the railways which were carrying coal south from the Tyne were even couched in terms of the traditional appeal to protect the country's maritime strength. Coal could in fact be carried to London cheaper by rail than it could by coastal barge. Over the next thirty years the railways elbowed their way into this valuable trade and by 1880 were accounting for about 62 per cent of it. This was really the limit of the railways' encroachment on the East Coast coal trade because from this time a series of developments swung the carrying advantage back to sea again. Faster, larger colliers were designed and unloading facilities were improved at the London end; a number of new industries established themselves on the Thames; and the various London gas companies responded to the surge in demand for gas that came around the turn of the century as the working classes began to adopt it for cooking as well as lighting. By 1902 the South Metropolitan Gas Company alone was taking in about a million tons of coal a year from this coastal traffic—three-quarters of its total requirements—and having it delivered to its own wharf via the Surrey Canal. By this time the industrial demand was also becoming important and over half the coal consumed in London for all purposes came by sea.

Quite as remarkable as the recovery of the coal trade—which probably accounted for over half the coastal traffic by the close of the century—was the manner in which coasters were able to extend their trade over a wide range of commodities. The railways were for once at a disadvantage in having lost flexibility in catering for trade between ports, especially the smaller ones, in contrast to the tramp vessels making up the coastal fleet. They were also meeting a competitor whose fixed and operating costs were both low and who was particularly well adapted to the carriage of bulky cargoes of low unit value. There was a sense in which this competition came to be a dominating factor in the fixing of railway rates, and it is conceivable that the rapid increase in the number of exceptional rates granted by the railway companies in this period can be explained in this way. Some of the shipping companies were showing just the kind of enterprise that the railways themselves had displayed in wrenching traffic from the canals. They were able to quote through-rates to inland towns by using short rail connections with the ports and doing it, for example, through South Wales ports serving upwards of 200 towns, for 10s. a ton less than the railway rate. On the other hand, the railways excelled in attracting passengers and they virtually annihilated the ordinary coastal passenger traffic by the end of the century. What sprang up in its place was a pleasure trade which by Edwardian times was beginning to exhibit some of the characteristic extravagances of that period: the cruise was becoming a popular pastime, with the Western Isles and round-Britain trips being encompassed in liners that were fitted out as well as anything on the North Atlantic.

Where some of the railway companies were able to compete and develop an ancillary traffic of great benefit to them was in the cross-channel shipping services. Even before this happened the London & Blackwall Railway had for a time run pleasure steamers from Blackwall to Margate before handing the whole business over to a steamship company. Before the end of that decade, in which furious efforts were made by the railway companies, three or four companies were successful in getting powers to operate their own. Most important of these was the London & South Western Railway, which the Railway Commissioners had noted as being ready to lend £50,000 to a steamship company in order to get a service established at Southampton. That was in 1847, the year before they got powers to take on the job themselves. The South Eastern Railway also came into this kind of business five years later, and the London, Brighton

o

& South Coast Railway, the London, Chatham & Dover Railway, and the Great Eastern Railway all did likewise in the years 1862–3. The year after that the Manchester, Sheffield & Lincolnshire Railway were authorized to operate, if they wished, all over the North Sea. The ferry between Tilbury and Gravesend was started by the London, Tilbury & Southend Company in 1852. Other railway companies entered the business later on in the Bristol Channel and on the Clyde. Such activities were of the greatest importance to those companies which took the initial steps without faltering. They were drawn into very heavy capital outlays in developing ports of great importance, not only for cross-channel and coastal work but for ocean-going ships. Harwich, Folkestone, Southampton were the focal points not only for heavy railway investment but sources of substantial profits, too. It may be noticed, incidentally, that the railway ferry services provided the opportunity for pioneering the use of turbines in marine engineering: the South Eastern's *Queen* was the first turbine steamer to ply the English Channel, in 1902.

All in all, coastal shipping withstood railway competition exceptionally well. It accounted for a falling proportion of the country's internal trade from 1845 onwards but in absolute terms its volume increased, particularly in the forty years after 1865. Though no satisfactory volume figures exist, it is clear enough from the statistics for entrances and clearances in British ports that the cargoes handled by coastal vessels more than doubled over the whole period down to 1914. It should be remembered that the tonnage around Britain's coasts, including trade with Ireland, was greater for much of the nineteenth century than that engaged in foreign trade, and it was of obvious significance for the prosperity of many small communities around the coast that the railway had definite limitations in competing with this ancient trade.

3   Road traffic and urban transport

We can now turn to the impact of the railways on road traffic and the interests involved in it. One of the striking things in the history of transport is the highly elastic response that has regularly recurred to relatively small changes in the cost of transport. It is noticeable, too, how often these marginal changes have been related to important changes in the quality of service. So it is now. The average fare per mile for travelling by coach at the end of the 1830s—inside—was about fourpence. This could be exceeded quite a bit wherever competition between coach companies was weak, or facilities were exceptional, as on mail coaches, which were charging fivepence around 1830. The fares charged by the main railway companies were pitched—with more of an eye perhaps on undercutting road competitors than on covering marginal costs—at about threepence for first class, twopence for second class, and a penny for third class passengers. In many cases the differences in fares appeared quite fractional, especially over short distances, and it is striking how the railways found that they could not charge the fares allowed by law but had to keep them firmly at or below coach fares if they were to keep the traffic they had won. Yet the real difference in costs was substantially greater than it appeared because railway travel was on the average at least twice as fast and, when competing with coaches being worked over bad roads, probably four times as fast; comfort and safety were also substantially improved. What this meant in practice is that, ignoring the qualitative improvement, travelling times and the cost of travel on the early railways were approximately half those on the roads.

The advantages of rail travel naturally increased disproportionately with distance and it was the long stage coaches which felt railway competition most promptly and lastingly. Coaching had reached its highest point of development in most parts of the country around 1830 (*see Map 14*, p. 212). After this, wherever the railway appeared the coaches were either driven off the roads or adapted to the railway's purposes. The 29 coaches which plied between Liverpool and Manchester in 1830 had been reduced to four within five months of the railway's opening and in another two years one only remained; within three months of the opening of the London & Birmingham Railway the 22 coaches that had been operating along this route were reduced to four. The number of coaches licensed to travel into the West Country as far as Taunton and Exeter before the Great Western Railway was built was 116 and between them they performed 807 journeys per week in 1834. The last of them disappeared in 1843, a couple of years after the Great Western's system was fully operational. Some coach proprietors issued defiant advertisements and sometimes risked horses, coaches, and passengers in hectic dashes ahead of the steam trains. On a Spring day in 1838, for example, the *Wonder*, a Shrewsbury coach, left Euston just as the Birmingham train departed and waited twenty minutes for it at the other end. Such exhausting gestures could not be repeated indefinitely and most coach proprietors began adjusting themselves to the new situation in a businesslike way. The early railways left gaps to be filled, just as the depleted lines of latterdays do, and coach services began slotting into place with a show of regret but more impressive alacrity. Dignified announcements told local newspaper readers of the proud names of coaches being withdrawn along with plans to run connections with the trains. The golden age of coaching was indeed brief, though it lingered for some years in the remote, mostly Celtic, fringes of the country.

What had to be adapted to new purposes when the stage coach disappeared was the vast underpinning structure of inns and posting stables that had lined its routes and concentrated thickly at its termini, especially in London. The business of travel by road has never been properly explored by historians but a glance at any leading directory of the period reveals

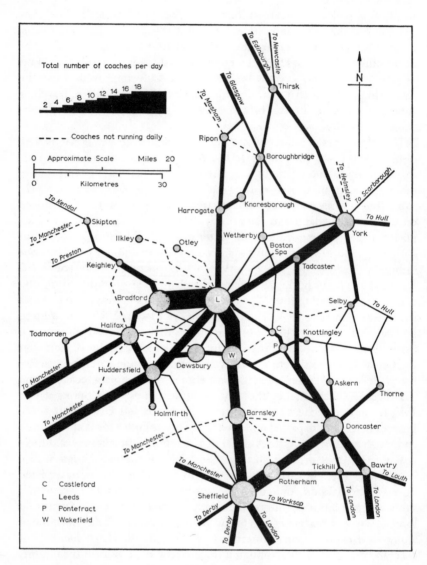

Map 14   *Coach services in West Yorkshire in the 1830s*

an extraordinarily intricate network of connections catering for many thousands of travellers each week to every part of the kingdom. About 800 coaches set out weekly from these London inns for the north alone in the late 1830s, and actually carried some 7,000 passengers. The coach-building industry which also supported this traffic was obliged to adapt to a railway demand, but the design of railway carriages had already been so markedly influenced by the architecture of the stage-coach that the technology of building them was little affected. What is more, the new demand for railway rolling stock more than replaced the custom of the coaching companies and the industry could not fail to benefit from the change.

The process of adaption extended also to the draught animals used. One interesting argument in favour of the railway which the railway economist, Henry Fairbairn, had included in his *Political Economy of Railroads* (1836) had been that replacing the live animal with the iron horse would economize on the land needed to grow its fodder. He reckoned that with some four million horses at work, each requiring as much land as could be used for growing food for four people, the coming of the railway would "therefore make room for human beings to a very considerable extent". He wrote at a time when the pressure of the population on the natural resources of the country appeared to be reaching a critical point. Yet the horse population was not decimated by the railways. The demand for sheer horse-power actually increased during the constructional phase, and the feeder services which the railways developed for themselves, as well as the great variety of uses to which horses could be put in the towns which the railways were helping to build up, led to a growth in their numbers for many years. The annual Cart Horse and Van Horse Parades held in London's Regent's Park before the last war were not archaic survivals of a vanished horse age. Coal, greengroceries, milk, and goods from leading West End stores were still being delivered by horse-drawn vehicles in large numbers even in 1939, and horse manure from the streets still made the cheapest fertilizer for suburban gardens. The great horse repositories to be found in towns all over the country have disappeared comparatively recently—one of the biggest, at the Elephant & Castle in South London, did not close down until the last war.

It is difficult to believe that the railways made any really serious inroads on road carriage in the early years. The institutional apparatus for the carriage of goods by road was probably even more complex than that for passengers, including every kind of conveyance from great stage wagons to nimble errand carts, almost all of it organized to a regular time-table. By the 1850s, certainly, these services had begun to melt away but long after this local directories were listing road carriers in substantial numbers who were still plying many of the old roads. Old habits did not change without big inducements in convenience and reliability as much as cost. The advent of the railways appears to have had a double effect. In step with the withdrawal of some of the long-distance services went an expansion of local traffic in the towns and as feeders to local railway stations. This was not altogether a matter of the triumph of the large carriers, like Pickford or Chaplin & Horne, over the small; nor of equal access for all carriers to the railway goods yards. The railways varied enormously in their attitudes towards them and were sometimes quite unscrupulous in taking their trade. This led to a good deal of rather inconclusive litigation and in one year, 1849, to a large deputation formed principally of carriers from Birmingham, Bristol, Liverpool, Leeds, Sheffield, Newcastle and Edinburgh which asked the Railway Commissioners to prevent the railways from discriminating against them under the law. Nowhere did the railways succeed in completely monopolizing this trade. The more effective response which road carriers were capable of making, of going in with the railway and picking up the subsidiary traffic which they were bound to create, was made by the biggest carriers without delay. Pickford's and Chaplin & Horne, for example, were specially inventive in dove-tailing their businesses with the railways—Chaplin himself so well that he became chairman of the London & South Western Railway. Pickford's lost on the canal side of their business but were soon co-operating with the railway to the extent of erecting the first exclusively goods station at Camden Town, and trying out new ways of transferring loads in bulk from road to rail and back again that have become in our own day the basis of the "liner" trains.

What is perhaps more surprising is that the railways failed to take over more rapidly the transport of perishable foodstuffs. Fish had found its way inland in surprisingly large quantities long before the railways, which certainly accelerated its supply and improved its quality. The modern port of Grimsby, for instance, was almost literally the creation of the Manchester, Sheffield & Lincolnshire Railway, which having encouraged a few fishing smacks to migrate there from Hull in the 1850s, offered the town's fish merchants free travel in search of markets, and thus created outlets for the catch from a fleet of 340 smacks by 1873. By this time fish-trains (an innovation of twenty years before) were on regular schedules to the major inland cities.

Cattle, which had come to be moved round the coast by steamship to a considerable extent, were now increasingly transported by rail, and, whether slaughtered before embarkation or at the backs of urban butchers' shops, their carcases lost none of the weight which they shed on the roads. Yet one Smithfield salesman told the select committee on the London, Chatham & Dover Railway's bill for its metropolitan extensions in 1860 that 6,000 animals were being driven weekly across Blackfriars Bridge, and described how half of them thereupon trudged back again to destinations up to 80 miles away: nine-tenths of the meat needed by the summer visitors to Ramsgate and Margate followed them there on the hoof. London never completely lost its agrarian aspects throughout the century, though keeping pigs, sheep, and cows in closed yards or on any floor of a converted house died out fairly rapidly after the 1860s. This was hastened more by the cattle plague of 1866 than it was by the marketing of alternative supplies by rail. The milk trade was peculiarly resistant to the railways and even twenty years after this date over a fifth of London's milk supplies still came from its own cowsheds. In general, however, the railways soon enlarged the area of supply for all foodstuffs to the country as a whole; and with the advent of refrigeration in the 1870s foreign railways and steam-ships extended the process still more.

In catering for the supply of food to the towns the railways were respond-ing to a demand they had helped to create, for urban growth was itself one of the most conspicuous products of railway development. The railways were not a sufficient reason for the growth of Victorian towns but there can be little doubt that they were a necessary one. They made their growth possible, not only by enlarging the area from which they drew their supplies and into which they discharged their products, but by opening out new technical possibilities for their industry. In one sense they merely removed some of the deadweight from a more fundamental factor, the growth in the population: a doubling and a redoubling of the population of the country first between 1801 and 1851 and then between 1851 and 1911 provided one of the two basic conditions for the urbanization of Britain. Industrialization of the economy provided the other; it was the rôle of the railway to supply some of the impetus for this along with the one really strategic element in the communication of men, materials and social ideas. The railway, it might be said, transformed the whole production function of the towns. "All vitality is concentrated through those throbbing arteries into the central cities," wrote Ruskin in a nostalgic passage in his *Seven Lamps of Architecture* (1849); "the country is passed over like a green sea by narrow bridges, and we are thrown back in continually closer crowds upon the city gates".

The railways were not the only moving parts in these machines for living in—to vary le Corbusier's term for its individual component, the house—and even in the major cities they cannot be regarded as having provided an important function as urban transport until the later nineteenth century. The railways' prime function was to inter-connect the towns rather than to supply them with a useful means of internal transport. It is not before the 1860s that the railway had any importance as a means of suburban communication even in London, and it was not till the 1870s, when almost all the central termini had been built, that the full range of destinations for journeys to work demanded by the inhabitants of new middle-class suburbs became available. The Metropolitan Railway provided a completely intra-metropolitan service from 1863, and the South London Line, developed by two companies and open throughout four years later, were distinct overtures to the suburbs.

The South London Line was carried on viaducts and through deep cuttings

Map 15   *Metropolitan communications, 1895*

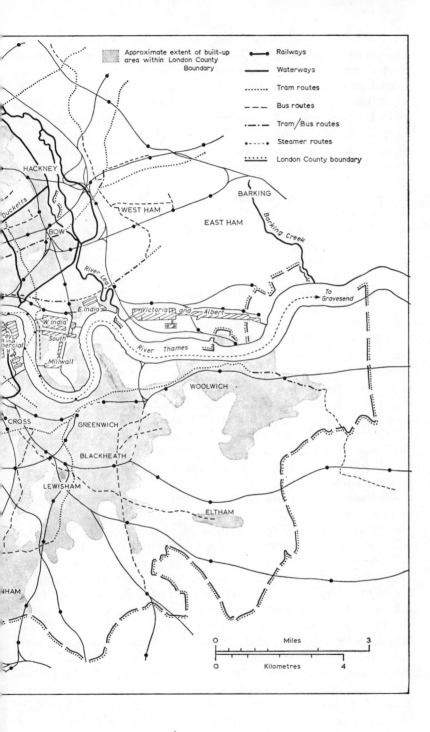

Approximate extent of built-up area within London County Boundary

	Railways
	Waterways
	Tram routes
	Bus routes
	Tram/Bus routes
	Steamer routes
	London County boundary

HACKNEY

Ducketts

WEST HAM

BOW

BARKING

EAST HAM

Barking Creek

River Lea

To Gravesend

E. India

W. India

Victoria and Albert

South

Millwall

River Thames

CROSS

WOOLWICH

GREENWICH

BLACKHEATH

LEWISHAM

ELTHAM

HAM

Miles 0 — 3

Kilometres 0 — 4

between London Bridge and Victoria via New Cross, Peckham, Denmark Hill, Brixton, and Battersea. The Metropolitan Railway had a different construction altogether. It had the distinction of being the first underground railway in the country (soon followed by the East London Railway which used the Thames Tunnel). The Metropolitan was joined below ground, quite literally, by another company, the Metropolitan District Railway—or District, for short. The original intention was that their identities should be merged but the Metropolitan shareholders were not ready to use their profits to subsidize the new company. The yawning cavities made in the streets for these lines were palpably costly. The District line had swallowed up the whole of its £3 million capital by the end of 1868 and one of its backers, Peto & Betts, the railway contractors, had failed eighteen months before for an even larger sum. The Metropolitan shareholders seemed justified: by the early 1870s their own company was carrying 40 million passengers a year and making about £400,000 out of it; the District was doing only half this business, even though its capital was barely a fifth smaller. The two companies bickered continuously but by 1884 the "Inner Circle" which they had formed between them, owning separate tracks and distinctive rolling stock, was complete, and the system extended both south and east to New Cross and Whitechapel, and west to Hammersmith. In 1890 the City & South London Railway was completed to Stockwell, the first railway in this country to be submerged at such a depth—over forty feet—in a tubular tunnel of cast-iron segments and to be operated entirely by electric traction. A third underground railway was built from Waterloo to the Bank in 1898, and from this point a new line, the Central London, tunnelled west to reach Shepherd's Bush two years later. From this date the "tube" was beginning to go in all directions and by 1910 it had extended to Clapham, and at its northern end to Finsbury Park and Hampstead.

The Underground, to use Londoners' own term for it, was an American enterprise developed by C. T. Yerkes and his Underground Electric Railways of London Ltd. It had an influence on suburban development to which it is impossible to do justice in a few words. With the surface and even the sub-soil so congested the modern metropolis depends increasingly on underground or overhead transport. Near Blackfriars, for example, a tier of four great structures were already packed into forty feet below street level by the end of the century: the low-level sewer; the river Fleet, now an underground sewer; the District Railway; a sub-way for gas, water, electric cables, telephone wires, and the like. There can be no question that London's Underground permitted a much larger and densely-packed concentration of people than could have been obtained on a civilized basis by almost any other means. It was always of far greater importance north of the river than south of it but wherever it extended it provided the principal commuter service to the City and West End during the interwar years. It is worth noting that it is the only form of transport first introduced in the nineteenth century which is still being extended in our own day—by the new Victoria Line, under construction between Victoria and Walthamstow since 1963.

Suburban services posed new problems of a kind which put at least two major companies in financial difficulties in this period and kept plans for suburban railways somewhat tentative. All the same, the main lines approaching London had to cross the suburbs at some point and railway stations planted hopefully in the fields were in time heaped up with houses for which a free first-class season ticket for the first year was not infrequently a house agent's, if not a railway company's, bait. The railways did not become the means of daily travel for the masses until the decade after this, when the Cheap Trains Act of 1883 made the running of workmen's trains at exceptionally low fares (which had been operating for twenty years before this on some lines) depend on the judgment of the President of the Board of Trade. The twopenny fare brought an entirely new travelling public on to the railways, but it was not only cheaper fares that were at work. Rising real wages, more regular employment, shorter working hours, and the pervasive desire for a castle on the ground all worked together. Nor was it the railways only that now accelerated quite dramatically the social transformation of the suburbs that had been going on since the middle of the eighteenth century, when the middle classes had begun to filter into them. The workmen's ticket that drove the middle classes still further afield was a facility of the tramways, too; nor was the ubiquity of the omnibus a factor of insignificance. (See Map 15, pp. 216–17.)

The railways, in fact, simply settled the general conditions in which more specifically urban transport could operate. The stage-coach, deprived increasingly of its long-distance traffic, either curtailed its operating radius until it could work profitably within the railway network or veered off to more circuitous, railway-free routes. The short stage-coach had probably always existed as a feeder to the main routes and the concentration of the population in the towns increased this rôle, though in central London the hackney coach monopoly which we noticed in an earlier chapter prevented short stage-coaches from operating freely. What helped to finish the short stage-coach was the hansom cab, which the ending of the hackney carriage monopoly in 1831 permitted to operate. Also helping to bring it to an end was the omnibus, which had had a desultory and over-taxed existence for over thirty years, and now came into popular use following George Shillibeer's attempt to imitate its recent success in Paris by running a spanking service from Paddington to the Bank in 1829. Steadily, the short stage-coach disappeared within fifteen years. Most omnibuses were twelve-seaters charging a standard 6d. fare, though competition reduced fares to a penny in some cases and improved design increased the capacity to 22 passengers.

Down to the 1850s, when well over a thousand omnibuses were in use in London, it was the standard vehicle for those who rode to work carrying perhaps three or four times as many passengers as the railways. Increased running costs and a general recoil from out-and-out competition brought conditions which in 1856 led to the formation of the London General Omnibus Company mainly with French capital and Anglo-French management, an undertaking which quickly bought up nearly 600 omnibuses and continued to dominate the industry for almost eighty years. Most of the remainder were formed into various working associations or "times" to minimize competition. By 1860 the London General's vehicles were carrying over 40 million passengers a year. By then, there were signs, however faint, of the rush-hour, with morning and evening cavalcades of buses so dense that reference to a timetable was already superflous: fourpence covered most suburban journeys and this was within reach of the better-paid clerk and artisan. Yet the horse-bus had a limited range and capacity and gave up its brief hegemony of the suburbs to the railways and to its street counterpart, the tramway, which had by the 1880s begun to dislodge the omnibus from many of the main streets outside the centre and forced it to pick its way through parts untouched by either of its competitors. It was the internal combustion engine that put it into major service again shortly before the first world war and enabled it in the end to vanquish all comers.

The tramway succeeded for the same general reasons as the railway, and when the horse was widely replaced by electric traction (mostly by the overhead wire system) from the 1890s it became in many places the suburban railways' most damaging competitor. It was then that the tram became, in Richard Hoggart's phrase, the gondola of the working classes, a vehicle capable of carrying an incredible work-load and becoming ingrained with a whole way of life. Its pioneer, the Oystermouth Railway, had been authorized in 1804 to run the eastern strand of Mumbles Head beyond Swansea, though not with the intention of becoming a passenger-carrying tramway. That function developed almost casually in the course of other business in 1807, and it had evaporated in the 1820s with the appearance of a turnpike alongside. The subsequent history of the tramway down to the 1860s became almost entirely European and American.

The tram was put on English streets for the first time at Birkenhead in 1860 by an American, G. F. Train, who also opened two somewhat calamitous and short-lived experimental lines in London the following year, but it was not till the end of that decade that the idea of a tramway system for London began to take firm hold everywhere, except in the central districts. Tramways then began to multiply rapidly and the Tramways Act of 1870 facilitated, and probably encouraged, their development all over the country —where they became an apparently immutable element in all scenes of provincial urban life, as much at home in the city-centre as on the outskirts. (*See Map 16*, p. 221.) The Tramways Act also gave local authorities both an absolute veto on local tramway development and the right to purchase at virtually scrap prices, though not to operate, tramways 21 years after being authorized. This, no doubt, was a lesson learned in the school of early railway development. Nevertheless, Huddersfield Corporation obtained powers

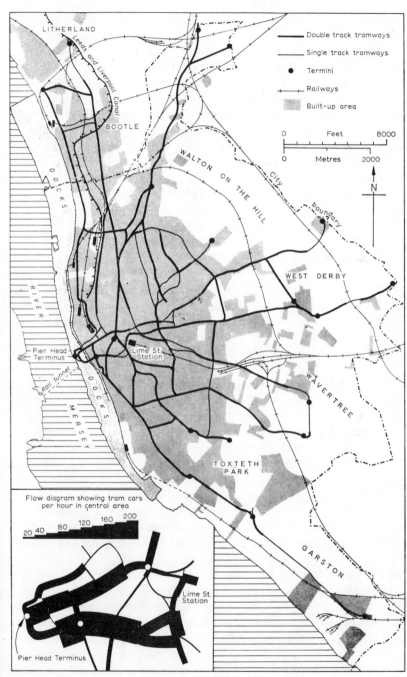

Map 16   *Liverpool tramways, 1905*

to operate their tramways in 1883. In London, the London County Council began to take over on the nail in 1891 and obtained powers to operate the trams itself, first south of the Thames and, after 1906, north of it too, using cheap fares as a means of syphoning off the working classes from the congested central areas. The municipal operation of tramways looked as if it would become almost conventional in the provinces also, and in many places their operating profits supplemented rateable incomes despite very low fares. By the outbreak of the First World War tramway systems in the country at large contained over 2,500 miles of actual route and were carrying around 3,300 million passengers annually. The war enabled them to touch a still higher peak of operations but this also demonstrated the paces of the motorbus and after the war it began to assert its superiority, allied with a new hybrid form of urban travel, the electric trolley bus.

4   Road administration

We come finally to the impact of the railways on the roads themselves. There can be little doubt that the turnpike trusts were generally in the most vulnerable position of all existing transport interests in the face of the railways. Perhaps they were the more so as their prosperity had seemed so secure in the span of years since Waterloo. This had been their heyday. The earlier strictures on the turnpikes, like Arthur Young's, had not been entirely dispelled but the turnpikes were widely held to be efficient, their "macadamized" surfaces poles apart from the miry or rutted tracks of earlier times, their grand routes underpinned at crucial points by great feats of engineering, and their administration a reproach to that of the parish roads. By 1837 their combined toll revenue had reached over £1½ million. They covered up to 22,000 miles of main trunk routes and cross roads, while the parish roads, which included most urban streets, about five times as many —figures which changed surprisingly little down to the end of the 1830s. Perhaps it should be added here that, all general impressions to the contrary, turnpikes were not common everywhere. In Middlesex almost a third of the roads were turnpiked in 1840 but in Cornwall, Cumberland, and Norfolk no more than 8 per cent of the roads were turnpiked.

There was a flicker of hope that steampower might have led to greater prosperity for the turnpikes rather than to their doom, with the invention of the steam-carriage. One was on the roads in 1821 and various attempts were made to improve designs over the next ten years. Three of them were running a regular service between Cheltenham and Gloucester in the spring of 1831, each carrying 36 passengers for half the ordinary coach fare and building up a total traffic over four months of between 3,000 and 4,000, before the weakness of the axles and the high tolls led their proprietor, Sir Charles Dance, to take them off the road. Two years later he showed his machine's paces on the London-to-Brighton run, which he did smoothly in under six hours in both directions. The device looked promising and Thomas Telford was prepared to say in 1833 that "with a well constructed engine of greater power, a steam-carriage conveyance between London and Birmingham, at a velocity unattainable by horses, and limited only by safety, might be maintained". It is significant that he forebore to mention the surface of the road. There was never any question of this being able to stand up so well to weight and speed as the smooth rail. It was a brilliant episode which had more promise than a rail-smitten generation could visualize, but it did nothing to make the turnpikes less vulnerable to competition from the railways.

The vulnerability of the turnpikes consisted in the very traffic they bore. They depended heavily on tolls taken from passenger traffic—one Worcestershire trust estimated the yield on each coach at £7–£14 a month in 1836 and there was nothing that they could do to prevent heavy loss of revenue once the railway—and in some places coasting vessels, especially steamers —provided an effective alternative to travel by road. As the stage-coach expired the trusts' toll revenues collapsed, falling by a third between 1837 and 1850. Their rising incomes before 1837 had camouflaged their inherent financial weaknesses. The arbitrariness of the legal rates meant that revenues were quite unrelated to costs, yet they were mortgaged heavily from the start. Some trusts had already paid no interest on their bonds for fifty years together. The trusts had usually weakened themselves too much already to enable them to overcome what Sir James McAdam called the calamity of the railways. Many of them, though by no means all, had mismanaged their funds in the period which was just closing by laying out too much on various capital works or by becoming administratively top-heavy: ironically, there was no way of cutting back to any extent on officials or pikemen when traffic declined. In some cases important offices had become sinecures and there is evidence that there was a certain amount of outright fraud, expecially over the administration of statute labour before it was abolished.

Like the canals, the turnpike trusts had tended to ignore some of the more important possibilities of forming regional groupings, either by working agreements or by thoroughgoing consolidation into larger trusts, nor was much done in these directions even when the outlook began to look really black towards 1840. There had been built up trusts to cover some sizeable territories, as in the Surrey and Sussex, Middlesex, Worcester, and Exeter Trusts, but all too often a scheme for rationalization could be rejected with some justification by trusts that were still solvent on the grounds that such a policy would make them insolvent; and there was always resistance from those having a vested interest in divided management. The financial condition of trusts that fell into debt for these reasons was usually also aggravated by the way in which unpaid interest was converted into interest-bearing bonds. The loss of statute labour also carried a financial penalty. What is indisputable in the situation is the impact which the railways had on the market price of any gates within their range: they simply began to let for less and less. Those in cities could still prosper to some extent, though the problem of the latter was how to collect all the toll that was due when side-streets offered ways round. In London this led to an enormous proliferation of gates during the 1840s, a mischief which had its impact on omnibus fares and the very pattern of development in the suburbs.

The turnpike trusts were by mid-century as much outdated as they were saddled by debt and their roads gradually passed under the control of local authorities dependent on rates levied on the whole community, not merely on the road-users themselves. By 1830 there were over a thousand independent turnpike trusts in existence, operating on terms virtually identical to those laid down in their several acts, and their standards of maintenance along with their use of statute labour had always varied widely. Ultimate responsibility for the upkeep of the roads under common law had never been shed by the parishes and as turnpikes began to decay Parliament had repeatedly looked into turnpike matters since 1806, and it clearly intended that this parish responsibility should revive. In an act of 1841 the magistrates were empowered at Quarter Sessions to order the levying of a special highway rate. This had predictable results. In South Wales especially, local people sensed injustice and expressed it, along with other grievances, in the Rebecca Riots of 1842–3. These did not subside until all offending gates in six counties had been demolished and contingents of Metropolitan Police and soldiers had been drafted into the area. After the riots and a royal commission, all turnpikes trustees in the region were discreetly dismissed and their responsibilities handed over to new county authorities which were ultimately responsible to the Home Secretary. The greatest wonder was that within thirty years or so these roads were free of debt as well as cheaper to use.

Elsewhere in the country the transfer of the turnpikes to local authorities was painfully slow, caught as it was in the great debate that surrounded so many questions of governmental reform in the mid-Victorian period, the question whether power should be centralized in Whitehall or left in the hands of the local community. By the 1860s there were signs of public impatience and a select committee of 1864 heartily recommended that they should be wound up without delay. The process proceeded piecemeal at a speed which accelerated in 1870–1 but took another decade or so to bring the remaining trusts below a hundred; the last of them (though not the last toll-road) expired in 1895. In London, all but one of the dozen toll-bridges —the London, Westminster and Blackfriars bridges, all rebuilt by 1870, were not among these—were freed from toll in 1878–80.

One reason for this sluggish operation in bringing the turnpikes to a formal end was that the administration of the parish roads themselves was so slow to evolve, and it was not until the year before the ending of the turnpike system that a satisfactory conclusion was reached. Every disturnpiked road added something to the local rates, and was understandably resisted wherever resentment over the payment of tolls was not greater still.

This phase in the history of the roads was even more protracted than that of absorbing the turnpikes. It had begun near the beginning of the century with the appointment of a number of county surveyors and the more widespread use of pauper labour, but there seems to have been little parliamentary attention given to them before 1835. The General Highway Act of 1835, which codified the whole law relating to parish roads, gave responsibility squarely to some 15,000 local vestries, with their salaried officials and hired labour (in place of the statute labour and team duty imposed under the Act of 1555), and permitted parishes counting over 5,000 inhabitants to elect a representative board of management—a Highway Board—having powers to nominate a surveyor and levy a rate. These authorities were too small for the job, some of them ludicrously so, but to have gone to the logical extreme demanded by the situation and given the administration of the roads into the hands of bodies large enough to attend to it effectively would have meant giving it to the Tory county magistrates, something which a Whig administration could not reasonably do, not least because this would have given new rating powers to a non-elective body—a procedure which belonged politically to the period of unreformed government, not to the new era. Since few, if any, Highway Districts were formed by the spontaneous combination of rural parishes and the District Surveyors envisaged as serving them failed to appear, the whole effort of road legislation for the next fifty years had to be aimed at correcting serious maladministration.

Down to 1862 a dozen bills were introduced on the subject but the administration of the roads was yoked firmly to the vestries, and the Highways Act of that year, which aimed at creating viable highway authorities compulsorily, was never carried into full effect. It produced a variety of responses all over the country and, if anything, created an even more chaotic situation than already existed. Highway Districts were created on all kinds of administrative basis, some 424 of them in the ensuing twenty years, but at the end of the 1870s there were 6,000 or more parishes still attending to their roads in their own vestries and relying on the parish surveyor to execute their wishes. Areas of local administration overlapped each other in great confusion and nothing short of a complete reorganization of county authorities could rescue the situation. Before that came about grants-in-aid were made for the first time in 1878 in an attempt to share the burdens of road administration evenly between parishes; ten years later the Exchequer contribution was increased under the Local Government Act of 1888, and at the same time the new county councils were made Road Authorities, responsible for all so-called main roads, comprising about 22,000 miles. The final act of reform did not come, however, until the Local Government Act of 1894, in which the public health legislation of the preceding half-century may be said to have culminated, and a new pattern of local government established; on its eve there were over 5,000 parishes still operating the vestry system of administering the roads. Strikingly enough, the total mileage of public

P

roads in England and Wales at the end of the century, about 120,000, was virtually the same as it had been before the railways began.

5   Street improvement

The failure to re-write the law pertaining to the roads in a more imperative mood was one of the more invidious aspects of the enthusiasm which was spent on the railways. They diverted attention from the roads to such an extent that not only their administration but their basic physical structure remained very much in the condition in which it had been on the eve of the railway age. The failure to develop a better road system for inter-urban communication was an insignificant one which a motorized age would find relatively simple to overcome. What was disastrous was the neglect of street improvement within the cities themselves at a time when urban growth was in full spate. The railways did not provide the only influence in this situation. Urban growth was everywhere happening so fast and on such a novel scale that it was literally too much for local authorities to handle with real command.

In London, the early impetus that had sprung as much from a desire to clear the slums as to make way for the traffic had almost spent itself with the labour (and dubious rewards) of cutting Victoria Street and New Oxford Street in the 1840s. The Metropolitan Board of Works, the first body concerned with the local government of the metropolis as a whole, and its successor, the London County Council, developed a new momentum, and concentrated chiefly on the West End. As we saw earlier, they thrust in new lengths of street at what seemed crucial points at great expense. It would be wrong to under-rate such achievements. The M.B.W. spent during its 33 years of existence, from 1855–88, £7 million on new streets, £5¼ million on street-widening, and £3 million on the Thames embankments; its successor spent no more than £20 million in the next half-century. It faced great problems in doing so, particularly in carrying out its programme of improvements authorized in 1872–7. These included the creation of Charing Cross Road and Shaftesbury Avenue (1886–7), in which its operations were greatly hampered by the high compensation it had to pay for the property taken, plus its inability to let or sell at the full market value all the plots fronting the new streets. It was obliged to re-house the working classes displaced by the demolitions—they were invariably numerous anywhere in Central London and most numerous where improvement was most urgent—and it was unable therefore to recoup the full value of the improvement. The L.C.C. could find no way round the problem of financing these improvements when they had been finished by levying adequate betterment charges on those whose property or business had been enhanced by them.

Such problems have a modern ring but it must be remembered here that operations like these had to be conducted at that time in the total absence of general legislation favouring the re-planning of built-up areas: the first Town Planning Act was not passed before 1909, and the only powers of that kind which local authorities could exercise without special legislation before then were derived from the Housing Acts. Nevertheless, substantial, if piecemeal, improvements were made, notably at the east end of the Strand and in the execution of Aldwych and Kingsway (1901–5). A cleverly engineered sub-way made a connection for trams with the Embankment and brought them to the surface towards the top of the new street without interfering with the flow of other street traffic. If it had to be judged in terms of communications alone, Kingsway would have to be written off as little more than an ostentatious piece of tinkering, just as the intrusions then being made into Nash's Regent Street (to be rebuilt entirely in the 1920s) are now to be regarded—architecturally speaking—as rather mischievous ones. Yet Kingsway came about, as much as anything, to rid London of more of its slums, and the extent of its success here may be judged by the fact that of the gross cost of £6 million as much as £4 million was obtained by recoupment. In the City of London, there was never any problem of recouping full site values—except, ironically enough, on Queen Victoria Street, the most promising of all—and the period from the 1890s to the 1930s saw an unbroken succession of street widenings and street rebuilding, including the important addition of another crossing of the river, below London Bridge. The Tower Bridge (1886–94), which never became as important to road traffic as its elaborate structure would suggest, cost over a million pounds and was financed out of the City's own funds. The corporation had coal duties and estate revenues to draw upon and these produced £2½ million for new bridges in the course of the nineteenth century. (*See Map 4, p. 58.*)

In other towns the same echo was heard, though the building of Corporation Street in Birmingham (1878–82) stands out sharply both as an example of bold initiative and of the financial problems entailed. It stemmed in both senses from the London & North Western Railway's station in New Street, which had been built on the site of a slum cleared for the purpose during the time of the railway mania. The railway was here literally the locomotive of change in the physical layout of central Birmingham, each line that entered it making its impact on the street system: the Great Western completely altered the area around its terminus at Snow Hill, the Midland likewise around Suffolk Street, and the London & North Western around New Street. Corporation Street, which cut into it almost at right-angles opposite New Street station, came relatively late in the day and would almost certainly not have come then but for the drive of Joseph Chamberlain, then mayor. There had been smaller schemes before this and there were to be even larger ones much later but the timing of Corporation Street depended above all on the culmination of forces of civic self-consciousness which Chamberlain was able to crystallize. Like many others, the Corporation

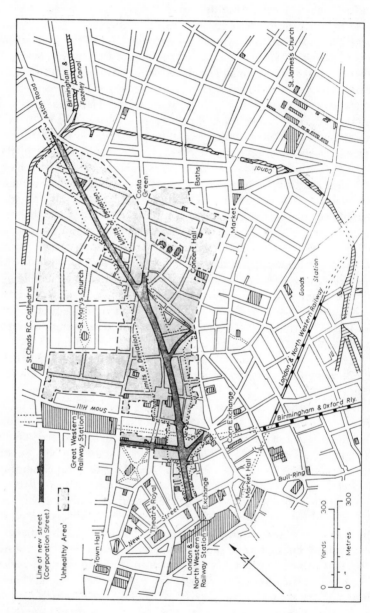

Map 17   *Plan of Corporation Street, Birmingham, 1875*

Street scheme—its main element was a street almost half-a-mile long—was related to slum clearance, over 43 acres of them, which it was estimated would cost £1,310,000 to acquire. Raising the money was not easy, partly because a government loan was not readily forthcoming. The Improvement Committee proceeded cautiously so as not to throw too much property on the market at the same time, and it might in fact have been difficult to do otherwise since its building, though conceived in prosperity, had to be continued during depression. The start of building operations came in the bad years 1878–9 and roused some solid opposition locally, which lasted until the financial success of the scheme no longer hung in the balance. This was not until 1892, and it was not before 1937–8 that the income from rents covered the capital charges in addition to recurrent expenses. Yet it was an improvement of incalculable importance for the city—as it became in 1889. (*See Map 17*, p. 228.)

In Manchester, where symptoms of economic stagnation during the years of the "Great Depression" of 1873–96 included a serious run-down in the occupation of warehouses at the centre, traffic problems were not alleviated at all by street improvement of any consequence. Despite its commercial difficulties, the congestion of traffic on the central streets depended as much on the movements of wagons delivering and collecting cotton from warehouses as it did on the convergence of large numbers of tram-cars on the same streets. Manchester's traffic problem became really acute just when municipal finances were very heavily committed in schemes for water-supply and the Ship Canal, and although capital was cheap enough there was a limit on how much could be done in the time. The railways, it is clear, simply led into this kind of situation by permitting economic resources to concentrate so tightly: they were not, however, exclusively responsible for it, nor were they capable of solving the problems it raised single-handed.

The new streets that were cut to the railway stations, as at Norwich and Bristol as well as Birmingham, were simply some of the opening exercises in the next phase of the development of urban communications. They are a reminder to us that the process of adaptation to which towns must submit is an endless one. Towns outlive the generations that built them and new technologies, especially of transport, soon make old structures obsolescent. Those who initiated the street improvements we have been considering here recognized this clearly enough and were also aware of the need to plan comprehensively. Their sense of comprehensiveness was not everywhere more limited than ours; their failures were certainly not any greater. The idea of a Greater London had formed by 1864, that of a Greater Birmingham by 1888: the editor of *The Builder*, advocating the first of these, wrote of the need for "a comprehensive *plan* [his italics] of the area occupied by London, with the largest estimated additions for the next century, designed and arranged for drainage and sewerage, water-supply, inter-communication. . . ." In London, where the problems of handling the daily journey to work of hundreds of thousands and presently of millions, have tended to dwarf those of any other city, no-one has ever had a really clear idea of how its traffic should flow. It was one thing to count the traffic of the present day. In a traffic census held in May 1891, the daily flow of passengers on foot and in vehicles entering the City of London alone was assessed at over a million; 92,000 vehicles, all horse-drawn, crossed its borders—including over 18,000 cabs and 10,000 buses. It was another thing altogether to anticipate its future growth.

Defoe's discovery of grave businessmen commuting on horse-back from Epsom at the beginning of the eighteenth century was a tiny hint of what was to follow. William Cobbett in his *Rural Rides* (1822) reported that "great parcels of stockjobbers" were staying at Brighton and "skipping backwards and forwards on the coaches" to their work in the City. The railways enormously enlarged these possibilities, so that by the end of the nineteenth century not only were clerks pouring in from Camberwell but merchants were steaming up daily from points along the Sussex coast. G. A. Sala, who lived at Brighton in the 1890s, described the town as the West End of London "maritimized". The rush-hour could already be defined even if the railway season-ticket zone of London could not. A Royal Commission did so in 1906, voluminously. A crude measure of the growing scale of the problem of shuttling workers about London, not only between suburb and city but between suburb and suburb, is contained in the commission's report: the number of passengers carried by the London railways, the trams, and two of the main fleets of buses in 1881 had been about 270 million; the comparable figure for 1901 was 847 million—more than doubling the average number of journeys made per head in twenty years. What the Royal Commission on London Traffic—probably the largest inquiry of its kind ever mounted—did was to demonstrate the inadequacies of London's traffic system. It could do nothing of itself to accelerate change in any direction, least of all perhaps in relation to street improvement outside the narrow box at the very centre. Here was the inner ring of boroughs where the major traffic problems of the next generation were already forming, where vestry finances were demonstrably inadequate for the job of driving new traffic arteries through neighbourhoods put together for quite different purposes. Neither metropolitan nor central government were prepared to embark on solutions to these problems. The one solution to the problem of avoiding congestion at the centre that was seized with any resolution was consequently a fugitive one—cheap fares and the spread of suburbia. This was also the unconscious strategy of the inter-war years and it was barely halted in the 1950s. The implications of that far-reaching process must be reserved for a later chapter, and in the meantime we must examine one major component in the country's great commercial supremacy, its shipping.

8

The development of overseas shipping

1 The growth of trade and shipping

Despite the extraordinary resilience shown by coastal shipowners in competition with the railways, their progress tended to be overshadowed by the more dramatic and far-reaching developments which were taking place at this time in ocean shipping. Indeed it can be argued that in the latter half of the nineteenth century it was shipping which showed the most striking progress in the field of transport as a whole. It was in this period that the real technological breakthrough occurred by which the ancient wooden sailing ship was replaced by the modern vessel built of steel and driven by steam. The importance of these changes must not be underestimated for without them it would have been virtually impossible to provide an efficient shipping industry with a greatly enlarged transport capacity sufficient to serve the growing requirements of both the British and world economies. Once again this country played a leading role in the changes which took place and it was the skill and ingenuity of Britain's industrial and mercantile classes which were largely responsible for the creation of the modern shipping industry.

The expansion of the British merchant marine can be seen from Table 2 below. From the 1840s onwards the British fleet grew steadily every decade and by 1910 it was over four times what it had been in 1840. During the same time total entrances and clearances of British vessels with cargo increased roughly ten times. For most of the time Britain possessed over one-third of the world tonnage and when allowance is made for steam tonnage, which ton for ton was much more efficient than sail by the end of the nineteenth century, British superiority was even more marked. Britain's share of the world's steam tonnage rose from 24·3 per cent in 1840 to a peak of 50 per cent in the 1880s. It was only towards the end of the nineteenth century when other nations, notably Germany and Japan, began to develop their fleets rapidly, that the rate of growth and relative importance of the British shipping industry began to decline. Even so, up to 1913 Britain was still by far and away the most important maritime country in the world. We owned nearly half the world's steam tonnage and our fleet was roughly four times as large as that of our nearest rival Germany. Roughly one half of the sea-borne trade of the world and two-thirds of Britain's trade was carried in British ships and in the 25 years before the First World War we built almost two-thirds of the new ships which were launched.

Table 2   *Merchant shipping tonnage of the United Kingdom, 1840–1910*

	U.K. fleet (million net tons)	*U.K. share of world tonnage*	*U.K. share of world steam tonnage*
1840	2·77	29·52	24·3
1850	3·57	39·47	23·0
1860	4·66	34·80	31·3
1870	5·69	33·94	42·3
1880	6·58	32·88	50·0
1890	7·98	35·83	49·2
1900	9·30	35·50	44·5
1910	11·56	33·37	40·0

The American tonnage employed on the Great Lakes has been included for the purpose of these calculations.

The growth of the shipping industry can be regarded as an automatic response to the rapid expansion in international trade which occurred during the period in question. From the 1840s world trade grew at a much faster rate than ever before; between 1840 and 1872–3 the increase in the

Table 3   *British and world trade, 1840–1913*

(Current Values £ million)

	British (including re-exports)	*World*
1840	152·6*	560
1850	186·4*	800
1860	375·0	1,450
1870	547·4	2,890 (1872–73)
1880	697·7	—
1890	749·0	—
1900	877·5	—
1910	1,212·5	
1913	1,403·5	8,360

* Declared value

value of world trade was over 400 per cent, and to 1913 1,400 per cent, compared with only 75 per cent in the first forty years of the nineteenth century. Much of this increase resulted from the spread of industrialization to countries outside Britain such as France, Belgium, Germany, the United States and later Japan. By the 1880s as much as 50 per cent of the world's visible international trade was done by four industrialized countries, namely Britain, France, Germany and America. As these countries came to concentrate more and more on the production of manufactured goods there was a constant search for new markets in the less developed regions of the world such as Latin America, Asia, Africa and the British Empire. Under western influence these regions were being opened up and their mineral and agricultural resources tapped, and in turn outlets were found for their primary commodities in the industrializing countries of Western Europe. The process was not, however, simply one of bilateral exchange between manufacturing countries and primary producers. The industrial countries themselves exchanged manufactured goods with each other in ever-increasing quantities whilst some of the more developed countries exported foodstuffs and raw material. The bulk of America's exports consisted of cotton and foodstuffs whilst Britain had a large and flourishing trade in coal down to 1914. The exchange of commodities on such a wide scale was facilitated by the fact that there were few artificial barriers on trade and nearly every country stood to gain in some way from the great commercial expansion of the nineteenth century. As a consequence the economic structure of many nations became increasingly interlocked by a system of multilateral trade and transactions, which replaced the earlier series of regional networks.

Britain provided the pivot on which this complex system of trading relationships revolved. It is true that by the end of the nineteenth century she was no longer the only economic power of any importance, but nevertheless down to 1914 she remained the world's largest and most influential commercial, financial and maritime country in the world. And as the leading industrial and commercial country she consumed ever-increasing quantities of raw materials and foodstuffs, a large proportion of which were imported, and exported manufactured products to all parts of the world. Over the period 1850 to 1913 for example, the volume of raw cotton imports rose from 664 to 2,174 million lbs, imports of raw wool from 74·3 to 806·4 million lbs, the import of grains rose sevenfold, and iron ore imports, which were negligible in the 1850s, exceeded 7 million tons by 1913. Outward cargoes increased no less rapidly though their physical bulk was not so great. The volume of iron and steel exports rose sixfold, cotton piece goods from 1,358 to 7,075 million yards and coal exports, which formed the backbone of the outward cargoes of tramp ships, from 3·2 to 73·4 million tons. These of course are only some of the more important items which required sea transport. Taken as a whole Britain's foreign trade (both imports and exports) almost quadrupled in value and probably more than trebled in physical bulk in the half century or so before 1914.[1] Though the pattern of trading relationships changed over time the larger part of Britain's trade was carried on with Europe, Asia, the United States and the Empire.

Thus the rapid expansion in British and world trade provided a constant source of employment for the enlarged fleet both in the home and in the cross trades. Many countries came to depend heavily on British shipping services for the carriage of their commodities and as a result some 20 to 25 per cent of the total British tonnage never touched home shores from one year to the next. In 1912 British ships carried 92 per cent of the inter-imperial trade, 55 per cent of the trade between Empire and foreign countries and 30 per cent of the inter-foreign trade. In addition the large-scale migrations from Europe to the New World provided an increasing volume of passenger traffic particularly on the North Atlantic route. In the ten years before the First World War an average of over one million emigrants left Europe annually for the United States compared with only 32,000 annually in the decade 1825–34. The immigrant figures of the United States give an indication of the size of the total traffic. Immigrants entering America rose from 5 million in the period 1815–1860 to 10 million between 1860 and 1890 and to 15 million in the years prior to 1914. Until the 1890s Britain and Germany provided the greatest sources of emigrants to the New World.

Unfortunately these crude statistics do not enable us to posit a very precise relationship between the expansion in trade and growth of tonnage though it is obvious that the connection is a strong one. Figures for an individual port however do bring out the point more clearly. Between 1857 and 1906 the value of cargoes dealt with in the port of Liverpool rose from £100 million to £277 million and the weight of these cargoes trebled. Liverpool also became the largest oversea passenger port in the U.K. and in the 25 years up to 1906 four million people sailed from there. To provide for this trade the tonnage owned by members of the Liverpool Steamship Owners' Association rose from 70,000 to 3,613,442 tons gross, comprising 22 per cent of the total steam tonnage afloat.

It would seem logical to conclude from this that the growth in trade was the major determinant of the rise of British shipping. Yet this line of reasoning is not altogether satisfactory. Undoubtedly the expansion in traffic potentialities provided a strong incentive to increase tonnage but it can be argued that in the first instance the line of causation ran the

[1] Indices of the volume of imports and exports are as follows: (1880 = 100).

	Imports	Exports
1850	28	32
1870	65	76
1900	166	140
1913	220	239

other way. Trade grew as and when transport facilities became available at a price which made it profitable to transport bulky goods, of low unit value, over long distances. This was particularly true of commodities such as grain and coal for which transport costs in the early nineteenth century might be as much as, if not more than, the cost of the commodity itself. Thus it was not until technical progress had reduced the unit cost of transport charges appreciably that it became relatively profitable to ship large quantities of bulky low unit valued commodities across the oceans. As Dr. Wickizer commented in 1938: "Shipping—together with railway transportation—created the world grain market and has been largely responsible for its vast expansion during the last century."

There is of course another point to bear in mind. The above argument does not offer a satisfactory explanation of why Britain secured a predominance in the mercantile field in the latter half of the nineteenth century. For until around the middle of the nineteenth century there was no clear indication that Britain's supremacy in this field was a foregone conclusion. Despite a rapid increase in the volume of trade after 1815 the British merchant marine was very slow to respond. In fact net registered tonnage actually fell in the years 1816 to 1825 and did not regain the 1816 level until 1838. Indeed, as Thornton says, "there was little to be proud of in the British mercantile marine. The ships were vastly inferior, as ships, to the American and no better than were being built in the Dutch ports or in the yards of the Hansa towns". Replacements and improvements were kept to a minimum and British shipowners, sheltered by the navigation laws, were content to cling to past traditions and techniques. On the other hand, foreign shipowners, particularly the American, took advantage of the situation. After the Napoleonic Wars the American merchant marine grew rapidly and offered an effective challenge to Britain. American ships were faster and less costly to operate than English vessels. American shipowners were quick to realize the commercial advantages of speed in the carriage of passengers, mails and certain classes of valuable cargo. Aided by the inexhaustible supplies of cheap timber they were able to build bigger, better and cheaper ships than Britain and in fifty years they contributed as much to the development of the sailing ship as the whole maritime world had contributed in three hundred. The years from 1800 to 1840 have been called the "most glorious period in American maritime history". During that time American ships carried around 90 per cent of the country's foreign trade and Yankee packets dominated many routes, particularly the North Atlantic where by 1850 they carried three-quarters of the emigrant traffic. British shipping was on the defensive in almost every trade and American tonnage assumed dimensions which very seriously threatened Britain's former position. Though the proportion of foreign trade carried in U.S. ships declined in subsequent years, America by 1860 had the largest fleet in the world, 5·3 million tons net against Britain's 4·7. It is true that some 2·7 million tons net were employed on the Great Lakes but the greater speed and carrying capacity of the American vessels partly compensated for the difference in tonnage employed in ocean commerce.

Though Britain still employed more tonnage in ocean commerce than any other country there is no doubt that the American fleet was vastly superior and, in view of the rapid advance made by that country in the first few decades of the nineteenth century, it appeared as if America and not Britain was destined to become the world's sea-power. Yet though British shipowners and shipbuilders had at first remained rather indifferent to the American challenge there are indications that by the late 1840s attempts were being made to recover lost ground. In fact Britain soon began to show a clear lead in the building of steam tonnage and by 1860 two-thirds of the steam tonnage employed in ocean commerce was owned in this country, whilst the Americans had about 14 per cent. Within the next decade the American mercantile marine had almost disappeared from the international scene and Britain was again in the ascendency. By 1874 the *Economist* was able to say "the steam mercantile navy of England is astonishingly pre-dominant, and there is no other State even beginning to approach us". The rapidity with which this transformation took place requires some explanation.

The relative stagnation of British shipping after 1815 has often been attributed to restrictive legislation which hampered individual initiative and protected British shipowners. The elaborate Navigation Code, passed in the seventeenth century to stimulate English shipping for defence pur-poses, still protected British shipowners from outside competition. The general aim of the Acts was to reserve the colonial and much of the foreign trade for British ships. Thus according to one authority British shipowners "long accustomed to handsome, if also rigid and cumbersome, protection from the Navigation Acts . . . tended to look to the government rather more than to their own enterprise for salvation". It is doubtful however if protection was as detrimental to British interests as is often suggested. Up to 1815, when Britain emerged from the wars without a rival, English shipping had developed more rapidly under the Navigation Acts than before and that expansion did not follow but outstripped the growth of commerce. Moreover, protection helped to increase rather than diminish Britain's share of world trade. On the other hand, after 1820 when the regulations were being liberalized by reciprocal treaties British shipping lost ground relatively and in the first decade after repeal (1849) failed to maintain its relative position. Whereas total British tonnage owned in 1861 was 52 per cent greater than in 1849, Norway and America had doubled the size of their fleets. In other words it seems improbable that British shipping would have benefited a great deal had protection been removed earlier. It was not the force of competition that laid the basis for Britain's eventual supremacy but the adoption of new methods of ship construction which conferred on British shipbuilders the advantages which America had hitherto held in this field. According to Harper "the theory that the invigorating influence of competition would have stimulated English ship-wrights to greater efficiency if they had not been stupefied by protection has little to support it. . . . English ingenuity eventually asserted itself in all fields of construction when steam and iron became the order of the day." On the other hand, it is possible that the Tonnage Laws (designed for taxation purposes) may have inhibited improvements in the design and construction of ships. Apparently these laws encouraged the building of short, deep, flat-bottomed vessels of low speed, "built by the mile and served out by the yard" rather than the larger, shallower and more speedy vessels which the Americans built. In 1836 new and more rational laws for tonnage measurement were instituted which gave more scope for improve-ments in design but unfortunately the legislation was not compulsory until 1854.

If the removal of protective legislation did not automatically produce the revival of British shipping, the American Civil War ensured the removal of Britain's leading competitor from the high seas. By 1865 the United States had sold over 750,000 tons of shipping to her competitors and American participation in the English carrying trade was much reduced. Altogether through losses and sales abroad the U.S. fleet was reduced by about 55 per cent and from that time onwards the American mercantile marine suffered an almost continuous decline until the twentieth century. After the Civil War America concentrated her attention on internal development and neglected her shipping industry. Yet again it would be misleading to lay too much stress on fortuitous circumstances. The repeal of the Navigation Code together with the collapse of Britain's most powerful rival undoubtedly made conditions more favourable for the advance of British shipping. But the most important long-term factor which made that revival possible was the change in the method of ship construction which allowed English shipowners to do without protection. As long as ships were built of wood and propelled by sail the Americans, and to a lesser extent the Scandinavians, held certain advantages. British shipbuilders were unable to construct wooden sailing ships as cheaply as their com-petitors since they lacked abundant supplies of good timber. At the turn of the century American building costs were some 25–30 per cent less than British costs. The adoption of new techniques however turned the balance in favour of Britain for "when the iron (or steel) steamship took the place of the sailing ship, British shipbuilders soon hopelessly outdistanced those of the United States. British iron manufacturing and engineering were further developed than those of any other country, and the trades were conveniently located so that shipbuilders could take full advantage of them when induced to shift from building sailing vessels to steamships". America was unable to compete with Britain in constructing iron hulls and by the 1860s American costs of construction were nearly one-third above those ruling in British yards. Thus it was technical changes in shipbuilding more than anything else which account for the rapid expansion of the British shipping industry.

2 Shipping technology

Technical progress which was to transform the shipping industry comprised two main features: first a change in the method of propulsion from sail to steam and secondly the use of new materials for shipbuilding, notably iron and later steel in place of wood. Though many experiments had been made with iron and steam in the early nineteenth century it was not until after 1850 that the new techniques were generally applied. In 1850 the majority of British ships were still very small vessels built of wood and driven by sail. Iron construction was neither common nor highly regarded and steam-ships were only used for certain classes of work. Apart from river, coastal and short sea trades the steamer was virtually confined to highly subsidized mail and passenger services to which the carriage of some fine cargo was purely incidental, and it was to be some time before the steamer was considered suitable for general deep sea trading. In fact many of the early steamship companies such as Cunard, P & O and the Pacific Steam Navigation Company could never have maintained operations but for the generous mail contracts given by the Admiralty. On the other hand, such endowments were not necessarily a benefit to the industry as a whole. Indeed one authority has argued that subsidies granted to Cunard injured the development of British shipping on the North Atlantic by deterring other enterprises and by enabling Cunard to club others out of the business who had more initiative. But although the Company was not a pioneer and refused to make improvements until forced to do so by competition, it is perhaps somewhat unjust to suggest as Meeker did, that Cunard "never originated anything but the art of securing mail contracts by private agreement on favourable terms".

The reliability and potentialities of the steamer were not of course in question. Successful voyages of paddle steamers across the Atlantic had proved beyond doubt the practical possibilities of steam for long distances. But at the stage of development reached in the late 1840s the steamer was far from being an economical proposition because of its high costs of construction and operation. The capital cost of each steamer in relation to the work it could do was in some cases as much as 50 per cent more than that of a sailing vessel. This would not have mattered so much had the cost of operating steam vessels not been so prohibitive. This was because in the early days of steam the volume of freight-earning capacity was sacrificed to the space required for engine, boilers and coal storage which on any but the shortest voyages practically monopolized the ship's carrying power. The marine engine was heavy in proportion to the power generated and it consumed inordinate quantities of fuel which meant there was little space left for the carriage of cargo. The first Cunard steamship, the *Britannia*, for example, had a total weight-lifting capacity of 865 tons, 640 of which were used for coal. Moreover, the earning capacity was further restricted by the fact that sometimes as much as half the total space in the ship was occupied by the engine. The coal problem was of course particularly acute on long distance voyages such as those to the Far East owing to the lack of coaling stations on route. As Blake points out in his history of *The Ben Line*, in some cases "The ordinary bunkers were not enough for the run from London to Singapore, and wooden pens had to be built upon the decks to hold reserves, even to the height of the boat-deck; and when these must be dipped into, all hands, the mates included, turned to with shovels and barrows."

It was clear therefore that if the steamship was to compete effectively with sail its costs of construction would have to be reduced and its efficiency raised appreciably. The most immediate problem was to increase the effective earning-capacity of the steamship and this could be done in one of two ways. Either the coal consumption and weight of machinery of the steamship could be reduced by introducing more efficient engines or the cargo carrying capacity could be raised by building much larger vessels. A partial solution to this complex problem lay in the use of iron instead of wood for ship construction. The construction of much stronger, lighter and eventually cheaper vessels was made possible by the adoption of iron as a shipbuilding material; an iron ship weighed about one quarter less than a wooden ship of similar dimensions. Even more important was the fact that iron enabled much larger vessels to be built and this was especially important as regards the steamer which had to carry large supplies of coal. Unfortunately iron was not widely adopted before the 1850s because of various difficulties. The iron hull of the ship was subject to fouling and corrosion which reduced the efficiency of the ship and shortened its life. An attempt to overcome this problem was made by building "composite" ships with wrought-iron frames and wood planking, though it was mainly the clipper sailing ships of the 1860s which were constructed in this way. The Admiralty and many shipowners were at first doubtful about the advantages of iron ships and the high cost and poor quality of some of the early ones deterred owners from ordering them. Moreover, most shipyards were accustomed to building in wood and were slow to adapt themselves to the use of iron which required different skills and techniques and far greater precision and accuracy of workmanship. There had been few improvements in shipyard practice and naval architecture in the eighteenth and early nineteenth centuries and the shipbuilders of the 1850s relied as much, if not more, on eyework and guesswork than rule or plan. Nevertheless, despite the initial difficulties in the way of the general adoption of iron, sufficient advance and experimentation had been made by the 1860s to prove the strength and seaworthiness of iron vessels, and the greater carrying capacity which could be achieved by using iron was clearly recognized. The most ambitious attempt to solve the problem of combining carrying power with bunker capacity on long voyages was made by Brunel when he built the *Great Eastern* (1854–7), a ship whose dimensions and weight were unparalleled. Commercially she was a failure but many valuable lessons in marine engineering were learnt from her construction. Though it was to be some years before vessels of that size were again built, the *Great Eastern* did demonstrate that large ships could be built of iron combining both strength and lightness, whilst the longitudinal method of building adopted served as a model on which later design and construction techniques were based. Furthermore, it provided valuable experience in working with new tools and new methods of handling materials, and in the problems involved in launching large ships.

By this time many of the difficulties relating to iron construction were being solved and henceforth iron construction became the order of the day. Yet despite the greater potentialities of iron construction the steamship still remained at a competitive disadvantage with sail, particularly as there was a considerable improvement in the efficiency of the sailing vessel at this time. Even by 1865 the steamship had not touched the fringe of the business engaged in the carriage of bulky commodities and British sailing tonnage was six times greater than that of steam. Nor could the steamship hope to compete until something was done to reduce operating costs and increase earning power. It was obvious therefore that this could only be accomplished if the iron ship was fitted with an efficient high-pressure marine engine together with adequate boilers, condensers and screw propellers which would allow vessels to carry large cargoes and travel economically, quickly and safely over long distances. Until a solution to this complex marine engineering problem was found the sailing ship remained the chief carrier of the world's commerce.

The first major advance in marine engineering came in the 1860s with the perfection of the compound engine which had been first applied successfully to a sea-going ship in 1854. The compound engine had in fact been patented as early as 1804 but for many years prejudice against the use of higher boiler pressures together with the absence of suitable boilers and surface condensers had held back further development in this field. It was not until the 1860s, by which time the technical difficulties had been largely surmounted, that it was possible to use a second cylinder in the engine. This enabled much higher pressures to be generated and as a result the amount of power derived from a given unit of steam was increased considerably. The efficiency of the new engine was further increased by the more widespread adoption of the screw propeller in place of the more vulnerable and clumsy paddle wheel. As a result of these improvements boiler pressures had been trebled or quadrupled by the early 1870s compared with twenty or thirty years earlier, whilst coal consumption was cut by about one half.[1] This had the combined effect of both reducing fuel costs and increasing freight-earning capacity. The reduction in coal consumption alone was an important economic gain since for the average tramp or cargo steamer fuel costs could be as much as 40 to 50 per cent of the total cost of a voyage. Such improvements made the steamer a much better commercial proposition for longer voyages and its future potentialities were revealed in 1865 when a Holt steamer, fitted with the compound engine, made a non-stop run of 8,500 miles from Liverpool to Mauritius. From that date the triumph of steam in the cargo as well as the passenger trade was only a matter of time.

Although by this time the steamship was beginning to make serious inroads into the traffic of sailing ships on some routes it did not really come into its own until the opening of the Suez Canal in 1869. This international waterway shortened the distance to India and the Far East by one half and one quarter respectively and made possible the economical operation of steamships on these routes. The main advantage over the Cape route was that steamers required far less coal for the journey and could bunker more frequently on route. Almost from the first the Canal became an all steamer route and it gave an enormous fillip to the adoption of the steamship and compound engine. In 1870, for the first time, the annual tonnage of steamships built in the U.K. exceeded that of sail (by as much as two to one) and only in two subsequent years did sail production exceed that of steam. During the 1870s the tonnage of steamships on the British register almost trebled. Many new steamship companies were formed whilst existing companies converted to steam and invaded some of the longer routes. Much of the high class cargo and some of the bulky commodities moving between India and Britain quickly passed into the hands of the steamers. The China tea trade, which was still dominated by the composite clippers when the Canal opened, had by the end of the 1870s been captured by steamships. By that time the steamer had obtained a practical monopoly in the carriage of mails, passengers and high class freight on all routes but the Australian, and some of the larger steamship lines such as P. & O., Cunard, White Star and Royal Mail were already flourishing institutions.

Nevertheless neither the compound engine nor the Suez Canal ended completely the life of sail. Not until 1883 did the tonnage of steam vessels on the U.K. register exceed that of sail and even by the end of the century sailing ships still accounted for almost one quarter of the British fleet. Many shipowners and merchants had an initial prejudice against steam despite its advantages. Moreover, though steamers were quicker, their freight charges were relatively higher which meant that the sailing ship remained a formidable competitor in handling cargo of low unit value and in all trades where speed was not an important factor. For many years

[1] In rough numerical terms steam pressures were raised from 25 lbs per square inch to over 100 whilst coal consumption was reduced from 4 or 5 lbs per horse power per hour to 2 lbs or less.

Q

after steam was in use on other routes sail continued to predominate on the Australian and South East Asian routes. As late as 1891 there were 77 sailing vessels loading wool in Sydney for London. The growth of bulk trade in grain and coal also gave sail a new lease of life. And indeed it was ironical that a number of sailing vessels ended their last days supplying the steam lines with coal at their outward bases. Despite the enormous increase in efficiency of the steamship it still consumed large quantities of coal which took up much valuable cargo space. Because of the space occupied by fuel and machinery the carrying capacity of the steamer before the introduction of the triple-expansion engine was about 16 per cent less than that of a sailing ship of similar dimensions. Thus running costs and freight charges still remained relatively high and could be undercut, particularly in times of depression, by sailing ships with their lower costs of operation. It should also be remembered that the sailing ship of the 1870s was vastly superior to that of thirty years earlier. It was faster, had double the space for cargo in proportion to its tonnage and could be manned and navigated by one half the number of men. Thus until further improvements were made in the efficiency of the marine engine the sailing ship could still offer an effective challenge to the steamship particularly in the carriage of cheap bulky commodities over long distances.

The perfection of the triple expansion engine finally signed the death warrant of sail. Its introduction was somewhat delayed however because it was not until the late 1870s that good cheap steel was available for the boilers. Iron-made boilers could not withstand the very high pressures which the triple-expansion engine possessed. In fact in 1874 the initial pressure of 150 lb per square inch was found to be too great for the iron-made boilers of the *Propontis* and consequently it had to be lowered to 90 lb. In 1887 the *Aberdeen*, built for George Thompson and Co., was fitted with similar engines as the *Propontis*, the difference being that the boilers were made of mild steel. On its first trip a pressure of 125 lb was reached and three years later 150 lb. By the early 1890s pressures of 200 lb per square inch were being achieved and fuel consumption was cut by nearly one half. Little more than one pound of coal was now consumed per horse-power compared with two or three in the compound engine and up to 10 lb. in the old low pressure single cylinder engine. The triple expansion engine not only effected a great reduction in fuel consumption and weight of the engine thereby enhancing carrying power, but it also permitted a speed which on average allowed a steamer to make three times as many voyages as a sailing ship within a given period of time. Moreover, further changes in marine technology, notably the turbine engine developed by C. A. Parsons, helped to secure the final predominance of steam. This engine made higher speeds possible than did the reciprocating engine and again cut down fuel consumption. Admiralty vessels ceased to be fitted with reciprocating engines after 1904 and in 1907 the Cunard line had the *Lusitania* and *Mauretania* fitted with turbines, after which they became the favoured form of propulsion for passenger ships. At the same time experiments were being made with the motor or diesel ship which eventually produced economies in ship operation as great, if not greater, as those brought about by steam. By 1914 however, only 3·4 per cent of the total world tonnage used diesel oil as a fuel and it was not until after the First World War that the marine internal combustion engine was adopted extensively for deep-sea propulsion duties.

3   The impact of technical progress

In the half century or so before 1914 the shipping industry passed through a technological revolution comparable to that which had occurred in many other British industries during the eighteenth and early nineteenth centuries. The transformation was most rapid from the 1870s onwards and within three to four decades the bulk of British shipping had been practically rebuilt. At the outbreak of war the British Mercantile Marine was the largest, the most up-to-date and the most efficient of all merchant navies in the world. Of the tonnage on the U.K. register in 1913, 85 per cent had been built since 1895, 68 per cent since 1900 and 44 per cent since 1905. The sailer and iron steamship had almost disappeared and had been replaced by steam vessels built of steel and driven by high-powered engines. The total number of sailing ships was still very large but their tonnage represented less than one tenth of the tonnage on the register. Most of them had finished their deep-sea life and were now employed in the coastal or short-sea trades. So great and far-reaching were the changes brought about by the new technology that it is difficult to summarize them in a few words. For technical progress not only produced remarkable changes in the size and carrying capacity of ships, in the costs of construction and operation and speed and safety of vessels, but it also transformed the whole structure of the shipping industry.

A remarkable increase took place in the size, speed and efficiency of British ships during this period. In 50 years or so boiler pressures were raised from 20 lb per square inch to 200 lb or more and coal consumption was reduced from around 9 or 10 lb per horse power per hour to nearly 1 lb in the early twentieth century. As a result the power of the marine engine increased by about 40 times. Until the middle of the nineteenth century a ship of 2,000 tons gross was considered to be a very large vessel even for the steamship lines, whereas by the early twentieth century the typical cargo steamer averaged around 7,500 tons. It was possible to build for less than twice the price of a typical clipper of the sixties a 10-knot cargo steamer carrying four times as much cargo and covering three times the mileage in a year's work. Generally speaking the annual carrying power of the modern steam cargo-boat was probably four times that of a sailing vessel of the same cargo capacity. The greater efficiency and reliability of the steamer enabled it to cover much more ground than the old sailing ship within a given period of time. In 1800 sailing ships were lucky if they made three voyages a year whilst by 1911 the average steamer made ten.

The most spectacular changes in size and speed of vessels took place of course in passenger liners. Transatlantic passenger steamers more than trebled in length, almost doubled in breadth and increased tenfold or more in displacement. The evolution of the Atlantic liner can be seen from comparing the dimensions and performance of three famous vessels.

Table 4 *Dimensions of the Atlantic liner*

Name of ship	1838 Sirius	1871 Oceanic	1907 Mauretania
Length (feet)	208	420	762
Gross tonnage	700	3,808	31,938
Horse power	320	3,000	70,000
Speed (knots)	7·5	14·75	25·0
Material	Wood	Iron	Steel
Engines	Paddle	Screw compound	Turbines Quadruple screws
Time taken to cross Atlantic	16 days	9 days 10 hrs 45 min.	4 days 10 hrs 41 min.

On average the travelling time across the Atlantic had been cut from 14 days in 1850 to 5 days and a few hours by the turn of the century. It was now possible to reach places like Australia and India within a matter of days instead of months when the sailing ship had been the only means of transport. At the same time the safety and comfort of passenger travel had increased enormously. Large modern liners with luxurious accommodation were very different from the uncomfortable and often unseaworthy emigrant "tubs" of the forties and fifties. By the late 1920s only 13 passengers a year were drowned on British ships compared with an annual average of 236 between 1847 and 1872. Part of this improvement was brought about by the growing body of legislation designed to improve the conditions of passenger travel, though some of the early steamship lines maintained a remarkable degree of safety from the very beginning. Apart from war disasters Cunard liners did not lose a single life or letter on the Atlantic route in the first hundred years of the company's existence.

Perhaps even more noteworthy was the rapid fall in ocean freight rates. Throughout the nineteenth century the cost of sea transport fell almost continuously but was particularly rapid in the latter half of the period, especially for bulky commodities. Atlantic grain freights fell from 8s. a quarter in 1863 to 1s. 3d. in 1901 whilst the cost of carrying a ton of textiles from Lancashire to Shanghai fell from 120s. to 40s. (1866–1913). Overall the reduction in freights was of the order of magnitude of 60 per cent in this period. Passenger fares tended to rise however, owing to the change in the nature of the service. The fall in the cost of operation of vessels was undoubtedly an important factor in bringing about the fall in freight rates. Between 1880 and 1900 for example, the cost of operating some of the Holt steamers was reduced by 73 per cent. On the other hand, too much importance can be attached to this factor. Part of the fall in freights in the latter half of the nineteenth century can be attributed to the secular (long-term) decline in prices, though it is not always easy to distinguish between cause and effect in this matter. Moreover, the downward shift in the freight curve not only reflected the impact of technical progress but also the increase in the utilization of existing ships. Improved techniques of navigation, better port facilities and the spread of the submarine telegraph—by 1887 there were more than 100,000 miles of cable laid—all helped to improve the efficiency of shipping by reducing the amount of time spent idle. Finally it can be argued that even if the shift to steam and steel had never been made these factors, together with the improvements which took place in the sailing vessels, would have brought about some reduction in the cost of sea transport though the change would not have been anywhere near so great.

The development of ocean shipping provided a considerable stimulus to economic development in general. In fact it probably had a greater impact than any other form of transport with the possible exception of the railways. By enabling the movement of large volumes of bulky commodities to take place at low cost it has been a powerful factor in unifying the world commodity markets. In the early days the carriage of such commodities over long distances was limited not so much by the lack of transport but because of its relatively high cost. For bulky commodities of low unit value such as grain, coal and timber transport costs might be more than the value of the commodity itself, in which case it would prove unprofitable to carry them unless there was an urgent demand. By the end of the nineteenth century, however, freight rates had fallen to one third or one quarter of their former level in some cases and hence formed a much smaller proportion of total costs. Low external transport costs raised the expected rate of return on primary products and this induced a rapid inflow of immigration and capital to the newer regions of the world. In other words, shipping had done much to open up large continental areas to the world market which had long been limited to the maritime fringes of these areas. As North says "it was water transport in which bulk shipment of commodities began, and it was the development of ocean shipping that was an integral aspect of the growing economic interdependence of the western world, the opening up of underdeveloped continents, and the promotion of settlement of empty lands. The declining cost of ocean transportation was a process of widening the resource base of the western world."

The British shipping industry played an important role in furthering the development of newer regions. For example, the rapid development of parts of Latin America in the latter half of the nineteenth century was due in no small part to British shipping and capital and the existence of a market in Britain for many of the products of that region. For much of the time the maritime contacts of that region were dependent on two or three major British shipping companies. The same could be said of the Far East where, according to Hyde, British shipping companies were instrumental in developing trade and fostering economic development. And if at times the profit motive was called in question, "let it be remembered", he says "that British shipping companies trading to the East brought, as a direct result of their own progress, stimulation of economic resources rather than stagnation, enlightenment and well-being rather than exploitation to those markets which they strove to serve."

It might well be argued of course that the recipients of the products of the primary producers stood to gain most from cheaper transport. New and expanding markets were opened up for the export of manufactured goods from the more industrialized countries of western Europe, whilst at the same time cheaper raw materials and foodstuffs improved the terms of trade of Britain and Europe and led to an improvement in the standard of living. In turn cheaper imports of primary products accelerated the redirection of resources from primary to manufacturing production in these latter countries. How far shipping was responsible for these changes and who the major beneficiaries were are obviously debatable points on which much ink has already been spilled. It would be out of place here to enter upon a discussion of such controversial issues. Suffice it to say that without cheap water transport world economic development would have been considerably less rapid.

As the world's leading maritime nation Britain undoubtedly stood to gain most. This country provided a large proportion of the world's shipping services down to 1914 and the international earnings from these services provided a welcome contribution to the balance of payments. Shipping credits were particularly important for they helped to cover the deficit on the merchandise trade account and/or provided further funds for investment abroad. Net shipping earnings rose from an annual average of £18·68 million between 1851–55 to £60·32 in 1881–85 and to a peak of just over £100 million in the years just before the First World War. In fact they formed the most important source of invisible earnings for almost two-thirds of a century and in a number of years they covered one half or more of the merchandise trade deficit.

Finally the shipping industry made a direct contribution to the growth of the British economy. The demand for ships, docks, warehouses, offices, etc. created increasing employment and investment opportunities for the British public. Apart from domestic building construction, shipbuilding constituted one of the largest sources of home investment, accounting at times for as much as one fifth to one sixth of the total gross fixed capital formation. Obviously it is impossible to measure the full repercussions of this investment, which indirectly generated a demand for a wide range of products and stimulated the expansion of many other sectors of the economy, particularly the iron and steel and marine engineering industries. Nor does it take into account the money spent on ancillary facilities such as ports and docks, investment in which was high throughout the nineteenth century.

4 Port and dock development

Indeed but for comparable developments in port facilities it would have been impossible for shipping to have functioned effectively. Though substantial improvements had been made during the industrial revolution few ports by the early nineteenth century possessed much dock and warehouse accommodation and certainly none that was adequate to meet the enormous requirements of the later nineteenth century. The great increase in the size of individual vessels and in the amount of tonnage entering the ports necessitated the provision of dock and warehouse accommodation, and loading and discharging equipment on a scale hitherto unknown, as well as suitable road and rail transport around the ports. Statistics for the port of London illustrate the scale on which accommodation was required. The total tonnage engaged in foreign trade entering London rose from 777,858 tons in 1820 to 4,089,366 in 1870 and to about 10 million tons in 1901, whilst the average size of vessels rose from around 200 tons in 1820 to 974 in 1901. The average size of the vessels using the port was really much greater than these figures suggest since the inclusion of the numerous voyages of small short-trade steamers has the effect of reducing the average appreciably. Thus in 1838 the largest vessel which the port had to accommodate was the *British Queen* of 2,016 tons gross, but by 1900 the *Celtic* belonging to the Oceanic Steam Navigation Company was more than ten times that size (20,904 tons). But it was not merely in terms of scale that port facilities had to match shipping. Each port had to be adapted to cater for the particular type of traffic which used it. In London and Liverpool, for example, a whole series of specialized docks had to be built equipped to deal with the wide range of commodities which entered these ports. On the other hand, some ports were much more specialized; in South Wales it was the coal export trade which largely determined the pattern of development, whereas in the case of Southampton special facilities had to be provided for large passenger vessels. Or alternatively, some ports such as Bristol were essentially receiving centres for imports which required different handling facilities from those at Cardiff, for example, where imports amounted to only about one quarter of the export traffic of the port.

Perhaps two other features are worthy of note. In the first place there was

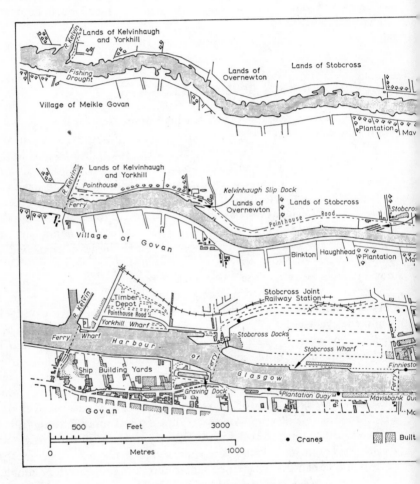

Map 18   *The development of the River Clyde: 1800, 1840, 1876*

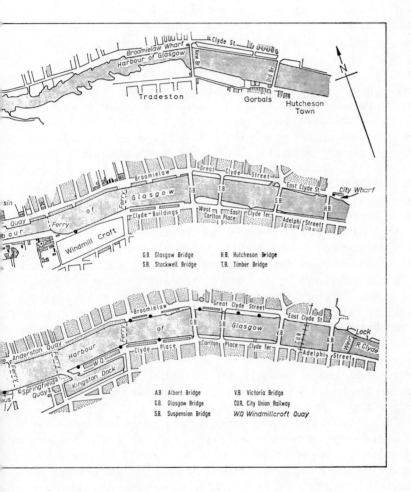

G.B. Glasgow Bridge   H.B. Hutcheson Bridge
S.B. Stockwell Bridge   T.B. Timber Bridge

A.B. Albert Bridge   V.B. Victoria Bridge
G.B. Glasgow Bridge   C.U.R. City Union Railway
S.B. Suspension Bridge   *W.Q. Windmillcroft Quay*

no proper planning and co-ordination of port development in the nineteenth century. This is perhaps hardly surprising in view of the variety of authorities responsible for port improvements. Municipal authorities, private companies, public trusts and the railways were all concerned in one way or another with the development of the ports. Such dispersion of control not only made co-ordinated activity between the ports difficult to achieve but in cases where a number of private companies were allowed to carry out work at the same port, as in London, fierce rivalry often ensued which tended to retard progress. However, three distinct trends in the evolution of control are apparent. One was the evolution of the private undertaking into the public trust. This occurred along the Tyne and the Tees in the 1850s and eventually in London in 1909 when the Port of London Authority was established. The second trend was the formation of the public trust in place of municipal control, notably in Liverpool and Glasgow in the middle of the nineteenth century. Lastly there was the progressive entry of the railways into the port business as for example at Grimsby, Barrow, Hull, Cardiff and Southampton. In fact, eventually the railways acquired control of a large number of ports and became one of the largest dock owners in the country.

The second important feature is that the incidence of port development was very uneven compared with the seventeenth and eighteenth centuries. Generally speaking it was the larger ports which received most attention. This of course is more or less what one would expect. Many of the smaller ports, like King's Lynn, Boston, Whitby and Whitehaven, declined in importance as the railway and the great ship brought a growing concentration of the country's trade around the already established centres of commerce and industry. By the early twentieth century 75 per cent or more of the total foreign trade (exclusive of coal and iron) was handled by 12 major ports. It was places such as London, Liverpool, Hull, Glasgow and Bristol where the greatest activity occurred, for they alone were able to offer the facilities required by the shipowners and traders.

The way in which the ports responded to the increased demands made upon them can best be illustrated by one or two examples. London deserves attention not only because it remained the country's largest commercial centre but also because it provides an excellent example of how difficult it was to keep pace with the growing volume of shipping using the port. Before the nineteenth century the port of London was in an extremely unsatisfactory state. The trade of the port had trebled during the course of the eighteenth century but little had been done to accommodate it apart from the provision of one small wet dock. The result was a great deal of unnecessary congestion and delay. "There was accommodation for 545 ships in the Pool, but as many as 775 were commonly found there, with sometimes as many as another 1,000 vessels thronging Limehouse Reach towards the lower Pool" (Bird). This position encouraged the promotion of a number of private dock companies and between 1800 and 1828 six docks, East and West India, London, Commercial, Surrey and St Katharine's were built in London. For a time the new port system served its purpose well but with the growing activity in London especially after 1830 the dock and warehouse accommodation soon became inadequate and further additions were necessary. Unfortunately, after the completion of St Katharine's Docks in 1828 few extensions or improvements were made for some twenty years partly because intense rivalry between the companies leading to rate reductions had seriously impaired their revenues.

The opening of two new docks, the Victoria in 1855 and the Millwall in 1870, only served to increase the competition since both were built by new companies. By this time however the companies were being forced to amalgamate. In 1864 the Commercial Docks in Rotherhithe were extended and their control amalgamated with that of the adjacent Surrey Docks. In the same year three separate dock undertakings, London, St Katharine's and Victoria, amalgamated to form the London and St Katharine Docks Company which eventually, in 1880, built the $1\frac{3}{4}$-mile Royal Albert Docks to accommodate the large iron ships. The East and West India Dock Company replied by building the Tilbury Docks in 1886. Despite amalgamation there were still four distinct dock companies none of which was in a position to raise the capital required for the drastic reconstruction of the port's facilities which the rapid development of ocean shipping made imperative if London was to remain the major port of the world. The port was already said to be losing trade owing to the failure to improve its facilities, and in a series of articles in 1894 *The Times* referred to "the deplorable and incontrovertible fact that no port of any considerable size in the United Kingdom is so grossly mismananaged as the Port of London". Larger docks and more warehouse accommodation were urgently required and ship-owners were demanding the deepening of the channels of the lower Thames. Divided control of the port and the weak financial position of the companies rendered this impossible, though it hardly required a full Royal Commission to prove something which had been known for years. The Commission in its report of 1902 recommended the setting up of a public trust to take over all the docks and control of the Thames tidewater. These suggestions were carried out by the Port of London Act of 1908. A Port of London Authority was established to take over the management of the entire dock area, consisting of a land area of 2,700 acres and a water area of 750 acres, together with 69 miles of tidal river from Teddington to the sea. Almost at once the new authority began to set about the urgent task of improving the port's facilities.

Liverpool's record was much better than that of London, possibly because the port remained under fairly unified control throughout the nineteenth century. Until the establishment of the Mersey Docks and Harbour Board in 1857 the management of the port was in the hands of the Corporation of Liverpool. Whatever shortcomings municipal control entailed the Corporation could not be accused of neglecting its duties with regard to dock

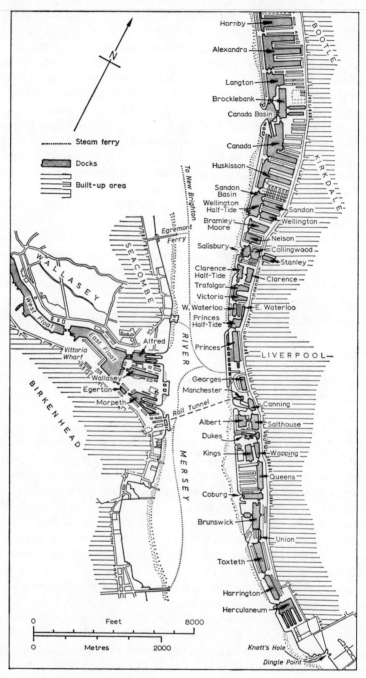

Map 19   *Liverpool docks, 1900*

accommodation. Liverpool in fact had one of the first wet docks in the world, built in 1715 by adapting the mouth of the old Pool. After 1750 the dock system was extended rapidly to meet the growing needs of the port's trade and shipping during the industrial revolution. Between 1760 and 1830 the Council's Dock Committee secured the construction of eight new docks which provided a fivefold increase in the dock space available. Even this however was not enough to satisfy requirements and by the early 1820s demand had already exceeded supply. Within the next twenty-five years the tonnage of shipping entering the Mersey trebled and much new accommodation was required. The Dock Committee had not however been slow to anticipate the demand for more docks. In 1824 the famous engineer Jesse Hartley had been given the task of preparing plans for more docks. He proved to be one of the most enterprising and successful dock contractors of the day and altogether he supervised the building of no less than eighteen docks, the last of which was completed in 1855. (*See Map 19*, p. 252.)

Despite the Council's strenuous activities in providing new dock facilities the management of the port came in for much criticism during the first half of the nineteenth century, which eventually led to the formation of a public trust. Many shipowners and traders complained that there was insufficient accommodation for their ships and goods. In some cases this was true. The Brunswick Dock for example, which had been built in 1832 to cater for the timber trade, soon became inadequate and vessels were delayed for an average of 30 days before entering the dock. Warehouse accommodation too was often inadequate and as a result cargo had to be left on the quays, which caused congestion and slowed down work. Another matter for concern was the Mersey channel itself. The Corporation it seems had devoted insufficient attention to the task of dredging, widening and deepening the river with the result that it was becoming increasingly difficult for some of the larger vessels to navigate it successfully. Vessels drawing up to 19 feet of water were unable to dock immediately they arrived and those drawing up to 24 feet could enter only on a very few days of the year. During the first six months of 1857, 112 vessels had been held up in the river through lack of sufficient depth of water and 225 were delayed through shortage of berthing space.

It would appear therefore that the port's customers had plenty of reason to complain. As a result of the growing dissatisfaction with the port's administration the Corporation's control was gradually weakened. Until the early nineteenth century the port was managed exclusively by the municipal officials but in 1826 the dock ratepayers (shipowners and merchants) managed to secure representation on the Dock Committee. In that year the Committee was reconstituted to include 15 members of the Council and a further eight elected by the ratepayers; the chairman continued to be appointed by the Council which retained the final right of veto. Though these changes did not seriously impair the Council's power the breach had been made and it was only a matter of time before the Council was dislodged from ultimate control. The strength of the opposition grew in the following years and further concessions were demanded. In part the opposition to the Council's control of the docks was associated with the question of Town Dues since a large part of the port's revenue was directed into the municipal coffers through the imposition of these dues. The Corporation was unable to satisfy its critics and eventually the pressure of outside interests forced the Council to relinquish all control over the port. In 1857 an Act of Parliament sanctioned the establishment of the Mersey Docks and Harbour Board, the first public trust for docks in England. The Board, consisting of 28 members, of which 24 were elected by the ratepayers, became responsible not only for the maintenance of the harbour and docks but also for conservancy services such as dredging, salvage, lighting, buoyage and general maintenance of the channel approaches.

Almost at once the new authority embarked on a policy of improving and extending the accommodation of the port. The first work undertaken on the Liverpool side was the construction of the Canada, Herculaneum and Waterloo docks in the 1860s; at Birkenhead, on the other side of the river, the Morpeth dock was extended and three new docks built. But despite all this new accommodation the growth of trade soon made further extensions necessary and so ambitious plans were drawn up to meet future requirements. These plans, the estimated cost of which was in the region of £4 million, covered the construction of five new docks and extensions to two existing ones as well as building a boundary wall around the dock estate itself. They were finally completed in 1888 with the opening of the Toxteth Dock. But even as this work was in progress the increasing size and draught of vessels called for yet further accommodation. In 1898 therefore, Parliamentary permission was sought for further improvements at the north end and for the remodelling of the southern system at an estimated cost of £3·5 million. The investment included new branches and more deep water quayage and two new docks at Birkenhead. Finally, much widening and deepening of existing docks was carried out. Before this work was finished plans had already been drawn up and sanctioned for the building of the famous Gladstone system of docks, which were to become the largest and best equipped in Europe. Work on this project was delayed however, and it was not until 1927 that it was finally completed. By 1914 the Board had provided Liverpool with one of the best systems of docks in the country and few complaints seem to have been made about the facilities offered. Throughout the entire period the authority had consistently followed a policy of constructing docks on a scale larger than was actually required at the time of construction and as a result Liverpool was able to accommodate practically any vessel whatever its size which chanced to sail up the Mersey. Moreover, the Board had not neglected its other duties of dredging and widening the approaches and generally maintaining the channel in good order. In all, the trust had spent £31·8 million by 1914 on new docks, and harbour and river improvements. During the period 1858 to 1908 the area of the dock estate had increased from 880 acres to 1171, the water area had more than doubled (207 to 418 acres) and the length of quayage had been increased by 12 miles. The success of the Board's policy can be judged from the use which was made of the port. In 1908 nearly 16 million tons of shipping entered the Mersey estuary compared with less than 4½ million sixty years earlier. Few ports could match this remarkable record of achievement.

Glasgow's problem was rather different from that of either London or Liverpool. (*See Map 18*, pp. 248–9.) Until the Clyde channel was deepened it was impossible for ships of any size to reach the city. The citizens of Glasgow were determined however not to remain for ever in the shadow of Port Glasgow further west, and from 1792 onwards strenuous efforts were made to dredge and deepen the Clyde so as to allow ships of any size to use it. Between 1770 and 1857 no less than £2·7 million was spent on river and harbour improvements and by the time the Clyde Navigation Trust took over the administration of the river and harbour in 1858, "Glasgow had created a river out of a ditch". By this time the river could accommodate most vessels and Glasgow city was already a flourishing port of call and an important centre for shipbuilding. The effect of making the Clyde navigable can be seen by the extensive trade handled in the city; by 1856 the revenue collected by the Crown from Glasgow's trade amounted to almost £2·8 million whereas prior to the river improvements it had been practically negligible.

When the Clyde Trustees took over, their main task was to provide suitable accommodation for the vessels using the port. As yet there was no proper dock accommodation except for one small private dock belonging to Tod & Macgregor. Additional quays were therefore built on both sides of the river and in 1867 the first public dock, the Kingston Dock, was opened. This was followed by a whole series of improvements and new docks including the first public graving dock at Plantation (1875), the Queen's Dock opened in 1880, the Prince's, 1897, and the Rothesay Dock completed in 1907. During the last quarter of the nineteenth century the harbour area was more than doubled and by 1900 Glasgow had a water area of 240 acres and 11 miles of quayage. Altogether up to 1914 some £10 million had been spent on river facilities and harbour improvements, a sum which was well invested. By their effort the citizens of Glasgow and later their trustees had made Glasgow one of the leading commercial and shipbuilding centres of the country.

Glasgow, Liverpool and London were not the only ports where extensive construction was being carried out during the nineteenth century. The same story could be told for a dozen other ports which were actively developing their facilities to cater for the needs of modern vessels. The dock area of Hull (the third British port) for example, was almost trebled in the period 1863 to 1885. Southampton was expanding rapidly as a passenger port, a development which was materially assisted by the London & South Western Railway Company after its acquisition of the docking facilities in the early 1890s. The great expansion of the coal export trade necessitated heavy investment in dock facilities in South Wales and North East England and here the railways played a prominent part in development. Some of the smaller ports too were following a similar pattern of progress though on a less elaborate scale. Grimsby, for example, was rapidly developed as a grain and fish port in the latter half of the nineteenth century with the assistance of the Manchester, Sheffield & Lincolnshire Railway. Similarly the Furness Railway was instrumental in developing the docks at Barrow.

Some idea of the magnitude of the investments involved can be gained from the following figures. Altogether some £153 million (at 1900 prices) were invested in docks and harbours of Great Britain between 1860 and 1914, an average of £2·8 million per annum. Investment tended to move in fairly long waves with heavy concentrations in the 1880s and early 1900s when port investment was dominated very much by activity in the London basin.[1] The accumulated investment in port facilities was substantial in some cases. By 1938 Liverpool had invested £45 million, the Clyde Navigation Trust £12 million and Bristol £9 million. At the same time the railways had contributed £66 million to the development of Britain's ports.

Whether these large sums were spent wisely or whether more should have been spent is of course another matter. It can be argued that some of the money was wasted due to the lack of planning. London provides a typical example of the way in which a lack of co-operation between rival dock companies could lead to a mis-allocation of investment resources. Another instance is the case of Barrow where, in an attempt to rival Liverpool, the Furness Railway spent £2¼ million on docks which were never fully utilized. There is also evidence to suggest that, despite the large investments made, facilities at many ports still lagged behind requirements by the early twentieth century. The President of the Chamber of Shipping, W. J. Pirrie, complained that dock and harbour authorities had not assisted shippers as much as they could have by anticipating the requirements of trade. This was certainly true in the case of London and, as we have seen, it was one of the main reasons why the P.L.A. was set up. The Tyne dock too was said to be completely inadequate and wherever possible shipowners avoided it. How far this state of affairs was general throughout the country is impossible to say. But according to Sir Douglas Owen, the leading authority on the subject, the position was far from satisfactory. He believed that in general "the country's docks are obsolete. They are for the most part of insufficient or barely adequate depth, while some of their locks are too short, and no longer suited in the slope of their walls, to the box-like sides of the modern vessels. Their quays are often not wide enough and the sheds which stand on them are of insufficient area." Only further research will tell us whether these assertions were correct or not.

[1] Total investments by decades are as follows: 1860–9 £21·5 m., 1870–9 £23·7 m., 1880–9 £33·2m., 1890–9 £29·4 m., 1900–9 £35·5 m. These figures were kindly supplied by Dr. C. H. Feinstein of Cambridge University. They also include a small amount of canal investment.

9

The organization and profits
of British shipping

1 Organization and finance

Perhaps even more remarkable than the physical growth of the mercantile
marine in the nineteenth century were the changes which took place in
the structure and organization of the shipping industry. In fact the organization of British shipping altered more radically in this period than at any
other time. The size of ships and individual fleets grew rapidly, the ubiqui-
tous general trader was replaced by specialized vessels and the method of
ship ownership and operation changed significantly especially in the latter
half of the century. To a large extent this transformation was brought about
by the expansion of trade and the accompanying improvements in shipping
technology which gradually rendered the older forms of organization and
operation obsolete.

In the eighteenth and early nineteenth centuries ships could hardly be
classed as liners, tramps and tankers as they are today since such distinctive
types of vessels did not then exist. The small firm or partnership often with
trading connections, and the single-owner undertaking operating perhaps
one or two vessels provided the bulk of the world's shipping services.
Probably most British ships at this time were used to serve the requirements
of their owners. It has been found, for example, that the majority of
Liverpool's sailing vessels were owned by merchants who imported goods
on their own account in ships belonging to them. Men such as John Gladstone, Charles Tayleur, John Bibby, the Brocklebanks and Sir John Tobin
were both merchants and shipowners, but shipowning tended to be an
ancillary or complementary function to the main business which was
trading. Shipowning as a specific occupation did exist of course; Duncan
Dunbar of London was one of the wealthiest and most prominent of the
individual shipowners of the early nineteenth century. He built up a large
fleet and some of his vessels were maintained on regular services. But

R

generally speaking this was the exception rather than the rule. The majority of ships which were used specifically for earning freight money were hired out by the voyage or for a period of time to load cargo and carry it between such places as the charterer required. These were the famous general traders and their counterparts can be found in the tramps of the twentieth century. There were very few regular services operating to a fixed schedule between specific ports, apart from the constant traders or East Indiamen, since the volume of trade on any one route was usually insufficient or too irregular to justify the provision of such services, whilst the sailing ship was generally too erratic and unreliable in its movements to maintain them. In any case, since more often than not merchants appear to have provided their own ships for carrying cargoes, there was probably little immediate demand for the provision of regular liner services.

With the rapid growth in the volume of trade and passenger traffic after the Napoleonic Wars it became increasingly possible to establish more regular services on some routes, especially on those which were favoured by Government mail contracts, such as the North Atlantic. Many of the early steamship companies, such as Cunard, P & O, Royal Mail and the Pacific Steam Navigation Company, established regular scheduled services from the beginning of their careers, though it is as well to remember that the embryonic liner services of these companies were often only maintained by means of the generous mail contract subsidies, since the early steamships were very uneconomical to run. Naturally the greater reliability and speed of the steamer encouraged the formation of regular services though it is a mistaken notion to assume that steam alone created the distinction between the liner and the tramp vessel.[1] The famous Yankee packets and clipper ships of the middle decades of the nineteenth century maintained fairly regular services on the North Atlantic and Australian routes. Moreover it should not be forgotten that in the last glorious days of sail many of the crack vessels were liners or at least regular traders and some of them belonged to substantial fleets.

During the middle decades of the nineteenth century there was a gradual trend away from casual ownership and operation of vessels by merchants and individuals towards larger undertakings which specialized in shipping exclusively. Most of the early steamship companies of the 1830s and 1840s were of this nature and as we have seen they maintained regular liner services. Some of these companies, which were eventually destined to dominate the British liner fleet, grew rapidly in the prosperous mid-Victorian period. The Pacific Steam Navigation Company, which was

[1] The term "liner service" often leads to some confusion owing to the fact that many shipping companies are referred to as "Lines". Essentially a liner service provides a fixed service, at regular intervals, between specified ports for the carriage of both cargo and passengers. Although many liner vessels carry both types of traffic there is a fair degree of specialization between passenger and cargo liner services. Tramp vessels, on the other hand, run to no fixed schedule. They are hired for a voyage or a fixed period of time to carry (mainly) cargo wherever the charterer may specify.

started on a very modest scale in 1840, had by the early 1870s a fleet of
119,870 tons gross and an authorized capital of no less than £4 million.
But for the most part the majority of British ships at this time were still
owned and operated by individuals with mercantile connections; shipowning was by no means a specialized business and many owners continued
to hold business interests outside the field. The old firm of Brocklebanks
for example, were merchants, shipbuilders and shipowners and it was
some time before they concentrated exclusively on the latter of these
functions. Similarly the Bibby family found their interests in iron, copper
and brass more pressing than shipping activities and it was not until 1864
that the two sides of the business became independent of each other. The
Rathbones of Liverpool provide another good example of the dual function
of trading and shipowning undertaken at this time. Primarily the Rathbones
were merchants who ran ships for their own use but in time they developed
a lucrative business acting as shipping agents and hiring out their ships to
other traders. Nor was it uncommon for shipping concerns to grow out of
trading interests established after the middle of the century. The famous
Booth Line of Liverpool can be traced back to the trading venture started
by Alfred Booth in 1863. Nevertheless there was an increasing tendency in
these years towards the separation of the mercantile and shipowning
functions of the business. This trend was greatly accelerated in the latter
half of the century, and by the early twentieth century few of the large or
medium sized shipping concerns were engaged directly in trading on their
own account. Perhaps the main exception to this general rule was in the
timber trade. Up to 1860 at least, and possibly beyond, timber importers,
in order to satisfy their own needs, increased their participation in shipping
and by the middle of the nineteenth century practically all the leading
Liverpool timber importers had substantial shipowning interests.

Though by the middle of the 1860s Britain and Europe were probably
linked with every other continent by regular shipping services, the greater
part of the world's commerce was still carried by the general trader since
the steamship had barely touched the fringe of the trade in bulky commodities by that time. It was only in the last two or three decades of the century
that the differentiation between liner and tramp services was completed.
The rapid expansion of trade together with perfection of the steamship
made possible the extension of liner services by companies owning large
fleets. Liner services of course were most prominent in the field of passenger
traffic and it is not therefore surprising to find development was most
rapid on the North Atlantic route where passenger traffic was heaviest.
In the 1870s Thomas Ismay's White Star Line was a pioneer in providing
fast ships with luxurious accommodation for passengers and in the next
few decades a network of regular liner services for both cargo and passengers
was established by British companies to many areas. During these years an
increasing proportion of trade was carried by liners; between 1870 and 1914
the bulk of the trade of Liverpool passed from ships engaged in general

carrying trade of the world chartered by merchants for particular voyages into the hands of regular lines having sailings at fixed dates to specific ports. On routes other than the Atlantic, cargo liners, built specifically for carrying regular cargo, were more common since passenger traffic was not as predominant as on the Atlantic route. By 1914 the large liner companies such as P & O, Cunard, Union-Castle, Royal Mail and White Star were household names and had become famous throughout the world for their regular and reliable services.

The modern British shipping industry was not of course built up solely by the great liner companies. Much of the heavy, dirty work was done, by the "blunt-nosed tramps that prowl the seven oceans for profitable employment" (Gregg). With the reduction in operating costs and increase in freight-earning capacity during the latter half of the nineteenth century the steam tramp rapidly replaced the general sailing trader as a conveyor of bulky commodities, particularly those of a seasonal nature which were unsuitable for liner services. The tramp was a cargo vessel, often chartered to third parties for the carriage of one or two commodities between specified points. Such vessels were tied to no specific trade or route and were free to go anywhere and carry anything which would pay. They formed a world pool of tonnage on which all countries could draw to meet the immediate needs of the moment. By the turn of the century tramp ships were predominant in the movement of the great seasonal cargoes of rice, cotton, wheat and wool to Europe whilst on the outward journey from Britain their holds were filled with coal. Coal exports gave British tramp shipping a decided advantage for no other country possessed a combination of two-way traffic to such a marked degree. From the 1880s onwards what might be called a specialized class of tramp developed to cater for specific needs such as the carriage of oil, frozen meat, iron ore and lumber. In 1880 the first shipment of frozen meat from Australia was landed in London and by 1914 about 200 specialized steamers with a carrying capacity of 15 million carcases were engaged in the frozen meat trade. These years also saw the birth of the oil tanker. At first oil was carried in barrels until it was discovered that bulk carrying in specially designed tankers saved nearly $1\frac{1}{4}d$. a gallon in transport costs. After this it was difficult to keep pace with the demand for tankers and by 1912 there were over 300 such steamers on Lloyd's Register for the carriage of oil in bulk.

Though liners and tramps provided two distinct services it is not always possible to make a precise differentiation since many vessels were frequently used interchangeably. In times of scarce tonnage tramps might be chartered by liner companies, and less frequently by industrial concerns, to perform regular sailings. Occasionally the large liner companies, such as P & O in the 1880s, built a few tramp steamers for their own use. Conversely liner companies, particularly cargo liners catering for the transport of manufactured goods, might take on berth cargoes at cut rates to fill space on the homeward voyage. In 1924 for example, 80 per cent of the grain exported from New York moved in liner vessels. For this reason it is difficult to classify tonnage exactly into specified categories. Nevertheless it does seem that in the past the importance of tramp operations has been overstated partly because many regular cargo boats were placed in this class. At one time it was thought that by 1914 tramp vessels dominated world trade and accounted for some 60 per cent of the total U.K. tonnage. More refined estimates show however that, in the case of Britain at least, liner services predominated by the early twentieth century. At the most, tramp vessels including tankers accounted for no more than one third of the British fleet whilst the remainder consisted of cargo, passenger and mixed liner vessels.

The change in the pattern of services was accompanied by a growing divergence in the size of individual fleets between tramp and liner owners. In 1850 there was little to choose between one undertaking and another; most of them including the regular steamship lines were small, operating perhaps half a dozen vessels and often not more than a couple. Sixty years later there was a marked difference in the size of companies. They ranged from the enormous passenger liner companies owning up to a million tons gross in some cases down to the small tramp steamer companies with only a few vessels. Generally speaking passenger liner companies were larger than either cargo liner or tramp companies. In 1912 24 British passenger liner companies operated 844 ships of 4,182,828 tons gross and had a paid-up capital of £22·2 million. In contrast nearly 100 cargo-boat companies with a paid-up capital of £10·3 million owned only 514 vessels of 1,746,609 tons gross. Variations in size were not determined solely by differences in the nature of the traffic or type of service offered. Many of the large companies had started off as very small concerns and the expansion of their fleets reflected the steady increase in trade. The fleet of Holt's Blue Funnel Line was increased from 29,000 to 325,000 tons gross between 1884 and 1907 to cater for an increase of nearly 600,000 tons of cargo, whilst the fleet of the Booth Steamship Company quadrupled within the space of 15 years (1895–1910) for similar reasons. Moreover, the existence of many small undertakings was an indication of the ease with which new firms could enter the tramp trade.

In the last couple of decades before 1914 the rapid increase in the size of many liner companies was brought about partly by a grouping or fusion of interests in the shipping world. Combinations among shipping companies were a common feature during this period and in part reflected the tendency towards larger units in industry in general. Intense competition between lines was another factor leading to a fusion of interests whilst at the same time shipowners were anxious to increase their strength and resources through amalgamation in order to meet the challenge of the large shipping groups which were growing up abroad, particularly in Germany and later in America where the formation of the International Mercantile Marine Company in 1902 was seen as a direct threat to British interests. The concentration movement began in earnest towards the end of the century. In 1900 two well-established lines, the Union Steamship Company and the Castle Line, merged their interests after a period of intense rivalry. Two years later Blue Funnel acquired a controlling interest in China Mutual, their former competitors in the eastern trade. During the following decade most of the larger liner companies, such as P & O, Cunard, Royal Mail and Furness Withy, were rapidly absorbing other companies. Cunard acquired a large interest in the Anchor Line (1911), Furness Withy secured Houlder Bros. (1911) and the Warren Line (1912), whilst in 1914 P & O made the largest catch of all when it amalgamated with the British India Steam Navigation Company. The combined group had a capital of £15 million and controlled nearly one and a quarter million tons gross of shipping. Perhaps most spectacular of all however was the Royal Mail grouping. In 1903 Sir Owen Philipps, already an established figure in the shipping world, became chairman of the Royal Mail Steam Packet Company, the oldest British steam line trading to South America. He rapidly raised the line to pre-eminence in the shipping world and brought many other companies into the Royal Mail group. The acquisitions included such notable concerns as Elder Dempster, the Pacific Steam Navigation Company, Union-Castle and the Glen, Nelson and Shire lines. Philipps was familiarly known as the "Colossus of the Seas" for by 1914 he controlled one of the largest shipping groups in the world. The amalgamation movement was accelerated during and soon after the First World War when many firms were acquired at inflated prices. By the early 1920s about one quarter of the U.K. tonnage was owned or controlled by one of the Big Five groups of P & O, Royal Mail, Cunard, Ellerman and Furness Withy whilst almost three quarters of the British liner tonnage was owned by seven large shipping companies. As we shall see this grouping, together with the conference system, provided a serious barrier to reform in later years.

The changes in the structure of the shipping industry were of course accompanied by certain changes in the pattern of ownership and methods of finance. To operate a regular liner service successfully, particularly for passenger traffic, a large number of vessels are required together with a fairly elaborate business organization the capital cost of which is likely to be heavy. In contrast the tramp owner or even the small cargo liner company can maintain services with only a few vessels at a relatively small capital cost. This has meant that not only has the scale of operations of the liner companies increased much more rapidly than that of the tramp owners but also the method of ownership and finance has differed somewhat. In the early days of steam when most undertakings were comparatively small the ability to expand operations was limited to the amount of finance which could be raised from the individual participants in the business. Most vessels were owned by individuals or partnerships, or by small syndicates taking shares in different ships, the management of the vessels being entrusted to a member of the group with special qualifications. The high risk factor involved tended to encourage a dispersion of ownership and hence the value of a ship was divided into a certain number of shares the most common denominators being 8ths or 64ths. In some cases all the shares of a ship might be owned by the same person or partnership but as a rule it was more common for one person or concern to hold shares in a number of different ships. Charles Tayleur of Liverpool both as an individual and as a member of his firm had a share interest in no less than 24 different ships between 1815 and 1835 whilst the *Druid*, a Liverpool vessel built in 1823, was owned by as many as 36 different people. Usually, however, the number of people with a share interest in the same ship did not exceed half a dozen and in many cases was probably a good deal less. The money to build the vessels was drawn largely from inhabitants living in the vicinity of the ports and since most vessels were owned by merchants or traders it seems plausible to assume that the profits of trading provided the major source of finance for the construction of ships.

This pattern of ownership was probably adequate for the early nineteenth century when the scale of operations was relatively small and when most of the finance for the construction of ships was provided by wealthy merchants engaged in business around the ports. And indeed the relative ease with which capital could be raised locally by private negotiation probably accounts for the continuation of the system far into the nineteenth century. In the middle of the nineteenth century many of the steamship companies and practically all the undertakings running sailing ships used this method. But with the rapid increase in the size and cost of fleets the 64th principle or variants thereof gradually became unworkable for steamers of any size. The amount of capital required was beyond the resources of a few individuals situated in a given region and since the value of each share tended on average to rise as ships became more costly to build, it was found increasingly difficult to raise the necessary capital. The shares of the Clyde Screw Steam Packet Company (formed in 1853) were as much as £400 each and shares of this value could hardly be expected to attract the investor with only a small amount of capital at his command. The question of finance apart, the 64th system was unsatisfactory; not only did it mean that each vessel had to be dealt with as a separate entity but it also led to an unnecessary fragmentation of ownership which was particularly unsuitable for firms engaged solely in the business of shipping. Even merchant shipowners found the 64th share system unsatisfactory as their demands for shipping space increased. Thus with the rapid growth in the timber import business in the first half of the nineteenth century there was a distinct trend towards single ownership of vessels. Of a total of 465 vessels in which the leading Liverpool timber merchants had shareholdings between 1820 and 1856, just over 75 per cent were owned outright either by one individual or a partnership.

To overcome these difficulties a number of the more ambitious steamship companies were organized on a joint-stock basis, which made it easier to raise capital from a wider field. The only snag here was that, unless incorporation was acquired by means of a Royal Charter or private act of Parliament, which under the existing law was the only way whereby the privilege of limited liability could be secured, the shareholders of the concern were liable to the last penny in the event of failure. But incorporation with limited liability by this method was a difficult and expensive process which only a few companies, such as the P & O, the Royal Mail and the Pacific Steam Navigation, could afford. Fortunately the pressure exerted by potential investors brought about a drastic reform of the company laws in the 1850s and early 1860s which greatly facilitated the formation of limited liability companies. At first however many shipowners were reluctant to take advantage of the reform and clung to the old methods of ownership. Indeed so attached were some shipowners to traditional methods that a variation of the 64th principle, the single ship company, was devised. This became very popular in the 1880s when whole fleets of vessels belonging to the same company were registered in almost as many companies as there were ships. They were still being registered a decade later and at least one of the more famous companies, Houlder Brothers, used this form of ownership extensively until the end of the century.

But as the size and capital cost of ships increased such primitive forms of organization eventually became obsolete. The advantages to be derived from incorporation encouraged many concerns to convert their businesses into limited liability companies from the 1860s onwards. This was particularly true of the liner companies who were anxious to secure more money for expansion. By 1885, 19 companies with a total loan and share capital of £15 million controlled almost one fifth of the total steam tonnage of the United Kingdom. Shipping shares were becoming more widely dispersed and investment was no longer confined almost entirely to the mercantile community around the ports, though doubtless this element still predominated. The spread of ownership was facilitated by a reduction in the value of individual shares to £10 or less which, it was said, encouraged even servant girls and small greengrocers all over the country to put their small savings in tonnage. Whether this assertion is true or not remains to be seen but it is notable that even as early as 1874 the P & O had no less than 2,000 shareholders of whom one-third were women. Of course such wide dispersion of ownership was mainly confined to the larger liner companies who managed to gain direct access to the organized capital market by securing a quotation on the London or provincial stock exchanges. The majority of shipping concerns, though they eventually became incorporated, remained private affairs with no access to the money market. In fact by 1914 the private company still predominated whilst many tramp ships were still owned by individuals or partnerships. By this time the 64th system of ownership and the single ship company were almost, though not quite, defunct.

Despite the obvious broadening of the basis of ownership of many shipping firms in the latter half of the nineteenth century it would be misleading to suggest that this led to any great divorce between ownership and control even in the case of the large liner companies. Much of the expansion of the shipping firms continued to be financed by ploughing back profits made in good years. Between 1881 and 1914 the Booth Steamship Company earned £2,162,684, five-sevenths of which was re-invested in the company. Shipowners were notoriously reluctant to call on outside sources of finance and the descendants of the original founders of the firms often maintained a preponderating influence in the affairs of their concerns. It was not until 1880 that Cunard first offered shares to the public and even after that the greater part of the capital of the firm, and with it the control, remained in the hands of three families. Many of the great companies of the early twentieth century continued to be dominated by powerful individuals or family oligarchies. Names such as Alfred Jones, Owen Philipps, Thomas Ismay, the Booths, the Bibbys, the Brocklebanks, and Ellerman spring easily to mind. These men controlled and directed the policy of their respective companies and often wielded their power in a way which was not in the long-term interest of the companies concerned. As we shall see in a later chapter when we resume the story of shipping it was the tradition of internal financing and family control based on a reluctance to let in outside interests that was eventually to prove a handicap to the industry in the more difficult and competitive climate after the First World War.

2 Prosperity and depression

For most of the nineteenth century accumulated profits provided the major source of finance for the expansion of shipping concerns. Yet reliance on internal resources could be a risky business since shipowning was by no means always a profitable occupation despite the rapid expansion in seaborne trade in the half century or so before 1914. In fact in the 45 years prior to 1914 the number of bad years exceeded the good by two to one. Profits, particularly of tramp vessels, often fluctuated violently from one year to another and one year's trading provided little indication of how the next would go. A tramp steamer company which recorded a net profit of £8,946 in 1910 could earn as much as £49,385 in the prosperous year of 1912. Liner company profits probably fluctuated less violently but the changes were often substantial. The Anchor Line, for example, made a profit of £157,458 in 1900–1 but eight years later (1908–9) the return had fallen to £68,306. The comments of the chairman of the German Levant Line in 1902 illustrate the rapidity with which fortunes could change: "1901 was a very unfavourable year for the shipping trade, the very antithesis, in fact, of the year 1900. Seldom has a sharper contrast developed so suddenly, as occurred between the brisk demand for vessels in the middle of the year 1900 and the superabundant offers of available tonnage in the autumn of 1901," Such sudden changes in fortune must have made it very difficult for shipowners to plan their expansion in advance.

Shipowners frequently complained about the unprofitable nature of their trade and it would be interesting to see how often their complaints were supported by the facts. Unfortunately it is difficult to speak with any degree of precision about the profitability of British shipping in this period. There is no reliable series of profit figures for shipping companies until the early twentieth century and even this refers only to a selection of cargo-boat companies. The only other worthwhile source of information we have is the Isserlis index for tramp freights which is available from 1869 onwards. It is dangerous however to attach too much importance to the tramp index as a measure of prosperity of the shipping industry as a whole. Though freight rates were determined largely by market forces for much of the nineteenth century, the tendency for liner rates to be regulated by conference agreements after 1881 means that the tramp index provides a less accurate guide to the fortunes of this section of the industry. Nor does the index enable us to say anything about the passenger side of the business since this section of the industry was influenced by quite different forces. Furthermore it must be pointed out that freight rates generally were falling almost continuously throughout the latter half of the nineteenth century and it is not always possible to determine how far this was due to changes in the supply of and demand for tonnage or whether it merely reflected a secular downward movement in the cost of transport due to technical progress. Until the end of the nineteenth century the latter factor was probably quite important in the long run, in which case the tramp index can only provide a useful guide to the short-term fluctuations in the prosperity of the shipping industry. With these warnings in mind we may take a brief look at the fortunes of the industry. The discussion will be mainly confined to the later nineteenth century as the almost complete lack of reliable data precludes any comment prior to 1850.

From the scraps of information available it would appear that the 1850s and 1860s were a relatively prosperous period for British shipping despite the fact that shipowners contended they were being ruined by the repeal of the navigation laws. When he died in 1862 Duncan Dunbar left £1½ million "the larger proportion of which was made", says Lindsay, "since the Free Trade sun had been allowed to shine on his ships". The rapidly expanding P & O Line also seems to have done quite well in these years. Between 1856 and 1874 the company made a profit of nearly £3 million and only in one rather exceptional year, 1866, was a deficit recorded. Of course there were depressed years even in the mid-Victorian golden age. The cessation of the Government's tonnage demands after the Crimean War left the market in rather a depressed state for a year or more. But generally speaking the market seems to have been more buoyant and the fluctuations less violent than they were to become in later years.

The opening of the Suez Canal in 1869 produced a minor boom in the early 1870s. Profits of some steamship owners were said to range from 25 to 45 per cent and many new companies were formed to take advantage of the favourable conditions. The boom soon overreached itself and by January 1874 freight rates in nearly all quarters were said to be very dull. In that year the Union Steamship Company failed to pay a dividend for the first time in 15 years. Conditions remained relatively depressed for most of the 1870s as more efficient tonnage, which had been ordered in better years, floated onto the market. The rate on rice from Burma to England dropped from 120s. 6d. in 1872 to 30s. in 1878, a fall of over 70 per cent. Apart from a slight revival between 1879 and 1881 and again in the latter half of the eighties shipping freights continued to fall until near the end of the century with troughs in 1886 and the early nineties which coincided roughly with the phasing of the so-called Great Depression (1873–96) in trade and industry. Overall, freight rates fell by about 50 per cent between 1869 and 1896. Obviously shipowning was by no means as unprofitable as the tramp index suggests. From time to time the market became glutted with tonnage and profits were depressed as in the early 1890s but there was certainly no long-term continuous decline in profits. Prices and costs were falling steadily throughout this period and hence it is no surprise to find that the freight index fell too. Under the impact of technical progress operating costs fell rapidly and the cost of steamer construction fell by nearly one half in the years 1878–96. Liner companies, particularly those which specialized in the passenger trade, probably did quite well since their earnings were less subject to the vagaries of the trade cycle; moreover passenger fares were relatively stable and liner companies were able to benefit more fully from falling operating costs. The earnings per gross ton of the White Star Line were well maintained throughout the period 1876–96 whilst the earnings of the P & O in the depressed year of 1894–5 compared very favourably with those of the much more prosperous year of 1911–12. On the other hand, one has to be careful about making generalizations of this sort since the earnings of one or two companies do not necessarily provide a reliable guide to the state of the industry as a whole. Whereas in 1894 the Union Steamship Company made a loss of £15,000 the Castle Line recorded a profit of no less than £27,000. A rough index of shipping earnings calculated by Cairncross does seem to indicate however, that shipping earnings were maintained at a consistently high level during this period and they were often above those of the years 1871–3. In the absence of further information it seems safe to conclude that shipping was more profitable in this period than often imagined.

Towards the end of the nineteenth century freight rates rose rapidly, reaching a peak in 1900, and it would be hard to find any year during the century comparable in respect of the volume of trade and the large profits earned. This boom was largely due to governmental demands for tonnage which arose from the Spanish-American and Boer Wars.

Altogether the British Government chartered nearly two million tons gross of shipping and many new companies were formed to take advantage of the situation. The sudden cessation of Government demands in 1901 made the prosperity short-lived, and in the following year the leading shipping journal, *Fairplay*, estimated that 80 per cent of British shipping companies were said to be largely unprofitable. Depressed conditions continued until about 1911 and in the commercial crisis of 1907–8 freight rates fell to the lowest point for over 100 years. This in fact constituted one of the first major international shipping depressions and at one point almost two million tons gross of shipping were laid up, over half of which belonged to this country. After 1908 freight rates began to rise slowly but even as late as 1910 the position had not improved very much. *Fairplay* estimated that 90 per cent of the cargo boats were not worth more than half their book value and that freights in many cases were not covering working expenses. Apart from the early 1930s the years 1902–10 constitute one of the worst periods in the history of the shipping industry. Liners as well as tramps were affected. For much of the time freight earnings barely covered operating expenses plus normal depreciation charges and many companies failed either to pay dividends or set enough aside for depreciation. The Houlder Line, for example, made a loss of £5,155 in 1907 and in the six years 1906–11 the company paid no dividends and set aside nothing for depreciation. Cargo-boat companies probably fared worst of all for, if allowance is made for interest on loans and depreciation at the rate of 5 per cent per annum, most of them were making losses between 1904 and 1911. During the latter half of 1911 recovery was rapid and in the next two years profits in some cases exceeded those of the boom years at the turn of the century. The extent of the recovery can be gathered from the fact that over half the earnings of 98 companies in the period 1904–13 were made in the last two years.

In view of the fairly buoyant nature of the economy in general during the early twentieth century the depression in shipping requires a brief word of explanation. The slump of 1901–2 can be explained as a natural reaction to the boom of the previous years. The rather more severe slump of 1907–8 was partly due to the economic crisis of that year when trade and passenger traffic fell appreciably. But the fact that the depression in shipping lasted for nearly a decade with little respite suggests that there was a more fundamental cause. The major factor seems to have been a rapid increase in world tonnage in excess of immediate requirements. Other countries, especially Germany and Japan, were rapidly building up their fleets and in the years 1897 to 1907 world tonnage launched was at a much higher level than in the previous decade. In the first decade of the twentieth century world tonnage increased at a faster rate than in any decade of the nineteenth century; by 1914 the world fleet was 70 per cent greater than in 1900 compared with an increase of 62·2 per cent in world trade. Moreover, because of the greater speed and carrying capacity of the new tonnage the efficiency of the fleet was considerably greater than before and this in turn accentuated the discrepancy between the demand for and supply of tonnage in this period.

3   Conference agreements and passenger pools

Fluctuating freight rates and increasing competition encouraged British shipowners to find some form of defence mechanism with which to protect themselves. By establishing conferences for freight cargo and agreements in the passenger trade to maintain rates and share traffic on the major routes of the world it was hoped that a greater degree of stability could be achieved than might otherwise obtain. Shipping conferences or agreements had of course existed in the days of sail when shipping brokers attempted to form rings to fix rates on the more regular trades. Few of them were very successful, however, partly because they lacked an efficient weapon with which to enforce their regulations. It was only in the latter half of the nineteenth century, when the large liner companies attempted to protect themselves from the indiscriminate competition of the tramp vessels, that they rose to importance. To avoid confusion, freight conferences and passenger agreements will be dealt with separately.

The shipping conference is a combination of shipping companies established to regulate and restrict competition in the carrying trade of a given route. Unlike passenger pools they originated in Britain. The first modern freight conference was established in August 1875[1] in the U.K.–Calcutta trade because of a drastic fall in freights on the far eastern routes. Two years later the deferred rebate was introduced which entitled shippers to a 10 per cent rebate of freights paid on a given route provided that they patronized the Conference exclusively. The Calcutta Conference became the prototype for many others which were subsequently formed; in 1879 the China Conference was formed followed by the Australian in 1884, the South African in 1886, the West African and the North Brazilian in 1895, and the River Plate Conference in 1896. By 1913, except for the British coasting trade and the North Atlantic trade, the conference system regulated most of the cargo exported from the United Kingdom, the major exception being coal. Many of the conferences had by this time become international in scope. On the other hand, in the import trade, which consisted largely of bulky commodities often carried by tramps, conference arrangements were far less prevalent.

Most of the conference members were liner companies and few attempts were made at internal regulation of the tramp trade before 1914 except for the Baltic and White Sea Conference negotiated in 1905 by tramp owners

---

[1] A freight tariff for a projected North Atlantic Conference was framed as early as 1869. There is evidence to suggest that some early Glasgow steamship owners fixed rates by conference.

engaged in the northern lumber trade. Tramp ships were difficult to organize not only because of the irregular nature of their employment but also because many tramp owners were also merchants and freight contractors which resulted in a certain conflict of interests in the dual capacity. Most conferences were separate entities though members often belonged to more than one. Their area of operation was usually strictly defined, but overlapping did occur and intra-conference agreements were not unknown. As a rule most of them placed emphasis on maintaining freight stability by agreeing to charge uniform, fixed or more often minimum, rates of freight and the loyalty of the shipper was secured by means of the deferred rebate. More elaborate agreements covering pooling of freight money, the sharing of traffic and regulating sailings became more common as foreign owners joined them. For example, cargo was allocated in the Bombay–Japan Conference formed in 1888, whilst in the conference agreement formed to regulate the trade between America and Brazil the Lamport & Holt Line, the Prince Line and the joint service of the Hamburg American and Hamburg South American companies were each allowed 24 sailings per year from New York. Generally speaking however, these latter regulations were probably a more important feature of the passenger agreements.

It is difficult to say precisely what effects the conference agreements had and the question is still a controversial one even today. Two sides of the question require examination: whether any benefits accrued to the shipowner and to what extent, if any, the shippers suffered at the hands of the conference members.

As regards shipowners it is probably true to say that rates were maintained at a more stable though higher level than they would have been in a free market especially in times of slack trade. Shipowners were able to earn a higher margin of profit and provide improved services as a result. Thus a year after joining the Far Eastern Conference Holt's, the Liverpool shipowners, had earned on average rates some 16⅔ per cent higher than previously. Competition was not eliminated altogether but it became a matter of service rather than price. As Hyde has written: "The Conference agreements did much, by reducing the extent of competition in freight rates and by maintaining competiton in service, to buttress the British shipowner against the pressure of foreign subsidies." On the other hand, the stability of rates under conference lines was by no means perpetual. Frequent rate wars broke out either within the conference or because of intrusion from without. Thus in 1887 a fierce rate war broke out on the Far Eastern route when the China Shippers Mutual Steam Navigation Company left the conference. Freight rates (outward to China) fell by 50 per cent and as a result the conference collapsed and was not reformed until the 1890s. Conferences in fact very often found difficulty in maintaining their rates particularly in times of surplus tonnage. Shortly after the Boer War, excess capacity developed resulting in numerous rate wars between lines plying from America and Britain to Australia and on the South African route with heavy losses to the shipowners concerned.

It was often alleged that the conferences used their monopoly power to exploit the shipper, and the rebate system has frequently been attacked both by traders and Governments. Conferences, it was maintained, led to excessive rates being charged from British ports whilst Continental and American quotations were much lower. This was found to be the case in the West African trade which was dominated by two firms, Elder Dempster and the German Woermann line, acting in conference. Until 1907, when freights were adjusted, it was found to be so much cheaper to ship goods to West Africa from Hamburg than from Liverpool that it paid to send British goods to the German port and then ship them from there, even in Elder Dempster steamers. Yet though the merchants' complaints are obviously not without foundation it is possible that critics of the system have exaggerated the position unduly. Foreign shipowners often did quote lower rates for similar services, or what seemed to be similar services, but very often they were special combined rail and sea rates which had no equivalent in this country. In any case the potential monopoly power of the conference was limited in many ways and in the last resort the shipper could use his own powers of retaliation. If a conference pressed its monopoly powers unduly shippers could combine together to exercise a countervailing power, they could establish their own shipping organizations or they could transfer their custom to non-conference ships including tramps. The unorganized tramp or non-conference ship offered a permanent source of threat to the monopoly power of the conference and it seems unlikely that the latter could have maintained excessive rates for long since entry into the industry was reasonably easy. As Gregg pointed out: "If piece cargo rates on liners are raised unduly above the general level, soon a dingy freighter will be announced on berth to take cargo over the same route at quotations at or under those of the more pretentious vessels." R. P. Houston of Liverpool was a regular pirate or conference "buster" and a type of shipowner the organized lines dreaded. After fighting his way into the Plate trade he commenced (July 1902) a service to South Africa in opposition to the conference line and for 18 months an expensive rate war ensued. In fact non-conference competition, rate wars and competition in service did much to weaken the possibilities of abuse by the conferences. Furthermore it can be argued that the monopoly of a conference of individual lines was far better than that of one line. The Chamber of Commerce of Sekondi for example, were of the opinion that the conference of two firms in the West African shipping trade had provided better facilities than Elder Dempster had done when she once held the monopoly in this field.

It will be clear from what has already been said that any firm conclusion as to the effects of the conference system is out of the question. The subject remains a controversial one even today. It has been shrouded in secrecy by the firms concerned and only a thorough examination of their archives will reveal the truth. Merchants themselves were never in agreement on the issue as the Royal Commission on Shipping Rings, appointed in 1905 to investigate the situation, found out. Some of the smaller merchants whom one would have expected to have suffered dearly at the hands of the conferences, spoke in favour of the system emphasizing the improvements in regularity and speed of service that had been made. Conversely a number of the larger traders such as John Holt who were, it was alleged, accorded preferential treatment by the conferences, denounced the system outright. After a long and exhaustive inquiry in which the Royal Commission was presented with an enormous amount of conflicting evidence which filled four large folio volumes, a majority and minority report were issued in 1909. Neither of these reports appeared unduly worried about the monopoly power of the conferences. The majority felt that it had neither been excessive nor open to abuse and were of the opinion that collective bargaining by shipper organizations could neutralize any undue power that conferences might possess. Even the more critical minority report did not advocate the prohibition of conferences or even some of their worst practices nor did it offer any radical suggestions as to how the system might be improved. That the shipowners got off so lightly might suggest that there was nothing seriously wrong with the system. Alternatively it may be that the Commission was so confused by the wealth of conflicting evidence at its disposal that it was incapable of drawing any definite conclusions from it. But one should be wary of making hasty judgments along these lines. As the late Miss Leubuscher has pointed out it is difficult to accept the face value of the Commission's conclusions because for one thing the members were greatly influenced by the opinions of Sir Alfred Jones who alone was allowed to give evidence *in camera*, none of which was published. The majority report she says "is proof that he was able to convince the majority of the commissioners of the usefulness, the indispensability of the conference system, including deferred rebates". And secondly, the reason why no drastic proposals were made was because the commissioners were determined to avoid at all costs recommending any measures which would involve extensive State interference in the affairs of the shipping industry. In the light of these unusual circumstances it is difficult to accept the judgments of the Commission as conclusive proof of the benefits of the conference system.

Restrictive agreements were not confined solely to freight traffic, for pooling arrangements in the passenger trade became common in the late nineteenth and early twentieth centuries. They were mainly concentrated on the North Atlantic and Mediterranean–U.S. routes since the bulk of the long-distance passenger traffic lay on these routes. Few passenger agreements existed outside this region though to some extent the competition for passenger business between companies operating elsewhere was controlled indirectly through the numerous freight agreements. Passenger agreements, both in their origin, scope and organization, are somewhat different from freight conferences and therefore merit special attention.

Generally speaking ocean passenger fares have been fixed in a similar manner to freight rates depending on what the traffic will bear. Competition however has been a less important factor in influencing the course of ocean fares partly because tramp competition is virtually non-existent in this field and partly because the quality of service rendered has been a more prominent feature than in the case of cargo shipments. Competition in the passenger trade has therefore been more often one of service rather than one of price. Consequently the desire to eliminate cut-throat competition has not always been the major factor determining the formation of passenger agreements though the threat of rate wars may have been an important element in maintaining them in existence once established. In fact their origin stems from the desire of the rapidly growing German liner companies to secure a greater share of the North Atlantic passenger traffic which, until the 1880s, had been dominated by the British lines. In 1885 an agreement was concluded between the two major German lines, the Hamburg American and the North German Lloyd, and the principal lines of Holland, Belgium and France, to maintain minimum fares and share the continental passenger traffic to North America. At first the British lines refused to join but Herr Ballin (who in 1886 became head of the Passenger Department of the Hamburg American Company) coerced them into joining by attacking the Scandinavian emigrant traffic, another preserve of the British companies. Though initially the agreement seems to have been fairly successful, at least as regards the stability of fares, the Conference never worked very smoothly largely owing to a lack of co-operation on the part of the members. The two German companies were not entirely in agreement over policy matters and the major British line, Cunard, left the Conference soon after joining.

In 1892 a more ambitious pooling arrangement was established for the steerage traffic between Europe and North America (both directions) between the two German lines and Red Star and Holland America of the Netherlands. In time most of the major lines engaged in the North Atlantic passenger trade, including Cunard and Anchor, joined the agreement. Ultimately by means of renewal, the agreement ran for just over 20 years until the war put an end to it. Of course the scope of the original agreement was much enlarged in later years and many separate agreements were made covering various classes of traffic. By 1913 there were some 12 separate agreements covering 30 companies in the Atlantic passenger traffic including the Mediterranean Steerage Conference established in 1908.

The provisions of the passenger agreements were far more elaborate and complicated than those of the freight conferences and it is only possible to outline the salient points. Usually minimum fares were established in both directions for all classes of traffic. The steerage traffic and quite often the cabin traffic was pooled. Members who exceeded their allotted quota

S

of traffic in any one year were required to pay to the other lines, who did not reach their quotas, an agreed amount per excess passenger. Consistent maladjustment between the actual traffic carried and the prescribed quotas was rectified either by manipulating fares or by revising the quotas. As far as it is possible to discern, the pooling agreements covered only European passenger traffic to and from North America, and British ports were excluded though provision was made in the original agreement to include them.

It is difficult to assess what impact the pooling agreements had for comparatively little is known about them. It is almost certain that they achieved a greater stability in passenger fares though they were probably maintained at a higher level than under free competition. In 1896, for example, the average fares for second class and steerage passengers were 180 and 110 marks respectively whereas by 1913 they were 210 and 140 marks. It did, however, ensure the companies a more secure return and no doubt permitted an improvement in the quality of service. As the *Shipping World* remarked: "As a working agreement between the several companies concerned . . . it has built up transatlantic traffic, both passenger and cargo, in a way that would otherwise have been impossible." On the other hand, the agreements did not always work very smoothly. From time to time disputes arose between the members, especially between the German and British lines, regarding the division of traffic or the fares charged, and occasionally threats to the interests of the members came from outside lines as in 1909–10. Rate wars were not uncommon and they sometimes had disastrous results as far as profits were concerned. The Cunard company was a particularly unsatisfactory member according to the Germans since she was always causing trouble. In May 1903, for example, Cunard withdrew from the agreement on the grounds that the company had been ignored in connection with an agreement between the newly formed International Mercantile Marine Company of America and some of the continental companies which provided for mutual assistance in any controversy with outsiders. Immediately a fierce rate war broke out in the North Atlantic passenger trade and by 1904 steerage fares had been reduced by two-thirds. Peace was eventually restored in October 1904 but not before the companies had sacrificed most of their profits for that year. Cunard's profit balance dropped from £248,563 in 1903 to £61,588 in 1904. It is probable that the German lines suffered the worst for they depended more on passenger traffic than most. Altogether it has been estimated that the crisis cost the member companies nearly £1 million. Yet the agreement proved its worth in the crisis of 1907–8; passenger traffic to North America fell by 60 per cent but fares were maintained and a serious rate war avoided.

As regards the division of traffic it seems that the German and other Continental lines rapidly increased their share of the passenger traffic between 1880 and the turn of the century though this was not entirely due to the pooling arrangements. By 1903 the bulk of the Continental passenger traffic to North America was in the hands of four companies, North German

Lloyd, Hamburg American, Red Star and Holland American. The two German lines alone controlled over one third of the steerage traffic, and their gain was mainly at the expense of the British companies. Had the British lines, and especially Cunard, shown a greater willingness to work with the Pool in the early years no doubt they would not have been left out in the cold. On the other hand, after 1903, when the British companies played a more positive role in the pooling arrangements, they maintained their position fairly well whilst the Germans appear to have lost ground in both cabin and steerage traffic to non-British lines. Thus the British lines (including the Canadian) held 33·9 per cent of the westbound steerage traffic in 1903 and 1913 as against 41·4 per cent in 1883, whilst the two German lines accounted for 30·8 per cent in 1883, 35·9 per cent in 1903 and 28·0 per cent in 1913. Overall, one might conclude that, although the British lines lost the predominant position they held in the Atlantic passenger trade in the 1870s and early 1880s, they were by no means crushed by the force of foreign competition. In fact in the early twentieth century they were able to maintain their relative position better than their closest competitors, the Germans, who tended to fall foul of non-British competitors. During these years the continental traffic increased as a proportion of the total passenger traffic carried by the British companies and by 1913 even the chairman of Cunard (A. A. Booth) was praising the benefits of the international conference system.

10

Transport under wartime conditions

1 The basis of wartime control

The demands and requirements of the First World War produced a complete revolution in the economic and civil administration of Great Britain. Initially however, Churchill's dictum "business as usual" caught the popular imagination and the Government was extremely reluctant to interfere with the normal channels of trade. The result was that during the first year or so of war the traditional policy of "muddling through" was adopted and Government control of economic activity was implemented on an *ad hoc* basis as and when the need arose. Gradually however it was realized that for the exacting criteria of war conditions the free economic system "produced too little, it produced the wrong things and it distributed them to the wrong people" (Salter). Thus the Government was eventually obliged to become a "giant practitioner in industry" and to control and regulate the economy on a scale hitherto unknown. By the end of the war private business interests had been almost completely subordinated to national interests and the British economy had been transformed from a highly competitive condition to one in which competition was narrowly circumscribed by Government demands and decrees.

The importance of the railways to the successful functioning of the economy in time of war had been recognized long before 1914. The Regulation of the Forces Act of 1871 had provided the State with powers to assume control of the railways in the event of war and, accordingly, on 4 August 1914 the Government commandeered the railway network by Order in Council. The State however took no part in the actual management or day-to-day running of the railways. This task was entrusted to the Railway Executive Committee, composed of general managers of the main railway companies, and it was made clear at the time that there was no intention of superseding the existing management by a permanent body of control. On the other hand, the State undertook responsibility for compensating the railway owners for any loss incurred by them during the period of control. The railway companies placed their organization at the disposal of the Government for the movement of troops and supplies without payment and, in return, they were guaranteed their net income of 1913. On this basis the railway companies secured a good bargain since 1913 was a prosperous year when total net revenue amounted to just over £46 million. In effect the Government, under the terms of the agreement, undertook to pay the Railway Executive Committee, on the basis of provisional estimates, monthly instalments of compensation to the companies. And as the Government met all the expenses of the railways out of the receipts the prosperity of the system became not a matter of indifference to the State.

During the course of the war the original agreement with the railways was modified, or rather enlarged upon. In 1915 the Treasury made an allowance for arrears of repair and renewal of rolling stock and for deferred maintenance work. The following year the Government agreed to pay 4 per cent annual interest allowance on all capital invested in new railway property, for, prior to this agreement, fixed charges on new capital had all been paid out of net income. Subsequently a further important revision was made concerning stocks, whereby the railways were guaranteed a stock of materials at the end of hostilities equivalent to their pre-war holdings. Finally, the obligation to guarantee practically all the increase in wages of the railwaymen completed the Government's financial control over the railways.

In contrast to the railways, ocean-going shipping was controlled in a very loose and haphazard manner in the first two years of war. Ideally the State should have become the sole importer at the outbreak of war and at the same time taken over the whole of the mercantile marine so that the demand for and supply of tonnage could be co-ordinated centrally. Far less than the ideal policy was adopted however, partly because a shortage of tonnage was not at first envisaged. Instead a piece-meal system of control was instituted, the logical outcome of which was the creation of a separate Ministry of Shipping in December 1916. Until that time the Government relied on a policy of requisitioning certain tonnage or ship space to meet its immediate requirements. Ships required for fighting purposes or troop transport were taken over almost immediately, the Government assuming all expenses of operation. For the carriage of essential commodities such as wheat, meat and sugar, the Government either requisitioned ships outright or acquired a proportion of space on vessels operating in certain trades. In 1915 for example, all refrigerated space was requisitioned and later grain space on the North Atlantic route was acquired leaving the balance of space for the use of the owners. The latter remained responsible for the operation and expenses of running the ships and for the services rendered they were paid fixed rates of hire (or Blue Book rates as they were called) which were determined by a committee of shipowners on which the Government was represented. As control was gradually extended attempts were made to improve the efficiency of shipping. In November 1915 a Port and Transit Executive Committee was established to improve the turn-round of shipping at the ports and in 1916 greater efforts were made to co-ordinate tonnage by the Shipping Control Committee. By 1916 some form of control had been imposed on nearly all shipping and about 37 per cent of the British tonnage had been requisitioned.

In many respects this system of partial control was highly unsatisfactory; indeed it can be argued that it raised more problems than it solved. The policy of requisition was by no means uniform and the impact of control fell unevenly on shipowners, who did their best to avoid it. This is not surprising since the free market rates soon outstripped the Blue Book rates which, though generous, gave an annual average profit return on the book value of ships of 5 per cent less than pre-war. Consequently shipowners whose vessels were not requisitioned were able to take advantage of the high freights in the free market, and, as the demand for tonnage rose, many speculative ventures were encouraged to enter the industry to profit from the situation. In one year alone, 1915, as many as 94 shipping companies were formed in Great Britain. It has been estimated that in the first 26 months of hostilities the total net profit of British shipping amounted to as much as £262 million. The high freights from which these profits accrued rather than the injustice suffered by owners of requisitioned vessels inspired the demand for more comprehensive control. By the end of 1915 free market rates were in some cases more than 100 per cent above the pre-war levels and the rapid rise in the cost of living was attributed largely to this factor. As one historian of the war period has observed: "Government action was forced by public indignation directed against the 'profiteers' as a result of soaring prices".

Though the Government was somewhat reluctant to take further action it was becoming quite clear towards the end of 1916 that, in view of the increasing shortage of tonnage and high freights and prices, a more comprehensive system of control would have to be established over the shipping industry and over the import trade. Moreover, the extension of submarine warfare during 1916 was making it increasingly difficult for British shipping to operate without protection. Already by August 1916 enemy submarines had sunk $1 \cdot 7$ million tons gross of British shipping only part of which had been replaced. Three months later the total reached $2\frac{1}{2}$ million tons and within the next few months sinkings rose rapidly from 160,000 tons in December to 545,000 tons in April 1917. In view of these developments further action could be delayed no longer.

The year 1917 was remarkable for the speed with which control was extended not only over the shipping industry but also over many other aspects of economic activity. At the end of 1916 the Ministry of Shipping was established whose Controller, Sir Joseph Maclay, a leading shipowner, was given almost unlimited powers of control over the industry. In the course of the next few months the new Ministry brought practically the whole of the British ocean-going tonnage, liners as well as tramps, under requisition at fixed rates of hire. This was followed by what was probably one of the most revolutionary steps of all—the national shipbuilding programme, the ships built from which were run entirely on Government account. At the same time measures were taken to protect shipping from enemy submarines. In the summer of 1917 a general plan for convoy organization was drawn up and by the following year nearly 90 per cent of the total overseas traffic of the U.K. was being convoyed. The convoy system proved remarkably successful and, had it not been for the intransigence of the Admiralty, it might have been introduced a lot earlier and spared the Allies the loss of much tonnage. Losses from enemy action dropped by half within just over a year and 99 per cent of the 17,000 vessels escorted in ocean convoy arrived safely. The control of shipping was finally completed at the end of 1917 when it was extended internationally by the formation of the Allied Maritime Transport Council whose job was to sift, co-ordinate and adjust to the capacity of available tonnage, the national import programmes of the Allies. By the end of the war this international authority was controlling about 90 per cent of the shipping tonnage of the world. By this time too the Government had become the largest and almost sole importer in the country. Thus in the last few months of war some 90 per cent of the imported supplies of Great Britain were bought, transported and distributed under official arrangements and about 96 per cent of the cargo was carried at fixed Government rates.

Control over other forms of transport was far less extensive and elaborate than that of the railway and shipping industries. The complex nature of the coasting trade with its many small vessels would have involved an inordinate amount of detailed administration and for this reason the Government feared to venture into the field. Thus apart from the requisition of certain vessels for Admiralty service the coastal shipping retained its freedom, though a partial system of control was eventually introduced in January 1918. Railway-owned canals were taken over with the railways on the outbreak of war but the independent waterways remained free until March 1917 when most of them were brought under the Canal Control Committee of the Board of Trade. Little attempt was made to control road transport until towards the end of the war when a Road Transport Board was set up to determine measures to ensure the most economic use of this form of transport.

To all intents and purposes control of the nation's transport system was complete by the last year of war. But Government control was not as revolutionary as it might seem for in no case could it be regarded as an act of expropriation. Certainly the State had wide powers at its disposal and could more or less direct the railways or shipowners to do anything that was required of them, but it owned none of the assets of the undertakings concerned. This meant that the Government had to rely on the existing

organization and personnel to carry out its orders. The day-to-day administration and operation of the railways and shipping lines were left in the
hands of the owners, and indeed the Government actually appealed to the
shipowners whose ships were requisitioned "to continue to carry on with
those same vessels the business which they, the shipowners, are alone
capable of carrying on". In other words war-time operation was essentially
a partnership between the State and private enterprise and the success with
which British transport performed its duties depended a great deal on how
smoothly the partnership worked. The ease with which co-operation was
actually achieved was in no small part due to the degree to which the industries were organized, together with the willingness with which the
owners responded to the State's demands. Had the owners not been prepared to sacrifice their private interests to the national cause there is no
telling what the outcome might have been.

2   The achievements of wartime operation

Transport played a significant part in the victory of the Allied Powers and
there is little doubt that the contribution of British transport was the most
important and most successful of all. Even motor transport played a small
though significant role for as Lord Curzon remarked: "The Allies floated
to victory on a wave of oil". But the shipping industry probably takes pride
of place in wartime operations. In fact it would be no exaggeration to say
that the decisive factor in the First World War was the possession by Great
Britain of a shipping fleet far larger than was required for her own essential
needs. Without British shipping, war could never have been waged on the
scale it was, for the transport demands of the other Allies far exceeded their
own shipping resources. In any case direct military requirements alone
provided a serious drain on the resources of the industry for by October
1918 practically 30 per cent of British tonnage was earmarked for naval
and military service. The transport of troops was on a scale hitherto unknown. Two million American troops alone crossed to Britain and France
in British ships and in all the Transport Authorities of the Admiralty
provided tonnage for 23·7 million individual passages, equivalent to roughly
24 times the average annual immigration into the United States during the
ten years prior to the war. In addition transport was found for 2·2 million
animals and 500,000 vehicles. The task of supply was even greater, for the
Allied Powers were heavily dependent upon British tonnage for supplies
of war materials, food and other essentials. Of the tonnage in the French
import service at the end of the war 45·4 per cent was British and in the
Italian service the proportion was just over 50 per cent. France received 20
million tons of munitions, supplies and military stores and 11 million tons of
coal from this country alone during the course of the war. The total volume

of military stores (excluding food and materials for munitions) carried to all war theatres in British ships amounted to no less than 50 million tons which was equivalent to one year's British imports under normal conditions. These figures are by no means complete—they do not include for example Britain's own tonnage requirements. Nevertheless they give some idea of the magnitude of the transport movements by sea which took place in these years.

This "extraordinary achievement", to use Fayle's words, could never have been realized had it not been for the great effort on the part of the Ministry of Shipping and shipowners to organize and redistribute the nation's ships so that they could be utilized in a manner most conducive to the successful operation of the war. Control by requisitioning was essential for this purpose for it was the only way in which the demand for and supply of tonnage could be centrally co-ordinated and hence used to its best advantage. It enabled, for example, ships to be transferred from the longer to the shorter trades thereby allowing more cargo to be carried in a given period of time. Over half the tonnage in the Indian trade, 75 per cent in the Australian, 80 per cent in the South Africa and nearly 100 per cent in the Far Eastern was withdrawn and redirected in this way. Much of it was re-employed on the North Atlantic route where three times the quantity of cargo could be carried by the same tonnage compared with the Australian trade. Moreover, the concentration of shipping on this route enabled Britain to take advantage of the exporting capacity of North America and at the same time obtain the benefit in the form of additional imports of the increased number of voyages. Furthermore, great efforts were made to speed up the turn-round of shipping in the ports and to ensure that ships were properly loaded so as to avoid waste of carrying power. The extent to which this policy was successful may be gathered from the fact that by the end of 1917 every 100 tons of shipping on the British register that entered our ports brought in an average of 150 tons of imports compared with only 106 tons in the six months before 1914. In the following year Britain was able to import 31 million tons of cargo with only $6\frac{1}{4}$ million tons gross of shipping whereas in 1913 it had taken twice this amount to bring in an additional four million tons. Had it not been for this amazing improvement in overall performance the transport requirements could never have been met. Moreover these services were provided at a cost much lower than in the free market. After 1915, when Blue Book rates were applied more extensively, freight rates rose much less rapidly than in the early part of the war. By 1918 Blue Book rates were only about 50 per cent above the 1915 level compared with a rise of 300 per cent in the open market rates.

The achievements of the railways were equally commendable. The amount of work they had to cope with during the war was enormous and it was to the credit of the administration that so much was accomplished under such trying conditions. "The success that has attended the operation of the railways throughout the war", said the Select Committee on Transport of 1918, "has been superior to that witnessed in any other of the belligerent countries", and "affords conclusive proof both of the adequacy of the arrangements which had been made in advance, and of the capacity of those who had been concerned with their execution. There has been little dislocation notwithstanding that in addition to a very large Government traffic the volume of civilian traffic both of passengers and goods has been heavier than in pre-war days, that large numbers of the staff have been inexperienced, and that considerable demands have been made upon the railways for rolling stock and materials of all kinds for use with armies abroad."

Unfortunately comprehensive traffic statistics are not available for the war period. It does appear however that most of the railway companies were carrying a much greater volume of traffic than ever before. Apart from ordinary civilian traffic the railways were obliged to carry troops, munition workers and Government supplies for the service of the war machine, and, in addition, much of the traffic which before the war had gone by water was directed to the railways for reasons of economy or security. The burden was not of course distributed evenly among the companies for lines which were of particular strategic value suffered the worst. The Great Northern for example became a great conveyor of war traffic; its goods traffic increased by 125 per cent over the corresponding pre-war period and 60 per cent of its passengers consisted of servicemen. The largest movement of troops was probably made by the London and South Western railway since it provided the major link to the continent through Southampton. The company carried no less than 20 million soldiers during this period, and the port of Southampton provided the main gateway for the flow of troops and military equipment to the Allied front. Altogether well over 7 million troops passed through the docks during the war, whilst 15,661 ships were loaded and unloaded. Another busy network was that of the Great Eastern Company. Between August 1914 and March 1919 nearly 13,000 special trains were run on the company's system for the conveyance of troops and in all the company carried 10·5 million troops. For other government traffic the company put on 11,000 special trains, in addition to which they conveyed many thousands of consignments of war traffic by ordinary goods train services. Owing to the unusual size and weight of some of this traffic special arrangements had to be made for it since the pre-war rolling stock was not always suitable for carrying such things as aeroplanes, tanks, heavy guns and armour plates.

Despite the immense burden few railways broke down under the strain and their task was accomplished with less manpower and rolling stock and with a minimum loss of life and injury. Indeed the number of passengers injured on the railways in these years was (barring 1915) the lowest on record. Yet throughout this period they suffered a constant drain of personnel as men left the service to join the forces. Altogether about 30 per

cent of the pre-war staff of 600,000 were released from the railways for
national service of some kind. Many of the places left vacant were filled by
women and non-railway workers who, although not lacking in willingness,
often did not possess the skill and physical strength of the men they
replaced. The drain was not confined to manpower, for large quantities of
railway equipment such as locomotives, rolling stock, rails and sleepers
were sent to the war theatres abroad. Altogether over 30,000 wagons and
nearly 700 locomotives were dispatched to France and other Allied
countries. Moreover, the repair of much rolling stock had to be neglected
since railway workshops were engaged in munition production. For these
reasons a serious shortage of rolling stock developed towards the end of
the war. Nevertheless despite these difficulties many companies were able
to carry more civilian traffic than ever before though perhaps not under
quite the same conditions of comfort. The Great Central's ordinary
passenger traffic increased by more than 8 million in addition to which it
found room for $2 \cdot 6$ million troops.

That the work was achieved at all was in no small part due to the drastic
revision and reorganization of railway services which were made at this
time. Everything possible was done to discourage inessential passenger
travel; fares were raised by 50 per cent, cheap travel facilities were withdrawn except for workmen and an appeal was made to the public to avoid
travelling by rail. Train services were ruthlessly cut and a number of
unimportant lines and stations were closed. By the end of 1916 the London
and North Western alone had cancelled 500 trains and shut down 44
stations. Trains running over parallel routes at the same hours were cut
out, and on main routes and branch lines every train that could be spared
without seriously inconveniencing the public was taken off. As a result
the number of passenger trains run was reduced by nearly 40 per cent with
a proportionate saving in rolling stock and manpower. Unified working
also made possible substantial improvements in the handling of goods
traffic. Steps were taken to eliminate the light loading of wagons and to
concentrate loads by allocating traffic between certain points to specific
routes. Congestion at sidings and terminals was lessened by regulating as
far as possible the flow of traffic to coincide with the rate at which it could be
dealt with at the receiving points. A considerable amount of through
running was arranged for locomotives hauling troops and supplies though
the extent to which this could be accomplished depended very much upon
the railway workers' ability to identify and handle the track and rolling
stock of companies other than their own. To obtain more effective use of
the available wagon capacity a pooling of railway-owned goods wagons
was brought into operation. By this system wagons previously returned
empty were reloaded at or close to the point of discharge. Thus the number
of wagons running empty was greatly reduced and the train mileage
correspondingly cut down. Particular attention was paid to coal which
before the war constituted about one third of the total railway traffic. In

conjunction with the Coal Controller a careful enquiry was made into the movement of coal in the United Kingdom. As a result a Coal Transport Reorganization Scheme, designed to eliminate all unnecessary hauling of coal, was drawn up and put into operation in 1917. This arrangement was very successful for it is said to have saved about 700,000,000 ton miles per annum and it reduced considerably the pressure on railway rolling stock.

Outstanding as the wartime achievements may seem the price the British transport system had to pay for them was a heavy one. In some respects the problems and difficulties which had to be confronted in the immediate post-war period were as great as any which had been encountered in wartime. Most forms of transport were in poor physical shape and some had lost considerable amounts of traffic. The canals and the coastal shipping trade had lost as much as one third of their traffic to the railways. The shipping industry had suffered heavy physical losses and faced severe competition from abroad at a time when the volume of international trade was much diminished. The railways themselves were not only short of rolling stock but part of their track and equipment was badly in need of repair. Apart from material losses there was a basic issue of policy to be decided, namely whether the benefits of unified control in wartime should be continued in peace-time by legislation designed to effect a reorganization of the transport undertakings of the country. To appreciate the problems involved and the method in which they were handled we must now turn our attention to the reconstruction period.

3   Problems of reconstruction

The British shipping industry suffered a setback in the First World War from which it never fully recovered. Total losses amounted to $7\frac{1}{4}$ million tons gross (38 per cent of the 1914 tonnage) and though part of this had been made good by replacement there was still a net deficit of 3·5 million tons gross. Other countries suffered far less severely. Only about one quarter of the world's fleet was destroyed by enemy action, most of which had been replaced by the time of the Armistice. Thus total world tonnage was more or less the same as in 1913 whereas the British fleet had declined by 14 per cent and it now contributed 5 per cent less of the world fleet. During the war many countries had taken the opportunity to expand their fleets and extend their shipbuilding capacity often in excess of immediate needs. The most notable example was that of America where tonnage rose by 144 per cent and shipbuilding capacity was increased fourteenfold. Altogether the capacity of the world's merchant shipbuilding yards doubled during the war compared with an increase of only one quarter in Great Britain.

The position was in no way relieved by the state of trade at the end of the war. By the Armistice there was hardly a single item in our export trade of which the volume of shipment was not well below the level of 1917. Coal exports, the backbone of our outward cargoes, had fallen drastically whilst the transit trade had almost disappeared. Imports of many bulky commodities were much lower in volume particularly wool and cotton; in 1918 the tonnage entering British ports with cargoes was only 47 per cent of that in 1913 and it was not until 1923 that the pre-war level was exceeded. Many of the trade losses were only temporary, of course, and could be expected to revive as soon as normal conditions returned. Yet in many cases British shipowners had lost services to foreign competitors whilst under Government control. American, Japanese and neutral shipowners took every advantage of Britain's position during the war and about 25 new liner services were started by foreign shipowners to replace suspended British services.

On the other hand, British shipowners could not complain financially, for they were able to make substantial profits, especially in the early years of war. No accurate figures are available of the total profits made by the British industry during this period but sample surveys of companies imply that they were fairly large. For example, liner companies owning 5 million tons of shipping increased their reserves by nearly £24 million between 1914 and 1918, whilst it has been estimated that in 1916 the net earnings of British shipping amounted to £188. During 1917 the almost universal application of Blue Book rates and a more stringent Excess Profits Duty curtailed the scope for excess profits. Yet despite this and the fact that by the end of the war the costs of replacement had more than doubled, the industry had made enough to cover replacement costs and pay dividends on a pre-war scale. It is true that British shipowners were at a disadvantage compared with some foreign, especially neutral, owners, who were able to make larger profits in the free market. Yet the disparity in earnings is unlikely to have been large and as one recent student of the industry has pointed out: "if shipowners had treated their profits during the war as a windfall to be preserved for fleet replacement, instead of doubling their dividends and using their liquid resources to buy the ships and goodwill of other lines at inflated prices, they would have been at least as well placed at the end of the war as any of their foreign rivals". This policy was carried even further in the immediate post-war years with disastrous consequences for British shipping.

In view of the difficulties facing the industry it is not surprising that shipowners were anxious to secure their release from Government control so that they could restore their position. Their views found full expression in the report of the Departmental Committee on Shipping and Shipbuilding (Booth Report, 1918): "We believe that the continuance of Government operation and control is bound to extinguish private enterprise and lead to State ownership", which the Committee felt "would be a dangerous experiment and blunder of the worst kind". The fears the shipowners had regarding the possibility of nationalization or the existence of a permanent State-operated fleet were not without justification. During the war some influential people, including Sir Leo Chiozza Money, had advocated nationalization and there is evidence to suggest that the War Cabinet had given the matter serious consideration at one point. Generally speaking, however, the idea attracted little enthusiasm; even the Labour Party was lukewarm towards it and the National Seamen's and Firemen's Union rejected it outright. Lack of support undoubtedly inspired the Government to reject nationalization a fortnight before the Armistice and tenders were immediately invited for the purchase of Government ships. Within a few days of the Armistice being declared the principle of State ownership and construction of ships together with any prospect of a reorganization of the merchant fleet had been abandoned for good.

Whilst endorsing the views of the shipowning community the Government was somewhat doubtful about the expediency of releasing shipping from all control immediately. Despite the reduction in trade the Booth Report had envisaged a shortage of tonnage for a short period after the war and the Government was anxious to ensure sufficient tonnage for its own needs without having to pay highly inflated market rates of hire. Thus although ships were steadily derequisitioned during 1919 a modified form of control was maintained. All ships remained subject to licence and the Government continued to direct vessels and requisition space in many trades. Altogether, in the twelve months from March 1919, approximately 25 per cent of the U.K. imports were brought in at Blue Book rates which were roughly at bare cost, and another 25 per cent were imported at rates far below the free market level. In short, the freedom of British shipping was still fairly limited in 1919 and in some trades, e.g. the North Atlantic, free chartering was reduced to a relatively small number of transactions. There is no doubt that the Government secured a good bargain since market rates rose to unprecedented heights during 1919–20.

Unfortunately the partial control of shipowners' activities during 1919 did not prevent a boom in the shipping market which was without parallel in the history of the industry. The boom was not confined to shipping alone but pervaded all sectors of the economy and in some respects was a natural reaction as the pent-up demands of wartime were unleashed. Yet as far as shipping was concerned there was, in theory at least, little reason for one since in relation to the volume of trade the world was already overstocked with tonnage by 1919. Unfortunately the tonnage surplus was concealed by large demands for tonnage for reparations and troop repatriation, by delays in repair of ships, and above all by chronic congestion at British ports which reduced the efficiency of shipping by about 30 per cent. Added to this was the fact that shipowners, both at home and abroad, were anxious to restore or build up their fleets with the result that they frantically bought up any tonnage which came on to the market. Thus as soon as the general release from control began in the spring of 1919 an orgy of speculation ensued and freights and ship values were driven up to extraordinary heights. Free markets rates doubled or trebled in some cases during 1919 and shipping values appreciated by about 42 per cent. The price of *Fairplay's* new ready cargo steamer rose from £169,000 at the end of 1918 to £259,000 at the peak of the boom in March 1920. The flotation of shipping companies, issues of fresh capital and amalgamations and absorptions became almost a daily event in the latter half of 1919 and shipbuilders rapidly expanded their yards to meet the demand for new tonnage. The speculation was based upon false hopes and the artificial nature of the boom was revealed in the spring of 1920 when the bottom began to fall out of the freight market. By this time the Government was able to meet its requirements in the free market at Blue Book rates or even below. Under these conditions the reasons for control disappeared and in the summer of 1920 the last vestiges of control were swept away.[1]

The artificial nature of the boom soon brought about its own collapse. Encouraged by the high freights shipowners ordered far more tonnage than was required. About 11 million gross tons of new shipping were constructed between July 1919 and July 1921 yet by the latter date the volume of international trade was barely 80 per cent of the 1913 level. Under the impact of excess tonnage freight rates fell by 80 per cent within 18 months and they continued to fall until the mid-twenties as more tonnage came on to the market. Freights in fact returned almost to their pre-war level even though operating expenses remained about two or three times above 1913. Thus in 1921 the industry was already in the depths of depression. There was some 10 million gross tons more shipping available compared with 1913 and half of it, including two million tons belonging to Britain, was laid up in the various ports of the world.

The post-war boom undoubtedly accentuated the difficulties of the industry in the inter-war years. The speculation of 1919–20 denuded both the shipping and shipbuilding industries of their accumulated reserves in a frivolous manner. Such speculative transactions, the dissipation of cash reserves, and the handicap of increased interest liabilities consequent on the issue of bonus shares and the heavy watering of capital, left the British shipping and shipbuilding industries without the reserves necessary to meet the post-war problems. It brought into existence a far larger amount of tonnage than was required and much of it was launched after the boom had collapsed. Even more disastrous was the fact that many British ship-owners had saddled themselves with large blocks of Government and ex-enemy tonnage which Lord Inchcape sold on behalf of the State to shipowners. Much of the 2·5 million tons of ex-German tonnage was of pre-war vintage and British owners could more profitably have spent their reserves on new ships—or better still not have spent the reserves at all. It has been estimated that in the immediate post-war years British shipowners

---

[1] The Ministry of Shipping was not dissolved until March 1921 as it was involved in certain winding up operations.

spent £55 million on ships which were far from suitable for future purposes. In fact British shipowners burnt their fingers badly in the post-war boom and the painful lessons of the period were to be brought home fully in the inter-war years.

The coastal shipping trade suffered a partial eclipse between 1913 and 1918 when the volume of coastwise shipping fell by about 50 per cent. There were a number of factors which caused the decline including the loss of vessels in war, the employment of ships on Admiralty service or in the near Continental trades and deteriorating port facilities. By far the most important factor, however, was that of railway competition. During the war the Government had diverted much water-borne traffic to the railways whose rates remained unchanged despite the fact that their expenses had risen by about 200 per cent. The operating costs of the coasting trade had risen by a similar amount but, unlike the railways which were under control, their charges were adjusted accordingly. Coasting rates which had once been competitive with railway rates were by the end of the war anything from 100 to 200 per cent in excess of comparable railway rates. Thus by the end of the war it was impossible for coastal shipowners to resume profitable operations over many routes where railways competed directly.

For most of the war the Government left the industry very much to its own devices and only introduced a temporary and limited form of control in 1918. In August 1919 the Government made a half-hearted attempt to relieve the difficulties of coastal shipowners by the introduction of a temporary subsidy scheme. But it did little to revive the industry and was abandoned in June of the following year. The only remaining solution seemed then to be a reform of the railway rates. These were raised by appreciable amounts in 1920 and the revised charging powers embodied in the Railways Act of 1921 were designed to afford some slight measure of protection to the coasting trade.

The measures which the Government took to assist the industry were relatively ineffective. Though a partial recovery did take place in the immediate post-war years the industry was still heavily depressed in 1921 when about half the ships in the trade were said to be laid up. There was now little hope for a sudden revival for during the inter-war years trade conditions were generally depressed and railway and road competitions increased rather than diminished. Nevertheless, coastal shipowners showed remarkable powers of resiliency; after 1922 there was steady and almost continuous increase in the volume of coastwise shipping though by 1938 it was still slightly below the 1913 level. The crisis however had an important and in some ways favourable effect on the industry. It forced out of business a number of small and inefficient firms many of which were taken over by larger more dynamic rivals such as Coast Lines of Liverpool which by the early 1920s dominated the coastal shipping trade of Great Britain.

Despite the limited attempts of the Canal Control Committee to revive

T

the traffic on the canals the volume of tonnage carried fell by about one third between 1913 and 1918. In August 1920 the independent waterways were returned to their owners and a committee was set up to review the post-war situation. The committee in its report advocated the formation of seven regional groups each under a public trust which would be financed by the State and local authorities. Unfortunately no attempt was made to implement these recommendations, and during the inter-war years the canals were left to fend for themselves. As a result few improvements were made, traffic continued to stagnate and a number of the navigations fell into disuse or closed altogether. Admittedly the prospects of revival were pretty grim in view of the fierce competition in inland transport during the years 1919–39. Yet the few renovations which were made to the canals during these years do indicate that canal transport was not quite obsolete.

The reconstruction and decontrol of the railways proved to be a far more difficult problem than that of water transport. The immediate task was to make good the forced neglect of physical assets in the previous four years and to resume normal services as soon as possible. As we have seen many normal passenger services and facilities were suspended during the war and maintenance and repair of track and rolling stock had been partly neglected owing to a shortage of labour or because railway workshops were engaged in munitions production. Consequently by the Armistice British railways had 20 per cent of their locomotives, 5 per cent of their wagons and 10 per cent of their carriages awaiting repair. Moreover, the railways were suffering from considerable shortages of rolling stock particularly wagons of which there was a deficit of about 80,000 in 1918.[1] But generally speaking physical reconstruction was a comparatively simple and short-term problem[2] compared with the financial problem and the even greater question of the future organization of the railway system. In order to gain time to consider these matters fully the Government, in 1916, had decided to extend the period of control and guarantee of receipts of the companies for two years after the war. This was a disastrous step as far as the Government was concerned because the railways soon ran into financial difficulties after 1918. During the war years the State had made a profit of about £20 million on railway operations but the failure to adjust charges in relation to costs soon reduced this profitability. In the years 1919, 1920 and 1921 the Government had to compensate the railway companies at the rate of £34, £41 and £51 millions respectively.

By the Armistice the Government had failed to produce a plan for the railways. In some respects this delay is not really surprising since many suggestions had been offered as to what should be done and the Government was torn between a variety of solutions. On one point at least most

[1] In the spring of 1918 the wagon position had become so serious that the Board of Trade was given powers to take possession of privately owned wagons.
[2] Broadly speaking normal train services were resumed by the end of 1919. Maintenance and repair work took somewhat longer and the railways were still short of some kinds of rolling stock in 1920 and 1921.

people were agreed: the railways could not return to the wasteful competition and duplication of facilities of pre-war days. The benefits of unified control in war-time had proved beyond doubt that the railways had something to gain from reorganization. The acting chairman of the Railway Executive Committee was known to be in favour of a large measure of co-ordination[1] and in 1918 the Select Committee on Transport came to a similar conclusion. "From a purely technical view, it appears, therefore, to be desirable that there should be unification of ownership", for "so long as the companies remain as separate corporations, it will be difficult to apply either method of securing economies to the fullest possible extent." If the solution of the problem was fairly straightforward the means by which it was to be achieved presented greater difficulties. There were three possible choices: the railways could be nationalized outright, they could revert to their pre-war position, or the companies could resume full control but with a far greater degree of State direction than hitherto. The last of these alternatives was eventually adopted but not before serious thought had been given by the Government to the possibilities of nationalization. A number of influential people apart from the socialists were in favour of nationalization of the railways and on more than one occasion both the Prime Minister and Winston Churchill hinted strongly that it would be a possible solution. After careful consideration the Cabinet rejected nationalization in the summer of 1920. Despite the delay it seems very unlikely that nationalization had much chance of being adopted. For one thing it would not have been a very popular policy with the majority of the electorate who were by this time heartily tired of war-time regulation and government interference, and consequently many tended to sympathise with the railway-owners' belief that "controlled private management is better than uncontrolled State ownership". In any case the cost of acquiring the system would have been substantial and the Government was not prepared to saddle itself with an industry the fortunes of which were rapidly deteriorating. Moreover the disappointing results of the State railway systems in many foreign countries inspired little enthusiasm for nationalization in Britain. State control therefore appeared to be the only and least objectionable alternative.

Despite the uncertainty about the future of the railways the Government was forced to take action early in 1919 owing to the rapidly worsening financial position of the railways. It was estimated at the time that the railways were spending £17 or £18 for every £14 or £15 they earned. In the light of this the Government confirmed its two-year extension of the guarantee made in 1916 and introduced a Bill to establish a Ministry of Transport

[1] In an interview with the *Daily Dispatch* Sir Herbert Walker made the following comment: "I cannot think that our railways will ever again revert to the independent and foolish competitive system (of before the war) . . . If we are to get the really useful and tangible result of what has been done in the war . . . if we are to prove that the experience gained has been beneficial there must be vastly more co-ordination between the various companies". *Railway Gazette*, 22 June 1917, p. 726.

which became law on 15 August 1919. To some extent the Act was nothing more than a reasonable compromise until something better could be arranged. The new Ministry acquired considerable powers and duties relating to railways and other forms of internal transport.[1] It was to retain control of the railways until 15 August 1921 and the financial guarantees were to remain for that period. Sir Eric Geddes, the first Minister of Transport, was the man responsible for planning the reorganization of the railways.

But for the time being the most important clauses of the Act were those conferring powers on the Minister to alter railway rates and charges after reference to the newly established Rates Advisory Committee. If many of the powers in the Act were never used, those relating to the fixing of charges and rates were worked to exhaustion in an effort to establish the charging policy of the railways on an economic basis. During the war only two main increases had been made in passenger fares and none at all in freight rates with the result that costs of operation had increased out of all proportion to rates and charges. From an analysis of the statistics it appears that falling net receipts were a direct function of increased costs which were in the main due to wage advances. The only practical thing to do therefore was either to reduce wages or raise charges and as the latter seemed to be the more politically acceptable solution it was adopted. The Minister of Transport therefore directed the Rates Advisory Committee to make revisions in railway rates to cover estimated deficits of between £40 and £50 million which were likely to accrue in the years 1919–20 and 1920–1. As a result of the Committee's reports two increases in freight rates and one in passenger fares were made in 1920.

The revised charges failed to improve the financial position of the railways. Total net receipts fell from £12·8 million in 1919 to £5·7 million in 1920 and in 1921 a real loss of £10·3 million was made. Interim increases in railway charges were of little value in checking falling revenue at a time when costs were still rising since they were usually out-of-date by the time they were made. By September 1920, when the final increase was made, goods rates were still only 112 per cent above the pre-war level whereas the increase in costs was roughly double this figure. Despite the deflationary trend in the economy after the middle of 1920 revenue was adversely effected by stoppages in the coal trade in 1920 and again in 1921, by the general trade recession which set in during the closing months of 1920, and by the amount of maintenance expenditure which was on an abnormal scale, largely because the arrears from previous years were being worked off.

Meanwhile the Government had been considering plans prepared by the Ministry of Transport for the reorganization of the railway system. In the summer of 1920 these were published in the form of a White Paper. It was proposed to organize nearly all the existing railway companies into a few large groups the object of which was to ensure that "direct competition

[1] Most of these powers were of course transferred from the Board of Trade.

between the groups would be as far as possible eliminated". The most important clause was that relating to the financial side of the new system: "The rates and fares shall be fixed at such a level as, with efficient and economical management, will in the opinion of a prescribed authority enable the railway companies to earn a net revenue substantially equivalent, on some pre-war basis to be settled in the Act, to the combined net revenue of all the companies absorbed in the group." Under the new plan the Government was to have a fairly large measure of control over the railway system of Great Britain.

The time between the issue of the White Paper at the end of June 1920 and the introduction of the Railways Bill in May 1921 was utilized in conducting lengthy discussions between railway and trade interests and the railway trade unions in an attempt to secure a substantial measure of agreement on the proposed new policy. Opposition came from many quarters and as a result the plan was considerably modified. Furthermore the Government was awaiting the report of the Rates Advisory Committee on the general revision of rates and charges which did not appear until December 1920. The recommendations of the Committee were, for the most part, embodied in the Railways Bill.

Though the Minister of Transport, when introducing the Bill in the House of Commons, stated that he had secured a wide measure of support for it, the debate on the measure was long, controversial and at times very critical.[1] Motions to reject it came from both sides of the House. As a result considerable modifications were again made the most notable being that the Scottish companies were no longer to stand apart from the English ones. Finally, on 19 August 1921, four days after the Government had ceased to control the railways, the Bill became law. In many ways the Railways Act of 1921 was the most constructive piece of railway legislation since the Act of 1844. It introduced for the first time in British railway history a serious attempt to grapple with the problem of scientific planning of the railway system and swept up masses of unco-ordinated legislation which had accumulated since railways were first sanctioned by Parliament.

The Act was divided into six parts, the most important being the first three covering reorganization, regulation and charging powers of the railways. Practically the whole of the system was formed into four main groups (the London, Midland & Scottish, the London & North-Eastern, the Southern and the Great Western railway companies) which remained in being until nationalization. The amalgamations were effected with great rapidity indeed and by 1923 four great companies emerged in place of the 100-odd companies which had previously existed. The scheme of grouping was designed to produce geographically compact systems which would

[1] Something of the size and scope of the measure can be gathered from the fact that the full report of the debates covered over 200 pages in Hansard (amounting to some 177,000 words); over 130 were filled from the Standing Committee's amendments alone and the final Act was exactly 90 pages.

eliminate as far as possible competition between the groups. A further consideration was that each group should be financially viable. It was for this reason that the Government's original proposal of a seven-group system with the Scottish companies standing alone was abandoned in favour of four larger companies in which the Scottish lines were grouped longitudinally with the English. (*See inset to Map 13*, pp. 152–3.) In many respects the grouping was merely a logical conclusion to the practice of the railway companies in the past "the object being economy and administrative efficiency". To achieve this object the Minister of Transport was given important regulatory powers over the railways to require or authorize the companies to conform to measures of general standardization of ways, plant and equipment, and to adopt schemes for co-operative working or common user of rolling stock, workshops, manufactories, plant and other facilities. In return the companies were awarded £60 million as "a full discharge and in satisfaction of all claims".

That part of the Act dealing with railway charges was the longest and most complicated section but undoubtedly the most important. The previous system of regulating rates and charges was swept away and an entirely new method adopted in accordance with the report of the Rates Advisory Committee on the general revision of rates and charges. This Committee was to remain in existence until it had completed a revised classification for goods traffic. A Railway Rates Tribunal was established by the Act and given wide powers and functions in all matters relating to railway charges. The Tribunal was to approve a new schedule of rates submitted by the amalgamated companies which were to come into force on the appointed day (1 January 1928) until which time the railways were allowed to retain their old charges. The Act of 1921 in no way guaranteed the earnings of the railway companies but it did initiate a new policy in that charges to be fixed in the first instance would be such that, together with other sources of revenue, they would yield, with efficient and economical working and management, an annual net revenue equivalent to that of 1913.

It was obvious that it would take some time before the revised classification and charges scheme could be completed and in fact it was not until 1928 that the new system became fully operative. The new classification followed very closely the recommendations of the Rates Advisory Committee which was satisfied that the former method of classifying goods met with general approval of the trading community. The major difference was that the new classification for merchandise was enlarged to 21 classes in place of eight under the old classification of 1891–2. After lengthy negotiations with interested parties the new classification was published in June 1923. On the other hand the general principles determining the class in which goods should be placed for purposes of charging remained broadly the same as before and were set out in section 29 of the Act. Value and bulk in relation to weight continued to be the main criteria for determining

classification though other factors such as risk of damage and cost of handling were not to be ignored. Traffic not covered by the General Merchandise
Classification was grouped into eight separate categories covering passengers, and other miscellaneous items such as returned empties, and the
carriage of animals and perishable commodities.

The drawing up of a new set of charges was a more complicated task and
it was not until 1927 that the Tribunal completed its work. The Act of 1921
attempted to make rate making more scientific and flexible than was previously the case. Under the old procedure maximum scales were fixed
within which the companies were in theory free to charge what they liked
but this freedom was greatly curtailed by the Act of 1894 because the railways
had to prove that any increases in charges were reasonable. In practice this
restriction was less onerous than it sounded for the companies still retained
their freedom to lower rates and standard class rates became the exception
rather than the rule.[1] By the new legislation this system was abolished.
Charges—known as "standard charges"—were approved by the Tribunal in
relation to the new classification and the companies had to maintain
these standard rates without variation either upwards or downwards
"unless by way of an exceptional rate or an exceptional fare continued,
granted or fixed under the provisions of this Part of the Act, or in respect of
competitive traffic in accordance therewith". Any alteration of the standard
charges had to be approved by the Tribunal.[2]

The companies were still allowed to quote exceptional rates but the Act
was designed to reduce these to a minimum. Exceptional rates of not less
than 5 per cent and not more than 40 per cent below the standard rates
were permitted without the approval of the Tribunal; outside these margins
the consent of the Tribunal had to be obtained. A greater degree of latitude
was allowed as regards passenger fares since the companies could fix fares
below the standard in such circumstances as they sought fit. The trader
or railway user was afforded ample means of protection against the railways
with regard to charges. Not only were the old laws of undue preference and
unfair discrimination strengthened by the 1921 Act but any "certified" person or recognized trader was allowed extensive rights of appeal to the Rates
Tribunal with regard to the making, cancellation or alteration of any railway
rates.

Perhaps the one really new feature of the Act of 1921 was the principle of
standard revenue. Charges fixed by the Tribunal were to be such that the
companies would be able to earn their net revenue of 1913. Each company
was expected to pay its way independently and the standard revenue eventually fixed by the Tribunal was £51·4 million divided in the following proportions: Southern Railway, £7·1 million; L.M.S., £20·6 million; G.W.R.,

[1] By 1913 80 per cent of the rates quoted were exceptional.
[2] The distinction between charges for conveyance and charges for terminals was retained. Conveyance rates were tapered and continuous and uniform mileage rates were
adopted throughout.

£8 · 5 million and the L.N.E.R., £15 ·2 million. There was of course no guarantee that the railway companies would receive this amount but in reviewing annually all charges the Tribunal was obliged to modify them according to whether or not the standard revenue had been realized during the period since the last review.

These then were the salient features of the Railways Act of 1921.[1] It represented the first real attempt to consolidate and codify the existing mass of legislation relating to the railways and in this respect it was successful. The Act was intended to secure the benefits of unification, codify the system of charging and increase its flexibility, and allow the railways to earn their pre-war net revenue. How far these aims were achieved in practice will be seen in the next chapter. For the moment it might be useful to comment on one or two of the defects of the legislation.

Essentially the Railways Act of 1921 was a compromise, a sort of "half-way house" between public ownership and private control and as such inherited the limitations of the former without losing all the defects of the latter.[2] As one writer later observed: "The four-group system possessed the inherent diseconomies of competition without its alleged virtues, the extortions of monopoly without its potential savings". The full benefits of unification could never be realized with four distinct groups; competition, though greatly reduced, still remained acute at some of the frontier towns between respective territories such as Birmingham, Sheffield, and Leeds.[3] The amalgamations were not scientifically planned on a geographical basis since one of the principal objectives was to leave the old companies intact. The result was that the territories of each group overlapped with one another. For example, the London, Midland & Scottish extended to Bristol, Bath and Swansea which was part of the Great Western Railway's system whilst in turn the Great Western encroached upon L.M.S. territory as far as Birkenhead and Warrington. Such duplication of facilities and additional expenses involved in administration and accounting undoubtedly hindered the realization of the very economies the Act was designed to achieve.

Probably the greatest weakness however lay in the new methods of charging. Despite the intention of the framers of the Act rate-making remained almost as unscientific and inflexible as it had been in the late nineteenth century. No provision was made for basing rates on the full economic cost of the service rendered. Granted, the difficulties of ascertaining indirect

---

[1] The last three parts of the Act dealing with wages and conditions of service, light railways and general matters will not be discussed here.

[2] One contemporary commented on the White Paper proposals as follows: "These 'outlines', if ever adopted in legislative form, would constitute an attempt to combine private ownership and responsibility with public control in a bastardised scheme of quasi-nationalisation fatal to railway progress". H. J. Jennings, "Our Insolvent Railways", *Fortnightly Review*, 1920, p. 477.

[3] Acworth maintained that "the effect of the new statutory grouping is to leave the bulk of the territory of Great Britain non-competitive, but the bulk of the traffic competitive". W. M. Acworth, "Grouping under the Railways Act, 1921", *Economic Journal*, March 1923, p. 31.

costs were overwhelming, but the accepted notion of cost-pricing as formulated by the Rates Advisory Committee provided little scope for eliminating the heavy cross subsidization which had prevailed in the nineteenth century. "It will suffice", the Committee said, "if the out-of-pocket costs of carriage are covered and a balance remains to contribute to the general costs, provided that there is other traffic which can bear rates high enough to meet the remainder of the general costs." In fact the Act did little to revolutionize charging. "It provided less rather than more of the flexibility sought by the Government in 1920 and it utterly failed to enable the railways to meet the competition which began to assail them long before Part 3 of the Act came into operation" (Harrison). In view of the complexity of railway charging it was utterly impossible to expect one single Tribunal to review charges annually and at the same time produce a greater degree of flexibility, and it was fortunate that the railways still retained their powers to make exceptional rates at a time when they were most needed. Finally, the Act still retained many of the nineteenth-century restrictions such as common carrier obligations and prohibition of undue preference which in the inter-war years were to prove a far greater handicap to the railways than ever before. Such factors were not wholly responsible of course for the declining fortunes of the railways in these years but there is no doubt that an Act designed largely for nineteenth and not twentieth century conditions did little to improve the situation.

11

Railways and shipping in the inter-war years

The First World War comprised a watershed in the history of British transport, for after 1919 great changes took place in the transport system. The
railway and shipping industries no longer continued to be the pace-setters
they had been in the nineteenth century and their fortunes steadily deteriorated. The canals continued to stagnate and it was not long before the urban
tramways were being called to share a similar fate. At the same time two
new forms of transport, the early origins of which lie in the pre-war period,
appeared on the scene. One of these was motor transport, a vigorous and
rapidly expanding industry, which provided fierce competition for established internal transport operators. The other was air transport, an expanding but extremely unprofitable undertaking. Each of these will be discussed
in turn but first let us take a look at the problems of railways and shipping.

The difficulties facing the railway and shipping industries in the inter-
war years were determined mainly by two factors. First, they were affected
adversely by the less favourable economic conditions obtaining in these
years compared with pre-1914 and, second, they encountered increasing
competition in the transport field. For much of the inter-war period parts
of the British economy were in a relatively depressed state and unemployment rarely fell below the one million mark. This is not really very surprising in view of the fact that the world economy as a whole was far less
buoyant after the First World War particularly in the disastrous years of the
Great Depression, 1923–33. But although the British economy continued to
expand in the inter-war period, it is apparent that certain sectors were
affected adversely by unfavourable trends in the international economy.
In the first place Britain's importance as an economic power, already
on the wane before 1914, declined rapidly after the war partly because
of the growing economic strength of foreign countries, particularly the

United States and Japan, both of which had largely escaped the harmful effects of the war. Thus Britain no longer maintained her influential rôle in the world economy as formerly. Second, Britain's prosperity in the nineteenth century had depended to a great extent on the ease with which she could buy and sell commodities in the world market. The international economic mechanism had worked in her favour simply because it had permitted the free exchange of commodities and capital. But there was always the danger that when things began to run less smoothly Britain would find herself in difficulties. And this is precisely what happened after the war. Though an attempt was made to reconstruct the international economic system on the old model it lacked any real stability. Trade was hampered by a growing network of commerical restrictions as each country tried to cope with problems of unemployment and to satisfy nationalistic ambitions arising from the war. Thus economic insecurity provoked policies which were incompatible with economic interdependence. Consequently the system gradually disintegrated and finally collapsed in ruins in the crisis of 1929–33. Britain lacked either the power or the will to prevent the collapse and henceforth self-sufficiency became the order of the day. The result was that more barriers were placed in the way of international economic co-operation and formerly interconnected markets were severed. For a country so dependent on trading links as Britain such events were disastrous.

But Britain's economic problems were not determined solely by forces outside the country. Even before 1914 her economy rested on insecure foundations. The industrial supremacy of the nineteenth century was based on a narrow range of industries such as coal, iron and steel, machinery and vehicles, ships and textiles, in which a competitive advantage was enjoyed. By 1911–13 two-thirds of Britain's exports belonged to these groups and nearly 70 per cent of all her exports went to agricultural countries. This overcommitment to producing traditional goods for traditional markets was to have severe repercussions in the inter-war years for it was these very industries and markets which were the most vulnerable. After 1920 the staple trades and the agricultural markets were no longer the most buoyant. Many countries had already begun to produce the staple goods, especially textiles, before 1914 and the war intensified the trend towards self-sufficiency as Britain's customers were cut off from their normal sources of supply. Moreover some of the basic goods were being replaced by substitutes; oil, for example, was competing with coal, and rayon with cotton textiles. Thus Britain was placed in the unenviable position of trying to find outlets for the type of goods the demand for which was steadily declining. Coupled with this was the fact that many primary producers were in difficulties because of falling agricultural prices and were therefore no longer in a position to buy the same quantity of goods from Britain as formerly. As a result of these changes Britain's exports stagnated and this had a major retarding affect on the growth of the British economy. In turn the stagnation in exports can be attributed to the failure to diversify the economy and alter the pattern of trading channels. It is not without significance that nearly five-sixths of the unemployment of the 1920s was caused by the fall in exports of the six leading staple export trades. Fundamental adaptations of the economic structure were required to meet new circumstances and the failure to make the necessary adjustments rapidly enough placed Britain in an extremely unfavourable position.

Such changes were bound to affect the transport system which formed an integral part of the British economy. Both the railways and the shipping industry had grown up to serve the needs of the rapidly expanding economy of the nineteenth century based upon the staple industries. Their services had been geared to the requirements of these industries and when contraction set in the transport system was affected likewise. Within limits adjustments could be made to transport services but in part such adjustments depended upon the rate at which the economic structure as a whole was adapted to meet the changed conditions. In addition, the transport system faced another problem, that of competition from without. In the case of the railways it came in the form of motor transport which proved to be more suited to meeting the requirements of the growing sector of the economy. The shipping industry had to cope with competition from foreign ship-owners who were often more enterprising. Thus economic difficulties and increasing competition provided a formidable challenge to both the railways and the shipowners in these years. How successful they were in meeting this challenge depended very much on the rate at which they adapted their services to accord with new conditions. In short, adaptability was the key to survival in the inter-war years.

1   Road and rail competition

Though the railways remained throughout this period the most important conveyors of freight traffic, they had come to the end of their rapid expansion. Financially they were much worse off than before the war. The companies both individually and collectively never earned their standard revenue as laid down by the Act of 1921. The nearest they ever came to it was in 1929 when almost £45 million was reached, but after that the surplus of earnings over operating expenses never again exceeded £40 million and in 1932 it was barely half of the standard. The worst group was the London & North Eastern which for most of the 1930s barely earned half its standard revenue of £15·2 million; the most successful company was the Southern whose revenue in 1937 fell short of the target by just over half a million pounds.

The fall in revenue reflected the steady contraction in railway traffic which began soon after the First World War (see Table 5). As regards freight the

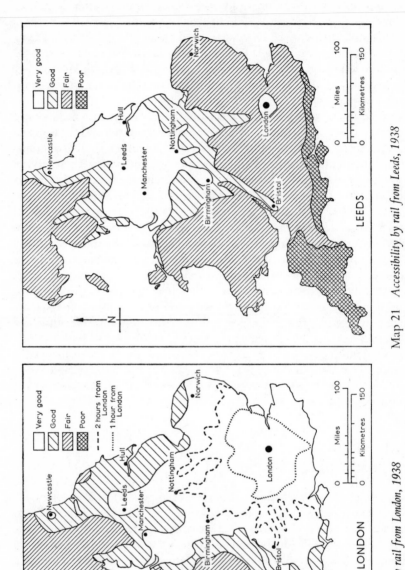

Map 21 *Accessibility by rail from Leeds, 1938*

Map 20 *Accessibility by rail from London, 1938*

decline was greatest between 1924 and 1933 when the depths of depression were reached, after which there was a partial revival until 1938 when once again there was a sharp contraction in goods traffic. In no year did the volume of freight traffic attain the 1913 level; even in 1937 the quantum of merchandise conveyed was only 74 per cent and the volume of minerals and coal 83 per cent of the 1913 figures. The position is less clear with regard to passenger traffic owing to the frequent changes in the form of official statistics. The number of passenger journeys rose to a peak in 1920 after which there was a significant decline. However it seems unlikely that total passenger traffic ever fell much below the pre-war level and by 1937 the railways were probably carrying a greater number of passengers than in 1913.

Three factors precipitated the fall in railway traffic: fluctuations in the level of economic activity, especially in the basic industries; the change in the pattern of internal trade; and the rise of a new form of transport. The railways suffered severely in the sharp contractions in trade which occurred in the early 1920s, in 1926 because of the general strike, in the

Table 5   Railway traffic, 1913–1937

000 tons	1913	1924	1933	1937
General merchandise (Classes 7–21)	67,755	60,943	42,479	50,319
Minerals (Classes 1–6)	71,067	65,393	43,117	58,683
Coal	225,601	209,161	165,452	188,149
Number of passenger journeys (including season ticket holders): millions	1,549·8	1,746·9	1,575	1,819

early 1930s and in 1938. The position was aggravated by the fact that the railways had been developed to serve the basic industries of the nineteenth century such as coal, steel, textiles and shipbuilding which were the most severely depressed industries in these years. This meant that the railways lost much of their former heavy traffic, especially coal and minerals which were largely immune from road competition. Many of the regions in which old industries were situated, e.g., the northeast and northwest of England and the southwest of Scotland, became depressed areas and the railway facilities within them became partly redundant and much less remunerative than before 1914. Moreover, the counter-balancing development of the "newer" or "lighter" industries in the south and midlands did not compensate the railways as might be expected. Not only was the volume of traffic originating from them less than that of the older industries but many of the new factories were situated nearer their markets and consequently their products required less haulage. In any case, some of the newer goods required more expensive handling facilities (e.g., collection and delivery

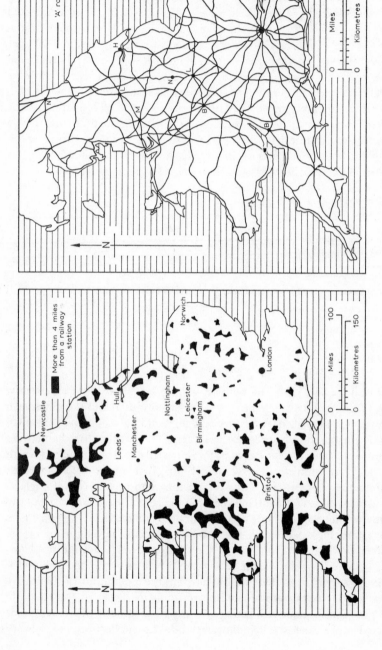

Map 23   *The national road network, 1938*

Map 22   *Distance from railway stations, 1938*

services) and tended to be more attractive to the road haulier. Concomitant with the rise of the newer industries there was a change in methods of trade and in social habits which brought a change in the type of transport services required. There was a tendency after the war for consumers and traders to purchase a greater range of goods in smaller quantities at more frequent intervals. The demand for transport services therefore altered accordingly. Merchandise traffic by goods train, for example, tended to be consigned in smaller lots more frequently. In Manchester it was found that the proportion of very small lots, 28 lbs or less, forwarded from certain rail depots doubled between 1924 and 1932. This type of traffic was less suited to a railway system designed for nineteenth century purposes. In any case some of it required special and expensive handling facilities and this limited the scope for technical improvements, e.g., the use of larger wagons. Possibly some of the new traffic would have provided a good return had the railways been adapted to meet its needs (e.g., use of containers and railhead system of distribution) but since at the time it proved to be a more attractive proposition to the road haulier the railway companies were less inclined to adapt their system for it.

The drop in railway traffic, however, was much greater than can be accounted for by fluctuations and changes in the pattern of trade. The rise in motor transport which was particularly rapid after 1922 made serious inroads into railway traffic. Table 7 in Chapter 12 gives an idea of its growth. Unfortunately, it is impossible to say exactly how much traffic the railways lost to road transport partly because the statistics relating to road traffic are incomplete. In 1937 the total number of rides taken on public service vehicles (buses and coaches) amounted to 6,664 million but at least half this total comprised very short distance or local journeys where rail facilities were non-existent. Of the remainder only a small proportion consisted of long-distance trips so that it was on the short or medium distance routes where the motor bus could offer a more convenient and cheaper service that the railways lost most of their passenger traffic to the road. It is probable that motor transport deprived the railways of more than 200 million passengers.[1] For freight traffic, Walker has estimated that in 1936 road hauliers carried 100 million tons of which about 45 to 50 million, or roughly one half, represented traffic which would otherwise have gone by rail. Since nearly 178 million tons of a total railway freight traffic of 281 million tons was in coal in which road competition was negligible it follows that road competition for general merchandise must have been fairly severe.

The contraction in railway traffic was more serious for the railways financially than the figures would at first suggest. There are a number of reasons to account for this. The railways for the first time experienced a decline in all classes of traffic. Before the war passengers and freight traffic hardly ever moved in the same direction except at times when all traffic was expanding. Thus for every contraction in tons conveyed the number of

[1] This makes no allowance for journeys made in private cars.

U

passenger journeys increased and vice-versa. After 1920 there were few contra-cyclical movements in traffic; a general contraction took place in both passenger and freight traffic and there was no contra-cyclical action in one sector to offset the fall in the other. Secondly, one has to remember that the effect of a transfer of traffic from rail to road harmed the railways much more than it benefited road transport for the simple reason that the variable costs of road operators were much greater than those of the railways. Since the costs of maintaining a railway system are relatively high[1] and inflexible in the short run, unit costs tend to vary inversely with the volume of traffic. In other words, any reduction in the volume of traffic will produce a greater fall in revenue than in operating expenses. This is just what happened in the inter-war years with the result that the railways' operating ratio, that is working expenses as a proportion of receipts, rose from 60 per cent pre-war to 80 per cent. The position was made worse of course by the fact that motor competition forced the railways to reduce their charges which adversely affected net revenue since comparable reductions could not be made in expenditure. It was this factor probably more than anything else which accounted for the poor financial position of the railways in these years.

Motor transport proved to be a serious competitor in terms of both price and service. For passengers the private car or public service vehicles provided a more convenient, often speedier and more reliable form of transport particularly on short distance or cross-country routes where the railways suffered the most severe losses in passenger traffic. On long-distance journeys the railways retained the bulk of the traffic though even here the introduction of long-distance limited-stop buses was beginning to carry competition further afield by the early 1930s. As a result of rapid technical improvements motor buses could be operated successfully at a fare of slightly less than 1d. per mile by the mid-1920s, compared with the ordinary 3rd class rail fare of 1$\frac{1}{2}d$. per mile. In addition bus operators could often afford to give appreciable reductions on return tickets.

Competition in freight transport proved to be the most formidable as far as the railway companies were concerned. Though vehicles owned by public carriers formed the smallest group numerically they offered the most serious source of competition since the majority of the privately-owned fleets were used largely for local collection and delivery services. Road charges were generally lower than the competitive railway rate though not for all classes of traffic. This arose not merely from the fact that operating costs of road vehicles were relatively low but also because road charges were based on the cost of service performed. Railway rates on the other hand were determined more by the value of goods conveyed rather than the cost of carrying them. This meant that road charges were lower than

[1] Today, for instance, it has been calculated that the total cost of providing the route system (i.e. excluding sidings, stations and depots etc.) amounts to nearly one quarter of the total revenue of British Rail.

railway rates for valuable or high-class merchandise and higher for less valuable or low-classed commodities. Road hauliers therefore tended to confine the scope of their operations to the dense traffic routes where full loads of fairly valuable merchandise could be obtained leaving the railways to deal with that traffic which was least attractive to them. The position has been summarized by Walker as follows: "Road competition was 'unfair' because the railways, by law, must charge rates which are higher than road costs for some classes of merchandise and lower for others; rates which do not make allowance for the differences in the cost of working traffic over one route compared with another, and rates which discriminate less between the large and the small consignment than road charges do. The results of such competition are inevitable. Road transport takes that traffic for which costs by road are low in relation to railway rate; the large consignments and the full loads to big centres whence a load back can always be obtained. The railways are left with the traffic for which the railway rate is low compared with cost by road, small consignments, traffic to the minor centres from which a return load cannot always be got and freight to remote areas generally." Broadly speaking, road competition, on the basis of a single outward load, was effective within a range of up to 75 miles, but if return loads were secured it was effective for much longer distances. As a result road hauliers were prepared to cut their rates drastically to acquire back-loads since if costs were covered on the outward trip any additional revenue earned was a contribution to profits.

Apart from the price advantages, traders have often been induced to consign their goods by road because of the added attraction of better service. Road transport offered a more reliable, safer and often quicker service than the railway particularly for short distances or cross-country routes. Packaging and loading arrangements were less complicated than by rail, and goods could be carried from door to door without transhipment. Road transport, moreover, was able to provide a more flexible type of service particularly in cases where traders required rapid delivery of goods at unusual times of the day. The lorry worked to no fixed time schedule and could be despatched as and when required by the traders whereas the railways had to conform to a tight schedule since any delay was bound to disorganize the whole system of operation. The balance of advantage in terms of service was not of course all one way. The railway companies could provide transport facilities to any part of the country whereas the road haulier was sometimes limited in his field of operation. On some of the main line routes the railways in fact gave a more reliable and speedier service particularly for bulk consignments since there was little limit to their haulage capacity whereas road hauliers were at times unable to provide all the capacity required. Since the ports and many factories were provided with on the spot railway facilities firms found it convenient to consign their goods by rail especially where export shipments were concerned. The railways also provided empty wagons for the convenience of traders and offered extensive accommodation for storing goods which road transport was incapable of doing.

There can be no doubt that the railways found themselves in a very difficult situation in the inter-war years. On the one hand, they faced contraction and fluctuation in their basic heavy traffic due largely to the prevailing economic conditions whilst on the other, they encountered rigorous competition from a more flexible form of transport which sought to rob them of some 'of their most valuable traffic. The solution to these problems did not lie entirely outside the powers of the railways. It has been suggested, however, that the railways were conservative and unenterprising and failed to take steps to meet the needs of the new situation. To some extent this is true particularly in the early years after the war when they were engaged with the problems of reconstruction and amalgamation. On the other hand it is perhaps a little unkind to suggest that they were "helpless spectators of their own defeat". In a number of ways the railways attempted to resuscitate their declining fortunes. They were not wholly responsible for the fact that the remedies adopted were largely without effect.

2   Technical change and efficiency

One of the chief aims of the Act of 1921 was to secure economies and improve efficiency through amalgamation. Sir Eric Geddes, the first Minister of Transport, estimated that these economies would be in the region of £20 million per annum. In evidence before the Royal Commission on Transport, traders alleged that the economies had been relatively insignificant whilst the companies on their part maintained that they had been large and progressive. A number of independent estimates have been made, all of them different and none of them very reliable. However we do know that operating expenses fell by about £29 million between 1924 and 1938 and allowing for price changes this amounts to a saving of around £19 million. On the basis of 1928, Broster estimated that by 1938 economies were running at about £15 million per annum. If the savings were less than had been anticipated they were by no means insignificant though it is unlikely that all of them arose from amalgamation.

The companies in fact did a great deal to secure as many of the benefits as partial unification would allow. Substantial economies were made by reducing administrative expenses, standardizing equipment, rationalizing construction and repair shops, closing down unprofitable branch lines, improving methods of traffic working and by more extensive common use of rolling stock. In 1935 for example the L.M.S. was working with 24 per cent fewer locomotives compared with 1923. By reducing the number of types of equipment, reorganizing the workshops and repair shops and by introducing new locomotives among other things the company was estimated to be saving about £2 million per annum. During the 1930s extensive pooling agreements of receipts arising from competitive traffic were made between the companies. In 1934 pooling arrangements covered about 53 per cent of the receipts and by the end of the decade inter-company competition had been effectively terminated for good.

The railways also improved their facilities appreciably especially in the 1930s. The speed and frequency of the main line passenger trains was increased through the reorganization of timetables and improvements in equipment. On the London to Manchester run of the former London & North Western the overall average speed including stops, rose from 44.4 m.p.h. in 1900 to 58 in 1938. During the 1930s the L.M.S. introduced 66 new express services at average speeds of 60 m.p.h. or over throughout the length of the journey. The most progressive company in this respect was the L.N.E.R. which in 1935 streamlined its services to the North, and one of the company's locomotives, *Mallard*, achieved the world speed record in 1938. By then there were 107 trains scheduled to run at speeds of 60 m.p.h. or over as against 25 in 1934 and four in 1914. Travelling time on a number of longer routes were reduced appreciably by cutting out intermediate stops. For example, 105 minutes was clipped off the London to Glasgow service and 135 minutes was knocked off the London–Edinburgh run. Passengers also benefited from improved cross country services, better and more comfortable rolling stock, cheaper fares and the increasing interchangeability of facilities by road, rail and air.

The trader was not neglected in these improvements. Express freight trains carrying bulk consignments were introduced. By rearranging the marshalling system and running trains through to their destination the L.M.S. had by 1938, 57 scheduled daily non-stop freight runs over 90 miles and seven over 150. Truck and train-loading were improved, larger wagons more widely used and nearly all railway-owned wagons were fitted with oil-axle boxes to permit faster running. New forms of co-ordinated road/rail transport were developed by the introduction of the container which allowed the advantages of high speed and low rates for bulk traffic of the railway to be combined with door-to-door delivery without unloading. By 1938 there were 15,500 containers in use on the railways compared with 350 in 1928. Collection and delivery services were speeded up by the use of motor vehicles and by concentrating these services more at central depots under the railhead system.

The most spectacular improvements however occurred on the Southern Railway, the only company to undertake a large-scale programme of reconstruction and modernization. Before amalgamation few attempts had been made at electrification except for the North Tyneside suburban lines and 83 miles on the Southern Region network. After the war the Southern Railway, the smallest of the four groups, was the most enterprising in this respect. Passenger traffic, from which the bulk of its revenue was derived, was hit badly by motor transport, and the company decided to combat this by undertaking a large-scale programme of capital investment designed to increase the frequency and reliability of services and at the same time reduce the costs of operation. Only 17 per cent of the track mileage was electrified in 1929 but in the following decade rapid progress was made, the company taking full advantage of the financial loan of £32 million made available for major schemes of modernization under the Railways (Agreement) Act of 1935. By 1936 electric mileage exceeded steam passenger mileage for the first time and in 1938 it was around 60 per cent of the total. With nearly one third of its route mileage converted, the Southern Railway constituted one of the largest electrified systems in the world. At the same time an extensive programme of modernization was carried out on the track and equipment in order to eliminate some of the antiquated stock inherited in 1923. Much of the old rolling stock was either scrapped or renovated and 520 new locomotives were built. In addition £7 million was spent in modernizing and enlarging the Southampton docks which the company owned. By the end of the 1930s the standard of equipment on the Southern was well above the average and, according to White, "there were no such antiquities as the ex-North London four-wheel sets which were still trundling disgruntled commuters up the Northern heights in 1935".

The benefits of modernization were enormous both for the company and the railway user. Though the company had spent nearly £21 million on its electrification project it was able to treble its suburban services for an extra working cost of only £164,000. Electric services were more frequent, more punctual, faster and cleaner than the steam ones they replaced. The volume of traffic increased enormously and many of the south coast towns enjoyed better train services than ever before. In the 1930s passenger journeys on electrified lines rose by 12½ million whereas, rather significantly, those on the remaining steam services fell by nearly one million. "It was only electrification and the reduced operating costs which allowed better services at cheaper fares. By those means rail transport was once more in a competitive position and new traffic was created."

Such bold experiments were not repeated elsewhere. The Southern group and the London Passenger Transport Board accounted for 800 of the 990 route miles electrified in Britain by 1939. Of the remainder well over one-third was accounted for by the Tyneside lines, together with three lines in the Manchester region which were converted in the 1930s. Up to the end of 1938 only five per cent of the total route mileage in Great Britain had been electrified, a lower proportion than in almost any other country. In view of the advantages of electrification it is surprising that the policy was not more widely adopted. In 1931 the Weir Committee reckoned that main line railway electrification was a policy worthy of serious consideration and estimated that operating expenses would be reduced by £17 million in so doing. This estimate was probably on the low side. It took no account of the possible increase in traffic and on the basis of the Southern returns, operating expenses had been reduced by one third to one half on the electrified sections. The other companies defended themselves by arguing that the Southern stood to gain more because of its greater proportion of passenger traffic, that the initial cost of electrification was extremely high and that it might lead to a loss in coal traffic. None of these reasons is entirely convincing. Admittedly the capital cost of electrification was high—£261 million according to the Weir Committee—yet between 1923 and 1939 the railways spent some £300 million on renewals and reconstruction of rolling stock, track and stations, a substantial proportion of which could no doubt have gone towards electrification. General apathy, an insufficient knowledge about the benefits to be derived from electrification and the opposition of coal-owners on the railway-boards probably provide a more realistic explanation for the failure to extend electrification. Perhaps too the very fact that considerable improvements were made in the performance of steam locomotives lessened the attraction of the new source of power to a generation of railwaymen brought up on "steam".

There can be no doubt that the railways did a great deal to improve the efficiency of their undertakings especially during the 1930s when the impact of road competition became more acute. Capital expenditure of the four companies rose by £67 million between 1923 and 1936. Yet was it sufficient, or rather was the money spent in the right way? The answer is probably in the negative. Most of the money was invested in existing technique, that is the renewal of existing equipment, rather than in new technology; the diesel locomotive, for example, was almost completely neglected in favour of steam, and apart from the Southern Railway, little interest was shown in electrification. Moreover, many of the improvements that were made only touched the surface of the system and much more was required if the railways were going to restore their fortunes and at the same time compete effectively with road transport. This is particularly so in the case of goods traffic where freight handling remained hopelessly antiquated and inefficient even by 1939. Bulk consignment of freight moving at high speed in through trains was the exception rather than the rule. Average truck and train loads were incredibly low and the speed of freight trains was often farcical. The average speed of some goods trains was less than one mile per hour whilst in 1931 the average load of trucks carrying merchandise was 2·83 tons compared with a capacity of 10 tons. In any case many of the wagons in use were far too small for economical handling; 20-ton wagons, for example, represented less than 3 per cent of the total mineral wagons.[1] Only Britain tolerated the small privately owned rail wagon which cost the railways enormous sums for superfluous shunting alone.

In all fairness the railways were not wholly to blame for this predicament.

[1] Considerable savings could be made by adopting the 20-ton in place of the 10-ton wagon. For a capital cost increase of 50 per cent the earning capacity is doubled whilst current maintenance costs would be reduced by 25 per cent per ton-mile, shunting would fall and locomotives could haul pay-loads up to 25 per cent greater.

Indeed under the conditions prevailing it is sometimes surprising to find that they achieved so much. The railways suffered from the legacy of the past in that they developed at a time when few other forms of transport were available and railway users came to rely on them for the provision of any service however uneconomic and however wasteful of the resources of the system. Hence, of course, the opposition to reform. The position is well illustrated by the development of freight transport. The railways were eventually obliged to provide conveyance for freight in any quantity to a multiplicity of stations and depots, much of the traffic moving in single wagon consignments. The *Beeching Report* describes the consequences of this and is worth quoting at length: "As a result the wagon became the unit of movement and through working of trains was largely suppressed. Instead, nearly all freight moved by the staging of wagons from marshalling yard to marshalling yard, with variable and accumulative delays in them, so that the overall journey was bound to be slow and unpredictable."

"Thus, in order to provide for a large measure of rail participation in country-wide collection and delivery of small consignments, which the railways were never particularly well suited to do, and which they only did because the horse-drawn cart was worse, the railways threw away their main advantages. They saddled themselves with the costly movement of wagons in small numbers over a multiplicity of branch lines, where there were too few wagons moving to make good trains. At the same time, they sacrificed the speed, reliability, and low cost of through-train operation even on the main arteries."

"The slow and semi-random movement of wagons, and their dispersal over many small terminals where they cannot be collected or delivered very frequently, has necessitated the provision of an enormous fleet of wagons. Also, because of their random motion, all these wagons have to be capable of coupling and running with one another and of going almost anywhere on the system. This compatibility requirement, combined with the size and cost of the fleet, has been an obstacle to technical progress, since the new always has to mate with the old. In consequence, evolution of improved rolling stock has been very slow."

In this way the railways sacrificed their main advantages to the convenience of traders many of whom have strongly opposed reform.

One of the biggest obstacles to reform has been the privately-owned wagon. Nearly half the wagons used on the railways were privately owned and the determination of traders to cling to their independent fleets has involved the railways in much expensive empty running and unnecessary shunting. In this respect coal-owners have been the worst offenders. Johnston suggests that "nothing has so retarded progress on the railways as the retention of the privately owned coal wagon, estimated to have cost £20 million a year for wholly avoidable shunting, and encumbering the tracks, to the restriction and retardation of other traffic". Many of the wagons were too small and antiquated, lacking proper brakes and oil-axle boxes which permitted faster running. Coal-owners remained wedded to the practice of "carting coal in bath-tubs", that is in the small 10-ton wagon instead of the larger more economical 20-ton truck. It is true that drastic reconstruction of the sidings and terminals would have been required before any large extension of the 20-ton wagon would have been practicable, yet in the retail coal trade the organization was such that even the 12-ton wagon was sometimes too large.

One of the chief methods adopted by the railways to combat road transport was to "get on the road" themselves. This policy of course was nothing new. Even before amalgamation the old companies had owned a number of motor vehicles and some of the first bus services had been started by them. But it was not until 1928 that the four companies obtained general road powers after which they "displayed almost feverish activity" in acquiring an interest in road transport. Initially the railways confined their attention to passenger services. Few new undertakings were established, for the method they adopted was to acquire substantial financial interests in, or working agreements with, the larger and more reputable road companies such as Scottish Motor Traction, Crosville, Ribble and the North-Western Road Car Company or to operate services in conjunction with municipal authorities. By the end of 1931 the railways controlled or were associated with nearly 50 per cent of the total buses on Britain's roads. In road haulage, where the structure of the industry was far more atomistic, the scope for acquiring financial interests in existing undertakings was far less. Apart therefore from the purchase of Pickfords and Carter Patersons, the two oldest and largest undertakings, the railways limited their action to buying vehicles to provide their own feeder services. By 1938 the four companies owned over 10,000 goods vehicles compared with just under 4,000 in 1929.[1]

It is somewhat doubtful whether the railways gained much from investing in their competitors. Although it produced a greater degree of co-ordination between road and rail services on the passenger side the extent of their interests was too small, especially on the freight side, to have much effect in limiting the degree of competition. The railways rarely held sufficient shares in road undertakings to give them a controlling voice so that it was impossible for them to determine the policy of road transport in their own interests. On the other hand, the capital invested was quite substantial—£4·6 million in their own road vehicles and probably a further £10 million in subscriptions to omnibus undertakings—and one feels that it would have been better applied to the electrification of suburban lines. This conclusion is justified if for no other reason than the fact that road transport undertakings of the railways brought in little additional revenue. In 1936, for example, road transport operations carried out by the railways made a net profit of only £122,000.

[1] It is interesting to note that the railways still owned about 24,000 horse-drawn vehicles.

3   Railway costs and charges

Whatever improvements the railways had made in their services it is unlikely that they could have prevented motor transport from capturing part of their traffic. Price was often the crucial factor and, as we have seen, road transport was able to undercut the railways both in passenger and merchandise traffic.[1] To combat this the railways adopted a policy of reducing their own rates and charges. Soon after 1920 standard rates and charges for both passengers and goods were reduced in stages so that by the end of 1927, before the new rate-making procedure was put into operation, passenger fares had been reduced to 50 per cent and freight rates to about 55 per cent above the pre-war level. In some cases rates for freight traffic were cut by about 40 per cent in order to retain traffic. During the late 1920s and early 1930s a remarkable growth in special fares and rates took place. On the passenger side monthly return fares at single fare plus one-third became general in 1933 and a wide range of cheap return tickets and other concessions were introduced so that eventually few passengers were paying the full standard fare. It has been estimated that in 1936, 93 per cent of the passengers (including workmen and season-ticket holders) were travelling at reduced fares and only 7 per cent at standard fares compared with 68 and 32 per cent respectively in 1924. A similar procedure was adopted for freight traffic. Contrary to the intentions of the 1921 Act the number of exceptional rates increased rather than diminished after 1928, though many of the old exceptional rates had to be incorporated into the new rate structure since the task of revision proved to be too large. Thus by 1948, 72 per cent of the railway receipts from freight traffic were derived from goods conveyed at exceptional rates compared with 68 per cent in 1935 and 50 per cent in 1928. In addition, a new form of sub-standard rate, the agreed charge, was introduced in 1931 and given legal recognition by the Road and Rail Traffic Act of 1933. These charges were negotiated individually with traders, the main advantage being that the railways usually gained the whole of the traffic of any trader with whom an agreement was made. They were never used very extensively however, and in 1948 only 7 per cent of total freight revenue earned came from agreed charges.

Despite these changes the average level of fares and rates did not fall as far as might be expected. The receipt per ton mile for general merchandise fell by about 2 per cent per annum and that for minerals and heavy goods by about 1·6 per cent. The average fare per passenger mile dropped from 0·744d. in 1931 to 0·612d. in 1936. To argue that these reductions were insufficient to allow the railways to compete effectively with road transport is somewhat misleading. Granted that short of reducing their charges to the

[1] Here of course we are merely concerned with public service facilities. It goes without saying that the railways could not have prevented people from travelling in their own cars or traders using their own vehicles for carrying goods.

same level as those of road transport, which would no doubt have involved the railways in conveying traffic at a loss in many cases, it was impossible for the railways to meet competition on an equal footing. But this does not alter the fact that selective price changes could have enabled the railways to retain that kind of traffic which was the most profitable and dispense with the rest. A selective and flexible pricing policy was the key to the whole problem since the development of road transport had raised the elasticity of demand for railway services to a level considerably higher than that prevailing under the pre-war monopoly conditions. Thus the important point is whether the actual reductions in charges were made in a way to secure the best results. Quite clearly this was not the case. Many of the changes were made indiscriminately and failed to differentiate sufficiently between good and bad traffic. Had greater attention been paid when making the concessions to the variations in the elasticity of demand for the transport services in question and the costs of operation, the outcome in the long run might have been more satisfactory. As it was many of the reductions were less than useless in helping the railways to pay their way. In some cases charges were too high and in others too low.

On the passenger side, where, except for short distance journeys, the price elasticity of demand was relatively low compared with the freight side, railway fares were often too cheap. Broster calculated that an average fare of $0 \cdot 904d$. per mile would have maximized net revenue. But the average passenger fare was much lower (around $0 \cdot 65d$. per mile) than this simply because the railways were pre-occupied with maximizing gross revenue; in so doing they automatically sacrificed their net revenue since the additional expense incurred in meeting the requirements of concessionary passengers and in providing special services e.g., holiday specials, often outweighed the gain in receipts. As one contemporary observed "in recent years these reduced fare facilities have been very extensive indeed and so fully made use of as almost to embarrass the companies who in some cases have had to devise special methods of handling the traffic". If the aim had been to maximize net revenue on passenger services the pricing policy would have required revision as follows. On the short-distance or cross-country routes where the railways suffered their worst losses there was a strong case for pricing the traffic out of the market, the assumption being that much of the traffic would have been lost anyway whatever concessions had been made since motor transport offered a more convenient and of course cheaper form of travel. If this had been done it would have been possible to cut out many of the services which were already uneconomic. Passenger fares could also have been raised on long-distance journeys for it was here that the elasticity of demand for railway services was lowest since the possibilities of substitution with an alternative form of transport were still fairly limited before 1939. On the other hand, the greatest reduction in fares should have been made on medium distance journeys between large towns, e.g., Liverpool–Birmingham and Leicester–Manchester, for the traffic flows on these routes were both dense and profitable yet at the same time most vulnerable to motor transport in the long run.

The situation is rather more complicated in the case of freight traffic. Merchandise traffic, which it has been assumed was the most profitable, was lost because charges were too high compared with those of road transport. On the other hand, the railways retained the bulk of the heavy traffic, which contributed little to overheads, since they provided the cheaper and better service. If this hypothesis is accepted (though there is reason to believe that much of the newer merchandise traffic was far less profitable than commonly supposed) then it would appear that the rate adjustment policy of the railways was incorrect. Exceptional rates were granted for almost everything regardless of variations in costs of operation and in the elasticities of demand or the degree of competition. Thus the rates for general merchandise were reduced only slightly more than those for heavy goods whilst the proportion of the higher-classed merchandise charged at exceptional rates was still less than the proportion of the lower-classed traffic, the traffic, that is, least affected by road competition. If the railways had reduced charges even further on the good merchandise traffic (that is the most profitable and least costly to handle) and raised it on the bad they would have maximized their net revenue and at the same time offered a greater challenge to their competitors. For heavy classes of traffic, particularly coal, where the elasticity of demand was low and road competition negligible, an increase in rates would have allowed a greater contribution to be made towards indirect costs.

The railway companies themselves, it seems, were in no doubt as to the expediency of adopting a policy of discriminating or differential charging. In a Memorandum addressed to the Minister on 26 January 1932 it was emphasized that "An increase of rates on the classes of traffic which for the most part cannot be diverted to road transport has always been recognized as a necessity which might be forced upon the railway companies if the diversion of traffic to road proceeded unchecked, as has in fact been the case. It is the logical and inevitable result of continued diversion." If so why was more attention not paid to simple economic principles when charges were adjusted?

To a large extent the companies were prevented from operating their undertakings as commercial concerns by the statutory obligations with which they had been encumbered. In framing standard freight charges the basis remained the "time-honoured" principle of low rates for the cheaper commodities and higher rates for the more valuable traffic. "It might well be, of course, that certain low-valued commodities were cheap for the railways to carry and certain high-valued commodities expensive; but such an indirect correspondence between charges and costs was likely to be fortuitous". In contrast charges by road were determined in a competitive market on the basis of cost plus profit; there was no uniform classification and charges varied widely from one haulier to another. The consequences of this difference in pricing policy have already been noted. For the valuable, easily handled commodities moving over dense traffic routes the road haulier was able to offer a rate which easily undercut that of the railways whereas for the less valuable, bulky or bad mixing cargo the haulier had no alternative but to charge a high price. Moreover, in contrast to the railways who were legally obliged to offer reasonable facilities and practise no undue discrimination, road hauliers were completely free to vary their charges so as to bring about an even flow of traffic over time and "the relationship between outward and inward rates will tend to be such as to induce a volume of traffic moving in one direction equal to that moving in the opposite direction".

The divergence between charges and costs which arose through basing railway rates on a value system of classification was partly overcome by granting special rates and fares. Though the consent of the Rates Tribunal had to be obtained for cuts in the standard rates of more than 40 per cent, this barrier to rate reduction was more apparent than real. If the Tribunal was convinced that any rate was fixed too high in relation to costs then it was unlikely to refuse a reduction unless it considered that by so doing the company's revenue position would deteriorate. In any case many of the exceptional rates that were made fell within the statutory limits. On the other hand, the delay in adjusting rates by this procedure was often sufficient to allow road hauliers with their ability to quote snap rates, to step in and collect traffic from under the noses of the companies. The Tribunal would have offered of course a more serious obstruction to rate adjustment in an upward direction as it would have encountered strong opposition from the railway users. Since the railways only ever applied for one increase (in 1937) the point is not worthy of further consideration.

It was suggested earlier that in making their concessionary rates and fares the railways failed to discriminate sufficiently between good and bad traffic. This was partly the result of the influence of the obligations to maintain equality and avoid undue preference which the railways had inherited from the nineteenth century. The railways were legally obliged to grant the same facilities and rates to all traders consigning similar goods under similar conditions. In other words it was difficult to discriminate between one trader and another. It was impossible, for instance, to grant a special rate to induce part of a particular traffic moved by road to transfer to rail since it would create an element of preference. Only when the bulk of such a commodity was going by road did it become profitable to offer special rates by which time it was probably too late to attract the traffic back to the railways. Moreover, the obligations made the railways cautious in granting exceptional rates since "it was difficult to see the end of the chain reaction that might be triggered off by a single concession to a single trader", though traders had in the first instance to justify their complaints of undue preference before the Tribunal. The position was aggravated by the fact that the railways, unlike their competitors, had to publish their rates and charges. This enabled traders to compare charges and seek concessions wherever possible, regardless of whether they were being discriminated against, which meant that a greater degree of uniformity was imposed on railway charges than the clause of undue preference demanded. Many traders in fact sought reductions to which they had no legal right for, as Savage points out, "traders came to expect the railway companies to quote the same rate for similar services all over the country, rates which the railway companies might only be able to grant at a considerable loss to themselves".

In addition to the above restrictions on their freedom the railways suffered other disabilities from which their competitors were largely free. They were required to secure the safety of the travelling public and provide facilities for the conveyance of workmen and members of the Forces at cheap rates. The rates of pay and conditions of service of their employees were laid down by Act of Parliament and accounts and returns had to be submitted for inspection annually. Finally the railways were obliged to perform common carrier duties. The companies did not contend that all these factors were disadvantageous, but merely stated that there were differences which existed between road and rail some of which had harmful economic effects. Taken together, however, they undoubtedly constituted a heavy burden and limited the degree to which the railways could meet the competition of road transport on a commercial basis.

It is somewhat surprising to find that the companies had few suggestions to make to the Royal Commission on Transport as regards the possibility of removing the disabilities. They did of course argue that it would be easy for Parliament to remove many of the statutory obligations but felt that such action would create confusion and produce strong opposition from railway users. They decided instead therefore that their difficulties could be alleviated by regulating road transport. As we shall see later their wishes were granted by the Acts of 1930 and 1933.[1] At the same time various suggestions were made concerning the co-ordination of inland transport facilities which it was hoped might do something to reduce the competition of road transport. Neither did much to improve the position of the railways. Though the legislation of the early 1930s curtailed the freedom of road transport it still remained competitive, whilst the proposals for co-ordination came to very little. Consequently the railways turned their attention to the only other solution. They decided to make a bid for freedom and in November 1938 launched their Square Deal campaign. This campaign was designed to secure the removal of the restrictions under which they laboured so that they would be in a position to compete effectively with road transport. The negotiations arising out of these demands resulted in the report of the Transport Advisory Council[2] in April 1939 which

[1] See chapter 12
[2] Established by Part III of the 1933 Act to assist and advise the Minister of Transport on transport facilities generally including co-ordination.

recommended the removal of legislation governing classification, standard charges, exceptional rates and undue preference. The Government accepted the committee's recommendations but the outbreak of the Second World War prevented action being taken.

It can be seen therefore that the railways were at a serious disadvantage compared with road transport operators. The latter, unfettered by statutory restrictions (at least until the 1930s) were able to run their concerns on commercial lines. As a consequence they were able to take the pick of the traffic leaving the railways to convey the least profitable traffic on the least profitable routes. It can be argued, however, that the railways, imbued with the legacy of the past, tended to take an unrealistic attitude to the new conditions. As Savage has suggested, the companies interpreted their obligations too rigidly. The provision of reasonable facilities, for example, did not stop the railways from curtailing economic services or closing branch lines though little was done in this respect.[1] Admittedly the restrictions on charging powers were formidable though they were by no means as inflexible as the companies imagined. Neither the value system of classification nor the legal restraints on undue preference prevented an application for a revision of rates on the grounds that one route or service was more costly to operate than another. That they did so rarely can be ascribed to their inability to define or determine precisely the costs of operation for any particular service. Even had the legal restraints not existed therefore it is unlikely that the railways would have been able to base all their charges on sound economic principles.

The failure to determine costs of operation was perhaps the most serious feature of inter-war railway history since amalgamation had increased the urgency of taking such a step. The grouping was so arranged that each amalgamated company had to pay its way. The element of cross-subsidization was greatly increased since the good lines were lumped with the bad. Many of the uneconomic units or sections were therefore maintained on a subsidized basis within the groups and became a burden on the system as a whole. A thorough analysis of costs and traffic flows would have shown what parts of the system were obsolete and required a surgical operation. Of course such an analysis was never undertaken partly because the Act of 1921 provided little incentive to do so. But all the blame cannot be attributed to the Act. There is no doubt that the task itself would have proved too large and unattractive to "a generation of railwaymen who had learnt to put more emphasis on the technical problems of railway operating than on the commercial problem of competing for net revenue". After all it is only recently that it has been accomplished. Inevitably the belated diagnosis will now entail a much bigger surgical operation.

[1] 1059⅓ miles of track were closed in this period but most of it consisted of very small branch lines or sidings.

4   Stagnation of British shipping

Compared with the period before 1914 there were few good years for British shipping in the inter-war period. Though the 1920s were relatively more prosperous than the 1930s, freight rates and profits tended to decline or remain depressed for most of the period. The tramp freight index fell from 602 in March 1920 to 112 in 1928 (1869=100) whilst tramp ship voyage profits per ton dropped from £3·8 in 1920–21 to £0·7 in 1928–9. With the onset of the world economic depression the position became much worse. The freight index fell by one quarter between 1929 and 1933 (115 to 85) and tramp profits were practically eliminated. At the latter date nearly one fifth (12·6 million gross tons) of the world's tonnage and one sixth (3 million gross tons) of the British fleet stood idle. Many companies were barely able to cover their running costs and as a result large arrears of depreciation accumulated, amounting to £10,589,000 for British tramp companies alone in the six years 1930–35. Though tramp owners suffered more severely than liner companies no section of the industry escaped the consequences of the depression. After 1935 a slow recovery took place and 1937–8 was the only year in which prosperity of the industry was in any way comparable to the immediate pre-war years.

Moreover, it was in this difficult period that Britain lost her supremacy in shipping. Though the growth and importance of the British mercantile marine had been declining slowly before 1914 it was not until after the First World War that the change became appreciable. Between 1914 and 1938 British tonnage fell both relatively and absolutely. Whereas in 1914 British tonnage amounted to 18·9 million tons gross or 42·8 per cent of the world total, by 1938 it had fallen to 17·8 million gross tons, equivalent to only 26·0 per cent of world tonnage. During the same period world tonnage (including British) rose from 45·5 to 66·9 million gross tons, an increase of 46 per cent, compared with a fall of 5·8 per cent in the British fleet. The share of world trade by value carried in British ships dropped from 47·5 per cent in 1912 to 39·5 per cent in 1936.

For much of the inter-war period the world was over-stocked with tonnage in relation to the volume of seaborne trade and it was only in 1937 that a shortage of carrying capacity began to be felt. This was the product of three factors: the increasing tonnage built abroad, the rapid increase in efficiency of ships, and the fall in growth of world commodity trade. The post-war boom created far more tonnage than was required and by 1923 there was 39 per cent more tonnage in existence to deal with 6 per cent less seaborne trade. After 1924 the position improved somewhat owing to a significant recovery in world trade but even by 1929 there was still excess carrying capacity. The depression (1929–33) however, provided a further setback. The volume of world trade fell by about 25 per cent and in 1932 it was about the same level as in 1913 whilst the volume of tonnage available was 48 per cent greater. Freights fell well below pre-war levels in most trades and around 20 per cent of the world fleet was laid up. From 1934 onwards a recovery in international trade coincided with a stabilization in world tonnage and by 1937 capacity was in reasonable balance with the volume of world trade. However, these figures probably understate the true position considerably for they make no allowance for improvements in efficiency. Technical progress—e.g., the use of oil-fired ships and diesel propulsion and improved methods of ship construction—greatly increased the speed and carrying capacity of shipping in the inter-war years. The League of Nations estimated that the freight-carrying capacity of the world's shipping probably doubled between 1914 and 1939 and roughly half of this may be attributed to the improvement in efficiency. If this is correct then it seems to suggest that much of the active tonnage was considerably under-utilized. Thus in 1933 the League of Nations reported that "There appears to be a surplus of considerably over 50 per cent of the ocean-going tonnage. . . . Partially employed tonnage is a very much heavier charge upon shipping companies than tonnage actually laid up." As far as British shipping was concerned the utilization of ships fell by 25 per cent between 1913 and 1937.

It is obvious therefore that the difficulties experienced in these years were by no means peculiar to this country alone. The root cause of the depressed conditions was a basic maladjustment between the carrying capacity available and the volume of freight to be carried. Yet in some respects British shipping was more vulnerable than that of other nations to the changes in trading conditions. In the nineteenth century Britain had supplied many countries with the bulk of their manufactured products and shipping services and so long as those countries remained dependent on the British economy there was no great cause for alarm. As other countries developed their indigenous resources however they tended to rely less on Britain for the satisfaction of their needs. After 1914 this trend was greatly accelerated for during the period of hostilities not only were foreign consumers cut off from their traditional sources of supply but also the seeds of economic nationalism were scattered widely and took root firmly in fertile ground. As a result the inter-war years witnessed the steady growth of economic restrictions designed to foster domestic production of the very products Britain had once supplied, thus curtailing the outlets for British exports. The position was further aggravated by the fact that the British economy was by 1914 over-committed to producing basic products the demand for which steadily declined in the inter-war years. At the same time vigorous attempts were made to build up national fleets abroad in order to reduce the dependence on British shipping. In these changing conditions it is not surprising that Britain began to lose her dominant control of the high seas.

The stagnation in British trade offered little opportunity for increased shipping activity in the home trades, the most important source of employment. World seaborne trade, though less buoyant than before the war, remained constantly above the 1913 level for much of the inter-war period.

In contrast the volume of British trade attained the pre-war level in one year only, that of 1923. For the rest of the period it remained well below the pre-war volume and in the 1930s it rarely exceeded three-quarters of the 1913 level. The most significant change, however, was in the relationship between imports and exports; while exports fell sharply imports tended to increase and imports as a proportion of total British trade rose from 37 per cent in 1913 to 57 per cent in 1937. This proved to be a double disadvantage for British shipowners. In the first place the fall in exports reduced the possibilities of employment for both liners and tramps. The rapid contraction in the coal export trade, from 76·7 million tons in 1913 to 38·2 million in 1938, removed one of the major competitive advantages of British tramps and was probably the chief factor in the decline in the size of the tramp fleet.[1] But the collapse of the coal trade was not the only reason accounting for the dwindling importance of tramp shipping which bore the brunt of the difficult conditions of these years. This sector of the industry never fully recovered from the partial eclipse it had suffered during the war and its difficulties were intensified afterwards by a diversion of cargo to the liner trades, the rise of industrial carriers and specialized types of ships and by the competition of foreign tramp tonnage which was increasing in these years. The liner trades suffered from both a decline in mechandise exports and emigration. Non-coal exports dropped from 16·9 million tons in 1913 to 9·8 million tons in 1933 and for the rest of the 1930s (except 1937) remained at just over 11 million tons per annum; emigrant traffic from the U.K. fell sharply after 1914 and in the first post-war decade was a mere 40 per cent of the pre-war rate. Secondly, though imports rose the increase in volume was insufficient to compensate for the fall in exports whilst the increasing use of c.i.f. shipments by foreign shippers reduced the opportunities for employment of British shipping in the inward trades. Moreover, nearly one half the increase in total imports consisted of oil, which provided employment for a type of ship largely neglected by shipowners in this country. In effect this aggravated the imbalance between inward and outward shipments which had existed before the war, the only difference being that the surplus of export cargoes was replaced by a surplus in the inward direction. Altogether the proportion of British vessels sailing in ballast increased by over 6 per cent (1913–37) and this adversely effected the profitability of British shipping.

Though the contraction in British trade obviously restricted the growth of British shipping it does not fully explain why the industry stagnated or

[1] Definitional difficulties render it impossible to make an accurate estimate of the decline in tramp shipping in the inter-war years. Jones maintains that the British tramp fleet fell by roughly 60 per cent between 1914 and 1938. This however is based on the assumption, which we questioned in an earlier chapter, that the tramp fleet formed nearly two-thirds of the total British fleet in 1914. On the other hand, Kindleberger has suggested that there was no decline at all in the tramp fleet. Both these estimates are fairly wide of the mark. It is almost certain that the tramp fleet declined during this period but the order of magnitude was probably no greater than 30 per cent if that.

lost its relative position. The growth in shipping abroad indicated that there were plenty of outlets for expansion in non-British trades had British shipowners taken the trouble to exploit them. Yet apart from Germany, Britain was the only country which showed a net decrease in tonnage over the period 1914 to 1938. During this time the tonnage on the U.S. register more than quadrupled, Japanese tonnage trebled whilst the fleets of Norway, Italy and Greece more than doubled. Though international trade was less buoyant than before the war it rose steadily between 1924 and 1929 and again in the later 1930s, and foreign shipowners took every opportunity to exploit any profitable outlets available. Thus they not only secured the lion's share of the new trades but also encroached severely on carrying trade of British shipowners. In fact on nearly every route, except the direct Empire routes, the share of trade carried in British vessels fell, in some cases significantly. For example, the share of the seaborne trade between foreign countries carried in British ships fell from 30 per cent in 1912 to 12 per cent in 1936; the share carried from foreign countries to the U.K. from 66 to 51 · 6 per cent and that between Empire and foreign countries from 55 to 38 per cent. Overall, the proportion of world seaborne trade carried in British shipping dropped from just under 50 per cent pre-war to 39 · 5 per cent in 1936. The only consolation was that by the 1930s British vessels were carrying a higher proportion of water-borne trade than their proportion of world shipping, compared with 1913.

In part of course the change in the position of the British mercantile marine reflected a trend already apparent before 1914. As other nations followed the British pattern of industrial development it was only natural that they should wish to expand their fleets to carry their own goods. Given these circumstances it was hardly to be expected that Britain would retain her nineteenth-century supremacy in the mercantile field. From the 1890s onwards British shipowners were experiencing serious competition from the nascent fleets of Japan and Germany and though the latter was incapacitated to some extent by the war, Japan's fleet continued to expand rapidly. Consequently by 1939 two-thirds of Japan's trade in the Orient and a similar amount of the trade between Japan and Australia was carried in Japanese ships, trades which two generations before had been almost monopolized by British ships. The war of course provided an enormous stimulus to the establishment of national fleets especially in those countries which had relied heavily on British shipping services before 1914. America provides a typical example. As we saw earlier, the American mercantile marine declined rapidly after the Civil War and by 1914 only a very small proportion of American trade was being carried in American ships. During the war the fleet was greatly expanded and henceforth a much greater proportion of American trade was carried in native ships to the detriment of British shipowners. By 1936 the proportion (by value) of water-borne trade of the U.S. carried in British ships was 25 ·5 per cent as against 54 ·5 per cent in 1912–13.

Although the growth of foreign shipping can be regarded as a logical result of economic development there is no doubt that the impact of war and the difficult political and economic conditions obtaining after it encouraged the adoption of nationalistic policies designed expressly to achieve a certain degree of self-sufficiency. Shipping and shipbuilding came to be regarded as 'key' industries and conscious efforts were made by foreign countries to build up or maintain war-expanded fleets. To this end, says the historian of inter-war shipbuilding, L. Jones "a variety of uneconomic expedients were adopted: national and municipal subsidies, operational subsidies, mail contracts, grants in aid for the replacement of obsolete tonnage, relief from the burden of rates and taxes, loans for the modernization of plant, and differential building subsidies". Aid to shipowners was by no means new but its scale and scope were vastly extended in the inter-war years and in some countries this was accompanied by nationalization, flag discrimination and government control of trade and foreign exchange.

It is difficult to assess the damage inflicted by nationalistic policies practised abroad. Britain did not suffer alone from these economic policies,[1] but since this country had more to lose it can be argued that the impact was more severe here than elsewhere. The adoption of the British practice of selling exports c.i.f., discriminating trade policies and economic restrictions in general made things more difficult for British shipowners since they tended to divert a greater proportion of seaborne trade to foreign ships. As the Imperial Shipping Committee said in 1939 "there is a strong *prima facie* case for the conclusion that in general the effect of foreign exchange control is to increase the proportion of trade carried under the flag of the country exercising the control."

Similarly the operation of uneconomic Government-owned shipping services in some countries, e.g. America and Australia after the war, and the nationalization of the Russian fleet were also unfavourable to British shipping. On the whole, however, such policies did not constitute a serious threat to our mercantile marine. Far more important was the financial assistance which many countries gave to their fleets in the inter-war years. The types of subsidy varied a great deal from country to country but broadly speaking they took the form of either operating subsidies or financial assistance to shipowners for new construction.

There can be little doubt that British shipping, which remained virtually unassisted until the 1930s, suffered, in some cases severely, as a result of liberal financial assistance granted by foreign governments to their maritime

[1]The Special Committee on Tramp Shipping appointed by the Council of the Chamber of Shipping in October 1933 observed in its report that "the decline in world trade is largely due to artificial restrictions imposed by Governments in the interests of home industries and agriculture, or the maintenance of budgetary and exchange stability. Such restrictions are almost universally harmful to shipping." L. Isserlis, "British Shipping since 1934" in *Britain in Recovery* (1938), p. 329.

industries.[1] In particular the rapid expansion of the Italian and Japanese fleets and the maintenance of the German fleet in the 1930s were largely due to subsidies. Generous financial assistance allowed some foreign shipowners to renew parts of their fleet with the most efficient ships available. This was particularly so in the case of Japan where between 1932 and 1936 three 'scrap and build' schemes were carried out. Altogether some 500,000 tons of old shipping were scrapped and 400,000 tons of new built including 48 fast ships of the most up-to-date type. By the end of 1936 Japan possessed more ships under five years old in proportion to its tonnage than any other country in the world. On the other hand, it is easy to exaggerate the impact of subsidization on British shipping. Subsidized competition was mainly confined to the liner trades and the effects were therefore more serious for a country such as Britain with a large proportion of liner tonnage than for tramp or tanker owners. Although British ships certainly lost trade to their subsidized competitors it is only correct to point out that shipowners who received little assistance from their governments, e.g., Denmark, Norway, Greece and Sweden, were equally competitive if not more so. In fact non-subsidized fleets expanded faster than any others in the inter-war years and they secured an increasing share of world trade both by conquering new fields and invading former British preserves. The unsubsidized Norwegian fleet, for example, succeeded in trebling its share of the American trade between 1920 and 1938 at a time when the British participation was declining rapidly. The table below shows how after 1929 non-subsidized foreign ships accounted for a large part of the fall in the proportion of British ships entering home ports.

Table 6   *Entrances at British ports (percentages), 1913-1937*

Identity of vessels	1913	1929	1937
British	65·8	65·0	55·8
Subsidized foreign	7·5	14·2	17·2
Non-subsidized	26·7	20·8	27·0

Another factor which was unfavourable to British shipowners was the higher operating costs of British ships compared with those abroad. Apart from the U.S.A., British operating costs before 1914 were probably the highest in the world and remained so in the 1920s partly because of higher crew costs. In particular the running costs of British tramp shipping were much higher than those of the chief foreign competitors, especially the Greeks. In the 1930s it was estimated that the costs of operating a Japanese cargo liner were about 10 to 15 per cent below the comparable British vessel and this differential was further increased by Japan's subsidy policy. Crew costs were well below the British level in many countries especially in Greece, Yugoslavia, Finland, Italy and Russia whose tramp shipowners provided serious competition in the inter-war years. Some levelling-up

[1] By 1933 foreign subsidies were running at the rate of £33 million a year.

did take place in these years, however, and by 1936 crew costs in the Netherlands, Germany and France were above the British and those of Norway just below.

Though the handicaps suffered by British shipowners in the interwar years were great, they did not necessarily constitute an insuperable barrier to progress. It has been argued that the difficulties could have been alleviated in part if shipowners had been willing to adapt themselves to the changing conditions. Openings in non-British and non-liner trades were available had the trouble been taken to exploit them, whilst the adoption of faster and more efficient vessels, e.g., oil-driven ships, would have reduced British costs and enhanced the competitive power of our ships. Adaptability was the key to survival in the inter-war years and the failure of British shipowners to respond rapidly enough to the new opportunities was one of the reasons for the stagnation of the industry. As Sturmey has remarked: "If enough British owners had responded in this way no decline in the position of the British fleet in the inter-war years need have occurred."

The most notable development in marine technology in the early decades of the twentieth century was the use of oil as a fuel. Before 1914 only 3·4 per cent of the total world tonnage was driven by oil, but after the war oil fuel made rapid headway. Between 1918 and 1938 the proportion of world tonnage using oil as a fuel, both in the internal combustion engine and for steam-raising, rose from 18 per cent to 52·8 per cent. Oil was far superior to coal in many ways: it was not only cleaner and easier to handle but it provided a 50 per cent increase in heat value for the same bunker space and therefore allowed more room for cargo. When used in the motor ship it was even more efficient. One ton of oil used in a diesel engine did the same amount of work as 2 tons of oil and 3 tons of coal employed in conventional steam boilers. Most British shipowners, however, were slow to change over to oil partly because of the plentiful supplies of coal. By 1939 only one-quarter of the British fleet used diesel propulsion compared with around one-half of the Scandinavian and Dutch fleets. The non-subsidized Scandinavian and Dutch shipowners made full use of modern and efficient vessels to enable them to compete with subsidized and low-wage lines and with the British fleet. Scandinavian tonnage rose from 3·6 million tons in 1919 to 7·6 million tons in 1939 and Norway in particular succeeded in capturing a substantial proportion of trade once held by British ships. British shipowners were not opposed to all change, of course, but it is surprising how often they failed to provide the right type of vessel even when fleet replacements were made. For example, between 1926 and 1389 the P. & O. replaced their Far Eastern fleet with new vessels but unfortunately they maintained a speed of 17 knots compared with 20 or more knots of the vessels of the North German Lloyd and the Lloyd Triestino.

Similarly Britain failed to exploit fully the opportunities offered by the growing trade in oil. During these years the seaborne trade in fuel underwent an appreciable change. The coal trade fell from 174 million tons in

1913 to 142 in 1937 whilst world oil shipments increased from 14 million tons to 84 million tons in 1937 and by the late 1930s accounted for about one-quarter of the total tonnage of world seaborne trade. This created a demand for a specialized tanker fleet which rose from 1·5 million tons in 1914 to 10·7 in 1938. Before the war the bulk of the tankers had been owned by the oil companies but subsequently an independent tanker fleet grew up which by the later 1930s was supplying roughly one half (4·9 million tons) of the oil companies' requirements. Logically, one would have expected British tramp owners, who were hit badly by the contraction in the coal export trade, to have adopted tankers. In fact tankers were largely neglected in this country and by 1939 Britain owned only one-quarter of the world tanker fleet as against one-half in 1913. Enterprising foreigners such as the Norwegians profited from the situation at Britain's expense. By 1939 Norway's independently-owned tanker fleet was twice as large as that of the British and in 1936 Norwegian tankers carried one quarter of the total petroleum imported into Britain.

There is no doubt that in many respects British shipowners were far less enterprising than their foreign rivals. This conservatism can possibly be regarded as a natural reaction to the difficult conditions of the inter-war years. It may also be argued that Britain suffered from the disadvantage of an early start in that a large amount of capital was invested in ships which became partly obsolete in the inter-war years, but which were costly to scrap, whereas many foreign owners started almost from scratch and were able to invest in the most up-to-date tonnage. Basically, however, the explanation lies in the different attitudes adopted by British and foreign shipowners. The fault of the British shipowners was not that they failed to invest but that their investments were made unwisely. In the post-war boom and during the 1920s resources were used to build traditional types of ships which were often unsuited to the new conditions. This policy was a reflection of the shipowners self-satisfaction with their past performance which made them unwilling to explore new possibilities. To quote Sturmey: "There was an attitude of complacency, that the British industry was best by definition, had the most suitable ships and generally knew best, together with an introverted concern with servicing British trades which was in marked contrast to the extrovert attitude of younger shipping enterprises in other countries."

The structure of the British shipping industry was largely responsible for this insular attitude. The divisions into which the industry grew up before 1914 (liners, tramps and tankers) were maintained rigidly in the inter-war years whereas some large shipowners abroad, especially Norwegian, owned all three classes of vessel which helped to provide a greater spread of risks. The large liner companies in Britain came to be dominated by family groups, the management of which was unduly conservative and unsuited to meeting the new conditions after 1918. The tradition of self-financing was maintained and outside capital for modernizing the fleets was rarely sought for fear of letting in "foreign" control. Moreover, most of the British liner companies continued to operate within the scope of the conference agreements which did much to deaden individual initiative and reduce the incentive to increase efficiency. Foreign shipowers on the other hand, were far more accustomed to breaking the conference rules whenever there was a chance to promote cheaper and more efficient services outside them. In short, the group structure based upon family control which arose in the conference system "resulted in an industry heavily biased towards maintaining the *status quo* and ill-adapted to showing flexibility to meet the enormous changes of the inter-war period" (Sturmey).

It is possible of course to argue that British shipbuilders were partly to blame for the shipowners' neglect of the latest and most efficient vessels. In 1913 British supremacy in the shipbuilding field was unquestioned, for at that time we produced around 60 per cent of the world output. After the war there was a significant decline in the proportion of tonnage constructed in Britain as other nations expanded their shipbuilding facilities. Most serious was the fact that many British shipbuilders became high-cost producers during this period since they failed to modernize their yards to take account of technical changes. By 1939 many of them were badly out of date both as regards equipment and methods of construction. "In the main, continental and American builders possessed modern well-equipped yards, whereas in Britain a number of yards dated from the days of wooden ships. Many British yards had not been designed to meet modern requirements, they just grew up from small yards where wooden ships had been built, and were enlarged from time to time as vessels increased in size and complexity. Others were sited on narrow river frontages in circumstances which did not permit of drastic remodelling and reconstruction. The organization of work was carefully considered abroad and so planned that a minimum of work was carried out on the berths." (L. Jones). Possibly the lack of initiative displayed by British shipowners provided little incentive for the shipbuilders to change their methods though there is no reason why they should have failed to satisfy the demands of foreign owners. In so far as this was the case British shipowners may be said to have suffered at the hands of the shipbuilders. This was particularly true in the case of the motorship, the development of which was neglected whilst "On the Continent", says Jones, "no efford was spared to perfect the internal-combustion engine, and while British engineering skill was concentrated on steam, continental, and particularly Scandinavian and German firms, gained a notable lead in the construction of motor-ships. Consequently, diesel machinery cost very much less on the Continent." On the other hand, it can be argued that if British shipowners were penalized by British shipbuilding methods they could always resort to building abroad. To some extent this is what they did especially after 1934 when an increasing proportion of new tonnage was built abroad. In 1938 shipbuilding imports accounted for 16·7 per cent of the tonnage built for British owners. Earlier delivery was one of the major reasons for contracting abroad and there is little evidence to suggest that British shipowners were ordering the type of vessel which was not readily available in this country.

In view of the difficulties of British shipping after the war and the lavish financial assistance given to foreign shipowners it is surprising that the British Government did comparatively little to assist the industry. But apart from the loans guaranteed for shipbuilding under the Trade Facilities Acts in the 1920s and the advances made to the Cunard Company for the completion of the *Queen Mary* in the early 1930s, neither shipping nor shipbuilding received any aid in the form of direct operating and construction subsidies until 1935. This was not simply because the State was completely indifferent to the fate of the industry but rather because British shipowners were generally hostile to state aid or interference. The attitude of the shipping community was summed up by the president of the Chamber of Shipping in 1928 when he observed that "British Shipping has no protection, not even in the coasting trade, and it seeks none; it is prepared to meet all competition that is fair and square." Moreover, it was recognized that to be really effective any action would require international co-operation, a thing which had been very difficult to achieve in the past.

The severity of the depression itself brought about a change of attitude. Tonnage laid up in British ports increased from 630,000 tons in 1929 to 3,610,000 in 1932 and both liner and tramp owners found themselves in grave difficulties. The liner companies, with their larger financial resources and conferences to maintain rates, were able to weather the storm more easily though they did not escape unscathed. In 1931 the Royal Mail Group, controlling 2 million gross tons of shipping, about one sixth of the British liner tonnage, collapsed with liabilities of over £20 million. But the tramp section of the industry was almost crippled by the crisis. Tramp freights fell to one half their 1921 level and three quarters of the 1929 level and many companies found it impossible to pay dividends or provide for depreciation. In 1934, 45 tramp shipping firms made a total profit of only £88,000 on their voyages. Consequently at the end of 1933 the Chamber of Shipping set up a Special Committee on Tramp Shipping which requested the Government to grant a temporary subsidy to that section of the industry. The Government consented and in 1935 the British Shipping (Assistance) Act was passed providing a subsidy of £2 million and a "scrap and build" scheme.

The "scrap and build" scheme was designed to assist both the shipbuilding and shipping industries by reducing redundant or excess tonnage and encouraging shipowners to modernize their fleets. For every ton of new shipping built owners were required to scrap two tons and one ton for every ton modernized; in return the Treasury advanced money or guaranteed loans up to a maximum of £10 million which it was estimated would be sufficient to build 600,000 gross tons of up-to-date cargo vessels. The scheme proved to be largely a fiasco. Shipowners were opposed to the scheme from the first partly because it did not meet their original demands and partly on the grounds that it was of greater benefit to the shipbuilders. Only 50 new vessels of 186,000 gross tons were actually built for which £3½ million was advanced out of a permitted total of £10 million; and 97 vessels of 356,625 gross tons were nominated for demolition, no applications being made for modernization. It appears that the financial provisions of the Act were not sufficiently attractive to encourage large scale scrapping and as freight rates began to improve from 1935 onwards owners were induced to hang on to their old tonnage for future employment. Moreover, as British shipowners were allowed to acquire foreign vessels for scrapping the "chief beneficiaries were the foreign owners of ancient ships who were able to sell them above scrap prices to British owners".

The subsidy provisions of the Act were probably more successful. The amount of assistance was not to exceed £2 million a year and was to be reduced progressively as freights returned to their 1929 level. The money, however, was only provided on condition that the tramp shipping industry took action to reduce competition and improve the level of freights. Accordingly a Tramp Shipping Administrative Committee was formed and co-operation was obtained from shipowners in all the main tramp-owning countries except Japan. Minimum freight schemes were eventually established in three major trades, the Argentine, Australian and North Atlantic. By the end of 1937 freights had improved sufficiently to permit the abandonment of the subsidy provisions.

It is difficult to say how effective the subsidy and freight agreements were in reviving the fortunes of the tramp owners. No doubt the payments (£4 million) provided a useful windfall to tramp owners and possibly, as Gripaios suggests, prevented complete financial disaster. The freight agreements reduced the severity of competition and produced a noticeable increase in freights on the three major routes covered by them. On the other hand, it is as well to remember that insufficient routes were controlled to make the scheme really effective. In any case a general recovery in trade conditions and freight rates was already taking place when the agreements were instituted. Nevertheless the shipowners were evidently satisfied with the position for they continued the agreements on a voluntary basis after 1937.

Apart from this State-sponsored scheme there were few other successful experiments made in international co-operation. Attempts to regulate coal and timber freights on the lines of the earlier agreements came to very little largely because of the uncompromising attitude of the Russian Government. The only other agreement worth mentioning is the Oil Tanker Pool established in May 1934. This provided for the laying up of surplus tonnage and the compensation of its owners out of a levy imposed on tankers in operation. The scheme was simple and relatively effective. By the end of 1934 the rate for Gulf–U.K./Continent clean oil trade had been raised from 8s. 6d. to 12s. 6d. a ton. A scheme to form a Deep Sea

Tramp Compensation Pool on similar lines proved abortive owing to inadequate support. The failure to achieve a wider measure of international co-operation either on a voluntary or compulsory basis must be considered as one of the factors which helped to prolong and intensify the difficulties of the shipping industry in the inter-war years.

12

The development of
motorized transport

Undoubtedly the most revolutionary development in the whole field of transport in the first half of the twentieth century has been the growth of motor transport. Within the matter of a few decades the motor vehicle had become an integral part of the British transport system and it produced significant changes in the economic and social life of the country. In fact not since the railways has any form of transport had such far-reaching effects. Not only did motor transport create a wide range of new opportunities but it also brought with it many problems, solutions to some of which have still not been found today.

1   The rise of the motor industry

One of the chief features of the motor vehicle has been the rapidity of its technical development. According to Buchanan: "The general form of the motor car was sketched out within ten years of the first invention. Within the next twenty-five years most of the derivations were worked out, and by 1930, with its capabilities clearly demonstrated, the motor was widely absorbed into the life of the country." In the initial stages of development of the internal combustion engine, foreign engineers took the lead. It was in the middle of the nineteenth century that the first internal combustion engines were produced by the Germans and French. An engine was first fitted to a car by the Frenchman, J. J. Etienne Lenoir in 1860; this was soon improved upon by the Germans, Otto and Langen, and the Frenchman, de Rochas, and came into common use during the 1870s. All of these were gas engines using coal or producer gas as a fuel. A few years later, in 1878, the German Benz applied the petrol engine to a road vehicle and this marked the beginning of the modern industry. Soon afterwards several firms were set up both in Great Britain and abroad to produce cars experimentally. Daimler began the manufacture of motor cars in Germany in the late 1880s, followed by the Frenchmen, Panhard and Levassor, and in 1896 Daimler and Lanchester began to manufacture as public companies in this country. Thus by the turn of the century technical developments had proceeded far enough to permit the manufacture of mechanically propelled road vehicles.

Though the French and the Germans had taken the lead in developing the motor car it was the American manufacturers who exploited the invention commercially before 1914. This in part was due to the fact that the American engineering industry, based upon interchangeable and standardized parts, was ideally suited to the manufacture of motor vehicles. Thus almost from the very beginning the Americans set out to produce a cheap standardized vehicle for the mass market and by 1915 nearly three quarters of the American output consisted of cars under £200 each. Production was concentrated in a few large, well-equipped and efficiently run plants; in 1912, when annual production was approaching the half million mark, seven manufacturers accounted for half the total production. In Britain progress was much slower and the pattern of production quite different. It is true that a large number of firms entered the industry between 1900 and 1914 including such famous names as Rolls-Royce, Napier, Albion, Crossley, Austin, Standard and Vauxhall, but none of them managed to produce a cheap car suitable for the mass market. In fact up to 1914 no British firm ever produced more than one car per man per annum whereas as early as 1903–4 Ford of America was turning out 1700 cars with a labour force of 300 men. The only model to be produced on a large scale in this country was the Ford 'T' which was manufactured in Manchester shortly before the First World War by an offshoot of the famous American firm. British firms were too small and too many in number to produce as efficiently, and engineers employed in them were obsessed by the technical product rather than by the technique of production. Consequently few attempts were made to standardize the product and frequent and costly changes in design occurred. By 1913 no less than 198 different models of British cars had been placed on the market, less than half of which were still in production.

Thus by the outbreak of war motor transport was only in its infancy in this country. Annual production of cars and commercial vehicles was less than 34,000, equivalent to about seven per cent of the American output. Though the total vehicles in use rose rapidly between 1909 and 1914 there were only 265,182 (excluding motor cycles) on the roads by the latter date. The private car was still very much a luxury item which only the wealthier classes could afford and as yet motor traffic had scarcely begun to have any effect on other forms of transport apart from the horse-drawn carriages of the upper orders. In the words of Brunner: "The wealthy were replacing their carriages by luxury cars, the doctor sold his gig and bought a coupé or two seater, the farmer found a Ford a quicker means of getting to the local market than his old market cart, and the pony-trap of the prosperous middle-class was being scrapped in favour of the more popular automobile. The same process was going on with commercial vehicles, although in the main the horse was holding its own for the heavier work."

Despite the fact that the motor vehicle provided a useful auxiliary form of transport in the First World War the growth of the industry was retarded for the simple reason that most of the car producers were forced to turn over to the production of aircraft engines, shells and other such weapons of warfare. Consequently by the end of hostilities American manufacturers had achieved a position of unchallenged supremacy in the field. Their output rose from just under half a million vehicles in 1913 to well over two million in 1920; in contrast British output had hardly increased at all during this period. Nevertheless the war opened the eyes of many manufacturers to the benefits to be derived from streamlining methods of production and the car producers were not the least to gain from these changes. As soon as the war was over manufacturers set about the task of meeting the urgent domestic demand for cars. Large capital expenditures were made on re-equipping plants and considerable efforts were made to improve methods of production so that cars could be produced more cheaply. William Morris had already begun production of his small family car when in 1921 the Austin Motor Company introduced its Austin Seven. This was to become the most famous of the cheap small cars which were to enlarge the the scale of the industry by increasing its effective market. Production of such cars grew rapidly in the 1920s as new models were introduced and prices fell accordingly. A private car which cost £500 in 1922 could be bought for £325 in 1926 and the price of commercial vehicles fell by £100 during the same period. This rapid fall in price and the improvement in the technical performance of motor vehicles together with the rise in real incomes were undoubtedly the main factors contributing to the growth of motor transport in the inter-war years. Though in scale and efficiency of production British car producers remained far behind the Americans they were able to produce a type of vehicle acceptable to the British public. From the early 1920s the expansion of the market can be largely attributed to the increasing sales of small cars and commercial vehicles and by the outbreak of the Second World War motor transport was no longer a luxury confined to the few. By that time over three million mechanically propelled vehicles were in use compared with only just over 330,000 in 1919. The growth in the different classes of vehicles can be seen from Table 7.

Table 7   *Motor vehicles in use, 1904–1938*

	Cars (private)	Buses and coaches	Goods vehicles	Total (all vehicles including motor cycles and taxis)
March 1904	8,465	5,345*	4,000	—
1910	53,196	24,466*	30,000	143,877
1914	132,015	51,167*	82,000	388,860
1918	77,707	41,815*	40,700	229,428
1921	242,500	82,800*	128,200	845,799
1929	980,886	49,889	329,794	2,181,832
1932	1,127,681	47,121	370,100	2,227,099
1938	1,944,394	53,005	494,866	3,084,896

* These figures include hackney carriages and taxi-cabs.

2   Structure and organization of road transport services

In the early years the development of motor transport services for public use was even more haphazard and chaotic than railway development in the nineteenth century. Entry into the industry was virtually unrestricted until the 1930s and there was no shortage of enterprise in the pioneering days. Competition was fierce and many small scale operators hopeful of making a fortune went to the wall in the process. Such features were common to both the road haulage and road passenger sectors of the industry. However the structure and organization of the two sides differed considerably and in view of this difference it is necessary to trace their development separately.

(a) The motor bus and the development of public road passenger transport

The first bus services began around the turn of the century but for some years development was slow and patchy. Many of the pioneer bus companies failed commercially partly because of the lack of experience of some of the operators and partly because of the high operating costs and technical problems of the early vehicles. The turning point came in 1905 when the London General and a number of other horse-bus operators in the city decided to experiment with motor traction. By the beginning of 1908 London had 1,000 motor buses running on the streets compared with only 20 three years earlier. But the early buses were not an unqualified success by any means. Costs of operation and maintenance remained high and break-downs were still frequent occurrences. Indeed such was the state of some of the vehicles that there was no guarantee that a passenger starting a journey by motor bus would finish it by the same means. Moreover competition between the old and new forms of transport in London was fierce and although this tended to bring about a reduction in fares it also led to dangerous driving and poor service.

But conditions slowly improved, more especially from 1910 onwards when the London General introduced its famous 'B' type buses which were much more reliable than the previous models. By 1913, 2,500 of the total of 3,522 buses running in London were of this type and the bus had driven practically all the horse services out of business. At the same time a considerable degree of unification had taken place in London's passenger transport services which had the effect of reducing considerably the amount of competition. Various agreements were made between the London General and other companies and in 1912 the Underground Group, which already had considerable transport interests in the London area, acquired control of the London General. Thus by the outbreak of war London's passenger transport had become fairly monopolistic and it was not until the arrival of the independents in the early 1920s that competition again became fierce.

In the provinces development occurred a little later though by 1914 many companies had begun to operate bus services. The British Electric Traction Company, for example, was running through its subsidiary British Automobile Traction Company, a number of bus services in various towns including London and Birmingham. In the Midlands the Birmingham and Midland Motor Omnibus Company (Midland Red) extended its motor services rapidly in the years immediately prior to the war whilst in the northwest region a number of companies, including Crosville Motor Company, Cumberland Motor Services and Lancashire United Transport & Power Company, were operating fairly extensive bus services. In fact by 1913 the motor bus had, in some large towns, virtually swept the horse bus from the roads, though it was still regarded as a feeder to the railway lines and trams.

The war brought a momentary check to expansion. Many services had to be suspended since vehicles were taken over for military purposes and petrol and labour were in short supply. Conditions immediately after the war however proved extremely favourable to development. The technical performance of motor vehicles had by this time been improved considerably and there was an urgent demand for the new form of transport. Demobilization made available large supplies of skilled labour and at the same time the home market was flooded with ex-service vehicles. Thus thousands of officers and men returning from the army with gratuities to spend, bought ex-army vehicles at low prices or new ones on easy purchase terms from motor manufacturers anxious to extend their market and began operating bus services in various parts of the country. Many new undertakings blossomed forth and within the short space of three years, 1919–21, the number of hackney carriages licensed in Britain doubled, reaching 82,800 in the latter year.

Y

Apart from the slump of 1921 conditions continued to favour rapid development in the decade after the war. Considerable improvements took place in the technical performance of the vehicles in this period and as a result operating costs were reduced substantially. The most important improvement was the adoption of the pneumatic tyre which made for higher speeds, lower fuel consumption and smoother running than was possible with the solid type. In the early days tyres had been an expensive item in the running costs of vehicles; in 1906 it cost 4d. per vehicle mile for solid tyres on a four-wheeled London bus whereas by 1932 the cost on a six-tyred London bus on pneumatics was less than 0·10d. per vehicle mile. Such improvements soon enabled the bus to emerge as a rival to the tram and later the railway. The field of operations was greatly extended not only in the towns and between urban areas; at the same time a vast array of new services on rural and long-distance routes came into being, many of which competed with each other. In addition many small firms started excursions and trips or hired out their vehicles to interested parties. In fact between 1919 and the early 1930s almost the whole of the present pattern of bus and coach services came into existence.

Four distinct types of operators emerged in the course of the 1920s—the municipal authorities, the territorial or associated companies, the independents and the railways. The first of these groups, the local authorities, were slow to adopt motor buses no doubt partly because they had invested heavily in tramways and also because before 1930 they had to acquire powers to run bus services by special Act of Parliament. Nevertheless many authorities began to introduce bus services after 1914 either in areas not served by the tram or on abandoned tramway routes. By 1928, 90 municipalities were operating bus services compared with only 18 in 1914. Most of the services were of a local nature for the authorities were usually restricted to operating within their own boundaries by the terms of the private Acts. As a rule they usually had a quasi-monopoly within their own territory though agreements were often made with private operators for the provision of extra services. Many authorities had inter-running arrangements with other operators, both municipal and private, and in some cases routes were allocated between the respective parties. As early as 1914 the Midland Red and Birmingham Corporation concluded an agreement whereby the company agreed to restrict its activities to operations outside the city boundary. In some cases joint or mixed undertakings were established to operate urban bus services. This happened in Keighley, Yorkshire where in 1932 the Keighley–West Yorkshire Services Ltd. was formed to operate services of the Keighley Corporation and West Yorkshire Road Car Company Ltd in that area. In terms of the number of vehicles owned and passengers carried municipal operation was far less extensive than that of the private operators. In 1933 local authorities accounted for only 12·8 per cent of the total vehicles owned by all operators and 23·4 per cent of the passengers carried. On the other hand the size of the individual fleets was relatively large averaging

53·9 vehicles (1931) compared with an average of 6·3 for all other operators.

Private bus operation was in the hands of two distinct groups—the associated companies, usually the larger undertakings belonging to one of the big holding companies, and the independents, or smaller concerns who remained outside the control of the territorial companies. The principal holding groups were the British Electric Traction, Thomas Tilling and Scottish Motor Traction which by the mid-1930s held extensive interests in about 50 of the largest operating companies. Altogether they eventually controlled about 40 per cent of the total buses in the country and probably accounted for around 50 to 60 per cent of all passenger journeys.[1] Nearly all the companies within the groups were large—owning well over 100 vehicles each—and in the inter-war years they grew rapidly either by adding to their fleets or by absorbing independent companies. For example, the fleet of the Midland Red (B.E.T. group) increased from 92 to 1,224 vehicles between 1919 and 1938. Many of the independent operators were swallowed up by the associated companies in the 1930s; in 1932 the North-Western acquired 12 companies and three years later Crosville absorbed 35. Both these companies belonged to the Tilling group. Generally speaking the associated companies concentrated on long-distance stage work and express services. Most of the companies within the groups were based on a large town centre and their area of operation was defined by a complex set of territorial agreements between the companies. Eventually the whole of Great Britain was divided by written agreements between the associated companies.

The railways also became associated with the large holding companies by acquiring an interest in the undertakings under their control. Prior to the 1923 grouping nearly every railway company had taken an interest in running bus services. The leader in this respect was the Great Western, which had pioneered bus services at the beginning of the century, and by 1928 the company had a fleet of 300 vehicles. However until the railways obtained general road transport powers in 1928 their holdings were not extensive and the buses they owned were used largely as feeder services to their main transport system. Subsequently the four railway companies acquired substantial financial interests in road transport mainly by investing in the larger associated companies. By 1933 they had sunk £9½ million into bus undertakings as against £13½ million invested by the road combines, and it has been estimated that in so doing they secured an interest in some 40 per cent of the buses operated by these companies. Nevertheless large as their interest was it gave little direct control over road concerns since in no case did the railways hold more than 50 per cent of the voting shares of the companies concerned.

The remaining group, the independents or "pirates" as they were often

<hr>

[1] This excludes operations of the London Passenger Transport Board. The complex network of holding arrangements is detailed in C. I. Savage, *An Economic History of Transport* (1959), pp. 125–6.

called, consisted mainly of the smaller concerns not formally linked with the large groups of Tilling, B.E.T. and S.M.T. Numerically, independent operators formed by far the largest group, some 90 per cent of the operators coming under this heading, but they accounted for less than 15 per cent of the passengers carried outside London despite the fact that they owned nearly 40 per cent of the buses and coaches in the country. The majority consisted of small companies or partnerships with five vehicles or less each though a few concerns, such as Lancashire United with 196 vehicles, did not fall into this category. Many of these firms found it difficult to resist the pressure of the associated companies who, as we have seen, absorbed large numbers of their weaker brethren each year. In view of the voracious appetite of the large companies it may seem surprising that so many small concerns managed to remain in existence. The reasons for their survival are not difficult to find however. Although the intense competition drove many of them out of business or forced them to amalgamate with the larger companies the industry was an expanding one in the 1920s and there was still scope for new enterprise to flourish. Thus despite the fact that many of these businesses perished there was no shortage of new ones to take their place. Moreover some independents tended to concentrate their resources on excursion and contract work, a field neglected by the larger companies, whilst others opened up remote rural areas unsuited to the services of the bigger companies. They also played a large part in developing express coach services. These factors apart it is as well to remember that many of these smaller concerns had other commercial interests and in some cases bus operation was of secondary importance. Finally, independents often formed district associations to protect themselves and some of these combined to form a national body, the Motor Hirers and Coach Owners Association. But apart from this the independent operators did not show much enthusiasm for combined action and their best line of defence was to concentrate on those aspects of road passenger transport which were not of great concern to the larger territorial companies.

Thus by the early 1930s the road passenger transport industry could be divided into two broad groups; on the one hand there were the larger and more respectable operators which included the municipal authorities, the associated companies and the railways, and on the other, the smaller concerns consisting mainly of the independents. The small scale operator clearly predominated; in 1933, 4,890 operators or 82·6 per cent of the total had less than five vehicles each whilst at the other end of the scale two firms owned over 1,000 vehicles apiece. Yet though numerically small, the larger operators owned the majority of the vehicles. In fact one per cent of the operators controlled 52 per cent of all road vehicles whilst the other 99 per cent, all of which had less than 100 vehicles each, shared the rest between them. Yet despite the increasing degree of concentration the industry remained highly unstable especially in the 1920s, competition was fierce and conditions of services were far from ideal. It was largely the smaller concerns or independents however which provided the unsavoury characteristics of the industry and secured for the rest the odium they did not deserve. Hundreds of small scale operators with little capital and little idea of how to manage a transport undertaking entered the industry soon after the war. Many of them maintained services with broken-down vehicles driven by incompetent drivers; facilities for maintaining the vehicles were often non-existent, the buses being run until they dropped to pieces. The Commissioners of the Western Traffic Area found that the condition of a large number of vehicles in the region was "appalling". Conditions of operation and services were often equally as bad. Many road services were operated without proper time tables and very often at cut fares to secure support. Indeed time-schedules seem to have been a rarity in the early 1920s for of the 1,888 operators listed in the *Motor Transport Year Book* for 1921-2 only 200 had published time tables. Many of the small bus companies adopted such doubtful practices as "chasing", "hanging back", running only at peak hours or on special occasions, and generally "creaming" traffic on the road. Such intensive forms of competition were not only wasteful but constituted a menace to public safety. One of the worst areas was in the Potteries where, before the legislation of 1930, some 90 omnibuses had been licensed by Stoke-on-Trent Council to run on the main route seven miles long through the five major towns of the area. The vehicles were owned by 25 different companies which were divided into two rival groups, the "Association" and the "Alliance". The conditions prevailing were described in graphic detail by the West Midland Traffic Commissioners in their first report: "No timetable existed, and the vehicles shuttled up and down in a continuous game of leap-frog, with an average frequency of less than a minute at peak times. Coupons giving cheap fares all day long were instituted by the 'Association' and adopted subsequently by the 'Alliance'. As each group only accepted its own coupons, the habit of a vehicle of one group running close to the vehicle of another group was acquired in order to cater for its non-coupon holders. Competition between individual omnibuses accordingly became general, and convictions of both drivers and conductors for dangerous driving or obstruction were frequent."

The Potteries were no exception for the position was equally chaotic if not worse in many other urban areas when the independents got going. This was particularly true of the London region where until 1922 the Underground Group had managed to maintain a fairly tight control over passenger services. But in the latter half of that year the first of the independents led by Christopher Dodson's "Chocolate Express" began to run buses in the city. Within a short space of time hundreds of buses of all makes and colours had invaded the streets of the metropolis. By the end of 1924 no less than 200 operators owning 500 vehicles had entered the field. There was nothing to prevent operators who so wished from running buses at their own convenience on the best routes and at the peak periods only. Routes could be changed at will and many of the concerns tended to confine their activities to the routes and times which most suited them. Abuses such as "racing" and "chasing" were common and accidents were by no means rare occurrences. In fact the position had become so chaotic in the London area by 1924 that the Government was forced to take action to control the situation.[1]

(b) The expansion of road haulage

The actual development of the road haulage side of the industry displayed similar characteristics to that of road passenger transport. Before 1914 the industry was still very much in the teething stage. Some of the large and well-established carriers of the nineteenth century such as Pickford and Carter Paterson introduced motor vehicles shortly after the turn of the century whilst a number of privately subscribed companies were established to carry on business as motor haulage contractors. Typical representatives of the newcomers were the Road Carrying Company and H. Viney, both of Liverpool, and the Manchester Motor Transport Company each of which had a small capital and carried on operations with a few vehicles. Such experiments were not however always commercially successful for road hauliers experienced similar difficulties to those of the early bus operators. Perhaps the greatest handicap was the high cost of operation and the poor technical performance of the vehicles. In some cases vans showed running costs of 11d. per mile for the tyres alone.

After the war conditions were ripe for rapid expansion. The market was flooded with ex-army lorries and demobilized soldiers anxious to secure employment and make a fortune at the same time. The Ministry of Munitions helped the process by releasing 20,000 vehicles at very cheap prices and hundreds of ex-service men "with little capital, no trade and little business training, bought lorries and set themselves up as haulage contractors". As a result the number of goods vehicles on the road doubled between 1919 and 1921 reaching 128,200 in the latter year. The rates of expansion scarcely slackened in the 1920s for the ease with which entry to the business could be obtained and the increasing improvement in vehicle performance encouraged hundreds of new firms to enter the field each year. By 1930 there were nearly 350,000 goods vehicles on the roads. But like the internal air operators of the 1930s many of these were mushroom concerns which had a very short life though for every one which died a natural death there were probably two to take its place. During the 1930s the rate of growth slowed down and by 1938 there was just over half a million goods vehicles of all kinds.

The greater proportion of these vehicles, that is around three quarters of the total, were owned and operated by manufacturers and traders for the conveyance of their own products, or by contractors working exclusively for particular traders. Probably 80 per cent of the road-borne goods were

[1] This aspect will be dealt with in more detail later.

carried in traders' own vehicles. Many of them consisted of light vans and trucks engaged in retail delivery services such as milk, groceries and bread, a type of work previously carried out by the horse-drawn vehicle. Some large firms often owned whole fleets of trucks and lorries which were used for long distance delivery services of their own goods. There were obvious advantages in operating one's own vehicles despite the fact that it might be more costly in the long run. Apart from the factor of convenience it gave the trader direct personal contact with his customers and enabled him to provide more regular and speedier delivery services than was possible by public carrier.

Most of the remaining vehicles were operated by general haulage contractors who acted as public carriers. The public sector of the road haulage industry was notable for its almost complete lack of organization. Compared with the passenger side there were very few large groups and the average size of the unit was much smaller. "There is a forcible contrast", *The Economist* said in 1934, "between the more or less nation-wide financial interconnection of the leading road passenger interests and the unorganized and almost inchoate condition of the road haulage industry. The latter has no dominating 'group', and though a number of companies maintain regular services, the bulk of the business is of 'tramp' rather than 'liner' character." The average number of vehicles per operator was around three compared with an average of nearly nine on the passenger side, whilst half the firms engaged in haulage contracting exclusively owned only one vehicle. The contrast is even greater than these figures would suggest for, whereas a few large passenger firms owned the majority of the vehicles, this was not the case on the road haulage side. There was probably no more than a score of firms owning over 100 vehicles each. Generally speaking the only really large goods haulage concerns were those supplying regular trunk services such as Carter Paterson, Pickfords, and Norman E. Box, both subsidiaries of Hay's Wharf Cartage Company, McNamara and Company, Sutton and Company, Garlick, Burrell and Edwards Ltd., M.R.S. Ltd., and the Tillotson group. In the early 1930s the railways gained control of the first three concerns together with a number of smaller companies. Apart from these few large undertakings there were a number of medium-sized firms such as A. Smart of Leith with 60 vehicles and Chaplins of London, the descendent of the famous firm of horse carriers of the nineteenth century, which by 1939 owned 58 vehicles. But generally speaking the large or medium sized firm was the exception rather than the rule and right up to the Second World War the industry was dominated by the very small independent carrier.

As might be expected road haulage was a highly competitive industry especially before the institution of control in 1933. The small independent road hauliers were out to get what traffic they could and they were indifferent as to what methods they used to attract it. The owner driver was usually a newcomer to the trade with "little business experience, little knowledge of the cost of running a lorry for a series of years and no appreciable organization for obtaining traffic". Competitive rate-cutting therefore became a marked feature of the industry and there was practically no uniformity in road haulage charges. Though the basis of charging was usually cost plus profit such elementary economic principles were often ignored by the small haulier anxious to outbid his rivals. This was particularly the case for return loads for which he was almost forced to accept any rate that might be offered, and he was certainly tempted to canvass for traffic at a rate which would obtain the traffic irrespective of whether the transaction was a paying proposition in the long run for himself. Unfair competition of this sort was common and not necessarily confined to the smaller firm though it was the larger and more reputable concerns trying to provide regular and reliable services at reasonable rates who complained most bitterly about it to the Royal Commission on Transport (1928–31). But undercutting was definitely more prevalent with the small haulier simply because he had little to lose by doing so and also because he did not maintain a very high standard of business behaviour. In fact the only way in which many of them were able to keep going was by paying low wages, working drivers excessively, neglecting the maintenance of their vehicles and refusing to depreciate their assets correctly. One of the most revealing features of the early reports of the Licensing Authorities is the frequent complaints made about malpractices. The Commissioner for the South Eastern Traffic Area found that at times drivers were worked to such a state of physical exhaustion "as to render their driving a menace to other road users". But by far the worst abuse was the road hauliers' failure to maintain their vehicles in a roadworthy condition. Sometimes as many as 50 per cent of the vehicles examined were found to be defective in some respect and it was usually the small contractor who was the culprit. In the Northern Traffic Area it was found that "the majority of small owners have little knowledge of the machines they operate and make no serious effort to maintain them in a roadworthy condition". Similar reports were made from other areas. The South-Eastern Commissioner was appalled by the fact that a large percentage of carriers had no proper system of maintenance. It was the practice, he said, to run vehicles until they broke down with the result that " . . . steering gear and brakes were found to be in a dangerously defective condition in many cases, through sheer neglect of simple adjustment."

Not all the small hauliers were as disreputable or as irresponsible as the Royal Commission would have us believe. Much of the evidence on which the Commission based its conclusions was drawn from the railways and the larger and more organized sections of the road haulage industry and could hardly have been free from a certain element of bias. Nevertheless the Licensing Commissioners' reports do tend to confirm the belief that it was the small haulier who was responsible for the unsatisfactory state of the industry. An attempt was made however to eliminate some of the worst abuses, such as back-loading at cut rates, by establishing clearing houses the purpose of which was to put the trader in contact with the haulier, and in so doing relieve the haulier of the job of canvassing for return loads. By 1930, 165 clearing houses had been established, 108 of which were in the provinces, 11 in Scotland and the rest in London. Unfortunately the clearing houses themselves were not free from abuse. Some of them were established by disreputable persons intent on making a quick profit. They obtained their traffic by under-quoting the organized hauliers and railways and then beat down the owner-driver to the cut rates less clearing house commission. As a result their terms were often onerous and many small hauliers avoided using the clearing houses. It is extremely doubtful, therefore, whether the clearing houses led to much improvement in the situation.

In contrast few complaints were made about the larger haulage undertakings which were said to be "highly organized, with audited accounts and a proper sense of their responsibilities both towards their employees, their clients and road users generally". A number of them such as Carter Paterson, Pickfords, McNamaras and Chaplins were road carriers in the days of the horse-drawn vehicle and had already established reputable and efficient business concerns before the advent of the motor car. Most of them ran regular services over a wide area at economic rates and maintained a network of branches throughout the provinces for the purposes of soliciting traffic. Sutton and Company of London, for example, had over 600 branches and agencies in the provinces and operated daily services to Bath, Birmingham, Bournemouth, Brighton, Nottingham and Bristol. Similarly McNamaras ran scheduled nightly services from London to Birmingham, Bristol and Liverpool as well as local delivery services in the London region and they were also contractors for the carriage of the Royal Mail. If some of these companies adopted the more unsavoury practices of the small hauliers it was only because they were forced to do so for want of a better alternative.

3   The consequences of motor transport

Motor transport probably had a greater economic and social impact on Britain than any other industry during the inter-war years. Never before in fact had one industry produced such profound changes in so short a period of time. As one contemporary observed: "The rapid development of mechanical road transport has been one of the outstanding events of the post-war period and in a single generation it has reacted in a marked degree on the whole economic and social life of the country." It greatly facilitated the movement of goods and people and created new employment and investment opportunities which did much to relieve the gloom and tension of those years.

Both motor transport and motor manufacturing experienced rapid and

almost continuous growth throughout this period. Starting from almost
nothing they rose to become one of the most important sectors of the British
economy. By the late 1930s around 1·3 to 1·5 million people derived their
livelihood from the manufacture, operation and servicing of motor vehicles.
There was relatively little unemployment in contrast to the position in
other industries; the percentage of insured tram and bus workers recorded
as unemployed between 1923 and 1936 never rose above seven per cent and
in January 1929 it was as low as 2·4 per cent. Men were always eager to get
a job on the buses and as late as 1937 "when two vacancies were advertised
on the buses 20 men applied". It is difficult however to measure the full
repercussions especially of the manufacturing side where Britain improved
her performance considerably in the 1930s. By the end of that decade the
manufacture of motor vehicles and cycles employed nearly 400,000 men
and it was the fourth largest industry in the country and the second largest
motor industry in the world. Annual output of vehicles rose from 95,000
in 1923 to a peak of 511,000 in 1937 and in the latter year exports were more
than twice those of 1929, accounting for nearly one fifth of total production
(including chassis). The industry's contribution to the country's economic
development must surely have been substantial. Apart from the direct
employment and trade effects the industry also generated a demand for a
wide range of other products such as machine tools, aluminium, steel,
glass, magnetos, rubber and above all petrol, and at the same time made an
important contribution in furthering the techniques of mass production.

Yet though the industry created a vast range of new jobs it should also
be remembered that it robbed some of the older forms of transport of their
employment-creating opportunities. Nearly all forms of internal transport,
railways, trams, canals, coastal shipping and horse-drawn vehicles, suffered
in some respect from road competition. How many men for example lost
their jobs as drivers of horse carriages, not to mention the horse grooms and
stable lads? The number must surely have been large for the horse vehicle
was literally swept off the streets by the car. The number of horse-drawn
carriages fell from 437,000 to 23,013 between 1903 and 1933 and by the end
of the 1930s they had become a curious relic of the past. The tram was to
share a similar fate though its decline was not quite so precipitous and total
extinction did not come until after the Second World War. Nevertheless
the tram's fate was sealed soon after the First World War when the bus
emerged as a serious rival. For a short time the tram maintained its ground;
passenger traffic reached a peak in 1919–20 and then remained almost stable
until 1927–8 when 4·7 million passenger journeys were made. But the
operating performance of the bus improved considerably in the 1920s and
with its many advantages of low capital cost, mobility, flexibility in operation,
speed, frequency and comfort, the tramway companies, mostly municipal
authorities, had no alternative but to abandon their networks in favour
of bus services. Thus after 1929 traffic carried by trams fell steadily and by the

early 1930s buses were carrying more passengers than their competitors. Between 1924 and 1933 one third of the route mileage was abandoned; many authorities dispensed with trams altogether in the last years before the war and only a few cities such as Glasgow, Liverpool and Blackpool continued to build new rolling stock. By 1938 passenger traffic on municipal tramways had fallen to one half the 1929 level and passengers travelling by bus were three times as numerous. Thus it was only a matter of time before the tram became a museum relic like the horse-drawn carriage. Needless to say the trackless trolley or trolley bus, a hybrid vehicle powered by electric current, failed to secure a strong foothold save in a few areas.

As we have already seen, the railways were affected increasingly by road competition in the interwar years though there was never any question of their services as a whole being abandoned. For the most part it was in urban areas and on the short to medium distance journeys (up to 75 miles) that road transport offered the most serious threat. In the Metropolitan Area of London for example, it was road transport which showed the most striking gains in traffic between 1906 and 1936. During this period the number of passengers travelling by rail increased by 72 per cent compared with 287 per cent by road (including trams and trolleys) and by the latter date three times as many people travelled by road as by rail though the average rail journey was considerably longer. As distance increased the degree of competition tended to diminish. The L.M.S. found from a detailed analysis between pairs of stations that for the years 1923–7 receipts from passengers (other than workmen and season ticket holders) fell by 27 per cent for distances up to 10 miles, by 23 per cent for 11 to 20 miles, and 9 per cent for 21–50 miles, whereas for journeys above 50 miles they increased by two per cent. This probably holds true for merchandise traffic as well though here the range of competition may have been greater since speed was not so important as in the case of passenger traffic. In 1929 an official of the Great Western estimated that within the area covered by one of its main lines, roads carried 57·8 per cent of the traffic up to 40 miles, but only 18·5 per cent of that over 40 miles. Thus it was on the shorter-distance journeys that railway traffic was most vulnerable, though one should bear in mind that both these estimates are for the 1920s. In the following decade competition was being pushed further afield and keen competition between road and rail was developing for traffic travelling over distances of between 75 and 100 miles. Nevertheless, by and large the railways retained their hold over long-distance traffic right up to the war. Exactly how much traffic road transport took from the railways is difficult to say. Possibly by the middle of the 1930s the railways had lost 50 million tons of freight to the road and 200 million passenger journeys or more. But these are at best tentative guesses. Even if complete statistics were available for road traffic it would not be possible to give precise estimates of the loss since private transport remains an unknown quantity. In any case it is not simply a matter of comparing road traffic figures with those of rail and drawing conclusions about railway losses therefrom. Much of the road traffic was new and had never existed before the advent of the car whilst the railways were not the only victims of this new medium of transport. Hence any attempt to make an accurate calculation of the railway losses is impossible.

That motor transport became a serious competitor to the older forms of transport is not surprising when one considers the advantages the business community must have derived from it. There is no doubt that in many cases it was able to offer a much more flexible and convenient form of transport for the distribution of goods. It made possible direct door-to-door delivery with a minimum of transhipment and often it could provide a more frequent and speedier service than either the railway or horse-drawn vehicle. In retail distribution a much greater range of action was now possible since previously the speed of the horse vehicle had limited deliveries to a fairly narrow area. Thus many housewives enjoyed for the first time the luxury of having their purchases delivered, as the larger shops and department stores began to provide delivery facilities for household goods of a durable nature. At the same time the baker, butcher, grocer and milkman improved their existing delivery facilities by replacing horse-drawn vehicles with motorized ones.[1] The manufacturer and merchant also found the motor vehicle a great convenience. For one thing it permitted a much greater degree of direct contact between the various channels of distribution and it also enabled a greater volume of trade to be done within a given period of time. As early as 1908 a witness to the Tariff Commission reported that one miller who had adopted motor vehicles had trebled his business simply because he had been able to increase his range of action. The farmer too, was quick to take advantage of road transport. In 1924 the railways were carrying nearly 75 per cent of the agricultural produce of the country but by 1938, when road haulage served nearly every farm in the country, some 60 per cent of the commodities produced and consumed by farmers were transported by road. For the carriage of perishable commodities such as milk, fruit, vegetables and flowers, the motor vehicle proved to be a godsend. The farmer or market gardener had no longer to worry about getting his milk or perishables to the station. As Mowat has pointed out, the transport of milk was virtually revolutionized in this period. "By about 1930 the old traffic in milk churns on country branch lines had practically ceased. No longer did the farmer drive to the station and unload his churns; instead the churns were picked up by lorries from a stand at the farm turning, and taken to a creamery, and the milk sent in glass-lined tanks to London or elsewhere, by train or road."

Motor transport was also a powerful factor in the location and pattern of distribution of industry. The location of factories was no longer tied so firmly to areas where railway facilities were available since the motor vehicle allowed a much greater freedom of choice in this matter. Thus many of the

[1] On the other hand it is perhaps interesting to note that it was in this period that the second daily delivery of milk tended to disappear.

new or light industries such as chemicals and electrical and vehicle manufacturing grew up in the industrial suburbs of northwest London and in the
Midlands, away from the coal, iron and rail nexus in the north. Moreover
the pattern of location within the "newer" areas differed from that of the
old industrial centres. Whereas railway transport had tended to encourage
the development of factories grouped around nuclear points with radial
distribution of goods from the centre, motor transport, with its greater
flexibility and ease of movement, made possible the building of factories
along arterial roads with no specific focal point. In the long run this brought
about a greater diffusion of industry and population which, though it had
advantages, eventually produced the rather undesirable feature of ribbon
development against which the Government was forced to take action in
1935.

Evidence suggests however that it was the personal habits of the people
that were most affected by improved communications. Never before had the
British public travelled so frequently and so regularly as in the years between
the wars. The frequency of travel in London, for example, increased three-
fold between 1906 and 1936 and a large part of this increase was accounted for
by the use of road transport. Much of the movement was of a short-distance
kind but this should not detract from its importance, for it was facilities for
this type of travel which had been generally inadequate before the advent
of the internal combustion engine. The private car and the poor man's bus
enabled a much greater proportion of the population to afford the luxury
of travel. Jaunts to the seaside and trips into the country became a popular
activity for all classes and rapidly replaced the Victorian fireside weekend.
Social intercourse was no longer restricted by lack of communication, for
the motor car greatly facilitated the contacts between town and country.
The week-end shopper from up country and the village lad invaded the
cities to get a glimpse of the bright lights whilst in turn the urban dweller
sought to escape from the confines of the town whenever possible. Perhaps
the impact was greatest on the countryside. The rural dweller was no longer
so cut off from the rest of the community and motor transport may have
helped to check the drift to the towns by making those who lived in the
country more satisfied with their lot. Better communications made it
possible to improve the delivery services of goods and newspapers as well
as enabling rural inhabitants to mix with their town cousins more frequently, which was a far better solution than bringing the town to the
country. In fact motor transport opened up all sorts of new and exciting
opportunities to countless numbers of people and it did much to relieve
the tension and strain of these otherwise depressed years.

But if people were travelling about more frequently it was not always
simply for the pleasure of doing so. For many it was simply the case of making the journey to work and back again. This became increasingly common
as people tended to live further away from their place of work. The great
nineteenth-century flow of population from country to town had already

been checked and a reverse movement was taking place. This movement of population from the city centre to the outskirts did not of course originate with the motor vehicle. Indeed it had already begun well before the end of the last century for, with increasing congestion in the towns and improved local transport facilities, mainly railways and trams, city dwellers were encouraged to move to residences in the suburbs. This drift from the centre to the fringes was greatly accelerated in the early twentieth century, and in the inter-war years it became the most prominent feature in the distribution of population. Almost all the major urban conurbations, which accounted for about one half of Britain's population, experienced this centrifugal movement. Numbers in the centre remained constant or even declined whilst all the growth took pace in the suburbs. Thus the inner centres of the seven largest urban areas, London, Manchester, Birmingham, West Yorkshire, Glasgow, Merseyside, and Tyneside showed a decline in population of 2·5 per cent (1921–38) whilst the suburbs expanded by 32 per cent. Altogether Britain's population increased by 3·44 million during this period, 75 per cent of which accrued to the suburbs of the 27 major conurbations. This outward flow of population brought a striking expansion of new housing estates and streets in the surrounding suburbs and since many of the people who moved out to these new areas continued to seek employment in the inner zones, they were therefore dependent on some form of transport.

Though road transport became increasingly important in determining the dispersion of population it was by no means the only factor which facilitated such development. The trams and suburban railways had played an important part in earlier years and in London the railways continued to dominate the scene because of the longer distances involved. Even before 1914 London had developed an extensive suburbia, and in the interwar years new urban centres were created on the edge of the old suburban ring. Thus the boundaries were gradually pushed out to Becontree in the east, Ilford and Wanstead in the northeast, Hendon and Edgeware in the northwest, South Harrow and Hayes to the west and Morden and Cheam in the south and southeast. At the same time a number of older, semi-rural communities such as Hounslow, Kingston, Croydon and Eltham continued to expand and helped to complete the ring of satellite towns spread over a radius of 10 to 15 miles from the city centre. Some of these new areas became partly self-supporting communities and their very existence created a heavy local demand for transport facilities for shopping, amusement and inter-urban travel services which the local bus or private car performed admirably. Even so a large proportion of the inhabitants continued to work in the metropolis and without the suburban rail services this would not have been possible, for it was too time-consuming and inconvenient to commute each day by road from places like Romford, Dagenham and Thames Ditton. Nevertheless motor transport still had a part to play in this daily migration, since dispersion of population within these satellite towns was only practicable if easy access to the local railway station was available to the inhabitants.

Similar developments were taking place in most of the larger provincial towns or urban communities though on a somewhat smaller scale than around the metropolis. In places such as Manchester, Liverpool, Birmingham and Glasgow people were constantly moving out towards the fringes in order to escape the filth and grime of the cities. Here the private car or the local bus played an important part in facilitating the process since, compared with London, suburban railways were less extensive and commuting distances were noticeably shorter. Yet both in London and the provincial towns better transport facilities were by no means the only factor in the growth of suburbia. Rising real incomes and shorter working hours made it possible for many people to live some distance away from their place of work for the first time. And of course the provision of new housing on the outskirts was an essential prerequisite for this development. The rapid growth of Essex as a commuters' paradise owed much to the London County Council's building programme of the 1920s; by 1932 the Council was accommodating no less than 103,328 people on its estate at Becontree. In the following decade Manchester was actively developing the Wythenshawe estate on the south side of the city for its overspill population. Such planned enterprises were still a novelty but the provision of housing either planned or otherwise was nonetheless essential before urban dwellers could hope to uproot themselves and move out beyond the inner walls of the city.

Though no doubt some people stood to lose, on balance the community secured a net social benefit from motor transport. It would be difficult to find any section of society which was not affected in one way or another. The social habits of the people, the pattern of trade, the location of industry, sport and entertainment were all affected by this new medium of transport. Even religion took to the road by fitting motor vans out as mobile chapels. But its impact was much greater than the superficially visible marks which it left for all to see. Psychologically the impact ran deeper for it brought a new element of hope and a new element of choice to the lives of many families. Indeed the very fact that the choice now lay between producing babies and buying baby Austins was sufficient to undermine the rigid and dull monotony of Edwardian society. But at the same time it brought new pressures to bear on society, and the social system as a whole was faced with new problems some of which will be investigated in the following pages.

4   The problem of public control

Whatever its benefits, and there is no doubt that they were considerable, motor transport was far from being an unmixed blessing. It created all sorts of new problems or intensified old ones, some of which are still with us today. As we have seen, the structure of the industry both on the passenger and goods side was unsatisfactory and left much room for improvement. The question was what form of control was necessary to achieve the most orderly pattern of development without at the same time restricting the growth of the industry unduly. The rapid growth of motor traffic also brought mounting congestion on the roads, a solution to which was urgently required if movement was not to be brought to a standstill. Above all there was the question of the relation of motor transport to other forms of internal transport. To what extent was co-ordination between competing interests desirable in the national interest? It was in an attempt to find an answer to some of the problems arising from the growth of road traffic that the Government set up a Royal Commission on Transport in August 1928. This Commission duly issued three reports between 1929 and 1931 in the last of which it made a fairly extensive survey of each branch of internal transport. This in fact was, and still is, the first comprehensive survey of the whole field of internal transport, and though many of its recommendations were subsequently ignored its proposals for the regulation of motor transport became the basis of public policy in the early 1930s.

(a)   A solution to London's transport problem

Long before the Royal Commission issued its findings, attempts had been made to regulate the growth of passenger traffic in the London Area. By the early twentieth century the condition of London's traffic had become one for great concern. The unco-ordinated development of trams, buses, tubes and suburban railways was leading to unnecessary waste and duplication of services and at the same time adding to the confusion of the traffic on the streets. As early as 1903 a Royal Commission had been appointed to review the situation and in its report two years later it emphasized the neglect of planning London's transport system. It recommended that greater unification should be secured by the establishment of a Traffic Board which would exercise some sort of overall authority over London's transport services. Nothing was done to implement the proposals but subsequently numerous committees (1913–19) were set up to investigate the same question, and each of these reached similar conclusions. All of them recommended some form of central authority to own, operate or at least supervise passenger transport in the London Area. The urgency of dealing with the problem was left in little doubt by the Committee of 1919: "The immediate creation by Parliament of a London Traffic Authority can alone remedy the present intolerable conditions".

Yet legislative action was not forthcoming, partly because by this time some attempt to secure a degree of unification had been made by the private transport undertakings themselves. The initiative in this respect was taken by the Underground Group under the energetic leadership of Albert Stanley (later Lord Ashfield). From 1909 onwards this group began acquiring control of various transport concerns including tramway and electric railway interests, certain bus services in the outer districts and the London General in 1912. By the end of the war the Combine (Underground Group) had secured a partial monopoly of London's transport services, for only the Metropolitan Railway, the main line railways, fourteen local authority tramway systems including that of the L.C.C. and a number of independent bus proprietors remained outside the group's network. But monopoly soon gave way to competition again with the arrival of the independent bus companies in the second half of 1922. Within a matter of months London was flooded with omnibuses and by the end of 1924 some 500 independent vehicles were operating in the area. Traffic obstruction and wasteful competition became so serious as a result of this invasion that in 1924 Parliament was forced to take action. The London Traffic Act of that year gave the Minister of Transport power to regulate or prohibit motor bus traffic on certain restricted streets whilst the licensing authority for the area, the Metropolitan Police Commissioner, could prescribe approved routes for the operation of buses. The London and Home Counties Traffic Advisory Committee was set up to assist the Minister of Transport in carrying out the Act.

The legislation was fairly effective in stabilizing the number of omnibus companies in the London area. By the end of 1925 practically every street in the Metropolitan Police District had been declared restricted and few new operators were allowed to commence services. The Underground Combine assisted the process of consolidation by acquiring control of many of the smaller independent companies. By 1930 only 199 omnibuses owned by 54 operators remained outside the two large groups, the Underground and the London Public Omnibus Company. This latter company owned some 234 vehicles and had been established in 1927 to combine the remaining independents under one management. For a time it competed fiercely with the Combine but eventually both companies agreed to co-ordinate their services.

It was soon obvious however that the 1924 Act would never provide a lasting solution to London's traffic problem. For one thing the legislation did little to ease the problem of street congestion. Furthermore it did not eliminate completely the competition in services and towards the end of 1927 coaches were beginning to operate on short-distance routes in London in a manner which brought them into competition with the ordinary stage omnibuses. It is true that coaches had been brought within the scope of the Act of 1924 but owing to certain legal ambiguities in the phrasing of the legislation it was found difficult to exercise any effective control over their activities. Thus competition continued, and even increased again in the later 1920s, and with mounting street congestion it was essential that some more permanent solution should be found. To relieve the latter problem, for example, it was desirable to extend the underground rail services but whilst wasteful competition remained at street level it was difficult to attract capital to undertake the necessary alterations. As Lord Ashfield

z

pointed out, what was required was the unification of the transport system so that services could be co-ordinated and investment allocated into the most appropriate channels. The London and Home Counties Traffic Advisory Committee came to much the same conclusion. After a series of public enquiries into the state of traffic and transport facilities in various sectors of London the Committee, in a report published in 1927, declared emphatically that "No lasting solution of the London passenger transport problem can be secured as long as the present competitive methods are pursued. . . . The unified management of the underground and other local railways, tramways and omnibuses would provide the only permanent solution of the whole problem." Both Lord Ashfield and the Committee were of course only repeating what had been stated on numerous other occasions but the force and authority with which they presented their arguments served to convince other influential people that some such solution could not be delayed much longer.

Delay appeared inevitable however, for by the autumn of 1928 it was clear that the Government would not be able to find time for a public bill before the Election. Whereupon the four main line railway companies arranged with other transport interests for a pooling of revenues in respect of traffic in the London region whilst the London County Council and the Underground Group united to promote private legislation to effect a partial scheme of co-ordination. Though permissive in character the Bills presented would have enabled the parties to enter into agreements with each other and any other transport operator in the London area for the co-ordination of traffic facilities and for the establishment of a common fund and common management. Owing to strong opposition from Labour members these Bills were defeated but the return of a Labour government in 1929 cleared the way for a much more ambitious scheme of control. In 1933 the London Passenger Transport Bill, conceived by Herbert Morrison as Minister of Transport in the previous Labour government, received legislative sanction. This finally put an end to the competition in London's transport services.

The Act of 1933 was the first attempt to create an organized body charged with the responsibility of providing adequate travelling facilities in the Metropolitan Area upon a remunerative basis and at reasonable, economic fares. The London Passenger Transport Board, which came into existence on 1 July 1933, was the largest transport undertaking in the world. It consisted of seven members (including the chairman) appointed by a group of "Appointing Trustees" and its primary duty was to secure the provision of an adequate and properly co-ordinated system of passenger transport for the London area and avoid all unnecessary and wasteful services. To accomplish this task the Board was given a monopoly of passenger transport services except those by private car, taxis and main line railways. This of course involved the authority taking over all the existing transport undertakings for which it issued £113 million in transport stock in exchange for the original shares. Over an area of 2,000 square miles the Board had the right to operate passenger services, and apart from the outer quarter of this area where it was subject to the licensing regulations of the Metropolitan Traffic Commissioner, no one could operate a bus or coach service without the Board's written permission. Provision was also made for co-ordinating the services of the Board with those of the suburban main line railways and a scheme was drawn up to pool all receipts from traffic originating or terminating within the Board's area. The Board had almost complete financial autonomy and it was under an obligation to secure economic self-sufficiency.

Under the able leadership of Lord Ashfield and Frank Pick, both of the Underground Combine, the Board lost no time in getting down to the task of improving London's transport facilities. The process of unifying transport services, which had been initiated earlier by the private undertakings, was completed and henceforth a much greater degree of co-ordination was effected between alternative transport services and with the main line railways. This made possible a considerable extension and modernization of London's passenger transport facilities. During the 1930s the tube system was extended and many of the stations reconstructed and modernized, trolley buses were substituted for tramcars amd many new additions were made to the bus services. A vigorous attempt was made to standardize the rolling stock and this involved scrapping many of the buses which the Board had inherited from the former companies. Altogether some 1,300 new vehicles had been introduced by the end of 1937. The Board also began the slow process of removing anomalies from the fare structure and reducing the basis of charging to uniform principles. How far the Board was able to pass on to the public the benefits of unification is difficult to say for one of the results, intended or otherwise, of unification is that some services are subsidized by others. By the end of 1935 only 43 per cent of the Board's services earned revenue in excess of operating costs and overhead charges whilst 34 per cent earned less than their direct cost of operation. Nevertheless it would seem that the Board was able to make sufficient economies to enable it to lower fares without seriously endangering its revenue position. In the first three years no less than 6,258 road service fares were reduced whereas only 1,390 were increased. Moreover the public no doubt enjoyed a substantial improvement in the quality of service as a result of the Board's work. Taken all round this experiment in public enterprise proved remarkably successful in coping with London's difficult transport problem. Even by 1938 the Board's achievements were such that one writer had no hesitation in stating that "sufficient progress has been made in nationalisation to demonstrate positive advantages in the planned provision of transport as against regulation by spasmodic and necessarily limited competition". Despite the success the experiment was not repeated elsewhere though a number of local authorities and private operators negotiated voluntary co-ordination agreements in the 1930s. Tentative proposals were in fact made for the formation of regional boards in areas such as Merseyside, Manchester, the West Riding and Tyneside but these failed to take concrete shape.

(b)   Regulation of road passenger transport

Outside London, passenger transport services remained almost free from control until 1930. It is true that under the Town Police Clauses Acts of 1847 and 1889 local authorities had power to license vehicles to ply for hire but this amounted to very little in the way of formal control. Moreover the way in which these licensing arrangements were administered varied from area to area depending on the inclination and interests of the locality concerned. Many local authorities had no licensing powers and those that did often failed to exercise them; in the southwest of England only 53 out of 177 local authorities exercised their licensing powers and of that number many did so only to a limited extent. Some authorities licensed any vehicle that was put on the road whilst others used their powers to protect their own transport interests. In effect there was almost a complete lack of uniformity in licensing arrangements which could hardly be said to act as a check to the growth of the industry. As a rule operators could usually get a license to ply for hire quite easily and no conditions were attached to the licenses granted. The result, as we have seen already, was that in the decade after the war conditions in the industry became chaotic in many areas. Hundreds of small operators, with poor vehicles and no proper service schedules, competed fiercely against each other for traffic and almost no attempt was made to co-ordinate their services.

By the later 1920s there was a widespread feeling that some greater degree of control over the passenger transport industry was urgently required. According to the Thesiger report of 1953 this "remarkable unanimity" of opinion was based on the belief that uncontrolled development of passenger road transport was becoming contrary to the interests of everyone concerned. It is true that unregulated competition was not producing the best results. The public suffered from irregular and unreliable services and there is no question that they would have benefited from a greater degree of co-ordination of the facilities available. These factors alone would have justified the need for more control. But it is misleading to suggest that the question was beyond dispute. Conditions in the industry were not quite so bad as they were made out to be and one has to remember that competition had provided the public with a choice of road transport facilities at fares lower than might otherwise have obtained. Much of the criticism of the industry came from vested interest such as the municipal authorities, the railways and the more reliable road operators (territorial bus companies) and it was these groups who presented their case most forcibly to the Royal Commission on Transport. No evidence was taken from the independents or from the public. Thus it is not surprising that the Commission's findings should reflect the opinions of the organized pressure groups. It was this apparent unanimity of opinion which accounts more than anything else for the alacrity with which Parliament accepted the Commission's recommendations and put them into effect even before the final report had been published.

The Road Traffic Act of 1930 substituted a fairly rigid form of control in place of the loose system of licensing previously exercised by the local authorities. Semi-independent tribunals, consisting of one full-time and two part-time members were set up in different areas of the country (11 for England and two for Scotland).[1] By means of an elaborate licensing system covering vehicles, services and employees the Commissioners were empowered to regulate the conditions in and entry into the industry. Before a vehicle could be operated for public hire three types of licences had to be acquired. A certificate of fitness was required for the vehicle in question[2] whilst the driver and conductor each had to obtain a personal licence which guaranteed their competence as transport personnel.[3] These licences were non-discriminatory in nature and anyone who satisfied the required conditions could obtain them. It was the third one—the road service licence —which was the most important for without it no vehicle could be used for any sort of service except private contract work. Moreover it was by means of this third licence, which was issued in a discriminatory manner, that the Commissioners were able to regulate entry into the passenger transport business.

The discretionary powers of the Commissioners to grant or refuse road service licences were quite wide and conditions could be attached to them when granted. Applications for such licences were heard at a public sitting of the Commissioners to which both supporters and objectors were invited. When considering an application for a road service licence the Commissioners were to take into account the suitability of the route and the extent to which it was already served, the extent to which the proposed service was necessary or desirable in the public interest, the needs of the area as a whole in relation to other traffic and the prospects for co-ordination of transport facilities within the area as a whole. Of course if an applicant could not show proof of support for his proposed service it was highly unlikely that he would be successful. When granted the Commissioners were obliged to attach certain conditions to the licences to ensure that fares were reasonable and at such a level as to prevent wasteful competition with alternative forms of transport, that copies of timetables and fare tables were available for public inspection and that passengers were only picked up and set down at specified places. The passengers' safety and welfare were also to be taken into account and if desirable the Commissioners could vary the conditions they attached to the licences. In practice licences were generally issued for three years; renewal was not automatic and they could be revoked or suspended within the current period if necessary. Appeals against decisions could be made to the Minister of Transport who in cases of dispute had the final word.[4]

[1] There was only one full-time Commissioner for the Metropolitan Area. In 1933 the number of areas for England and Wales was reduced to ten.
[2] A vehicle licence could be refused on the grounds that the owner was not a fit person to hold one.   [3] All bus drivers were obliged to pass a driving test.
[4] Local authorities were subject to these licensing arrangements.

Though the conditions on which licences were to be issued were embodied in the Act the Commissioners and Minister of Transport refused to lay down any general criteria as to when a road service licence should be granted or refused. It was held that cases varied so widely that each had to be considered on its own merits and any attempt to define general principles would lead to unnecessary inflexibility. The Traffic Commissioners had no precedent to fall back upon and it quickly became apparent from the early hearings that applications were being judged on the basis of priority, protection and public need.

From the start the Act was interpreted as giving the established operator priority over the new applicant and the existing operator the right to protection from competition. Provided that an established operator had been performing a reasonable service prior to 1930 the Commissioners had no alternative but to let him continue. In fact to facilitate their proceedings in the transitional period the Commissioners were empowered during the first four years to grant public service licences to all vehicles operating prior to 1931, without a certificate of fitness having first been granted. Once licensed, operators might be protected in several ways from competitive road services. As a rule whenever more than one operator performed a service in the same area or on the same route the Commissioners allocated services on a non-competitive basis. Obviously this neat division of function could not be applied in every case since a great deal of overlapping was bound to occur especially on routes traversed both by stage and long distance operators. A different form of protection had therefore to be devised to safeguard local services from the competition of the express services. This form of protection seldom led to an outright refusal of an applicant to run long-distance services; instead certain conditions were attached to the licences. The latter might be precluded from picking up or setting down passengers in the territory of the local service operator or, alternatively, fares might be fixed in such a manner as to favour the short-stage operator in his own area. Protection from the irregular or seasonal operator might also be afforded by placing restrictions on the number of vehicles used, the journeys made, the number of passengers carried or the fares charged. Likewise the Commissioners also sought in some cases to protect alternative forms of transport such as tramways and railways from the competition of the motor bus.

A recent student of the licensing system has intimated that the third principle, that of public need, has been passed over in favour of priority and protection. He also argues that the licensing system has been detrimental to the transport industry as a whole. By restricting entry to the industry and safeguarding the existing operator it "put a premium upon inefficiency by linking most operators in a pricing system based upon the protection of those with the highest costs". The large territorial bus companies, which have the highest overhead costs, have steadily expanded their monopoly of public service operation at the expense of the smaller independent concerns. Thus the competitive thrust of the latter has been sacrificed and this has led to inertia in the industry. Similarly it is argued that the railways have been protected unduly and "there was no sign of a determined counter-attack with services adapted to meet growing competition". These are sweeping criticisms and it will not be possible to examine them all in detail.[1] They stand out in sharp contrast to the high praise accorded by the Thesiger Committee in 1953. "The system", they believed, "has in fact succeeded—indeed it would be no exaggeration to say that it has handsomely succeeded —in achieving its objectives." It had, the Committee were told, "achieved an orderly growth of the industry whilst preserving the essential features of fair competition". Under the system, the road passenger industry had proved to be a progressive and not a static industry. There was little public dissatisfaction with road passenger services operated under the control of the Licensing Authorities and the system had proved strong and flexible enough to cope with great difficulties and changes. Obviously both views cannot be correct and it remains for us to examine the broad consequences of the legislation.

There can be no doubt that the licensing system restricted the growth of the industry though at the same time it created a greater degree of stability throughout. The total number of public service vehicles rose by only just over 3,000 between 1931 and 1938 whilst the number of operators fell from 6,434 to 4,798. As a result the average number of vehicles owned by each operator rose from 7·1 to 10·4. The most noticeable feature was the rapid growth of the larger concerns at the expense of the smaller. By the beginning of 1938 over 60 per cent of the buses and coaches were owned by firms possessing 100 vehicles or more compared with around 47 per cent in 1931, whilst the percentage owned by the smaller operators (less than ten vehicles) fell from 29 to 22 per cent over the same period. This change can be attributed to the fact that many of the smaller and less desirable concerns were either disfranchized by the Commissioners or alternatively they were absorbed by their larger neighbours. Nevertheless a large number of very small concerns still remained since the Commissioners sought to protect the established operator both small and large alike. Perhaps one of the most serious criticisms of the Act was that it had little to say about the structure of the industry. In fact, economic principles were almost wholly ignored when framing the legislation and the Commissioners were given no powers to reorganize the industry so that the units which remained in being were the most economic. Nor for that matter was much attention given to the question of which type or size of operator could best perform a particular service. This was a serious defect since it is possible that some of the smaller concerns with relatively low overhead costs were best suited to providing services in rural areas where traffic was fairly sparse. Thus apart from

[1] In all fairness it should be pointed out that these criticisms apply to the period after 1945 though many of them are, according to the author, relevant to the 1930s. John Hibbs, *Transport for Passengers* (Hobart Paper 23, 1963), p. 45.

the changes we have already outlined the structure of the industry remained much as before with a few large concerns dominating the industry, a large number of small operators and the municipal authorities in between. In this respect therefore the legislation of 1930 stands condemned.

After the institution of licensing it was much more difficult for the newcomer to enter the passenger transport field and in fact few entirely new concerns were established in the 1930s. To obtain a licence the newcomer had to prove that there was a volume of traffic which he could carry but which was not actually being carried at the time of his application. But possessing no vehicles or records the applicant obviously found it very difficult to substantiate his case especially when confronted by the opposition of rival concerns and alternative transport interests. It was far easier for an existing operator to obtain permission to run additional services than it was for the newcomer to gain access to the industry. Consequently the growth in motor transport facilities in the 1930s was largely provided by existing operators extending the range of their activities. Moreover it was easier for the established operators (more especially the large territorial bus companies) to divide the market up amongst themselves, a practice which found favour with the Traffic Commissioners. This in itself was not necessarily a bad thing since it assisted the elimination of much wasteful competition which had previously existed. The position in the Potteries for instance improved beyond all recognition when the two rival groups agreed to co-operate. Nor is there any firm evidence which suggests that the larger companies were inefficient or that they abused their privileged position. Though competition was naturally reduced, service facilities undoubtedly improved during the 1930s and it can be maintained that the larger company was in a better position to provide some of the more unremunerative services by cross-subsidization. In any case competition was not eliminated entirely except perhaps on some of the long-distance routes, for in the larger urban areas duplicate services were continued much as before, the main difference being that they were now on a controlled basis.

On the other hand it is possible to argue that by restricting the entry of the newcomer the consumer suffered since he was being deprived of transport facilities he might otherwise have enjoyed. The importance placed upon the principles of priority and protection meant in practice, as Savage has observed, that public inconvenience had to precede the recognition of public need. No doubt a certain amount of hardship did occur since the Commissioners had to be convinced that there was a sufficient demand for new services or the extension of existing ones before additional licences were granted. But there is no evidence to suggest that the public suffered unduly in this respect and when account is taken of the improvement in facilities which occurred in the 1930s it is difficult to reach any other conclusion than that the public secured a net gain from the licensing system. In nearly every case the Traffic Commissioners were able to report that there had been a remarkable improvement in the standard of equipment and in the comfort and cleanliness of public services vehicles. They were no longer worked to a standstill before repair and "dirty interiors, unhealthy fumes, bad springing and noisy machinery are now a rare occurrence in public service vehicles, while the safety of the public is increased by constant supervision of the maintenance of steering, brake gear, and general improvement". The public also enjoyed the benefits of safer and more reliable services and the advantages which followed from the much greater degree of co-ordination of timetables and fare schedules. In the East Midlands Traffic Area alone 600 time and fare tables were co-ordinated to the advantage of operators and public alike within the first year of the licensing system. The South Wales Commissioner reported a similar success. "We have been able to effect co-ordination of the services on practically every route in the area and to put an end to the highly dangerous practice of racing between public service vehicles which was so prevalent before the Act." In fact perhaps the most remarkable feature is the frequency with which the Commissioners reported that services had been co-ordinated and the attention paid to the closer integration of rail and road services and their respective timetables. No doubt much more could have been done towards co-ordinating transport services in general in the 1930s but this should not preclude us from recognizing the achievements which took place in this period.

Finally there remains the question as to what effect the licensing system had on alternative forms of transport. Under section 72 of the Act the Commissioners were directed to consider what other forms of transport were available when adjudicating applications for road service licences. It is unlikely that this had much effect on local systems of tramways and trackless trolleys. The degree of protection afforded was equivalent to that given to local bus services but as Chester has pointed out there was a limit to the amount of protection that might be granted and local authorities could not demand it as a right. Indeed the very fact that the tramway routes were being abandoned so rapidly in favour of bus services is evidence enough that the Commissioners were in no way inclined to bolster up a declining industry. Possibly the Act gave a new lease of life to the trackless trolley not merely because the amount of bus competition was reduced but also because trolley services did not come under the control of the Traffic Commissioners. Nevertheless trolley buses never became very popular and most of them were owned by the local authorities. The railways were able to secure a greater measure of relief from bus competition possibly because they were one of the most vocal elements at the Traffic Court hearings. Generally speaking it was on the long-distance routes where they managed to restrict the extension of bus services though it is a mistake to assume that this seriously reduced the amount of competition between the competing forms of transport. Against local services the railways gained little relief and in the matter of fares, which usually favoured the buses, the railways attempted with little success to have them increased. Thus there is no reason to suppose that the railways were sheltered excessively from motor bus competition or that protection led to inertia on the part of the railway management. In fact, after the licensing system was introduced the railways were more enterprising both as regards fares and facilities than at any time during the decade after the First World War.

(c) The restriction of road haulage

The report of the Royal Commission on Transport in favour of the licensing of road haulage operators was not followed by legislation immediately. This was partly because it was felt at the time that the Commission had not investigated the problems of the industry thoroughly enough and also because the Commission's recommendations, especially those relating to an increase in road taxes, aroused opposition from many road hauliers. Consequently a Ministry of Transport Conference (the Salter Conference) was convened in 1932 with a view to establishing what would be a fair basis of competition and division of function between rail and road transport of goods, particularly as regards the incidence of highway costs and the nature and extent of regulation which should be applied to goods transport by road and rail. In their report of the following July the Conference considered that some regulation of road haulage was necessary and that it should be enforced through a licensing system. To alleviate the twin evils of overcrowding and unbridled competition, entry into the industry must be restricted for "unrestricted liberty on entry" they felt, "was fatal to the organization of the industry in a form suitable to a carrier service purporting to serve the public". On the other hand it was realized that road transport must be left flexible enough to adapt to changing needs and therefore a distinction was made between the public carrier and the ancilliary haulier who ran vehicles for his own convenience. All should be licensed but the public haulier would be subject to more restrictions than the latter. In particular, wages and conditions of service should be controlled, which would put road haulage on a more equal footing with the railways. When it came to considering the division of function between road and rail the Committee were understandably vague. They felt that the licensing system, coupled with a reallocation of the incidence of highway costs (the general effect of which would be to make road hauliers meet a greater share of their track costs) would tend towards a more economically sound division of function between road and rail goods transport. But it is clear a few lines later on in the report that they were doubtful as to whether this would really do the trick. "We conceive that, in the main, transport will divide itself between road and rail as the demand of those who require it, and the facilities offered by those who provide it, determine. We believe that the best division of function will be obtained mainly through the deliberate effort of those engaged in road and rail transport to co-ordinate their services and give the public the full advantages of complementary service."

The decision to legislate against the expansion of road haulage was based therefore on three principal factors. It was argued both by the Royal Commission and the Salter Conference that the industry was unstable because of excessive competition and low rates, that this in turn led to the neglect of maintenance and hence a high rate of accidents and finally that transport in general would benefit from a greater degree of co-ordination between road and rail. It has recently been shown however that on none of these heads could the restriction of road haulage be justified. Accident rates were not excessive, freight charges were not unduly unstable in view of the economic conditions of the time and co-ordination was largely a myth for it was never really achieved. The main reason why restriction gained such wide currency was partly because evidence about the conditions of the industry was drawn largely from vested interests such as the railways and larger road hauliers who were anxious to limit the indiscriminate competition of the small road haulier. Moreover, as Hart points out, much of the evidence presented was based on general impression rather than established fact and cannot be regarded as authoritative. On the other hand a case can still be made for some form of control. Though conditions in the industry were not as bad as the opposition factors made them out to be, it should be remembered that the industry had been unstable from the very beginning, in fact long before the depressed conditions of the early 1930s. Wasteful and excessive competition was certainly prevalent much of the time and as the Licensing Authorities testified in their reports the standard of conduct of many of the operators was deplorably low. Thus some form of control, though not necessarily that adopted in 1933, could be justified on these grounds alone. In the second place, in so far as control could bring about a more equitable distribution of costs between road and rail then it could be claimed that it was a step in the right direction. Finally though co-ordination between alternative forms of transport was never realized it is perhaps unfair to criticize too severely the efforts to find a solution to a fairly new problem.

Whatever the pros and cons of the situation the recommendations of the Salter Conference were implemented by the Road and Rail Traffic Act of 1933 and the Finance Act of the same year. Higher duties were imposed on heavy goods vehicles and a licensing system established which was to be administered by the chairmen of the Traffic Commissioners appointed under the Act of 1930. All owners of vehicles used for goods haulage were required to hold a carriers' licence of which there were three main types. An "A" licence entitled the holder to carry goods for hire or reward whilst the "C" licence was only issued to the trader who carried his own goods. The intermediate "B" licence could be used for both purposes. Once granted few restrictions could be placed on "A" and "C" licences but the "B" licence-holder was subject to special conditions regarding the type of traffic he carried and the area in which he operated.[1] All licencees had however to

[1] Each licence had a limited currency: "A" licences ran for two years, "B" for one year and "C" for three years. In 1938 the currency of "A" and "B" licences was raised to five and two years respectively but "C" licences remained the same.

fulfil certain statutory conditions relating to the fitness of vehicles and the observance of regulations concerning speed, loading and drivers' hours. Provision was also made for the regulation of drivers' wages. The Act also established a Transport Advisory Council to assist the Minister of Transport in connection with his duties in relation to the means of and facilities for transport and their co-ordination, improvement and development.

The Licensing Authorities' powers of control over road haulage were less extensive than those of their counterparts on the passenger side. They had, for example, no power to regulate the charges of road hauliers. Traders were considered to be protected against excessive charging by the freedom to operate their own vehicles, whilst there was as yet no proper structure of haulage rates over which public control could have been exercised. In the matter of granting licences the Authorities' powers were also limited. Provided the "safety" conditions were fulfilled "C" licences could not be withheld from ancillary users. On the other hand, after the expiry of the first licensing period,[1] the issue of "A" and "B" licences was subject to the discretion of the Authorities who had to be convinced that there was a need for additional facilities and that the existing transport capacity was not adequate to meet it. In other words applicants for licences had to produce evidence to support their cases before the Court of the Licensing Authority to which objections might be made by persons already providing transport facilities of any kind. Appeals against the Courts decisions might be made by any interested party to a specially constituted tribunal.

As in the case of passenger transport the main effect of the licensing system was to freeze the *status quo*. The entry of newcomers to the industry was severely restricted and it was more difficult for existing operators to increase the size of their fleets. Thus, during the later 1930s the growth in road haulage slowed down appreciably; it was moreover confined entirely to private carriers' vehicles ("C" licences) for after 1935 the number of "A" and "B" licence-holders and the vehicles operated by them actually fell. Despite a number of amalgamations the structure of the industry did not change significantly and by the Second World War it was still dominated by the small man. By June 1938 the average vehicle holding (all classes) was only 2·11 and even in the "A" class it was not more than 3·5. Thus apart from one or two large holdings, including the railways, the bulk of the firms in the industry had less than five vehicles apiece. To some extent this lack of concentration may be attributed to the licensing system since it had the effect of protecting the already small established operator, whilst the Authorities had no power to coerce firms to amalgamate their activities. In fact the road haulage industry itself maintained that the system sometimes denied the carrier with a sound and efficiently conducted business the opportunity of expansion which would normally result from his efficiency. "It is impossible", the British Road Federation claimed, "to expect that,

[1] Those in business during the year the Act was passed were automatically allowed licences for the first period.

under such insecure conditions, operators can either maintain or build up organizations on efficient and economically sound lines, and it is equally out of the question for any industry so hampered to achieve a satisfactory degree of co-ordination with others enjoying a much greater permanency." There is no doubt a strong element of truth in this allegation but it is only fair to point out that even without control concentration would not have proceeded very far in an industry in which the small unit was economically extremely viable.

Informed opinion has generally inclined towards the view that regulation has been detrimental to both the public and the road haulage industry. Gilbert Walker has argued that the licensing system inhibited both change and enterprise in road haulage and as a consequence the consumer was denied the benefits of competition. It is quite true of course that newcomers found it difficult to enter the industry, and before they could run additional vehicles established operators had to prove that the existing requirements for transport were not being met satisfactorily. In other words the burden of proof ultimately lay with the consumer and the Licensing Authorities tended to take the view that a degree of inconvenience had to be present before public need could be legitimately justified. This interpretation merely reflected a recognition on the part of the Authorities that facilities in excess of requirements were wasteful and should be eliminated. Up to a point this interpretation was beneficial since it meant that resources could be saved if overlapping and duplication were reduced. On the other hand it could be economically wasteful and inconvenient to the traders concerned if applications for additional road facilities were rejected simply on the grounds that alternative carriage facilities already existed. This sometimes happened when the railways objected to the provision of additional road haulage capacity. If they could prove that it was technically possible for them to carry the traffic for which additional facilities were demanded then the authorities were inclined to reject the applications even though the railways charged a higher rate for their services. This was not only unfair to both applicants and consumers alike but it also tended to make a mockery of the intentions to co-ordinate transport services as a whole. However there is no definite evidence which suggests that the Authorities favoured the railways unduly in this respect. Indeed in some cases the Authorities were clearly on the side of road transport which they thought ought not to be discouraged.

It would be wrong to create the impression that the licensing system was unduly rigid in its application and that it led to an unnecessary reduction in the amount of haulage capacity available to the public. The Commissioners recognized that competition still had a part to play in goods transport and it was only the "more extreme manifestations of wasteful competition" which the licensing system was designed to restrain. There is no evidence that this created a real shortage of road transport facilities. Though a reduction occurred in the number of "A" and "B" vehicles this was not necessarily an indication that less transport was being provided. On the contrary it was simply that the haulage capacity was now being used more efficiently and therefore less vehicles were required. Prior to licensing there had been a considerable reserve of under-utilized capacity some of which was still not being claimed officially in the later 1930s. "There is abundant evidence that a very large amount of claimed tonnage has never been taken up, because the licensees have been unable, notwithstanding the improvement in trade, to find work for it." It was of course more difficult to get permission to increase capacity but few traders who really required additional facilities were left without them. This point was confirmed by the Metropolitan Commissioner who was anxious to establish the fact that "in cases where traders requiring to use transport are really in need of additional facilities, experience does not show that they have much difficulty in getting them, or in supporting applications by those whose function it is to provide and operate vehicles. Any real need can be, and is being met." In any case if traders were deprived of public haulage facilities there was nothing to stop them from obtaining permission to run their own vehicles.

Finally it should be pointed out that the licensing system brought about a considerable improvement in the standard of performance of most road operators. In respect of the mechanical fitness of vehicles control it did nothing but good though perhaps this is hardly surprising since the standard was so deplorably low on first examination. Within the first sixteen months the Licensing Authorities issued no less than 24,642 notices of prohibition. As time progressed operators also became more accustomed to observing the other safety regulations relating to speed, loading and hours of driving. Even so there was still room for much improvement and in their last report before the war the Authorities called attention to the continued widespread disregard of the statutory conditions attached to licences, especially those relating to hours of work and rest and the falsification of drivers' records. Nevertheless, generally speaking it would be true to say that a more responsible body of road haulage operators was emerging in the later 1930s who were at last showing signs of co-operating among themselves to achieve things which were outside the domain of the Commissioners' powers. A typical example was in the matter of rates, over which the authorities had no jurisdiction. Various bodies representative of the road hauliers began to apply their energies to this problem and by 1937 there were at least ten associations and rate committees in the Yorkshire Area alone actively engaged in trying to find a solution to this question.

5   Towards a national highway policy

Among the problems arising from the growth of motor traffic was that of how to adapt the road system to meet the needs of the new form of transport.

Highways had been somewhat neglected after the arrival of the railways and though by the early twentieth century Britain possessed an intricate network of roads they were for the most part "of tortuous alignment, of indifferent character, and of infinite variety of width and gradient". However suitable these roads may have been for the slow moving horse-drawn vehicles of Victorian England—and there are grounds for believing that they were not entirely adequate since street congestion was not unknown in some of the larger towns such as London—it was obvious that they could not cater for the great expansion in traffic and the different requirements which the heavier and faster motor vehicle created. It was the persistent demand for better facilities on the part of the motoring public which eventually forced the government to take action on a national scale.

For the greater part of the nineteenth century, highway policy had been largely the responsibility of the local authorities and the annual cost of the roads had been defrayed almost entirely out of local funds. In many respects this basis of highway administration was unsatisfactory. Local authorities were reluctant to spend heavily on large-scale improvements and it was extremely difficult to achieve any sort of co-ordination in road improvements owing to the multiplicity of authorities concerned with the matter. At the turn of the century the English highway system was in the hands of nearly 2,000 separate local authorities which in itself ruled out any possibility of a unified road policy for one region let alone the whole country. It soon became obvious therefore that local authorities left to themselves would never be able to cope with the problem of increasing traffic and so in 1909 the first step was taken towards a national highway policy. By the Development and Road Improvement Funds Act of that year a Road Board was set up for the purpose of improving the facilities for road traffic. A special Road Fund, financed from the proceeds of a motor vehicle duty and a tax levy of 3d. per gallon on petrol, was also established, from which the Board was empowered to make grants to highway authorities for the construction of new roads or the improvement of existing ones.

The practical results of this first experiment in national highway finance were disappointing and the motorist certainly did not get value for the money he paid in taxes. Between 1909 and 1920 when the Road Board was wound up, the motoring community paid just over £23 million, only £7 million of which was actually spent on the roads. The bulk of this money was expended on improvements in road crusts and in this respect the Board did a good job for the menace of road dust created by the motor car was finally eliminated. On the other hand, few new roads or major street improvements were made. The Board interpreted its powers narrowly and largely confined its activities to making grants to local authorities to cover part of the cost of their expenditure. Only two important schemes of arterial road construction were initiated by the Board, namely the Great West Road and the Croydon By-pass, neither of which were finished during the

Board's tenure of office. To be fair the Board itself was not wholly to blame for the failure to do more. For one thing its resources were limited and in the latter part of the war payments into the Road Fund were suspended altogether. Thus the Fund received only £16 million of the motorists' contributions. Furthermore the Board was not allowed to spend a penny without Treasury approval and the latter, as watchdog of the Government's purse, was in no way inclined to sanction lavish expenditure on roads which still came low down on the official scale of priorities. On the other hand the Board was clearly reluctant to undertake constructive works and from the onset declared its intention not to "embark on the direct construction of new roads or appoint any staff for the purposes of road construction". This attitude was no doubt in part due to the fact that few of the members of the Board had a direct interest in the roads. Indeed the chairman, Sir George Gibb, was a prominent railway magnate!

By the end of the war the rapid growth in motor traffic had made the problem of catching up on arrears of expenditure even more imperative. In December 1918 therefore the Treasury set aside £8$\frac{1}{4}$ million to assist highway authorities to undertake some of the backlog of maintenance which had accumulated in the previous four years. In the following year the basis of road administration was changed. The Road Board was wound up and its powers transferred to the newly created Ministry of Transport. The Finance Act of 1920 abolished the petrol tax[1] and levied heavier duties on motor vehicles the proceeds of which were to be given to a new Road Fund which the Minister of Transport could utilize for improving or constructing roads either directly or by way of grants to local authorities. For the purposes of allocating maintenance grants the Ministry made a classification of some of the main roads of Great Britain. Class I roads were the main traffic arteries which were entitled to receive a grant of 50 per cent towards the cost of maintenance, and Class II roads were routes of lesser importance the grant for which was 25 per cent. In 1929 these grants were raised to 60 per cent and 50 per cent respectively whilst "scheduled" but unclassified roads qualified for a grant of 25 per cent. Of course central grants only formed a small proportion of the total expenditure on roads and the local authorities, who remained the principal highway administrators, had to find the rest from their local rates. In 1930, when classified roads became the sole responsibility of the County Councils, Classes I and II accounted for a mileage of 66,803 out of a total for Great Britain as a whole of 179,095 whilst a further 68,000 were designated as scheduled roads. (*See Map 23*, p. 304.)

Despite constant raids on the Road Fund by the Exchequer, for a decade or so after its establishment more was spent on the highways than was derived from motor taxation. Between 1920 and 1930 the total expenditure on roads by central and local authorities rose from £26·6 million to £65·5 million whereas revenue from taxation increased from £4·3 to £41·0 million. The motorist could still of course argue that he was being robbed in some

[1] The petrol tax was reintroduced in 1928.

years when allocations from the Fund were well below the amount derived from taxation. The point is however a very debateable one for it revolves round the question of whether the motorist should make a direct contribution to Exchequer accounts. Nevertheless during the 1920s an attempt was made to catch up on some of the arrears, though many of the schemes instituted were designed to relieve unemployment. In the trade depression of 1920–21 a number of schemes were launched in cities such as London, Edinburgh, Manchester, Leeds and Sheffield comprising either the widening of existing radial roads or the construction of by-passes and ring roads. In 1924 £6¼ million was allocated for the Trunk Road Reconstruction Programme designed to improve certain bad sections of important trunk routes. Under this scheme certain main traffic arteries, including the Glasgow-Inverness road, parts of the Great North Road and the Holyhead Road were selected for complete reconstruction. By the end of the decade considerable sections of some of the major trunk roads had been reconstructed, and a number of new roads such as the Edinburgh–Glasgow and a new road from Liverpool to east Lancashire towns had been built. In addition 139 separate schemes for by-passes comprising a total mileage of 226 had been completed. Altogether some £28 million had been paid out of the Road Fund for new works.

And there the building programme came almost to a halt. A new trunk road programme drawn up in 1929 failed to materialize. The financial crisis of 1931 resulted in a postponement of all schemes not actually started and works in progress were curtailed. Contributions from the Road Fund were reduced and less than half the work originally contemplated was completed. For several years no major schemes were started though local authorities continued to maintain and improve their roads. Though an increasing proportion of expenditure was now required merely to maintain the upkeep of the roads many improvements were in fact made to existing roads in the 1930s and a number of by-passes and ring roads near large cities were built. But it was not until the later 1930s, when the Ministry itself became directly responsible for 4,505 miles of roads under the Trunk Roads Act of 1936, that schemes for major improvements were drawn up and ratified by the Minister. These envisaged a total expenditure of £131 million, £106 million of which had been accepted in principle at March 1939. By this time however it was too late; the war intervened and the bulk of the work had to be postponed. Thus for most of the decade expenditure on roads remained below the level of 1930 and contributions from the Road Fund diminished after 1932. From that date onwards the revenue derived from motor taxation consistently exceeded road expenditure both central and local combined.

It is quite clear that at no time did the road programme keep pace with the growth of motor traffic. The *Economist* was not exaggerating when in 1937 it reported that "at present, with the densest traffic of any country we are doing least to accommodate it". It was estimated that a thoroughgoing

AA

programme for the whole country would cost at least £800 million which was more than ten times the then current expenditure on roads. The absolute number of improvements in the interwar years might have been large but they amounted to very little. Surface improvements, reconstructions, ring roads and by-passes were all very useful but they only scratched the surface of the problem. At the crucial points the national road policy failed to solve the problem. In the first place no attempt was made to construct major trunk roads or motorways for fast moving traffic; altogether a mere 4 per cent was added to the road mileage over the period 1899 to 1936. Secondly, insufficient attention was given to relieving the bottlenecks created by motor traffic especially in urban areas. The result was that in relation to the volume of traffic road conditions definitely deteriorated during this period and in turn the cost to the community rose year by year. Sir Charles Bressey in his *Report on London Traffic* in May 1938 pointed out that there was a bottleneck on average every mile all the way from London to Birmingham. The problem of congestion was probably worst around the larger conurbations and according to one survey in the early 1930s it had already "become extraordinarily acute in every big city". In central London the average speed of movement by road motor vehicles was actually less in 1938 than it had been by horse vehicles thirty years earlier and one large concern handling goods estimated that deliveries cost less than half as much on Sunday when traffic was freer. The total cost of traffic delays in London alone were said to be in the region of £70 million per annum. This figure takes no account of the cost of road accidents to the community which were estimated to be about £60 million a year for the country as a whole.[1]

The legacy of these years is of course still with us today and it probably serves little useful purpose to dwell upon the failure to meet the requirements of motor transport. More to the point is to enquire why more was not done in these crucial years. Why did the national road policy fail to achieve anything really worth speaking of? In the first place of course it is essential to point out that there never was a proper national road policy. No single comprehensive long-term plan for road development was ever drawn up partly because few people were capable of conceiving what was really required. In theory the Ministry of Transport should have been the one to take the intiative in this matter but unfortunately its powers of control were limited. Technically all schemes were still initiated by the local authorities in their capacity as highway authorities and though the Ministry could dole out finance from the Road Fund towards the cost of their schemes it could do little either to encourage them to present schemes in the first instance or bring pressure to bear upon them to co-ordinate their programmes. Each authority retained considerable autonomy with respect to road policy and despite a greater degree of centralization of road powers in

[1] In the ten years ending 1938, 68,248 people were killed on the roads and 2,107,964 injured.

the 1930s there still remained a large number of local authorities responsible for the roads. Under these conditions it was impossible to achieve any unified programme of action without strong pressure from above. But as we have already seen this was the very thing that was lacking. Not only were the Minister's administrative powers limited but in the matter of finance he was subject to the dictates of the Chancellor of the Exchequer. Consequently central funds for road building were limited which meant that the local authorities retained the power of the purse and as a result they were in a strong position to ignore, if they wished, any direction from above. These factors apart it is unlikely that any long-term policy would have emerged in view of the low calibre of the Ministers of Transport[1] and the frequency with which they were removed from office in the interwar years. Perhaps even more important was the fact that spending on the roads both at the central and local level was determined largely by political considerations. Policy was influenced by matters unconnected with traffic requirements, such as unemployment, the financial situation and the pressure of railway interests. As a result there was a distinct lack of continuity both in the projection and execution of road schemes. Throughout the interwar years road improvements were accorded a very low priority and the rate at which they were made depended very much on the political and economic circumstances prevailing at that time.

[1] With the possible exception of the first Minister of Transport, Sir Eric Geddes.

13

The birth of civil aviation

The two new forms of transport, motor and air, which developed almost simultaneously in the early twentieth century had few features if any in common, apart from the fact that both were new. Spanning the heavens was for one thing a much more exciting and dramatic achievement than the experiments made with mechanically propelled road vehicles. After all, people had travelled on wheels for centuries but until the present century flying through the air had remained the exclusive preserve of the birds. In this age of space-ships one can imagine therefore the thrill and excitement which greeted the introduction of the first man-made flying machines. Naturally such contraptions were not without their sceptics and had it not been for the perseverance and fortitude of the pioneers such as the Wright brothers, Alcock and Brown, Charles Lindbergh, Ross and Keith Smith, Alan Cobham, Charles K. Smith and of course that famous aviator Amy Johnson it is doubtful if commercial air services would ever have become a practical possibility. These people had no counterparts in the nineteenth century; their task was far more difficult than that of the railway and steamship pioneers and was in many ways comparable to that of the astronauts today.

In turn the use of the aeroplane for commercial purposes demanded a class of men with unusual faith and courage who were ready to risk their savings and sometimes their lives in developing a form of transport in which the hazards were great and the rewards few. There were no fortunes to be made in aviation as there were in developing motor transport. Indeed few if any British air operators ever made a real profit in the inter-war years. To a great extent this was due to the difference in the type of market they served and the nature of the service offered. There was already a large and growing internal demand for surface transport which could be easily tapped by the motor vehicle simply by virtue of the fact that it offered a highly competitive and reasonably safe alternative form of transport. The aeroplane was in a far less favourable position. Its inability to compete with other forms of transport except in terms of speed, together with its limited carrying capacity particularly for cargo, narrowed substantially the area from which it could cream its traffic. Moreover, for some time the public distrusted this novel and somewhat dangerous mode of conveyance. For these reasons air transport remained a luxury for the privileged classes throughout the inter-war years.

Though the theory and principles of aerodynamics had been formulated during the nineteenth century by Sir George Cayley and others, it was not until 1903 when the Wright brothers achieved their notable success with an engine-driven aeroplane that flying was shown to be a practical possibility. Other experiments soon followed. In 1909 Blériot flew across the English Channel and in the same year J. T. C. Moore-Brabazon (now Lord Brabazon) became the first British person to fly in this country. A year later the Frenchman Paulhan won the £10,000 prize offered by the *Daily Mail* to the first man to fly from London to Manchester in 24 hours. The same newspaper offered another cash prize in the following year for a 1,000 mile race round Britain and four of the nineteen competitors managed to finish the course and collect their reward. Yet despite the steady technical progress made in the construction of "flying machines" which made these feats possible they were of little commercial use before 1914. Several aircraft were in fact built to convey people and actually used in experimental flights. But most of them ended in failure since the machines in question lacked the speed, carrying capacity and reliability necessary for successful commercial operation.

The First World War gave an important stimulus to the technical development of the aeroplane. Under military demands design of aircraft and the performance of the engines improved considerably during these years and by the beginning of 1919 the aeroplane had developed sufficiently to make regular flying a technical and practical possibility. Nor was Britain behind in developing aircraft for military needs as she had been in the initial stages of development before 1914. Indeed this country was one of the first to recognize the importance of military air power and by the end of the war Britain was in a unique position to develop the new form of transport. Britain had a separate Air Ministry (established in 1917) and one of the largest air forces in the world. Towards the end of the war Britain was producing 4,000 planes a month and the numbers employed in aircraft construction were larger than those of France and Germany combined. In fact plans were afoot for conducting a war in the air on a scale comparable to that of the Second World War.

The importance of aerial transport for civil purposes had also been recognized by the Government at a fairly early date in the reconstruction period. In May 1917 the Civil Aerial Transport Committee had been formed under Lord Northcliffe to consider the future possibilities of air transport in peacetime and to offer suggestions on how it could best be developed. This Committee issued two reports in 1918, one dealing with international questions and the other with a wide range of matters.

The Northcliffe Committee made many detailed recommendations but three stand out in particular. They suggested that private enterprise assisted by the State would be the best organ to develop civil aviation for commercial purposes. Powers of control over the new field of transport should be vested in the Air Ministry which would be charged with responsibility under the Aerial Navigation Acts of 1911 and 1913. Their third major recommendation —one which was to have important legal implications for the future of civil aviation—favoured support for the doctrine of the State's sovereignty within its internal air space. But the Committee emphasized that whatever line of policy was eventually adopted it was imperative for the government to act quickly and formulate a plan before the end of hostilities.

Unfortunately this last piece of advice fell upon deaf ears. This may seem surprising in view of the government's early recognition of the importance of the aeroplane. But it should be remembered that the government was anxious to end its commercial responsibilities after the war and was not eager to take up any new ones. Commercial aviation "must fly by itself" to use Churchill's phrase, if it was to fly at all. No clear plan was drawn up and private enterprise was left to get on with the job as best it could. Not until the four pioneering companies had suspended operations (early in 1921) did the government come to the rescue. On the other hand, the State did make certain preliminary arrangements for civil flying soon after the Armistice. It was realized that more elaborate provisions for the regulation of flying would be required than those formerly administered by the Home Secretary under the Aerial Navigation Acts of 1911 and 1913. Early in 1919 therefore a temporary Air Navigation Act was passed extending the powers of the Secretary of State for Air to include licensing of aircraft operations, registration, inspection and certification of aircraft, regulation of aerodromes and conditions for aircraft operation. At the same time a Department of Civil Aviation was set up within the Air Ministry with a Controller-General whose responsibilities included the administration of the Air Navigation Acts. This new department immediately drew up a detailed list of air navigation regulations which came into force on 1 May 1919, the date on which civil flying was made legally permissible. These were subsequently embodied in the Air Navigation Act of 1920 which replaced and consolidated the provisions of the Acts of 1911, 1913 and 1919. The Act also embodied into British law the International Convention for Aerial Navigation passed by the Paris Peace Conference of 1919, which guaranteed to all aircraft of the contracting countries freedom of passage over their internal air space. Unfortunately this was later to prove something of a stumbling-block to the development of certain air routes on account of the nationalist policies adopted by some of the countries, including of course Germany, not represented at the Convention.

1 Early air transport companies

Though civil flying had been made legal in May 1919 little was achieved in that year except for one or two pioneer flights, notably the first flight across the Atlantic by two R.A.F. pilots John Alcock and Arthur Whitten-Brown in June of that year, and a few scheduled flights by small-scale operators. Early in 1919 two companies, Aircraft Transport & Travel Company Ltd. and Handley Page Ltd., both subsidiaries of successful aircraft construction companies, were preparing to establish, with converted military aircraft, scheduled air services to the Continent. Both companies, however, were waiting to see what assistance would be forthcoming from the government. When it became clear that the government was unwilling to assist the new industry, the two companies began their operations to Brussels and Paris in the summer of 1919 on the basis of provisional flying arrangements with Belgium and France. Though they got off to a fairly good start the winter of 1919–20 proved disastrous. Traffic fell sharply in these months and the regularity of services was reduced. By February 1920, Aircraft Transport & Travel had only completed 293 out of 358 scheduled flights. In the summer of 1920 traffic improved again and Handley Page began a service to Amsterdam in conjunction with the Dutch airline K.L.M. Unfortunately two more British airline operators, S. Instone & Company Ltd. and the short-lived Air Post of Banks, in addition to two French ones, were attracted to the London–Paris route. Consequently by the winter of 1921, with falling traffic and increasing competition, the companies were finding it very difficult to keep going in the face of heavy financial losses. A. T. & T. had been operating at a loss since its inception and it is probable that the other companies fared no better. One by one they were forced to suspend operations and by the end of February 1921 Britain's civil aviation had ceased altogether.

The reasons for the failure of these early air transport companies are not difficult to find. Undoubtedly severe competition especially from the heavily subsidized French airlines, was largely responsible for their failure. Handley Page, for example, was forced to give up the passenger traffic to Paris as they could not possibly operate at a fare below £10 10s. whilst the French were charging only £6 6s. On the other hand, subsidized foreign competition was not the only reason. It was inconceivable that the London–Paris route could support six airline operators, subsidized or not. A. T. & T. estimated that with a fare of £5 on the London–Paris run they would be able to break even with a load factor of 100 per cent. In practice of course load factors were well below this and freight and mail revenue was insufficient at this time to make up the difference. Moreover, many of the earlier aircraft used, the stick and string biplanes converted from military to civil use, were unsuitable for successful commercial flying. They required an excessive amount of technical maintenance which reduced their degree of utilization thus increasing overhead costs. Other factors which affected the fortunes of the companies adversely were the poor navigational aids and inadequate and highly seasonal nature of the demand for this novel and still dangerous form of travel. Given this set of unfavourable factors it is not surprising that the early small-scale operators with high overhead costs and small load factors made substantial losses on their operations.

Fortunately for British civil aviation the government came to the rescue just as the last company was expiring. In March 1921 a temporary subsidy scheme devised by the Cross-Channel Subsidies Committee under Lord Londonderry was adopted. The maximum liability under the scheme was to be £88,200 with a guaranteed minimum payment of £30,000 to each company. The Air Council was to approve schedules, freight charges and types of aircraft used and to guarantee the companies a clear profit of 10 per cent on gross receipts. By the following year the same Committee had drawn up a permanent subsidy scheme which came into operation in April 1922. This new scheme was based on the rather optimistic assumption that traffic figures would be double those of the summer of 1921. The Air Ministry gave its approval for three British firms to operate in competition on the London-Paris route and subsidies were paid both on a block and per capita basis. Assistance towards payment of insurance premiums was made and the companies concerned were permitted to receive up to half their fleet from the Air Council on a hire-purchase basis. In October of the same year the scheme was again revised. By this time the government had at last realized the futility of excessive competition on the same routes and henceforward routes were allocated to the airlines on a non-competitive basis. The hire-purchase scheme was discontinued and subsidies granted on a lump sum basis with fines for the non-performance of certain minimum conditions.

Until the formation of Imperial Airways in 1924, therefore, the Government's policy was to subsidize individual airlines operating on specified routes. Two of the former airlines, Handley Page and Instone's were revived by the subsidy and in April 1922 they were joined by Daimler Airway[1] (a branch of the London car-hire firm) and in 1923 by the British Marine Air Navigation Company Ltd. By the beginning of 1924 these companies were operating four main routes:

(1)   London to Paris with an extension to Zurich, by Handley Page.
(2)   London–Brussels–Cologne with an internal line between London and Manchester, by the Instone Company.
(3)   London to Amsterdam with extensions to Hamburg and Berlin and an internal link to Manchester, by the Daimler Airway.
(4)   London–Southampton and thence to the Channel Isles and Le Havre, by British Marine Air Navigation Company.

The passenger traffic of these airlines to the continent doubled (5,692 to 11,648) between 31 March 1922 and 31 March 1924 and an increasing proportion of the total traffic was being carried by British companies. By the end of 1922 British companies were carrying 65 per cent of the passenger

[1] This firm had acquired the business and aircraft of Aircraft Transport and Travel Ltd.

and 41·6 per cent of the freight traffic on the London-Paris route. Freight and mail traffic were also increasing slowly but, contrary to original expectations, these formed only a small proportion of total traffic.

Despite the fairly substantial increase in total traffic, civil aviation was far from being a profitable venture in the transitional period. None of the operators made a profit even with the subsidy payments and it is quite obvious that but for these the companies would not have been able to maintain services at all. Even the Daimler Airway, which relied on Government assistance for over 80 per cent of its income (a higher share than any other company), made a net loss of £17,303 on all its operations up to March 1924. Altogether in the first four and a half years the gross losses (that is, excluding subsidy payments) of the pioneer airlines amounted to more than half a million pounds and their total revenue was less than one third of the total expenditure. To offset the deficit the airlines received £378,851 in subsidies and gifts from the government. If British aviation had been established on a slightly more secure basis it was at no inconsiderable expense to the taxpayer.

Again one of the reasons for the financial failure was excessive competition particularly from the French companies. In the first year of subsidized operations on the London–Paris route there was three times the 1921 capacity available to carry much the same volume of traffic. The French were still paying much more to their airlines than the British Government—in 1921-2 the French subsidy was £1,328,000 compared with £85,000 paid by Britain—so that the French airlines were in a better position to undercut their British rivals. On the other hand, competition became less severe later on when the revised subsidy scheme allocated routes to particular companies. As the figures for passenger traffic show, British companies were able to hold their own in this period as regards the U.K. Continental traffic.

Probably the main factor militating against success lay in the nature of the early undertakings. They were far too small to permit economical operation and yet too large, or rather too many in number, in relation to the existing level of traffic. Load-factors were generally well below the breakeven point even on the more lucrative London-Paris run. Most modern short or medium haul airlines operate with break-even load factors of about 60 per cent. The break-even point of the early airlines was of course much higher than this but in practice rarely attained. On the London–Paris run for example the break-even load factor with a single fare of £6 6s. was estimated to be 80 per cent, but this figure was rarely achieved. At times load factors were very low indeed; in the first ten months of its existence the average monthly load factor of the Daimler Airway was only 29·8 per cent. On the other hand, though break-even load factors were not often obtained in this period, "it is doubtful", as Birkhead pointed out, "whether even 100 per cent load factors could have eliminated operating losses equal to six times revenue".

A further disadvantage was the high operating and heavy maintenance costs of the aircraft used. Generally speaking the early aircraft were very inefficient, with low capacity and high maintenance charges resulting in high operating costs, compared with modern aircraft. Though operating costs were falling fairly rapidly—they were reduced by about one third in the 1920s—aircraft still remained very expensive to run even by the late 1920s. Yet perhaps the real clue to the failure lay in the nature of the traffic. Passenger traffic had originally been regarded as a subsidiary element and high quality freight and mails were intended as the staple cargo of the airlines. In actual fact the reverse took place. Post Office mail contracts tended to be irregular (and subject to a special surcharge) whilst freight traffic involved expensive collection and delivery services and foreign airlines captured the bulk of this traffic. Consequently British airlines came to rely on passenger traffic for the bulk of their revenue. Unfortunately the latter traffic was highly seasonal in nature, far more so that it is today, with winter traffic often falling to negligible proportions. It was in these "off-peak" periods that the bulk of the losses occurred.

Finally it might be asked why, given the existence of so much excess capacity, the airlines were not able to attract sufficient traffic to fill it? The answer is largely because of the unreliability of services especially in bad weather and in winter, the greater risk involved and the high fares charged which discouraged demand for air transport. The last of these factors was probably the most important. Air fares generally were well above those charged for surface transport and out of the range of any but the higher income groups. Even when fares were lowered on the London–Paris run the charge was around £12 return compared with £5 15s return by first class surface transport.

The airlines were therefore caught in a vicious circle. Their scale of operations was too small to effect any significant reduction in operating and overhead costs; yet given the volume of traffic the capacity available was too great. In these circumstances the only solution to the problem was the formation of one large company.

2   Imperial Airways

Despite improvements in the state of civil aviation after 1921 it soon became clear that the policy of subsidizing a number of small companies was far from satisfactory. Early in 1923 therefore a small committee under Lord Hambling (the Civil Air Transport Subsidies Committee) was set up to review the whole question and to suggest the best method of subsidizing air transport in the future at the least possible cost to the State. The Committee speedily published a short but important report in which it concluded that the only solution to the development of civil aviation on a reasonably secure basis was the creation of one large private undertaking with State backing. The idea of a large monopoly company was not new—Holt Thomas and others had suggested it in 1920—but at that time opinion generally was not in favour of such a scheme. It was not until the operation of individual airlines had proved unsatisfactory and the idea of a monopoly had been given semi-official blessing by a Government committee that the Government felt it expedient to act along these lines. Within just over a year after the publication of the Hambling report, the million pound monopoly, as it was called, became a practical reality.

The detailed negotiations prior to the formation of the company need not concern us here. All that need be said is that the report caused a great deal of interest and opposition and during 1923 the Air Ministry was engaged in reconciling the conflicting interests. By October 1923, however, all four companies were agreed upon one scheme. On 31 March 1924 the Government's "chosen instrument", Imperial Airways, was incorporated with a capital of £1 million having purchased the four vendor companies for £148,750. Sir Eric Geddes, a leading figure in the transport world, became the Company's first chairman.

In return for special privileges the new company had to comply with certain conditions. The company was granted a monopoly of subsidized air transport in that no company was to receive state aid in the next ten year period, which at least in theory meant that no independent airline would be able to undertake profitable operations. Annual subsidies, up to a maximum of £1 million over the 10-year period, were to be paid to the company on a descending scale beginning with £137,000 in the first year and ending with £32,000 in the tenth, by which time it was hoped the company would be self-supporting. In practice, as we shall see, things turned out quite differently. Annual subsidies increased rapidly till 1936 partly because of changes in official policy. Imperial Airways also undertook to fly an average of one million miles per annum over the whole ten year period, to maintain efficient air services on the routes of the former companies and to introduce such other services as in the opinion of the company might be commercially desirable. All aircraft and engines used were to be of British make and all aircraft were to be equipped with apparatus for safe and proper navigation.

The new company got off to a rather shaky start. A dispute with the pilots over terms of employment and the failure of the share issue in the June— 75 per cent of the issue having to be taken up by the underwriters—were not exactly encouraging. Furthermore, it took some months for the new company to formulate a plan of campaign consistent with the objectives laid down by the government. By early 1925 however Imperial Airways had completed a thorough investigation into the economics of air transport. It was quite clear that the existing fleet, consisting of thirteen oddly-assorted aircraft inherited from the four companies, was inadequate to undertake the services envisaged, or for that matter to produce a profit at the fares then charged unless load factors of 70 per cent or more were obtained. This was impossible at the existing rates—which were roughly 50 per cent to 100 per cent above those charged by surface transport—so that every mile flown in excess of the minimum required to earn the subsidy was a dead loss. In other words the amount of flying which could be carried out was limited by the amount of the subsidy so that there seemed to be little hope of achieving solvency unless drastic changes were made.

The conclusion reached from the survey made it plain that the single-engined aircraft would have to be replaced by new, larger and faster multi-engined machines capable of carrying far greater loads and flying over greater distances without refuelling. It was considered that small-scale operations involving shorthauls were uneconomic. The obvious solution, therefore, was to expand the scale of operations and the most promising main line expansion seemed to be on Empire routes, a plan which fitted in well with the government's revised objectives, namely the improvement of Imperial communications. A large expansion in Europe against the competition of heavily subsidized foreign airlines and surface transport was out of the question. From 1926 onwards therefore the Company began to make the changes foreshadowed.

At the time the Company was still operating the West European services of the pioneer companies. These faced severe competition from European airlines and the services lost money. Some of the services were gradually curtailed or abandoned altogether. The service to Amsterdam, for instance, was discontinued in 1927 and the route to Berlin handed over to the Deutsche Lufthansa airline; whilst in 1929 the service from Southampton to the Channel Islands was abandoned. By 1934 the Company was operating a minimum mileage in Europe itself mainly on the London–Paris–Cologne and London–Paris–Basle–Zurich routes. In fact it was hoped that all the European routes would be abandoned eventually but the Air Ministry refused to agree to this yet at the same time failed to provide sufficient funds to allow the airline to maintain competitive services. It is true that the subsidy agreement was revised in 1928–9 whereby the company was to receive £2,760,000 over the next eleven years instead of £806,300 over six years by the old contracts. Yet generally speaking, the government steadfastly refused to allocate more to the European services and in fact the total subsidy paid for these routes dropped sharply after 1929. Moreover, the Post Office provided little support in the way of mail contracts until the adoption of the Empire Mail Scheme in 1934.

As the European services were being contracted, Imperial Airways was steadily building up a network of Empire routes. The policy of concentrating development on these routes was not determined purely by the commercial considerations adopted by the company in 1926, for the government itself was becoming convinced of the importance of opening up Imperial communications by air.

By this time long-distance flights had become an established fact. As long ago as 1919 Alcock and Brown had navigated the Atlantic and the daring

Australian Smith brothers had flown from England to Port Darwin via India. Another notable achievement in long-distance flying was made in 1924 when three American airmen succeeded in circling the world. In the following year Alan Cobham piloted a craft carrying Air Vice-Marshal Sir Sefton Branker from London to Burma. Altogether Cobham covered a distance of 18,000 miles with the same machine. Soon afterwards Cobham and the Australian pilot Charles Smith made historic long-distance flights to Australia. The record of achievement was already an impressive one and the government not without good reason felt confident that the time had come to put air links with the Empire on a regular commercial footing. Accordingly in 1926 the government signed an agreement with Imperial Airways for a service between Cairo and Karachi as a first link of an England–India service. Soon afterwards the first stage of the flight began with a service between Cairo–Baghdad and Basra (1,100 miles). New "Hercules" planes with air-cooled engines were used on the route. Traffic increased rapidly and during the first year the service operated with 100 per cent regularity. In 1929 the route was extended eastward to Karachi and Delhi and westwards to Genoa where the train service to Basle provided the link-up with the European air network. A direct Empire service between London and Karachi via Egypt was attempted in this year but it did not become fully operative until the later 1930s.

In view of the initial success of the Indian service the government encouraged the company to direct its efforts to forging other Imperial links. Accordingly Imperial Airways drew up plans for an all-African service and for the extension of the Indian service to Australia. By 1932 the Capetown service was in full operation so that it was possible to fly from London to Cape Town via Paris, Athens, Alexandria, Nairobi and Johannesburg, roughly 8,359 miles in eleven days. The following year saw the extension of the Indian service to Burma, Malaya and Singapore and the African services to the Sudan, Uganda and Tanganyika. In December 1934 the London–Australian airmail service (via Singapore) was opened by arrangement with the Australian Government and Qantas Empire Airways, an associate of Imperial Airways. This was the longest air service in the world, covering some 11,600 miles. (See Map 24, p. 384.)

The same year saw the conclusion of agreements with the government for the introduction of the Empire Air Mail Scheme. First-class mail had been carried on most routes from the beginning and by 1935 about 200 tons of mail were being carried by air transport. But Post Office contracts tended to be irregular and all mail was subject to a special surcharge. The bulk of the overseas mail from Britain was still conveyed by surface transport which meant that there was still a large reservoir of mail for the airlines to draw upon. With this object in mind the government gave its approval to the Empire Air Mail Scheme. This provided for the conveyance by Imperial Airways, at flat rates of postage, of all letters, cards or letter packets exchanged between Empire countries which were on or could be served from Imperial routes. Some 30 countries were partners with the United Kingdom in the scheme and shared in the subsidy payments to the airlines. Two years later the special surcharge on European air mail was abolished and the "all-up" services started by British Airways.[1] The Post Office encouraged the reorganization of services by making it known that considerable regular loads would be sent by air providing suitable services were available. By 1939 the list of countries to which the "all-up" system applied both in Europe and the Empire was very extensive. The results of the reform were quite astonishing. In 1938 around 2,000 tons of first class mail were carried by air under the "all-up" system compared with 200 tons in 1935 and 28 tons in 1928. In fact by this time the bulk of first-class external letter mail had been transferred to the air[2] and most of it was being conveyed in British aircraft.[3] Indeed it is probable that British airlines carried a greater volume of air mail than those of any other country.

Much of the success of Imperial Airways in pioneering new routes could not have been achieved without the rapid technical improvements in aircraft which took place over this period. In turn the company's demand for better aeroplanes provided the requisite incentive to aircraft manufacturers to make such improvements. In the early days of flying before the formation of I.A. the aircraft used were single-engined monoplanes with limited accommodation for passengers and freight and cruising speeds of 85 m.p.h. or less. Their limited accommodation (generally a maximum of four passengers), unreliability and high costs of maintenance made them a distinctly uneconomic proposition. As we have seen the Company's declared policy was to order larger and more economical aircraft. This was encouraged by a revision of the subsidy payments in December 1925 which henceforward were paid on the basis of horse-power miles rather than machine-miles. In 1926 three big triple-engined airliners capable of carrying 19 passengers plus crew were put into service by Imperial Airways. By the early 1930s 13-ton four-engined machines with accommodation for 38 passengers and a crew of four and cruising at a speed of 105 m.p.h. were being put into service. A few years later airliners attaining cruising speeds ranging from 140 to 200 m.p.h. were available. On an overall average during this period vehicle size and carrying capacity roughly doubled, specific operating costs were reduced by about one third and speed increased by about two thirds.[4] Safety, reliability and standards of passenger accommodation also improved considerably. In 1933–34, for example, only 1·55 per cent of the services were cancelled as against 23·25 per cent in the year 1924–5. Technical improvements had made regular long-distance flying a practical proposition if not an economic one.

[1] For British Airways see below.
[2] To most regions outside Europe and the Empire an additional fee was still required so that most of the mail was still conveyed by surface transport.
[3] It should be remembered that first-class mail (letters, cards and small packets) accounted for only about 8 per cent of all mails despatched from the U.K.
[4] Improvements of similar magnitude took place in the next decade.

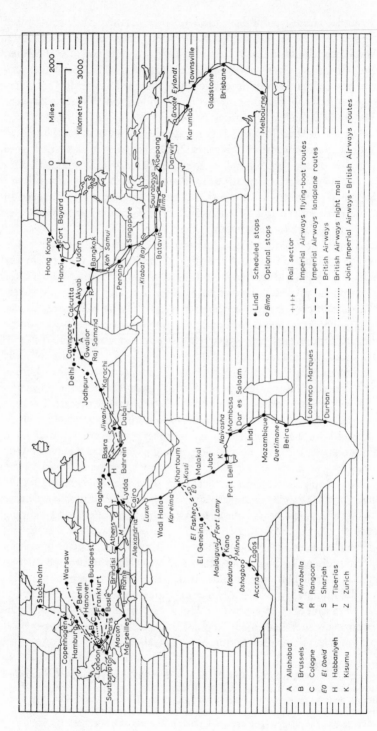

Map 24 *Overseas airway routes, 1939*

3   Reorganization

By the middle of the 1930s Imperial Airways had achieved a fair degree of success. Route mileage flown had increased from 1,520 in 1924 to 15,529 in 1935 whilst passenger traffic increased steadily from 10,321 to 66,324. The financial position also improved considerably in these years and I.A. progressed more rapidly towards financial autonomy than most of her foreign competitors. In 1935, when a profit of £140,705 was made, subsidies as a proportion of total revenue amounted to no more than 27·7 per cent compared with 69 per cent in 1930. Nonetheless without these subsidy payments —amounting to £561,556 in 1935—the company would have made substantial losses.

Despite the statistical success it can be contended that the company's policy of concentrating on Empire routes was not entirely satisfactory. Empire services were far less remunerative than the company or the government had originally anticipated partly because the total mileage flown on them in relation to the level of traffic was far greater than on the more lucrative European services. In 1936, for example, 55 per cent of the total passenger mileage flown by the company was on Empire routes but it accounted for only 10 per cent of the passengers carried. Furthermore, though the non-Imperial traffic of I.A. increased rapidly it is clear that the government's policy of fostering Imperial communications tended to retard development elsewhere, particularly in Europe. From 1927 the government set an upper limit to the total Civil Aviation Vote and since an increasing proportion of it was deliberately set aside for Empire services there was little which could be spent on services elsewhere. Non-Empire routes therefore remained neglected. In Europe there was no British service east of Cologne and not one British night airmail service out of the country. In fact in the first decade of its existence I.A. established only two new European services, London to Brindisi (via Paris and Rome) and London–Budapest (via Cologne, Prague and Vienna), both of which were unsubsidized. British services to South America, Scandinavia and West Africa remained non-existent. And it was not until June 1937 that the first commercial survey flights across the North Atlantic were made by the company, though a weekly service between New York and Bermuda in co-operation with Pan American Airways had been started somewhat earlier.

By 1935 therefore it was clear that the development of non-Imperial routes left much to be desired. Though the company's traffic was growing rapidly it was becoming increasingly difficult to develop new routes because of the magnitude of the task which it had undertaken throughout the Empire, and it was at this time that the company's preparations for the inauguration of the Empire Air Mail Scheme began to constitute a serious drain on resources. Furthermore, during the early 1930s a number of independent, unsubsidized companies such as Wrightways, Air Dispatch and Hillman Airways were beginning to establish cross-Channel services

BB

and modifying to some extent the traffic position of the company in Europe.

In 1935 a Standing Inter-departmental Committee was set up under Sir Warren Fisher to consider the question of international air communications with particular reference to the improvement of the European services. The Committee concluded that if profit were to be gained from the experience of the last few years the future policy of the government would have to be based on two major conditions. First it was essential that government support should be given to more than one company and secondly that each supported company should have its own delimited sphere of operation. The creation of British Airways (November 1935), a merger of a number of unsubsidized airlines, provided the government with an opportunity for a re-appraisal of its policy. The new company was accepted as the government's second "chosen-instrument" and Imperial Airways was pressed to relinquish that part of the company's concession which related to Europe north of a line London to Berlin. In fact the new company was soon entrusted with nearly all subsidized European services in northern Europe and with the development of services to West Africa and South America. At the same time the Air Navigation Act (1936) provided further financial assistance by raising the annual subsidy limit from £1 million to £1·5 million.

Despite many difficulties British Airways succeeded in filling some of the gaps left by I.A. Within the next two or three years a network of services were opened in Northern Europe and Scandinavia and regular night airmail services were started to the continent. Unfortunately political and other difficulties delayed the introduction of services to West Africa and across the Atlantic and neither of the two trans-Atlantic routes were really operating when war broke out. As regards traffic figures British Airways did quite well; the number of passengers carried rose from 15,500 in 1936 to 22,500 in 1938, whilst route mileage flown rose from 1,200 to 3,800 miles. The company was well-managed and efficient and though still making losses these had been halved by 1938. The financial position of the company would no doubt have been better had it not been for the uncompromising attitude of Imperial Airways together with the latter's support for Railway Air Services' "booking ban" boycott imposed in 1933.[1] It has been estimated that this cost British Airways and its allies some 80 per cent of their potential business until the ban was withdrawn in 1938.

Meanwhile inquiries and investigations had been going on into the position of Imperial Airways which were to lead eventually to further far-reaching changes in the structure of civil aviation. During the early 1930s considerable dissatisfaction had been expressed regarding the activities of Imperial Airways, and, as we have seen, the government was obliged ultimately to sponsor a second company to develop those routes which had been neglected. However, this change of policy did not silence the critics and in a

[1] See below.

House of Commons debate on civil aviation in November 1937 both the
Air Ministry and Imperial Airways were severely indicted by Robert Perkins
on several grounds including the general charge of inefficiency. The upshot
of the debate was the creation of a three-member committee under Lord
Cadman to investigate the accusations and to inquire generally into the
state of Britain's civil aviation.

In March 1938 the committee issued an extremely critical report. It was no
great surprise to find that Britain was generally behind in civil aviation except
on Empire routes. In Europe the mileage flown all the year round by Imperial Airways was less than it had been before the company was formed,
largely because the policy of concentrating on Imperial routes had led to
the neglect of services in other regions. Although it was admitted that
Imperial Airways' existing commercial service had been conducted fairly
efficiently the committee were extremely dissatisfied with the company's
relations with the Air Ministry and its dealings with staff and management:
"Not only has it failed to co-operate fully with the Air Ministry, but it has
been intolerant of suggestion and unyielding in negotiation." It was further
alleged that the company was operating obsolete aircraft whilst British Airways had found it necessary to buy foreign aircraft because there were no
suitable aircraft of British construction available. In the committee's opinion
the Air Ministry was partly to blame for the failure to plan properly the
future of civil aviation and aircraft construction. In the past both of these
had been treated as separate questions and there had been no consistent
policy directed to encouraging manufacturers to produce civil aircraft of the
types likely to be required by British airlines. Finally, as regards financial
assistance, the committee felt the subsidy limit of £1½ million annually
under the 1936 Act was quite insufficient: "If, as we assume, the Government
desire this country to take a leading place in civil aviation, much reorganization and additional expenditure of public money will be
necessary."

In view of the damning report it is not surprising that the committee's
recommendations were fairly drastic. Services, it said, should be established
at once to all major European capitals and plans laid for the development
of new routes to South America, the West Indies and West Africa. Both
companies would operate the external routes, British Airways to concentrate on European and South American routes and I.A. on the Imperial
services. For the lucrative London–Paris route on which both companies
then competed, it was suggested that a jointly-owned separate company
should be set up to take over the service. As regards staffing, the committee
recommended a full-time chairman for the company on the grounds that
"the responsibilities which now confront the Company have increased to
the point that they can no longer be borne for practical purposes by a
Managing Director". On the Air Ministry side the committee called for an
enlargement and strengthening of the staff, especially in the higher control
of the Department of Civil Aviation, and the appointment of an additional

Under-Secretary of State. Above all it was essential that the Air Ministry should formulate a co-ordinated plan for the development of both civil aviation and aircraft construction.

The government accepted most of the recommendations though not all of them were carried out in the way the committee envisaged. In 1938 the subsidy limit was doubled (to £3 million) and certain staff changes were made at the Air Ministry which proceeded to rush through plans for the development of a medium-sized, twin-engined, all-metal airliner suitable for British Airways' use. At the same time arrangements were being made for the joint operation of the London–Paris route. Hardly had these changes been made, however, than they became linked quite unintentionally with a proposal for the complete amalgamation of the two chosen companies. This proposal came from Sir John Reith who had been appointed the full-time chairman of Imperial Airways in June 1938. With his B.B.C. background Reith "brought to civil aviation . . . the gospel of a single chosen instrument exercising public responsibility for an industry dependent on public money" (Mowat). He worked from the start for the amalgamation of both companies into one national air corporation and in fact he himself claims that he accepted his new position on the understanding that this would take place. By the end of the year he had convinced both the government and the companies of the soundness of his scheme. In the following spring the government announced the purchase terms and in April 1940 British Overseas Airways Corporation, with Sir John Reith as its first chairman, replaced the two companies. Civil aviation had entered a new phase which the war soon brought to an abrupt halt.

4   Internal civil aviation

The establishment of air communications in Great Britain proved a far more difficult task than in the international field. In fact before the 1930s there were practically no regular commercial air services within the country. Several attempts were made in the 1920s to establish them but all ended in failure and in 1931 no internal air service was recorded whatsoever.

There are several reasons why internal civil aviation proved to be a non-starter in the 1920s. For one thing internal air operators probably had greater difficulties to contend with than external operators without the attendant advantage of a government subsidy. Lack of financial resources, unsuitable aircraft, shortage of experienced pilots, inadequate navigational aids, a scarcity of aerodromes, and adverse climatic conditions, not to mention the apathy of the public in general towards flying, all helped to retard development. But the most important reason for the slow development lay in the economics of the situation. The fairly short distances involved and the existence of a highly developed surface transport system limited the scope for internal air services within this country. As early as 1929 Fenelon observed that air transport showed to the greatest advantage when long distances were involved and speed was essential, where ground transport was hindered by geographical reasons and where sea crossings were involved. In Britain only the last of these factors operated to any great extent and it is significant that many of the internal airline companies of the 1930s, in fact the bulk of them at one period, were flying partly over water. In other words internal flying only really became attractive when it could offer appreciable savings in time over railway transport. In practice, as was discovered later, this was only possible on long journeys of around 200 miles or more and at air speeds of not less than 150 miles per hour except where a water crossing was involved. Other difficulties apart, the technical performance of the early aircraft ruled this out of the question.

In the late 1920s and early 1930s however conditions became somewhat more favourable for the development of internal air routes. With the expansion of international aviation many of the initial difficulties of aircraft operation were being solved and flying became more popular as the public gradually became less distrustful of the new form of transport. Secondly, the number of aerodromes increased rapidly after 1930, from 58 in 1931 to 95 in 1935, partly as a result of the municipal building policy inaugurated in 1929 at the instigation of the Air Ministry. Thirdly, rapid technical development in aircraft construction made possible faster and safer machines with substantial reduction in operating costs, whilst navigational aids under the Air Ministry's direction were improving albeit somewhat slowly. Moreover, in 1934, the Post Office took steps to utilize internal air services for the carriage of mail.

It is not surprising, therefore, that from 1932 onwards several companies began to initiate internal air services. One of the first was that of Hillman Airways Ltd which commenced a summer service between Romford and Clacton in 1932 and in the following year extended its operations to Paris. Many new companies were formed in that year including Blackpool and West Coast Services, Eastern Air Services, Jersey Airways Ltd, Spartan Airlines Ltd (London to Cowes), Northern and Scottish Airways and Highland Airways Ltd. The last of these companies secured the first internal mail contract from the Post Office (May 1934) for its service between Inverness and the Orkney Islands. No additional charge was made for the service and it was announced that in future the Post Office would be willing to use for the carriage of first-class mail, without extra charge to the public, any regular internal service which was capable of giving an acceleration in delivery.

In 1934 and 1935 more new companies were formed to carry on internal services but the most important development in these years was the penetration of the railways into air operations. The railways had acquired powers to operate aircraft in 1929 but did not enter the field until air transport began to threaten their own interests. In the spring of 1933 the first experimental railway air service between Cardiff–Halldon and Plymouth with an extension to Birmingham was inaugurated by Imperial Airways on behalf of the Great Western Railway. In March 1934 Railway Air Services Ltd was established with a capital of £50,000 for the purpose of providing such internal air services as the four British railway companies might require. The new company quickly established services on five important routes and at first these were operated on their behalf by Imperial Airways.

Thus by the middle of the thirties a network of internal air services had been established in Great Britain. In 1935 there were nearly a score of companies operating some 76 services. All the major town centres in Great Britain were provided with air services and most of the main islands had been linked to the mainland by air. (*See Map 25*, p. 391.) Miles flown and passengers carried increased from 28,396 and 3,260 respectively in 1932 to 3,463,000 and 158,000 in 1936 and in the latter year freight and mail shipments amounted to nearly 1,200 tons. The scope for further extension of services was already becoming somewhat limited however. In fact between 1935 and 1936 the route mileage operated actually fell and though it rose again in subsequent years it never recovered its former level. After 1936 the total miles flown and traffic carried levelled off and remained more or less stationary (*see Table 8*).

Despite the rapid increase in traffic, internal aviation was far from being a profitable venture; in fact internal air services were almost certainly less profitable than external ones, though it should be remembered that the former were not subsidized. Few financial details of the operations of the early companies are available except for those of Railway Air Services and if these are anything to go by the deficits must surely have been large. The total losses of the company increased from £14,541 in 1934 to £43,196 in 1935 and to £51,468 in 1937. In most years the company was losing around 80 per cent of its subscribed capital. The Maybury Committee found that most companies were making losses which in one case amounted to £44,000

Table 8   *Internal air operations, 1932–8*

	Route mileage	Miles flown	Passengers carried	Tons of freight and mail carried	Number of companies	Services operated
1932	—	28,396	3,260	—	5	—
1933	1,220	442,100	22,107	13·7	13	18
1934	3,265	1,559,000	72,441	402	15	34
1935	5,810	3,037,000	121,559	888	19	76
1936	4,019	3,463,000	158,000	1,200	16	54
1937	4,500	3,300,000	161,500	1,300	14	—
1938	5,300	3,267,000	147,500	1,200	16	—

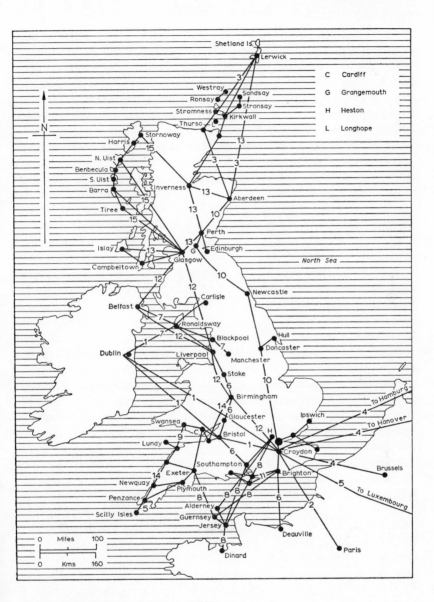

Map 25   *Principal internal air routes, 1939*

1 Aer Lingus Teoranta
2 Air Dispatch Ltd
3 Allied Airways (Gander Dower) Ltd
4 British Airways Ltd
5 Channel Air Ferries
6 Great Western and Southern Air Lines
   Ltd
7 Isle of Man Air Services
8 Jersey Airways Ltd

9 Lundy and Atlantic Coasts Air Lines Ltd
10 North Eastern Airways Ltd
11 Portsmouth, Southsea and Isle of
   Wight Aviation Ltd
12 Railway Air Services Ltd
13 Scottish Airways Ltd
14 Western Airways (unit of Straight
   Corporation Ltd)
15 Western Isles Airways Ltd

(in 1934). In fact few companies were able to cover more than 50 per cent of their expenditure.

The financial insolvency of these companies should occasion no great surprise in view of the experience of the pioneer companies a decade before in the international field. What is indeed surprising is the fact that the companies kept going at all in the face of such adverse financial results. Although conditions were improving in the 1930s it is quite evident that they were by no means sufficiently favourable to permit profitable operation. For one thing a large part of the traffic tended to be seasonal, chiefly because the airlines were unable to provide a transport service acceptable to the public during winter months or in bad weather, though some improvement in this respect occurred in the late 1930s. The use of poor aircraft, adverse climatic conditions, unsuitable aerodromes (Glasgow and Belfast, for instance, could not be used in all weathers), and inadequate ground organization and navigational aids made punctual, all-weather day and night services practically unobtainable. In 1935 probably less than one-ninth of the services were operated without a break. Regularity tended to decrease further north especially in winter when only about 60 per cent of the scheduled flights were carried out. Consequently services tended to be concentrated in the day-time and in summer months so that for much of the time equipment was not utilized. Most operators found it difficult to employ their aircraft for more than about 600 hours per annum despite the fact that to ensure profitable operation it was necessary to use them for at least double this length of time. It was estimated in 1935 that aircraft on internal routes were grounded for about 90 per cent of the time and that a 16-seater aircraft standing idle cost the operator 14s. per hour. Thus the amount of traffic when averaged over the year was spread very thinly and load factors were usually considerably less than 50 per cent. The average load factor of the private operating companies in the period 1924–39 was as low as 35 per per cent, roughly half that of Imperial Airways.[1] Since the revenue from the traffic had to meet both current operating costs and fixed charges for replacement, air fares were high and these discouraged traffic. Passenger fares ranged from 3d. to 10d. per mile compared with just over 1d. by rail and slightly less by road. Moreover, air journeys tended to be inferior in both speed and comfort to those of rail except perhaps over fairly long distances, say 175 miles or more, and even on these it is doubtful whether the time saved was worth the additional expense except where a proportion of the journey happened to be across water.[2] In practice most of the stages were much shorter than this and on many of them the average air speed was not much higher than the average speed of the best trains. The Maybury Committee found that the saving in time by air on the London–Liverpool

[1] The break-even load factor of internal operators was probably in the region of 100 per cent.
[2] The journey between town and aerodrome, which could take up to half an hour each way, greatly reduced the saving in time by air particularly on short and medium distances.

run (180 miles) was a mere 45 minutes and even on the London-Glasgow route (417 miles) the saving amounted to only just over two hours. In contrast, on the London–Birmingham run (101 miles) it was 17 minutes faster by rail.[1] Inevitably therefore, there was a limit to the extent to which air transport could be substituted for rail. On the longest and most difficult routes, particularly those involving a water crossing, the possibilities of substitution were greatest but the potential traffic thinnest; traffic was heaviest on intermediate stages between large towns, areas over which surface transport was most efficient and air transport least competitive.

The airlines would probably have fared better had they been able to carry more freight and mails. Unfortunately their ability to do so was limited. The aircraft were not designed to carry large freight loads and in any case in this field surface transport was even more competitive than on the passenger side. Passenger traffic therefore continued to bulk large and only urgent freight of high value went by air. As regards mail the airlines were again restricted in their scope by the mere fact that the bulk of the inland mail was collected by day and required night conveyance, a task which the airlines were least capable of performing. Thus in view of the difficulties involved in this respect and the excellence of rail facilities the Post Office was reluctant to entrust the airlines with more than a limited amount of mail to carry.

The position was of course aggravated by the atomistic nature of the industry and by the fact that competition between the airlines themselves and with the railways became more intense as time went on. In 1935 there were no less than 19 companies covering a route mileage of under 6,000 and carrying an average of less than 6,400 passengers each per annum. During the 1930s there was a substantial increase in route mileage flown in competition from 5·2 per cent in 1933 to 31·1 per cent in 1936. Nor did the policy of the Post Office with regard to mail contracts do anything to lessen the force of competition. The practice was to accept the lowest airmail tenders for short-term contracts which often meant that the tenders accepted were those which could only be carried out at a loss. This was certainly not a policy conducive to the long-term stability and progress of internal civil aviation.

By the mid 1930s it was quite evident that if internal aviation was ever to approach anywhere near solvency the existing structure of the industry would have to be altered radically. Most of the firms were small and unstable and lacked adequate resources to carry out efficient and profitable operations even under the most favourable conditions. The life of some of the companies was extremely short and many of them "flitted like brief shadows across the scene". By 1937, 12 of the 31 companies which had begun scheduled services had already disappeared. The Maybury Committee in their report felt that the conditions under which internal services had been

---

[1] The distances given are for the air routes and are measured between town centres and not between aerodromes. The distances by rail are 201, 402 and 113 respectively.

hitherto carried on offered no reliable guide as to whether profitable operations could be obtained. Accordingly they recommended the elimination
of cut-throat competition on the grounds that "so long as wasteful competition continues and services are unduly limited in their frequency,
regularity and convenience, it seems unlikely that air transport will pay its
way". The obvious solution to the problem appeared to be a consolidation
of interests.

In point of fact this is just what was happening. As early as October 1935
a merger was announced between Hillman Airways, United Airways,
Spartan Airlines and British and Continental Airways with the intention of
promoting a well-financed and compact organization called British Airways. The chief aims of the company were claimed to be the reduction of
competition and operating costs and the co-ordination of services as far as
possible. It was intended that the new concern should operate the main
unsubsidized services in Great Britain but in fact, as we have seen, British
Airways became the Government's second "chosen instrument" for the
development of international air routes. Consequently the company soon
devoted most of its energies to European routes and in July 1936 all its
internal services were taken over by Northern and Scottish Airways and
Highland Airways.[1] However, it was the railways, fearing the threat of air
transport, which took the major initiative in the process of consolidation.
From 1935 onwards they acquired a dominating interest in a large proportion
of the airline undertakings. By the end of 1938 only five important companies, the services of which for the most part offered little potential threat
to the railways, remained outside the direct control of the railways. Altogether 24 out of the 40-odd companies created between 1933 and 1939 had
either failed or been absorbed. But the number of companies still remained
high, partly because in 1938, as a result of agreements between the railways
and certain financial groups, several new companies were formed to take
the place of the older concerns.

It seems unlikely that the process of concentration brought much improvement in the situation. It certainly restricted competition but in whose
interests—the railways? Internal aviation still remained unprofitable. If the
financial results of Railway Air Services are anything to go by they were doing
just as badly as before, a loss of £42,000 being made in 1938. There were still
far too many separate concerns in a field where one would have been enough.
It might be argued that up to 1939 the railways had little time to reorganize
their new interests efficiently. Far nearer the truth might be the suggestion
that the railways had little intention of doing so. The railways were far more
interested in acquiring a controlling interest in the airline companies to
limit the competition than they were in promoting orderly expansion. This
negative attitude is reflected clearly in the action they took in 1933 to restrict
the growth of new airlines. The railways refused to recognize travel agencies

[1] In August 1937 these two companies amalgamated to form Scottish Airways based on
Renfrew with railway interests participating alongside Whitehall Securities.

which dealt in airline tickets other than those of Imperial Airways and foreign airlines.[1] The booking ban as it was called continued until 1938 when the government intimated that it would take action to curtail it if not removed. Moreover, if the railways had really been interested in consolidating air services under one large efficient undertaking it seems highly unlikely that they would have fostered the creation of new companies as they did in 1938. On the other hand, these criticisms may perhaps be a little unjust. The Cadman Committee felt that the railway companies, though no doubt influenced by a consideration of their own interests, were making a useful contribution to civil air development and had "provided capital and experience in a proper and constructive manner".

As we have seen the Maybury Committee were strongly in favour of restricting competition in internal aviation. The committee, however, virtually ignored the question of the reform of the structure of the industry and instead put forward their own plan to avoid the "indiscriminate multiplication of services". They recommended that a licensing scheme be instituted together with their proposed Junction Aerodrome Scheme by which selected routes would be regulated with a view to ensuring that suitable conditions might be secured for the operation of air services. It was proposed that the scheme should be applied as an experiment over a restricted number of key routes where everything would be done to make air transport as safe, regular and efficient as possible. Instead of indiscriminate services between various points in the U.K. there were to be intermediate services to and from the base point or junction situated in Manchester or Liverpool.[2] In effect this would cut down the route mileage between main towns from 2,900 to 960 miles. Although it would undoubtedly have involved slightly longer flights and a certain amount of double hauling it was reckoned that the scheme would help to raise the average load factors of the operating companies.

The government accepted the plan in principle but it was never put into practice since the airlines themselves opposed it. Eventually in 1938 the government gave belated acknowledgment to the difficulties of the industry. In that year a licensing system was established and the industry received a subsidy for the first time. An Air Transport Licensing Authority was set up and, from 1 November, air operators had to obtain a licence for all services in the U.K. on which passengers and goods were carried for payment. At the same time the Air Navigation (Financial Provisions) Act provided a sum not exceeding £100,000 per annum to assist the airlines, on the clear understanding that they should attempt to become paying propositions within a five year period. Only regular services licensed by the A.T.L.A. could receive the subsidy and initially eleven companies were eligible for it.

[1] Imperial Airways secured this favoured treatment partly because their services were largely non-competitive with the railways and partly because the company had a financial interest in Railway Air Services.
[2] The main centres included in the scheme were Belfast, Glasgow, Edinburgh, Newcastle, London, Southampton, Portsmouth and Bristol.

The subsidy was based upon capacity-ton-mileage[1] flown on approved services so as to encourage operators towards larger aircraft and higher frequencies.

The outbreak of war cut short the operation of the scheme so it is impossible to tell what effect it would have had. However it seems highly unlikely that it would have enabled the airlines to pay their way. Internal aviation was even less capable of flying by itself than international aviation where one company, Imperial Airways, held a monopoly of subsidized operations for much of the time. In view of this it seems extraordinary that the Government should have attempted to keep nearly a dozen companies afloat in the internal field. In fact in the case of many of the companies the subsidy payments alone would only have covered part of their deficits. The total payment to any one company was limited to a maximum of £15,000 per annum and, on the basis of 1937, this would have covered less than one third of the total deficit incurred by Railway Air Services.

[1] Being the pay-load capacity in tons of the aircraft used multiplied by the number of miles flown.

Epilogue

This book has brought the history of British transport down to the last war. It is a logical stopping-point, even though it is now thirty years ago. The facilities for travel and transport which were available then seem already to belong to quite a different era and to have more in common with the experience of the preceding century than they do with our own. There is some truth in this. The more primitive forms of transport had almost vanished and transport was also moving in a new element altogether. But the railway and the steamship were still in a dominating position, and although the use of motor vehicles was growing more rapidly than any other form of transport, the horse and even the handcart continued to have many commercial uses. The canal had already been drained of many of its transport functions generations before. Yet coastal shipping continued to have some importance. Travel had been made reasonably comfortable, cheap and fast at home, and most of the world brought within reach by aircraft, but virtually all these facilities were still being used far below their real potential. The travelling public had not yet moved very far outside the orbit of the daily journey to work, and only one-third of the population travelled away from home for an annual holiday.

The war altered the whole scale of this experience and widened its scope immeasurably. Other parts of the country and of the world came into view for the first time for hundreds of thousands of people, the very young as well as those on war service, and these perspectives remained. The war effort accelerated few basic changes in the technology of transport but it brought about a substantial growth in carrying capacity on land and sea, and enabled a few inventions that might have remained dormant in more peaceful conditions to develop to the point at which they could come into widespread use after 1945. The jet engine and navigational radar are but two examples. What the war also did was to make inordinately heavy demands on transport facilities without securing the means of maintaining their capital intact. Above all, the logistical problems of prosecuting the war to the full developed in the government not only a capacity for management but a sense of responsibility for providing a transport service on a peacetime footing.

In the last two or three decades transport has been subject to increasing state intervention. Wartime needs, of course, necessitated strict control over most branches of transport in the years 1940–6. But, unlike the situation after the First World War, this did not stop short of public ownership. The post-war Labour Government nationalized a large section of British transport, including the railways, airways, parts of the road transport industry and a variety of other transport services which had formerly belonged to the railways. During the 1950s and early 1960s the public sector diminished somewhat, especially following the denationalization of road haulage in 1953, while the private sector was allowed greater freedom. Nevertheless, structural reorganizations in the public sector occurred in 1953 and 1962 and control over private transport was maintained by various licensing arrangements, as for example in road transport and aviation. During the 1960s a spate of government papers on transport appeared out of which emerged the Transport Act of 1968. This proposed a further reorganization of public transport by which it was hoped to achieve a greater degree of integration in inland transport.

The different branches of transport developed in the manner one might have expected from the experience of the inter-war years. Soon after the war the financial position of the railways deteriorated and by the late 1950s and early 1960s large deficits were recorded. The rapid growth in road transport reduced the share of traffic carried by the railways considerably and they are now no longer the largest inland carriers. By the early 1960s British Railways accounted for less than 15 per cent of the inland passenger traffic compared with just over 30 per cent in 1938, while the proportion of freight carried by rail fell from 55 per cent in 1952 to 32·4 per cent in 1962. The relative loss on the passenger side was due primarily to the expansion in private motoring since the volume of traffic carried by public passenger transport began to decline slowly in the 1950s. These proportions would be even lower if allowance was made for air transport which became increasingly competitive with rail, especially on the passenger side and on long distance routes.

But the railways' financial problems cannot be attributed simply to loss of traffic to competitors because until the early 1960s the volume of traffic carried by the railways was actually higher than before the war. No doubt road transport creamed away some of the best traffic but it was only one of many factors which affected the fortunes of the railways. Among these might be included an inadequate pricing policy, lack of investment and innovation, the retention of excess capacity, social and legal restraints, and poor management.

The most rapidly expanding sector since the war has been air transport. The number of passengers carried by British airlines rose from 217,000 in

1938 to nearly 6·9 million in 1961. Freight traffic also expanded rapidly though it still forms only a small part of the airlines' business. For some years after the war air traffic was monopolized by the two large State Corporations (B.E.A. and B.O.A.C.), though in the later 1950s and early 1960s, when greater freedom was given to private operators, their monopoly became less secure. Generally speaking, aviation was more profitable than before the war though many of the independent airlines were far from viable propositions. In 1963 there were no less than 24 independent operators most of which were making losses, a situation curiously reminiscent of the internal airline market of the 1930s.

By contrast the post-war achievements of British shipping have been disappointing. Though the volume of world seaborne trade more than doubled between 1948 and the early 1960s, the British fleet did not participate in this expansion to any considerable extent. Most of the wartime shipping losses were made good by 1948 when the U.K. tonnage amounted to 16·1 million tons, compared with 16·9 million in 1939. But between 1948 and 1961 tonnage on the Register rose by only just over one quarter, to 20·3 million tons, whereas world tonnage more than doubled in the same period. In fact British shipping grew more slowly than the fleet of almost every other country. Consequently Britain's share of world tonnage fell sharply, from 27·5 per cent in 1939 to 22 per cent in 1948 and 15·8 per cent in 1961. This relative decline was due primarily to internal constraints on growth, for example the failure of British shipowners to branch out into new trades or develop new types of ships, rather than to the effect of trade changes, differences in costs, subsidies and discrimination, government policies or other factors which might distort the process of competition.

Many of the pre-war transport problems are still with us today and in some cases they are now more serious. These include traffic congestion in towns, pricing and investment policies, problems relating to the organization of transport, excess capacity, the vexed question of integration and a host of smaller issues. Despite the vast amount of study devoted to such problems in recent years we appear to be no nearer to finding adequate solutions. In part, no doubt, political factors have intervened to complicate the issue; the absence of a long-term transport policy, for example, has not helped matters. Moreover, current policy has often failed to take account of past mistakes. A notable example is that of the Air Transport Licensing Board which in the past few years has granted licences to a large number of small airlines few of which have any chance of commercial success. The experience of the 1930s indicates the folly of such a policy. What post-war experience had repeatedly shown is the historical complexity of our contemporary problems. To understand them fully it is necessary to study their beginnings. The transport system of modern Britain is still a growing organism and it will be as necessary in the future to study the legacy of the past as it has been in the past to plan for the future.

Bibliography

Transport history has only quite recently come to be recognized as a distinct field of study. Yet it contains a literature to be numbered in scores of thousands of items, the full extent of which has not yet been catalogued, nor brought within the compass of more than a couple of specialized bibliographies. It reaches into the general field of history at a great many points, as it does into the annals of the business world, of science and technology, of government, as well as entering into the whole field of English literature. It is plainly impossible in a volume of this kind to provide anything more than an introductory guide to such a large assortment of works. The bibliography which follows is therefore more in the nature of an extended reading list than anything else.

It will necessarily be patchy in its coverage if only because the available works are themselves very unevenly spread. For a long time attention has focussed sharply on a relatively small number of topics—chiefly on types of vehicles and their means of locomotion rather than on the circumstances which governed their development, the uses to which they were put, or their implications for the economy or for society. One consequence of this has been that—unlike the development of some other historical fields—the basic framework of the subject has been erected at the beginning. The chronology of the subject has been carried to a particularly refined pitch, for example, and a lot is known about the changing phases of its technology. This does not mean that there is nothing more to be found out in these directions—far from it—but it does mean that transport history has no really dark ages. What this kind of preoccupation has also helped to bring about, however, is the narrowing of the range of individual studies, with the effect of producing innumerable specialisms having too few points of contact between them. It has therefore produced a literature largely composed of monographs. The transport pioneer, the individual undertaking, a type of machinery, or a specific incident—these have hitherto been the most popular subjects for transport historians. This tendency is very conspicuous in

CC

this bibliography. Under Section 7—"Railways and the Transport System", for example, where larger questions are raised than can be answered within the experience of the individual firm or the particular pioneer, the list of work in print is very brief indeed. This has meant a big swing in the emphasis of the research that is now going on. The subjects most commonly offered for theses in post-graduate research, for example, are more generalized and concerned very often with comparisons between institutions and periods, if not with less institutionalized subjects altogether.

This is a subject, it must be recognized, of wide appeal and it is natural that it should evoke three or four kinds of response which show up very clearly in the literature: the technological, antiquarian, romantic, and academic. It would be foolish to confine oneself too much to a particular element in this literature if the object is to understand how and why transport has developed and to give it meaning. In this bibliography we shall be emphasizing the economic and business aspects of the subject because our book has been addressed principally to these fundamental matters but, even so, it is important not to overlook material that does not have obvious economic significance. We have tried to take account of some of this material.

It might be added that this is a field in which there has always been a profusion of periodicals, and now there are more than ever. The *Journal of Transport History* has been published twice a year since 1953 by our own university; *Transport History* has recently begun to appear three times a year. Apart from the numerous archaeological society transactions which often contain articles of importance to transport historians, and the other learned journals, there is a wide array of very ably edited periodicals which are making valuable contributions to the subject: *Institute of Transport Journal, Modern Transport, Railway Gazette, Railway Magazine, Fairplay, Shipping World, Shipbuilding and Shipping Record, Flight, Aeroplane.*

The bibliography contains some references to *Parliamentary Papers*, almost all of them printed reports and minutes of evidence from Select Committees or Royal Commissions, and a few statistical returns. They may be supplemented by P. Ford and G. Ford, *Select List of British Parliamentary Papers, 1833–1899* (1953), *A Breviate of Parliamentary Papers, 1900–1916* (1957) and *A Breviate of Parliamentary Papers, 1917–1939* (1951). For guidance in consulting this material, see the same author's *A Guide to Parliamentary Papers* (1956).

The sequence of the sections in this bibliography follows that of the chapters in the book. Unavoidably, there is some overlapping, but works once cited are normally referred to briefly or omitted altogether from later sections. There is a separate index under author's names at the end.

There are very few general accounts of the history of British transport. The most exhaustive is still W. T. Jackman, *The Development of Transportation in Modern England* (2 vols., 1916), which was reprinted in 1962 in a single volume with a bibliographical introduction by Dr W. H. Chaloner. It is primarily concerned with the evolution of the main forms of inland transport between the sixteenth and the middle of the nineteenth centuries and only incidentally with their relation to general economic developments. Some of the principal economic themes are better displayed in E. A. Pratt, *A History of Inland Transport and Communication in England* (1912), which covers a much wider field of transport and continues its history down to the date of publication. Both these books have very useful bibliographies and are the best general guides to the contemporary publications. There is also a brief but valuable essay and some 240 judiciously selected illustrations of the main aspects of transport history in Britain in Jack Simmons, *Transport* (1962). J. H. Appleton, *The Geography of Communications in Great Britain* (1962) deals well with internal transport from a geographical viewpoint. C. I. Savage, *An Economic History of Transport* (1959), is rather brief and is mainly concerned with the public regulation of road and rail transport in the nineteenth and twentieth centuries. Sir John Clapham's *An Economic History of Modern Britain* (3 vols., 1926–38) has the unique merit of analysing the transport developments of 1820 to 1914, including shipping, in their economic context; C. E. R. Sherrington, *A Hundred Years of Inland Transport, 1830–1933* (1933) is a much more modest exercise. A large volume of research in this field lies unseen in university theses and a list of those presented in British universities since 1911 is included in H. J. Dyos, "Transport History in University Theses", *Journal of Transport History*, iv (1960), and in a second list in vol. vii (1965). A notable series of articles on the sources of transport history has appeared in the same journal: L. C. Johnson, "Historical Records of the British Transport Commission", i (1953); Jack Simmons, "Railway History in English Local Records", i (1954); J. A. B. Hibbs, "Road Transport History in *Notices & Proceedings*", i (1954); Charles Hadfield,"Sources for the History of British Canals", ii (1955); D. B. Wardle, "Sources for the History of Railways at the Public Record Office", ii (1956); Rupert C. Jarvis, "Sources for the History of Ports", iii (1957); Jack Simmons, "The Scottish Records of the British Transport Commission", iii (1958); Rupert C. Jarvis, "Sources for the History of Ships and Shipping", iii (1958); Maurice Bond, "Materials for Transport History amongst the Records of Parliament", iv (1959); John R. Kellett, "Urban and Transport History from Legal Records", vi (1964). For a brief survey of the materials of the subject, see H. J. Dyos, The "Literature of Transport History", *Library Association Record*, lix (1957).

1   The transport system of pre-industrial Britain

There are several contemporary writings commenting on transport conditions in Restoration and early Georgian England, of which the most useful are Christopher Morris (ed.), *The Journeys of Celia Fiennes* (1947), covering the years 1685 to 1703, and Daniel Defoe, *A Tour Thro' the Whole Island of Britain* (1725–7), which reappeared in plagiarized forms later in the eighteenth century, and in 1927 was reprinted from the original in a limited edition with an introduction by G. D. H. Cole and a set of Hermann Moll's maps dated 1724; the English and Welsh tours were also printed in the Everyman Library in 1928 and in the complete original form in 1962. See also J. D. Marshall (ed.), *Autobiography of William Stout of Lancaster* (1967). The general state of internal communications is well described in Joan Parkes, *Travel in England in the Seventeenth Century* (1925); some aspects of internal trade are well covered in N. S. B. Gras, *The Evolution of the English Corn Market* (1915); J. U. Nef, *The Rise of the British Coal Industry* (2 vols., 1932); R. B. Westerfield, "Middlemen in English Business", *Transactions of the Connecticut Academy of Arts and Sciences*, xix (1915); G. E. Fussell and Constance Goodman, "Eighteenth century traffic in livestock", *Economic History* (supplement to *Economic Journal*), iii (1934–7); and A. R. B. Haldane, *The Drove Roads of Scotland* (1952). Easily the most authoritative source of information on market towns, fairs, and internal trade in agricultural products generally for the period immediately preceding that treated in this chapter is Alan Everitt, "The Marketing of Agricultural Produce" in Joan Thirsk (ed.), *The Agrarian History of England and Wales*. Vol. IV; *1500–1640* (1967), chap. viii. Mrs Thirsk's own contribution to that volume on "The Farming Regions of England" is an admirable complement to it.

The state of roads and road legislation down to 1720 are well described in S. & B. Webb, *The Story of the King's Highway* (1913). C. J. Hartmann, *The Story of the Roads* (1927) gives a good deal of space to early developments; J. W. Gregory, *The Story of the Road* (2nd ed., 1938) makes a justifiable attempt to put the history of English roads into a larger historical context. For a description of the English roads of the Middle Ages see F. M. Stenton, "The Road System of Medieval England", *Economic History Review*, vii (1936). Dorothy Ballen, *Bibliography of Road-making and Roads in the United Kingdom* (1914) is one of the only two exhaustive bibliographies that exists for any branch of British transport history.

The history of river improvement in the seventeenth century is described in general terms in the invaluable study by T. S. Willan, *River Navigation in England, 1600–1750* (1936) and in numerous detailed case studies by the same author, of which the most important are: *The Navigation of the Great Ouse* (Bedfordshire Historical Record Society, Vol. xxiv, 1942); "The River Navigation and Trade of the Severn Valley, 1600–1750", *Economic History Review*, iii (1937–8); and "Yorkshire River Navigation, 1600–1750", *Geography*, xxii (1937); "River Navigation and Trade from the Witham to the Yare, 1600–1750", *Norfolk Archaeology*, xxvi (1938). See too: F. S. Thacker, *The Thames Highway* (1914); W. B. Stephens, "The Exeter Lighter Canal, 1566–1698", *Journal of Transport History*, iii (1957); H. C. Darby, *The Draining of the Fens* (1940); A. W. Goodfellow, "Sheffield's Waterway to the Sea", *Transactions of the Hunter Archaeological Society*, v (1943); G. G. Hopkinson, "The Development of Inland Navigation in South Yorkshire and North Derbyshire, 1697–1850", *ibid.*, vii (1956); B. F. Duckham, *The Yorkshire Ouse: The History of a River Navigation* (1967). S. W. Skempton, "The Engineers of the English River Navigations, 1620–1760", *Transac-*

tions of the Newcomen Society, xxix (1953), is a valuable study of river navigations as a phase in the development of civil engineering. The early history of pound locks and mitre gates, among other hydraulic matters, is interestingly illuminated by A. G. Keller, *A Theatre of Machines* (1964).

The organization of coastal shipping is covered by T. S. Willan, *The English Coasting Trade, 1600–1750* (1938). The best brief introductions to the general development of overseas trade and of the shipping industry are, respectively, G. D. Ramsay, *English Overseas Trade during the Centuries of Emergence* (1957) and C. E. Fayle, *A Short History of the World's Shipping Industry* (1933). T. S. Willan, "The Foreign Trade of the Provincial Ports" in his *Studies in Elizabethan Foreign Trade* (1959) and A. A. Ruddock, *Italian Merchants and Shipping in Southampton, 1270–1600* (1951), illustrate important aspects of earlier developments. G. N. Clark, *Science and Social Welfare in the Age of Newton* (2nd ed. 1949) includes some interesting reflections on the navigational advances of the period. Ralph Davis, *The Rise of the English Shipping Industry* (1962) is a penetrating and comprehensive analysis of technological and organizational changes in the seventeenth and eighteenth centuries; the former are also clearly described in C. Singer, E. J. Holmyard, A. R. Hall, and T. I. Williams (eds.), *A History of Technology*, Vol. III (1957), Part IV, where certain other technical aspects of communications down to 1750 are covered. The best history of an individual port in this period is C. N. Parkinson, *The Rise of the Port of Liverpool* (1952).

2 Transport and the industrial revolution (1)

There are numerous works on the economic background to the transport developments of this period, of which the most helpful brief statements are the most recent, by Phyllis Deane, *The First Industrial Revolution* (1965); and M. W. Flinn, *The Origins of the Industrial Revolution* (1966). David S. Landes' forthcoming *Unbound Prometheus: Technical Change and Development in Western Europe since 1750* will provide an analysis of the historical processes described in Deane and Flinn within the larger context to which later chapters of this volume refer. Among older books that may still be relied upon for their factual content are: W. Bowden, *Industrial Society in England towards the End of the Eighteenth Century* (1925); P. Mantoux, *The Industrial Revolution in the Eighteenth Century* (1928); T. S. Ashton, *An Economic History of England. The Eighteenth Century* (1955); W. H. B. Court, *A Concise Economic History of Britain from 1750 to Recent Times* (1958). Two regional studies of exceptional importance in relating transport developments to industrial, commercial and demographic changes are J. D. Chambers' *The Vale of Trent, 1670–1800* (1957) and T. C. Barker and J. R. Harris, *A Merseyside Town in the Industrial Revolution: St Helens, 1670–1900* (1954). For a general review of transport itself in this period see H. L. Beales, "Travel and Communications", in A. S. Turberville (ed.), *Johnson's England* (1933). W. E. Minchinton's paper "Bristol—Metropolis of the West in the Eighteenth Century",

Transactions of the Royal Historical Society, 5th Series, iv (1954) is essentially argued in terms of communications.

The most searching and exhaustive history of shipping yet written, in four volumes, is by W. S. Lindsay, *History of Merchant Shipping and Ancient Commerce* (1874–6). Two short works that deal reliably with the technology of shipping are Charles E. Gibson, *The Story of the Ship* (1958); and C. Hamilton Ellis, *A Picture History of Ships* (1957), which treats the sailing ship quite well. Björn Landström, *The Ship* [1961] is a simplified visual history of maritime architecture. The most authoritative treatment of marine insurance is Charles Wright and C. E. Fayle, *A History of Lloyd's* (1928). H. Moyse-Bartlett, *A History of the Merchant Navy* (1937) pays a lot of attention to the period before 1815. On the early developments in steam navigation the following are the most important contributions: A. C. Wardle, "Early Steamships on the Mersey, 1815–1820", *Transactions of the Historic Society of Lancashire and Cheshire*, xcii (1940); H. S. Irvine, "Some Aspects of Passenger Traffic between Britain and Ireland, 1820–1850", *Journal of Transport*, iv (1960); H. P. Spratt, *The Birth of the Steamboat* (1958).

The history of ports down to the nineteenth century, despite the large number of university theses devoted to them, is far from replete. The only attempt so far made to review and measure their progress as a whole in this period is a brief article by D. Swann, "The Pace and Progress of Port Investment in England, 1660–1830", *Yorkshire Bulletin of Economic and Social Research*, xii (1960); Professor Swann has since written on "The Engineers of English Port Improvements, 1660–1830" *Transport History*, i (1968). A more rounded account of the circumstances prevailing in one port is given in the same volume of this journal by Gordon Jackson under the title "The Struggle for the first Hull Dock". James Bird's *The Major Seaports of the United Kingdom* (1963), though containing some exhaustive information and valuable bibliographies, is concerned more with their individual amenities today than it is with their historical formation. Bird has also written *The Geography of the Port of London* (1957), which is useful chiefly on account of its meticulous topography of dockland. Sir Joseph G. Broodbank's classic *History of the Port of London* (2 vols., 1921), though primarily a study of the Port of London Authority since its creation in 1909, contains some valuable chapters on early developments. On the history of the London docks, see W. M. Stern, "The First London Dock Boom and the Growth of the West India Docks", *Economica*, xix (1952), and for a marvellously scrupulous history of dock labour the same author's *The Porters of London* (1960). R. Smith, *Sea-Coal for London* (1961) looks at the Coal Factors' Society which handled virtually all London's supplies in this period.

Two older books, Finden's *Ports, Harbours, Watering-Places, and Coast Scenery of Great Britain* (2 vols., 1844)—so often pillaged for its numerous engravings., —and L. F. Vernon-Harcourt's technical treatise, *Harbours and Docks* (2 vols, 1885), provide a good yield of historical information, but Henry Rees, *British Ports and Shipping* (1958) is useful as an historical synopsis. C. Northcote

Parkinson, *The Rise of the Port of Liverpool* (1952) is the best short history of a single British port before 1793. W. E. Minchinton *The Port of Bristol in the Eighteenth Century* (1962) along with A. F. Williams, "Bristol Port Plans and Improvement Schemes of the 18th Century", *Transactions of the Bristol and Gloucestershire Archaeological Society*, lxxxi (1962) give an excellent idea of port problems. Among other studies of particular ports the following are the most informative: Rodwell Jones, "Kingston-upon-Hull: A Study in Port Development", *Scottish Geographical Magazine*, xxxv (1919); W. G. East, "The Historical Geography of the Town, Port and Roads of Whitby", *Geographical Journal*, lxxx (1932); J. H. Andrews, "The Thanet Seaports, 1650–1750", *Archaeologia Cantiana*, lxvi (1954); E. A. G. Clark, *The Ports of the Exe Estuary, 1660–1830* (1960); James Guthrie, *The River Tyne: Its History and Resources* (1880); W. H. Jones, *History of the Port of Swansea* (1922). For more data on these matters, see Royal Commission on the Condition of the Harbours, Shores and Navigable Rivers, *Parl. Papers*, 1845 (665), xvi and 1846 (692, 756), xviii. Rupert C. Jarvis has written two highly expert articles on the historical materials that exist for further research in this field: "Sources for the History of Ships and Shipping", *Journal of Transport*, iii (1958) and "Sources for the History of Ports", *ibid*. (1957). A more esoteric but fascinating study of the coastline is contained in Alan Stevenson's seemingly definitive work *The World's Lighthouses before 1820* (1959).

Urban transport is best approached through general studies of particular towns, of which some of the most helpful in this context are: Mrs Dorothy George's classic *London Life in the XVIIIth Century* (1925); O. H. K. Spate, "The Growth of London A.D. 1660–1800" in H. C. Darby (ed.), *An Historical Geography of London before A.D. 1800* (1935); Conrad Gill, *History of Birmingham* (1952), Vol. i; Leon S. Marshall, "The Emergence of the First Industrial City: Manchester, 1780–1850" in Caroline F. Ware (ed.), *The Cultural Approach to History* (1940). There is a useful treatment of the expanding suburbs and their dependence on new lines of communication in H. J. Dyos, "The Growth of a Pre-Victorian Suburb: South London, 1580–1836", *Town Planning Review*, xxv (1954). For the changing street pattern of London there is Sir John Summerson's incomparable study, *Georgian London* (1945), and some splendid contemporary writings, of which John Gwynn's *London and Westminster Improved* (1766), and James Elmes' *London and Its Environs in the Nineteenth Century* (1829), are two of the most illuminating. The relations between street improvement and slum clearance are touched on in H. J. Dyos, "Urban Transformation: A Note on the Objects of Street Improvement in Regency and Early Victorian London", *International Review of Social History*, ii (1957).

The only book which offers a general review of the nature of the road system and its use in this period is John Copeland's *Roads and Their Traffic, 1750–1850* (1968), which has brought together a lot of scattered information, though this does not wholly replace either S. and B. Webb, *The Story of the King's Highway* (1913), or W. T. Jackman, *The Development of Transportation in Modern England* (1916), to which has been added in the 1962 edition a most valuable bibliographical essay by W. H. Chaloner. For the study of local road systems there is no substitute for large-scale county maps, of which one illustration is given in this book in Map 5, which is based largely on C. Greenwood, *Map of the County Palatinate of Lancaster* (1818). Greenwood completed a whole series of maps covering the counties of England and Wales in the course of the next ten years or so. The best brief guide to this source is R. V. Tooley, *Maps and Map-makers* (1949), especially chap. viii; see also Thomas Chubb, *The Printed Maps in the Atlases of Great Britain and Ireland. A Bibliography, 1579–1870* (1927). The development of the turnpike system as a whole remains curiously obscure at several points and surprisingly little has been published even on its regional and local aspects. Happily, some of the most carefully researched papers that have been written do refer to areas of economic importance, of which the best are: W. Harrison, "The Development of the Turnpike System in Lancashire and Cheshire", *Transactions of the Lancashire and Cheshire Antiquarian Society*, iv (1886); G. H. Tupling, "The Turnpike Trusts of Lancashire", *Memoirs and Proceedings of the Manchester Literary and Philosophical Society*, xciv (1952–3); Arthur Cossons, *The Turnpike Roads of Nottinghamshire* (1934); W. B. Crump's *Huddersfield Highways through the Ages* (1949); and the chapter by C. R. Elrington on "Communications" in W. B. Stephens (ed.), *A History of the County of Warwick*, Vol. vii: *The City of Birmingham* (1964). P. L. Payne has written a model for others to use in interpreting the abundant turnpike records in existence in his "The Bermondsey, Rotherhithe and Deptford Turnpike Trust, 1776–1810", *Journal of Transport History*, ii (May 1956), and F. H. W. Sheppard has provided a rare and brilliant insight into the relations between turnpike trusts and local government in his *Local Government in St. Marylebone, 1688–1835* (1958). For relations between the turnpikes and agrarian discontent, see David Williams, *The Rebecca Riots* (1955). Far less digested but still informative are the few records of turnpike trusts yet published to any extent: F. A. Bailey, "The Minutes of the Trustees of the Turnpike Roads from Liverpool to Prescot, St Helens, Warrington and Ashton-in-Makerfield, 1726–89", *Transactions of the Historic Society of Lancashire and Cheshire*, lxxxviii (1936) and lxxxix (1937); A. E. and E. M. Dodd, "The Old Road from Ashbourne to Leek", *Transactions of the North Staffordshire Field Club*, lxxxiii (1948) and lxxxiv (1949). There is no general guide to the local sources of turnpike history, but Jackman's bibliography does include a quite invaluable list of British Museum manuscripts. For the richest imaginable goulash of original materials on tollroads in print—a collector's item—see Mark Searle's *Turnpikes and Toll-Bars* (2 vols., 1930).

There is an enormous volume of evidence in print pertaining to travelling conditions. For road travel there are the exhaustively anecdotal but irreplaceable books by C. G. Harper of which the following are representative: *The Brighton Road* (1892); *The Dover Road* (1895); *The Great North Road* (2 vols., 1901); *The Holyhead Road* (2 vols., 1902); *Stage-Coach and Mail in Days of Yore* (2 vols., 1903). Among the many monographs on coaches and coaching, some of the older books are still the most valuable. Stanley Harris, *The Coaching Age* (1885); and W. Outram–Tristram, *Coaching Days and Coaching Ways* (1893) are both chatty and nostalgic without any serious sacrifice of historical meaning; W. C. A. Blew, *Brighton and Its Coaches* (1894) is a very readable encyclopaedia. One of the most vivid and scrupulous modern introductions to the history of coaching is E. W. Bovill's *The England of Nimrod and Surtees, 1815–1854* (1959) which may be supplemented by his *English Country Life, 1780–1830* (1962). Leslie Gardiner's *Stage-Coach to John O'Groats* (1961) contains much road lore and is chiefly directed at admirers of the "golden age of coaching"; Charles R. Clear, *John Palmer, Mail Coach Pioneer* (1955) is written by an admirer of Palmer. Easily the most scholarly work on the élite of the coaching world is Edmund Vale, *The Mail-Coach Men of the Late Eighteenth Century* (1960). The only explicit attention to have been given to the slowest but most convenient form of urban transport of the time is Harold W. Hart, "The Sedan Chair as a Means of Public Conveyance", *Journal of Transport History*, v (1962). The same author has assembled some interesting data on fares and journey times in another place: "Some Notes on Coach Travel, 1750–1848", *Journal of Transport History*, iv (1960). Thomas Burke's *Travel in England* (1942) has two lively chapters on Georgian and Regency modes of travel, and many of the excerpts from travellers' tales in Jack Simmons, *Journeys in England* (1969 ed.) come from the eighteenth and early nineteenth centuries. Among foreign observers' reports of British roads that are worth turning to are: Baron Charles Dupin, *Voyages dans la Grande-Bretagne en 1816, 1817, 1818 et 1819* (3 vols., 1820–4); Rev. Charles Moritz, *Travels, chiefly on Foot, through Several Parts of England, in 1782* (originally published in Berlin but reprinted in John Pinkerton's *A General Collection of the Best and Most Interesting Voyages and Travels in All Parts of the World* (17 vols., 1808–14), vol. ii). Sir Herbert Fordham has written copiously on road books: *The Road-Books and Itineraries of Great Britain, 1570 to 1850* (1924); "John Ogilby, 1600–1676" and "*Paterson's Roads*: David Paterson, his Maps and Itineraries, 1738–1825" in *Transactions of the Bibliographical Society*, v–vi (1924–5 and 1925–6). Edwin F. Gay, "Arthur Young on English Roads", *Quarterly Journal of Economics*, xli (1927) is a sobering corrective to any over-hasty reading of Arthur Young, especially his *A Six Months' Tour through the North of England* (1771); William Marshall's various *Rural Economies* of different parts of the country, which throw a more discriminating light on conditions, appeared between 1787 and 1798.

On road vehicles, Ralph Straus, *Carriages & Coaches. Their History and Their Evolution* (1912) is a little wayward but gives sound factual information. On the more technical level there is the brief primer by J. W. Burgess, *A Practical Treatise on Coach-building Historical and Descriptive* (1881); and Hugh McCausland's pictorially pleasing *The English Carriage* (1948); Cecil Robertson, *Coach Building —Past and Present* (c. 1930) establishes, perhaps unconsciously, the lineage between the horse-coach and the modern motor car.

For information about the carriage of goods by road it is necessary to consult Jackman, Copeland, and a variety of studies concerned chiefly with the production and distribution of bulky commodities. For example, A. H. John, *The Industrial Development of South Wales, 1750–1850* (1950); M. W. Flinn, *Men of Iron: the Crowleys of the Early Iron Industry* (1962); T. S. Ashton, *Iron and Steel in the Industrial Revolution* (1924); R. A. Lewis, "Transport for Eighteenth Century Ironworks", *Economica*, xviii (1951); B. L. C. Johnson, "The Foley Partnerships: the Iron Industry at the End of the Charcoal Era", *Economic History Review*, 2nd Series, iv (1951–2). T. S. Willan, "The Justices of the Peace and the Rates of Land Carriage, 1692–1827", *Journal of Transport History*, v (November 1962) is an extremely rare attempt to estimate transport costs in the period, recently amplified by W. Albert, "The Justices' Rates for Land Carriage 1748–1827, reconsidered", *Transport History*, i (1968).

The history of postal services since the sixteenth century is comprehensively treated in Howard Robinson, *The British Post Office* (1948); K. L. Ellis, *The British Post Office in the Eighteenth Century* (1958) is a piece of administrative history, valuable for its exposition of the internal workings of the Post Office.

The problem facing road engineers are probably best approached through the technical treatises of the generation following them, and for this purpose Thomas Aitken's *Road Making and Maintenance* (1900); and H. Law and D. K. Clark, *The Construction of Roads and Streets* (1901), both of which include some historical data, are very helpful. John Loudon McAdam's principal utterances on these matters are collected together in his *Remarks on the Present System of Road Making* (1816), and *Observations on the Management of Trusts for the Care of Turnpike Roads* (1825). The achievements of bridge-builders may be gauged in the same way by referring to the two volumes of plates accompanying the symposium published by John Weale on *The Theory, Practice and Architecture of Bridges* (4 vols., 1843). The best general history of bridges in this country is Eric de Maré, *The Bridges of Britain* (1954), which is beautifully illustrated. Over half of Charles Welch, *History of the Tower Bridge* (1894) is given to the much earlier history of London Bridge and some space is also spared for the other Thames bridges. A rather rare modern study of the building of a single bridge is Patricia Carson, "The Building of the First Bridge at Westminster, 1736–1750", *Journal of Transport History*, iii (1957). David Lampe deals well with the building of the Thames Tunnel in *The Tunnel* (1963). For biographical details of John Metcalfe it is still necessary to go to Samuel Smiles' *Lives of the Engineers*, Vol. iii (1878), which, despite its well-known heroic tendencies, does give a surprisingly full and reasonably accurate account of him. L. T. C. Rolt's magnificent study, *Thomas Telford* (1958) makes reference to Smiles superfluous, but there is more to be told about Telford's activities on the Holyhead road in Mervyn Hughes, "Telford, Parnell, and the Great Irish Road", *Journal of Transport History*, vi (1964). Roy Devereux, *John Loudon McAdam* (1936) has wide historical gaps. Robert H. Spiro, Jr., fills some of these admirably in a number of articles, of which "John Loudon McAdam and the Metropolis Turnpike Trust", *Journal of Transport History*, ii (1956) is the most important.

3   Transport and the industrial revolution (2)

The most authoritative contemporary accounts of inland waterways are
John Phillips, *General History of Inland Navigation* (1792)—the cheap 4th edition
of 1803 lost its map in the abridgement but included up-to-date information
on current developments—and Joseph Priestley, *Historical Account of the Navigable Rivers, Canals, and Railways of Britain* (1831); the best early advocate of canals
is the anonymous collection of writings (possibly made by Thomas Bentley)
entitled *The History of Inland Navigations* (1766, 1769, and 1779). One of the most
helpful maps of the canal system at its height, including railways and details
of mineral deposits of every kind, is J. Walker's six-miles-to-the-inch *Map of
the Inland Navigation, Canals and Rail Roads . . . throughout Great Britain* (1830).
There are useful regional maps of canals on a slightly smaller scale without
supplementary detail in J. Cranfield and M. Bonfiel, *Waterways Atlas of the
British Isles* (1966). The leading modern authority on the history of canals is
Charles Hadfield, whose *British Canals* (2nd edition, 1959) is easily the best
introduction to the subject; his *The Canal Age* (1968) glances at some foreign
canals but does not noticeably enlarge our knowledge of British ones, nor
set them at all securely in their historical context. The same author is in the
course of writing a series of exhaustive regional studies of which the first four
to appear are *The Canals of Southern England* (1955), *The Canals of South Wales and the
Border* (1960), *The Canals of the East Midlands* (1966), and *The Canals of the West Midlands* (1966); among Hadfield's articles "The Grand Junction Canal", *Journal of
Transport History*, iv (1959), and "The Thames Navigation and the Canals, 1770–
1830", *Economic History Review*, xiv (1944–5), are the most important. L. T. C.
Rolt's *The Inland Waterways of England* (1950) is full of canal lore and technology,
extremely well illustrated, and contains the largest key map to the canal
system which is available. The histories of particular undertakings have been
explored by: T. C. Barker, "The Sankey Navigation: The First Lancashire
Canal", *Transactions of the Historic Society of Lancashire and Cheshire*, c (1948),
"Lancashire Coal, Cheshire Salt and the Rise of Liverpool", *ibid.*, ciii (1951),
and "The Beginnings of the Canal Age in the British Isles" in L. S. Pressnell
(ed.), *Studies in the Industrial Revolution* (1960); H. Pollins, "The Swansea Canal",
Journal of Transport History, i (1954); H. Clegg, "The Third Duke of Bridge-
water's Canal Works in Manchester", *Transactions of the Lancashire and Cheshire
Antiquarian Society*, lxv (1955); A. T. Patterson, "The Making of the Leicestershire Canals, 1766–1814", *Transactions of the Leicestershire Archaeological Society*,
xxvii (1951); H. Household, "The Thames & Severn Canal" *Journal of Transport
History*, vii (1966). For river navigations in this period, see T. S. Willan, *The
Navigation of the River Weaver in the Eighteenth Century* (1951) and A. C. Wood,
"The History of Trade and Transport on the River Trent", *Transactions of
the Thoroton Society*, liv (1950).

The primary authority on canal technology is H. R. de Salis (a director of
the leading canal carriers, Fellows, Morton & Clayton Ltd.), whose *Bradshaw's
Canals and Navigable Rivers of England and Wales* (1904) is an exhaustive handbook

and guide to its subject; its glossary of canal terms is the best in print. J. S. Jeans' *Waterways and Water Transport* (1890) also contains much technical and historical information and has the unusual merit of placing British water-ways in an international context. Relatively little has been published in the last fifty years on the engineering and business aspects of canals, though they have been covered to some extent in biographical studies. The starting point for these is Samuel Smiles' very readable *Lives of the Engineers* (2nd edition, 5 vols., 1878), which is usually sound on the main outlines and on technical matters—the author was Secretary to the South Eastern Railway —but its faintly moralistic tone sometimes engenders fiction: he deals with Brindley, Smeaton, Rennie, Metcalfe, and Telford. More reliable studies are Sir Alexander Gibb, *The Story of Telford: the Rise of Civil Engineering* (1936); L. T. C. Rolt's wider study *Thomas Telford* (1958); W. H. Chaloner's *People and Industries* (1963), which reprints the author's meticulous articles on Bridge-water, Telford, and McAdam, and Hugh Malet's *The Canal Duke* (1961), an attractive study of the man as well as the entrepreneur. There is also Jack Simmons' penetrating miniature of William Jessop in his *Parish and Empire* (1952), Charles Hadfield's "James Green as Canal Engineer", *Journal of Transport History*, i (1953), and C. T. G. Boucher, *John Rennie, 1761–1821* (1963); H. G. W. Household's "Early Engineering on the Thames and Severn Canal", *Transactions of the Newcomen Society*, xxvii (1949–51) contains some valuable technical data on both engineering and contracting which are not avail-able elsewhere. On canal folk see George Smith, *Our Canal Population* (1875).

Parliamentary papers pertaining to the canal era are very few. The number of bills for canals, railways, docks, turnpikes, and enclosures in each year, and the aggregate capital involved, are listed in the *Lords' Committee on the Resumption of Cash Payments*, Parl. Papers, 1819 (30), xcviii, Appdx. G.6. For a comparison of the annual value of canal and railway property in 1842, see *Parl. Papers*, 1845 (102, 165), xxxviii. Though unreliable on finance, the earliest return from all inland navigation and canal companies, including gross tonnage and revenue at decennial intervals between 1828 and 1868, is in *Parl. Papers*, 1870 (184), lvi. The *Fourth Report, Royal Commission on Canals*, Parl. *Papers*, 1910 (Cmd. 4979), xii also contains summaries of canal history. Other references are mentioned in Section 5 below.

4   The creation of the railway system

The literature of the history of the railways is immense. An exhaustive guide to it is George Ottley, *A Bibliography of British Railway History* (1965), which has almost 8,000 entries arranged topically and cross-indexed—an indis-pensable asset for all reference libraries: its author is now planning biblio-graphies of railway company prospectuses, historical sources, and periodical literature. There is a useful critical bibliography of books (though not articles) on railways in the United States and the Commonwealth as well as the United Kingdom in E. T. Bryant, *Railways: A Readers' Guide* (1968).

There are surprisingly few reliable books devoted specifically to the growth of the railway system as such. Easily the most concise, lively, and authoritative is Jack Simmons, *The Railways of Britain* (2nd ed., 1968), which also contains the most helpful general bibliography (especially of maps) yet available. Michael Robbins, *The Railway Age* (1962) is another stylishly robust essay covering wide ground, including some railway development overseas and a curious and informative list of sources. The first volume of C. E. R. Sherrington, *Economics of Rail Transport in Great Britain* (2 vols., 1928), contains a well-ordered historical account of the subject. By contrast, the largest work available, Hamilton Ellis, *British Railway History* (2 vols., 1954–9), is inclined to melodrama and facetiousness and is singularly weak on economic factors, but it is packed, all the same, with information that is hard to come by in any other form: one drawback to using it is its poor index. A simple but by no means simple-minded introduction to railway history is J. B. Snell, *Early Railways* (1964); similarly, P. Thornhill, *Railways for Britain* (1954) is elementary but supported by good sketch maps. Quite invaluable as detailed guides to the early period are two works by a Railway Superintendent, H. G. Lewin, *Early British Railways, 1801–44* (1925) and, on a different plane of excellence, *The Railway Mania and its Aftermath, 1845–52* (1936)—which has recently been reprinted though without its indispensable maps. C. E. Lee, *The Evolution of Railways* (2nd ed., 1943) scrupulously examines the evidence on the beginnings of railways and can be supplemented by his various articles on wagonways and plateways in the *Transactions of the Newcomen Society*, xxv (1947) and xxvi (1949). J. U. Nef, *Rise of the British Coal Industry* (2 vols., 1932) is helpful, especially bibliographically, on wagonways; and E. Hughes, *North Country Life in the Eighteenth Century: the North East, 1700–50* (1952) puts them even better into their historical context. Sir Arthur Elton, "The Pre-History of Railways", *Proceedings of the Somersetshire Archaeological Society*, cvii (1963) is interesting on Allen's railway at Bath; C. F. Dendy Marshall, *History of British Railways down to the Year 1830* (1938) is sumptuous but not absolutely reliable. For the most detailed tour of wagonways and early railways as they were in 1826–7 it is necessary to go to C. von Oeynhausen and H. von Dechen, *Uber Scheinenwege in England* (1829); for a brief translation of some of the authors' other published observations, see E. A. Forward, "Report on Railways in England, 1826–27", *Transactions of the Newcomen Society*, xxix (1958). For some insight into the factors affecting the adoption of steam-power, see Jack Simmons, "For and Against the Locomotive", *Journal of Transport History*, ii (1956). Tables of locomotive performance and other experiments on some 58 railways are included in the valuable work, F. Whishaw, *The Railways of of Great Britain and Ireland* (1840–1).

Biographies of companies and lines are very numerous and extremely patchy in quality, chiefly owing to a preoccupation with their technical aspects and a neglect of their corporate development, local context, and larger historical influences: some of the commonly neglected issues are mentioned in Michael Robbins, "What Kind of Railway History do we Want?", *Journal of Transport History*, iii (1957)—a paper which nevertheless tends to perpetuate the emphasis on individual undertakings. The following representative list will be found to include some of the most helpful writing on matters of fact or on the types and phases of railway development: C. J. Allen, *The Great Eastern Railway* (4th ed., 1967); D. S. Barrie, *The Taff Vale Railway* (2nd ed., 1950); C. R. Clinker, *The Leicester & Swannington Railway* (1954); and *The Birmingham & Derby Junction Railway* (1956); G. Dow, *Great Central* (3 vols., 1959–65); Edwin Course, *London Railways* (1962); H. Ellis, *The South Western Railway* (1956); D. J. Hodgkins, "The Origins and Independent Years of the Cromford & High Peak Railway", *Journal of Transport History*, vi (1963); R. W. Kidner, *The South Eastern Railway* (1953) and *The London, Chatham & Dover Railway* (1952); E. T. MacDermot (ed. C. R. Clinker), *History of the Great Western Railway* (3 vols., 1964); C. L. Mowat, *The Golden Valley Railway* (1964)—a little gem; G. D. Parkes, *The Hull & Barnsley Railway* (2nd ed., 1948); Harold Pollins, "The Last Main Line to London", *Journal of Transport History*, iv (1959); M. Robbins, *The North London Railway* (4th ed., 1953); J. Simmons, *The Maryport & Carlisle Railway* (1947); C. H. Grinling, *History of the Great Northern Railway* (3rd ed., 1966); W. W. Tomlinson, *The North Eastern Railway* [1915]. On light railways the most important work is W. J. K. Davies, *Light Railways: Their Rise and Decline* (1964). For narrow-gauge railways, there are: C. E. Lee, *Narrow-Gauge Railways in North Wales* (1945); and J. I. C. Boyd, *Narrow-Gauge Railways in Mid-Wales* (1952). For diagrams (first devised by Charles E. Lee for *The Railway Gazette*) showing the family trees of the railway groupings of 1921 see the appendix to G. Ottley, *A Bibliography of British Railway History* (1965).

In some ways the most valuable method of handling the institutional and economic aspects of railway development has been through their regional study. *A Regional History of the Railways of Great Britain* has been launched with several useful volumes: D. St J. Thomas, *The West Country* (1960); H. P. White, *Southern England* (1961) and *Greater London* (1963); K. Hoole, *The North East* (1965); D. I. Gordon, *The Eastern Counties* (1968). The *Victoria History of the Counties of England* [the V.C.H.] is also now making this approach conventional: H. C. Darby in *Cambridgeshire*, Vol. ii (1948); J. Simmons in *Leicestershire*, Vol. iii (1955); C. R. Clinker in *Wiltshire*, Vol. iv (1959); H. W. Parris in *York* (1961); C. R. Elrington in *Warwickshire* [Birmingham], Vol. vii (1964); S. A .H. Bourne, M. J. Wise and P. L. Clark in *Staffordshire*, Vol. ii (1967). Since 1956 the *Railway Magazine* has been publishing studies of railway development in towns: Bristol (1956), Manchester (1957), Liverpool (1959), Preston (1960).

One of the best approaches to the subject is through the lives of the engineers themselves. Samuel Smiles' writings on the Stephensons are misleading as studies of personality though not seriously inaccurate on broad matters of fact. Better far is L. T. C. Rolt, *George and Robert Stephenson: The Railway Revolution* (1960), which is not only a mature evaluation of father and son in relation to each other but an acutely observed study of the indispensable human dimension in the building of the system; the same author's *Isambard Kingdom Brunel* (1957) is a very sure-handed treatment of a more complex and in many ways more interesting figure. O. J. Vignoles, *Life of Charles Blacker Vignoles* (1889) is by comparison a weak eulogy of a not unimportant engineer; Joseph Devey, *The Life of Joseph Locke* (1862) is a worse study of a more important figure. There is an incomparable work giving an insight into the motives of the leading railway promoter of early days in Sir Alfred Pease (ed.), *The Diaries of Edward Pease, the Father of English Railways* (1907). For some light on the reception given by landowners to the railways see David Spring, "The British Landed Estate in the Age of Coal and Iron, 1830–1880", *Journal of Economic History*, xi (1951); for a still more positive response to railway opportunities, see J. D. Marshall's penetrating study, *Furness and the Industrial Revolution* (1958). Joan Wake's corrective study, *Northampton Vindicated: or Why the Main Line Missed the Town* (1935) tends still to be overlooked: V. A. Hatley's two articles, "Northampton Re-vindicated: more light on why the main line missed the town", *Northamptonshire Past and Present*, ii (1959), and "Northampton Hoodwinked? How a main line of railway missed the town a second time", *Journal of Transport History*, vii (1966) take the story still further.

On the amalgamation of companies and the ebb and flow of parliamentary control, the most generally useful work is still E. Cleveland-Stevens, *English Railways: their Development and their Relation to the State* (1915), and this may usefully be supplemented by H. M. Jagtiani, *The Rôle of the State in the Provision of Railways* (1924); but for a more sophisticated examination of some aspects of their interplay, particularly of the contribution of the Board of Trade, there is Henry Parris, *Government and the Railways in Nineteenth-Century Britain* (1965). For James Morrison's views see his *Observations Illustrative of the Defects of the English System of Railway Legislation* (1846). Easily the most thoroughgoing contemporary advocacy of State ownership of the railways, including a valuable historical review, which was published as a reminder of the powers to nationalize that then existed, is William Galt, *Railway Reform: its Importance and Practicability* (1865); for a later statement of the issues, see James Hole, *National Railways* (1893) The modes of handling railway bills are set out unequivocally in the first volume of O. C. Williams, *The Historical Development of Private Bill Procedure and Standing Orders in the House of Commons* (2 vols, 1948). The legislative history of companies can be traced in *Index to Local and Personal Acts, 1801–1947* (H.M.S.O., 1949). A short cut through the general legislation is given by James Bigg, *A Collection of Public General Acts for the Regulation of Railways*, which went through ten editions between 1845 and 1864.

Among contemporary writing, John Francis, *A History of the English Railway* (2 vols., 1851) is one of the very best informed, though partisan; Dionysius Lardner, *Railway Economy* (1850) was not written from close practical acquaintance with railways but is an interesting reflection of current opinion; so, too, is Herbert Spencer, *Railway Morals and Railway Policy* (1855); F. S. Williams, *Our Iron Roads* (1852) and *The Midland Railway* (1876) are outstanding examples of the merits and demerits of history written at close range. The most comprehensive and readable account of railways to appear in the nineteenth century is Sir William Acworth, *The Railways of England* (1889). Of incomparable importance for reference are *Herapath's Railway Magazine* (1835–1903), the *Railway Times* (1837–1914), and, under slightly varying titles, Bradshaw's *Railway Manual and Shareholders' Guide* (1848–1923): each contained a detailed map, and that for 1914 forms the basis in this book for Map 13.

5   The economics of railway operation

For a general analysis of some of the economic problems discussed in this chapter one must still resort to the older texts. Some of these are in fact quite good. The following should be consulted: Sir William Acworth, *The Railways and the Traders* (1891), and *Elements of Railway Economics* (1911); E. A. Pratt, *Railways and the Nation* (1908), and *A History of Inland Transport and Communication in England* (1912); C. E. R. Sherrington, *Economics of Rail Transport in Great Britain* (1928); A. W. Kirkaldy and A. D. Evans, *The History and Economics of Transport* (4th ed. 1927). Particular topics may be studied in greater depth by consulting the following sources. For monopoly and amalgamation there is the contemporary work by W. A. Robertson, *Combination among Railway Companies* (1912); and the official *Report of the Departmental Committee on Railway Agreements and Amalgamations*, Cd. 5631 (1911). A general but very useful review of the problem is given by W. G. Scott, "Competition and Combination in Railway Transportation in Great Britain", *Proceedings of the Royal Philosophical Society of Glasgow*, xli (1909–10). Most books say something about the State and the railways but for a general survey the reader should consult E. Cleveland-Stevens, *English Railways, their Development and their Relation to the State* (1915); and the more recent treatment by C. I. Savage in his *An Economic History of Transport* (1959), ch. iii. On pricing policy there are some quite good studies: the contemporary work by E. A. Pratt, *Railways and their Rates* (1906); and more modern accounts in A. M. Milne and A. Laing, *The Obligation to Carry* (1956) and A. A. Harrison, "Railway Freight Charges", *Journal of the Institute of Transport* (1957).

The operating efficiency of Britain's railways in the late nineteenth century attracted a good deal of contemporary attention and resulted in a number of studies the chief of which were E. B. Dorsey, *English and American Railroads Compared* (1887); G. Paish, *The British Railway Position* (1902), and W. Bolland, *The Railways and the Nation* (1909); whilst a number of articles on efficiency and the collection of statistics by Acworth and others appeared in the *Journal of the Royal Statistical Society* in the years just before the First World War. Most contemporary writers were extremely critical about railway management and operation and probably they overstated their case. Recently interest in this theme has been revived and although the railways cannot be given a clean bill of health the following studies do give a more balanced account of the position. See in particular C. P. Kindleberger, "Obsolescence and Technical Change", *Bulletin of the Oxford Institute of Statistics*, xxiii (1961); and D. H. Aldcroft, "The Efficiency and Enterprise of British Railways, 1870–1914", *Explorations in Entrepreneurial History*, v (1968). The efforts made by the Railway Clearing House to standardize various aspects of railway operating practice have recently been dealt with extensively by P. S. Bagwell, *The Railway Clearing House in the British Economy, 1842–1922* (1968).

Despite the mass of railway records available in the archives of the British Railways Board nobody has yet produced a good business history. There are of course a large number of company histories but most of them are written by railway enthusiasts who tend to avoid discussing the financial and economic problems of the companies concerned. Most of them however do contain some interesting snippets and they cannot, therefore, be ignored altogether. Two of the more useful ones are G. Dow, *Great Central*, Vol ii;. *The Dominion of Watkin* (1962); and O. S. Nock, *The London and North Western Railway* (1960). An excellent regional study of transport including railways is that by T. C. Barker and M. Robbins, *A History of London Transport:* Vol. i, *The Nineteenth Century* (1963).

A handy summary of railway statistics for the period 1850–1912 can be found in *The Jubilee of the Railway News* (1914). These have been abstracted, of course, from the Board of Trade's *Railway Returns*.

Very little has been written on the maritime activities of the railways. There is, however, quite a good summary of the chief developments in *The Jubilee of the Railway News* (1914). Useful information on cross-Channel passenger services can be found in C. Grasemann and G. W. P. McLachlan, *English Channel Packet Boats* (1839); E. W. P. Veale, *Gateway to the Continent* (1955); R. Bucknall, *Boat Trains and Channel Packets* (1957). Early developments in the Irish services are dealt with in H. S. Irvine's "Some Aspects of Passenger Traffic between Britain and Ireland, 1820–50", *Journal of Transport History*, iv (1960). Railway freight steamer services have been almost entirely neglected except for B. F. Duckham's "Railway Steamship Enterprise: The Lancashire and Yorkshire Railway's East Coast Fleet, 1904–14", *Business History*, x (1968), though it is somewhat limited in scope. Most of the railway company histories contain marine reviews though few of them examine the economic aspects in any great depth.

On the running of the railways themselves there are several treatises, of which *Modern Railway Administration: A Practical Treatise by Leading Railway Experts* (2 vols., 1925); and H. F. Sanderson, *Railway Commercial Practice* (2 vols., 1952), with a supplementary volume on the Transport Act, 1953 (1955), are relatively handy. J. Macaulay (ed.), *Modern Railway Working* (8 vols., 1912–14) is more exhaustive and pertains very usefully to the period before grouping. On locomotives, rolling stock, fast runs, and so on, the following represent the best of a very numerous class of books: D. K. Clark, *Railway*

Machinery: A Treatise on the Mechanical Engineering of Railways (2 vols., 1855), of which the second volume contains nothing but plates, and *Railway Locomotives: Their Progress, Mechanical Construction and Performance* (2 vols., 1860); T. Tredgold (ed. W. S. B. Woodhouse), *The Steam Engine* (2 vols., 1838–9); C. J. Allen, *Railways of Today* (1930); P. Ransome-Wallis (ed.), *The Concise Encyclopaedia of World Railway Locomotives* (1959); Hamilton Ellis, *Railway Carriages of the British Isles from 1830 to 1914* (1965); G. Behrend, *Pullman in Europe* (1962); J. R. Day and B. G. Wilson, *Unusual Railways* and J. R. Day, *More Unusual Railways* (1960)—two studies of unconventional means of propulsion; E. Foxwell and T. C. Farrer, *Express Trains* (1889); O. S. Nock, *The Railway Race to the North* (1959). On all these matters E. L. Ahrons, *Locomotive and Train Working in the Latter Part of the Nineteenth Century* (6 vols., 1951–54) is entirely authoritative.

6   Railways and the expansion of the economy

It is impossible to assess the full impact of the railways on the economy and on society without the widest reading, and a touch of subjective evaluation as well as statistical measurement. The general economic context of railway development is clearly stated in S. G. Checkland, *The Rise of Industrial Society in England, 1815–1885* (1964) and, very much more briefly, in J. D. Chambers, *The Workshop of the World, British Economic History from 1820 to 1880* (1961). G. R. Porter, *The Progress of the Nation* (2nd ed., 1847) and J. S. Jeans, *England's Supremacy: Its Sources, Economics, and Dangers* (1885) present two different ways of looking at closely related events at the time, and W. L. Burn's brilliant work. *The Age of Equipoise* (1964), not only reveals the diversity of the factors at work at the height of the railway age but contains a warning not to become over-selective in studying them. G. Kitson Clark, *The Making of Victorian England* (1962) is one of the best antidotes to this. In many respects, Sir John Clapham's *An Economic History of Modern Britain*. Vol. i, *The Early Railway Age* (1926) and Vol. ii, *Free Trade and Steel, 1850–1886* (1932), is still the most inquisitive and balanced account of the economic world most closely surrounding the railways. A single example of a business undertaking closely related to railway developments, George Spencer & Company, is developed by P. L. Payne, *Rubber and Railways in the Nineteenth Century* (1961). It is impossible to pursue the repercussions of the railways on individual firms any further here.

A bold attempt to assess the overall contribution which the railways made to Victorian economic expansion is B. R. Mitchell, "The Coming of the Railway and United Kingdom Economic Growth", *Journal of Economic History*, xxiv (1964). Some measure of the new sophistication that is increasingly being used by economic historians to measure with precision the rôle of railways may be had by glancing at American railways through the eyes of R. W. Fogel, *Railroads and American Economic Growth* (1964)—but see the valuable assessment by Marc Nerlove, "Railroads and American Economic Growth", *Journal of Economic History*, xxvi (1966). Another article in the same volume, "United States Transport Advance and Externalities" by S. Lebergott, indicates the measurable quantities entailed in such studies. A brief general assessment of the influence of the railways in Britain, using entirely different standards of measurement, is Eric L. Waugh, "Railroads and the Changing Face of Britain, 1825–1901", *Business History Review*, xxx (1956). Some indication of the extent of the contribution which railway-building abroad was making to British economic expansion is contained in W. O. Henderson, *Britain and Industrial Europe, 1750–1870* (1954), and analysed by A. K. Cairncross, *Home and Foreign Investment, 1870–1913* (1953). For more statistical material on railway growth it is possible to go to the annual returns made by the railway companies to the Board of Trade from 1847, the basic elements of which have been included in B. R. Mitchell and Phyllis Deane, *Abstract of British Historical Statistics* (1962), chap. viii. G. L. Boag, *Railway Statistics* (1912) is concerned mainly with concocting traffic figures; C. D. Campbell, "Cyclical Fluctuations in the Railway Industry", *Transactions of the Manchester Statistical Society*, 1928–9, deals with the period since 1870 and is valuable. A great deal of other numerical data is to be found among the company reports referred to in their standard histories and, annually from 1848 to 1923, in *Bradshaw's Railway Manual and Shareholders' Guide*. Among the "Accounts & Papers" of *Parliamentary Papers* are vast quantities of statistical returns touching many aspects of railway development, as for example those included in the return made of every railway in the United Kingdom in *Parl. Papers*, 1849 (145), xvi. For the gist of this, presented interpretatively, see H. Scrivenor, *The Railways of the United Kingdom Statistically Considered in Relation to their Extent, Capital, Amalgamation, &c.* (1849); also W. F. Spackman, *An Analysis of the Railway Interest of the United Kingdom* (1845). Samuel Salt, *Statistics and Calculations Essentially Necessary to Persons Connected with Railways or Canals* (1845) speaks for itself. E. D. Chattaway, *Railways: Their Capital and Dividends* (1855–6) is an extremely brief but valuable synopsis of its subject. The most careful estimate of railway capital formation available is presented by A. G. Kenwood, "Railway Investment in Britain, 1825–75", *Economica*, xxxii (1965).

Three other modern works that make distinguished contributions to the appraisal of railway construction and finance in relation to general levels of economic activity are R. C. O. Matthews, *A Study in Trade Cycle History: Economic Fluctuations in Britain, 1833–42* (1954); J. R. T. Hughes, *Fluctuations in Trade, Industry and Finance: A Study of British Economic Development, 1850–1860* (1960); and, more generally, W. W. Rostow, *British Economy of the Nineteenth Century* (1948). D. Morier Evans, *The Commercial Crisis of 1847–8* (2nd ed., 1849) gives a contemporary view of the railway mania in financial terms, and John Francis, *A History of the English Railway* (2 vols., 1851) a more human one. For modern views of what happened and why, see E. V. Morgan, "Railway Investment, Bank of England Policy and Interest Rates, 1844–48", *Economic History* (Supplement to the *Economic Journal*), iv (1940), and C. N. Ward-Perkins, "The Commercial Crisis of 1847", *Oxford Economic Papers*, ii (1950). A. C. O'Dell, *Railways and Geography* (1956) is a very helpful study of the geographical factors in railway development.

There are numerous studies of various aspects of the forming of railway companies and the contribution this made to capital markets. The main pioneering work, not yet superseded, is C. C. Wang, *Legislative Regulation of Railway Finance in England* (University of Illinois Studies in the Social Sciences, Vol. VII, March–June 1918), which deals mainly with share and loan capital, and with accounts and auditing. It may be supplemented by two valuable articles by H. Pollins: "Aspects of Railway Accounting before 1868" in A. C. Littleton and B. S. Yamey (eds.), *Studies in the History of Accounting* (1956) and "Railway Auditing: a Report of 1867", *Accounting Research*, viii (1957). On this matter there are some valuable minutes of evidence to the three reports of the Select Committee on Railways, *Parl. Papers*, 1849 (H.L.21), xxix. Pollins has advanced in some directions the early work done by B. C. Hunt, *The Development of the Business Corporation in England, 1800–1867* (1936), which was much concerned with railway developments, with two more articles of importance: "The Marketing of Railway Shares in the First Half of the Nineteenth Century", *Economic History Review*, vii (1954) and "The Finances of the Liverpool & Manchester Railway", *Economic History Review*, v (1952). No more research of consequence has been done on railway finance beyond the important addition made by S. A. Broadbridge, "The Early Capital Market: the Lancashire & Yorkshire Railway", *Economic History Review*, viii (1955). Several of these and other articles have now been collected together in M. C. Reed (ed.), *Railways in the Victorian Economy. Studies in Finance and Economic Growth* (1969). Virtually no work has yet been done on the re-investment of undistributed profits. On the history of corporate enterprise and the part railways played in it, see: C. A. Cooke, *Corporation, Trust and Company* (1950); G. H. Evans, Jr., *British Corporation Finance, 1775–1850: A Study of Preference Shares* (1936); W. A. Robertson, *Combination Among Railway Companies* (1912). On weaknesses among the manipulators of railway capital, see: D. Morier Evans, *Facts, Failures and Frauds* (1859); Michael Robbins, "The Redpath Frauds on the Great Northern Railway", *Railway Magazine*, ciii (1957); R. S. Lambert, *The Railway King, 1800–1871* (2nd imp. 1964). Herbert Spencer's *Autobiography* (2 vols., 1904) gives some unexpected as well as predictable views on both the practical and political aspects of railways. His *Railway Morals & Railway Policy* (1855) is an indictment of waste and duplicity which first appeared in the *Edinburgh Review* and caused a stir. J. S. Jeans, *Railway Problems* (1887) is mostly concerned with finance.

On the organization of railway contracting there is less to read than there ought to be, partly because so few business historians have yet interested themselves in the vast archives that exist in this field. One valuable attempt to explore a corner of it is presented in two articles by Harold Pollins, "Railway Contractors and the Finance of Railway Development in Britain", *Journal of Transport History*, iii (1957), and the same author has also dealt objectively with the question how much early railways cost to build in "A Note on Railway Constructional Costs, 1825–1850", *Economica*, xix (1952–3). One competent business portrait, of Thomas Brassey, appears in R. K. Middlemass, *The Master Builders* (1963). Brassey's son alluded to these matters in *Work and Wages* (1872). More illuminating is [Sir] Arthur Helps, *The Life and Labours of Thomas Brassey* (1969 ed.) and the introduction by J. Simmons. Peto deserves more objective treatment than he gets in H[enry] P[eto], *Sir Morton Peto* (1893); and F. McDermott, *Life of Joseph Firbank* (1887) has got plenty of flavour but no filling. For a leading contractor to the Welsh railways, there is the study of David Davies: I. Thomas, *Top Sawyer* (1938). See also [F. R. Conder], *Personal Recollections of English Engineers* (1868). There is a vivid reconstruction of the navvy's world in Terry Coleman, *The Railway Navvies* (1965) and one rare attempt at defining its social structure in J. A. Patmore, "A Navvy Gang of 1851", *Journal of Transport History*, v (1962), which is about the Knaresborough Viaduct project. R. A. Lewis, "Edwin Chadwick and the Railway Labourers", *Economic History Review*, iii (1950) deals most interestingly with the reform of living conditions. A glimpse of navvies at work is given in Henrietta Cresswell, *Winchmore Hill, Memories of a Lost Village* (1912).

For some inkling of the professional approach of the contemporary engineer, see L. T. C. Rolt, *The Mechanicals* (1967), which is a sound history of the Institution of Mechanical Engineers since its formation in 1847, and the work by the authoritative engineering writer, W. Bridges Adams, *Roads and Rails and their Sequences, Physical and Moral* (1862). He also wrote an article, with a wealth of technical detail and probably the best drawings of different types of rail ever published, entitled "The Construction and Duration of the Permanent Way of Railways in Europe", *Proceedings of the Institution of Civil Engineers*, xi (1851–2). For the engineering of the early railways, there is Nicholas Wood, *A Practical Treatise on Railroads* (1825); and L. Hebert, *A Practical Treatise on Railroads and Locomotive Engines* (1837), which is profusely illustrated.

The organization of railway employment deserves much more research. W. F. Mills, *The Railway Service: Its Exigencies, Provisions and Requirements* (1867) is an excellent starting-point for it: it contains information about the numbers and types of railway workers, their working conditions, and a wide range of social amenities open to them. G. Turnbull "A Note on the Supply of Staff for the early Railways *Transport History*", i (1968), shows how the railways drew labour from road hauliers. An early discursive work based on the running of the London & North Western Railway is [Sir Francis Head], *Stokers and Pokers* (1849); its more informative successors are Sir George Findlay, *The Working and Management of an English Railway* (1889); and G. P. Neele, *Railway Reminiscences* (1904). Roger Lloyd, *Railwaymen's Gallery* (1953) contains, among less useful things, brief studies of a couple of railway managers and of the navvy; H. Holcroft, *The Armstrongs of the Great Western* (1953) offers a brief insight into one of the many minor dynasties of the railway world; L. T. C. Rolt, *A Hunslet Hundred* (1964) and E. Mountford, *Caerphilly Works, 1901–64* (1965) explain the technicalities and achievements of locomotive works: Dionysius Lardner, *Railway Economy* (1850) is stuffed with expertise—and some of the expert's failings—about how railways ought to be worked.

One topic not dealt with in this volume is railway accidents. A somewhat melodramatic treatment of them is John Thomas, *Obstruction—Danger* (1937), but a much more sober assessment is L. T. C. Rolt, *Red for Danger* (2nd ed., 1966). O. S. Nock, *Historic Railway Accidents* (1966) is also of use. The series of reports made by the Board of Trade and later by the Ministry of Transport, and published from 1839 to 1938–39 in *Parliamentary Papers* comprise a rich source of detailed information on the industrial sociology of railways that has scarcely been touched.

On labour relations there is very little beyond P. W. Kingsford, "Labour Relations on the Railways, 1835–1875", *Journal of Transport History*, i (1953), but there are several histories of trade unionism on the railways: on the National Union of Railwaymen there are two large works—G. W. Alcock, *Fifty Years of Railway Trade Unionism* (1922) and Philip S. Bagwell, *The Railwaymen* (1963); on the Associated Society of Locomotive Engineers and Firemen, there is the more modest J. R. Raynes, *Engines and Men* (1921); and N. Mc-Killop, *The Lighted Flame* (1950). G. D. H. Cole and R. P. Arnot, *Trade Unionism on the Railways* (1917) is now largely outdated. An unusual study of the way in which the railways were used to quell popular disturbance is F. C. Mather, "The Railways, the Electric Telegraph, and Public Order during the Chartist Period, 1837–48", *History*, xxxviii (1953).

For the impressions and demands which railways made on individual communities it is necessary to look in many different places, including local newspapers and national periodicals. *Punch* caricatured the locomotive and its deific demands during the railway mania with real brilliance, and in quieter days joked endlessly about railway travel: *Mr. Punch's Railway Book* [1905] is more important historically than it appears, as are Emett's quaint little books of his *Punch* drawings—*Sidings and Suchlike* [1946], and suchlike. The *Illustrated London News*, especially down to the 1870s, contains quantities of drawings and news reports on railway development. There was in the 1840s a spate of railway periodicals on which hardly anything has ever been written except for unpublished bibliographies, but note C. E. Lee, *The Centenary of "Bradshaw"* (1940). There are several anthologies, of which Stuart Legg (ed.), *The Railway Book* (1952) Kenneth Hopkins, *The Poetry of Railways* (1966) and, above all, B. Morgan, *The Railway Lover's Companion* (1963), are the best. The railways made innumerable subjects for artists, notably: J. C. Bourne, whose *Drawings of the London and Birmingham Railway* (1839) and *The History and Description of the Great Western Railway* (1846) give the most vivid picture of the making of an early railway; W. P. Frith, whose painting of Paddington station at the beginning of the 1860s is a kind of social kaleidoscope, interpreted by Tom Taylor, *The Railway Station* (1862). Frith's own memoirs and some of his paintings were reprinted in Neville Wallis, *A Victorian Canvas* (1957); and Gustave Doré, whose engravings of London railway and street landscape appeared in *London: A Pilgrimage* (1872), ed. Blanchard Jerrold. F. D. Klingender, *Art and the Industrial Revolution* (1947), of which an elegant new edition by Sir Arthur Elton appeared in 1968, is rich in railway material.

On railway architecture there is a growing literature and the best starting-point is C. Barman, *Introduction to Railway Architecture* (1950); Henry-Russell Hitchcock's *Early Victorian Architecture in Britain* (2 vols., 1954) is by far the most authoritative treatment and includes the railways. O. L. V. Meeks, *The Railway Station* (1957) is also valuable. The only full-length study of a single British railway station is Jack Simmons' noble historical portrait *St. Pancras Station* (1968), which is valuable, among many things, for the use it makes of the unique data on operation.

To see what the countryside was like before the railways came it is best to begin by consulting W. G. Hoskins, *Making of the English Landscape* (1955). There is a forthcoming study of the impact of the railways on the towns by John R. Kellett, to be entitled *The Impact of Railways on Victorian Cities*. On railway towns as such there is very little. An important pioneering work here is W. H. Chaloner, *The Social and Economic Development of Crewe, 1780–1923* (1950). On Swindon there are three articles of value: two of them by D. E. C. Eversley: "Engineering and Railway Works" in *V. C. H.*, Wiltshire, Vol. iv, ed. R. B. Pugh and Elizabeth Crittall (1959); "The Great Western Railway and the Great Depression", *Birmingham Historical Journal*, v (1957); the third is by Kenneth Hudson, "The early years of the railway community in Swindon" *Transport History*, i (1968). See also H. B. Wells, "Swindon in the 19th and 20th Centuries" in *Studies in the History of Swindon*, ed. L. V. Grinsell and others (1950). Two valuable studies of seaside towns made prosperous by railways are: E. W. Gilbert, *Brighton: Old Ocean's Bauble* (1954); D. S. Young, *The Story of Bournemouth* (1957). J. A. R. Pimlott, *The Englishman's Holiday* (1947) deals with the general contribution of the railways to leisure pursuits, including excursions, but on this topic there are two commemorative studies of Thomas Cook, the travel agent: W. F. Rae, *The Business of Travel* (1891); and John Pudney, *The Thomas Cook Story* (1953). For some impression of the impact of the railways on the holiday industry, see the guide published by Walter Hill & Company, *The Holidays, 1898: Where to Stay and What to See* (1898). For further references to the enormous literature of urban history, into which the influence of the railways enters at so many points, see H. J. Dyos (ed.), *The Study of Urban History* (1968), especially Chapter 1. On some of the particular social repercussions of railways in London, see also the articles by the same author: "Railways and Housing in Victorian London", *Journal of Transport History*, ii (1955); "Some Social Costs of Railway Building in London", *ibid.*, iii (1957); "The Slums of Victorian London", *Victorian Studies*, xi (1967), which includes an extensive bibliography. For a different kind of impact, that on the reading public, see Kathleen Tillotson, *The Novels of the Eighteen-Forties* (2nd ed., 1956). As an example of contemporary observation of the influence of building and running railways in a particular community, there is Earl of Bessborough (ed.), *Lady Charlotte Guest: Extracts from Her Journal, 1833–1852* (1950), which concerns Merthyr Tydfil. The topography of the railways can only be followed adequately with the aid of the Deposited Plans, but Edward Churton, *The Railroad Book of England* (1851) provides at least a view of the country through which they passed, and the various editions of *Bradshaw's Tours* around the same date do likewise. The Ordnance Survey, which had covered the whole country by 1870 (and is now being reprinted commercially), is indispensable if railways are to be followed on the ground, especially the modern one-inch maps—though there are snags about these which Professor Simmons explains in the appendix to his *The Railways of Britain*, along with other words of advice about finding one's way about British railways.

Charles E. Lee, *Passenger Class Distinctions* (1946) deals with the relative comforts and costs of going by rail; and H. J. Dyos, "Workmen's Fares in South London, 1860–1914", *Journal of Transport History*, i (1953) follows this up in more detail. On tourism there is a chapter in L. J. Lickorish and A. G. Kershaw, *The Travel Guide* (1958). But to discover what it was really like to travel on steam trains, it is necessary to go to museums or to apply the methods of the industrial archaeologist. On museums, see Jack Simmons' *Transport Museums* (1969). On the methods of industrial archaeology, see J. P. M. Pannell, *The Techniques of Industrial Archaeology* (1966)—a book by an engineer who remembered his railway days. It has a good bibliography.

7   Railways and the transport system

Hardly anything has been written specifically on the impact of the railways on other forms of transport beyond the more general works already mentioned in the last few sections. Jackman, Pratt and Clapham are of special value in this respect, and there is a useful discussion of the relative advantages of roads, canals, and railways in the carriage of goods in A. W. Kirkaldy and A. D. Evans, *The History and Economics of Transport* [1915]. Among contemporary writings there were some that did deal with these matters, such as Henry Wilson, *Hints to Road Speculators, together with the Influence Railroads will have upon Society* (1845); and William Sheardown, *The Great North Road and the Great Northern Railway* [1863]. But more generally these questions arose only by implication in the general advocacy of railways or in discussions of their failings, and of these the following give a good idea: T. Gray, *Observations on a General Iron Rail-Way* (1820) and four later editions; Henry Fairbairn, *A Treatise on the Political Economy of Railroads* (1836); James Morrison, *The Influence of English Railway Legislation on Trade and Industry* (1848); Robert Ritchie, *Railways; Their Rise, Progress and Construction* (1946); F. S. Williams, *Our Iron Roads* (7th ed., 1888); W. Bridges Adams, *Roads and Rails* (1862); William Galt, *Railway Reform: Its Importance and Practicability considered as affecting the Nation, the Shareholders, and the Government* (1865), which provides a valuable critique of high-cost railways.

The main place in which to look for the reaction of other transport interests to the railways is not in the published literature of the railways but in the unpublished minutes of the select committees examining railway bills, and there is no way of reaching these without research. More explicitly, there is a certain amount in the printed *Parliamentary Papers*, among which the following are the most important reports and returns. On turnpikes: Select Committee on Turnpike Returns, *Parl. Papers*, 1833 (422,703), xv; Select Committee on Turnpike Trusts & Tolls, *Parl. Papers*, 1836 (547), xix— which considered the expediency of abolishing the tolls; Select Committee on the Formation of Railroads and their Effect on the Interests of Turnpike Trusts, *Parl. Papers*, 1839 (295), ix; Royal Commission on the State of the Roads in England and Wales, *Parl. Papers*, 1840 (256), xxvii; County Reports of the Secretary of State [on Kent, Surrey, Sussex, and Hampshire roads only], *Parl. Papers*, 1851 (1376), xlviii, 1852 (1458-9, 1521), xliv; Select Committee on Abolition of Turnpike Trusts, *Parl. Papers*, 1864 (383), ix. On canals: Return from Inland Navigation and Canal Companies in England and Wales, *Parl. Papers*, 1870, lvi; Select Committee on Canals, *Parl. Papers*, 1883 (252), xiii; Returns relating to Canals and Navigations in United Kingdom, for 1888, *Parl. Papers*, 1890, lxiv; Royal Commission on the Canals and Inland Navigations of the United Kingdom, 1906-11, *Parl. Papers*, 1906 (Cd. 3183-4), xxxii, xxxiii; 1907 (Cd. 3716-19), xxxiii; 1909 (Cd. 4839-41), xiii; 1910 (Cd. 4979, 5083, 5204), xii; 1910 (Cd. 5447, 5653), xiii. On railway amalgamations and absorption of canals there are three sets of papers: Select Committee on Amalgamations, *Parl. Papers*, 1846, (200, 275), xiii; Select Committee on Railway Amalgamation, *Parl. Papers*, 1852-3 (79, 170, 246, 310, 736), xxxviii; Joint Select Committee on Amalgamation of Railway Companies, *Parl. Papers*, 1872 (364), xii.

For coach and wagon services, see John Copeland, *Roads and Their Traffic, 1750-1850* (1968), which includes a particularly informative chapter on steam carriages; on this there is also the authoritative monograph by C. St C. B. Davison, *History of Steam Road Vehicles*, (HMSO, 1953). It is also worth noting R. W. Kidner, *The Early History of the Motor Car, 1769-1897* (1946). All other references may be taken from Section 2 of this bibliography. Street and commercial directories yield a great deal of information on road traffic, but virtually no calculations have been made of the scale of this traffic for any part of the country in the railway period, nor has the economic history of road services been more than broached. The directory used here by way of example is *Robson's London Directory and Street Key for 1835*. There is an interesting evaluation of the rôle of Pickford's in E. Halfpenny, "Pickford's: Expansion and Crisis in the Early Nineteenth Century", *Business History*, i (1958-9). G. C. Dickinson, "Stage-Coach Services in the West Riding of Yorkshire between 1830 and 1840", *Journal of Transport History*, iv (1959), discusses most helpfully the impact of the Leeds & Selby Railway on local coach services. On the means of provisioning towns, some useful hints are given in T. C. Barker, J. C. Mackenzie and J. Yudkin (eds.), *Our Changing Fare* (1966); and expanded by Janet Blackman, "The Food Supply of an Industrial Town: A Study of Sheffield's Public Markets, 1780–1900", *Business History*, v (1963). The only Royal Commission ever to have investigated the communications and to a very limited extent the supply lines of a city is the Royal Commission on London Traffic, 1905–6, *Parl. Papers*, 1905 (Cd. 2597), xxx; 1906 (Cd. 2751–2, 2798, 2987), xl, xlii, xliii, xliv. This deals with every form of transport at a moment of transition from old to newer forms of locomotion and contains numerous short histories of them; it also contains some material on other cities, as for example the tramways of Liverpool. The main substance of the *Report* may be supplemented by the searchingly statistical *Annual Reports of the London Traffic Branch to the Board of Trade*. For many years exceptional in its coverage of urban transport, G. A. Sekon, *Locomotion in Victorian London* (1938), is now being superseded by T. C. Barker and Michael Robbins. *A History of London Transport*, Vol. i: *The Nineteenth Century* (1963), which provides a more complete picture of the whole range of urban communications in one place than can be found anywhere. W. Ashworth discerns various types of suburban development on the eastern edge of London and indicates the rôle which communications played in this in his contribution to the *V.C.H.*, Essex, Vol. v (1966), the essence of which is also available as a chapter entitled "Types of Social and Economic Development in Suburban Essex" in Centre for Urban Studies Report No. 3, *London: Aspects of Change* (1964). Harold Pollins also writes with some insight in this volume on "Transport Lines and Social Divisions". The same theme comes through in W. Ashworth, *The Genesis of Modern British Town Planning* (1954). For a detailed account of the way urban transport fulfilled its rôle in the spread of suburbia, see H. J. Dyos, *Victorian Suburb: A Study of the Growth of Camberwell* (1961). A more general study of considerable value in this respect is J. T. Coppock and Hugh C. Prince, *Greater London* (1964). D. A. Reeder, "A Theatre of Suburbs: Some Patterns of Development in West London, 1801–1911" in H. J. Dyos (ed.), *The Study of Urban History* (1968), relates transport developments very pertinently to other social changes. See also Michael Robbins, *Middlesex* (1953). For an analysis—perhaps the first of its kind—of traffic flows, it is still useful to return to G. Kemmann, *Der Verkehr Londons* (1892). Another foreigner's view, this time of classic quality, is offered by S. E. Rasmussen, *London, The Unique City* (2nd ed., 1948). For the more general contribution of railways to urban development, see Asa Briggs, *Victorian Cities* (revised edition 1968). The best portrait of an individual city is still Asa Briggs' *History of Birmingham*, Vol. II: *Borough and City, 1865–1938* (1952), in which the railways and street improvements are assigned their historical rôles with real discernment. A brief but valuable synopsis of Manchester's development in which transport figures importantly is W. H. Chaloner, "The Birth of Modern Manchester" in the British Association volume, *Manchester and Its Region* (1962).

The development of commuting is best approached through K. K. Liepmann, *The Journey to Work: Its Significance for Industrial and Community Life* (1944). Several travel surveys are now available to supplement it in detail: J. Westergaard, "Journeys to Work in the London Region", *Town Planning Review*, xxviii (1957–8); R. Lawton, "The Daily Journey to Work in England and Wales", *ibid.*, xxix (1959). Note, incidentally, the London Transport Executive, *London Travel Surveys* (1950, 1956) and *"Crush-Hour" Travel in Central London* (HMSO, 1958).

The literature on the means of commuting is now growing very fast, largely under somewhat antiquarian stimuli, but the following all have value either as general surveys, technical histories or as local studies of public transport: H. C. Moore, *Omnibuses and Cabs* (1902); C. F. Klapper, *The Golden Age of Tramways* (1961); John Hibbs, *The History of British Bus Services* (1968); C. E. Lee, *The Horse Bus as a Vehicle* (1962), *The Early Motor Bus* (1962); John Tilling, *Kings of the Highway* (1957); J. E. Ritchie, *Here and There in London* (1859) —for the economics of bus operation in Victorian London; *London General: The Story of the London Bus, 1856–1956* (1956); O. J. Morris, *Fares, Please: The Story of London's Road Transport* (1953); G. F. A. Wilmot, *The Railway in Finchley* (1962); C. E. Lee, "The English Street Tramways of George Francis Train", *Journal of Transport History*, i (1953); Wingate H. Bett and John C. Gillham, *Great British Tramway Networks* (4th ed., 1967)—a record of every tramway, and light railway ever planned, constructed, or operated; D. K. Clark, *Tramways: Their Construction and Working* (2nd ed., 1894); G. P. Rippon, *Street Railways in London* (1860); W. W. Duncan, *Duncan's Manual of British and Foreign Tramway Companies* (11th issue, 1888)—a valuable synopsis of financial and operating data; A. B. Hopkins, *Tramway Legislation in England* (1891)—an annotated list of Acts, Orders, and provincial undertakings owned by municipal corporations; P. W. Gentry, *The Tramways of the West of England* (1952); J. S. Webb, *The Tramways of the Black Country* (1954); S. E. Harrison, *The Tramways of Portsmouth* (1955); D. L. Thomson, *A Handbook of Glasgow Tramways* (1962); Ian Yearsley, *The Manchester Tram* (1962); D. L. G. Hunter, *Edinburgh's Transport* (1964); "Rodinglea", *The Tramways of East London* (1967); Allan A. Jackson and Desmond F. Croome, *Rails Through the Clay* (1962); Hugh Douglas, *The Underground Story* (1963); H. F. Howson, *London's Underground* (4th ed., 1967). For full details of the scope and operation of all forms of public transport in one large city at a single moment in time there is nothing better than the London County Council report, *Locomotive Service* (1895), of which the second part comprises a comprehensive map, redrawn in this volume as Map 15.

On street improvement, there is a complete compendium of schemes carried out under the M.B.W. and early L.C.C. in P. J. Edwards, *History of London Street Improvements, 1855–97* (1898), which may be supplemented by two unofficial commentaries on the way things were going: H. Clarke, *London Street Improvements* (1892); and A. Cawston, *A Comprehensive Scheme for Street Improvements in London* (1893). Sir Laurence Gomme, *London in the Reign of Victoria* (1898) has a useful chapter on this. For the relationship between the historical development of the street pattern and present planning possibilities, see *The City of London: A Record of Destruction and Survival* (1951), a report of the Improvements and Town Planning Committee of the Corporation of London. Ralph Turvey, *The Economics of Real Property* (1957) includes an excellent analysis of the financial difficulties of carrying out street improvement, then or since. For Corporation Street, Birmingham, see Briggs, *History of Birmingham*.

8 Development of overseas shipping

The published material on the shipping industry is almost as prodigious as that for the railways, but again much of it is of poor quality as far as the economic historian is concerned. There is still no definitive history of the nineteenth century but the following three works provide useful introductory reading: C. E. Fayle, *A Short History of the World's Shipping Industry* (1933); A. W. Kirkaldy, *British Shipping* (1914); and R. H. Thornton, *British Shipping* (1945 edition). Statistical data is presented in a convenient form by A. P. Usher, "The Growth of English Shipping", *Quarterly Journal of Economics*, xlii (1927–28). The trade side has received better attention; see in particular A. H. Imlah, *Economic Elements in the Pax Britannica* (1958).

For a more comprehensive treatment of individual topics the reader is obliged to refer to the more specialized texts. The impact of the navigation laws on English shipping is dealt with thoroughly by L. A. Harper, *The English Navigation Laws* (1939). There is a voluminous literature on technical developments. See in particular E. C. Smith, *A Short History of Naval and Marine Engineering* (1937); C. E. Gibson, *The Story of the Ship* (1958); and H. Moyse-Bartlett, *From Sail to Steam* (Historical Association pamphlet, 1946). The competition between sail and steam is analysed by G. S. Graham, "The Ascendancy of the Sailing Ship, 1850-85", *Economic History Review*, ix (1956–57). For technical progress in early steamship construction and the re-interpretation of some traditional views see J. R. T. Hughes and Stanley Reiter, "The First 1945 British Steamships", *The Journal of the American Statistical Association*, liii (1958). The most up-to-date material on the construction of ships, costs and shipbuilding in general can be found in K. Maywald, "The Construction Costs and the Value of the British Merchant Fleet, 1850–1938", *Scottish Journal of Political Economy*, iii (1956); and the work by S. Pollard "The Economic History of British Shipbuilding, 1870-1914", unpublished Ph.D. thesis (University of London, 1951); "Laissez-Faire and Shipbuilding", *Economic History Review*, v (1952–53); and "British and World Shipbuilding: A Study in Comparative Costs, 1890–1914, *Journal of Economic History*, xvii (1957). The Scottish side is surveyed briefly in R. H. Campbell, "Scottish Shipbuilding: Its Rise and Progress", *Scottish Geographical Magazine*, lxxx (1964). The question of subsidies is covered quite adequately by R. Meeker, *History of Shipping Subsidies* (1905).

The contribution of shipping to economic development is a subject which has attracted attention in recent years. D. C. North, "Ocean Freight Rates and Economic Development, 1750–1913, *Journal of Economic History*, xviii (1958);

and M. E. Fletcher, "The Suez Canal and World Shipping, 1869–1914", *ibid.*, xviii (1958) provide the general background. The following more specialized studies should also be consulted: R. G. Albion, "British Shipping and Latin America, 1806–1914", *Journal of Economic History*, xi (1951); K. H. Burley, "The Overseas Trade in New South Wales Coal and the British Shipping Industry, 1860–1914", *The Economic Record*, xxxvi (1960) and F. E. Hyde, "The Expansion of Liverpool's Carrying Trade with the Far East and Australia, 1860–1914", *Transactions of the Royal Historical Society*, vi (1956), and "British Shipping Companies in East and South-East Asia, 1860–1939", in C. D. Cowan (ed.), *The Economic Development of South-East Asia* (1964). A. H. Imlah, *Economic Elements in the Pax Britannica* (1958) shows how important shipping was as regards the British balance of payments.

The literature on coastal shipping is very scanty and the following sources can by no means be regarded as satisfactory: R. Smith, *Sea-Coal for London* (1961); Anon., *The Coastwise Trade of the United Kingdom Past and Present and its Possibilities* (1925); *The Isle of Man Steam Packet Co. Ltd.,: Centenary, 1830–1930* (1930); G. E. Farr, *West Country Passenger Steamers* (1956); "Coastwise Lines of Great Britain", *The Times Shipping Number* (1913); and P. T. Wheeler, "The Development of Shipping Services to the East Coast of Sutherland", *Journal of Transport History*, vi (1963). Port and dock developments have also been neglected by the historian. The only statistical study of investment is A. G. Kenwood, "Port Investment in England and Wales, 1851–1913", *Yorkshire Bulletin of Economic and Social Research*, xvii (1965) but the data need to be used with caution since they are in current prices. Sir Douglas Owen's *Ports and Docks* (1904) and Sir David Owen's *The Origin and Development of the Ports of the United Kingdom* (2nd ed. 1948) provide the general background. There are however quite a number of studies of individual ports though many of them are of poor quality. For London the standard history is Sir Joseph Broodbank, *History of the Port of London* (2 vols. 1921). Shorter accounts are by Sir David Owen, *The Port of London: Yesterday and Today* (1927); Sir Arthur Bryant, *Liquid History: To Commemorate Fifty Years of the Port of London Authority, 1909–1959* (1960); and L. Ford, "The Development of the Port of London", *Journal of the Royal Society of Arts* (1959). Sources for some of the other larger ports are as follows: J. Deas, *The River Clyde* (1876)—from which Map 18 in this book has been derived; W. F. Macarthur, *History of the Port of Glasgow* (1932); W. F. Robertson, "History of the River Clyde and the Port of Glasgow", *Dock and Harbour Authority* (1949); and "The Port of Glasgow: Review of Developments over the Last 200 years", *Ibid.* (1959–60); J. E. Allison, "The Development of Merseyside and the Port of Liverpool", *Town Planning Review*, xxiv (1953–54); Mersey Docks and Harbour Board, *Business in Great Waters* (1958); S. Mountfield, *Western Gateway: A History of the Mersey Docks and Harbour Board* (1965); R. P. Biddle, "The Port of Southampton", *Journal of the Institute of Transport* (1939); C. Wells, *A Short History of the Port of Bristol* (1909); W. H. Jones, *History of the Port of Swansea* (1922); and E. L. Chappel, *History of the Port of Cardiff* (1939). Useful descriptive material on the rôle of the railway in dock development is presented in

The Jubilee of the Railway News (1914). A good case study of the rôle of the railways in port development is that of Barrow which has been examined in some detail in S. Pollard and J. D. Marshall, "The Furness Railway and the Growth of Barrow", *Journal of Transport History*, i (1953) and S. Pollard, "Barrow-in-Furness and the Seventh Duke of Devonshire", *Economic History Review*, viii (1955).

9 Organization and profits of British shipping

There is no handy guide to the changes in the organization of British shipping. Much of the material presented in this chapter has been drawn from scattered sources. Some general comments on this aspect can be found in American texts: C. E. McDowell and H. M. Gibbs, *Ocean Transportation* (1954); H. C. Calvin and E. G. Stuart, *The Merchant Shipping Industry* (1925); and E. R. Johnson and G. C. Huebner, *Principles of Ocean Transportation* (1918). Fayle's *Short History of the World's Shipping Industry* (1933) summarizes the main changes. A. G. Course, *The Deep Sea Tramp* (1960) has useful comments on the history of some well-known companies. This should be read in conjunction with E. S. Gregg's "The Decline of Tramp Shipping", *Quarterly Journal of Economics*, xl (1926). A fairly comprehensive survey of the organization and structure of British shipping before 1914 is given in the *Report of the Departmental Committee on Shipping and Shipbuilding after the War*, Cd. 9092 (1918).

The best way of understanding the evolution of company structure is probably by studying company histories but unfortunately there are very few first-class ones available. F. E. Hyde's *Blue Funnel* (1957) and *Shipping Enterprise and Management 1830–1939: Harrisons of Liverpool* (1967) are exceptions and deserve close study. A further volume from the same stable also deserves careful study, S. Marriner and F. E. Hyde, *The Senior: John Samuel Swire 1825–98: The Management of Far Eastern Trade* (1967). This is in fact a complementary volume to Hyde's *Blue Funnel*. Though not of the same high standard, M. Murray, *Union-Castle Chronicle 1853–1953* (1953) and B. Cable, *A Hundred Years of the P. & O., 1837–1937* (1937) contain some useful material. For the 64th system see R. C. Jarvis, "Fractional Shareholding in British Merchant Ships, with Special Reference to the 64ths", *Mariner's Mirror*, xliv (1959). On the ownership and finance of shipping companies very little has been written though relevant comments can be found in most works. However, for the early years of the nineteenth century there is F. Neal, *Liverpool Shipping 1815–1835*, unpublished M.A. thesis, (University of Liverpool, 1962) which contains much useful information. The close connection between shipowning and trading is described in some detail by D. M. Williams, "Merchanting in the First Half of the Nineteenth Century: The Liverpool Timber Trade", *Business History*, viii (1966).

The standard work on freight rates still remains L. Isserlis, "Tramp Shipping Cargoes and Freights", *Journal of Royal Statistical Society*, ci (1938).

D. C. North, "Ocean Freight Rates and Economic Development 1750–1913", *Journal of Economic History*, xviii (1958) should also be consulted. E. A. V. Angier, *Fifty Years of Freight, 1869–1919* (1920) provides a year by year commentary on the freight market. Volumes 3 and 4 of W. S. Lindsay's *History of Merchant Shipping and Ancient Commerce* (1876) contain scattered references on company profits but for the most part the files of the shipping journal *Fairplay* have to be resorted to for this aspect. One individual study of note is that by T. E. Milne, "British Shipping in the Nineteenth Century: A Study of the Ben Line Papers" in P. L. Payne (ed.), *Studies in Scottish Business History* (1967). Fluctuations and profitability are dealt with generally by F. C. James, *Cyclical Fluctuations in the Shipping and Shipbuilding Industries* (1927); E. S. Gregg, "Vicissitudes in the Shipping Trade 1870–1920", *Quarterly Journal of Economics*, xxxv (1921); and D. H. Aldcroft, "The Depression in British Shipping, 1901–1911", *Journal of Transport History*, vii (1965).

The Conference system has not received the attention it deserves. D. H. Macgregor, "Shipping Conferences", *Economic Journal*, xix (1909) is mainly a commentary on the Royal Commission on Shipping Rings (1909), the evidence and reports of which still provide the best treatment of the subject available. Some valuable comments of an historical nature can be found in D. Marx, *International Shipping Cartels: A Study of Industrial Self-Regulation by Shipping Conferences* (1953). C. Leubuscher, *The West African Shipping Trade, 1909–1959* (1963) also contains interesting material on the workings of the conference system in that particular trade. Passenger pools have been completely ignored by British historians and the material presented in this chapter has been drawn largely from German sources. Details about foreign competition can be obtained from W. L. Hichens, "Anglo-Japanese Competition in the Shipping Trade", *International Affairs*, xviii (1939); and the *Report of the Select Committee on Steamship Subsidies* (H.M.S.O., 1902). The impact of German competition on British shipping is covered by D. H. Aldcroft, "The Mercantile Marine", in D. H. Aldcroft (ed.), *The Development of British Industry and Foreign Competition, 1875–1914* (1968) which also contains a discussion of the neglected subject of passenger pools.

10   Transport under wartime conditions

There is a fairly extensive literature dealing with the rôle of transport in the First World War. The standard work on shipping is C. E. Fayle, *The War and the Shipping Industry* (1927). This should be read in conjunction with J. A. Salter, *Allied Shipping Control* (1921), which covers the international aspects of the question. J. Russel Smith, *Influence of the Great War Upon Shipping* (1919) should also be consulted. A convenient summary of the steps taken to control shipping can be found in S. J. Hurwitz, *State Intervention in Great Britain* (1949), chap. xi; whilst chap. iii of S. G. Sturmey's *British Shipping and World Competition*

(1962) provides a very good account of the effects of war on Britain's maritime industry. The standard text on the railways is still E. A. Pratt's *British Railways and the Great War* (2 vols. 1921). But though comprehensive and reliable, Pratt's work has the obvious defect of being far too long and readers might do well to consult first the relevant section in F. H. Dixon and J. H. Parmelee, *War Administration of the Railways in the United States and Great Britain* (1918). The problems of coastal shipping are examined in D. H. Aldcroft, "The Eclipse of British Coastal Shipping, 1913–21", *Journal of Transport History*, vi (1963). The only easily accessible information on canals is in C. Hadfield, *British Canals* (1959).

Some of the volumes mentioned above also cover the events of the immediate post-war period. But for a more recent treatment of the problem of reconstruction see D. H. Aldcroft, "The Decontrol of British Shipping and Railways after the First World War", *Journal of Transport History*, v (1961), and "Port Congestion and the Shipping Boom of 1919–20", *Business History*, iii (1961). Information about the railway legislation of 1921 and its effects can be found in W. M. Acworth, "Grouping under the Railways Act, 1921", *Economic Journal*, xxxiii (1923); C. E. R. Sherrington, "Some Economic Results of the British Railways Act of 1921", *American Economic Review*, xiv (1924); H. C. Kidd, *A New Era for British Railways* (1929); W. E. Simnett, *Railway Amalgamation in Great Britain* (1923). A very useful survey of the long-term consequences of the 1921 legislation is given by W. G. Scott, "An Aspect of the British Railways Act, 1921", in H. A. Innis (ed.), *Essays in Transportation in Honour of W. T. Jackman* (1941, University of Toronto Press).

11   Railways and shipping in the inter-war years

A handy account of the problems of the railways in the inter-war years can be found in C. I. Savage, *An Economic History of Transport* (1959), chap. v; K. H. Johnston, *British Railways and Economic Recovery* (1949) provides more background material but is far less reliable. *British Railways in Transition* (1968) by D. H. Aldcroft analyses the problems of the railways and brings the story up to date. K. G. Fenelon, "British Railways Since the War", *Journal of the Royal Statistical Society*, xcvi (1933), provides a valuable statistical study of the railways up to the early 1930s and there is also some useful data in International Union of Railways, *The Main Line Railways of Great Britain, 1923–1930* (1931). However, there is no survey which covers the whole of the period and it is necessary, therefore, to consult the official *Railway Returns* (Ministry of Transport) for a complete run of figures. These should be used carefully since the basis of compilation was changed at least twice during the period and the data are not strictly comparable with those for the pre-war period.

There are a number of contemporary works on railways which are worth consulting though they are not always very accurate about financial and economic matters. The more useful include A. Brown, *The Railway Problem* (1932); K. G. Fenelon, *Railway Economics* (1932) and *British Railways Today* (1939), both of which are fairly reliable; W. J. Stevens, *The Future of British Railways* (1938), though the reader should be warned that this book is very misleading about financial aspects; C. Stuart-Williams and E. Short, *Railways, Roads and the Public* (1939); and W. V. Wood and J. Stamp, *Railways* (1928).

A good study on the relationship between trade and transport is that by T. Hultgren, *Transport and the State of Trade in Britain* (1953, Occasional Paper 40, National Bureau of Economic Research, New York). Earlier studies covering a similar field were made by C. D. Campbell, "Cyclical Fluctuations in the Railway Industry", *Transactions of the Manchester Statistical Society* (1929–30) and in greater detail in his *British Railways in Boom and Depression: An Essay in Trade Fluctuations and Their Effects, 1878–1930* (1932).

Finance and pricing policy of the railways have been covered quite well. T. Watson Collin, "Railway Finance in the Light of the Railways Act, 1921", *The Accountant*, lxxxvi (1932) provides a very good survey of the financial side. Two very useful contributions on pricing of railway services are G. Walker, *Road and Rail* (2nd. ed., 1947); and A. M. Milne and A. Laing, *The Obligation to Carry* (1956). The first of these is especially valuable since it deals with the whole question of competition between the railways and road transport in a very scholarly manner. Other useful studies include: E. J. Broster, "Railway Passenger Receipts and Fares Policy", *Economic Journal*, xlvii (1947), and "Variability of Railway Operating Costs", *ibid.*, xlviii (1938); A. A. Harrison, "Railway Freight Charges", *Journal of the Institute of Transport*, July 1957; G. J. Ponsonby, "Freight Charges by Road in Competition", *Economic Journal*, xlviii (1938); W. V. Wood, "The Problem of Railway Charges", *Journal of the Institute of Transport*, May, 1936 and "Some Aspects of Railway Finance", *ibid.*, Nov. 1936. The legal disabilities of the railways in relation to pricing policy are discussed in most of the above studies.

Changes in technical progress have not been dealt with very satisfactorily. There are many books on locomotives and related aspects but few of these bring out the significance of changes in techniques. Probably the most useful is C. J. Allen's *Locomotive Practice and Performance in the Twentieth Century* (1949) though it is far from being ideal. Useful surveys of electric traction can be found in the Electric Traction Supplement of the *Railway Gazette*, 18 August 1939 and in E. C. Cox, "The Progress of Southern Railway Electrification", *Journal of the Institute of Transport*, Jan. 1937. An analysis of the factors influencing the rate at which diesel and electric traction were applied is given by D. H. Aldcroft, "Innovation on the Railways: the Lag in Diesel and Electric Traction", *Journal of Transport Economics and Policy*, iii (1969). A useful article on improvements in railway services is that by S. H. Fisher, "Acceleration of Railway Services", *Journal of the Institute of Transport*, Feb. 1939. But by far the most valuable is the article by W. L. Waters, "Rationalisation of British Railways", a paper presented to the American Society of Mechanical

EE

Engineers in May 1938. This attempts to measure changes in the efficiency of railway working since 1913.

With the regrouping most company histories terminate in 1923 though in recent years an attempt has been made to examine the post-war problems of the railways from a regional angle. The Southern Railway has received most attention. Two volumes deserving attention are those by G. T. Moody, *Southern Electric* (4th ed. 1968) and H. P. White, *A Regional History of the Railways of Great Britain*, Vol. II, *Southern England* (1961).

The shipping industry's problems are analysed vigorously in S. G. Sturmey's controversial book *British Shipping and World Competition* (1962), especially ch. IV; and L. Jones, *Shipbuilding in Britain—Mainly Between the Two World Wars* (1957) is helpful, for it deals with the problem from the shipbuilding side. Scottish shipbuilding has recently been examined by N. K. Buxton, "The Scottish Shipbuilding Industry Between the Wars: A Comparative Study", *Business History*, x (1968), though it does not add a great deal to existing knowledge about the industry. Tramp shipping, a rather neglected topic, is covered briefly in H. Gripaios, *Tramp Shipping* (1959); and E. S. Gregg, "The Decline of Tramp Shipping", *Quarterly Journal of Economics*, xl (1926). A thorough statistical analysis of the decline in Britain's seaborne trade has been made by H. Leak, "The Carrying Trade of British Shipping", *Journal of the Royal Statistical Society*, cii (1939). A useful survey of the main trends is given by P. Jaffé, "World Trade and British Shipping", in M. Abrams (ed.), *Britain and Her Export Trade* (1946). D. L. McLachlan gives a brief sketch of the conference system in "The Conference System Since 1919", *Business History*, iii (1961). For an excellent study of one particular trade readers should consult K. H. Burley, *British Shipping and Australia, 1920–1939* (1968).

12   The development of motorized transport

Motor transport has not received much attention from economic historians. There is no modern authoritative history of the road transport industry. Probably the most handy introduction is in C. I. Savage, *An Economic History of Transport* (1959), chaps. vi and vii. For the passenger side there is the recent volume by J. Hibbs, *The History of British Bus Services* (1968), but this is very inadequate and gives no indication of the growth dimensions of the industry. Road haulage, however, has been completely neglected. A number of general surveys are available but they tend to be of a rather chatty nature and occasionally inaccurate in detail. Moreover, they concentrate mainly on the passenger side. Among the most important are C. T. Brunner, *Road versus Rail: The Case for Motor Transport* (1929); C. D. Buchanan, *Mixed Blessing: The Motor in Britain* (1958); and L. A. G. Strong, *The Rolling Road: The Story of Travel on the Roads of Britain and the Development of Public Passenger Transport* (1956). A short historical account can also be found in the *Final Report of the Royal*

Commission on Transport, Cmd. 3751 (1931). The whole field of London Transport will be surveyed by T. C. Barker and M. Robbins in the second volume of their *A History of London Transport*. Some may wish to supplement their reading by looking at the manufacturing side. Here again the literature is not vast but two works in particular are worth mentioning: S. B. Saul, "The Motor Industry in Britain to 1914", *Business History*, v (1962); and P. L. Cook and R. Cohen, *Effects of Mergers* (1958), chap. v.

Statistical data on road transport operations is not very plentiful and, indeed, is almost non-existent for road haulage. Estimates of the number of passenger miles travelled and average fares charged on public passenger transport undertakings can be found in J. R. Stone and D. A. Rowe, *The Measurement of Consumers' Expenditure and Behaviour in the United Kingdom, 1920–1938*, Vol. II (1966). These estimates do not, of course, include journeys made in private cars, for which there are no figures. Capital formation in road transport is given in C. H. Feinstein, *Domestic Capital Formation in the United Kingdom, 1920–1938* (1965); whilst employment data can be found in the companion volume by A. L. Chapman and R. Knight, *Wages and Salaries in the United Kingdom, 1920–1938* (1953). These three volumes published by Cambridge University Press provide the statistical background to the study of inter-war transport as a whole and cannot afford to be ignored. In addition, there is some very useful statistical information on roads and road transport in *Basic Road Statistics* published annually by the British Road Federation.

The problem of regulating road transport has received more attention than the early development of the industry. On the passenger side D. N. Chester's *Public Control of Road Passenger Transport* (1936) is still indispensable, but for a more recent critical account see J. Hibbs, *Transport for Passengers* (Hobart Paper 23, 1963). The restriction of road haulage is covered by G. Walker in his scholarly volume *Road and Rail* (2nd ed. 1947). For a reinterpretation of the basis which determined the licensing of the 1930s see P. E. Hart, "The Restriction of Road Haulage", *Scottish Journal of Political Economy*, vi (1959). Even so, much of the information on the regulation of road transport has to be drawn from the *Reports* of the Licensing Authorities and Traffic Commissioners. Unlike most official reports these are often quite entertaining to read and they contain a great deal of information on the size and structure of the road transport industry, especially the passenger side, and on many other aspects of the industry.

There is a number of sources on road and rail competition and the question of co-ordination of inland transport. Apart from Walker's study cited above and the article by G. J. Ponsonby, "Freight Charges by Road in Competition", *Economic Journal*, xlviii (1938), the following sources should be consulted: H. O. Mance, *The Road and Rail Transport Problem* (1940); the Transport Advisory Council's *Report on Services and Rates* (H.M.S.O., 1937); C. Hurcomb, "The Co-ordination of Transport in Great Britain during the Years 1935–1944", *Journal of the Institute of Transport*, May-June 1945; and C. F.

Klapper, "Co-ordination—Cliché or Key to Progress?", *Institute of Transport Journal*, Mar. 1963.

Very little has been written about the social and economic impact of motor transport, except for the studies on suburban development. W. Ashworth shows the relationship between transport and suburban development in one particular region in his "Types of Social and Economic Development in Suburban Essex", in *London: Aspects of Change* (1964), edited by the Centre for Urban Studies. The relationships between building, transport and suburban growth are analysed in a wider context in H. W. Richardson and D. H. Aldcroft, *Building in the British Economy Between the Wars* (1968), chap. xiv. Useful background material on population movements and suburban development can be found in W. Ashworth, *The Genesis of Modern British Town Planning* (1954), and the *Report of the Royal Commission on the Distribution of Industrial Population*, Cmd. 6153 (1939-40).

Traffic congestion became a problem in the 1930s and gave rise to serious discussion. The extent of the problem was not measured very accurately, however, though most contemporary writings, for example, A. G. Pool, *A Survey of Transport in Sheffield* (1933), and Sir Charles Bressey's *Report on London Traffic* (1938) claimed that it was very acute especially in large cities. Since then there has been little serious study of the pre-war situation because the current problem has overshadowed that of earlier years. For the development of the road system and the failure to keep pace with the growth in traffic see *The King's Highway* (1949), the semi-autobiographical account by Rees Jeffreys. S. and B. Webb provide the nineteenth-century background in *English Local Government: The Story of the King's Highway* (1920). G. C. Gurnock, *New Roads for Britain* (1944); and G. Walker, "Highway Finance", *Journal of Industrial Economics*, June 1956, should also be consulted.

The following works dealing with particular aspects covered in the chapter on motor transport will also be found useful. J. Sleeman, "The Rise and Decline of Municipal Transport", *Scottish Journal of Political Economy*, ix (1962); J. M. Cummings, *The Rise and Decline of the Railway Bus* (1958); C. Klapper, *The Golden Age of Tramways* (1961); E. S. Shrapnell-Smith, "Five Decades of Commercial Road Transport with Inferences about its Future", *Journal of the Institute of Transport*, Feb.-Mar. 1946; R. Fulford, *Five Decades of B.E.T.: The Story of the British Electric Traction Company* (1946); and W. J. Crosland-Taylor, *Crosville: The Sowing and the Harvest* (1948).

13   The birth of civil aviation

The experiments in flying powered machines before 1914 can be followed in I. Edwards and F. Timms, *Commercial Air Transport* (1926), ch. i; and P. W. Brooks "Aeronautics", ch. xvii in *A History of Technology*, Vol. V. (1958), ed. C. Singer *et alia*.

The definitive history of commercial aviation still awaits an author. R. Higham's *Britain's Imperial Air Routes 1918 to 1939* (1960) provides a detailed account of Imperial Airways but tends to concentrate too much on political aspects. W. E. Wynn, *Civil Air Transport* (1945), is useful but limited in scope. There are however a number of very useful articles dealing with particular aspects of international aviation. Eric Birkhead's "The Financial Failure of British Air Transport Companies, 1919–24", *Journal of Transport History*, iv (1960) and "The Daimler Airway", *ibid.*, iii (1958) provide an excellent introduction to the pioneers in the field. R. Higham provides a good account of the problems of a later company in "British Airways Ltd., 1935–40", *ibid.*, iv (1959). A. J. Quin-Harkin, "Imperial Airways, 1924–40", *ibid.*, i (1954) is far less satisfactory. The following should also be consulted: G. E. Woods Humphery, "A Review of Air Transport", *The Journal of the Institute of Transport*, March 1933; D. O. Lumley, "The Development of Air Mail", *ibid.*, Jan. 1939, and F. Handley Page, "The Achievements and Possibilities of Air Transport", *ibid.*, June, 1930.

There is no book on commercial flying in Great Britain. For the beginnings of internal aviation see F. C. Shelmerdine, "Air Transport in Great Britain: Some Problems and Needs", *Journal of the Institute of Transport*, Dec. 1935. P. G. Masefield provides some very useful statistical material in "Some Economic Factors in Air Transport Operation", *ibid.*, March 1951. A comprehensive account of the growth of internal airline companies and the problems they faced can be found in D. H. Aldcroft, "Britain's Internal Airways: The Pioneer Stage of the 1930s", *Business History*, vi (1964) and "The Railways and Air Transport in Great Britain, 1933–1939", *Scottish Journal of Political Economy*, xii (1965). P. Brooks, *The Modern Air Liner* (1961) gives a comprehensive treatment of the technical developments of the aeroplane, whilst a potted summary of these is given by the same author in "The Development of Air Transport", *Journal of Transport Economics and Policy*, i (1967). Information on airports is conspicuous by its absence. Some useful material can however be found in L. A. Savile, "Aerodromes for Civil Aviation", *Journal of the Institute of Transport*, Feb. 1935; and P. W. Brooks, "A Short History of London's Airports", *Journal of Transport History*, iii (1957).

14 Transport developments since 1940

In recent years transport has become a popular field for scholarly study and as a result there is a fairly large volume of literature, much of it analytical, on post-war developments. A comprehensive survey of the literature cannot be made here, but the reader who wishes to study the more recent changes will find the following items very helpful.

Transport in wartime is covered thoroughly by the official history *Inland Transport* (1957) written by C. I. Savage. General surveys of the main developments since 1945 can be found in K. M. Gwilliam, *Transport and Public Policy* (1964); J. R. Sargent, *British Transport Policy* (1958); G. F. Ray and C. T. Saunders, "Problems and Policies for Inland Transport", ch. XI in W. Beckerman and Associates, *The British Economy in 1975* (1965); and E. G. Whitaker, "Transport— the Changing Pattern", *Institute of Transport Journal*, May 1962.

For information on individual sectors of transport the following studies should be consulted: D. H. Aldcroft, *British Railways in Transition* (1968); J. Hibbs, *Transport for Passengers* (Hobart Paper 23, 1963); H. E. Osborn, "Road Haulage and Roads", *Institute of Transport Journal*, July 1966; N. Cayzer, "The Challenge to British Shipping", *Institute of Transport Journal*, July 1963; S. G. Sturmey, *British Shipping and World Competition* (1962); S. Wheatcroft, *The Economics of European Air Transport* (1956), and *Air Transport Policy* (1964). Valuable economic studies of the road and rail problem are C. D. Foster, *The Transport Problem* (1963), which is mainly a theoretical work, and the series of articles in the *Bulletin of the Oxford University Institute of Statistics*, xxiv (1962).

Index to bibliography

The figures in brackets refer to the number of works cited

General index